A HISTORY OF THE HABSBURG EMPIRE
1273–1700

In preparation:

A History of the Habsburg Empire: 1700–1918
Jean Bérenger
Translated by C. A. Simpson

A History of the Habsburg Empire 1273–1700

JEAN BÉRENGER

Translated by
C. A. Simpson

LONGMAN
London and New York

Longman Group UK Limited
Longman House, Burnt Mill,
Harlow, Essex CM20 2JE, England
and Associated Companies throughout the world.

Published in the United States of America
by Longman Publishing, New York

Originally published as *Histoire de l'Empire des Habsbourg 1273–1918*
© Librairie Arthème Fayard, 1990

English translation © Longman Group UK Limited 1994

First published 1994

ISBN 0 582 09009 1 CSD
ISBN 0 582 09010 5 PPR

British Library Cataloguing-in-Publication Data

A catalogue record for this book is
available from the British Library

Library of Congress Cataloging in Publication Data

Bérenger, Jean, 1934–
[Histoire de l'empire des Habsbourg. English]
A history of the Habsburg empire / Jean Bérenger; translated by
C.A. Simpson.
p. cm.
Includes bibliographical references and index.
Contents: 1. 1273–1700.
ISBN 0–582–09009–1. — ISBN 0–582–09010–5 (pbk.)
1. Austria—History. I. Title.
DB36.3.H3B4713 1994
943.6—dc20   93–7777
                                   CIP

Set by 15A in 10/13pt Garamond
Produced by Longman Singapore Publishers (Pte) Ltd.
Printed in Singapore

Contents

List of Maps and Genealogical Tables

MAPS

GENEALOGICAL TABLES

Translator's Note

Personal names present the historian and translator with a particular challenge; ever present is the risk of imputing the wrong nationality or indeed of bestowing nationality where to attribute any sense of belonging to a particular nation would be quite inappropriate.

As translator, I have presumed to depart from the, it might seem, admirably simple and consistent system of the original text which gives all names in French, and have used instead the native forms of names, e.g. János Hunyadi rather than the awkward hybrid John Hunyadi. While this policy remains appropriate for those rulers whose native origins are too important not to be acknowledged, neutral English forms have been preferred in the case of the Habsburgs, even of those early members of the House before Maximilian I who might be considered to have been unambiguously German.

To avoid pedantry, certain exceptions have been made: Don Carlos, the son of Philip II and hero of Verdi's opera, is too familiar to English readers for the Spanish form of his name to undergo anglicization; the names of rulers not central to the narrative have been given in the English version most frequently encountered, e.g. William the Silent; among the Hungarian 'national' rulers, Matthias Corvinus is too well-known by that name to be referred to as Mátyás Hunyadi.

Foreword

The solemn funeral at Vienna, Easter 1989, of the empress Zita brought the Habsburgs to public attention once again through the media coverage granted by the Republic of Austria. Zita of Bourbon-Parma was born in 1892 and in 1911 married the great-nephew of the old emperor Francis Joseph, the archduke Charles Francis Joseph, who was to become heir presumptive to the imperial crown of Austria and the royal crown of Hungary following the assassination at Sarajevo of the archduke Francis Ferdinand on 28 June 1914. The funerary honours paid to a sovereign who with her young husband had tried to end the vain and bloody slaughter of the First World War might well have seemed a little nostalgic. Yet six months later, there appeared in Hungary a current of opinion in favour of placing the archduke Otto von Habsburg, the son of the late sovereign, at the head of the Hungarian Republic as part of the process of re-establishing the tradition of Hungary as a *Rechtsstaat* while renouncing the epithet 'People's' imposed by the all-powerful Communist Party and the ever-watchful Soviet Big Brother.

These two events showed the world that the House of Habsburg was still alive and that, like the Bourbons of Spain before 1976, it was still interested in politics and in the nations over which it had once ruled. In these circumstances, it does not seem inappropriate to set out the role which the Habsburgs played during the six centuries from 1273 to 1918 when they exercised their sovereign responsibilities.

It would of course be absurd to pretend that this study of political history in the *longue durée* was realized in a few months. Rather, writing it has been a matter of giving substance to the author's long-standing interest in Central Europe and European history. The bibliography is vast, the quantity of documents in archives immeasurable. To aid the reader wishing to acquire deeper knowledge of the themes dealt with here, the author has supplied references to recent works and also to earlier ones available in the large public libraries but not to archival material, which does not have a place in a book such as this.

I wish to pay my respects to the memory of my master Victor-Lucien Tapié, too soon departed from the scene, who opened up the vista with his magisterial book *Monarchie et peuples du Danube*.* I thank my colleagues and friends, Francis Rapp (Strassburg), Daniel Tollet (Paris) and Charles Kecskeméti (UNESCO), who willingly undertook a critical reading of the manuscript, and likewise record my gratitude to my collaborator in Strassburg, Simone Herry, who carried out the difficult task of completing the index.

* Translator's note: published in English as *The Rise and Fall of the Habsburg Monarchy*, in the translation by Stephen Hardman, Praeger Publishers, New York, London, 1971.

Introduction

Originally from Alemannic Switzerland,* by the end of the thirteenth century the Habsburgs had extended their possessions in the Danube basin and would go on to affirm in the fifteenth century their European destiny, indeed, in the sixteenth century with Charles V, their pretensions to universal monarchy. It was inevitable, therefore, that after the death of Charles the Bold (1477) the Habsburgs would clash with French interests since they were the heirs of the Burgundian Valois. Apart from short-lived alliances, from 1477 to 1918 it is rare to find France and the Habsburgs on the same side. In France it is difficult to speak of the Habsburgs without passion and hostility.

The French kings accused the Habsburgs of wanting to surround France – this was Richelieu's particular obsession – and later, during the Third Republic, the French charged them with being party to pan-Germanism. At the same time 'liberal opinion' saw the Habsburgs as the defenders of Catholicism, of obscurantism and of reaction in the face of a Prussia with pretensions towards 'enlightenment' and 'progress'. This thesis was put forward repeatedly in government circles from Belle-Isle under Louis XV to Napoleon III. It was in the nineteenth century that mistrust and misunderstanding reached their peak when liberal historians supported the politicians in charging the Habsburgs with having created and maintained in Europe a form of state far removed from the ideals of the French Revolution.

The reason for these accusations was that the Habsburgs have always been indifferent to the idea of the nation-state, preferring instead the concept of a supranational monarchy where loyalty to the sovereign forms the fundamental bond between peoples and takes the place of patriotism.

This concept, which was carefully defended by the successors of Joseph II (1741–90), might seem the very opposite of enlightened but it had the advantage of not identifying the Habsburgs with any one privileged culture

* Translator's note: Alemannia was the territory between the Rhine, the Main and the Danube later forming part of the duchy of Swabia; Alemannic Switzerland is that part of Switzerland inhabited by German speakers.

or nation. Rather it allowed them to respect all the vernacular languages, cultures and the autonomy of the peoples who had voluntarily placed themselves under their tutelage. This attitude was a better guarantee of what is now termed 'the right to difference' of minorities, even though centralization as practised in Spain in the Golden Age could, in theory, have been possible;[1] however if the prestige of the dynasty meant that such centralization was feasible, the wisdom and structure of the government certainly did not permit it.

Whenever the Habsburgs took any steps along the path towards unification, difficulties arose as, for example, in the baroque age when Ferdinand II and Leopold I wanted to impose not a single language but a single confession with a view to adapting to Central Europe and the German world the model which a little earlier had succeeded in the Iberian peninsula. While the members of the orthodox Church in Hungary accepted the union of Brest-Litovsk,[2] the Protestants there took up arms, relying on the Turks and the French for support until they obtained confirmation of their privileges and succeeded in ruining the Habsburgs' plans for confessional unity.[3] Joseph II likewise encountered serious opposition when he decreed the Germanization of all his states.[4] Finally, the arrangement which resulted from the Compromise of 1867,[5] known as Austro-Hungary, was probably an error in so far as Francis Joseph preferred a two-tier centralization – very strict in Hungary, more flexible in Cisleithania – to a federal system more in keeping with tradition. Indeed, the Compromise appeared to favour two cultures, the German and the Hungarian, on the lines of Chancellor Beust's quip, 'You look after your hordes and we'll look after ours'.

This attitude kept the Habsburgs from creating 'an Austrian nation', despite the efforts of the archdukes Charles and John, the younger brothers of the emperor Francis I who, during the Napoleonic Wars, would have liked to mobilize public opinion. Rather the sovereign was content with an imperial hymn, the work of Joseph Haydn. The idea of an Austrian nation – still the subject of debate – became a reality only in the second half of the twentieth century.[6]

The Habsburgs' strength and their weakness was either to rule over nations already in existence – the Castilian, Hungarian, Polish and Bohemian nations[7] – or to govern states which were only fragments of much larger nations – Naples and Milan within the Italian nation, Styria, the Tyrol and Lower Austria within the German. The German nation, Robert Minder has recently shown,[8] was divided between strong particularist tendencies and universalist sentiment which harmonized well with the idea of the Holy Roman Empire and its universalist vocation, desirous of encompassing all the Christian West. A nation of great importance, the German nation was divided in the early Middle Ages into tribes (*Stämme*) – the Bavarians, the Swabians and the Saxons – who formed principalities, were endowed with one language but each used a dialect very different from that of its neighbour. The Habsburgs had to be content with the 'colonies' (Lower

Austria, Carinthia) and with frontier districts (Styria, the Tyrol) since they were never able to lay hold of the duchy of Swabia, which belonged to the Hohenstaufens. For this reason, from 1440 to 1866 the Habsburgs' real vocation was to gather together peoples and princes who retained their autonomy but who for a time would unite to confront an external danger, for example, the Turks and the French. Yet the Habsburgs still had to respect the delicate balance which found its expression in German public right issuing from the treaties of Westphalia and in the German confederation of 1815. Each time the Habsburgs like Charles V and Ferdinand II tried to unify the Germans through religion, they encountered opposition from their most loyal allies – Maurice of Saxony in the sixteenth century, Maximilian of Bavaria in the seventeenth – until finally they were excluded from Germany in 1866 by Wilhelm I of Prussia and his minister Bismarck.

The 'historic nations' existed before the House of Austria.[9] As early as the tenth century, the Poles, Czechs, Hungarians and Croats had succeeded in creating embryo states after the character of the Frankish monarchy, each forged around a national dynasty, the Piasts, the Přemyslids and the Árpáds. Once they converted to Catholicism – to the Latin form of Christianity – these princes were able to give themselves legitimacy in the face of the Empire and the Ottonians. The princes were supported by a service nobility. The peoples continued to use their language whereas the Church and the royal chancelleries converted to Latin. The vernaculars meanwhile were maintained in the oral tradition and reappeared at the end of the Middle Ages when national consciousness emerged among the ruling classes. Marxist theories which are content to bring up to date nineteenth-century ideas that national consciousness is a new phenomenon do not seem to give adequate account of the underlying realities of the past in Europe.[10] A nation's existence was not bound to the creation of a capitalist bourgeoisie. A language, culture, elites (clergy and nobility), and the presence of invasive neighbours (the Germans for example), were enough to develop national consciousness. The weakness of these countries was tied to the progressive enfeeblement of the power of the monarchy, the development of the power of the barons (the great feudal lords) but above all the absence of rigid rules of succession, such as the 'salic law' in France which permitted the easy transmission of the crown to a foreign dynasty, either through election or the marriage of the legitimate heiress. It was precisely through marrying such heiresses that the Habsburgs made their fortune and like twentieth-century multinational companies, they had the wit to take out options in different kingdoms and so were frequently in the position of reaping the fruits of their matrimonial 'investment policy'.

The result was a mosaic of states over which the sun, in the sixteenth century, never set since the Habsburg empire embraced not only their Central European patrimony but also the monarchies of Spain and Portugal and their colonial empires. This arrangement might appear implausible but, allowing for the problems presented by communications and local particularism, it was in fact quite workable. As Pierre Chaunu has repeatedly

3

observed, among institutions there is only one choice – between a system which does not function and one which functions badly. As long as the Habsburgs admitted the malfunctioning of their empire, they succeeded in their enterprises despite the condescending and pitying remarks of French diplomats. Yet as soon as they wanted, like Joseph II, to introduce rational principals and to imitate the French system – which responded to quite a different logic – everything quickly fell apart; in the case of Joseph II only the rapid departure of this too well-intentioned monarch made it possible to save the whole.

Another tradition of the House of Austria made its mission easier: the German tradition rejected the right of seniority when it came to granting the younger sons (cadets) responsibilities and duties. In the Middle Ages, the Habsburgs long hesitated between two concepts of the law of succession: the exclusion of the cadets and the division of the patrimony. In the end they found a middle way, creating apanages under the firm authority of the head of the family and in doing so they satisfied their subjects' taste for autonomy, eased decentralization and improved the efficiency of the administration, while maintaining the cohesion of the whole. When in the sixteenth century they extended their empire over part of the globe, they were able to overcome numerous administrative difficulties by using Habsburg archdukes and archduchesses for some of the tasks of government. The viceroys created the illusion that the legitimate sovereign, the 'natural lord', was present in the country, whether in the Netherlands, the Tyrol, Styria, Portugal or much later, in Hungary. Serious family disputes were rare, with the exception of the fifteenth century and the beginning of the seventeenth.[11] That there were sufficient cadets made possible the many marriages with foreign princes (in the eighteenth century this was a fundamental aspect of Maria-Theresa's diplomacy) and the placing of archdukes on episcopal thrones in order to strengthen imperial influence in Germany. This was how it came about in the seventeenth century that many of the bishops of Strassburg were members of the House of Austria.

One of the major departures from traditional dynastic policy was in the nineteenth century, when most of the archdukes were held aloof from the business of government and were restricted to employment in the army in the second rank. This change was the result of the head of the family's mistrust of his cadets because of their divergent politics. The House of Austria had within it strongly contrasting personalities; there were liberals like the archduke Charles,[12] the archduke John,[13] and much later the archduke Maximilian, the future emperor of Mexico, not forgetting the archduke Rudolf, romantic hero of the tragedy at Mayerling,[14] but there were also reactionaries like the archduke Albert, son of the archduke Charles,[15] and Francis Ferdinand, the archduke and heir apparent who was assassinated at Sarajevo,[16] to say nothing of the feeble-minded who could not reasonably be trusted with political responsibilities, such as Francis Joseph's father, the archduke Francis Charles.

One of the secrets of the Habsburgs' success was that they knew how to cooperate with the dominant forces in society – the Church, the nobles, then the great bourgeois businessmen – while progressively creating a class of new men – functionaries and career officers – and meanwhile accommodating themselves to universal suffrage and the social democrats prepared to maintain the monarchy on condition that it grant more autonomy to the various ethno-linguistic groups.

The collapse of the Habsburg monarchy in 1918 has for a long time seriously begged the question of whether a dispassionate history of the monarchy could be written to the point where Charles Kecskeméti could elaborate the notion that such a history is impossible,[17] that all that has been produced is a collection of chauvinistic histories aimed at settling old scores with neighbours. Such pessimism is perhaps a little extreme. For if it is true that since the Stalinist era, the national schools have, under cover of national history, strengthened the questionable tendencies of the debates initiated in the successor states, these tendencies nonetheless have evolved considerably since 1970 with on the one hand German historians now able to approach the history of Bohemia without resentment,[18] whereas on the other hand Czech historians, like Josef Macek,[19] have developed much greater serenity and take into account their country's diverse schools of history.[20] There has been much of worth also written by historians of the English-speaking world,[21] Americans of Central European origin like István Deak and the late Robert Kann,[22] as well as distinguished British colleagues like R. J. W. Evans,[23] P. G. M. Dickson,[24] and Derek Beales, who is in the process of revising the history of Joseph II. All these historians have in common a deep sympathy for the peoples of Central Europe and their problems and know their languages and archives while maintaining a certain detachment, a 'distance' with respect to the old quarrels and are quite without any of the spirit of 'local politics' which hangs over the current school of Austrian history.

The history of the Habsburgs presents another difficulty; it cannot be simply a collection of biographical notes like the dictionary which does a splendid job at providing such entries.[25] Nor can it be just a history of the family, or to be more precise, 'the House'. Despite the importance of marriages and inheritances in the Habsburgs' remarkable destiny, it would be foolish to write simply a social history since the relations of the dynasty with its subjects need to be taken fully into account. It is in precisely this area that research is growing and becoming more complex and so this present work is not concerned simply with Central Europe and what the French call Austria, but what here will be called, after the practice of Austrian historians, the 'Danubian monarchy'.

Since the House of Austria fostered universalist ambitions, this study will encompass more than simply the House's relations with the Germans of Austria, the Czechs, the Hungarians, the Poles, the South Slavs, the Romanians and Italians. Rather the field of inquiry in the Middle Ages will be extended in order to understand better the universal monarchy of Charles V and the ruling House's collection of possessions at the time when it reigned both at Vienna and at Madrid, but without going so far as to write a summary of the history of Spain, something which a number of experts have already done splendidly and will continue so to do.[26]

Consequently this social history of a sovereign house doubles as a political history but with due reference to cultural and economic history. The goal is to approach an understanding of why the original construction functioned, contributed to the European equilibrium and eased the evolution of many small nations and why in 1918, without having lost esteem, it was condemned by the victors, who were unable to substitute a system which was either more just or more effective.

This work will be divided into four parts, corresponding to the four phases of the development of the House of Austria: a German monarchy in the Middle Ages; a universal monarchy in the early modern period; a great European power in the age of the Enlightenment; and after Sadowa, a regional power which until the end in 1918 preserved its multinational character.

NOTES AND REFERENCES

1. Pierre Chaunu, *L'Espagne de Charles Quint*, 2 vols, Paris, 1973.
2. Ambroise Jobert, 'L'union de Brest,' in *De Luther à Mohila: la Pologne dans la crise de la chrétienté (1517–1648)*, Paris, 1974, pp. 321–43.
3. Jean Bérenger, *Les Gravamina: doléances de la Diète hongroise (1655–1681)*, Paris, 1973.
4. François Fejtö, *Joseph II: un Habsburg révolutionnaire*, Paris, 1949.
5. Louis Eisenmann, *Le Compromis austro-hongrois*, Paris, 1903.
6. Félix Kreissler, *La Prise de conscience de la nation austrichienne, 1938–1946–1978*, 2 vols, Paris, 1980.
7. From the German word *böhmisch, Böhme*, which does not distinguish between Slavs and Germanophones, both being equally *regnicolae*.
8. Robert Minder, *Allemagnes et Allemands*, 3 vols, Paris, 1954.
9. Friedrich Engels contrasted nations without a state, like the Slovaks and the Slovenes, and nations with a recognized state-right, like the Hungarians and the Czechs; see Jean Bérenger, 'L'Empire austro-hongrois', in Maurice Duverger (ed.) *Le Concept d'empire*, Paris, 1980, pp. 331–5.
10. Jenö Szücs, *Nations und Geschichte: Studien*, Budapest, 1981; Szücs defends a highly coloured thesis.
11. See the celebrated play by Franz Grillparzer, first performed at Vienna in the Burgtheater in 1839, *Bruderzwist im Hause Habsburg*, which portrays the quarrel between Rudolf II and his brothers.
12. Jean Tulard, 'Archiduc Charles', in *Dictionnaire Napoléon*, Paris, 1987.
13. Jean Tulard, 'Archiduc Jean', in *Dictionnaire Napoléon*, Paris, 1987.
14. The best work on archduke Rudolf is Brigitte Hamann's *Rudolf, Kronprinz und Rebell*, Vienna, 1978.
15. Brigitte Hamann, 'Erzherzog Albrecht, die graue Eminenz des Hauses

Habsburg', *Politik und Gesellschaft im alten und neuen Osterreich*, vol. 1, Vienna, 1981.
16. Jean-Paul Bled, *François-Joseph*, Paris, 1987, pp. 7–9.
17. Charles Kecskemeti, *Études Danubiennes*, 1988, vol. 2, pp. 89–105.
18. Jörg K. Hoensch, *Geschichte Böhmens: von der slavischen Landnahme bis ins 20. Jahrhundert*, Munich, 1987.
19. Josef Macek, *Histoire de la Bohême*, Paris, 1984.
20. Richard Plaschka, *Von Palacký bis Pekař*, Vienna, 1957.
21. Jean Bérenger, 'L'Empire des Habsbourg de 1526 à 1918', *Bulletin bibliographique, Revue historique*, vol. CCLX, 1978, pp. 179–211.
22. Robert A. Kann, *A History of the Habsburg Empire, 1626–1918*, Berkeley, Calif. and London, 1974.
23. R. J. W. Evans, *The Making of the Habsburg Monarchy*, Oxford, 1979.
24. P. G. M. Dickson, *Finance and Government under Maria-Theresa, 1740–1780*, 2 vols, Oxford, 1987.
    Derek Beales, *Joseph II*, 2 vols. Cambridge: vol. 1, *In the Shadow of Maria Theresa (1741–1780)*, 1987; vol. 2 in preparation.
25. Brigitte Hamann (ed.) *Die Habsburger: ein biographisches Lexikon*, Vienna, 1988.
26. John Lynch, *Spain under the Habsburgs (1516–1700)*, 2 vols, Oxford, 1981.

CHAPTER ONE

The Origins

Rudolf of Habsburg, at the time of his election as king of Germany in 1273, was head of a House which traced its origins back to the eleventh century and which had considerable possessions in Alemannic Switzerland and Upper Alsace. The heart of these domains was the present-day canton of Aargau, the fortress of Habichtsburg mentioned as early as 1020 and which yields by contraction the name Habsburg. The cradle of the House of Austria is situated in what was once the kingdom of Lotharingia, at the very heart of Europe and the crossroads of commerce and culture.

Shortly after the royal election of 1273, the Habsburgs ordered the deliberate embellishment of their origins since they were pained by their relative humble extraction and parvenu status. For the past century, however, medieval scholars have managed by their patient labours to separate truth from fiction.

MYTHICAL ORIGINS[1]

Since the Habsburgs could not link themselves to the leading German imperial dynasties, the Saliens or the Staufens, the legend gained ground at the beginning of the fourteenth century that they were descended from the Colonna, a Roman patrician family claiming links via the counts of Tuscany with the *gens Iulia* and so with Julius Caesar. As late as 1450, the Habsburgs still believed this legend, which strengthened their claim to the German throne at the time of their exclusion by the House of Luxemburg: it was a theory entirely compatible with the late medieval way of thinking.

In the fifteenth century, another theory appeared which made the Habsburgs the descendants of the Pierleoni, the counts of Aventine, and through them of the *gens Aniciana*. This new legend had the advantage of demonstrating the 'sanctity' of the Habsburgs since the Pierleoni counted among their members pope Gregory the Great (590–604) and St Benedict

(480–543), the founder of the Benedictine order. This theory was first propounded in 1476 by Heinrich von Gundelfingen and was connected to the revival of the political power of the papacy.

During the same period the legend of the House's Frankish origins also appeared. This connected the Habsburgs directly with the Merovingians, going back in a general way through their successors, the Carolingians.* These Frankish ancestors also enabled the Habsburgs to claim that they were descended from the Trojans. This theory was bound up with anti-Roman and anti-Italian prejudices and was not without ulterior political motives. It was championed by the emperor Maximilian I who used it to present himself as the legitimate heir to the Merovingian and Carolingian kingdoms of Gaul and Germany and also to justify his expansion into Western Europe and his claims to the Burgundian patrimony. Maximilian I encouraged numerous works on the subject – illuminated manuscripts, treatises on heraldry and illustrated genealogical tables. During the Renaissance, the theory found a huge response among the first German nationalists, but later went out of fashion as the conflict in Germany between France and the House of Habsburg gave way to Austro-Prussian rivalry.

A theory was then used which first had been developed in 1649 by the French scholar Jérôme Vignier; the Habsburgs were descended from the dukes of Alsace, from Eticho† and his successors, who in the early Middle Ages ruled over Alsace and Swabia. This 'House of Alsace', which dated back to the seventh century and a certain Archinoald, the Mayor of the Palace under Clovis II, was the cradle of the Habsburgs and the dukes of Lorraine. This theory conferred an obvious advantage in 1736 when the Habsburg archduchess Maria Theresa married the duke of Lorraine, Francis Stephen (Francis III) : the new Habsburg – Lorraine dynasty was nothing other than a restoration of the 'House of Alsace' founded by Eticho. Marquard Herrgott (1694–1762), the scholarly monk of Sankt Blasien, compiled a great genealogical history of the House at the request of the emperor Charles VI (16851740), the last male descendant of the House of Habsburg, in order to justify the marriage of his daughter and heir to Francis Stephen of Lorraine. This work, which drew on new methods of textual criticism, was based chiefly on the *Acta Murensia*, the annals of the abbey of Muri in Aargau which date from the twelfth century.[2]

While the theory of the House's Alemmanic origins would later find favour under the climate of social and intellectual conservatism prevailing in the first half of the nineteenth century, the other theories were felled during the age of the Enlightenment, demolished by the critical philosophy which took hold during the reign of Joseph II (1780–90). The pious legend

---

* Translator's note: the Merovingians, who derived their name from their supposed founder in the fifth century, Merovaeus, were the first dynasty of Frankish kings and rose to prominence under Clovis I (481–511). They were finally supplanted by the Mayor of the Palace, Pepin the Short (751), the father of Charlemagne and first of the Carolingian or (Carlovingian) dynasty.

† Translator's note: Eticho, otherwise known as Adalricus, died *c*.683.

of the Habsburgs' ancestral saint, Morand, and of the saints of the Pierleoni family celebrated during the baroque period collapsed before the advance of rational criticism; duke Eticho alone withstood scrutiny and was evoked in the imperial Schloss Luxemburg outside Vienna which was rebuilt by the emperor Francis I in the style of a medieval German castle: Eticho with the emperor Rudolf head the procession of great ancestors.

During the same period, prince Lichnowsky, the court historiographer, put an end to all these fables with the publication of his great work on the Habsburg family, *Die Geschichte des Hauses Habsburg* (1836). He dismissed the medieval historians' mania for hunting out, regardless of reality, ancestors among the *gens Iulia*, *gens Aniciana* and the Scipios, while some scholars without a qualm even went back as far as Hector. A scrupulous historian, he overlooked the fact that this had been the fashion among humanist scholars; in the sixteenth century, the House of France had itself sought out Trojan ancestors. He concluded that

For the conscientious historian, one fact should suffice: if since the tenth or eleventh century a family has been classed among the most powerful and most esteemed lines, then it should be counted among the higher nobles and there should be no question but that its ancestors belonged to the earliest Carolingians and that it should be held equal to the descendants of the Mayors of the Palace and their family. All the rest is superfluous, a man belongs to the higher nobility and that is enough.[3]

The Habsburgs' official circle once more went beyond historical evidence to trace the dynasty's origins back to the Carolingian age and the roots of German history.

It took the catastrophe at Sadowa and the unification of Germany to the benefit of Prussia and the Hohenzollerns to make Habsburg historiography keep to a reasonable version of the facts. In 1889 Franz von Krones in his *Grundriss der österreichischen Geschichtsforschung* presented a definitive condemnation of all the fine fables, even if no one managed entirely to disprove the Carolingian origins of the House.[4]

In the twentieth century, the Austrian historian Alphons Lhotsky, the director of the Viennese equivalent of the French Ecole des chartes,* had rejected the whole mishmash of legends, but like his colleague Anna Coreth admitted nonetheless that they had served the Habsburgs' political ends well and had nourished their skilful propaganda in the age of retreat.[5]

* Translator's note: the School of Archivists in Paris.

THE HISTORICAL ORIGINS[6]

Historical scholarship has not succeeded in making the Habsburgs' origins completely clear. They may have been descended from Gontran the Rich, the duke of Lower Alsace, who for being a traitor was deprived of his estates in 952 by Otto the Great. An amnesty might explain why part of the confiscated domains was returned to the Habsburg patrimony. The Habichtsburg domain was an allodial land* within the kingdom of Burgundy which was outside the direct authority of the emperor Otto. The advantage of this hypothesis is that it bolsters the Habsburgs' claims to membership of the family descended from Eticho but it also has the unfortunate result of making their ancestor a traitor and so rather detracts from the illustrious House's distinguished image.

It was, however, in Aargau that Gontran the Rich's son Lancelin (the diminutive of Landolt) was based; possibly he had acquired the Habichtsburg domain through marriage. What is certain is that one of Lancelin's sons, Radbot, married Ita, the daughter of the duke of Lorraine, while another son, Rudolf, married a certain Kunigunde from the family of (Hohen) Zollern and the eldest contracted a marriage with one of the daughters of count Berchtold of Villingen.

The most notable figure of this generation was Werner, bishop of Strassburg, thought by some to have been yet another of Lancelin's sons, and so a Habsburg, but by others to have been the son of the duke of Lorraine and Ita's brother. Certainly, if the latter theory is correct, Werner would have been in a position to obtain an amnesty for the grandsons of the errant Gontran the Rich. Bishop Werner was a childhood friend of the emperor Henry II and took an active part in his election. He supported the policy of expanding the empire towards Burgundy as his interests coincided with those of the Habsburgs and the emperor Henry II.

The Habichtsburg fortress was built at precisely this time (1020), its construction giving rise to the first legend concerning the House of Habsburg. The somewhat bellicose bishop Werner advised his relative Radbot, the feudal lord, to fortify his residence because it was not surrounded by any kind of rampart and Radbot promised to achieve this in one night. The following morning, the fortress was surrounded by his people, knights in armour positioned at regular intervals taking the place of towers. Bishop Werner deigned to show his approval and advised his relative to make the most of this living wall since no other was more trustworthy.

The same legend, scholars have pointed out, was told in connection with the emperor Frederick I Barbarossa (1152–90) and also the landgrave of

* Translator's note: the term allodial, derived from the Old French alôd meaning complete possession, refers to land which, unlike a fief, is the absolute property of its owners, free from feudal dues and taxes.

Thuringia. It was used by the Habsburgs at a time when they were subject to severe criticism in Swabia and throughout the whole Empire. In its original form handed down by Matthias von Neuenburg, the legend concerned neither bishop Werner nor count Radbot but told of two brothers from Rome who had crossed the Alps. The point of the legend remains the same: a prince's best protection lies in the affection and loyalty of his subjects. The Habsburgs, right to the very end, put this maxim into practice and enjoyed a genuine popularity, at least among their German subjects.

The family's power is evident from the advantageous marriage alliances made by the grandsons of Gontran the Rich and is confirmed by the number of religious foundations which its members established in the region during the first half of the eleventh century. While Habichtsburg was being built, Radbot, encouraged by his wife Ita and perhaps also by Werner, the bishop of Strassburg, founded the Benedictine abbey at Muri in Aargau which became the family monastery and guarded the House's *memoria* from its earliest days. Werner, thought to be the founders' son, became abbot of Muri and put it in the van of Cluny reformism.

Rudolf, Radbot's brother, founded the abbey of Ottmarshein in Upper Alsace, between the Rhine and the eastern fringe of the Hardt forest. The church at Ottmarsheim is reminiscent of Charlemagne's palatine chapel at Aix-la-Chapelle. Was this not a manifestation of the already immense ambitions of a rich and powerful family?

For two centuries the Habsburgs did not cease bolstering their position in the region: Alsace, Breisgau, Alemannic Switzerland. Around 1180 they founded the convent at Hermetswyl not far from the abbey at Muri, two foundations which both survived into the nineteenth century.

In 1090 Otto, a grandson of Radbot, was the first to take the title count of Habsburg. As a vassal of the emperor Henry V, he took part in the campaign against the king of Hungary, Kálmán (St Coloman), and is mentioned as 'count Otto of Havichsburg' in an imperial document, which bears a date, from Pressburg (Poszony, now Bratislava). This seems to be the first appearance of the family in that part of Europe.

Alsace continued to be the base of the Habsburgs' power. They secured for themselves the *avouerie** of the abbey of Murbach, which possessed extensive domains in Upper Alsace as well as the landgraviate of Upper Alsace which confirmed their political power over the region.

In the course of the twelfth century their destiny became linked to that of the Hohenstaufens and they appeared increasingly often at the imperial court and took part in military expeditions. The Habsburgs were able to amass untold inheritances with the support of the imperial authorities, because the active policy pursued by the Hohenstaufens entailed the rapid extinction of many lines, including some to which the Habsburgs were

---

* Translator's note: the term *avouerie* refers to the recognition by the holder of a fief of the feudal lord (seigneur) from whom he holds his land.

heir. They thus found themselves on the way to establishing with the Hohenstaufens' permission what amounted to a principality. The wealth of the 'poor counts' was apparent in 1212 when Rudolf the Old paid the duke of Lorraine 1 000 marks for the account of the young Frederick von Hohenstaufen (Frederick II, emperor of the Holy Roman Empire 1220–1250) whereas of the sum total of 3 200, the archbishop of Mainz, the bishop of Worms and four other lords gave only 700 marks.

Rudolf the Old, the grandfather of the future king of the Romans, Rudolf the Founder, in 1198 took the side of the Ghibellines, abandoning for good the Guelph cause.[7] This change of allegiance finally settled the Habsburgs' destiny. When Frederick left Sicily, Rudolf the Old was among the feudal lords from Germany who supported him without hesitation and Frederick II became godfather to the young Rudolf, who was born on 1 May 1218.

The death of Rudolf the Old inevitably retarded the rise of the House as he followed the custom of the German princes and divided his patrimony between his two sons, Albert IV and Rudolf III. It was the latter who founded the cadet branch of Laufenburg which later rejoined the Guelph party, while Albert IV remained loyal to the Hohenstaufens but died in 1249 after leaving for the crusades and left his son Rudolf the Founder, to become reconciled with the House's cadet branch, or 'branch of counts'. Not until the seventeenth century did the House abandon its opposition to the principle of primogeniture, which was contrary to the old Germanic law, and in the meanwhile proceeded repeatedly to divide its patrimony among its male heirs.

KING RUDOLF I, THE FOUNDER (1218–91)[8]

Rudolf IV, count of Habsburg, who acceded to that title in 1249 upon the death of his father Albert IV, is better known in general history as Rudolf I of Germany and king of the Romans. He is in fact the first of his House about whom very much is known, as much from chronicles as from iconography. One contemporary chronicle describes him thus:

Tall, he had long legs; of a delicate constitution, he had a pale complexion, a long nose, short hair, long and slender hands; he was a man moderate in his appetites and with respect to food, drink and other matters he was intelligent and wise.

This account agrees with that of another chronicler, who wrote that Rudolf was 'from his youth of great valour, intelligent, strong and favoured by fate; of tall stature, he had a pointed nose, a grave and dignified expression appropriate to his great strength of character'.[9]

The stone effigy on his tomb in the cathedral at Spire where the medieval German kings and emperors are buried agrees fairly with these written descriptions. It breathes energy and integrity, with perhaps a certain severity of expression which is not at all incompatible with a measure of humour – if the stories about him passed down by tradition are to be believed. When the royal remains were exhumed in 1900, those of Rudolf the Founder corresponded to the traditional image: a man of great height, elegant and well proportioned.

The descriptions of his character are similarly attractive for they were idealized after his death: Rudolf was, it would appear, generous, simple, good, pious and modest, in short he embodied all the virtues of the *miles christianus*, of the Christian knight, which concealed his ruthlessness and ambition. The alliance which he concluded with the great cities (in particular Strassburg and Zurich) helped to forge the image of a popular and pious sovereign. This was how he would appear in the Viennese tradition of the nineteenth century; 'half emperor Francis, half saint Florian' is how he was summed up by the creator of the role of Rudolf in Franz Grillparzer's play *König Ottokars Glück und Ende*.[10] He became in due course the model of piety which his descendants aspired to imitate and which Schiller celebrated in his ballad *Der Graf von Habsburg*.

His positive traits – his humanity and piety – have been greatly exaggerated by Habsburg propaganda. Comparison with the emperors of the early Middle Ages and with his son Albert could not but be to Rudolf's favour. A generation after his death a series of anecdotes celebrated his affable character and reflected the burghers' gratitude to the man who had put an end to the 'terrible time without an emperor'. The frugal, rather down-to-earth Swabians appreciated his practical side, illustrated by the story of how Rudolf advised the burghers of Strassburg to sell their fish in Cologne and to buy wine in exchange since fish was scarce in Cologne and wine at that time was short in Strassburg. The Rhineland patricians trusted a prince wise enough to forgo vainglorious campaigns into Italy as being costly and vain. The Habsburgs' enemies, however, were able to develop the image which hardly flattered the feudal aristocracy of 'a king of shopkeepers'. Even Dante (1265–1321), the champion of the Guelphs in Italy and the defender of the imperial cause south of the Alps, reproached Rudolf and his son Albert for having neglected their obligations and, contrary to tradition, for having let their greed keep them north of the Alps: they had neglected 'the garden of the Empire' in order to round off their own patrimony and to establish their own territorial power.

Rudolf I is considered first and foremost as the founder of *pietas austriaca*, that genuine piety which characterized the House right until the end of the Austrian monarchy.[11] Over the centuries, two legends have contributed to the image of a particularly pious prince. The first is an expression of his devotion to the Blessed Sacrament and is the basis of the Habsburgs' *pietas austriaca*. It was first recounted in the fourteenth century by a Swiss chronicler, the Franciscan Johann von Winterthur. One day

14

Rudolf met a priest carrying the *viaticum* to a dying man and he offered him his horse to help him cross the ford of a river which was in full spate. Afterwards he presented his mount to the priest since he no longer dared to ride, let alone hunt with or go to war on, a charger which had had the great honour of carrying the Lord. The legend was later embroidered so that the priest became the future archbishop elector of Mainz. In time the story changed so that Rudolf had dismounted as a matter of course when he recognized a priest carrying the Blessed Sacrament. During the Counter-Reformation, the Habsburg rulers showed special devotion to the Eucharist, the visible sign of the Real Presence: it was not unusual to see the emperor on foot and bare-headed following a procession of the Blessed Sacrament, to see a humble vicar carrying the *viaticum* to the sick. In the nineteenth century, the emperor Francis Joseph maintained the tradition: in 1854 in the Prater he left his carriage and renewed this ancestral gesture. It is probable that Rudolf's surrender of his charger originally signified a renunciation of war and a desire to reign as a just and peaceful sovereign. Much later it came to show an adherence to the Tridentine doctrine of the Real Presence, solemnly reaffirmed in opposition to Protestant theories of Holy Communion.

The second legend tells how Rudolf, after his election as king of the Romans, was to invest the peers of the kingdom of Germany but at that moment, the royal sceptre could not be found. Looking up, he noticed the crucifix on the wall, grabbed and kissed it, declaring 'Here is the sign of our redemption – let it now be our sceptre!'; Rudolf's first act of government thus took place beneath the sign of the cross. He was also associated with a miraculous vision: during the coronation, he saw a cloud in the form of a cross over the cathedral at Aix-la-Chapelle where the ceremony was being held. His contemporaries connected these signs with a desire on the part of the new sovereign to set out on a crusade or, at the very least, to leave for Rome to be crowned emperor and to re-establish his monarchical authority in Italy. The conclusion that was later drawn was that the Habsburgs' rule was placed under the sign of the victorious cross and that the dynasty was the legitimate heir of Constantine the Great, the first Christian emperor.

Rudolf's contemporaries were convinced that his election, which had put an end to an interregnum lasting a quarter of a century, was a providential sign: until late, simply a feudal warrior from southern Germany, unknown outside Swabia, Rudolf had shown that he intended to live as a Christian prince desirous of establishing within the Empire the rule of peace, order and justice for which his subjects longed after a long period of civil war.

He had already had the chance to learn the trade of a king and to prove himself a shrewd politician. At thirty-two he had succeeded his father as count of Habsburg and was fifty-five in 1273 when he was elected king of the Romans. During his middle age he had strengthened the regional power bases of his House. Loyal to his family's alliances, he did not abandon the Hohenstaufens and accompanied Frederick II's grandson as far as Verona but was not at the young Conradin's side at the battle of Tagliacozzo which sealed the unfortunate prince's fate. As landgrave of Upper Alsace and master of the western part of Alemannic Switzerland, he alone could guarantee the security of the route leading from Strassburg to Italy through the letters of safe conduct which he issued to protect merchants in times of trouble.

The conflict with his uncle Rudolf of Habsburg-Laufenburg stirred up local wars but Rudolf was sufficiently canny to emerge victorious and to consolidate his possessions in the region. Most importantly he was able to recover part of the inheritance belonging to his mother's family, the powerful counts of Kyburg, despite the opposition of count Peter of Savoy.

He did not hesitate to do battle with the powerful bishops of Basle and Strassburg, Heinrich von Neuenburg and Walter von Geroldseck, in order to appropriate part of the Hohenstaufen patrimony which had been lost after the tragic death of Conradin.[12]

A prudent administrator, he was able to increase resources, introducing new taxes and administering them thoroughly. He was inspired by the model set by the Normans in Sicily and which had been perfected by Frederick II. The sums raised enabled him to purchase fiefs from his neighbours who had been ruined by poor management of their land.

The slow process of unifying the domains of the Upper Rhine remained unfinished, interrupted by the election of 1273. The domains of Upper Alsace, Breisgau and Alemannic Switzerland were not held by one tenant. Rudolf was unable to lay his hands on Colmar, Mulhouse and Kaiserberg, which remained free towns. Moreover, he was obliged to promise the electors, the Rhine princes, that he would restore to them the Hohenstaufen domains which he had appropriated. These feudal estates later presented an insurmountable obstacle to the Habsburgs' expansion in southern Germany.

Why did so great a feudal lord suddenly abandon the wise policy of adding to his patrimony?

THE LONG INTERREGNUM (1250–73)

Frederick II's death in 1250 provoked a major crisis within the Empire and the kingdom of Germany and marked the momentary victory of the papacy in the secular quarrel between the Church and the Empire.

According to the theory which had prevailed since the time of Otto the Great, the king of Germany as successor of the Roman emperor did not accede to his office until he had been solemnly crowned at Rome by the sovereign pontiff, the pope. This required the king of Germany to travel to Italy (*der Römerzug*) and to cooperate with the pope, who was supposed to hold spiritual power within the Empire while surrendering temporal power, i.e. the investiture of bishoprics and large abbeys, to the emperor. The two spheres were poorly defined, however and since Innocent III (1198–1216), the popes had claimed that the emperors were subordinate to them. The Hohenstaufens meanwhile were extending their influence into the Italian peninsula. At the end of the twelfth century, the Empire extended as far west as the Rhône and the Escaut and to the south embraced the Alps of northern Italy. The emperor Henry VI (1190–6) by his marriage to Constance, the heiress of the Norman kings of Sicily, became master of southern Italy and encircled the patrimony of St Peter menacingly. Henry VI wanted to recover the imperial crown for his own House but he died at the age of thirty-two before he could realize his plan, leaving behind him a three-year-old child, the future Frederick II.

Following Henry's premature death, the initiative rested with the Holy See. Otto of Brunswick, the son of Henry the Lion, disputed the imperial throne with Philip of Swabia, the uncle of Frederick II. The latter was elected king of Germany in 1212 with the support of Innocent III, who could no longer tolerate Otto of Brunswick, who had become too independent. The new king was crowned emperor at Rome in 1220. More concerned with pursuing his policy in the Mediterranean than with German affairs, Frederick II at first bestowed great privileges upon the ecclesiastical, and then the secular, princes (1228). These measures had serious long-term consequences for the constitution of the Empire.

Frederick II was not slow to enter into conflict with the Holy See; Gregory IX (1227–41) excommunicated him for being so slow to carry out his promise of departing for the crusades. Nevertheless he liberated Jerusalem by negotiation and without striking a blow (1229), and married Yolande, the heiress of the kingdom of Jerusalem, who gave birth to Conrad, the last of the Hohenstaufens.

Frederick II, while he had better relations with the patricians of the large towns in Germany, like his grandfather Frederick Barbarossa, clashed with the Italian towns and the League of Lombardy, which was allied with the Holy See and was the principal force of the Guelph party south of the Alps. Gregory IX excommunicated him for a second time in 1239. At the Council of Lyons in 1245, the pope, appealing to the theocratic conception of public right, took the initiative and deposed Frederick II. Despite serious reversals of fortune, Frederick II died undefeated on 13 December 1250 at Castello Fiorentino in Apulia and was buried at Palerma by the side of his parents.

His son Conrad IV (1250–54) continued the hopeless conflict; he had married Elizabeth of Bavaria, who gave birth to Conradin in 1254, while Manfred, Frederick II's illegitimate son, continued the conflict in Italy and Germany suffered a period of anarchy. After Frederick II had been deposed and excommunicated, the Guelph party put forward a succession of anti-kings, Wilhelm of Holland (king of the Romans 1246–57), Alfonso X of Castile (king of the Romans 1257–72) and Richard of Cornwall (king of the Romans 1257–72), but not one of the three enjoyed any real authority over the German princes.* Italy was the centre of activity.

Pope Urban IV (1261–64) appealed to Charles of Anjou, the brother of St Louis, and invested him with the kingdom of Sicily. Charles fought Manfred relentlessly, eventually defeating and killing him at the Battle of Benevento (1266).

The last hope of the Ghibelline party and the Hohenstaufens rested with the young Conradin, who entered Rome in triumph in 1268. Defeated at Tagliacozzo, he was betrayed to his enemy Charles of Anjou and was executed at Naples.

The German towns and princes were tired of anarchy; once again a suitable candidate had to be found for the throne of Germany after the death of Richard of Cornwall. The king of Bohemia, Otakar II Přemysl,[13] was judged too powerful by the other German princes and at this point Rudolf, the count of Habsburg, began negotiations with the assistance of the burgrave of Nürnberg, Frederick of Hohenzollern. His advanced age by the standards of the time conferred on him authority and his ties with the Hohenstaufens assured a measure of continuity, but most importantly he was neither too rich nor too powerful. Rudolf had the qualities of 'a new man' who would not upset the wealthy princes, jealous of their authority.

Rudolf negotiated expertly. He secured the support of the electors of Saxony, Brandenburg and the Palatinate, giving them his daughters in marriage and pursuaded the others to recognize the acquisitions which he had made, more or less legitimately, during the interregnum. What also proved decisive was that pope Gregory X (1271–76) was determined to re-establish order north of the Alps and Rudolf promised him that he would organize a crusade once he was crowned emperor at Rome.

Rudolf, 'the candidate of the union', was obliged, however, to undertake an altogether different policy since he realized that his power was threatened by the ambitions of the king of Bohemia, Otakar II Přemysl. He forwent the traditional journey to Italy which had marked the death knell for the authority of most of his predecessors. He was never emperor and was satisfied with the royal crown, which was quite an advance for a count of Habsburg. But most importantly he directed his efforts to the east of Germany, abandoning all vain fantasies of taking Italy. This was a decisive choice because in practice he put an end to the universalist aspects of the imperial power and made the Empire essentially a German monarchy. He moved the Habsburg patrimony's gravitational centre towards Danubian

---

* Translator's note: in the double election of 1257, three of the seven electors chose Richard of Cornwall (1225–72), the younger brother of the King of England Henry III, while the rest elected Alfonso X of Castile (1221–84), the candidate put forward by the Ghibelline anti-papal republic of Pisa. Alfonso continued to press his claim to the imperial title after the election of Rudolf of Habsburg, only finally renouncing it in 1275.

Europe: curtailed in Swabia by the pledges that he was obliged to swear at the time of his election, he pursued his family policy in the eastern marches of Germany, thus sealing the destiny of his House. As for the dreams of Italy, these were not resurrected until the Renaissance and, most remarkably, the eighteenth century.

From 1273 onwards the Habsburgs, with their bent towards financial gain and their taste for conquest, were to come into contact with a world very different from that in which they had originated and the Rhineland lords were to become Danubian princes. The royal election of 1273 set the seal on the Habsburgs' European destiny.

NOTES AND REFERENCES

1. Adam Wandruszka, 'Römer, Trojaner oder Alemannen?', in *Das Haus Habsburg: eine europäische Dynastie*, Vienna, 1956, pp. 26–35 (hereafter Wandruszka).

2. Marquard Herrgott, *Monumenta Augustae Domus Austriae*, 3 vols, published in folio by Martin Gerbert, Sankt-Blasien, 1750–60.

3. Prince Lichnowsky, *Geschichte des Hauses Habsburg*, quoted from Wandruszka, p. 32.

4. Franz von Krones, *Grundriss der österreichischen Geschichte*, Vienna, 1889, pp. 302–10.

5. Alphons Lhotsky, 'Apis Colonna, Fabeln über die Herkunft der Habsburger', *Mitteilungen des Instituts für österreichische Geschichtsforschung*, vol. 55, Vienna, 1945.
   Anna Coreth, 'Dynatisch-politische Ideen Kaiser Maximilians I', *Mitteilungen des österreichischen Staatsarchivs*, vol. 3, 1980.

6. Wandruszka, pp. 37–45.

7. In the quarrel between the papacy and the Empire that divided Germany and Italy, the Guelphs were the supporters of the papacy while the Ghibellines upheld the supremacy of the emperor.

8. Oswald Redlich, *Rudolf von Habsburg*, Vienna, 1903; 2nd edn, 1965.

9. Quoted by Wandruszka, p. 46.

10. Grillparzer, *König Ottokars Glück und Ende*, a tragedy in five acts, first performed at the Burgtheater, Vienna, 1825.

11. Anna Coreth, 'Pietas Austriaca: Wesen und Bedeutung habsburgischer Frömmigkeit in der Barockzeit', *Mitteilungen des österreichicshen Staatsarchivs*, 7, Vienna, 1954; reissued, 1984.

12. Taken prisoner at Tagliacozzo, Conradin was executed on the orders of Charles of Anjou, brother of St Louis, in Naples in 1268. This was the end of the House of Hohenstaufen and the German domination of southern Italy.

13. Jörg K. Hoensch, 'Böhmen als přemysliden Königreich', in *Geschichte Böhmens: von der slavischen Landnahme bis ins 20. Jahrhundert*, Munich, 1987, pp. 87–96.

CHAPTER TWO

The Early History of Austria and its Neighbouring Lands

Some account should be given of the lands which the Habsburgs gradually placed under their control. The hub of these lands is the Vienna basin from which radiate the eastern Alps and the Hercynian massifs of Bohemia, then the Danube – the major route of communication in this part of Europe – which has inevitably established a direct link with the Carpathian basin, the most vital part of which is the great Hungarian plain, the Alföld, sometimes Austria's bulwark, sometimes its partner and sometimes set in total opposition.

A transit zone subject to invasion, after the Roman era the region was never really dominated by one ethno-linguistic group: herein lay its weakness when confronted by the ambitions of the Germans and later, though to a lesser degree, by Russian imperialism. The various ethno-linguistic nuclei, however, completely resisted assimilation despite some fleeting attempts at Germanization. It was the Habsburgs' good fortune that it was the most Germanized part of the Danube region – the Vienna basin and the eastern Alps – that they first acquired.

Although this region has always been open to invasion because of the great axes of penetration, the theory so readily put forward of 'backwardness' with respect to Western Europe is not supported by any natural determinism; the natural potential of the region is just as good as that of Western Europe.

DANUBIAN EUROPE: AN OPEN COUNTRY

The region's relief is made up of four major mountain ranges: the Bohemian massif and three alpine chains; the eastern Alps continuing into the Carpathians, and the Dinaric Alps. Alpine pasture is rare, the greater part of the uplands and slopes being covered by forest. The northwest Carpathians are characterized by longitudinal folds so that Slovakia does not present a barrier but rather serves as a refuge and transit zone. The Carpathians to the south surround the great depression of Transylvania formed by hills 400–500 metres high; the mountain range consists of the crescent formed by the principal chain with the massif of Bihor joining the horns of the crescent. As in Slovakia, agriculture rests within a framework of great forests interrupted by farm clearings and pastures where hamlets have been established. As in the Alps there is a series of craters which causes the Pannonian and Transylvanian basins to be extended and reduces the chain in the sub-Carpathian Ukraine to a thin line no more than 500 metres high. This narrow ridge, called the Mukačevo, has great historic and strategic significance. Volcanic massifs appear in the craters, extend from the metal-bearing Slovak mountains to Transylvania and generally have fertile soil particularly suited to viticulture.

The Dinaric range by contrast is a collection of long stony or wooded plateaux fringed by escarpments which are difficult to traverse; furrowed by folds, in some places crossed by gorges, it ends at the Adriatic in a great wall of limestone. In 1918 a single-track railway crossed the Dinaric range to serve a coastline as long as the Atlantic coast of France. Tall massifs are rare and the inhabitants live concentrated in the depressions or *poljés* and in the great tertiary basin of Sarajevo. To the west the Dinaric range meets the Carinthian Alps around Ljubljana in Slovenia. This configuration has serious results: relations with Mediterranean Europe are difficult, although the inhabitants have always sought to increase cultural contacts with the Graeco-Roman world and its successors; the values of the Latin world have often had to take a circuitous route and since the eastern Alps present a much easier obstacle to cross, have travelled via the Germans before arriving late and much altered.

The Austrian Alps have many longitudinal valleys and cover a surface area of 50 000 sq km (64.4 per cent of the territory of Austria). As the limestone pre-Alps form in effect a pole of repulsion (clear from the toponomy – the Dead Mountain, the Sea of Stones), the two outer ends are better favoured. The Vorarlberg resembles the pastures of the foothills of the Swiss Alps; to the east the Austrian Alps are heavily wooded and since the end of the neolithic period have been an active mining centre. The iron mine of Erzberg in Styria has been worked as an open-cast mine since the third century BC. The Austrian Alps are joined to the Vienna Forest which dominates the Austrian capital. The igneous High-Alps are less wooded but have vast pastures which are the setting for intense pastoral activity. The mass of the population is concentrated in the valleys and basins; the great valley of the Inn, the great Drava basin at Klagenfurt in Carinthia, the small basins of the Mur valley. Innsbruck, a large city with 140 000 inhabitants, is at the west and north–south crossroads of the Austrian Alps (the mouth of the Brenner).

The Danube valley is flanked to the north by a complex collection of ancient landforms – the Bohemian massif. The Austrian part of this complex is the Waldviertel, an area of igneous rock, mostly wooded with scattered clearings of reclaimed land. As it extends into Czechoslovakia, the Waldviertel becomes the Bohemian Forest, one of the four mountainous massifs which make up the quadrilateral of Bohemia and enclose the great central depression. These four massifs are similar to the German mountain range with wooded summits and the population concentrated in hamlets. The relief is broken by rift valleys and by great depressions filled with lava or loess (the region of Karlovy Vary (Karlsbad) in the metal-bearing mountains; Krusné Hory). The mountain range is industrialized with silver mines and uranium at Jáchymov (Joachimsthal) while the inner depressions are the cradle of the Czech textile industry (Librec).

The low regions are the Vienna, Pannonian, Transylvanian and central Bohemian basins and the Moravian depression which links the valley of the Danube through its tributary the Morava to the valley of the Odra and the Great Polish Plain. The basins of Olomouc and Brno are dominated by a succession of basins and mountain chains. These low regions offered better opportunities for development and were the site of the densest concentrations of settlements. The Vienna basin to the east of the capital is a semicircular crater and is simply the extension of the Pannonian basin, with neither the hills of Burgenland nor the Austro-Hungarian political border breaking its unity. To the east of the Danube stretches the great Hungarian plain (Alföld) at an altitude of 120 metres, featureless and covered with great sheets of loess, the source of its fertility. East of the Tisza there are more dunes and the natural vegetation is that of steppe. Transdanubia by contrast offers a great variety of landscapes; hills covered by loess, a little massif (the Mecsek) while the limestone Bakony dominates lake Balaton: a real inland sea within Hungary and a holiday resort, the waters of lake Balaton generate a micro-climate despite their shallowness. The landscape of Transdanubia reoccurs in Slovenia at the foot of the Dinaric range. There once again the political frontier is unrelated to geography or population. The presence of loess gives the region great natural fertility. Only the great river banks of the Tisza and Danube which are badly drained and prone to flooding – sometimes quite catastrophic – have not attracted settlement.

The Bohemian basin is also a complex structure. The ancient underlying plate for the most part has come to the surface, yielding wooded crests and the coal-bearing basin of Kladno, a priceless factor in Bohemia's industrialization. The area to the north-east is covered by marl and loess, producing a countryside of compact and fertile fields where wheat, beet and hops are grown. The ancient underlying plate to the south-west is generally covered by loess and is similarly fertile. With the exception of some peaks, the balance of agriculture in the whole basin is clearly positive. Bohemia and Hungary as well as part of Lower Austria have always been considered a prosperous agricultural region with a continental climate and various slight differences which taken as a whole are favourable to agriculture; cereal crops can be combined with stock-rearing, industrial cultivation and, on favoured ground, viticulture. Although Danubian Europe has often suffered from wars and plagues, it has dreaded famine far less, at least within the framework of the old economy which, without too much difficulty, provided people with bread, wine and meat. The climate and adequate fertile soils act as a unifying element although there are regional differences according to latitude. The average temperature in January is below zero (1.6°C in Prague) but the summers are hot, the average temperature for July wavering between 21°C and 24°C in the Pannonian plain; it has been possible to attempt cotton-growing in southern Hungary but by contrast the summers in Bohemia are much fresher. Everywhere vine-growing has been successful on well-exposed slopes with favourable soils (the volcanic soils on the northern bank of lake Balaton and the Tokay region). Rain is heavy everywhere in summer but diminishes progressively towards the east. Danubian Europe enjoys a temperate climate; the differences are not extreme but rather more pronounced than on the Atlantic coast.

Fertile plains, a favourable climate, mountains rich in fuel (the wood from forests) and in minerals (sufficient coal for the first industrial revolution) and easy communications (except with Mediterranean Europe): Danubian Europe has always been open not only to invasion but also to multiple cultural influences. The Mukačevo threshold did not always withstand the waves of horsemen from the steppe, attracted by the fertile open spaces of Pannonia; once over the rocky bar at Belgrade the plain has been prey to invaders from the Balkans for whom the final barrier has been the incomplete rampart of the Carpathians. This is why Moravia and Silesia in the very heart of Europe many times broke the flood of Tartar horsemen. If Central Europe has been the route of invaders it has also been the route of fruitful exchanges because of the Danube, which diminished in importance as the region's main artery only after the railway network was established. The two major capitals, Vienna and Budapest, have developed on advantageous sites: Vienna for contact with the plain and the rampart of the Alps, Budapest for contact with the valleys of Transdanubia and the Alföld at a point where the Danube is easily crossed. Since the last century, these two capitals have been the point of departure for a star-shaped railway network, with the premier line of the Austrian network using the Moravian corridor to link Vienna with Berlin via Prussian Silesia. As for the Alps and the ancient massifs of Bohemia, their longitudinal valleys mean that they have never presented an obstacle to the passage of people and goods and with Transylvania have served as a refuge for the Hungarian nation during its greatest misfortunes.

It is human migration which remains the leitmotiv of the region's history, the constant ebb and flow which hardly covered the groups which had settled previously, at least after the collapse of the Roman Empire and the disappearance of the Romanized populations. The invasion of the Huns almost completely eliminated pre-existing cultures. Only the eastern Alps, the Dinaric range and perhaps the Transylvanian Alps have preserved a part of their most ancient heritage: the Celts in Noricum, the Illyrians in

Dalmatia and on the edges of Pannonia, the Dacians in Transylvania. The early attempts at Christianization were swept away by the flood of barbarians and Danubian Europe remained a missionary region to the first millennium. For this reason it is necessary to skip the history of the Celts and Romans and to describe briefly the civilization existing before the great changes brought about by the barbarian invasions.

PATTERNS OF SETTLEMENT BEFORE THE GREAT INVASIONS[1]

Excavations have revealed that the region was occupied before paleolithic times (the cave of Mixnitz in Styria). Finds in Upper Austria show that in neolithic times (3 500 BC) lake towns had been built around the Mondsee. These civilizations were not at the same high level of development as contemporary civilizations in Egypt and the Near East but their communities were already sedentary and were making pottery with a linear decoration.* They knew how to cultivate the land, raise cattle, sheep, pigs and goats, to spin and to weave. They were integrated within the trade route for amber which was collected on the shores of the Baltic and sold throughout Europe.

In the course of the second millennium BC, the Bronze Age, humans abandoned polished stone in favour of bronze weapons and jewellery; finds from this period have been made in Bohemia, Transdanubia and on the fringes of the Vienna Forest and there is an increase in the number of tombs. Towards 1100 BC people stopped burying their dead and instead burnt them, keeping their ashes in urns which were collected together in vast open spaces (the Urnfield culture). Three centuries later, around 800 BC, iron weapons and tools appeared. The golden age of the Hallstatt culture of Upper Austria lasted from 800 to 400 BC and was based on the salt trade which expanded to a scale hitherto unknown. Excavations at Hallstatt, near Bad Ischl, have disclosed more than 2 000 tombs. These seem to have belonged to a Veneto-Illyrian people who came to dominate the whole of Central Europe and northern Italy, leaving their mark in certain place names (Carnuntum, Karawanken, Noricum). Their level of culture seems to have been superior to their political organization since c.400 BC these 'Illyrian' peoples became subject to the Celts, who came from Western Europe, followed the route along the Danube and settled first in a block in Bohemia to which they gave their name (Boii). A second wave travelled up the Po valley

* Translator's note: the *Linearbandkeramik* (LBK) is the linear pottery which gives its name to the Danubian culture of the period.

and overran the Austrian Alps while the Illyrian peoples took refuge in the Vorarlberg and the northern Tyrol.

The invasion seems to have had a profound effect upon the anthropological character of the inhabitants of these regions (Bohemia and Austria). What is certain is that these Celts left enduring evidence of their presence in the region's toponomy – the Danube and the Inn rivers for example. They founded numerous small towns – Bregenz, Wels, Vienna (Vindobona). They developed the local mineral resources and established trade links with the Greeks, Etruscans and peoples of the north, along the route of the rivers Morava and Oder, but above all they were agrarian farmers who also practised stock-rearing, hunting and fishing.

In the period immediately after the colony of Aquilea was founded (181 BC), the Celts of Noricum enjoyed good relations with the Romans and allied with them against the invading Cimbri and Teutons (113 BC). During the first century BC, at the time of Julius Caesar, the kingdom of Noricum tried to maintain the balance between the Romans and the Suevi under Ariovistus. This was the time of the Celts' first apparent retreat immediately before the dawn of the Christian era. The Celts from Bohemia settled in Transdanubia in *c*.60 BC and were replaced by a German people, the Marcomanni, whom the Romans knew as formidable neighbours. The Danube, however, with its unstable banks and its marshy fringes, presented a natural barrier which was difficult to cross and which the Romans exploited and reinforced, as they did the Rhine in Western Europe.

The conquest of the Alpine lands by the Romans dated from the reign of Augustus and the inhabitants of Noricum readily opened their land to the legions. The famous disaster of Varus's legions in the Teutoburger Wood (*c*.9 BC) had a decisive effect on the course of European history. The Romans had established themselves in a block to the west of the Rhine and to the south of the Danube but had left the forests of Saxony, Thuringia and Bohemia to the German peoples. Roman civilization never had a direct influence there. When, in the second century AD, Trajan conquered Dacia, the valley of the Tisza, for example, escaped Roman colonization while the lands corresponding to the greater part of present-day Austria, Transdanubian Hungary and the former Yugoslavia were well acquainted with the *pax Romana*.

The Romans organized the regions they had annexed into five provinces, *c*. AD 150, as follows:

1. Noricum, corresponding to the Alpine lands.
2. Pannonia bordered to the north by the Danube, to the west by Noricum and to the south by Dalmatia; it was divided by Trajan into Upper and Lower Pannonia with capitals at Vindobona (Vienna) and Sirmium (Sremska Mitrovica) respectively.
3. Dacia, corresponding to Transylvania and Romania, bordered to the west by the Tisza, to the south by the Danube, to the north by the Carpathians and to the east by the Dniester; inhabited by the Thracians

who had achieved a high level of civilization, the kingdom of Dacia constituted a grave threat to the Romans who under Domitian bought peace by paying tribute to the Dacian king Decebalus; for this reason Trajan decided to conquer Dacia and to turn it into a province (*c.*107 AD) where he established the XIII legion, countless auxiliaries and Roman colonies; in 129 AD Hadrian divided the province into Upper Dacia (Transylvania) and Lower Dacia (Lesser Wallachia).

4. Moesia, corresponding to present-day Serbia and Bulgaria.
5. Dalmatia.

Romanization took place slowly and in stages. Funerary inscriptions from the first century AD found in the neighbourhood of Wieselburg (Lower Austria) give Latinized Illyrian and Celtic names alongside Roman ones. In the mountainous regions, the local population kept their own customs and beliefs; Roman influence was strongest in the towns. It was through the towns and their municipal administration that the local populations became assimilated – the imperial functionaries acted as a role model for the local notables – while the principal Romanizing element outside the towns was the army whose legionaries were recruited throughout the provinces of the Empire and were gradually assimilated to Roman ways. In the third century AD, it would seem that the process of Romanization was complete.

The Roman administration's first concern was to secure the safety of the frontiers and links with Rome. For this reason the Romans constructed along the Danube a string of forts which were linked by a road to Lorch, Mautern, Traismauer, Tulln and Klosterneuberg. Particularly important were the forts at Vienna, Carnuntum and Aquincum (present-day Oduba in the northern suburb of Budapest). They were Roman forts constructed to the classic design and were strongly fortified, each protecting a legion (the XIV at Carnuntum, the X at Vindobona). The camps were strictly for the army but were surrounded by the houses of the legionaries' families, merchants and artisans. In the course of the second century AD, the Roman emperors granted these conurbations the rights accorded to cities. A hundred decurions appointed for life formed a kind of patriciate which each year chose a commission of four members and a quaestor in charge of finances. This was why Trajan did not hesitate to cross the Danube and conquer Dacia.

The Roman empire did not restrict itself to defensive action alone. In the first century AD, the prince of the Marcomani became an ally of Rome but after AD 150 the Marcomani found themselves under increasing pressure from the advancing Barbarians; in AD 171 they broke through the Danube line, laid waste Transdanubia, Styria and Carniola, crossed the Alps and attacked Aquilea. It took the emperor Marcus Aurelius eight years to drive them back (171–9) after which the line of defence along the Danube was strengthened. To replace the population lost through the invasion and to rebuild the ruins, Rome for the first time appealed to German colonists, a move which changed the composition of the population of Pannonia. It was the governor of Carnuntum, Septimus Severus, who in AD 193 marched on Rome, seized supreme power and founded a new dynasty.

At the beginning of the fourth century, Diocletian (emperor AD 284–305) reorganized the Empire, dividing the large provinces and separating civil and military power. He also strengthened the Danubian navy and garrisons, creating a new legion. Constantine (AD 274–337) then divided the vast empire into a hundred provinces, thirteen dioceses and four prefectures. Christianity first appeared in these regions at this time and gradually replaced the old Celtic beliefs and the martial cult of Mithras, which had been brought from the East by the legionaries and protected by their power. Diocletian's persecution of the Christians produced countless victims (including St Florian) but the new religion flourished after 313, when every Roman city became an episcopal see. Recent excavations have revealed countless cult centres – basilicas, chapels and necropoles. The fourth century, however, marked an irreversible decline in these frontier regions; the towns emptied, the countryside fell increasingly under the domination of the German colonists, while the legions were recruited from among the barbarians. The Empire became less and less able to withstand the blows inflicted by the Germans fleeing the pillaging nomads from the steppes. For the next five centuries Danubian Europe was the scene of great upheavals which left little of the Roman past remaining.

THE TRIBES PRIOR TO THEIR SETTLEMENT IN THE DANUBIAN REGION

This section is concerned with the Slavs, Germans and Hungarians who were all considered as 'barbarians' by the more-or-less Romanized peoples of the Empire.

The Germans were the closest and the least restive. Their origin remains uncertain. One theory holds that they were a people from the North who during the Bronze Age adopted an Indo-European language, while another asserts that they were from eastern Russia, the original point of departure for the Indo-European family. On the eve of the invasion they were divided into three groups: the Goths, who moved from the Baltic into the Ukraine; the Vandals, Burgundii, Alemanni and Franks to the west; the Angles, Saxons and Lombards to the north, on the edge of the Baltic. Although a common German culture did exist, the Germans' shared language and culture could not give rise to any 'national sentiment'. The Germans did not have a state or towns but rather communities (tribe, clan, family) which formed the framework of their political and social life. The tribe was governed by an aristocracy based on birth, which owned the greater part of the land; beneath them was the mass of freemen, who served as warriors; finally there were the slaves, who formed the bottom layer but who could be emancipated. The Germans were chiefly soldiers and peasants. They had a basic love of nature and its forces; their religion was simple, involving various sacrifices on a fixed date near a tree or spring. The warriors did not believe in death and the dead had to keep to hand their tools, weapons and finery. Those who died on the battlefield were certain to share in the life of the gods. Their contacts with the Roman world were longstanding (dating back to the first century AD) and ambiguous. Since the time of the Roman historian Tacitus (c. AD 55–117), the author of the *Germania*, a myth of a virtuous 'good savage' had grown up. As they swarmed across the *limes* some were already enrolled in Rome's service, first as auxiliaries, then as legionaries and finally as colonists. Other barbarian peoples, often partly Germanized, came into the regions, which explains the weak resistance presented by the inhabitants.

The Slavs originally came from the region between the Dnieper and Vistula rivers, a land of forests and marshes with little relief. They were bordered to the west by the Germans, to the north by the Finns and to the south by Iranian and Tartar peoples. Their language shows that they were Indo-European but they did not constitute so homogenous a group as the Germans. The South Slavs were very different from the Eastern Slavs (the Russians) and the Western Slavs (the Poles and Czechs): the South Slavs were tall in stature and suggested a southern type. Cut off from the North Sea and isolated from other tribes by vast forests, the Slavs were untouched by Hellenic and Latin culture (and still less by the culture of the steppe peoples, the Scythians and Sarmatians. They were unacquainted with the art and language of their southern neighbours. Their language, however, contains ancient borrowings from the Germans: terms connected with government, commerce, war and agriculture as well as the word for book. These words which are found in all the modern Slav languages were borrowed before the Slavs were scattered, i.e. before the sixth century AD. The Slavs were primarily farmers and according to the Latin chronicler Jordanus were of Goth origin, 'for them the forests and marshes took the place of towns'. They were organized in tribes made up of clans. A Slav clan was a social group consisting of many families and possessing communal means of production. The head of this large family was either the oldest man or the widow of the chief. In certain instances the chief of the clan was obliged to consult the community of freemen. All the patrimony acquired through the group's work belonged to the clan and it could not be disposed of without the consent of all. Through the development of trading links, certain clans became more powerful than others and gathered other clans around them and in this way formed tribes. The oldest name for a tribal chief was *joupan*.

Pagan Slav society was divided into three classes: at the top was an aristocracy composed of clan chiefs and a certain number of their immediate relatives, beneath them came a large class of freemen and peasants, and at the bottom were the slaves, prisoners of war, debtors and the descendants of slaves. Their religion was grounded in animism and the cult of the dead. They believed in demons to whom the souls of the dead became attached. Gradually they passed from demonology to a kind of pantheism. They did not have a priestly hierarchy.[2]

The Slavs and Germans were sedentary farmers, pagan, indeed 'barbarian' but not fundamentally different from the peoples of the Roman Empire. They took flight in the face of a grave threat, the horsemen of the steppe, the Turks and Mongols whose way of life was totally incompatible with that of the sedentary agriculturalist since the nomad shepherd needed space for his flocks and had no understanding of the value of towns, villages and dwellings. The arrival of these nomads – who were raiders to boot – represented a tremendous set-back for Europe and posed a considerable threat to settlers everywhere. Most of these peoples from the steppe disappeared without leaving any trace (the Huns, the Avars). Only the Hungarians who belonged to the Avars ended up settling and becoming farmers.

The Hungarians' origins have for a long time been obscured by the myths which they fostered about their relationship to Attila, the king of the Huns dubbed 'the scourge of God'. Patient research by archaeologists has confirmed the facts established by comparative linguistics. The Hungarians are of nordic not Asiatic origin and for a long time before their migration had been living in northern Russia. In the second millennium BC the proto-Hungarians were settled north of the Urals, where they lived as fishermen and nomadic hunters. The Ural tribes divided into a Finnish branch along the shores of the Baltic (the Estonians and Finns) and an Ugric branch which continued to migrate towards the middle course of the Volga. The distant cousins of these proto-Hungarians, the Ostiaks and Vogouls to the north of Siberia, still use a hunting vocabulary which is close to Hungarian; all these Finno-Ugric languages have similarities in their structure, which is very different from that of Indo-European languages. In their new home the proto-Hungarians acquired basic agricultural techniques and it was only as a result of contact with Turcic elements that they became nomadic raiders, just at the time of their final settlement in the Danubian plains. They then integrated with this steppe civilization, which had had no contact with the Slavs and which produced the works of art that can still be admired in the Hermitage, St Petersburg. The National Museum at Budapest contains the weapons and harness of a horseman who was buried with his horse.

At this early period the real link between the Hungarians was language rather than 'race' as their tribal organization permitted the integration of groups and subjects who requested it. Indeed, the Hungarians placed themselves under the protection of neighbouring peoples who were for the moment more powerful.[3]

The Slavs, Germans and Hungarians, however, did not follow the route into Central Europe nor cross the *limes* simply because they were pushed forward by other migrants coming from the East. After AD 376 when the Goths crossed the Rhine, there was another great moment in world history when in 896 the five Hungarian tribes crossed the threshold of Mukačevo. For more than five hundred years, successive invaders advanced, jostled and destroyed the fragile empires built by their predecessors on the ruins of Roman civilization.

THE BARBARIAN INVADERS[4]

This is not the place to trace in detail the history of the half-millennium which, while it might appear momentous, was in fact featureless. It will be enough to take several dates marking the stages in the settlement of the peoples who were to make Danubian Europe their homeland.

In 376 the Ostrogoths crossed the Danube. Driven forward by the Huns, they left southern Russia and sought refuge from the emperor of the West, Valens (ruled 365–78). Two hundred thousand barbarians crossed the Danube and the emperor Theodosius I (ruled 392–4) finally accepted them as members of the 'federation'. St Ambrose, the archbishop of Milan (died 397), summarized the situation thus:

The Huns have leapt over the Alans, the Alans over the Goths, the Goths, driven from their fatherland have driven us into Illyricum and this isn't the end of it all.

The real threat to the Roman provinces were the power struggles and the religious conflicts but above all the advance of the Huns.

The Huns were Tartars related to the Turks. For a long time before their arrival in Europe, they had threatened the security of the Chinese Empire: it was to keep them out that the Han emperor Shih Hwangti (ruled 221–210 BC) built the Great Wall of China. After having been defeated by the Mongols, the Huns left the frontiers of the Celestial Empire and turned towards the West. Since the Scythians occupied Turkestan, they carved out a route across the Russian plains, destroying the empire of the Alans, crossing the Volga and the Don c.370 and making contact with the Germans. The Huns were nomadic shepherds who were looking for pasture for their flocks but they also had a taste for adventure and for raiding. Their chariots served as their dwellings and they spent their life on horseback, handling the sword and lasso with skill. They were the natural enemies not only of the Roman Empire but also of all sedentary barbarians.

In 405 the Huns settled in the Danubian plain, provoking indirectly the invasion of Gaul by the Vandals (406). They organized their empire, incorporating the Germanic populations within their bands. For a while these fearsome nomads tried to follow a sedentary way of life but in 439

Attila became king of the Huns. Viewing his settlement in Hungary as temporary, he launched an attack against the Roman Empire. At first he threatened the Eastern Empire (443–50) and Theodosius II paid him tribute. He then turned against Gaul and after his defeat on the Catalaunian Fields, near Troyes (451), he invaded Italy. His empire, however, broke up; after his return to Pannonia, he died and his sons quarrelled over their inheritance. The Germans rose in rebellion and the Huns had to withdraw to the shores of the Black Sea. The barbarians had been halted for the first time but Danubian Europe had been ruined during the Huns' occupation. Forest once again took hold of lands which had been reclaimed over centuries, re-covering fields and places only lately occupied.

Last to come were the Bavarians, Germans who probably came from the steppes of southern Russia and who occupied the regions abandoned by the Huns. The description of them furnished by St Severinus is without any redeeming features; to a Roman and a Christian, the barbarians were a people governed by their unrestrained appetites and very different from the much earlier picture of the Germans drawn by Tacitus. Odoacre, knowing that the Romanized populations would be too weak to resist invasion, ordered them to leave their homeland. After 570, the Bavarians occupied the Tyrol, part of the Austrian Alps and the Danubian plain.

In 565 the Avars settled in the Danubian plain. They were Turcic tribes, the Ouigours, subject to the Mongols, related to the Huns or Avars. The Avar confederation dominated the steppes of the Volga until 555 when they offered their services to the Byzantine empire; the emperor Justinian (ruled 527–65) paid them tribute to fight his enemies, the Slavs and the Bulgars. In 565 when they ceased receiving payment from Justinian, they settled in the Danubian basin between the Danube and the Tisza, pushing the Lombards towards Italy. The Avars' success would seem due to the political genius of their khan, Bajan, who took Sirmium and negotiated tribute payments with Byzantium before besieging Thessaloniki. In 617 the Avars laid waste to the outskirts of Constantinople but shortly afterwards their vassals revolted; the Bulgars seized their independence and the northern Slavs created Great Moravia. Avar domination played an important part in establishing the Slavs in the regions where they are in the present time – either where they were before the Avars advanced or where the Avars settled them on the frontiers of their short-lived empire.

The sixth century saw another important event when Slav tribes left their original home and occupied the lands left vacant by the departing Germans. They colonized eastern Germany as far as the Elbe; from the territory of present-day Saxony, Lusatia and Silesia, in the course of the sixth century they occupied Bohemia and western Slovakia. Fleeing before the advancing Avars, the Slovenes (also Slavs) settled in Carniola and pressed on as far as the Vienna basin, taking advantage of the space left by the Roman populations: they came to a halt when they encountered a solid block of Germans (Bavarians). In 568 the Avars for a while subjected the Slavs to their rule. What is important is that the northern Slavs and the

Slovenes were finally settled in these regions. In the seventh century, they recovered their autonomy from the Avars who had been defeated by the Byzantines (626).

The first Slav principality emerged *c.* AD 630. A Frankish chief, Samo, created an embryo Slav state which disappeared after his death in 658. In the course of thirty years, he had extended his sovereignty over the Czech and Moravian tribes. His capital was in the Morava valley but the confederation he had created quickly returned to being subject to the Avars.

The Croatian tribes coming from Galicia* settled the region between the rivers Drava and Sava and were welcomed as liberators by the Slovenes. The Slavs, who were organized into tribes, were not yet ready to form coherent states. They risked being absorbed by their better-organized German neighbours. In the course of the eighth century the Slovenes of Carinthia were converted to Catholicism by German missionaries, from the Salzburg bishopric, who proceeded to found monasteries.

In 791 Danubian Europe became a zone of Frankish influence. Charlemagne, king of the Franks and Lombards, completed the work begun by the duke of Bavaria and St Boniface; he undertook a campaign against the pagan Avars, who again were posing a threat to the Church and to his empire. Leaving his base in present-day Lower Austria, in a second campaign (796–7) he drove the Franks to the edge of the Tisza where they seized the Avar camp; this defeat marked the end of the Avar empire. In the ninth century the first Slav empire was born and in 805 the last Avars, fearing their former subjects, sought Charlemagne's protection. Thus a once powerful and formidable nation disappeared. They were probably nothing more than a thin governing stratum which the Slavs absorbed. The theory that they were the ancestors of the medieval Vlachs and the modern Romanians is difficult to substantiate.

Charlemagne turned the conquered territories into a mark and distributed the lands among Bavarian clerical and lay landowners, who alone were in a position to repopulate the region quickly. Numerous serfs were sent there and settled in isolated households while the Slav inhabitants were swiftly Germanized. The land was organized according to the Bavarian model (legislation, division into counties) while the bishop of Passau extended his authority over the new 'eastern mark' and the number of churches and monasteries increased. In 798 Salzburg was raised to a metropolitan see in order to coordinate the task of rebuilding the culture in these regions. Charlemagne may with reason be considered the founder of modern Austria; although German in its language and culture and Catholic in its religion, its ethnic composition was a mixture of Romanized Celts, Bavarians and Germanized Slavs.

Great Moravia emerged during the eighth century.[5] It was a large Slav state which embraced all the western Slavs and held the tribes of Bohemia subject to it. It was centred on the Moravian–Silesian passage. The Franks,

* Translator's note: the region in Poland and western Russia.

in order to bolster their supremacy, introduced Catholicism; the first church was built c.830 at Nitra. Prince Rastislav (846–70), who had been enthroned by the king of Germany, Ludwig the German (843–76), turned towards Byzantium in a bid to escape Frankish subjugation. He complained that the missionaries did not explain 'the Faith' to his people in their own language. The Eastern Church responded by sending two missionaries, the brothers Cyril and Methodius, who in 863 arrived in Moravia. Originally from Thessaloniki, the brothers brought with them an alphabet adapted from the Greek to fit the Slav language (the so-called glagolitic alphabet), and translated the New Testament. Methodius organized the Church, introducing Eastern, or Orthodox, ritual. The papacy at first supported the work of the Byzantine missionaries but after Methodius's death in 885, his disciples were banished and the Latin liturgy was re-established in 900. It was a decisive moment for the subsequent development of the western Slavs; they would remain faithful to Roman Catholicism and to Latin Christianity. After 894 and the death of Svatopluk (who had regained power in Moravia in 872), the unity of Great Moravia like the security of the eastern mark was threatened by the advent of new pagan invaders, Hungarian nomads who represented the final wave of invaders coming from the steppe and threatened the region of modern Austria, destroying the Slav empire (902–7).

The Hungarians[6] were the last group of invaders to appear and they replaced the Avars. Forced from the Russian steppe by the Petchenegs, the five Hungarian tribes, crossed the Carpathians in 896 and went down the steep Tisza valley. Accompanied by the Khazars, Árpád's bands numbered c. 300 000 men. They occupied the central Danubian plain and Transylvania without difficulty but met resistance from the peoples of Transdanubia and the mountains of modern Slovakia. In 906 Árpád overran the Moravians and subjugated the Slovakian tribes. After ten years, Hungary was conquered. The Slav population quickly submitted and easily assimilated to Hungarian society.

For almost a century, the Hungarians kept their traditional way of life. Each year they organized expeditions to supply themselves with slaves and booty. In spring, they gathered at Székesfehérvár in Transdanubia, to the north of lake Balaton, and launched their attack upon the former Carolingian empire, which was then in complete disarray. They spread terror throughout southern Germany, extending their raids as far as Burgundy. Their large expeditions and raids were, however, stopped by the reorganization of the German kingdom and the victory of the king of Germany, Otto I, at the Battle of Lechfeld, in Bavaria (955). The Hungarians were by this time sufficiently established in their new land to give themselves over entirely to an existence as sedentary farmers and to abandon, perhaps rather half-heartedly, their profitable raids. It was only at the close of the tenth century that they assumed the final form of a Christian kingdom completely integrated within Latin Christianity, becoming, with the kingdom of Poland, one of the eastern marks bordering the Eurasian steppes and the

Byzantine world, and permanently cutting off the south Slavs from the western Slavs.

Danubian Europe around the first millennium had, then, almost taken on its lasting appearance. A balance was established among the Slavs, Hungarians and Germans, with the latter occupying the Alpine lands, where they organized the vassal states of the kingdom of Germany.

THE EASTERN MARK[7]

Otto I, king of Germany, created an eastern mark immediately after achieving his decisive victory over the Hungarians at Lechfeld. Resuming the work begun by Charlemagne, Otto chose to create a mark and to support the Hungarian state which was being organized on the Danubian plain. Henceforth the kingdom of Germany was protected by Austria and Hungary, an arrangement which would prove effective in the face of the Mongols and, much later, against the Turks. In 1002 the Vienna region was annexed to the mark. From 976 Carinthia separated itself from Bavaria and established itself as a mark which in the eleventh century annexed Istria, Friuli and the Verona district. Carniola also established itself as a mark in the eleventh century. In 1074 the Lower Austrian frontier reached as far as the Leitha. For a quarter of a century, the quarrel between the papacy and the German emperors over appointments to ecclesiastical sees paralyzed any political expansion towards the East.

Government of the mark, which was called in German *Ostrarrichi* (*Œsterreich* which the French turned into *Austriche*, then *Autriche*) was entrusted to a certain Liutpold (or Leopold), the forefather of the Babenbergs, the true creators of Austria. He installed himself in his fortified castle at Melk on the banks of the Danube where at the present time stands the magnificent Benedictine monastery overlooking the entrance to the Vienna Woods and the Wachau; he had control of the two East-West routes by land and water. The role of margrave (or marquis) was basically military as he was obliged to defend the country against its venturesome neighbours, the Czechs to the north and the Hungarians to the east. During this period one of the constants in Austrian history appeared; Austria's relations with its Slav and Hungarian neighbours.

During the eleventh century, the margrave was simply a great feudal lord among the other great lay and ecclesiastic lords, hereditary counts holding fiefs from the Carolingian era and the abbots of the great monasteries founded to safeguard the settlement, reclamation and Christianization of the mark. Austria became involved in the quarrel over ecclesiastical appointments since the Babenbergs generally supported the pope against the emperor Henry IV and endorsed the Gregorian reformation, founding the convents at Klosterneuburg and Heiligenkreuz near Vienna and endowing the Benedictines at Melk. They managed to crush the all-powerful great feudal lords. After Henry IV died, the German princes wanted to elect the margrave Liutpold, the late king of Germany's brother-in-law, a great honour which Liutpold declined in order to be free to dedicate himself to his Danubian principality. His forty-year reign (1096–1136) contributed to the establishment of Austrian power. A popular ruler, his tomb quickly became a place of pilgrimage. He was formally canonized in 1485 and in 1665 became the patron saint of Austria, like St István (Stephen) in Hungary and St Václav (Wenceslas) in Bohemia.

The emperor Frederick Barbarossa invested Liutpold's successor, Henry Jasomirgott with the mark, which was raised to the rank of a duchy (1156). The new duke also obtained the *privilegium minus* which gave the Babenbergs the right to inherit the mark and to nominate a successor should the male or female Babenberg line die out. Austria thus ceased to be simply a fief of the Empire and became a practically independent principality: no law could be put into effect without the duke's agreement; Austria received immunity from taxation; the obligation to carry out (unpaid) military service was limited to the territory of Austria. Shortly afterwards, the king of Bohemia, Vratislav, received the same privileges for his land. It was at this time that the new duke chose Vienna as his residence and founded the Scottish monastery there.

In 1192 Henry VI, Frederick Barbarossa's son, granted Styria to Leopold V as a fief, thus inaugurating the policy of peaceful reunion which gradually gathered together the Alpine provinces under the sovereign authority of Austria. Leopold VI continued the policy of consolidating his princely domain in the face of the great feudal lords while maintaining an alliance with the Hohenstaufens. Frederick II dreamt of raising Austria and Styria to the rank of a kingdom, just as his grandfather Frederick Barbarossa had raised Bohemia. The Babenberg line, however, became extinct in 1246 with the death of duke Frederick and the question was raised of who should succeed him. The Babenbergs over three centuries had turned a deserted mark into a principality that was prosperous and held in esteem by its immediate neighbours and by the other German princes in so far as the Austrian dukes had had the wisdom to avoid becoming involved in the great political quarrels which had shaken the Empire and dissipated the strength of the German kings. While aristocratic families like the Starhembergs and the Puchheims, the 'twelve apostles', were still great at the time of Frederick's death, they no longer challenged the prince's authority. The royal domain represented an essential economic and political base for the prince: at that time taxation hardly existed and the prince was obliged 'to live off his own'. The Babenbergs had followed a clever policy of close collaboration with the Church which lent them its support without placing them under its tutelage. They had opened the way for the Habsburgs.

Only the vicissitudes of thirteenth-century German political life combined with their ambition might have seemed to destine the Habsburgs for their future role as the dukes of Austria and Styria.

NOTES AND REFERENCES

1. Hugo Hantsch, *Die Geschichte Œsterreichs*, 2 vols, Vienna, Styria, 1951, vol. 1, pp. 13–39: *Die Welt des römischen Reiches* (hereafter Hantsch).
2. A. Fichelle, 'Le Monde slave', in *Histoire universelle*, vol. 2, pp. 1109–28, *Encyclopédie de la Pléiade*, Paris, 1957.
3. Ervin Pamlenyi (ed.) 'La préhistoire ougrienne', *Histoire de la Hongrie*, Roanne, 1974, pp. 39–51 (hereafter Pamlenyi).
4. Ferdinand Lot, *Les Invasions barbares*, Paris, 1949.
   Pamlenyi, pp. 24–35.
5. Jörg K. Hoensch, 'Auf dem Wege zur Staatsbildung', in *Geschichte Böhmens: von der slavischen Landnahme bin ins 20. Jahrhundert*, Munich, 1987, pp. 32–43.
6. Pamlenyi, pp. 47–51.
   Denis Sinor, 'The earliest period of Hungarian–Turkic relations', in G. Ranki (ed.) *Hungarian History–World History*, Budapest, 1984. pp. 1–12.
7. Hantsch, 'Die deutschen Marken des Ostens', vol. 1, pp. 40–54.

CHAPTER THREE

The Acquisition of Austria (1278)

The Habsburgs acquired Austria through a process customary in the Middle Ages and set down in the framework of feudal law: when the male line of a princely family died out, the sovereign was authorized to grant the domain as a fief to whoever struck him as most capable of assuming the obligations of a vassal. In 1246 the death of the last Babenberg, Frederick the Quarrelsome, in battle against the Hungarians raised two problems: the question of who should receive Austria as a fief from the emperor and the danger that either the Slav kingdom of Bohemia or the kingdom of Hungary might annex what had formerly been the *Östmark*, the Eastern March.

Austria, to its great misfortune, suffered an interregnum at the same time as the Empire and monastic chroniclers were quick to realize that not only feudal anarchy but also more seriously their Czech and Hungarian neighbours threatened the country and its people. They repeated the lament, 'Austria, alas, has been deprived of its prince and rightful heirs to the woe of the land and its inhabitants'. A little later a feudal lord, Ulrich von Liechtenstein, described in his chronicle the grave consequences of the interregnum:

After (the duke Frederick), great was the wretchedness in Austria and Styria. More than one who had lately been rich found himself poor. There were untold injustices; the countryside was ransacked day and night which is why many villages were deserted. The rich took goods from the poor and lost their dignity.

Frederick had left just one niece, Gertrude, who was married to a Bohemian prince shortly to become the margrave Hermann of Bade. In 1156, through the *privilegium minus*,[1] the Babenberg dukes had secured Austria's exemption from the general provisions of feudal law so that a woman could be the legitimate heir. However, the sons of Frederick's two sisters, Margaret and Constance, were also in a position to put forward claims to the patrimony. Once again there was a need for a strong imperial authority able to impose a solution but the Hohenstaufens had concerns elsewhere and were indifferent to the fate of the German world's eastern marks; they were confronted by the local barons and the kings of Bohemia and Hungary.

FEUDAL SOCIETY AND ITS TENDENCIES TOWARDS ANARCHY

Hermann von Altaich (d.1275) described without mincing his words the failings of a decentralized society where, during a disputed succession, the state is generally weak and all but non-existent:

No one can describe or recount such sufferings as were endured by the two provinces during the six years following the death of duke Frederick, for all the nobles, and perhaps the common masses just as much, did what they wanted without fear of God or man. Those who did not manage to flee to a secure place or a cave were captured, brutally treated, killed or tortured with unimaginable and hitherto unknown torments.

Von Altaich's account describes a genuine breakdown of the feudal society which, after the model of the Frankish kingdoms, had become one of the common characteristics of Danubian Europe. The Slavs and Magyars had progressively abandoned the tribal structure in favour of the German model which had prevailed to the end of the Carolingian era.

A measure of specialization in labour had confined the peasant to the production of material goods while those who fought, who prayed and who traded lived directly or indirectly from the peasants' toil. The mounted warrior was provided with land and could support himself, his horse, squire and family from its revenue. By an inevitable process, he also became the lord of the manor, the feudal lord, in German *der Grundherr*, in French *le seigneur*. The priest was assimilated to the warrior and became a landowner. Only the merchants remained on the margin, neither peasant nor lord, living in the modest small towns which had withstood the great invasions.

This specialization conferred some benefit on the peasant since the lord of the manor guaranteed his security, but it was accompanied by the pronounced polarization of society with the warrior as the noble at one end of the heirarchy and the peasant at the other as the common man. A great number of the clergy and the princes' immediate servants were assimilated to the nobility: these were the famous German *ministeriales*,* while in

---

* Translator's note: the *ministeriales* emerged as a social group distinct from the serfs within the great ruling and ecclesiastical households during the eleventh century. Still unfree, they performed specialized tasks as warriors and in administration. See Timothy Reuter, *Germany in the Early Middle Ages*, (London, 1991), pp. 231–2.

Hungary all freemen were considered nobles. Merchants and artisans at first were assimilated to the peasantry but gradually acquired privileges in those market towns under the prince's protection.

The fundamental socio-political unit was the manor (German, *Grundherrschaft*, French *seigneurie*) which lasted until the revolutions of 1848. Relations between the lord of the manor and the peasants were based on servitude, the grant of a plot of land and the lord of the manor's role as the guardian of his peasants. The condition of servitude was a continuation of the practice of the ancient societies; it was a legal status which progressively fell from use in the course of the Middle Ages. The number of slaves, which had been so great under the 'barbarians', was reduced and presently included only household slaves (*familiares*). The rest, like the free peasants, held a tenure and increasingly became assimilated to the tenant class. The low density of population made a man an item of value and the lord of the manor entered into a contract with a colonist-farmer who was prepared to bring his land into cultivation. The colonist received a basic house, meadows, fields and the right to use the woods. In return he would apply himself to developing the land and would pay the lord of the manor a portion, fixed in advance, of his harvest. This contractual arrangement could be annulled by either party. The peasant was thus assured of his existence and the feudal lord of his income. Tenure became hereditary. The peasant became *de facto* proprietor of his house and fields and the lord of the manor owned the land and was content to levy a portion of his peasants' harvest without the worry of having to work it. The vast extent of his domain offset the small amount of the levy.

In Austria in the tenth century the lord of the manor was also transformed into the protector of the peasant, whom he was pledged to defend, thus taking the place of 'public power'. This role of protector spread progressively over the whole of Danubian Europe. The tenant was under obligation to assist the lord of the manor, paying tax and providing labour services. He took an oath to the lord, who promised him protection. The lord of the manor in turn pledged his loyalty and homage to his own feudal lord, the margrave of Austria, the duke of Styria or the duke of Bohemia. This personal link of man to man was the very basis of feudalism. It spread to Hungary where the service nobility established by St István was gradually transformed into a feudal nobility dominated by the barons, who possessed vast domains and were surrounded by a clientele of less wealthy freemen (the lesser nobility). The barons often created what amounted to principalities based on their own wealth and encroachment upon the royal domain.

Added to the lord of the manor's obligation to protect his subjects' person and goods was the right to exercise justice at the manorial level. He could punish his peasants, a right which became the right of high and low justice. Gradually he came to exercise criminal and civil justice over all the inhabitants of the manor. This encroachment upon royal power gave the nobility an extraordinary amount of power which lasted until the modern era. From the thirteenth century, princely jurisdiction was for the mass of commoners exercised only over the criminal cases, and then only on appeal. Only the nobles were truly accountable to the princely courts.

Another characteristic of feudal society in Central Europe was that the clergy was assimilated to the great landowners. Bishoprics and Benedictine abbeys were often princely foundations richly endowed with lands, for example the abbeys of St George at Prague, at Melk in Lower Austria and Pannonhalma in Hungary. These great abbeys played a role in the economy. They contributed to the reclamation and development of the land but most importantly had a cultural role since they enjoyed the right of patronage over countless parishes and took part in the evangelization of the population through the parish priests whom they planted throughout the countryside. In addition they spread Latin culture, maintaining the liturgy and gradually imposing the Latin rite upon the masses, who had until lately been pagan or else favoured the Slavonic liturgies. They kept and copied sacred texts and Latin literature. In a world where the secular clergy were still too small in number and bishoprics were few and far between, parishes depended on the goodwill of the feudal lords, who were obliged to found more parishes and to endow pastors with benefices. The abbeys under these circumstances played an important role in drawing Danubian Europe into the sphere of Christian Latinity; first came the Benedictines, then the Cistercians, while in the thirteenth century mendicant orders operated in the towns. The Church in the early Middle Ages was able to take root only because it had assimilated the ruling class, the feudal lords and warriors, and because it was richly endowed with lands, then the only base of power and prestige. Among the Slavs and Hungarians, it was the kings who led the conversion to Christianity; conversion was a political decision intended to preserve the principle of national independence in the face of the German Church which, supported by its own political apparatus, urged further conquest the better to Christianize the pagans.

Conversion to Christianity had a natural corollary: in the tenth century the nations that were settled in Danubian Europe formed states with monarchies after the Frankish model, where one family more powerful than the rest monopolized the royal title and shared power with the magnates of the kingdom while the Church, as in the Frankish kingdom from the time of Clovis, associated its destiny with that of the national dynasties. Charlemagne, in German *Karl der Große*, the name of the great king of the Franks and emperor of the West, became in Slavonic *Kral* and in Magyar *Király* and so gave the Czechs and Hungarians their word for 'king'.

Austria, Styria and the other Alpine provinces, however, were unable to form a sovereign kingdom and were coveted by the local great feudal lords as well as by other kings. Philip, the archbishop of Salzburg, took part in the scramble and reclaimed a number of domains over which he claimed to have inalienable rights. This was why the local nobility quickly realized the threat from outside and challenged the claims made by foreigners. Their efforts were in vain: Otakar II Přemysl created an empire stretching from Saxony to the Adriatic (with the exception of the lands of the king of

Hungary) and for the first time realized the union – albeit temporary – of Austria and Bohemia, to the benefit of the Slav kingdom which was then a formidible power in that part of Europe.

OTAKAR II PŘEMYSL AND THE KINGDOM OF BOHEMIA[2]

In the course of the ninth century the Slavs occupying the quadrilateral of Bohemia gradually became separate from Great Moravia. In the tenth century, the Czech tribe around Prague regrouped and formed a national state under the authority of a national dynasty, the Přemyslids, who counted among their number Otakar II. The Czechs stopped bringing into cultivation the surrounding mountains and instead devoted themselves to the more fertile lands of the central depression.

The supposed founder of the dynasty, Přemysl the Ploughman (Přemysl Oráč), was little more than a mythical hero. The first known prince was Borivoj, who in 875 was baptized in Moravia and in 890 began to build the first church in the country. In 895 his sons Spythinev and Vratislav took an oath of loyalty to Arnulf of Carinthia, then king of east Francia and later emperor (896–9). Spythinev encouraged the evangelization of his subjects, a policy which was continued by Vratislav (905–21).

His son Václav, who assumed power in 924 at the age of seventeen, had received a Christian education. He reigned for only five years but he made a lasting mark upon national history as he proved to have the qualities of a statesman. He stifled the intrigues within his entourage, who had remained for the most part pagan: conversion to Christianity for them signified subordination to their powerful German neighbour, while for Václav it represented the best way to preserve his independence. He maintained friendly relations with king Henry I 'the Fowler' (919–36, previously Henry duke of Saxony) who offered him the royal crown. However Václav, though, was assassinated c.935 by his brother, Boleslav I 'the Cruel' (duke of Bohemia, 929–67), and was later canonized, becoming the patron saint of Bohemia (St Václav). Boleslav I depended on the national and anti-Catholic party, which was unhappy about the political alliance with Germany, but this combination of forces brought the Czechs little benefit. After fifteen years of warfare, Otto I 'the Great' (king 936–73, crowned emperor 962) defeated the Czechs and imposed vassal status upon them. Bohemia henceforth would be a fief of the Holy Roman Empire, unlike Hungary which was never incorporated into the *Reich*. The dukes of Bohemia were obliged to appear at the court of the German kings, to follow them to war and to accompany them to Rome.

The Prague bishopric was founded in 973 by the king of Germany, not by duke Boleslav II (the son of Boleslav I). The Přemyslids, however, retained the royal rights. In the eleventh century Bretislav, duke of Bohemia (1034–55), who dreamt of reviving Great Moravia, tried to cast off German suzerainty, but the emperor Henry III (1039–56) crushed the Czechs and Bretislav was obliged to go to Ratisbon in 1041 to seek pardon and to ask to be invested with Bohemia. Consequently Bohemia supported Henry III against the Hungarians and Henry IV (1056–1106) against pope Gregory VII (c. 1020–85, also known as Hildebrand) in the quarrel over investitures. As reward, Wratislav was awarded as a personal title the status of king. Later, in 1212, Otakar I obtained the title of king from Frederick II in return for having supported the Hohenstaufen cause (Golden Bull of Sicily). Bohemia would henceforth be an autonomous state, the succession would be the concern of the kingdom and the king of the Romans alone, and the emperor would automatically grant the investiture of the new sovereign; the king of Bohemia would appoint the bishops and would put no more than 300 soldiers at the disposal of the king of the Romans for the journey into Italy. As the king-duke of Bohemia was also the grand cupbearer of the *Reich*, he was, from the beginning of the eleventh century, an elector; although he was not German, he thus took part in making a political choice of prime importance for the kingdom of Germany. At the end of the thirteenth century, under Rudolf I of Habsburg, the electoral title of king of Bohemia was beyond dispute (the royal crown of St Václav (Wenceslas) is a masterpiece of fourteenth-century jeweller's art).[3]

The Golden Bull of emperor Charles IV (1356), which finally regulated the election of the king of the Romans, confirmed the position of Bohemia. Its king became the foremost lay elector and kept the use of royal rights, its inhabitants escaping the jurisdiction of the courts of the Empire (the privilege of *non evocando* and *non appellando*). The Prague See was raised to the rank of a metropolitan see and ceased to be subject to the archbishop of Mainz. The archbishop had the honour of crowning the king and as the first holder of the title, Ernest of Pardubice, was the confidant of Charles IV, he became the second most eminent person in the state.

The right of succession under the Přemyslids was very complicated. The duke before his death appointed the oldest and held to be the most competent among his relatives, while his children would receive apanages.* In the twelfth century this system led to serious quarrels over the succession, which enabled Frederick Barbarossa, the emperor, to make several interventions. The idea of primogeniture emerged under Otakar I: the king had his eldest son elected during his own lifetime. The brutal death of Václav III in 1306 raised, however, a new problem concerning the succession because the male line of the Přemyslids died out with him. The

---

* Translator's note: apanage refers to a portion of the royal domain given to the cadets of the royal house as compensation for their exclusion from the crown.

king of the Romans, Albert of Habsburg, granted Bohemia as a fief to his son Rudolf but the operation failed and his successor, Henry VII (Henry of Luxemburg), granted Bohemia as a fief to his own son, John of Luxemburg (1310, John 'the Blind') who married Eliška Přemyslovna (sister of Václav III). The new Luxemburg dynasty, which had possessions in the Netherlands, posed far less of a threat to the Czech state as it was completely assimilated to French culture and could counterbalance German influence. It quickly proved to be a true national dynasty like the Angevins (the Anjou dynasty of Naples), in Hungary. Moreover, the Czech nobility readily paid homage to the new king. The Luxemburg dynasty continued for more than a century, in 1347 achieving union with the imperial crown and in the fifteenth century embodying in the person of Sigismund the union of the crowns of Hungary and Bohemia and the Empire, a foreshadowing of the political configurations of the modern period.

The kingdom of Bohemia consisted of the incorporated provinces as well as the Czechs' fatherland. The margravate of Moravia came under the Poles c.1000 and was annexed in 1029 by duke Bretislav of Bohemia, who gave it as a fief to his son. Moravia henceforth was part of the kingdom of Bohemia and often served as an apanage for the cadets of the Přemyslid House. A fief of the Empire under Frederick Barbarossa, it was made a dependency of the Bohemian fief under Charles IV of Luxemburg. Possession of the duchy of Silesia was disputed between Poland and Bohemia; in the tenth century Silesia was half Czech, but at the end of the twelfth century it was annexed by Poland and Upper Silesia was divided into numerous principalities. In 1327 it was conquered by John of Luxemburg, who wanted to defend his rather questionable rights (i.e. homage paid in the past by certain princes of Upper Silesia) while the duke of Breslau ceded Lower Silesia to him. Charles IV completed the acquisition of Silesia, which kept its status as an autonomous principality and vassal of the king of Bohemia. Lusatia had been acquired in the eleventh century when in 1076 the emperor Henry IV gave it as a fief to duke Wratislav of Upper Lusatia (Bautzen and Görlitz). A sister of king Otakar II, however, brought it to the margrave of Brandenburg as part of her dowry. After the death of the last Ascanian, the margrave Waldemar (1319), the king of Bohemia, John of Luxemburg, recovered Upper Lusatia; his son Charles IV bought back Lower Lusatia in 1367. The principality of Eger was given by Ludwig of Bavaria to John of Luxemburg as a pledge valued at 20 000 silver marks in return for Bohemia's support in the imperial election. Eger was placed under the king's authority and was totally exempt from taxation; it was never again tied to the kingdom whereas Moravia and Silesia were fiefs of the crown of Bohemia and enjoyed autonomy within the kingdom and are often referred to as incorporated provinces.

The kingdom of Bohemia's administration was modelled on that of the Franks. The sovereign (the duke, then later the king) governed with the aid of his relatives and grand officers whose duties were chiefly at court: the chamberlain, the marshal, the esquire trenchant, the cupbearer as well as the grand judge, the grand huntsman and the master of the horse. The office of chancellor appeared *c*.1150 and was replaced in the thirteenth century by that of protonotary. Under Otakar II Prague became the administrative centre, to be precise the seat of the supreme court of law presided over by the grand judge, the court of appeal of the provincial courts and also the special tribunal for the aristocracy to which all the judges of the supreme tribunal belonged. In the course of the Middle Ages, the chamberlain assumed an increasingly important role as he was responsible for the good administration of the royal domain; in the thirteenth century an assistant officer of the chamber was concerned with jurisdiction over the towns and Jewish communities. Indeed, the chamberlain had control of the royal finances. The grand burgrave of Prague had control over the burgraves of the circles. In imitation of the Frankish system, the territory was divided into cantons (Czech, *župa*). Each canton was placed under the supervision of a castle governed by a burgrave (*župan*; Latin *comes*) who was appointed by the duke and was often drawn from among the regional nobility.

The burgrave's duties were military and administrative. He was assisted by a chamberlain, a steward (responsible for the management of the royal domains) and a judge who was president of the district court. Since the noble families monopolized the office of burgrave, Otakar II regrouped the cantons into circles (Czech *Kreš;* German *Kreis*), which until the twentieth century remained the basic administrative districts. Each circle's court was installed in the main seat of the circle and Otakar II appointed for each two judges (*popravči*) drawn from among the barons of the region; they were responsible for administering criminal jusice and maintaining order. The circle's finances were entrusted to a special receiver.

Otakar II was a formidible opponent; the only other ruler in the region who approached him in might was the king of Hungary, Béla IV, whose domain, while in theory vast, was for the moment weakened by the Mongol invasion.

THE KINGDOM OF HUNGARY

In 896 Árpád and his followers, around 300 000 Magyars and Khazars, without difficulty occupied the Danubian plain, but it was only at the end of the tenth century that Hungary assumed the semblance of a Christian kingdom and gradually became integrated with the West. Its political organization was the work of its king István (997–1038).*

* Translator's note: the dates of István's reign are often given as 1000–38, the date of his coronation by tradition being Christmas Day 1000.

Hungary lay between the expanding German and the still vigorous Byzantine empires; István, who had been baptized in 985, realized that he could not postpone his country's conversion to Christianity. His genuine espousal of Christianity was a political act no less than had been the Czech princes' conversion at the beginning of the tenth century. To prevent Hungary from becoming a dependency of the German Empire, István who married a Bavarian princess, Gisela, turned to the Holy See for support, declaring himself to be its vassal. Hungary never became a province of the Empire although some emperors became kings of Hungary. Pope Sylvester II sent him the crown which, with a Byzantine diadem, constituted the celebrated 'Holy Crown of Hungary', the essential symbol of Hungarian statehood. From this period onwards the rulers of Hungary took the title of 'apostolic king'.[4]

Following the final abolition of the tribal system, István organized his country after the Frankish model. The territory of Hungary was divided into counties or comitats, areas of *c.*3 000 sq km around a royal castle entrusted to a royal agent, the count or *ispán*. Appointed by the sovereign and also subject to dismissal by him, the count was the military chief (he commanded the other royal castles of the comitat), and the judge-delegate. The maintenance of these fortresses and their garrisons was entrusted to the lands and peasants of the royal domain. István, like the Frankish kings, governed with the aid of grand officers who had duties both at court (grand cupbearer, grand pantler, master of the horse) and in the administration (treasurer, grand judge and perhaps already at this time, palatine). The king reserved a special place for priests; the chancellor, in principle, was always a prelate assisted by clergymen for the simple reason that for five hundred years Latin was the written language to the exclusion of all others and the clergy were the experts in Latin. István organized the Church, endowing it with important domains, but kept the right of patronage for the crown. He created eight dioceses dependent on two metropolitan bishoprics, Kalocsa and Esztergóm (Latin, Strigonium; German, Gran), the latter with Szekesféhérvár being the king's preferred residences. The first bishops were generally foreigners, Germans or Italians. The Church also received the right to collect the tithe throughout the kingdom. Created by a king confronted by a people for the most part pagan, the Church from its earliest days maintained the habit of submission of political authority. István encountered opposition from a party of aristocrats still attached to paganism and the tribal organization and who were in addition hostile to foreign influences. Many uprisings followed: the revolts of Koppany in 998 then of Ajtony in 1002. Half a century later, difficulties over the succession provoked a fresh anti-Christian uprising. István was without a direct heir since his son Imre (Emmerich) had died in 1031. Passing over his brother and his brother's sons, he chose as his successor his nephew Pietro Orseolo, the son of his sister and Otto Orseolo of Venice. Pietro was supported by the Church and the emperor Henry III, who supplied arms to establish him on the throne (1044). The Hungarians, however, rose up against him once again in 1046, dethroned and blinded him according to Byzantine practice. He died from his wounds. István's cousin, András I (Andrew, 1047–60) subdued the agitators, who were using religious motifs to destroy István's political achievement, and restored order. Presently, those who were opposed to German and Roman influence turned for support to Byzantium, which had broken with Rome in 1054. They gave the Holy Crown to the brother of Géza I, László (Ladislas, 1077–1095), who succeeded in converting Hungary to Christianity, passing strict laws against the last adherents of paganism. While remaining completely loyal to the Roman Church, he maintained good relations with Byzantium, arranging the marriage of his daughter to the future emperor of Byzantium, John II Comnenus. Like István, László was later canonized and also became the national saint of Hungary. Intervening in Croatia, he prepared the union of the kingdom of Croatia-Dalmatia with Hungary, thereby opening up for his country a direct route to the Adriatic.

Linked to the religious question was the other great problem facing the Hungarian monarchy – to maintain a balance of power with the aristocracy. The nobility created by István was in principle a service nobility but in practice there was a tendency for offices to become hereditary and the magnates tried to surround themselves with a clientele of freemen. László favoured the development of towns as a way of curtailing the great increases in the authority of the nobles and created royal free towns while his son Kálmán (Coloman, 1095–1116) arranged the return to the royal domain of those fiefs left without an heir. To maintain a better level of surveillance over the more far-flung provinces, Kálmán instituted governors (the *voïvode* in Transylvania, the *ban* in Croatia) whose duty was to oversee the counties. In 1104 he forswore the right to appoint bishops and promised to respect the freedom of episcopal elections. After Kálmán's death, Hungary suffered a period of troubles over the succession; royal authority was not restored until king Béla III (1172–96). He allowed the aristocrats to keep those lands which they claimed but stood firm on the issue of military service. To increase the revenues of the crown, which until then had come only from the royal domains, he introduced the first royal taxes: customs, tolls and rights over markets and fairs. Trouble with the nobility came to a head under András II (1204–1235). After the king's return from the crusades (1218), the nobles rebelled and in 1222 obtained a Golden Bull which bears many similarities to the *Magna Carta* imposed upon the English king John (1215): it served as the basis for noble liberties within the kingdom, guaranteed the rights of freemen and the inhabitants of towns, promised the regular convocation of representatives of the nobility (the Hungarian Diet) and gave them the right to take up arms against royal power (*jus resistendi*) if the king did not respect their privileges.

In the thirteenth century, the great problem confronting the Hungarian state and society was to confront the last wave of invaders from Central Asia, the Mongols. Gengis Khan had founded an empire that stretched from China to Russia. After his death in 1227, his steppe empire was divided among his sons who for thirty years continued with its expansion. No army was capable of resisting these horsemen armed with bows and arrows and many peoples fled before the invading forces. Among these fugitives were the Cumanians (*Kunok*) who were settled by king Béla IV in the part of Hungary between the Danube and the Tisza which still bears their name (*Kunság*).

The Mongols' advance seemed irresistible. The Bulgars' Volga kingdom fell in 1237, Russia was conquered 1237–40 and in 1241 it was Poland and Hungary's turn to suffer the Mongol hordes. In April 1241 they overran Silesia, Moravia and Hungary, wiping out the royal army at Mohi, pillaging the land and slaughtering the inhabitants. Béla IV took refuge in Dalmatia. Central Europe was saved by chance: the Grand Khan, Gengis Khan's successor, died and the Mongol chiefs returned to Central Asia to decide the succession and never again set out. It remained for Béla IV to rebuild the ruins: this is why he is often considered 'second founder' of his country. Hungary had had to pay a high price for being 'the thoroughfare of Christendom' whereas Austria and Bohemia had been spared the Tartar-Mongol invasions (the Tartar auxiliaries then worked for the Mongols whose vassals they were). The summer of 1241 had serious consequences for the country's development.[5]

To prevent the recurrence of such disasters, Béla IV fortified and granted privileges to towns like Visegrád, Pressburg and Buda which became the capital and royal residence. He gave the barons permission to build fortresses on their lands and to fortify the small towns which depended on them. From this period onwards the barons added military power to their economic power, which rested on their possession of large domains. Henceforth they constituted a formidable political force capable of counterbalancing the power of the king.

It is impossible to quantify the extent of the catastrophe. In an attempt to repopulate the country, Béla IV, 'the second founder', appealed for large numbers of foreign colonists; Germans and Vlachs in Transylvania, Ruthenians and Slovaks in Upper Hungary. In this way, the non-native nuclei, the Slavs and Romanians, were strengthened and much later, in the nineteenth century, would complicate the nationality question. Most importantly, the gap left by the Hungarians and Magyarized Slavs made possible the first German expansion. The Saxons received extensive privileges in Transylvania where they constituted a privileged *natio* alongside the Hungarians; peasants from Middle Germany, between the Rhine and the Elbe, peopled entire villages and maintained their language and original culture.

THE ACQUISITION OF AUSTRIA BY OTAKAR II PŘEMYSL

Paradoxically it was Béla IV who tried to obtain pledges and gave his vassals in eastern Hungary permission to carry out raids against Austria and Styria during which peasants were taken away and held captive on the Hungarian barons' estates which, following the Mongol invasion, needed to be repopulated.

The feudal lords of Styria saw as the only course open to them to place themselves under the protection of the powerful Přemyslid dynasty of Bohemia. Interpreting somewhat freely the privilege granted by Frederick in 1156, they claimed the right to choose their duke's successor in the event of the extinction of the male line of the ruling house and accordingly decided upon Otakar, the son of the king of Bohemia and margrave of Moravia. Otakar promptly married the duchess Margaret, the widow of Frederick the Quarrelsome, despite the difference in their ages (she was forty, he was twenty-two). Naturally for political reasons, Otakar had first sought the pope's permission. He then concluded an agreement with Béla IV whereby he ceded to Hungary the eastern part of Styria as far as Semmering.

Finally in 1260 Otakar II, who meanwhile had become king of Bohemia, resolved the conflict in his own best interests and after defeating the king of Hungary, István V, at Kroissenbrunn, forced him to cede to him Austria and the whole of Styria. The king of Bohemia had achieved his purpose by combining many factors: first and foremost a clever marriage strategy, dubious judicial titles, the support of the local nobility, which preferred a Slav suzerain to a Hungarian king, all combined with undeniable military and economic power.

Nine years later the Spanheimer line was extinguished with duke Ulrich, who since 1268 had made Otakar heir to his entire estate. Carinthia thus passed under the authority of the king of Bohemia who found himself master of the area of present-day Austria with the exception of the Tyrol. In 1271 the governor of Styria appointed by Otakar, Ulrich von Dürrenholz, managed to conquer Carniola and installed himself as the captain-general of Friuli.

On the eve of the election to the German throne, Otakar's position in Central Europe was remarkable. This energetic and ambitious prince had created for the first time in history a state stretching from the Sudeten mountains to the shores of the Adriatic and had united under his sceptre the north Slavs (the Czechs) and the south Slavs (Slovenes of Carniola). His position within the Empire was second to none and no one dreamt of opposing so powerful a monarch. Austria benefited from his rule because his authority was so great that he could impose order on the vassals and procured peace for his subjects, especially for the abbeys and towns. Otakar understood the importance of urban culture and consequently introduced more privileges favouring the merchants and artisans. Although he undertook a crusade into eastern Prussia and founded Königsberg, he did not especially favour the Church. Most importantly, however, the lords who had summoned him were ready to submit to his authority and he had no qualms about retrieving those ducal domains which they had appropriated during the time of troubles. This uncompromising policy earned him many enemies among the great feudal lords of Austria who waited for the first chance to cast off his too burdensome tutelage.

In 1273 Austria, like the Empire, found itself at a critical juncture. How the Austro-Bohemian state founded by Otakar II might have developed is a matter for speculation but it is reasonable to suppose that such a combination would have been to the long term advantage of the kingdom of Bohemia, the Slav Přemyslid dynasty and the Czech nation. Bohemia's peculiar character was already sufficiently strong to effect a union in its own best interests and to prevent German expansion into south-east Europe; Austria might have lost its character as a German province. This was how the cards were stacked as far as the success of Rudolf was concerned.[6]

RUDOLF OF HABSBURG'S INTERVENTION[7]

Otakar II, angry that such a nonentity as the count of Habsburg should present himself as a rival candidate for the throne of Germany, did not even take part in the royal election of 1273 since the German princes had blocked his candidacy, not because he was a Slav but because they feared that the demands he would make upon them would be too great.

Rudolf of Habsburg, after receiving in 1274 assurance from the pope of his unconditional support, turned his attention towards the eastern part of the kingdom of Germany. Instead of summoning his vassals to accompany him on the traditional journey into Italy to be crowned emperor at Rome, he preferred to devote his energy to restoring order and royal authority north of the Alps. Otakar II had set himself up as succesor to the Babenbergs in a way which was hardly in accordance with feudal law and his right to hold Austria, Styria, Carinthia, Carniola and Friuli was open to dispute: he held Carniola and Friuli only through force of arms and by conquest, while his marriage to Margaret, the widow of the last Babenberg, provided him with only a weak title to Austria and Styria which had never been seriously confirmed during the Great Interregnum. Rudolf as the new king of Germany was therefore quite warranted in summoning Otakar II before the Diet to justify himself and to obtain, legitimately this time, the right to hold all the Austrian provinces as a fief. This procedure was quite regular and was not unusual at that time: the kings of France acted in the same way. There is nothing to prove that had Otakar II appeared in court, Rudolf I would have refused to recognize the existing situation since his adversary governed his new acquisitions as a good Christian prince.

By refusing to appear, Otakar II made the most serious mistake of his reign. Angry at the election of 'a poor count of Habsburg' – it was he who coined the phrase – he considered it beneath his dignity to answer this summons from a new sovereign whom he did not recognize. He did not understand that the situation in Germany had changed considerably and that the Interregnum was at an end. He did not even condescend to reply to the first summons to appear at Würzburg. He answered the second summons by sending to Augsburg his best adviser, the eloquent Werner von Seckau, whose Latin speech, however, did not prevent the Diet from pronouncing a sentence of condemnation: Otakar II held the Austrian fiefs illegally and Rudolf was charged with carrying out the sentence.

It was then that the 'Lion of Bohemia's' difficulties began. Frederick, the archbishop of Salzburg, took sides against him. The wealthiest Styrian feudal lords, including the Liechtensteins, met at the monastery at Rein on 19 November 1276 to swear loyalty to Rudolf of Habsburg. Urged on by the papacy, which was hostile to Otakar, the mendicant monks rose against him. Suddenly, his government seemed tyrannical and his officers were put to flight while even Werner von Seckau abandoned him.

Rudolf of Habsburg once more employed his political acumen. He sought support from all quarters and had the wit to buy off potential opponents. He married his son Albert to Elizabeth, the daughter of the powerful count of the Tyrol, Meinhard II, to whom he granted Carinthia as a fief. He also concluded an alliance with the king of Hungary, László IV, holding out to him the possibility of recovering eastern Styria. Finally he obtained the support of the powerful duke of Bavaria, Henry, giving him his daughter in marriage with the region of present-day Upper Austria as a pledge for her dowry. He was then in a position to lead an army of 3 000 knights from the Rhineland, Swabia and Franconia. The foundations of the Habsburgs' real power in Germany were sketched out for the first time: the support of the papacy, the backing of the majority of the imperial Diet, the alliance with Bavaria, the accord, albeit a fragile one, with the Hungarians, and most importantly the deployment of diplomacy and armed forces.

After the count Palatine captured Klosterneuburg (Lower Austria), Rudolf's army laid siege to Vienna, his support increasing all the while. Otakar II then agreed to negotiate beneath the walls of Vienna and signed a peace treaty, based on compromise, with Rudolf (26 November 1276): Rudolf agreed to invest him with the kingdom of Bohemia and the margravate of Moravia, both fiefs of the Empire, and a double marriage was planned between their children whereby Jutta of Habsburg would bring as part of her dowry the northern part of Lower Austria (modern *Waldviertel*) thereby extending the kingdom of Bohemia right to the gates of Vienna. Otakar II, however, did not favour this compromise, which cost the Habsburgs dear, seeing in it only the loss of a significant part of his recent acquisitions rather than the enlargement of the kingdom of Bohemia. As a contemporary commentator observed, since it was by taking hold of the Babenberg inheritance that Otakar had become powerful, he could not countenance so considerable a retreat.

For this reason, he chanced his luck for the last time. He sought allies, turning to Poland in a direct call upon Slav solidarity. He enlisted Saxon and Bavarian knights in his army and prepared to reconquer his lost provinces by force. Rudolf I meanwhile, following the signing of the peace, had reorganized the imperial army. In 1278 his troops had a more pronounced 'Danubian' character: Austrian and Styrian knights were ranged *en masse* beneath his banner. He also received valuable support from László of Hungary. The decisive blow came on 26 August 1278, at Dürnkrut in the Marchfeld where the Morava river opens into the Danubian plain.

THE BATTLE OF DÜRNKRUT AND ITS CONSEQUENCES[8]

The Battle of Dürnkrut was a remarkable cavalry battle in which both opponents employed all their forces and engaged all their being. Otakar II died in combat, slain by his cupbearer, Berthold von Emerberg, who wanted to be avenged upon the king of Bohemia for having ordered the execution of his parents. Few medieval battles had such serious consequences as that at Dürnkrut. It marked the end of the dream of a great Slav kingdom, the salvation of German Austria but also the starting-point for the Habsburgs' fortunes in the part of Europe where they would one day rebuild the Austro-Bohemian state of Otakar. The destiny of the Czech nation would henceforth be confined to Bohemia and Moravia, even though, in the fourteenth century, the kingdom of St Wenceslas would expand towards the north and east. In the future the House of Habsburg became the House of Austria, assured of a European destiny.

Rudolf I decided to follow up the victory at Dürnkrut and promptly continued the offensive in the direction of Moravia and Bohemia. As master of the situation, he endeavoured to act with moderation; he granted the kingdom of Bohemia as a fief to Václav II Přemysl, his son-in-law and Otakar II's legitimate heir, and set aside the case of Moravia.

With respect to the Alpine provinces, Rudolf was inspired by the policy of the Hohenstaufens, who had wanted to take hold of that region of the Empire, and kept the Babenberg patrimony for his own House, thus using the royal crown of Germany to increase considerably the Habsburg family patrimony. Formally, Rudolf governed Austria just as in 1282 by virtue of his royal prerogative. He passed laws, renewed and extended privileges, secured the loyalty of the barons. He travelled continuously in Austria and Styria and made Vienna his residence, granting it the status of a free city (*Reichsstadt*). Before the Diet of Augsburg in December 1282, he granted Styria and Austria as fiefs to his sons Albert and Rudolf, without appropriating them personally. In 1286 he rewarded his ally the duke of Tyrol by granting him the duchy of Carinthia as a fief.

Austria therefore became a possession of the Habsburgs in 1282 and would remain without interruption under their rule until 1918. The Habsburgs had time to establish themselves there and perhaps loyalty to the monarchy was strongest in Austria, where they were viewed as the 'natural lords' of the land in a way which happened much later in the Tyrol. Although foreign, the new dynasty was able to make itself accepted once the generation which had lived through the conflict over the succession had died out. The changes of fortune which the Habsburgs suffered in the fourteenth century, however, forced them to retreat temporarily from their new domains.

Rudolf, after ensuring for his descendants a substantial patrimony, devoted the final years of his reign to founding a royal dynasty. His efforts, though, were in vain. He was unable to secure his son Albert's election during his lifetime and did not have himself crowned emperor because he was not prepared to take the risks entailed in travelling to Italy. He preferred to consolidate his patrimony in Alemannic Switzerland and to maintain civil order in northern Germany. He died at Spire, where he was buried beside the medieval rulers of Germany. The electors, who now feared the considerable might of the House of Austria, preferred Adolf of Nassau to Rudolf's son Albert, whom they believed to be too adventurous but he would take his revenge some years later.

Rudolf I's achievement was considerable. He had restored order in Germany, shattered the imperial ambitions of the king of Bohemia, shown himself to be a statesman and most importantly had founded the House of Austria by exploiting circumstances to his own best interests. Through him, a powerful line from Alemannic Switzerland had made a decisive entrance into the history of Europe.

NOTES AND REFERENCES

1. Hugo Hantsch, *Die Geschichte Œsterreichs*, 2 vols, Vienna, Styria, 1951, vol. 1, pp. 77–9: *Die Welt des römischen Reiches* (hereafter Hantsch).
   Wilhelm Erben, *Das Privilegium Friedrichs I für das Herzogtum Œsterreich*, Vienna, 1902.
2. Jean Bérenger, 'Que sais-je?', in *La Tchécoslavaquie*, Paris, no. 1726, 1978, pp. 13–16.

Karl Bosl, *Handbuch der Geschichte der Bömischen Länder*, 4 vols, Stuttgart, 1976–4, part 1.

Josef Macek, *Histoire de la Bohême*, Paris, 1984, pp. 15–56.

3. Prince Charles Schwarzenberg, *Die Sankt Wenzels-Krone*, Vienna, 1960.
4. Magda von Bárány-Oberschall, *Die Sankt Stephans-Krone*, Vienna, 1961.
5. Ervin Pamlenyi (ed.) *Histoire de la Hongrie*, Roanne, 1974, pp. 72–95.
6. Hantsch, vol. 1, pp. 110–17.
7. Adam Wandruszka, *Das Haus Habsburg: eine europäische Dynastie*, Vienna, 1956, pp. 57–62.
8. Hantsch, vol. 1, pp. 110–17.

CHAPTER FOUR

The Period of Establishment (1291–1439)

Albert had been left an important inheritance by his father, Rudolf, and was without question endowed with the qualities of a statesman. He was not, however, able to pursue the apparently irresistible rise of the House of Habsburg as he roused great envy among his old and new subjects, including the other great princely houses of the Empire. The reign of Albert of Habsburg ended in tragedy in 1308 and left behind a sense of failure. It took his descendants more than a century to consolidate their position and to prepare a new ascendancy which would endure.

THE FAILURE OF ALBERT V OF HABSBURG (1291–1308)[1]

Trained by his father, Albert shared responsibilities with him after the 1273 election. Father and son possessed similar talents. Like Rudolf, Albert was good at analyzing a situation, had great determination and was similarly unscrupulous when the interests of his House were at stake, but he could also be moderate when circumstances demanded. He was patient but could take and carry out a decision swiftly and effectively. However, he lacked the human warmth and sense of humour which had made Rudolf so popular. Friends and opponents had to recognize from the beginning that they were dealing with a strong personality and an ambitious prince who had never made any secret of his pretensions to the imperial crown. His appearance was far from prepossessing after he lost an eye in 1295. He made many enemies inside his entourage and his brother-in-law, the king of Bohemia, Vacláv III, often exhibited great hostility towards him. During the whole of his reign, Albert faced a three fold struggle: in his old domains, in Austria and for the royal title.

In the Upper Rhine, Rudolf I's policy of acquisition provoked a spirited response. As early as 1291 the three Swiss cantons, Uri, Schwyz and

Unterwalden, formed a Perpetual League, the nucleus of the future Helvetic Confederation. The League, while not expressly directed against the Habsburgs, sought to guarantee its members liberty in the face of a new sovereign. Later it played a part in weakening the Habsburgs' position in that part of Europe. In October 1291 an alliance was concluded between the canton of Zurich and the Habsburgs' old enemy, the count of Savoy, thereby weakening Albert's position in his struggle for the royal title in Germany.

There was a feeling throughout the whole Empire that the House of Habsburg had become too powerful. The electoral princes, just as they had previously rejected Otakar, the king of Bohemia, as a candidate, warded off Albert 'the Austrian', who now possessed a vast and powerful territory and was in a position to exercise his hegemony over the Empire. It was for this reason that they preferred count Adolf of Nassau, a feudal lord who had modest possessions also in the Rhineland. This interlude allowed Albert to consolidate his position within his own domains. By accepting his rival's election, he gave proof of his political wisdom.

In his eastern domains, the nobility and the urban patriciate contested the authority of the new duke of Austria and Styria. They looked on him as a 'stranger' and criticized him for his 'Swabian' entourage. While Rudolf had made many concessions to his new subjects, Albert was firmly resolved to strengthen his power and to recover the liberties granted him by his father. He showed his political and military strength when he crushed the rebellions of the Styrian (1292) and Austrian nobles (1295–6). He took his enemies by surprise, defeated them and imposed rigorous terms while granting a general pardon to the vanquished rebels. To demonstrate his attachment to his country he renounced the Christian names traditional in his House and christened his sons Frederick, Leopold and Henry to give them a more 'Austrian' air.

Albert of Habsburg also concluded an alliance with the king of Hungary, András III, giving him his daughter in marriage. Having thus secured his back in the Danubian region, he was free to attack Adolf of Nassau, whose relations with the princes had rapidly deteriorated to the point where the electors deposed him. Albert attacked, defeated and killed Adolf at Göllheim and then had himself elected king of the Romans by the same princes who seven years before had been so unenthusiastic about his candidature.

The princes' fears were justified: Albert proceeded to make a concerted effort to reduce their powers in order to establish strong monarchical power in Germany. Albert concluded an alliance with Philip the Fair of France, which was sealed by the marriage of Philip's daughter, Blanche, to his son Rudolf. He sought to lay hold of Bohemia after the death of his brother-in-law, the last Přemyslid, and then tried to put his hands on Thuringia, the mark of Misnia and even the county of Holland, in an attempt to surround Germany with possessions belonging to the House of Habsburg. He also wanted to be crowned emperor at Rome and for this reason he maintained a distance between himself and Philip the Fair. If Albert, then aged fifty, had succeeded, he would have brought tremendous glory to the imperial crown and the House of Habsburg.

His murder put a brutal end to the efforts of two generations of sovereigns: on 1 May 1308, on his way from Reuss, not far from the Habichtsburg castle, Albert was assassinated by his nephew John, later dubbed 'the Paricide', who was helped by three local noblemen. It was a violent reaction on the part of the nobles, who felt frustrated by their king's energetic policies. John believed that Albert would remain firm over the issue of primogeniture and that the family patrimony would not be further divided. He believed that he had been unjustly disinherited by his uncle and that according to feudal law he was entitled to take justice into his own hands. Albert's death was a disaster for the House of Austria and for Germany.[2] The power of the Habsburgs in the Upper Rhine started to decline. The electoral princes refused to elect a Habsburg again as the family had proved too venturesome, and chose instead count Henry of Luxemburg, who was able to manage the succession in Bohemia to his advantage and so excluded the Habsburgs for two centuries.[3]

THE RENUNCIATION OF THE GERMAN THRONE

Albert of Habsburg's sons, Frederick and Leopold,[4] who ruled Austria and Styria jointly, sought to continue their father's policy. First they took open vengeance on Albert's murderers and so added to the tension between the Habsburgs and their Swiss subjects, who rose against their legitimate feudal lord: in 1315 at Morgarten the Swiss confederates defeated in open country the knights loyal to the Habsburgs.[5] In addition, the premature death of Henry VII of Luxemburg in 1314 gave them hope of recovering the royal crown. The electors kept at bay the king of Bohemia, John of Luxemburg, thinking him too young and too powerful, and divided their votes between Frederick of Habsburg and his first cousin, Ludwig of Bavaria. For the first time in German history, the two most powerful Houses of southern Germany entered into competition. The war lasted eight years and ended in 1322 at the Battle of Mühldorf with the defeat and capture of Frederick by Ludwig of Bavaria. Leopold continued the struggle but Frederick, while captive, signed a treaty renouncing the throne of Germany. The death of the two brothers in 1326 set the seal on the duke of Bavaria's triumph and the withdrawal of the Habsburgs from the competition for the imperial crown.

For the Austrian historian Wandruszka[6] the three dates 1308, 1315 and 1322 – the death of Albert of Habsburg, the defeats at Morgarten and Mühldorf – marked a decisive turning-point in the destiny of the

Habsburgs since they lost their former dominant position in Alemannic Switzerland and withdrew into their Austrian patrimony without having realized the great Austro-Bohemian complex which, from the sixteenth century, would be the base of their European power. Frederick was able to make himself accepted by his Austrian subjects. He founded many more churches and monasteries in Styria and Austria and prepared the ground for the dogged policy of his immediate successors, Albert II and Rudolf IV.

THE ACQUISITION OF THE ALPINE PROVINCES
(1335–1365)[7]

Albert II the Wise followed a less aggressive but nonetheless very clever policy. To his vassals, he was 'the prince of peace' and countless stories reflect his popularity. Through the alliance concluded at the beginning of his reign with John of Bohemia, he was reconciled with Ludwig of Bavaria by the treaty of Haguenau (6 August 1330) which in 1335 enabled him to acquire Carinthia and Carniola, both of which naturally went with Styria; these three provinces much later formed Inner Austria and brought guaranteed access to the Adriatic. When the line of counts of Tyrol-Gorizia died out in the male line, Ludwig of Bavaria granted the two provinces as a fief to Albert II as recompense for his definitive renunciation of the German crown. The Tyrol meanwhile remained in the hands of Margaret, the only daughter of the late count Henry, who married in succession John of Luxemburg, son of the king of Bohemia and then the eldest son of the emperor Ludwig of Bavaria. She had only one sickly son, Meinhard III who, with the blessing of the emperor Charles IV of Luxemburg, married Albert II's daughter – a move which smoothed the way for the eventual reattachment of the Tyrol to Austria in 1365 after Meinhard III's death. The king of Bohemia's claims to Carinthia had meanwhile been quashed following Albert II's military success and through the diplomatic support of the emperor Ludwig of Bavaria, who did not want to strengthen the House of Luxemburg. After 1339, Austria entered a period of peace.

Between 1348 and 1349 no less a social crisis hit Austria with the arrival of the Black Death. In Vienna, although the House of Habsburg itself did not lose any members, the capital and its outskirts lost 40 000 inhabitants. The Austrian historian E. Zöllner estimates that the losses were on a similar scale to those suffered by other European countries – between 25 and 35 per cent of the total population.[8] Urban development and the drive to colonize were interrupted despite the privileges granted to peasants wishing to settle in a town. The people were incapable of explaining the phenomenon and were seized by panic, all the more so since 1348 was marked by a series of earth tremors. The wrath of God was seen in all these disasters: the Jewish communities were quickly singled out as the scapegoat and held responsible for the spread of the epidemic. Just as in the rest of Germany, popular movements threatened the lives and goods of the Jews, who were blamed for economic but primarily religious reasons. Albert II had to intervene to protect his Jewish subjects from popular anger and so inaugurated the policy which his descendants followed right to the modern era.

In 1355 Albert II settled the matter of who would succeed him by rejecting the principle of primogeniture and declared his four sons, Rudolf, Frederick, Albert and Leopold, equal heirs, exhorting them 'to remain united through brotherly love'. The nobility of the country was declared the guarantor of the application of the edict of 25 November. Instead of dividing the Habsburg patrimony, the four brothers were named co-regents. This notion of the unity of the House of Habsburg would persist into the modern era and avoided partition (as in Germany) and absolute submission to the head of the family (as in France).

Albert II died in July 1358 and was buried at the Carthusian monastery of Gaming which he had founded in 1332. For twenty years he had survived an attack of paralysis, perhaps brought on by an attempt to poison him, and it was his eldest son Rudolf, then aged nineteen, who became the head of government.

RUDOLF IV, THE FOUNDER (1358–65)[9]

During his brief reign, Rudolf IV governed alone as his brothers were too young to take part in government and it is open to question whether this energetic and intelligent prince would in practice have tolerated a co-regency.

He was convinced of the exalted mission of his House, which he believed was destined to hold the royal crown, although temporarily deprived of it by the House of Luxemburg, and he did not hide his admiration for Rudolf I. Like his great-grandfather and namesake, Rudolf IV was a realistic statesman and despite his youth did not let himself get drawn into adventures in pursuit of his goal. He was shrewd enough to concentrate his efforts on his Austrian inheritance and to surround himself with good advisers; his chancellor Johannes Platzhein from the Swabian lesser nobility, count Ulrich of Schaunberg and the burgermeister of Vienna, Johannes Tirna. At the beginning of his reign, Rudolf IV took three measures intended to ensure the independence of Austria until circumstances were more favourable: in 1358 he promulgated the *Privilegium majus* which was nothing but a 'patriotic forgery';[10] on 21 March 1359 he issued the fiscal ordinance; he reconstructed St Stephen's cathedral at Vienna, laying the first stone on 11 March 1359, thereby earning his epithet 'the Founder'.

The Golden Bull issued by his father-in-law Charles IV of Luxemburg in 1356 was seen as an insult to Austria and the House of Habsburg. The emperor saw the necessity of bringing some order to the electoral procedure and took advantage of the unchallengeable authority which he enjoyed to regulate the election through a constitutional decree. Henceforth the election of the king of Germany, which carried the prestigious title of king of the Romans, would be restricted to seven princes chosen from among the most powerful and wealthiest in Germany who would also carry out the important offices at court: chancellor, almoner, cupbearer, master of the horse, etc. Charles IV designated three ecclesiastical electors – the archbishops of Mainz, Trier and Cologne – and four lay electors – the count Palatine of the Rhine, the margrave of Brandenburg, the duke of Saxony and the king of Bohemia. He thus ensured that his House had a preponderant role in German politics, although the Slav kingdom was only on the margins of the German world: Austria was totally excluded. This blow was all the heavier for the Habsburgs since the Golden Bull of 1356 was effectively in force until the dissolution of the Holy Roman Empire in 1806 and underwent modification only in the seventeenth century when two new electors were added.

For this reason Rudolf IV tried to strengthen Austria's autonomy in relation to the Empire, inventing the *Privilegium majus* to countervail the *Privilegium minus* granted to Austria in 1156 by Frederick Barbarossa and confirmed by Frederick II of Hohenstaufen in 1245. If the duke of Austria could not secure the title of elector, he would at least arrogate extensive privileges. Present day historians agree that the *Privilegium majus* was a forgery made up by Rudolf IV's chancellery. In it Austria was described as the 'shield and heart of the Holy Roman Empire': in the future its duke would furnish a dozen men-at-arms only if the emperor went to war; a supplementary contingent would be provided only voluntarily so that the duke of Austria might be recognized as a prince of the Empire. He would no longer go to the emperor's court to pledge his loyalty and homage: it was for the emperor to come to Austria to receive the homage of his vassal. He could not be summoned before a tribunal of the Empire and was accountable to no one for his actions. If he came in person to the imperial Diet, his place was on the emperor's right, immediately after the electoral princes. This fierce affirmation of Austrian sovereignty had as its corollary that there would no longer be fiefs of the Empire within Austria and that all the lay lords would pay homage to the duke. All the courts in the country depended on his authority and the duke claimed for himself all the royal rights (forest hunting, fishing, protection of the Jews and Lombards); no subject had the right to make an appeal before a tribunal of the Empire.

Two principles laid down in the *Privilegium fridericianum* had serious consequences for the future and show that its author had a conception of the state which was quite modern. All the present or future acquisitions constituted a domain which could not be divided, the *dominium Austriae*. For the first time there appeared the notion that Austria was identified with the basic patrimony of the Habsburgs. At the same time, Rudolf IV established a strict law of succession; the patrimony was governed by the eldest duke and after his death by the eldest of his sons and, if a male descendant were lacking, the eldest daughter succeeded. In the absence of direct heirs, the duke bequeathed the domain to whomever seemed best. It was, then, the idea of sovereignty stemming from Roman law which inspired Rudolf IV; the emperor no longer had any authority over Austria and the Empire was already perceived as a confederation of sovereign principalities.

Naturally Charles IV could not confirm so revolutionary a text which was as prejudicial to his authority as to the interests of the Empire. He saw in it evidence of his son-in-law's disproportionate pride and an attempt to shatter the unity of the Empire. He was no more appreciative of the titles which his son-in-law arrogated as compensation for the lack of an elector's cap; grand huntsman of the Empire, archduke Palatine and duke of Swabia, a title which had disappeared in the thirteenth century after the extinction of the Hohenstaufens. The emperor ordered the destruction of the seal of the Austrian chancellery, which depicted Rudolf with a royal crown, and Rudolf fell into disgrace with his father-in-law, who hitherto had always shown him a measure of affection. Charles IV deprived him of the office of grand bailiff of Alsace, took the side of those princes of the Empire who had holdings in Austria, supported the Swiss against their natural lord and, to cap it all, refused to grant him the Tyrol as a fief.

The reform of the Austrian fiscal system was followed shortly afterwards by other measures intended to make Austria a rich and powerful country, a base for the Habsburgs' recovery of royal power. Rudolf tried to diminish the feudal lords' authority over the towns by developing municipal liberties. He reorganized the Viennese guilds and secured the creation of a bishopric at Vienna, albeit one modest in size and revenues. A short time before his death in 1365 he founded the university of Vienna modelled on that at Prague. Rudolf IV's epithet was not undeserved: Vienna was already one of the great commercial centres of Central Europe and the cathedral of St Stephen remains one of the most beautiful Gothic buildings in the German world.

Part of his long-term plan remained to acquire territory. His most important acquisition without question was when he annexed the Tyrol in 1363 and so assured a link between the eastern and western part of the Austrian domain, between the old and the new patrimony. The Tyrol assumed considerable strategic significance since the Habsburgs henceforth possessed Alpine provinces and their domain stretched from the Vosges to the Carpathians. They were masters of the southern boundary of the Empire, controlling the routes into Italy. Rudolf IV was in fact the first Habsburg to pursue a policy directed towards Italy, extending his authority over Friuli and the bishopric of Trent. It was, moreover, at Milan that he died prematurely, while negotiating the alliance with the Viscontis which would sanction the marriage of his brother Leopold to Virida Visconti.

It is not premature to describe Rudolf IV as a 'prince of the Renaissance'. He endeavoured to demonstrate his power and exhibited an immoderate desire for glory and fame. He had a quite modern notion of the state based on the theories of Roman law and possessed a great imagination as well as a profound conviction that the House of Habsburg was called to an extraordinary destiny. During his brief but brilliant reign, for the first time it was a matter of the *archidux* (archduke) and *domus Austriae* (House of Austria). As his only heirs were his two young brothers Albert III and Leopold III, aged fifteen and fourteen respectively, he was obliged to renounce the principle of primogeniture affirmed in the *Privilegium majus* and resorted to the system of co-regency defined by Albert II in 1355, until the patrimony was parcelled out among the many branches.

ACQUISITIONS AND PARTITIONS (1365–1439)[11]

The two brothers had very different characters: Albert was unadventurous, shy, even timid,[12] while his brother Leopold was ambitious and had an irascible temperament.[13] Their collaboration, however, was to prove fruitful even if their objectives remained modest in the face of the House of Luxemburg, then at the zenith of its power within the Empire, and the House of Anjou (Angevin), which brought a new brilliance to the kingdom of Hungary after the extinction of the Árpáds.

In 1368 the Habsburgs acquired the town of Freiburg im Breisgau, which they kept until 1798, and were entrusted by Charles IV with the landgraviate of the Breisgau. In 1369 they finally managed the succession to the Tyrol to their benefit, warding off the claims of the Wittelsbachs since Charles IV, fearing Bavarian more than Habsburg pretensions to the imperial throne, preferred to see the Tyrol joined to Austria rather than Bavaria. By the treaty of Schärding, the Wittelsbachs renounced their claims in return for financial compensation. In 1382 the town of Trieste found itself under threat from the Republic of Venice and turned to the Habsburgs for protection. The acquisition of Trieste brought the Habsburgs an outlet on the Adriatic for their domain, albeit a small one, and provided access which would prove very useful in the future. Earlier they had inherited feudal lordships in Istria, while the purchase of the county of Feldkirch in the Vorarlberg assured better communications between the Tyrol and their old patrimony.

This policy of acquisition, as cautious as it was, suffered a fresh arresting blow in 1386 in Alemannic Switzerland. At the Battle of Sempach,[14] the confederate forces crushed the cavalry of Leopold III, who was killed in the engagement and was buried in the abbey of Königsfelden, which had been erected on the site of his grandfather's murder in 1308. Thus two Habsburgs had fallen victim to their Swiss subjects. It was clear that expansion, even the Habsburgs' continuance in Alemannic Switzerland, was seriously in doubt. According to the terms of the treaty of Neuberg in 1379, the two brothers had resigned themselves to the division of their patrimony, contrary to the provisions made by their father and eldest brother. Albert received Lower Austria, while Leopold III claimed Styria, Carinthia, Carniola and the Tyrol as well as the old patrimony. Historians speak of the 'Albertine branch' and the 'Leopoldine branch' until the reunification of the patrimony in the fifteenth century.

The result of this partition became apparent in the next generation. During the reign of Frederick IV of the Tyrol, the younger son of Leopold III, known by his nickname 'Frederick of the empty purse', the ruin of the Habsburgs' ancestral possessions became a matter of fact.[15] For having helped the anti-pope John XXIII flee from Constance, Frederick was placed under a ban of the Empire by Sigismund of Luxemburg and the Diet pronounced the confiscation of his lands. Aargau, the cradle of his House, was occupied by the confederates while his enemies from Breisgau and Switzerland concluded an offensive alliance in order to prevent fresh expansion in the region by the Habsburgs. When, after some years of captivity, banishment and exile, Frederick IV was able to return to the Tyrol, his ancestral domains in the Upper Rhine were politically no more than a field of ruins. They became an administrative dependency of the Tyrol and under the name of Further Austria (*Vorderösterreich*) were governed from Innsbruck until 1648 when Upper Alsace fell under the sovereignty of the king of France.[16]

After 1411 the Austrian patrimony was divided, not into two, but three: after the death of Leopold IV the domains of the Leopoldine branch were divided between his two younger brothers, Frederick IV, who received the Tyrol, and Ernest, the 'Iron duke', who inherited Inner Austria. This redivision of territories into three groups was not without basis; there were definite geo-political reasons with the dangers then emerging at the beginning of the fifteenth century. The Albertine branch faced a Bohemia overturned by the Hussite revolution, which threatened the northern borders of Lower Austria. The Leopoldine branch with Inner Austria was confronted by the threat from the Turks, a new phenomenon which would presently come to the fore and threaten the existence of the peoples of southern Hungary and Croatia. As for Frederick IV, his failure over the Swiss cantons and the progressive elimination of the Habsburgs from Alemannic Switzerland have already been discussed.

Given the relative weakness of the dynasty, it is not surprising that the decline of princely power was accompanied by the return in full force of the local nobles who regularly met in the provincial Diets and developed their own administration. In these circumstances, the sudden success of

Frederick III, son of Ernest the 'Iron duke', might appear unexpected. Not without his weaknesses, which will be analyzed later, he was nevertheless the first Habsburg to have himself crowned emperor; he introduced the imperial title permanently into the House where it remained, apart from a brief interlude 1740–5, right until 1806.

NOTES AND REFERENCES

1. Alphons Lhotsky, *Geschichte Œsterreichs (1281–1368)*, Vienna, 1967, pp. 43–168.
2. Bruno Meyer, *Studien zum habsburgischen Hausrecht*, Zeitschrift für Schweizerische Geschichte, vol. 1; 1945.
3. Hans Hirsch, 'Deutsches Königtum und römisches Kaisertum', in Heinrich von Srbik (ed.) *Œsterreich, Erbe und Sendung*, Vienna, 1936.
4. Brigitte Hamann (ed.) 'Friedrich' and 'Leopold', in *Die Habsburger: ein biographisches Lexikon*, Vienna, 1988.
5. Bruno Meyer, 'Die Entstehung der Eidgenossenschaft, der Stand der heutigen Anschauungen', *Schweizerische Zeitschrift für Geschichte*, vol. 2, 1952.
6. Adam Wandruszka, *Das Haus Habsburg: eine europäische Dynastie*, Vienna, 1956, p. 73: from this point, the House of Habsburg became the House of Austria.
7. Otto Brunner, 'Œsterreiche, das Reich und der Osten im späteren Mittelalter', in Srbik (ed.) *Œsterreich, Erbe und Sendung*.
   Erich Zollner, 'Ausdehnung der habsburgischen Hersschaft', *Geschichte Œsterreichs*, Vienna, 1961, pp. 128–45 (hereafter Zollner).
8. Zollner, p. 168. The epidemic of 1381 claimed 18 000 victims in Vienna.
9. Ernst Karl Winter, *Rudolph IV von Œsterreich*, 2 vols, Vienna, 1934–6.
10. Alphons Lhotsky, *Privilegium majus*, Vienna, 1957.
11. Hugo Hantsch, *Die Geschichte Œsterreichs*, 2 vols, Vienna, Styria, 1951, vol. 1, pp. 173–85.
12. Alfred Strnad, *Herzog Albrecht III von Œsterreich*, doctoral thesis, Vienna, 1961.
13. J. Egger, *Geschichte Leopolds III*, Vienna, 1869.
14. Xavier Weber, *Der Sempacher Krieg*, Lucerne, 1936.
15. J. Riedmann, 'Herzog Friedrich IV', in J. Fontana (ed.) *Geschichte des Landes Tirol*, Innsbruck, 1985, vol. 1, pp. 437–59.
16. Völker Press, 'Vorderösterreich in der habsburgischen Reichspolitik', in Völker Press and Hans Maier (eds) *Vorderösterreich in der frühen Neuzeit*, Sigmaringen, 1989, pp. 1–41.

CHAPTER FIVE

The Hussite Revolution and its Consequences

The Hussite revolution might appear a marginal phenomenon since Austria was not directly touched by the Hussite heresy and the Habsburgs were not immediately confronted by a revolution that first and foremost affected Bohemia. The crisis, however, was a major one in the history of Danubian Europe and reveals much. It was a decisive moment in the history of the Czech people, whom the Habsburgs were shortly to rule, and appears as a general rehearsal for the great religious crisis of the sixteenth century; it was, in a way, the first major dispute in modern Europe.

The great Czech historian František Palacký thought that the Hussite revolution was a religious, national and social movement,[1] while contemporary Marxist historiography has seen it as indicative of the underlying contradictions of feudalism. Whatever the case, it is interesting to see how a theological quarrel and the growth of a heterodox doctrine could degenerate into a revolution which still marks Czech national consciousness.

CHARLES IV AND THE APOGEE OF THE KINGDOM OF BOHEMIA (1346–78)[2]

After the difficulties stemming from the extinction of the national dynasty, the Přemyslids (Václav III died without a male heir in 1308), Bohemia was granted as a fief by the emperor Henry VII of Luxemburg to his son John the Blind, the hero of the Battle of Crécy (1346), who married Eliška Přemyslovna. For the moment, the Habsburgs were kept from Bohemia, which under the Luxemburg dynasty experienced one of the prosperous periods in its history, especially during the reign of Charles IV.

Charles of Luxemburg, son of John the Blind, was an extraordinary character: lord of the Empire, as a relative of Charles V of Valois he had been raised at the court of France and was culturally French yet later also felt great affinity with his Slav subjects. Experienced in politics, educated, with a gift for the arts and letters (he wrote his autobiography in Latin), brave in combat (he was wounded at Crécy), Charles IV was of a pious and pacific temperament.

He was successful in his bid to be elected king of the Romans and so made the king of Bohemia the head of the Holy Roman Empire and Prague the imperial residence. He then took three decisions of momentous importance for the future of Bohemia. First, he obtained from pope Clement VI the elevation of the Prague bishopric to a metropolitan see, which made it independent of the German bishops. Second, in 1348 he founded the university of Prague, the first institution of its kind in Central Europe which made it no longer necessary for students to go to Paris or Italy and conferred important intellectual prestige upon the town. Third, in the same year, he founded *Nové Město*, 'the new town' of Prague, with a view to developing a Czech burgher class.

He embellished the capital and had a stone bridge constructed across the Vltava which still carries his name and unites the royal town (*Hradčany*) with the two burgher towns (the old and new towns). He had the choir of St Vitus's cathedral reconstructed, the central building of the *Hradčany* with the royal palace and the abbey of St George. The work was directed by the French architect Matthias of Arras and, after his death in 1352, was continued by his Czech pupil Petr Parleř of Schwäbisch Gmünd. Charles IV was the second founder of Prague, which became the third leading city of Europe after Constantinople and Paris. It was during his reign that the essential elements of the modern urban landscape were put in place and the city did not grow noticeably until the urban expansion of the nineteenth century.

Charles IV effected the unification of the 'historic' kingdom which, besides Bohemia proper, now included Moravia, Silesia, the two Lusatias and the region of Cheb (in German, Eger). He created a crown of Bohemia (*corona regni Bohemiae*), with the crown of St Wenceslas as its symbol, like the crown of St Stephen in Hungary. This reform showed that the state was already seen as more than a simple patrimonial and feudal monarchy. When in 1356 he promulgated the Golden Bull, which reorganized the college of electors of the Holy Roman Empire, Charles IV assured a dominant place for the king of Bohemia, who became first among the lay electors of the German monarchy and guaranteed the complete autonomy of Bohemia in relation to the Empire.

Charles IV's relations with the barons of the kingdom were difficult and he was obliged to promise them extensive privileges. They were required to give only such military service as was necessary for the defence of the country and the nobles acquired immunity from taxation since the cost of the assistance which they gave the king when needed, fell back on the peasants. The royal exchequer annexed those domains only where the line of heirs had died out. Offices were reserved for natives of the kingdom alone, a measure directed against the policy of systematic immigration favoured by the previous kings of Bohemia.

The Přemyslids had attracted German colonists into the northern regions of Bohemia and Moravia to cultivate under-populated and under-developed woodland regions. They gave them lands, forests and mines as well as urban privileges and exemptions. The municipal law in medieval Bohemia was German in inspiration and the charters of exemption were based on the law of Magdeburg or Nürnberg (as in the case of the old town of Prague). The result was a customary law different from Slav customary law; courts of appeal, for which the royal chamberlain was responsible, had to be established at Litoměřice, Jihlava and Olomouc. The industrious German colonists certainly gave the Czech economy a vigorous push forward but generally they refused to assimilate with the Slavs. The colonization of the Germano-Czech confines and of the capital (the old town of Prague was essentially German), although peaceful, represented a serious long-term danger. The Hussite revolution was not, as is often claimed, an exclusively anti-German movement, but it was nevertheless exacerbated by conflicts between the two communities.

The other serious socio-political problem of the fourteenth century was the price paid for the progress of the Church. Through countless donations, the Church had become the largest landowner in the kingdom. It owned 30 per cent of land under cultivation and the aristocracy wanted to recover its share. Premonstratensians, Cistercians and the canons regular of St Augustine owned vast domains which they ran rigorously, with the result that the peasants were ill-disposed towards them because they raised much higher levies on their tenants than did the lay feudal lords. The Church was increasing its power to control: an inquisitor was installed at Prague as early as 1343 since the German colonists had responded favourably to heresy. Finally the privileged orders viewed with disquiet the development of the tendency affirmed by the papacy at Avignon to appoint directly the holders of benefices to the detriment of natives of the kingdom. There was a visible sign of the malaise: the archbishop of Prague, Jan of Jenštejn (1378–96), entered into open conflict with king Václav IV, son and successor of Charles IV. The prelate wished for close collaboration between the bishops and lay feudal lords; he preferred to withdraw to Rome, then to abdicate.

The university of Prague fostered a current of dispute while maintaining relations with the Italian intellectual world and placing emphasis on the vernacular language. Charles IV favoured such a development authorizing sermons in Czech which were well received by the elites. Moreover, the Augustinians and Carthusians helped to create devout circles which practised an altogether more internal and personal piety.[3]

It was in this climate that Jan Hus was able to expand his activities and to adapt to the particular conditions of Bohemia the theories of the Englishman John Wyclif, who condemned the wealth of the Church and demanded the translation of the Bible into the vernacular so that it could be put at the disposal of all the faithful. Wyclif, of course, was condemned in England by a synod of the Church in 1382, but his ideas spread abroad and at the beginning of the fifteenth century had won over the majority of the 'Bohemian nation' at the university of Prague.

THE WORK OF JAN HUS (1370–1415)[4]

Hero, martyr, symbol of Church reform, Jan Hus was typical of a generation of restless and dissatisfied clergy. Born in 1370 to a poor family in Bohemia, he was led to become a clergyman out of ambition and studied at Prague. In 1393 he took his bachelor of arts degree and in 1396 his master of arts. Ordained in 1400, he became a bachelor of theology in 1408 but never became a doctor. In 1401 he was chosen as dean of the faculty of arts at the university of Prague and proved to be a good teacher. He was entrusted with the direction of the chapel of St Bartholomew in the Staré Město, where he introduced sermons in Czech and was very popular with the people of the capital. Hus was not a systematic theologian but he picked up the old criticisms against the Bohemian clergy and combined them with nationalist fervour and the ideas of John Wyclif. It was only in 1410 that Jan Hus openly took sides with the ideas of Wyclif and appealed to Christ against the Church visible. Since he refused royal mediation, all that was left was to appeal to the council. Václav IV, though moderate at first, opposed the new ideas and had burnt at the stake three artisans for whom Hus then said the mass for the martyrs. In 1412 Hus's work *De Ecclesia* was published as well as some writings in Czech and enjoyed a great success. He left for Constance in 1414 in order to appear before the Council. Arrested shortly before he arrived – since the safe conduct granted by Sigismund of Luxemburg was no more than a simple passport – he spent six months in prison and made a poor defence before the judges who were, even so, in favour of reform. They extracted thirty propositions from his *De Ecclesia* and gave him the chance to retract them. In order to avoid embarrassing his Prague supporters, he refused and made an appeal to Scriptural authority, but in so doing pronounced his own death sentence. Jan Hus was burnt at the stake in Constance in June 1415, the first martyr of a movement that would produce many more and would serve as a model for Martin Luther.

The symbol of Hussitism was communion in both kinds (*sub utraque specie*), hence the name *Utraquist* that is sometimes given to the movement's followers. To receive from the chalice suddenly seemed an unprecedented clerical privilege, while its extension to all the faithful appeared a sign of change, of a return to Scriptural authority and an affirmation of equality between clergy and laity. Jan Hus's supporters railed against the clergy for being landowners and so attracted the support of the aristocracy in Bohemia. Indeed, the aristocracy had lost the right of patronage – and so its control of the secular clergy – two generations earlier as a consequence of the extension of canon law.

For this reason, 452 barons and knights delivered a protest to the Council of Constance in 1415. Only a small minority of nobles remained faithful to the Roman Church and gathered around a young baron, Ulrich von Rožmberk. In 1417 the university of Prague declared itself the supreme authority of the Church (in Bohemia) and approved a programme of four points which constituted the essential 'Hussite' doctrine:

1. communion in both kinds
2. freedom to preach
3. the practice by priests of poverty according to the model in the Gospels
4. the punishment of mortal sins, to which was added the restoration of the vernacular.

In 1419 the movement assumed the aspect of a revolution and Václav IV decreed the banishment of all Utraquist priests. The movement was precipitated by the king's death in September. The throne remained empty because Sigismund, Václav's brother and king of the Romans, refused any compromise; in 1420 he proclaimed a crusade against the Hussites. The capital became the bastion of the revolution; the people sacked the churches and monasteries loyal to Catholicism. The German burghers fled while a radical movement, the Taborites, overwhelmed the Hussite movement.

The millenarians who proclaimed the immediate arrival of the Antichrist and the imminent beginning of the Apocalypse wanted, while they waited, to gather 'the elect' and to establish a kind of evangelical communism. They abandoned the liturgy and held their goods in common. In the Tabor, to the south of Prague, revolutionary clergymen were to be found along with the poor from the urban proletariat. The arrival of Jan Žižka, a nobleman acquainted with their ideas, enabled them to organize themselves as a military force. The Taborites were the armed force of the Hussite revolution against king Sigismund's crusaders. Žižka was a self-confident fanatic. He invented the tactic of a camp with mobile barricades. In 1421 he defeated Sigismund's army at Kutná Hora using campaign artillery for the first time in Central Europe. The majority of the Taborites elected a bishop, Mikuláš of Pelhřimov, who reduced the liturgy and dogma to its basis in the Gospels while distancing himself from small extremist groups, for example the Adamites, who advocated total sexual license.

The Taborite movement was organized as a federation of towns since Žižka himself held fast to the society of orders and depended on the urban governing classes. In the spring of 1421 Prague organized a Confederation of towns which demanded precedence at the Diet. A Taborite, Želivsky, put himself at the head of a republican dictatorship supported by the artisans and their employees. He controlled Nové Město, expelled the Germans and united Staré and Nové Město. This episode came to an end in November 1421, and Prague became a royalist town supporting Mikuláš Korybut, Sigismund's rival candidate for the throne of Bohemia.

The question of the king arose because the legitimate sovereign, Sigismund of Luxemburg, was the Hussites' enemy. From 1420 the country was governed by the Diet, the nobles and towns being opposed to the king and Catholicism. In 1421 the Diet elected a directory that was made up of twelve members, each 'circle' providing one director, and took the place of royal power. The great innovation was the presence of the royal towns at the Diet. Bohemia was governed by the nobles and towns, who shared sovereignty, while the clergy were completely excluded as an order.

The Hussite revolution unleashed upon the country seventeen years of civil war in which both sides committed atrocities. It was the conservatives who began the terror (drownings, burials in the redundant wells at Kutná Hora), but quickly the urban population destroyed the monasteries, hacked to death or burnt those clergy who remained Catholic. Violence was loosed over the countryside; the towns, while remaining German and Catholic, joined the movement for fear. The Jews were also persecuted because they were not Utraquists. As for the crusaders, who were often simply self-seeking adventurers, they too left the Jews with sad memories. Žižka died in 1424 and Procope succeeded him at the head of the Hussite army.

Procope, who was from a German family from Prague (his grandfather founded the Chapel of Bethlehem), tried in 1429 to negotiate a compromise. Two years later the Council of Basle declared that it was ready to negotiate after the failure of the 'fifth crusade'. A Hussite delegation sent to Basle negotiated the Compactata of Basle (1433) which split the movement, the high Utraquist Church approving and the Taborites rejecting the Compactata. In 1434 an army of barons and people from Prague defeated the Taborites, the more moderate among whom negotiated with the Utraquists to settle a new formulation of the four articles, which were reduced to just communion in both kinds.

The struggle for the reform of the Church ended in a minor reform of the original liturgy in Bohemia and the division of the Czech Church which lasted until 1620. Only the expropriation of Church property was lasting. The metropolitan see of Prague remained vacant until the sixteenth century while the Utraquist church was governed by a consistory sitting at the university.

The question of the king was decided in 1436. The Diet of 1434 had drafted a convention for Sigismund who recognized communion in both kinds and the administrative autonomy of the Utraquist Church. The king of the Romans made his entry into Prague in August 1436, a few months before his death, which posed afresh the question of the king. The German historian K. Bosl concluded:

The internal quarrels of the society of orders had been settled in 1436 in favour of the barons but the conflict with the Crown over the exercise of power was not decided. It continued over two centuries and did not reach a conclusion until the decisive victory of the king at the Battle of the White Mountain (1620).

The Hussite revolution had also revealed a powerful nationalist current of anti-Germanism as well as tendencies towards messianism among the humble levels of the urban population. The result was that the power of the king was eclipsed by the privileged orders who increasingly governed through the Diet. The phenomenon was not peculiar to Bohemia: it was apparent also in the Alpine provinces where the power of the Habsburgs was greatly weakened, while in Hungary feudal anarchy gave way to a more coherent system in which the orders had preponderance but did not succeed in resolving satisfactorily their relationship with the executive power. Three possible solutions quickly emerged: a national monarchy where one of the country's great feudal lords was invested with royal power; a multinational monarchy entrusted to the Habsburgs; finally a multinational monarchy under the aegis of the Jagiellons, the ruling family of Poland whose principal merit was that they ruled without really governing, making their lands aristocratic republics. All three solutions were tried in turn according to the circumstances and in the sixteenth century the Habsburgs finally imposed themselves.

THE NATIONAL MONARCHY

After the death of Sigismund of Luxemburg, the Bohemian Diet was deeply divided; although it elected as king the late king's son-in-law Albert of Habsburg, the Utraquist party would have preferred to invest Kasimierz IV Jagiełłończyk, the younger brother of Władysław Jagiełłończyk, the king of Poland. The sudden death of Albert of Habsburg in 1439 scotched his House's chances as he left only a child still in his cradle, Ladislav the Posthumous. Bohemia and Moravia subsequently experienced forty years of anarchy with neither king nor central government, the two parties, confronting each other; there was a Habsburg, Catholic party led by Ulrich von Rožmberk, and a national, Utraquist party with Jiří of Poděbrady (George of Podebrady) at its head.

Jiří of Poděbrady belonged to a great family from eastern Bohemia which was on good terms with Jan Žižka. Born in 1420, he had always lived in an atmosphere hostile to Sigismund and the Catholic Church. Captain of a circle at twenty-four, he was made regent of the kingdom by the Utraquists while the young king Ladislav was held at Vienna by Frederick III. He assumed the title *gubernator*, according to Hungarian practice. In 1448 he drove Ulrich von Rožmberk from Prague and so provoked the flight of the Catholic authorities (the chapter of the cathedral of St Vitus and the three burgermeisters). In 1450, victorious over the Catholic party, he was recognized by Frederick III, then by the Diet of the kingdom. The death of Ladislav the Posthumous in 1457 served to change the situation. Although always suspected of having had the young Habsburg poisoned, Jiří of Poděbrady was elected king of Bohemia on 2 March 1458, against the foreign candidates. He arranged for two Hungarian bishops to come to crown him and swore in secret to restore the kingdom to Catholicism.

At that time, around 50 per cent of the Bohemian crown's subjects were Catholic; although the majority of inhabitants of the kingdom proper were Utraquists, the population of Silesia had remained entirely Catholic as had the greater part of Moravia, differences which could only make worse tensions between the kingdom and its incorporated provinces and explain the serious difficulties which 'the king of the Hussites' encountered.

Poděbrady wanted to fend off attack by seeking an alliance with Poland and above all France. In 1463 the Czech chancellery conceived a project for reaching perpetual peace among all the sovereigns so that a crusade could be launched against the Turks, who had taken Constantinople in 1453. This project, which did not involve the Holy See, was the idea of Antonio Marini from Grenoble, who became an adviser to the king of Bohemia. In 1464 a Czech embassy was received with all due courtesy by Louis XI of France, but without any result.

Despite his evident goodwill, Jiří of Poděbrady never returned Hussite Bohemia to the concert of Christian rulers. Pope Pius II, Aeneas Sylvius Piccolomini, knew Central Europe well and remained stubbornly opposed. In 1462 he denounced the Compactata of Basle, pronounced an interdict over Bohemia and in 1465 entrusted the crusade against the Czechs to the king of Hungary, Matthias Corvinus (Matyás Hunyadi), another champion of national monarchy. Corvinus received support from the Catholic lords; the grand burgrave Sidonius of Sternberk gathered sixteen barons into the League of Zelená Hora and declared Matthias king of Bohemia in 1470. He spread his authority effectively only over Moravia and Silesia which his supporters, the Catholic barons and their clientele, controlled; he was never able to take Prague.

At the time of his death in 1471, Jiří of Poděbrady had secured the election, not of one of his three sons as king, but rather of Władysław Jagiełłończyk, son of the king of Poland and, through his mother, grandson of Albert of Habsburg. Władysław would wage war against Matthias Corvinus but after the latter's death in 1490, he finally received the crowns of both Bohemia and Hungary. Jiří of Poděbrady was the last native head of state in Bohemia until 1918.

CONFESSIONAL PLURALISM

It was the Church that was most harmed by the Hussite revolution. Besides losing its land-holdings and being evicted from the Diet, it found its influence reduced to certain regions within the kingdom (Moravia and Silesia), and was obliged to share the monopoly which hitherto it had enjoyed in the medieval West where 'heresy' had had no place. The Utraquist Church had the right to exist side-by-side with the Catholic Church.

The archbishop of Prague, Jan Rokyčana, friend of Jiří of Poděbrady, was never confirmed in his office as archbishop by either the pope or the Council. He was satisfied with the office of administrator and kept himself at the head of the Hussite clergy through a delegation of the Diet, which declared him supreme head of the Utraquist Church in the temporal domain. Nobles and towns appointed priests to their parishes and fixed their stipends since the tithes had been abolished. As the Utraquist administrator and the Consistory sat in the Old Town of Prague it was known as the 'Lower Consistory' in contrast to the Catholic 'Upper Consistory', which continued to sit in the castle.

There were appreciable differences between the two Churches. The Utraquists had suppressed the religious orders, rejected the notion of purgatory and gave little importance to the intercession of the saints. They recognized the pope as having only limited authority in spiritual matters. Finally the liturgy was transformed and simplified. Great emphasis was placed upon prayers and singing in Czech in order to allow the faithful much greater participation. Communion, of course, was distributed in both kinds while the number of feast days was reduced and ceremonial was simplified. This tendency would prosper during and after the Protestant Reformation.

There were, however, many tendencies within the Utraquist Church itself and its radical wing was divided at the roots into communities which, in addition to rejecting the Roman Church, rejected the Utraquist Church as an institution; these communities proclaimed popular reform and social equality, in short the realization of the kingdom of Christ on earth. Their chief theoretician was Petř Chelčický who, until his death (1460), lived under the protection of the Taborites in southern Bohemia. One section of the faithful formed the community of the 'Brothers of Chelčický', apostles of non-violence who would later form the Unity of Moravian Brethren.

The Hussite revolution thus gave birth, in the heart of the Christian community, to three tendencies – traditional Catholic, moderate Utraquists and heterodox communities – and the Habsburgs inherited a difficult situation when they ascended the throne of Bohemia; all the more so since confessional pluralism was closely tied to the dominance of the orders and the political claims of the Diet.

NOTES AND REFERENCES

1. František Palacký, *Geschichte von Böhmen*, 5 vols, Prague, 1844–67.
2. Ferdinand Seibt, *Karl IV: ein Kaiser in Europa, 1346–1378*, Munich, 1978.
   A. Pludek, *Český kral Karel*, Prague, 1979.
   A. Blaschka (ed.) *Vita Karoli Quarti* (autobiography in Latin), Prague, 1979.
3. Eduard Winter, *Frühhumanismus: seine Entwicklung in Böhmen und deren Bedeutung für die Kirchenreformbestrebungen im 14. Jahrhundert*, Berlin, 1964.
4. F. M. Bartoš, *Husitska revoluce*, 2 vols, Prague, 1965–66.
   Robert Kalivoda, *Revolution und Ideologie: der Hussitismus*, Vienna and Cologne, 1976.
   Ferdinand Seibt, *Hussitenstudien*, Munich, 1987.
   František Palacký (ed.) *Documenta magistri Johannis Hus, vitam, doctrinam, etc., illustrantia*, Prague, 1869.

CHAPTER SIX

The Strengthening of the Power of the Nobility

In Danubian Europe, unlike Western Europe, the general trend of development at the end of the Middle Ages did not favour monarchical power and the reinforcement of the state apparatus. The Hussite revolution, it has been seen, resulted in the emergence of a noble republic. In Austria the division of territory contributed to the growth of federalist sentiment and a provincial administration under the control of the nobility. In Hungary, after the reign of Matthias Corvinus, the first truly modern prince in this part of Europe, the reaction was all the more pronounced and the nobles' triumph all the more complete.

THE SOCIETY OF ORDERS AND THE POLITICAL POWER OF THE NOBILITY

In the fifteenth century there appeared what the Hungarian historian Lajos Elekes has termed the 'Diet system of orders',[1] where in contrast to what had happened in the thirteenth century, the barons shared power with the other privileged orders – the simple country gentlemen, clergy and towns. The rise of the free towns proved decisive in the development of this system. Before this period, the landed lesser nobility should be considered as an element outside the governing class, even though the government of the free towns was oligarchic in character, since it rested in the hands of a patriciate made up of merchants and landowners. The order of towns represented interests different from those of the landowning lords and found itself virtually in opposition to the barons.

The barons always formed the most important order in the state, even though protocol in Hungary and Austria placed them after the clergy. Their economic power remained great because of their estates; whether in Bohemia, Hungary or Austria, the barons held sway in the countryside. They were rich enough to raise troops when needed but, in the system of

Diets, they shared administrative tasks with the lesser nobility. Through their wealth in land and property, their offices, alliances and clientelle, the feudal lords – magnates in Hungary, members of the *Herrenstand* in Austria and the *pani stavu* in Bohemia – were as distinct from the mass of simple country gentlemen as were the lords from the gentry in England.

The lesser nobility, under its order's slogan, 'the same noble liberty', strove to achieve its own political aspirations; it was unanimous in its opposition to the barons but its unity was quite relative and there were considerable differences in material standing within the group. The advance of the lesser nobility as an order was accompanied by the decline into poverty of a relatively large number of those country gentlemen who had owned only one domain. At the same time, it made it easier for a section of the large landowning families to enter the ranks of the barons and did not prevent modest landowners – the prime force within the movement – from becoming, in the long term, large landowners. At the time when the orders took shape, the lesser nobility held a relatively high social position within the population (much more so than in Western Europe); it embraced a section of large landowners, almost as rich as the barons, and families little different in their way of life from well-to-do peasants. The rich among them claimed their part in the government of the state while the poor were careful to avoid paying tax so as not to fall into the rank of the common people and so be liable for contributions (only the common people paid tax to the state). The prime purpose of their collaboration was to restrict the omnipotence of the aristocracy.

There were two ranks of nobility in each country; in Austria, Styria, Bohemia and Moravia there was an order of feudal lords, the members of which usually held the title *lord of.* . . . It was only much later that the titles *count* and *baron* multiplied in imitation of Western practice. In Hungary the upper rank of the nobility was formed by the order of magnates who were often satisfied with the title *master* (Latin *dominus*; Hungarian *úr*). The country gentlemen in Hungary constituted the *noblesse ordinaire*, in Hungarian the *Közepnemesség*, which is often translated as the *petite noblesse* and the *gentry* by analogy with the French and English case respectively. This group is most akin to the Polish *szlachta*, the great mass of nobles, freemen, descendants of all those who, in the early Middle Ages, had escaped the condition of servitude but among whom there was considerable disparity in wealth.

In Austria, Styria, Bohemia and Moravia, the country gentlemen formed the order of knights (the *Ritterstand*) who bore the title of *nobleman* (*Edler von . . .*) and whose origin was more complex since a number were descended from the *ministeriales*, the serfs, soldiers or stewards of a baron or margrave who, through their political services, had little by little wiped out the blot which their servile condition originally constituted. Others were descended from freemen who had joined a baron's clientele in order to obtain protection and to avoid complete ruin.

Unlike the nobility of Western Europe, the Eastern nobles were never organized into a real corporation. There was never a crisis comparable to that in France when Louis XIV's minister Colbert ordered the revision of proofs of nobility – a measure which cost the Breton nobility dearly. A new member was admitted by his peers only if he satisfied certain genealogical and economic criteria; he would enjoy privileges but would also take on responsibilities. Above all, each order carefully catalogued its members. There was no question of demanding public recognition on the basis of a vague reputation or, for a foreigner, of being admitted without the consent of one's peers. The nobility was not a closed group but admission to its ranks was strictly controlled.[2] Countless marriage alliances within the same order as a matter of course ensured a much greater overall cohesion, especially for the aristocracy.

The Church, well before the arrival of the regime of orders, had formed a body apart, in Hungary as much as in the other countries; it could not recruit solely by nepotism for clerical celibacy made a straightforward hereditary system impossible and the game of succession from uncle to nephew was moderated by elections within the chapters and by appointments made by the king. The Church was a corporation which adapted itself perfectly to the system of orders. As for the exercise of power, except in Bohemia, there was in the end a twofold movement; on the one hand the lower clergy were excluded, and on the other, the higher clergy were assimilated to the barons through the size of their land-holdings and the importance of their revenues. Only in Hungary did the law governing patronage, which king István had reserved for himself, force the claimants to important and middling benefices (i.e. bishoprics and canonicates) to enter, for a while at least, the service of the central power.

Be that as it may, what marked the composition of the orders was the predominance of landed proprietors who might hold many estates (aristocrats) or one or two estates (gentlemen), enjoy usufruct (prelates) or be landed proprietors from the towns.

The political expression of the orders' real power was the Diet, the advance of which was linked not only to the weaknesses of royal power but also to the new demands of political life. It was clear that the army of knights in armour, gathered under the banner of the barons, was obsolete. The military history of the period 1346–1444 records a long series of disasters for the heavy cavalry, whether at Crécy (1346) or Agincourt (1415) in France or in Eastern Europe at Nicopolis (1389), during the Hussite wars and at Varna (1444). The artillery and well-disciplined infantry put an end to the masses of knights who no longer saw war as a sporting adventure but as a subtle art tied to good organization. The Christian princes quickly realized that they would have to appeal to professional soldiers, especially to confront the Turks who were real professionals and for whom conquest was a natural activity. This entailed deploying regular and considerable financial resources which could be provided neither by the royal rights nor from the revenues from the royal domain nor through the extraordinary assistance which feudal custom provided. However,

taxation could not be carried out without the consent of a king's subjects
and this entailed the frequent and regular summoning of the Diets which
represented the whole state territory. These Diets accepted local particulari-
ties but nevertheless rendered them subject to their authority as to a
homogenous legislation and dominated local organizations in Bohemia as
in Hungary where they strengthened the territorial and governmental unity
of the country. The homogeneity of the central government fitted in well
with local institutions, in particular the assemblies of the nobility at the
level of the *comitat* in Hungary and the *circle* in Bohemia.

The assemblies of the Estates were not representative bodies elected in
the modern manner. It was no longer the case that every member of an
order made an appearance. Members of the aristocracy everywhere took
part in person; indeed the legal definition of a Hungarian magnate was that
he was invited in person by a letter from the king since the order was
successor to the barons of the king's court in the early Middle Ages where
to serve the Council (*concilium*) was among the feudal obligations. The
representation of the lesser nobility, however was much harder to regulate.
In Bohemia and Austria, no precise rule was established. Invited collectively, the lesser nobles very often were not interested in sessions taking
place in the capital (Vienna, Prague, Graz) where attendance entailed heavy
expenses that they could not always meet. Precise rules were arrived at in
the course of the fifteenth century in Hungary. Although for a while the
Polish solution was tried, which required all the gentry to be present on
horseback, king Matthias asked them to elect two deputies from each
county, thereby reinforcing the authority of each county assembly. Within
the order of clergy in Hungary, the opposition between the higher clergy
and the humble prebendaries became gradually more entrenched; while the
bishops were treated like the magnates, the chapters were invited to elect
representatives.

In Styria and Austria, the abbots who represented the prelates as a whole
were invited in person and their order was officially called 'the order of
prelates'. In Bohemia the representation of the clergy was not restored until
after 1620 when it was based on the Austrian model. In most countries
(Austria, Styria, Moravia and Bohemia) each order negotiated separately
the questions on the agenda. In Austria there was opposition among the
'three higher orders', the nobles and prelates on one side and on the other
the representatives of the towns, who were consulted only over financial
and administrative questions which concerned them and did not have a
voice in deliberations over the question of general policy. In Hungary, the
multiplication of elected representatives (gentry, chapters and, of course,
royal towns) led to the organization of two tables: a 'royal table', where the
magnates and bishops sat and the palatine presided, and the 'table of
regnicolae', where the deputies of the nobles, the chapters and the towns sat
and a magistrate of the royal court presided. This opposition gave rise after
1608 to a true bicameral system, similar to that in England, which lasted
right until the revolution of 1848.

Why did the towns succeed in raising themselves to the rank of the fourth order? This was a complex phenomenon in which the sovereign's protection and the legitimate ambitions of the urban patriciate played their part, but these political factors would themselves have been insufficient without the prodigious economic development that Danubian Europe experienced at the end of the Middle Ages and which the Black Death of 1348 could not impede. Production was progressively integrated within an exchange economy linked to the production of precious metals and the development of currency.

THE DEVELOPMENT OF THE ECONOMY IN THE FOURTEENTH AND FIFTEENTH CENTURIES

A crucial event in the history of Danubian Europe in the Middle Ages was the discovery and exploitation of deposits of precious metals within the boundaries of modern Czechoslovakia, in Bohemia, in Upper Hungary (Slovakia) and in Transylvania. In Bohemia, the silver mines at Jihlava (Iglau) were exploited and most importantly at Kutná Hora (Kuttenberg) which became the second town of the kingdom and in the present day bears reminders in its urban landscape of its magnificent past (the patrician houses and the church of St Barbara). As the king had claimed for himself the monopoly of casting and minting coin, trade in silver was forbidden and the whole output went into the production of coins. The miners and engineers were Germans from Saxony and Thuringia. In 1300 the royal mint at Prague began to mint silver pennies (in Czech, *groš*) which were used for foreign trade while pure copper coins were used for current transactions.

In the mining towns of Upper Hungary (Kremnica, Banská Štiavnice, Banská Bystrica) and Transylvania (Baia Mare), gold, silver and copper were mined. Here also the production and trade in precious metals was a royal monopoly. During the fourteenth century, this production was relatively large; it has been estimated that at this period output stood at 100 kg of gold and 10 tonnes of silver a year, about 33 per cent of the world production of gold and 25 per cent of the European production of silver. This precious metal made possible the minting of gold florins modelled on the Florentine pattern which, in the fifteenth century, were the most stable form of European currency. In the Tyrol, the mines at Schwatz also guaranteed a regular output of copper and silver, which soon made a fortune for the Habsburgs and for Jakob Fugger when he rented them after 1495.

The emergence of a real monetary economy had two important consequences. First, the condition of the peasantry improved, at least at the beginning. In Bohemia the feudal lord made a contract with the tenant farmer guaranteeing hereditary tenure and dues paid in money tended to replace dues in kind or labour (*robot*) and became feudal rent. The condition of an agricultural worker established on a small manor thus came very close to that of a peasant proprietor. Advances in technique – the practice of three-year rotation with fallow ground became widespread – also assured a better return. Since the Black Death had affected Central Europe, the sudden disappearance of a portion of the manual labour provided by the peasantry made the labour of the survivors all the more precious for the feudal lords, with the result that the noble proprietor endeavoured to look after his tenants. It is understandable that the peasants should have reacted so vigorously when certain feudal lords at the end of the fifteenth century wanted to re-establish the *robot* and became in turn cultivators drawing profit from the sale of agricultural products.

Second, and at the same time, city life grew in strength. Around 1380, Bohemia had thirty-five towns with more than 2 000 inhabitants and had presented the most dense urban network in the whole of Danubian Europe; the capital, Prague, had more than 30 000 inhabitants. In Hungary, the royal towns with privileges (about thirty) in *c.*1430 had between 3 000 and 5 000 inhabitants, while the capital, Buda, had 8 000. The proportion of artisans grew noticeably and towns ceased to pivot on agricultural production.

There should be no illusions about the 'liberties' which towns offered their inhabitants. Although their inhabitants escaped the 'tax collections' and authority of the feudal lords and represented a different world from that of the feudal estate, they were nevertheless subject to the authority of a patrician oligarchy that governed the city in its own interests. In Vienna the aldermen were generally merchants, landowners and some wealthy artisans owning several houses. These aldermen, like the Polls and the Klebers (aldermen 1208–1417), formed what amounted to dynasties. In Bohemia and Hungary they were generally merchants who were concerned with large-scale trade or else landowners. They were often of German origin and refused to share power with the artisans grouped into guilds. In the towns of Bohemia, the members of the guilds were Czech and social antagonism doubled as national antagonism which expressed itself clearly in the Hussite revolution. Everywhere it was difficult to acquire the legal status of a burgher and so to benefit from the privileges offered by the municipal law, based on the privileges of the German towns.

The rise of the towns nevertheless favoured the growth of large-scale commerce through the staple-right (*Stapelrecht*); every merchant arriving at Prague had to show his wares at the customs on the Staré Mesto and could leave again only if there was no local demand. Danubian Europe found itself integrated into the routes of international exchanges, especially because of the splendid access provided by the river Morava. The general principle of commerce was simple: in exchanges with the West and Germany, Danubian Europe, being less developed, exported agricultural goods and raw materials while it imported manufactured products, primarily textiles; it settled the deficit in the balance of trade with coinage; the produce of the copper and silver mines of Bohemia and Slovakia was thus introduced into the European commercial circuit – that is when it did not serve to nourish the papal treasury.

The history of Hungary's external trade illustrates how precious metals assumed a vital place in European economic life and how Eastern Europe became a favoured market for German industrial products; it should not be forgotten that in the fourteenth century, with the system of the entrepreneurial merchant, the fields of southern Germany were worked for the merchants of Ulm, Augsburg and Ravensburg.

The economic policy of the fourteenth century (in 1332, Bohemia and Poland agreed by the Višegrad settlement to boycott Vienna) also opened a direct route for German merchants who, via Wrocław (Vratislava/Breslau) and Brno, had direct access to Hungarian gold. Hungarian florins, which were valued greatly, spread within the European market while German manufactured products in exchange flooded the Hungarian market. From 1440 to 1460 the export of currency through the customs of Bratislava alone rose from 30 000 to 180 000 florins a year. According to the Hungarian historian E. Szcücs, in the course of the fifteenth century, 20 million gold florins went from Hungary to the West and contributed to the formation of banking capital in southern Germany (Augsburg, Nürnberg). The success of a man such as Jakob Fugger was not due to an economic miracle but to the easy exploitation of Eastern Europe. The growing deficit within the balance of trade (imports covered only 50 per cent) was due to the import of textiles (in 1457, 80 per cent of imports or 25 000 pieces of cloth), the rest was made up of hardware from Nürnberg (weapons and knives), spices and various wares. Half the export consisted of cattle, a quarter of raw copper and the rest of skins and fleeces. The deficit, however, did not cease to grow more marked as Hungary was unable to produce linens, silk and fustians to compete with the imported products. Hungary already found itself in the position of a 'colony' and to a certain extent played the role taken by Spanish America in the sixteenth century. Even in 1400, German and Italian business men passed through the intermediary of Hungarian businessmen at Bratislava and at Buda. Then, the capitalist class changed character; it was made up of patricians who invested their capital in business and German immigrants grown rich through commerce. Trading societies appeared whose principal activity was the export of fine wine and livestock and the import of cloth. While the Prague-Brno route was less secure because of the Hussite revolution, Vienna resumed its prime position in Hungarian commerce. In 1457, 42 per cent of the turnover was assured by four businessmen and their associates who imported cloth for around 70 000 gold florins. The remaining business was secured by small merchants who exported wine and imported cloth. Hungarian capital, however, was too weak to break the commercial and banking hegemony of the towns of Upper Germany. Annual imports reached 300 000 florins *c.* 1450 and a single Hungarian merchant found it difficult to mobilize a thousand florins. In 1518 a trading society at Košice with difficulty put together 5 000 florins, of which 1 500 came through municipal subsidy, at a time when the customs at Košice collected a tax at 1/30th (3.33 per cent) *ad valorem* and received 15 000 florins in a year. It has been calculated that in 1461 the taxable income of the whole bourgeoisie of Sopron was 26 174 florins while that of Augsburg was 472 026 florins. The Hungarian merchants were obliged to purchase on credit from their German colleagues in Brno and Vienna and their own capital sufficed only to pay customs and the cost of transport. Large-scale Hungarian commerce then depended on German credit. Sometimes the institutions from Upper Germany installed at Buda a factor who would even take Hungarian nationality. It becomes easier to understand how Jakob Fugger could go into partnership with the Thurzos to lease the mines of Upper Hungary and make substantial profits to the detriment of the Hungarian crown – and economy.[3]

It is also understandable why the growth of Hungarian towns was arrested in the fifteenth century. As the artisans were unable to compete with their German competitors, industry could not develop and capital could not accumulate. Indeed, the market economy passed into the hands of capitalists from Upper Germany or their Viennese associates. The towns also were not sufficiently large to fight the nobility on the political level and the experiment attempted by Matthias Corvinus (discussed below) rested on a fragile basis.

Bohemia kept more on the edge of the great routes and so found it easier to escape domination by German capital thanks to the Hussite revolution which, if seen as a national reaction, was in fact of great benefit. The principle of Bohemian external trade was little different from that of Hungary. As for importing goods, Prague merchants who had a quasi-monopoly of large-scale trade, imported salt directly from Austria and also Hungarian livestock as well as spices via Venice or Cracow. This urban development, however, whatever its importance, remained limited and did not prevent the landed aristocracy from retaining by far its preponderance in economic and political life.[4]

It is, moreover, interesting to note that the system became fixed after 1500 and that certain social groups, like the lesser nobility, tended to see their influence decrease while certain towns, too small and too poor, stopped regularly sending representatives to the Diet because the expense was too great. With the exception of the Tyrol, always cited as an example, the peasant communities were no longer invited to send their representatives, the noble landowners acting on behalf of their 'subjects'; revolts show that the peasants who then took part were not particularly satisfied with the re-emergence of these practices from the early Middle Ages. In 1478 the peasants in Carinthia revolted with a view to establishing their own confederation in place of the province's orders who were incapable of protecting them from the annual invasions by the Turks. If the revolt had succeeded, the resulting peasant federation would certainly have become 'the province', but the undertaking ran aground because the rebels were unable to achieve a military victory over the nobility. The Swiss example did not spread and there remained just four orders right until the end of the *ancien régime*.

THE ADMINISTRATIVE POWERS OF THE DIET[5]

The disputes within the House of Habsburg allowed the orders of the different provinces to defend their territorial community in the face of the sovereign House; in 1451 the orders of Lower Austria demanded that the young Ladislav the Posthumous, their natural lord, appear in court on behalf of his guardian Frederick III.

The Diets, the meetings of the orders of a province, turned from being an occasional occurrence into solid, quasi-permanent organizations, a development reflected in the orders' construction or provision of their own palaces (German *Landhaus*) and the creation of their own financial commission since the whole administration needed offices and archives. In 1513 the orders of Lower Austria acquired the former Liechtenstein palace in the Herrengasse in Vienna. The choice of site was not without significance; the *Landhaus* was close to the *Hofburg*, the sovereign's residence, and it was situated in one of the most prestigious streets of the Austrian capital where a number of great families had established their town residences. The Liechtenstein palace has, of course, been renovated and extended but the present-day palace, long the seat of government in Lower Austria, was rebuilt during the Metternich era, from 1837 to 1848, with due respect for the Gothic and Renaissance elements of the old building.

At the end of the fifteenth century, the orders of Styria had their own chancellery; from 1510 they bought a series of houses on the site of which they had lately built the *Landhaus*. In 1643 this complex was extended by the construction of the famous arsenal, made necessary by the proximity of the Austro-Turkish military frontier. At the present time it still stands as a monumental expression of the power of the orders in the baroque age.

In Carinthia, the orders easily played a leading role as the capital, Klagenfurt, was never a princely residence after its annexation by the Habsburgs in 1335; the orders took control of the administration and had their government palace built in 1574.

The government of the orders was divided into two clearly distinct activities: the plenary sessions of the Diet which were intermittent, and the permanent administration, which existed in the commissions and offices where clerks appointed by the Estates worked.

The Diets were summoned by the prince and could never legally summon themselves. An extensive examination of the archives reveals, however, that the practice of an annual session gradually was imposed in Austria and Bohemia while in Hungary the heavy machinery of the national assembly met less frequently because administrative tasks devolved upon the county assemblies.

A session of the Diet was a carefully regulated ceremony. The prince promulgated a patent of convocation, sent by the chancellery to all the members of each order. Despite the imperative nature of the convocation, there was clearly a discrepancy between the legal requirement and actual practice since a number of the gentry could appear in person only if they stayed several weeks in the capital. The session opened with the members solemnly taking their places while the king was generally represented by a great aristocrat, the imperial commissioner, charged with presenting the agenda or 'proposition' which was dominated by demands for contributions. The orders then retired to deliberate and draft their response, humble in form, often, at heart, very firm. If the prince was dissatisfied, he gave his reply and the negotiations could be prolonged right until he was satisfied with the Estates' final response. He then promulgated a decree of closure, or 'conclusion of the Diet', which had the force of law. It was then for the Estates to vote contributions and to levy them on different members, who were generally willing to comply after such lengthy bargaining.

The Diet selected from its midst a very important commission, the 'deputies', charged precisely with the apportionment of tax. In the fifteenth century, the amount of tax was set in proportion to the land rent which each feudal estate yielded. A second commission sat permanently between sessions (this was the 'commission of the Diet'), while a third examined the account of the Estates' treasury but this was less important. All the orders recovered their importance in the commissions because they each supplied precisely the same number of commissioners – two or three – so that there were as many prelates and gentry as great aristocrats. Clergy and patricians, given their experience in business and their education, could play a leading role.

Even in Austria the Diets had an essential role in so far as the prince depended on their goodwill for money as he could not live off just the revenues of his domain (forests, mines, landed property, customs and tolls, coinage, taxes on the Jews); the raising of contributions alone enabled him to follow an active foreign policy, while the system allowed the greater part of the administration to escape his control.

What of Bohemia and Hungary where the crown was elective and a new sovereign was elected only after he had made a contract in good and due form with the orders?[6]

Despite the sentiments of loyalty and attachment which the orders pledged to their natural lord, they were organized politically to defend steadfastly their interests in the face of the dynasty and the demands of an emergent modern state.

A true 'provincial' consciousness, that is a sense of belonging to a *Land*, appeared at the end of the Middle Ages. In Styria it was created by the *ministeriales* of the margrave, who identified themselves with the country, while in Lower Austria the feudal lords and their clientele felt distinct from the entourage of Rudolf of Habsburg. For the Austrian historian Otto Brunner, the orders did not represent the province, they in themselves constituted the province (*Landschaft*) and were the champions of provincial particularism. Right until the revolution of 1848, the existence of different provinces and of a provincial consciousness and the traditions of each *Land* were closely linked to the existence of the orders.

A phenomenon on a quite different scale appeared in Bohemia and Hungary, where the orders already possessed a true national consciousness albeit one which was tied to the nobility. With this in mind, it is easier to grasp the scale of the task facing the Habsburgs, who wanted to unite under their authority peoples so diverse and so little disposed to merge themselves into a unitary state.

NOTES AND REFERENCES

1. Lajos Elekes, 'Système diétal des Ordres et centralisation', in G. Szekely and E. Fugedi (eds) *Les États féodaux, la Renaissance et la Réformation en Pologne et en Hongrie,* Budapest, 1963, pp. 331–96.
2. V. Letosnik (ed.) *Die böhmische Landtafel: Inventar, Register, Uebersichten*, Prague, 1944.
3. Richard Ehrenberg, *Le Siècle des Fugger*, Paris, 1957.
4. Jenö Szucs, 'Das Städtewesen in Ungarn im 15–17. Jahrhundert', *Studia Historica*, no. 53, Budapest, 1963, pp. 97–164.
5. Otto Brunner, *Land und Herrschaft*, 4th edn, Vienna, 1959.
6. E. C. Hellbling, *Œsterreichische Verfassungs und Verwaltungsgeschichte*, Vienna, 1956.

CHAPTER SEVEN

Frederick III (1440–93)

The emperor Frederick III (1440–93) may be considered the second founder of the Habsburgs' European fortune, with the reign of his immediate predecessor, Albert V (1438–39), being seen as an extension of the reign of his father-in-law, Sigismund of Luxemburg. Frederick, duke of Styria, like Rudolf I before him, had the wit to take advantage of the relative weakness of his personal position to obtain the royal crown and to restore a tradition broken at the beginning of the fourteenth century by the tragic death of Albert I.

The success – albeit relative – of Frederick III can seem an aberration and liberal historiography has dealt harshly with the sovereign of Wiener Neustadt.[1] He was a gentle, other-worldly man, opposed to violence and self-possessed but nevertheless extraordinarily ambitious and convinced of the superiority of his House. Lacking the material means to realize his objectives, he suffered hardship on a number of occasions: despite having had the imperial title bestowed upon him, in 1485 he was driven from his capital by the king of Hungary; for five years, Matthias Corvinus occupied Vienna and Frederick III was obliged to take refuge at Linz.

His apparent weakness was, however, a virtue in the eyes of the electoral princes who were always made uneasy by an ambitious and powerful House with hegemonic tendencies, like the Luxemburg dynasty. Adam Wandruszka wrote that princely powerlessness in the face of the Diets reached its low point, and anarchy in Austria its high point, during the reign of Frederick III, although his obstinate policy brought rewards in the long term.[2] Convinced that right was on his side, he never lost heart. He anticipated the stubbornness of some of his successors, who in their turn would experience adversity: Rudolf II, Leopold I and Francis I (Napoleon's father-in-law), all suffered crushing reverses before triumphing over opposition.

In medieval eyes, he enjoyed a resounding success when he had himself crowned at Rome by the pope, an honour which his glorious ancestor Rudolf I had forgone. Frederick belonged to the Leopoldine branch of the House of Austria, the Styrian line that ruled from Graz. He was the son of

85

Ernest of Iron and it was the decline of the senior Albertine branch that brought him, after many set-backs, to the throne of the Emperors.

ALBERT V OF HABSBURG (1438–9)[3]

The Habsburgs benefited from the extinction in 1438 of the House of Luxemburg after the death of the emperor Sigismund. Albert V had married Elizabeth, the only daughter of the late emperor. Sigismund died on 9 December 1437 and his son-in-law without great difficulty received the impressive inheritance of the last Luxemburg. A few weeks after Sigismund's death, Albert V was elected, unopposed, king of Hungary, thereby opening the way for the Habsburgs and creating a precedent which served as the model for later bids by princes of the House of Austria. In March of the same year, Albert V had been elected king of the Romans, reviving the tradition broken at the beginning of the fourteenth century by the death of Albert II. In fact he accepted the crown without enthusiasm, aware of the enormous responsibilities which it brought and the modest means at his own disposal. In June he was also elected king of Bohemia by the lords of the Catholic party, while the Utraquist nobility and the towns favoured Kasimierz IV Jagiełłończyk, brother of the king of Poland and so, once again, sparked off civil war in Bohemia.

The election of Albert of Habsburg divided anew the kingdom of St Wenceslas; there was now a Habsburg party and a Polish party which faced each other on the battlefield near Tabor in the south of the country. The Polish party mobilized its troops 'in the name of the Czech and Slav language', but with the Habsburg party controlling Moravia, the Lusatias and Silesia, Bohemia was isolated. The premature death of Albert of Habsburg in autumn 1439 allowed the Utraquist party to triumph as Albert V's successor was yet to be born – for which reason he is known in history as Ladislav the Posthumous. From June 1438 to October 1439, for a little more than a year, Albert V had united the three crowns (Bohemia, Hungary and the Holy Roman Empire), an achievement that Rudolf I had not managed and which Ferdinand I would realize after 1531 when he became formally king of the Romans, or rather, after 1556 when he succeeded Charles V. It cannot be said that Albert V created a 'model', however, as his success was short-lived. His death brought everything to a halt (he contracted dysentery while on campaign in Serbia).

During a short space of time, Albert V had overseen the birth on the eastern flank of the Holy Roman Empire of a great power which might have been capable of breaking the Turks' conquering drive but which had a decidedly German character. Albert of Habsburg's Bohemian and Hungarian subjects regarded him as a German prince and the magnates quickly regretted giving him their votes. Might he have been capable of appeasing religious and national passions in the long run?

At the time of his accession he was already forty-one but his energy and wisdom were remarkable. He was as pious as he was courageous. The first task to which he applied himself was the defence of Hungary as he was aware of the danger presented by Ottoman imperialism in the Balkans. Despite the magnates' illwill, he called together a small army at the camp at Futak to relieve Semendria, which was besieged by sultan Murâd II. Already ailing, he decided to return to Vienna but time was running out: he died on the road to Komarno, by the Danube, on 27 October 1439. The chronicler Thomas Ebendorfer wrote:

Not only Austria but the whole of Germany lamented the sad end [of a prince] who was master of the world, a comfort to the unfortunate, a refuge to the oppressed and despairing, the shield of humble folk, scourge of the unbeliever, champion of the faith, worshipper of God and untiring promoter of His worship, father of the fatherland.[4]

A Czech chronicler paid him exceptional homage, 'He was a prince, gentle and just, although he was German'.

The late sovereign had a good understanding of the ills from which his age suffered and gave his attention to much needed religious reform. He lent the weight of his authority to monasticism; his chancellor and former tutor, Andreas Plank, founded at Vienna the College of St Dorothea (which, in the eighteenth century, played an important role in religious life in Austria) and installed canons regular of St Augustine at Dürnstein in Lower Austria. These attempts, however, were hindered by the lack of continuity; this was the case with the archbishop of Salzburg and the bishop of Passau. The tensions between the rigid discipline of the new foundations and the laxity of countless other abbeys became more apparent, to the great disgust of the poor and pious faithful. It would, however, be an exaggeration to speak of general decadence at this period in monastic life.

Albert V, a good Habsburg, also proved to be a patron of the arts and learning; under the influence of his chancellor Plank, who had studied at Padua, he showed an interest in humanism, which was already flourishing in the Italian peninsula, and applied himself to collecting humanist works. With the 110 manuscripts inherited from the Luxemburg collection, he founded a prestigious library.

THE SUCCESSION[5]

The sudden and premature death of Albert V in October 1439 again raised the eternal problems which a minority presented under the monarchical system. It was only in February 1440 that the late sovereign's son was born, Ladislav, who for the whole of his brief existence was a plaything of the factions. With the sovereign's death, the Leopoldine branch returned to the political scene after being for a long time marginalized with only regional importance in Styria and the Tyrol. Then in 1457, the Albertine branch was extinguished when Ladislav the Posthumous died at seventeen without having been able to recover the inheritance bequeathed to him by his father.[6]

The hopes of the Leopoldine branch also rested on a child, the archduke Sigismund of the Tyrol, whose father died in 1439, but most importantly on the two sons of duke Ernest the Iron, who were close in age but different in character.

Albert of Styria did not accept with good grace the arbitration of his uncle, Albert of Austria, who after the death of duke Ernest had entrusted the government of Styria to his brother Frederick and left him only the shreds of an inheritance when he had wanted shared sovereignty. In 1440 Frederick suddenly found himself faced with enormous responsibilities. The widowed Elizabeth of Luxemburg and her son Ladislav placed themselves under his protection, bringing with them the crown of St Stephen in contravention of all the fundamental laws of the kingdom of Hungary.[7] Frederick thus held in his hands valuable pledges over which the various parties proceeded to dispute as national feelings quickly came to the fore; the Hungarians wished to make the baby a Hungarian, the orders of Bohemia wanted to transform him into a Czech sovereign, while no one wanted him to become a Styrian prince.

Frederick was politically weak. A baron of Lower Austria, Ulrich Eyzinger, who appeared *parvenu* but as general steward of the domains was rich and powerful, demanded that Ladislav the Posthumous be handed over to him. Eyzinger had succeeded in forming a 'national' party supported by the city of Vienna and the nobility of Lower Austria. For the first time in Lower Austria's history, a league among the orders of the different countries was formed which took on the appearance of a confederation of dissatisfied nobles. The League of Mailberg succeeded in bringing together János Hunyadi, Jiří of Poděbrady, the Estates of Upper Austria, of Moravia and of Lower Austria in a configuration which foreshadowed the alliances at the beginning of the seventeenth century. Frederick then had to defend the interests of the House of Austria in the face of recalcitrant subjects who had at their disposal military and financial resources superior to those of their sovereign. The paradox is that he did not allow himself to be discouraged and continued to dream of a universal monarchy when he was not even master in his own home.

Frederick III was nonetheless convinced of his House's superiority to all other Christian dynasties and of the exceptional destiny to which God would one day call it. It was as the modest duke of Styria but the descendant of the illustrious Rudolf I that he adopted the famous Latin device *AEIOU* (*Austriae est imperare orbi universo*; it is for Austria to rule the whole world), which in the circumstances might have struck a Luxemburg, Valois or Wittelsbach as risible. However, Frederick was convinced that, if not he, then certainly an offspring of the illustrious House was destined one day to be crowned with the crown of the emperors at Rome and to restore the Holy Roman Empire in all its glory, quite simply because the House of Austria was destined by God for greatness.

Even so, in February 1440 it was the oldest of the surviving Habsburgs who was unanimously elected king of the Romans with the discreet blessing of pope Eugene IV. According to Aeneas Silvio Piccolomini, the future Pius II, Frederick III had been elected *against* his will, but this apparent modesty and his genuine weakness had probably worked in his favour with the College of Electors, always anxious to curb the emperor's power. Frederick, then, had benefited from the same prejudice which in 1273 had been to Rudolf I's advantage. The electors' choice was a historic one because the Habsburgs would keep the crown of Charlemagne right until the dissolution of the Holy Roman Empire in 1806.

Frederick III now extended his horizons to the whole of Europe. In 1444 he concluded an alliance with the king of France, Charles VII, because he questioned the ambitions of the Burgundians in Upper Alsace, where he drew the bands of brigands who continued to trouble France until the conclusion of the Franco-English treaty, which put an end *de facto* to the Hundred Years War. For Charles VII, the dispatching of large companies under the orders of the dauphin Louis, did not meet any desire for conquest but was rather an operation to release tension. The nobility, preoccupied with the danger presented by the Swiss cantons, supported the move. Eight days after the arrival of the future Louis XI, the initial objectives were attained but the presence of the brigands created a new situation as their leader appeared determined to direct his own policy like a war lord and Frederick III, acting in the name of his young relative Sigismund of the Tyrol, seemed not to be master of events. Finally, the Armagnacs left Alsace in the spring of 1445 but this affair left bad memories and German opinion long remained hostile to Frederick III for having appealed to *Welsche* troops.[8]

A more successful project was his marriage into the Portugese royal family at a time when the little Atlantic kingdom was in the process of strengthening its mastery over the sea and preparing to win for itself a colonial empire. In 1452 Frederick married at Rome the *infanta* Eleonora, niece of prince Henry the Navigator, who launched the Portugese *caravela* to uncover the shores of Africa. The marriage led to fruitful collaboration between German experts and the sailors of Lusitania. The empress Eleonora played a part in widening the horizons of her son, Maximilian.

THE IMPERIAL CORONATION (1452)[9]

Frederick III doggedly followed his imperial dream. Through the efforts of his chancellor Schlick, a lawyer from Eger who had been enriched and ennobled, he won the support of the Holy See. He was able to descend into Italy surrounded by countless knights, carrying out for the last time the *Römerzug* (Roman journey), the climax of which was the crowning of the king of the Romans by the pope. He and his young wife were crowned at St Peter's in 1452. He was the first and last Habsburg to be consecrated in this way – an honour which many, more powerful, German sovereigns had been denied. In 1529 Charles V was content with a coronation at Bologna at the hands of his old adversary, pope Clement VII, two years after his mercenaries had sacked the Eternal City.

Frederick III took advantage of this to confirm the *privilegium majus* which, while its authenticity was open to question, was nevertheless of real benefit to the House of Austria and its subjects in the hereditary lands as it conferred upon them a privileged position within the Holy Roman Empire. The origin of the *privilegium majus* was debatable in so far as it was an exorbitant extension of the *privilegium minus* which, though authentic, was deemed inadequate by Rudolf IV the Founder who had tried to obtain its extension by doubtful means from his father-in-law Charles IV of Luxemburg. Frederick III at least conferred on the *privilegium majus* a definite character of respectability in virtue of the principle according to which no one looks after one's interests as well as oneself.[10]

Again with an eye to adding to the glory of the House of Austria, he assumed the title thought up by Rudolf IV; in place of 'archduke Palatine', he satisfied himself with the title 'archduke' for the princes of his House, the title which the dukes of Styria as well as their descendants henceforth bore. This was how the practice arose which distinguished the members of the House of Habsburg from all the other princes of Christendom.

Certain Italian humanists, never at a loss for flattery, did not hesitate to compare Frederick to Caesar Augustus or Alexander, although the new emperor had nothing of the conqueror about him in spirit or physique. A statue made shortly afterwards shows an extremely tall man with sunken shoulders and a melancholy expression. From his mother, the Polish princess Kymburga of Masovia, he had inherited a heavy build and the prominent lower jaw that became a dominant physical characteristic of the Habsburgs; he wears the crown set square, without any majesty. The year after his coronation at St Peter's, when the new Alexander learnt of the capture of Constantinople by Mehmed the Conqueror, he shut himself inside his private apartments for several days to weep, but guarded against replying in earnest to the pope's appeals for a crusade.

Two characters close to Frederick III nonetheless wanted to breathe life once again into the imperial ideology; cardinal Nikolaus of Cusa, from the Rhineland and the Tuscan Aeneas Silvio Piccolomini. They hoped to prevent the decline of their familiar universe by restoring the prestige and authority of the two great powers of the triumphant Middle Ages, the papacy and the Empire.

Nikolaus of Cusa, bishop of Brixen (Bressaone, in the southern Tyrol), was one of the last great scholastic theologians and so one of the favourite targets of the humanists. The son of a boatman on the Moselle, he rose to the rank of cardinal through his great learning and powerful intellect. He issued stern warnings to the clergy in crisis in his *Concordantia catholica*.

Aeneas Silvio Piccolomini belonged to a patrician family from Sienna and was the model of a diplomat-prelate. Long periods of time spent north of the Alps, participation in various councils and his friendship with the Austrian chancellor Schlick made him particularly able to form a judgement. As the future pope and good neo-Ghibelline that he was, he thought that the Italy of rival cities would survive only if the Germans and the emperor re-established order there and if they ceased their indifference to the fate of the peninsula.

Piccolomini's views corresponded to Frederick III's deepest thoughts, as the emperor believed that only lack of courage kept the German nation from restoring the former glory of the Holy Roman Empire. If the House of Austria had sufficient strength to accomplish such a project, Frederick III was certain of success because he was ready to sacrifice Austria, Styria and the Tyrol in order to regild the blazon of the German nation and of the Empire.

The future pope, however, was under no illusions with regard to Frederick of Habsburg's weaknesses and lack of commitment and told one of Frederick's advisers: the fear of expense leads the majority of subjects to understimate the importance of the Holy Roman Empire for which they wouldn't give twopence; the burghers of the large towns, now experiencing full economic growth, think that they are the citizens of their own little urban republic and that the Empire brings them little; if Frederick aspires to universal monarchy, it is he who should pay the price as it is he who will draw all the advantages. But all this theorizing was futile: Frederick III was not master in his own house nor was he in a position to exercise his authority as the head of the House of Habsburg.

THE LEAGUE OF MAILBERG

Eyzinger and the orders of Lower Austria had formed the League of Mailberg with the avowed goal of the 'liberation' of Ladislav the Posthumous from the clutches of his imperial guardian. The League took into its service the Styrian *condottiere* Andreas Baumkirchner, who did not hesitate to attack Wiener Neustadt, Frederick III's favourite residence.

Although the assault was repulsed, the emperor suffered the humiliation of 'restoring' Ladislav to the party of the Estates. The young man, led in triumph to Vienna, became a plaything in the hands of the orders of Lower Austria, Bohemia and Hungary.

In 1456 Ladislav was taken away to Hungary by the magnate Ulrich of Cilli, leader of the clan hostile to the Hunyadi. The young king was party to the execution of László Hunyadi, the eldest son of the hero of Belgrade, then returned to Prague where, at the instigation of Jiří of Poděbrady, who sought an alliance with France, he was betrothed to Madeleine of Valois, daughter of Charles VII of France. Ladislav the Posthumous died suddenly on 20 November 1457 at the age of seventeen while the Czech capital was preparing to celebrate his marriage. General rumour, without any great basis, accused Jiří of Poděbrady of having had the young king of Bohemia and Hungary poisoned.

The unexpected death of the last surviving heir of the Albertine branch of the Habsburgs put an end for a while to the personal union of the hereditary lands, Hungary and Bohemia, which had been achieved by Albert V of Habsburg. The failure of the line postponed the possibility of forming a powerful confederation against the Turkish menace and left Hungary solely responsible for the defence of Danubian Europe. The particular – often short-sighted – interests of the nobles of the different countries forced another, apparently more modern solution – the creation of national monarchies – while Frederick III tried to collect together the inheritance of the Albertine branch as a prelude to the reunion of the hereditary lands under the authority of one prince. Could the emperor once more have united Bohemia, Austria and Hungary under one sceptre? Measured against this plan, his reign must be judged a failure. The protagonists each mistook their enemy, using their forces against their neighbour rather than against the Turkish menace.

FRATRICIDAL CONFLICT (1457–63)

Once again the question of the succession brought civil war to medieval Austria. The family regulations which had been followed since Rudolf I's accession, and which vacillated between old Germanic law and the more modern concept of primogeniture, were of little value. The famous *privilegium majus* confirmed the pre-eminence of the head of the House of Austria but in this particular case no authority could settle the question with a semblance of impartiality as the emperor, the arbiter recognized by feudal law, was both judge and party. The principle of excluding cadets was never again clearly affirmed because it was contrary to the judicial traditions of the German nobility.

The Estates were designated as arbiters but their one concern was to weaken the power of the prince, to share his territories and revenues. The verdict granted Lower Austria to Frederick and Upper Austria to Albert VI while the leading towns were to take an oath to three Habsburgs, the two brothers Frederick and Albert and also their cousin Sigismund of the Tyrol. In these circumstances the House of Austria could not but play a major role in the Empire, the Danubian region and in Europe.

Frederick III's political skill – not to say genius – lay in that he managed to survive between Jiří of Poděbrady and Matthias Corvinus who, according to the tradition begun by Otakar Přemysl and Béla IV, were in a position purely and simply to annex Austria to their kingdom.

Frederick also tried to play off Poděbrady against Matthias Corvinus, who was the more dangerous opponent. In dealing with Matthias, though, Frederick III held the trump card: he still had in his possession the crown of St Stephen which his rival, the elected king of Hungary needed if he was to be crowned and to exercise his legitimate power. Having failed to find sufficient support with Poděbrady to exercise his rights after his election by a clan of magnates, Frederick III preferred to negotiate with Matthias Corvinus in 1463 and to find a compromise that would take care of the future. He renounced his rights over Hungary and restored the royal crown; in return he received the lordships of Transdanubia, which corresponded roughly to modern Burgenland, and also an indemnity of 80 000 gold ducats, which Matthias paid out of the money provided by the pope for a crusade against the Ottomans. He kept the title of king of Hungary and also the right of succession if Matthias died without a legitimate male heir.

The agreement between Albert VI and Frederick III did not last the anticipated three years. The *Bürgermeister* of Vienna, Wolfgang Holzer, unable to put an end to the internal conflicts within the magistracy fell victim to the ambitions of Albert VI; Frederick III charged him with treason and condemned him to death. Jiří of Poděbrady, the Austrian nobility and Albert VI then joined together to attack Vienna and laid siege to the royal palace while the princes of the Empire dreamt of forcing Frederick III to abdicate. Only Albert VI's death (2 December 1463) saved the emperor from a humiliating defeat and put an end to the fratricidal strife.

Frederick was a pacific prince, as much by disposition as by necessity. The chronicler Arenpach described him as obstinate and doctrinaire, possessed of remarkable intelligence and with a near infallible memory. He was full of dignity, even if this did not correspond to any real power and he saw the imperial crown as an extraordinary advantage which was not to be compromised, no matter how adverse the circumstances. Albert had a totally different character; aggressive, he was always ready to launch an attack and to cover himself with glory on the battlefield. If Frederick was circumspect and avaricious, Albert was by contrast generous and quick to make decisions.

Thomas Ebendorfer observed that the Austrian people were the principle victim of this fratricidal quarrel which was continued by the nobility who refused to admit defeat, despite the death of their champion; calm only returned in 1465. Andreas Baumkirchner with his bands struck terror into Styria, pillaging and razing to the ground. After his capture and execution, his sons took advantage of Frederick's impassivity and continued to lay waste to the countryside on the pretext of avenging the late *condottiere*.

THE WESTERN FRONTIERS OF THE EMPIRE

In the West, the Holy Roman Empire and the Habsburgs' Rhineland patrimony were threatened by the ambitions of the Valois. From 1467 Charles the Bold ruled over Burgundy, Franche-Comté and the Netherlands, but he extended his authority over Alsace and Breisgau which had been given to him as a guarantee by the archduke Sigismund, and was waiting to attack the Swiss and Lorraine in order to reconstitute the Lotharingia of the early Middle Ages. For a while, he even dreamt of having himself elected king of the Romans. To succeed in his purposes, he needed allies to neutralize his most formidable opponents, the Swiss, and above all his cousin Louis XI, king of France.

The Habsburgs, especially Sigismund of the Tyrol, seemed to be the ideal partners. Sigismund the Rich, despite his epithet, was as generous as his cousin Frederick III was mean and never had any money, in spite of the Tyrolean silver mines. Disastrous management and the war against the Swiss had forced him to borrow, then to mortgage his domains. For this reason he thought it wise to turn to Charles the Bold for support.

With the consent of his vassals, for the Alsatian nobility were always seeking French support against the Swiss menace, Sigismund by the 1469 treaty of Saint-Omer ceded as a guarantee his domains of Alsace, Breisgau and the 'forest towns' in exchange for a loan of 50 000 florins. In fact Charles the Bold received more in terms of rights of sovereignty than he did real revenues, as these were already pledged to private citizens. He appointed a directory of five commissioners and a grand bailiff, Peter of Hagenbach; the coat-of-arms of Burgundy replaced those of the Habsburgs and the Estates met at Ensisheim and swore an oath to Charles the Bold. For the historian George Bischoff, there can be no doubt, 'the annexation of Burgundy was a matter of fact; Upper Alsace and the Sundgau formed until recently an autonomous unit, separated from the old *Vorlande* (further lands) in a manner comparable to that effected in 1648'.

Sigismund's volte-face was due to the support which he found among the towns of the upper Rhine (Basle, Strassburg, Colmar and Sélestat) and the Swiss cantons; Louis XI, for sure, played his part in the formation of this 'League of Constance' in 1474. Sigismund obtained 80 000 florins which enabled him to pay off the mortgage on his lands and the League declared war on Charles the Bold, whose imperial ambitions had become disquieting.

At the same time, Frederick III undertook negotiations with Charles the Bold, who proposed marriage between his only daughter Maria and the archduke Maximilian in exchange for the dignity of Vicar of the Empire and most importantly – for want of being able to claim the dignity of king of the Romans – the title of king of Burgundy. Although Maria of Burgundy was the richest heiress in Christendom, the marriage raised numerous difficulties, not least the future couple's extreme youth; Maria was born in 1457 and Maximilian in 1459. Frederick understood perfectly well that Charles the Bold was not a sincere friend of the Holy Roman Empire and that he coveted Lorraine, Switzerland, the lands of the Empire and was the mortal enemy of his cousin in Paris, Louis XI, who was still the emperor's ally. The Austro-Burgundian alliance signified the end of friendly relations between the king of France and Frederick III.

The betrothal was concluded in 1473 at Trier during a formal meeting between Frederick and Charles the Bold. Frederick perhaps did not foresee that this event was to prove heavier with consequences than any other during his reign; the young Maximilian, despite his father's caution, was able to make the most of circumstances. Thanks to a daring which bordered on folly, he preserved his wife's inheritance and founded an Austro-Burgundian House of Habsburg that quickly found its centre of gravity in Western Europe and finally possessed means in proportion to its ambitions. Yet more grave for the future was the fact that Maximilian's marriage clouded relations between the House of France and Austria for almost three centuries.

In the immediate future, in 1475, Frederick III found himself incapable of preventing Charles the Bold from attacking Lorraine, at the very moment when the Alsatians were shaking off the Burgundian yoke and executed Peter of Hagenbach, who was deemed a tyrant for having served the duke of Burgundy too well.

Salvation came from the Swiss confederation who were no more inclined to submit to the Valois of Malines than they had been to the Habsburgs. The year 1476 was decisive as the Swiss pikemen easily overpowered the heavy Burgundian cavalry, who had believed themselves invincible, and so confirmed the superiority of footsoldiers on the battlefield. The battles of Grandson and Morat marked the end of the hitherto unstoppable rise of Charles the Bold. In January 1477 the grandduke of the West died, wretchedly, in front of the walls of Nancy. The scene was set, or more precisely, the chapter opened for the Burgundian succession which set Maximilian of Austria against Louis XI, as both were claimants to the inheritance of Charles the Bold while Sigismund of the Tyrol tried to resume control of Further Austria. There he encountered opposition from the three orders (clergy, knights and towns), who were no less conscious of their political rights than were the orders of Styria and Lower Austria. The Burgundian occupation had contributed to the emergence of an Austrian Alsace.

THE ADMINISTRATION OF THE HEREDITARY LANDS

Despite the control which the assemblies of the Estates had over the administration, Frederick III secured some success in the government of the hereditary lands which, while limited, promised well for the future.

Well aware that the Church on the eastern fringe of the Holy Roman Empire had suffered since the early Middle Ages from inadequate pastoral administration and staffing, he tried hard to improve the situation; the hereditary lands were subject to the sees of Salzburg and Passau outside Austria and far too vast for the diocesan bishops to administer thoroughly. For this reason, as early as 1461, he secured from pope Pius II the foundation of the bishopric at Laibach in Carniola (now Ljubljana in the Republic of Slovenia). In 1469 the Holy See granted him the creation of two new episcopal sees, Wiener Neustadt, the emperor's favourite residence, and Vienna which already possessed a cathedral, the collegiate church of St Stephen, but not a bishopric. Faced with the ill will of the bishop of Passau, the jurisdiction of the bishop of Vienna was for a long time limited to the capital and its outskirts while the episcopal see itself was poorly endowed.

Frederick III also managed to acquire from the lord of Wallsee Rijeka, (Fiume, then called Sankt Veit am Pflaum) a still modest port which assured the House of Austria an additional outlet on the Adriatic and prepared for its later expansion in that direction.

THE CONFLICT WITH MATTHIAS CORVINUS (1480–90)

A serious blunder by Frederick III provoked armed intervention by Matthias Corvinus, who had not forsworn the dream of reassembling the monarchy of Albert V of Habsburg and Ladislav the Posthumous, even at the cost of neglecting the struggle against the Ottomans. The fall in 1471 of the chancellor Jan Vitéz of Sredna pointed dramatically to the new direction of Hungarian strategy; first to form a powerful Danubian federation, then to carry the offensive into the Balkans. Supported by the Catholic and conservative party, Matthias was able to extend his authority over Moravia and Silesia while Bohemia remained faithful to the Utraquist Church.

Johann Beckensloer, Vitéz's successor, quarrelled with Matthias Corvinus and in 1479 sought refuge with Frederick III who appointed him bishop of Vienna and had him elected coadjutor of the archbishop of Salzburg with the right of succession. Bernhard von Rohr, the acting archbishop, was presented with the *fait accompli* and, instead of yielding his place to his rival, appealed to Matthias Corvinus.

Corvinus invaded Carinthia, Styria and Lower Austria, where he found many supporters and accused the emperor of breaking the peace and negotiating secretly with the Porte. The armistice of 1481 was broken the following year by Matthias Corvinus, who had made new allies in Switzerland and Italy. The contest was unequal since the king of Hungary had at his disposal one of the best armies in Europe. After a long siege, he occupied Vienna in 1485 and took up residence there. In 1487 he also seized Wiener Neustadt and Frederick III had to flee to Linz. Maximilian was prepared to cede Lower Austria to Matthias Corvinus but the old emperor was intractable and it was only the death of the king of Hungary in 1490 that saved Frederick; Matthias did not have a legitimate heir and the magnates were weary of strong royal power.

It was no accident that Maximilian was at hand. He made good the rights of the House of Austria to the crown of St Stephen, rights which Matthias himself had recognized in the treaty of Sopron in 1463. He invaded Hungary but the expedition was cut short because of lack of money to pay the Austrian mercenaries. The treaty of Pressburg re-established the status quo, simply confirming the agreement of 1463. Electing Władysław Jagiełłończyk in 1491, the Hungarian orders re-established the personal union with the kingdom of Bohemia and restored peace to the Danubian basin. Frederick III could die in peace (19 August 1493) after forty-three years as king of the Romans. Since Maximilian had already acquired this title in 1486, the succession was assured and, for once, the death of an emperor did not create any difficulty.

The long history of Frederick III can appear confused and unattractive, a real slice of *histoire événementielle* where there is little to be debated but the dreams of the emperor constantly clashed with reality, as much because of the weaknesses of the House of Austria as the caution of the sovereign. At a time when princes were daring war leaders (Albert VI, his cadet, Charles the Bold, Matthias Corvinus and his own son Maximilian), he was reluctant to entrust the destiny of the House to the chances of arms and an engagement of a few hours on a battlefield. In this he resembled his contemporary and ally Louis XI. His brilliant opponents, including Matthias Corvinus, all achieved spectacular – albeit short-lived – successes. At a time when the life of princes could be brief, it fell to Frederick to outlive his contemporary rulers: his reign's strength lay in its very length combined with the strategic vision of his mission.

Such great principles were undoubtedly the mainspring of his action and later created the grandeur and success of his House. He was wedded to the imperial dignity, never moved from his principles, whether faced with the pretensions of a newcomer like Charles the Bold, who humiliated him with his ostentatious luxury at the time of the meeting at Trier, or the extravagant nobilities of Danubian Europe. By the marriage of his son with the heiress of the House of Burgundy, he had prepared the European destiny of Maximilian and the universal monarchy of Charles V. Even in the Hungarian question, he never renounced the rights of the House of Austria, which eased the election of Ferdinand in 1527.

His religious policy was very far-sighted. Had it fully succeeded, a better administered Church in Austria would, perhaps, have resisted the advances of the Lutheran Reformation. He had, in any case, undertaken a task which was to be achieved three centuries later by Joseph II.

Even if his character has hardly stirred the enthusiasm of historians, one must acknowlege his virtues of tenacity, patience and constancy amid the adversities which would establish the grandeur of his House. Phlegmatic, convinced of the divine mission of the House of Austria – it was during his reign that Austria gradually began to replace the Habsburg name – he always thought of the long term when confronted with the intense activity of his contemporaries, who were always inclined to talk a lot, wave their arms around and rush headlong into any dazzling adventure where success was by no means certain. Of remarkable sobriety, he disapproved of heavy drinkers at a time when drunkenness was an aristocratic virtue. Frederick III was a cold, introverted character. Finding the dangers and toil of warfare deeply repugnant, like Louis XI of France he used diplomacy rather than war to weave the complex web, which ensured that his descendants would one day dominate Latin Christendom.

NOTES AND REFERENCES

1. Joseph Loserth, *Geschichte des späteren Mittelalters (1197–1492)*, Vienna, 1903, passim.

2. Adam Wandruszka, *Das Haus Habsburg: eine europäische Dynastie*, Vienna, 1956, p. 91.

3. Günther Hödl, *Albrecht II: Königtum, Reichsregierung und Reichsreform 1438–1439*, Vienna, 1978.

4. Thomas Ebendorfer, *Kaiserchronik*, published by Bachmann, *Urkunden und Aktenstücke, Fontes Rerum Austriacarum*, II, 42, Vienna, 1879.

5. Heinrich Zeiszberg, 'Der Österreichische Erbfolgestreit nach dem Tode des Königs Ladislaus', *Archiv für Œsterreichische Geschichte*, 54, Vienna, 1876.

6. Heinz Dopsch, 'Die Grafen von Cilli – ein Forschungsproblem?', *Südost-deutsches Archiv*, 17–18, Munich, 1975, pp. 9–49.

7. It was forbidden to take outside Hungary the crown of St Stephen, the symbol

of the unity of the kingdom. Madga von Barany-Oberschall, *Die Sankt Stephans-Krone*, Vienna, 1961.

8. Georges Bischoff, *Gouvernants et gouvernés en Haute-Alsace*, Strassburg, 1981.
9. J. Markus, *Die letzte Kaiserkrönung in Rom*, thesis, Leipzig, 1900.
10. Alphons Lhotsky, *Privilegium Majus: Die Geschichte einer Urkunde*, Vienna, 1957.

CHAPTER EIGHT

Danubian Europe and the Threat from the Turks

It will already be clear from remarks in preceding chapters that at the end of the Middle Ages the internal balance of continental Europe was in the process of change: a people coming from Central Asia had gradually extended their domination over Anatolia and built a powerful, well-organized state to the detriment of the Roman Empire in the East. The Turks proved to be first and foremost good soldiers, combining indisputable military genius with great talents as organizers and administrators. Unlike the other conquerors coming from the steppe, the Huns, Avars and Mongols who one or two generations before had occupied the Danubian area, the Ottomans founded a state which endured. In the fourteenth century, they crossed the straits which separate the Black Sea from the Aegean and extended their rule over the Balkan peninsula; in a great movement with Constantinople as its pivot, they occupied in succession Greece, Thrace and Albania, then destroyed the Serb and Bulgar monarchies, reducing the Christian population to the condition of 'protected' subjects.

The Turks, while certainly not the barbarians described by the writers of the anti-Turkish propaganda which developed in the German world, brought with them a different civilization. Having converted to Islam in the tenth century at the time of their settlement in Iran, they posed a mortal threat to Christianity, although they were tolerant and let the Greeks and Bulgars practise the religion of their fathers. The Ottoman state was a Muslim state which accommodated only elites converted to Islam. The aristocracy was mercilessly eliminated to the benefit of the sultan's soldiers and officials, the timariots.

The urban landscape was likewise transformed: the principal churches were converted into mosques with towering minarets. The orthodox clergy was closely subordinated to the sultan and was deprived of its lands while the faithful were considered as second-class subjects and were compelled to pay a special tax, the *haraç* or poll tax.

The reasoning behind Ottoman imperialism combined with the Islamic notion of 'Holy War' (*jihâd*) required the continuous extension of the Empire's frontiers. Muslim expansion, which had been blocked in the ninth

100

century and had even been driven back in the Iberian peninsula, found a fresh wind which unsettled the Holy See and those rulers capable of looking beyond the internal quarrels of Latin Christendom.

The Italian maritime republics, Genoa and in particular Venice, found their vital interests threatened (they traded extensively with the East) and sought to come to terms with the Turks in order to be able to continue with the business that was the reason for their existence. The popes, on the other hand, tried to bring up to date the old idea of a crusade: since the little Christian nations of the Balkans were too weak to resist the Turkish advance, should not the powerful armies of knights mobilize themselves to come to their rescue? The Holy Roman Empire could take up arms, the Christian kingdoms of Eastern Europe – Hungary, Poland and Bohemia – could come together under one sceptre and the combination briefly realized by Sigismund of Luxemburg and his son-in-law Albert V of Habsburg – the union of the Holy Roman Empire, Bohemia and Hungary – could be perpetuated.

All these geo-strategic alliances ended in a string of crushing defeats, however: as the princes and Christian nations faced the superiority of the Turks, they were incapable of reaching agreement among themselves.

THE IRRESISTIBLE ADVANCE OF THE TURKS[1]

After defeating the Byzantines at Mantzikiert in Asia Minor (1071), the Turks pitched their tents and grazed their herds in Anatolia; the Greek population remained only in the cities on the coast. It was not until the fourteenth century that the conquerors crossed into Europe to lend strong support to the Byzantines in their fight against the Serbs. Settled at Bursa in western Anatolia, the descendants of Osmân went on to absorb the other Turkish principalities and quickly became a force all the more to be feared since they made themselves the champions of the Muslim cause. Osmân's grandson, Murâd I (1362–89), went on to make rapid progress through the Balkans; in 1361 the Turks conquered the whole of Thrace. The first coalition was formed, gathering together pope Urban II, Louis of Hungary, the rulers of Bosnia, Serbia and Wallachia, but was defeated near the river Mautza. As a result of this defeat, Murâd established his capital at Adrianople in 1365 and proceeded with the conquest of the Balkans; he defeated the Serbs in 1371, took Niš in 1375, Sofia in 1382 and Thessaloniki fell in 1386. The following year, Murâd decided to take revenge for what proved to be the short-lived success of the Serb and Bulgar coalition and prepared a great expedition against the Serbs, who were defeated at Kosovo, 28 June 1389. At the same time, the grand vizier crushed the Bulgars at Nicopolis. The whole of Bulgaria passed under Ottoman rule.

Murâd's son, Bâyezîd I, continued the conquest of the Balkans. In 1396 Bâyezîd inflicted a second defeat on the Christian armies. A 'crusade' was undertaken under the leadership of the king of Hungary, Sigismund of Luxemburg, and with 10 000 Frenchmen commanded by the duke of Burgundy, John the Fearless. The consequences were catastrophic: the kingdom of Hungary now found itself in the front line, under threat from the Ottomans. Even though the conflict between Bâyezîd and the Mongol khan Tamerlane temporarily postponed the immediate threat, no government could ignore the possibility of Turkish invasion; the game of diplomacy in Danubian Europe was noticeably modified by the need to find help to resist the enemy from the south. Various combinations were tried in the course of the fifteenth century.[2]

First, an appeal to all the forces of Christendom in the spirit of the crusades; this presupposed the pope's support and the goodwill of the other European princes and, while it appealed to the martial nobility, led to ill-disciplined troops being put into the field and frequently ended in disaster.

Second, the king of the Romans was made king of Hungary and Bohemia in order to combine the resources of Germany and Danubian Europe; this combination, realized by Sigismund of Luxemburg, prefigured the solution that triumphed in 1526 with Ferdinand of Habsburg but it had the disadvantage of subordinating the Czechs and Hungarians' interests to those of the Germans.

Third, the personal union of the great monarchies of Eastern Europe – Poland, Hungary and Bohemia – which were threatened in the long term by the Turkish peril and possessed similar political structures; from 1370 to 1382 the king of Hungary, Louis the Great, was king of Poland while from 1490 onwards the Jagiellons united Lithuania, Bohemia and Hungary under the Polish sceptre. This was a prudent solution as only a complex of states pooling their resources in pursuit of a common policy could simultaneously fight against the Turkish threat and German ambitions.

Fourth, the modernization of the state in order to build a powerful national monarchy capable of finding allies and resisting the Turkish peril with military force, indeed, the realization of a united Danubian Europe; this was the ambition of Matthias Corvinus.

Fifth, stirring up an enemy capable of proving a match for the Ottoman sultan, i.e. the *sofi*, the shah of Persia, since the two Middle Eastern empires were intractable enemies for religious reasons (Persia was shi'ite, the Ottoman empire was sunni); the borders between the two empires were uncertain and they were in dispute over Azerbaijan, the Lake Van region and Mesopotamia. Matthias Corvinus already nurtured the idea of a counter-alliance with Persia but this brilliant diplomatic coup led to no more practical results than the negotiations undertaken by Ferdinand I and Philip II of Spain with the shah of Persia (studied by Jean Aubin).[3] The distances were too great, the negotiators, generally mendicant monks, were not true plenipotentiaries, and there was the difficulty of coordinating military operations. Moreover the Europeans proved incapable of taking advantage of the Turks' decisive reverses in the East; on 20 July 1402 Timur Lenk, or Tamerlane, who aspired to the restoration of the empire of Genghis Khan, crushed the Ottoman army near Ankara. The sultan Bâyezîd was taken prisoner and his capital, Bursa, was sacked and occupied. Tamerlane did not cross the Straits but left for Samarkand, where he died in 1405.

'In the language of the devout, God protected Europe; in the language of the historian, we say that the evil genius of the Turks willed that Bâyezîd the Shaved, the conqueror of Nicopolis, should live during the same era as Timur the Lame.'[4] The Europeans, however, did not have the wit to take advantage of the opportunity offered to them. In five years, the Ottomans managed to reform their empire because European Turkey remained loyal and the Christians, Byzantines and the rest did nothing to drive them away. What is more, Mehmed I Kirişci (1405–21)* depended on an alliance with Byzantium to reconquer the Turkish emirates of Anatolia and to put an end to social agitation in the Asiatic part of his empire.

When Murâd II (1421–51) turned his arms against Byzantium in return for the support given to his father, he encountered several difficulties. He besieged the city protected by its high walls without success, ran aground on a fresh assault against Belgrade and met the stubborn resistance of János Hunyadi, the Hungarian *condottiere* from Transylvania.

János Hunyadi enjoyed the protection of the emperor Sigismund, who recognized his military talents and appointed him *vojvode* (governor) of Transylvania. Establishing himself as one of the strong men in the country after the death of Albert V of Habsburg, Hunyadi, full of ambition, understood that the Ottomans represented a mortal danger for his fatherland and for Danubian Europe in general. He succeeded in launching a crusade, gathering together on the Hungarian side the Germans, Venetians and Albanians under Skanderbeg: this led to the truce of Szeged (1444). The Christians were dissatisfied with the terms of the agreement; however and broke the truce, thereby provoking the wrath of Murâd II, who returned in strength and crushed them at the Battle of Varna (1444), where Władysław III Warneńczyk met his death. Nicopolis, then Varna: for the second time in half a century, a crusade ended in the slaughter of the flower of the Christian cavalry; why did the Ottomans enjoy such success?

---

* Translator's note: the dates of Mehmed I's reign are generally given as 1413–21; although Bâyezîd I died in 1402, it was not until 1413 that Mehmed I succeeded in defeating the other Ottoman princes and gaining sole rule.

THE BASIS OF OTTOMAN POWER[5]

The basis of Ottoman power was political and military. The Turks, although settled and Islamicized, remained basically steppe horsemen whose tactics took the European armies by surprise. In a series of swift, well-timed actions, they harassed the great battalions and still more the squadrons of knights in armour. They swarmed over their opponents, riddling them with arrows, disappearing as quickly as they had appeared and renewing their surprise attacks, until the enemy was completely demoralized for want of being able to engage in the man-to-man combat to which it was used. Attack at a gallop and archery were the basis of this tactic, which called for complete mastery of the equestrian art and the possession of bows which had been brought to perfection. It was only after sufficient preparation that the Turks embarked on an attack from the front with the squadrons of heavy cavalry, scattering the Christian cavalry who remained incapable of finding a way of parrying their adversaries' tactic.

The appearance of firearms in Europe could have sounded the death knell for the Turkish cavalry. This was certainly the case for the Turks in Central Asia, whose military superiority quickly collapsed when the Ottomans took part in the firearm revolution, swiftly adapting themselves and making use of artillery; to the detriment of Christendom, 'they adopted an entirely new method of combat'.[6]

The Ottomans in the fifteenth century had a remarkable ability to adapt. They had created an infantry which soon became invincible in open country, namely the janissaries. Concerned with how to supply their troops, they invented logistics at a time when the Christian armies were content to live off the land. Under Bâyezîd I, with Greek help, they developed a fleet modelled on the Venetian navy and soon just as effective; in 1499 it had 200 galleys and inflicted a severe defeat on the marines of *La Serenissima*.[7]

However, this was only a minor aspect of the ease with which the Ottomans at that time copied and borrowed from the peoples they conquered. A tolerant people they sought neither to convert nor to assimilate their subjects into an empire where, from the beginning, they were themselves a minority. Their success at building a state and civilization was remarkable and the speed of their achievement is still astonishing. Their scholars were exceptional, their technical skills surpassed those of Europe; the sultan's finances were more prosperous, the armies more modern and the towns soon became full of monuments which count among the most important in the world.

Power henceforth rested in the Turkish camp and, after the second Ottoman victory at Kosovo (1448), Murâd II died (1451). Christian Europe, on the defensive, was incapable of saving Constantinople; it might be asked whether Christendom had truly been concerned for the safety of that mighty city isolated in the midst of the Ottoman empire. In 1453 when

Mehmed II the Conqueror, aged only twenty-one, decided to launch a final assault, Europe sent help – just 700 soldiers – and Venice, installed at Pera on the other shore of the Golden Horn, declared itself neutral. On 29 May 1453 Mehmed II realized an old dream of Islam: he presided over prayers in Haqia Sophia, which had been converted into a mosque.

During this time, Frederick III disputed his inheritance with his brother Albert VI and wept in his rooms, but he alone cannot be held responsible for this disaster as the two Christian Churches, the Roman and the Eastern, had been unenthusiastic about the reconciliation initiated in 1439 by the Council of Florence. The fall of the Second Rome would subsequently weigh heavily on the destiny of the Habsburgs; at the beginning of the twentieth century, their Empire collapsed partly because of quarrels stemming from the break up of the Ottoman empire. As for the Hungarians, it was they who would play the role of *antemurale Christianitatis*, the bulwark of Christendom.[8]

JÁNOS HUNYADI, DEFENDER OF BELGRADE (1456)[9]

Having become captain-general during the reign of Ladislav the Posthumous, Hunyadi was in fact master of the country after Władysław III Warneńczyk's death during the disastrous battle at Varna (1444). He founded a national monarchy similar to that then being created by Jiří of Poděbrady in Bohemia. He had to rouse his compatriots to the defence of Belgrade which was once again threatened by the Ottomans.

Belgrade's strategic importance for Danubian Europe cannot be exaggerated. A fortress, situated at the confluence of the Sava and the Danube, it was the key to the Pannonian plain since it controlled access to the north–south, Morava–Vardar axis which passed across the Balkan massifs and led directly to the Aegean Sea and Thessaloniki. It was the last piece of the kingdom of Serbia to have escaped capture by the Ottomans. If Belgrade fell into the hands of the sultan, the route to Buda would be open to the Turkish armies; the Hungarian plain would be without serious protection against an invading army coming up through the Balkans. Equally, possession of Belgrade would provide a vital base for the complete reconquest of the Balkan peninsula.

János Hunyadi, with modest support from the Hungarian magnates, had resumed hostilities in 1454. In spring 1456 a Turkish army estimated at 140 000 men entered the field against Hungary. While Ladislav the Posthumous left to go hunting in Austria, pope Nicholas V sent a legate to mobilize the Holy Roman Empire, Poland and Hungary in a crusade against the Ottomans. The preacher St John Capistrano (canonized in 1724) toured the land to recruit volunteers; he gathered together a band of crusaders, badly armed, badly trained and of little military value, but even so the fortress of Belgrade was properly defended. Mehmed II lay siege to the town with 120 000 men, a powerful artillery and flotilla. Arriving on 3 July 1456, he made his assault on 21 July but two days later, wedged between the citadel and the relief army, the wounded sultan beat a retreat. Three years after the seizure of Constantinople, he admitted defeat. János Hunyadi wanted to make the most of this brilliant victory by pursuing the Ottoman army, but he died of the plague on 11 August 1456. The pope conferred on him the title *Christianae fidei defensor* (defender of the Christian faith) and gave orders that all the bells of Christendom should sound every day at midday in recognition of the intervention of Divine Grace; this is the origin of the Angelus, which the Christian peasants under Ottoman rule certainly ignored. It seems that Mehmed II regretted the death of his adversary. Pius II's spirit was broken when he saw his hopes of reconquering the Balkans vanish.

The victory at Belgrade at least brought Hungary a significant respite; until the rise of Süleymân the Magnificent the Ottomans did not again risk attacking Belgrade.

THE POLICY OF MATTHIAS CORVINUS[10]

In 1458 Matthias Corvinus, the younger son of János Hunyadi, was elected king of Hungary but his policy with regard to the Turks remained unclear. A true Renaissance prince, he never gave priority to the crusade, much preferring what was later termed *Realpolitik*, namely to consolidate first of all his power in Hungary.

At the beginning of his reign, Matthias became involved in the crusade which had been decided upon at the Council of Mantua in 1459. The Italian princes and Pius II understood that the victory at Belgrade was only a tactical success and that the Ottomans would resume their assault upon Europe. Frederick III quite simply refused to join in but the *vojvode* of Transylvania, Vlad III, known in history by the evocative name Vlad the Impaler, or better still as Dracula (the devil), took an active part. Strengthened by support from the West, he stopped paying tribute to the sultan in 1461, crossed the Danube and invaded Bulgaria during the winter campaign of 1461–2. In spring 1462 Vlad III defeated Mehmed II, although Matthias had not answered his urgent requests for help even though he was his relative and ally. It was only after the sultan invaded Bosnia that Matthias Corvinus took action. In the course of the campaign of 1463, he recaptured the town of Jajce but his attitude as a whole was ambiguous: he used the money for the crusade to compensate Frederick III in accordance with the treaty of Sopron and he removed Vlad III from the scene, having him arrested and imprisoned in Hungary.

In 1482 Matthias became involved in further timely action against the Ottomans after they landed in Apulia and took Otranto; separated from Albania by a narrow stretch of sea (the Straits of Otranto) this part of Italy was especially open to attack and Matthias, who had married a Neapolitan princess, believed that it was his duty to engage the Ottomans at once. The Turks were driven back to the sea, leaving behind nothing but bitter memories, still recalled in the present day in the martyrs' memorial at Otranto.

Once he had seized the throne of Bohemia, which had become an obsession of his middle years, Matthias was for a decade without the means to fight the Turks. The primate János Vitéz of Sredna had been adviser to János Hunyadi and as he originally came from Slavonia, he was well aware of the Ottoman threat. A pupil of the Italian humanist Pietro Paolo Vergerio, he gathered around him a group of scholars from whose midst emerged Janus Pannonius, probably a nephew of Vitéz. This court humanist circle launched the myth of 'Hungary, bastion of the East'. In the sixth of his elegies dedicated, naturally, to the king, Janus Pannonius showed that all the Christian nations foolishly made light of the Turkish peril: France slept, England surrendered to the delights of civil war, neighbouring Germany summoned powerless Diets and Italy cared only for trade.[11]

János Vitéz, who was both chancellor of Hungary and archbishop of Esztergom, was accused of conspiracy because he had gone to the Diet of the Holy Roman Empire meeting at Ratisbon to demand the German princes' assistance against the Ottomans. His action was an expression of the middle nobility's dissatisfaction with the policy of the king who, instead of fighting the country's mortal enemies, consumed men and resources in pursuit of a foolish dream – laying hold of the crown of Bohemia. The orders even went so far as to offer the crown of St Stephen to a Polish prince, Kazimierz IV Jagielloñczyk, who turned it down.

Matthias had other reasons to be cautious. He had repeatedly expressed his doubts about Christendom's capacity to defend itself:

If our era possessed one hundredth of the armies of Antiquity and if it had comparable mastery of the art of war, it is certain that the Turkish army would not have grown so large.

All the negotiations with the Imperial Diet met the polite indifference of the princes, for whom the Turks were still a distant menace; it was not only the emperor who was unconcerned at that time, but also the whole German world. Alone or dependent on an ill-assorted and poorly motivated coalition, Matthias would have borne the principal weight of the war effort even though the Hungarian forces were still insufficient to overcome the Turks, despite the spectacular advances made under Matthias's administration which made the country appear a great power.

THE HUNGARY OF MATTHIAS CORVINUS: A GREAT POWER[12]

As has already been stated, Frederick III did not at this time possess any real strength and during the period 1460–90 it was Matthias Corvinus's Hungary that was the great power in Central and Danubian Europe.

Matthias had made a serious effort to create a modern, centralized state. The principal instrument of his power was, both inside and outside the country, a permanent army of regularly paid mercenaries, 'the Black Army', which was made up of Czechs, Germans and Poles who had pledged loyalty to their employer. His army reached the then considerable number of 18 000 and was far larger than the permanent army of Louis XI. Made up of professionals, it easily outclassed the feudal bands and Matthias could dispense with the services of the ill-disciplined rabble which knew nothing of the new methods of warfare. This was why the barons resigned themselves to accepting the reforms which deprived them of part of their privileges.

After 1470, Matthias stopped summoning the Hungarian Diet where he had imposed a system whereby the lesser nobility were represented by elected delegates. For the only time in the history of Hungary under the *ancien régime*, direct tax became permanent and was collected annually; this was the *dica* which was raised on each peasant hearth and was similar to the *taille* which was yet to be introduced in France. It was levied at one gold florin per fiscal unit or *porta*, which corresponded to a large holding and generally to several farms. It seems that this direct tax was quite acceptable in a country where agriculture was prosperous, especially on the Great Plain.[13] With the revenues of the domain, the mines of Upper Hungary and the customs, which were raised at 1/30th *ad valorem* – hence its name 'the thirtieth' – Matthias's resources reached 2 million florins a year.

The king had the means to follow an ambitious policy but he was aware that his forces were no match for the 60 000 horsemen and 10 000 janissaries who were at the sultan's disposal. This was why he decided on a different course; first of all to extend his authority over the whole of Danubian Europe so that he could eventually launch a large-scale counter-offensive.

A DEFENSIVE STRATEGY

Like every strategic option, Matthias Corvinus's choice was open to question. It excited bitter criticism from the Holy See which was always ready to preach in favour of crusades but was never capable of establishing peace in Christendom and so of assuring the security of the crusaders. The diplomatic correspondence which the king of Hungary exchanged with the other Christian princes shows that Frederick III's tergiversation was an obstacle to the adoption of a more belligerent stance against the Porte.

In the long term, the defensive strategy was settled to Hungary's advantage. First, Matthias put in place a system of military frontier which János Hunyadi had already staked out. He built or rebuilt a series of fortresses covering the south of the country, which stretched from Wallachia to the Adriatic over 500 km of border. The work was begun in 1463, just after the recapture of Jajce, but this did not prevent the Turks from launching a series of raids from Bosnia where they were still firmly entrenched. These well-timed operations affected Croatia and Carinthia and brought despair to the peasants, who were the principal victims of the pillaging and fires. Frederick III, of course, did nothing to protect his subjects.

The frontier system still remained effective thirty years after Matthias's death, during the reign of Władysław II Jagiełłończyk (1490–1516). It was the latter's son, Louis II Jagiellon, who provoked Süleymân the Magnificent into resuming hostilities against Hungary at a time when it no longer was the great regional power that it had been under Matthias Corvinus. The internal crisis which followed the great peasant revolt of 1513 had broken his people's will to resist.

THE DECLINE OF HUNGARY UNDER THE JAGIELLONS (1490–1526)

The death of Matthias Corvinus marked a decisive moment in the history of Danubian Europe and the history of Hungary. It represented the abrupt end of the modern state which János Hunyadi's son had tried to construct. The nobles and the magnates, weary of central power, rejected both national monarchy (according to the model presented by the Hunyadis) and integration into the Habsburg monarchy (according to the model offered by Albert V). The rigorous system imposed by Matthias did not find favour with the magnates who considered the kingdom their property, while the nobles did not have a sufficiently developed sense of state to support for much longer heavy taxation and a centralized monarchy. The hour of the Jagiellons had finally come.

Since 1471 Władysław had been king of Bohemia where he had developed a reputation for moderation in a country long split by religious conflicts, although he was himself deeply devoted to Catholicism. His personal qualities of kindness, gentleness, openness of spirit and sense of humanity had won him the sympathies of the orders of Bohemia with whom he shared government. The accession of Władysław II marked the apogee of the orders' power in Hungary and a clear retreat for monarchical power. It led to two sets of tensions: on one side with the orders, between the nobles (who had been the principal beneficiaries of Matthias Corvinus's reforms) and the magnates, and on the other side between the orders and the peasant masses at the time when the feudal regime became more burdensome and when what Marxist historians call 'the second serfdom' made its appearance.

Danubian Europe did not exist on the edge of the great economic currents and the general trend there was similar to that affecting Western Europe in the second half of the fifteenth century: in the period 1470–1530 there was a slow and continuous rise in the price of cereal, considered as a measure of economic comparison. Between 1470 and 1530 the price of a sextary of wheat doubled on the Viennese market where it passed from 11 to $20\frac{1}{2}$ kreuzers (60 kreuzers = 1 Rhenish florin). Modern prices, of course, are not subject to exceptional rises caused by bad harvest or years of war. This slow and regular rise corresponds to a relative prosperity and progressive integration into a market economy. It encouraged the great landowners to turn towards the merchant economy and to become true capitalist entrepreneurs.[14]

The medieval system in which the feudal lord essentially rented out the land (in German, *Grundherr*) gave way gradually to a new way of working the land where the landed proprietor himself worked the agricultural land (in German, *Gutsherr*) and managed the estate either himself or indirectly through a steward.

In the old system, the peasants' dues were low since the only important market was in livestock. The tenant paid a very modest due in kind: not more than 1 florin for a holding of 30–50 hectares. Added to this were taxes paid in produce, in particular the tithe, which was generally paid to the lord as patron of the local church. These dues represented less than 10 per cent of the harvest. As for the *robot* (from the Slav word for work), it had practically disappeared in Austria and Hungary, where it amounted to no more than three to five days' work a year. Finally there were the gifts of honey, fowl, and so on, which the peasants were obliged to make on great feast days to furnish the feudal lord's table.

This situation was radically altered by the 'second serfdom'. The levy in kind certainly remained modest while the state tax did not burden the peasant's budget but these were in addition to the *champart* (levy in produce) and the *robot*. In Hungary the feudal lord exacted the *champart* at the rate of one ninth of the total harvest. With the tithe this amounted to 20 per cent of the harvest, that is one sheaf in five. This extension of the levy in produce provided the great landowner with a marketable surplus. Most importantly, however, the *robot* was used to develop the production of the lord's estate. As is indicated by its Latin name (*gratuiti labores*, free labour), it was work without pay and had to be rendered by the peasant. The yoked *robot*, which was owed by the ploughman, was distinct from the manual *robot*, for which the day labourer was liable. Thus the feudal lord had at his disposal not only manual labour at little cost but also harness for horses or oxen for carts or for ploughing.

The extension of the *robot* was linked to another operation: the recovery of small farms abandoned by the peasants. The land was divided into two distinct parts: the communal land or *rustical* left to the peasants, which was subject to all the levies and state tax, and the lord's estate or *dominical* made up of meadows, forests, ponds and land which could be cultivated. Finally the vineyards were governed by a special law (the *Bergrecht*), which was extended to Bohemia and Hungary. The peasant escaped the *robot* and was content to pay a levy in produce amounting to 10–20 per cent of the harvest.

The great peasant revolts at the beginning of the sixteenth century, which were to a large extent caused by the deterioration of the peasantry's condition, hastened the process of change.[15] The revolt of 1514 in Hungary and the Peasants' War in the hereditary lands in 1525 brought down upon the rural masses legislative vengeance. In Hungary the case is particularly clear; the crusade against the Turks preached by cardinal Bákócz enabled the peasants to arm themselves but they were then stirred up by the Franciscans and turned their arms against the nobility instead of marching against the Infidel. Castles were burnt and the nobility took vengeance in exemplary fashion. The leader of the peasants, György Dóza, was tortured to death and the Diet passed the law of 1514 which attached the peasant to the glebe and imposed on him one day's *robot* a week, i.e. fifty-two days a year. The nobility's point of view was set out by Werböczi in the *Tripartitum opus*,[16] which was published in 1516 but which did not have the force of law: the fixed levy no longer applied to a peasant with hereditary title to his land. Later provisions extended the law of 1514: in a land as ruined and thinly populated as Hungary after 1541, it was relatively easy to clear out and settle in more hospitable lands, the Military Frontier or Turkish-occupied Hungary.

The legislation of 1514 was only a pyrrhic victory: the peasants had become second-class citizens and cared little for the struggle against the Ottomans and thought that there was little to choose between one serfdom and another. Sometimes they fancied that the Ottoman yoke was lighter than that of the Hungarian lords and it was a people totally demoralized that confronted the great conflicts of the sixteenth century.

The social policy imposed by the nobility after 1490 had crushed the nation's spirit of resistance and Hungary ceased for the moment to be the surest bulwark of Christendom against Ottoman imperialism. Only the Military Frontier built by Matthias Corvinus was able to continue the illusion and to delay a fresh Turkish advance.

NOTES AND REFERENCES

1. Jean-Paul Roux, *Histoire des Turcs*, Paris, 1983 (hereafter Roux).
2. V.-L. Tapié, *The Rise and Fall of the Habsburg Monarchy*, London, 1971, pp. 39–49.
3. Jean Aubin, 'Per viam portugalensem: autour d'un projet diplomatique de Maximilien II', *Mare luso-indicum*, vol. 4, Paris, 1980, pp. 45–88.
4. Roux, p. 228.
5. N. Beldiceanu, 'L'organisation de l'empire ottoman', in Robert Mantran (ed) *Histoire de l'empire ottoman*, Paris, 1989, pp. 117–38.
6. Jean Bérenger, 'L'influence des peuples de la steppe (Huns, Mongols, Tartares, Turcs) sur l'emploi de la cavalerie', *Revue internationale d'histoire militaire*, no. 49, Paris, 1980, pp. 33–49.
7. Colin Thubron, 'La terrible menace turque', in *La Marine de Venise*, Paris, 1981, pp. 101–12.
8. The title accorded to Hungary by the Holy See after János Hunyadi's victory at Belgrade.
9. Ervin Pamlenyi (ed.) *Histoire de la Hongrie*, Roanne, 1974, pp. 120–4.
10. Isabella Ackerl, *König Mathias Corvinus: ein Ungar, der in Wien regierte*, Vienna, 1985, pp. 56–76.
11. Jean Bérenger, 'Conscience européene et mauvaise conscience à la cour de Mathias Corvin: la naissance du mythe de Dracula', *La Conscience européene aux XV et XVI siècles*, Paris, 1982, pp. 8–22.
12. Vilmos Fraknoi, *Mathias Corvinus: König von Ungarn*, Freiburg im Breisgau, 1891.
13. Jean Bérenger, 'Humanisme et absolutisme dans la Hongrie de Mathias Corvin', *Études finno-ougriennes*, 1974, pp. 264–80.
14. A.-F. Probram and R. Geyer, *Materialen zur Geschichte der Löhne und Preise in Œsterreich*, Vienna, 1938.
15. There is abundant literature on the 1514 Peasants' Revolt in Hungary. See in particularly Gustave Heckenast (ed.) *Aus der Geschichte der Ostmitteleuropäischen Bauernbewegungen im 16–17. Jahrhundert*, Budapest, 1977.
16. István Werbőczi, *Tripartitum opus juris consuetudinarii inclyti regni Hungariae*, 1st edn, Vienna, 1517.

CHAPTER NINE

The Renaissance North of the Alps

The tremendous intellectual development experienced by Italy at the end of the Middle Ages, which is sometimes known as humanism and sometimes as the Renaissance, was not slow to cross the Alps and to affect Danubian Europe. The route that it followed was curious, however; it first touched Hungary before it reached Vienna and the hereditary lands. The Holy Roman Empire experienced its own development for the great merchant cities of Upper Germany – Nürnberg and Augsburg – had direct economic and cultural contact with the great Italian cities, especially Venice, where German–Italian relations were given solid expression on the banks of the Rialto in the *Fondaco dei Tedeschi*.

HUNGARIAN HUMANISM[1]

Even Marxist historians have definitively rejected the notion of 'popular humanism' during the fifteenth century and agree that it was an elite phenomenon, tied to royal patronage and government circles, while the influence of Hussitism was negligible. The Hussites at most had given birth to a current of controversy, which in 1514 eased the success of György Dóza's peasants' revolt.

The emperor Sigismund introduced humanism into Hungary. After the Council of Constance, he summoned to Buda Pietro Paolo Vergerio, who remained there until his death in 1444 and founded a circle of Hungarian, Italian and Polish humanists, and established the first direct links with the humanists of the Italian peninsula. Author of a Latin *Historia* now lost, Vergerio had a decisive influence over János Vitéz of Sredna.[2]

A clergyman originally from Slavonia who carried out the duties of protonotary at the royal chancellery in Buda, Vitéz was a friend of János Hunyadi, who entrusted him with the education of his sons Ladislav and Matthias. In 1445 he was appointed bishop of Nagyvárad (Oradea), one of the most richly endowed sees in Hungary, where he created a humanist circle and a library which soon became famous and served as the model for the Corvinian, Matthias's great royal library. Vitéz had a series of manuscripts copied in Italy and as a genuine philologist took great pains over the quality of the texts; the Florentine bookseller Vespasiano dei Bisticci considered it a *bibliotheca bellissima* where no classical Latin text was lacking. Vitéz also proved no less distinguished as a writer and neo-Latin orator; his letters copied by a canon at Nagyvárad bear witness to this.[3]

His assistance in securing the election of his pupil Matthias as king in 1458 was rewarded in 1465 with promotion to the seat of Esztergom. The alliance of the Hunyadis and the humanist party soon made itself apparent in what amounted to a genuine absolutist ideology. Vitéz went on to install himself at Esztergom and had built a bishop's palace in the Italian style. He moved his library there while a humanist circle was established at Buda.

Among the many young men sent by Vitéz to Italy before 1465 was his nephew, Janus Pannonius, who went to Ferrara where he was received by Guarino. On his return he became the most celebrated of the Hungarian humanists and one of the greatest European poets. His complete works, re-edited in the course of the sixteenth century, have long been the object of Hungarian scholars' attention.[4]

János Vitéz had also invited foreign scholars, most notably the astronomers Regiomontanus and Martin Bylica. Originally from Königsberg in Franconia, hence the Latinized form of his name, Regiomontanus studied at Vienna, then in Italy, and was invited to Oradea to direct the observatory that Vitéz wished to establish there. He followed Vitéz to Esztergom, as did Martin Bylica, who was born at Cracow (Kraków) to a family of Italian origin. After beginning his studies at Cracow, Bylica continued at Bologna where he met Pannonius, who invited him to Hungary where from 1471 he followed his career after the king took him into his service.[5]

After Vitéz's disgrace, the court at Buda became the only humanist centre in Hungary. It developed relations with the literary world of Florence, with Marsilio Ficino and the neo-Platonist academy. A friend of Ficino, Francisco Bandini, became the protégé of Miklós Báthory, bishop of Vác, and of Petár Váradi, the new chancellor of Hungary and archbishop of Kalocsa. They made the court at Buda a neo-Platonist centre outside Italy. Finally, from 1480, Matthias engaged the services of Bonfini whom he made his historiographer. It was Bonfini who wrote the first history of Hungary in Latin, the *Rerum Hungaricum Decades*, composed in the style of Livy and Tacitus and intended to glorify the king and the nation.[6]

The Hungarian humanists were clergy, either native or foreign, who became prelates through royal favour, and whose role was at once cultural and political. Matthias offered them the positions in government of which Western humanists dreamt, from Erasmus of Rotterdam (?1466–1536) to the French humanist Guillaume Budé (1467–1540). In return they contributed to the royal propaganda and elaborated an absolutist theory of state.

THE POLITICAL WORK OF THE HUMANISTS AT BUDA[7]

Vergerio was the first to celebrate Hungary as the 'bastion of Christendom' in order to draw the great powers' attention to the gravity of the threat that the Ottomans posed to the future of Western Europe. In 1465 Janus Pannonius demonstrated that the European nations little appreciated the danger threatening the Danubian region and reminded them that Hungary stood alone in the front line. Ten years later, Marsilio Ficino (1433–99) put his pen in the service of Matthias's propaganda. In 1477 his biography of Plato was issued at Buda with a flattering dedication to the king; he did not send his book to Athens, then in ruins, but to Pannonia because there lived 'the great king Matthias, powerful and wise who in a few years would restore the temple of wise Pallas'.[8] With his *Exhortatio ad bellum contra barbaros* (*Exhortation to war against the barbarians*) he tried to interest the king in a crusade to save Italy from the Turkish peril. This address served as the introduction to his *Epistolae* of 1482, dedicated to Matthias, who had come to save the territory of Otranto by his energetic counter-offensive after the Ottoman landing. Ficino pointed to the existence of close solidarity between Italy and Danubian Europe. At the end of Matthias's reign, Bonfini developed the same theme in his history of Hungary setting out the decisive role which the Hungarians and the Hunyadi family had played in the defence of Christendom.

The humanists of the chancellery took part in defending royal policy in a yet more positive way, involving themselves in the Dracula affair. In 1463 Janus Pannonius composed a poem with the title *De captivitate Dragulae wajwodae Transalpini* (*The imprisonment of the Transalpine vojvode Dracula*) which is the origin of the legend of the vampire, and had his work circulated through a Viennese bookseller. He justified Matthias's policy of abandoning the crusade while describing with gusto the crimes (real or supposed) of the prince of Wallachia. By creating the black legend of Dracula, Pannonius explained his master's policy towards Vlad III and the Turks. The material furnished by the young humanist was taken up at once by Thomas Ebendorfer, who included it in his *Kaiserchronik* (*Chronicle of the kings of the Romans*). Thus Matthias became one of the first princes to use printing to affect public opinion and rally the Germans to his side in his interminable quarrel with Frederick III.

Bonfini in the *Rerum Hungaricum Decades* was quick to elaborate a theory of monarchical power and to write that Matthias was the 'living law' and consequently above the law and the embodiment of legislative power. He did not shrink from comparing him to Attila, Augustus and Trajan. He lent on the principles of Roman civil law at the height of the Empire. Matthias relied less on strength than on the revival of Roman law to establish his power over the orders who were wedded to national judicial tradition. In 1489 the chancellor Callimachus Experiens compared the new king to Attila who, for the Hungarians, remained a national hero and was

115

never thought of as the 'scourge of God': Matthias was portrayed as the 'living law'. Another humanist, Aurelius Brandolinus Lippus in his work dedicated to Matthias, the treatise *De comparatione rei publicae et regni* (*Monarchy and republic compared*), developed the notion of absolute monarchy: the king made the law according to his pleasure and embodied the legislative power. These analyses dating from 1489 are far bolder than those of the sixteenth-century French humanists: Jean Bodin never went so far,[9] and one must look at the most daring French and English theories of the seventeenth century to find such vigorous theorizing. It becomes, then, much more understandable that the orders preferred to end the experience of national monarchy and elected in 1491 Władysław II Jagiełłonczyk who for twenty years had given pledges of goodwill to the nobility of Bohemia.

The neo-Platonist circle at Buda even developed the myth of 'the sun, source of life, centre of the planets'. Towards the end of his reign, Matthias reached an almost perfect harmony with the ideologists, the humanists of the court putting absolutism on as exalted a level as it later held in the entourage of Louis XIV. This glorification was manifest in the culture of Matthias's Hungary in a series of spectacular projects which the country's later ills all but completely obliterated.

THE CORVINIAN LIBRARY[10]

Most impressive of all Matthias's achievements was the royal library which he created and which enjoyed considerable prestige, in Renaissance Italy no less than in the eyes of the Habsburgs; in the seventeenth century, the emperor Leopold tried to recover from Constantinople those works which had survived Süleymân the Magnificent's occupation of the royal castle at Buda. The history of the Corvinian library is closely bound to the reign of Matthias (Sigismund of Luxemburg's library had been scattered); it was started at the time of his accession and was dissolved some years after his death. One of the king's letters from 1471 explains that he had decided to collect manuscripts; he arranged to have them purchased in Italy and opened a workshop for copyists at the royal castle at Buda (there were few incunabula). His goal was to bring together the works of the Greek and Latin classical writers, the Church Fathers and the great medieval authors (among others, St Thomas Aquinas and St Bonaventura). It was an ambitious project and in this as in everything else he did, Matthias intended to surpass all his fellow monarchs.

At this period, the Corvinian was equal to the finest libraries in Italy. Apparently 3 500–5 000 volumes while the Vatican library founded by the pope had 3 500 in 1489, the Laurentine of the Medicis 1 017, and that of the duke of Urbino, 1 120. The Corvinian represented an investment of 1 million florins over thirty years, just 2 per cent of the sovereign's annual budget. The holdings were divided as follows: one floor of religious works, two floors of secular works (history one-quarter, philosophy and poetry one-tenth each). The holdings in Greek were considerable: the librarian Ugoletto had purchased a number of manuscripts from Turkish-occupied Greece – 200 in total between 1485 and 1490 – and Bonfini was charged with translating them into Latin. All this activity stopped after the king's death and the workshop of copyists was closed as Władysław II had neither the means nor the will to continue so ambitious a task.

As for Frederick III, he was content to acquire a part of the much more modest library of János Vitéz of Sredna. It was only in the sixteenth century that the Habsburgs had the financial means to be great patrons of the arts and learning.

MATTHIAS'S BUILDING PROGRAMME[11]

The great monuments erected by Matthias are yet more difficult to describe than the Corvinian library and only archaeology can reveal their importance. From Pressburg to Buda, all along the Danube, Matthias left his mark on the landscape.

He founded a university at Pressburg, the Academia Istropolitana, because Hungarian students had had hitherto to register abroad, at Cracow or Vienna; Prague was out of the question since the beginning of the Hussite revolution. About a hundred young men from the lesser nobility and the urban middle classes went to study each year at Vienna, in an establishment controlled by the 'enemy', Frederick III. Founded in 1465, the university of Pressburg had a brief existence but helped to acquaint the students of the faculty of arts with the *devotio moderna*, the spiritual movement born in the Netherlands which encouraged the Christian to personal examination and to surrender himself to Christ's mercy. In addition to the faculty of arts, essential for the teaching of philology and mathematics (Regiomontanus and Bylica gave courses there), the university had a faculty of law.

Some properties and canonicates of the collegiate church were assigned for the maintenance of the professors but the most urgent need was for new buildings where the university could be settled. The upper town which towers over the Danube, was chosen. Excavations have brought to light the remains of the university buildings in the the present-day Jirašek street. Houses dating from the fourteenth century, attached to the royal castle, were destroyed to make room for a complex made up of three ranges of two-storey buildings: originally part of the royal residence, Matthias gave them to the university. Without the guiding hand of János Vitéz of Sredna, and dependent on donations, the university went into decline after 1471. Matthias ceased to take an interest in it after 1485; he occupied Vienna and Hungarians could go there to study. The buildings were then taken over once again by the chapter. The primate's palace at Esztergom was destroyed during the sieges of 1595 and 1596 when the town was bitterly fought over by the imperial army and the Turks.

At Visegrád, at the foot of the old fortified castle, Matthias built a large villa in the Italian style; although at the present time it is in a sorry state, it bears witness to a remarkable breakthrough of *Quattrocento* architecture north of the Alps. The complex is without any suggestion of Gothic and the architecture shows the influence of Antiquity; the surviving decorative elements belong to the Pompeian style.

It was, however, the royal castle at Buda which received Matthias's complete attention. The devastation of the Second World War (the siege of Buda by the Red Army in the course of the winter of 1944–5) made possible important excavations before the task of reconstruction was begun. These excavations brought to light evidence of continuous building activity in the fifteenth century. Begun by Sigismund of Luxemburg, the construction was continued by Matthias. Outside his residence and the government agencies, the king installed his library, a workshop of copyists, of miniaturists and a press that was one of the earliest operating north of the Alps. The excavations have also confirmed what had previously been known only from chronicles and illustrations made before 1526. A series of pieces of red marble fashioned for inclusion in a building give firm evidence of the Renaissance character of the wing of the palace constructed, remodelled and decorated on the orders of king Matthias.

Although the royal workshops continued to operate after Matthias's death, the magnates and prelates assumed direction of artistic life. The Báthorys and the Gereb, relatives of the Hunyadi, built at Vác, Nógrád and Nyírbátor; the Zapolya family built in Upper Hungary (Spisska Kapitula), the Perényi at Siklós, Ippolito of Este and archbishop Tamás Bakócz at Esztergom and Eger, György Szatmari at Pécs. Among the numerous artists engaged in supervising these buildings at the beginning of the sixteenth century there were still many Italians.

It was from Hungary, through the sovereigns and aristocrats, that Renaissance art at the turn of the sixteenth century reached Poland, Silesia, Bohemia and Austria, while the patricians of the Hungarian towns in their turn felt the influence of the court.

MAXIMILIAN, RENAISSANCE PRINCE[12]

The conflict among Frederick III, Albert VI, the orders and Matthias Corvinus seriously hindered scientific and cultural advance at Vienna and Austria as a whole. The emperor did not have sufficient money to be a great builder and contented himself with altering the castle at Wiener Neustadt, where he had built the chapel of St George, a masterpiece of flamboyant Gothic architecture. Religious art, financed by numerous donors, also flourished; more and more churches were refurbished and decorated as witness to not only the fervour, but also the deep disquiet of Christians in the fifteenth century.

Frederick III did not care for Thomas Ebendorfer (d. 1464), who was one of the great figures at the university of Vienna. The last representative of scholasticism, he enjoyed a reputation towards the end of his life as a historian but had earlier been a professor of theology, a commentator on Isaiah and a preacher. Frederick III did support Aeneas Silvius Piccolomini, who settled in Vienna in 1437 and at first was very critical of Austria which he thought 'barbarian'; even so, he gradually introduced humanism there. In his two manuals of education (in German, *Fürstenspiegel*), his *Pentalogus* and his novels, he defended the new educational ideal based on classical culture and rhetoric. As he wrote with ease, his works enjoyed a wide circulation among the educated nobility while through his lectures he endeavoured to win over the world of the universities which approached the new ideal with caution.

While the archduke Maximilian was won over to the ideas coming from Italy, it was only after his accession at the end of the fifteenth century and so after a considerable delay that humanism was implanted in Hungary. In 1497, Conrad Celtes was summoned as professor to the university at Vienna, where shortly afterwards he founded a learned society (*Sodalitas literaria danubiana*, the Literary Society of the Danube) which counted among its members the poet Johannes Cuspinian and the mathematician Conrad Peutinger. The faculty of arts stole a march on the other faculties, philology and the exact sciences over theology: Vienna was integrated into the great intellectual movement which would overturn Europe and would respond to the challenge posed by Martin Luther. As for humanism, Maximilian was able to put it to the service of his own propaganda, lack of money preventing him from being a great builder and patron.

The best known surviving portrait of Maximilian is a charcoal drawing by Albrecht Dürer, made in 1518 during the Diet of Augsburg, when shortly before his death he tried to have his grandson elected king of the Romans. His daughter Margaret hated the portrait, perhaps because it accentuated too much the marks of old age apparent in this man of seventy-two and emphasized the prognathism which was not hidden by any beard.

Albrecht Dürer and the emperor Maximilian – two representatives of the Renaissance north of the Alps. Maximilian, however, never had the money or the time to build lasting monuments; a patron must have a more settled existence than that enjoyed by Maximilian, who was always on the move, rushing from one castle to another, always lying in wait for an attack. The only place where he made his mark was Innsbruck, where he remodelled the Hofburg from 1489 onwards: Maximilian was not Viennese. In 1490 he created the Neuhof, once a fortified town house which Sigismund had had extended bit by bit; to the north he had built a suite of *Prunksäle*, the Vordere Burg where he installed his second wife Bianca Maria Sforza and her entourage, while to the south he built an arsenal, the Aeussere Burg. Also at the Tyrolean capital he undertook the construction of a monumental tomb, but this was completed long after 1519 and bears no trace of the Renaissance. Despite its strategic position at the mouth of the Brenner, Innsbruck was never again an imperial residence, because the gravitational pull within the Austrian monarchy came from the Netherlands and Spain and even Central Europe after the division of 1555. This was why Maximilian's capital enjoyed but a brief hour of glory and ceased, after Maximilian's death, to lodge the imperial court except during various brief visits by Charles V; Ferdinand and his successors preferred Vienna or Prague.

The Renaissance in Germany, unlike in Hungary, was not an elite phenomenon tied to the court, but is better explained by the formidable prosperity which the towns of Upper Germany were then enjoying: Dürer did not work outside Nürnberg and Augsburg.

As for Maximilian, it is open to question whether he was, as the tradition fabricated by German romanticism claimed, the 'last of the knights', or indeed the first prince of the Renaissance. In common with all the sovereigns of his day, he delighted in physical exercise to display his strength, his skill at handling weapons and his mastery of the equestrian art. In his forties, he harked back to the successes of his youth at the castle at Wiener Neustadt and on his campaigns against France where he proved a modern tactician, using artillery and infantry and not relying, like his late father-in-law, on heavy cavalry. Around 1500, he had to change his way of life, perhaps because of an attack of syphilis in 1497 and certainly after a serious fall from his horse in 1501 which had lasting consequences. Morally Maximilian had understood well the lessons coming from the other side of the Alps. He was both an optimist and a pragmatist, quite amoral in matters of politics Machiavellian and without scruple. Of a sensual nature, he was very receptive to all forms of beauty, above all in the plastic arts (i.e. drawing, painting, sculpture and architecture). He was interested in all aspects of contemporary intellectual life and was ready to adopt ideas then in fashion, such as nationalism in politics, humanism in literature and philosophy, and 'capitalism' in the sphere of the economy. He was a true Renaissance prince, greedy for personal glory and exhibiting a frantic individualism. It was for this reason that he preferred, combining egotism and family tradition, to dedicate his limited resources to exalting his reign and the House of Austria, thus resuming the policy begun by Rudolf I.

The first work which celebrated the person and work of Maximilian was the *Historia* of Grünpeck who divided the life of his hero in two parts; his adventurous life in the Low Countries and his for the most part successful campaigns against the Swiss in 1499. Around 1500, Maximilian turned himself into a Renaissance prince, a 'universal man' of the kind glorified some years later by Balthazar Castiglione in his work which became the reference for all the European aristocracy, *Il Corteggiano* (*The Courtier*).[13] The prince took a keen interest in the arts and sciences and not only as a patron: he renounced jousts and military campaigns in order to raise himself to the level of a statesman.

The glorification of his reign reached its peak after 1512 when he entrusted his secretary Max Treitzsauerwein with the creation of a biographical monument with 118 illustrations (wood-engravings and etchings), the *Theuerdank*, which was published in 1517; it recounted the legendary history of a young prince, Theuerdank, who set out to rescue a young princess, the queen Ehrenreich whom he freed after countless trials. He could marry her only after going on a crusade, a project which Maximilian never realized. *Theuerdank* was only the first book in a series numbering twelve in total. In fact, only the triumphal procession, the tournaments, masked balls, triumphal arches, the holy family of the emperor Maximilian, the genealogy, the fragments of an autobiography in Latin, the books on artillery, on hunting, the 'white king' (*Weisskunig*) and the *Historia Frederick et Maximiliani* were published. These all made up the pieces of a veritable encyclopedia destined to glorify the House of Austria and to show Maximilian as the creator of a universal monarchy.

The imperial project was successful in so far as Maximilian passed into the German collective imagination as a great patriot and a victorious hero who had extended the patrimony of the Habsburgs.[14] That his reputation was not entirely unfavourable is additional proof of his qualities as a statesman, a prodigious man of action whose chief fault perhaps was to have 'too many irons in the fire'.

NOTES AND REFERENCES

1. Jean Bérenger, 'Les caractères originaux de l'humanisme hongrois', *Journal des savants*, 1973, pp. 257–88.
2. Vilmos Fraknoi, *Vitéz Janos*, Budapest, 1879.
3. Tibor Kardos, *A magyarorsagi humanizmus Kora*, Budapest, 1953.
4. *Iani Pannonii . . . opera omnia*, Vienna, 1569; reissued Budapest, 1972.
5. Jerzy Zathey, 'Martin Bylica, profesor Academie Istropolitany', in L. Holotik and A. Vantuch (eds) *Humanizmus a Renesancia na Slovensku*, Bratislava, 1967, pp. 40–53 (hereafter Holotik and Vantuch).
6. Antonio Bonfini, *Rerum Ungaricarum decades*, Ladislas Juhasz and Petér Kulcsar (eds), 5 vols, Budapest 1936–76.
7. Jean Bérenger, 'Humanisme et absolutisme dans la Hongrie de Mathias Corvin', *Études finno-ougriennes*, 1974, pp. 264–80.
8. Jean Bérenger, 'Conscience européenne et mauvaise conscience à la cour de Mathias Corvin: la naissance du mythe de Dracula', *La Conscience européenne aux XV et XVI siècles*, Paris, 1982, pp. 8–22.

9. Jean Bodin, *Les Six Livres de la République*, Paris, 1576.
10. Csaba Csapodi, *The Corvinian Library: History and Stock*, Budapest, 1973.
11. Holotik and Vantuch.
12. Gerhard Benecke, *Maximilian I (1459–1519): An Analytical Biography*, London, 1982.
13. Baldassare Castiglione, *Il Corteggiano*, Venice, 1522.
14. The success of his marriage policy was the origin of the universal monarchy of Charles V.

CHAPTER TEN

The Work of Maximilian I (1459–1519)

A young man burning with ambition as befitted his youth but without means, the archduke Maximilian made a good start to his career through his father's careful contriving: he married the heiress of the kingdom of Burgundy. This first success encouraged him to contract many other marriage alliances and to be active in all directions at the point when the House of Austria's interests had become European rather than narrowly local. While his numerous military interventions, with the exception of his very earliest in the Low Countries, rarely bore fruit, his clever marriage strategy allowed his grandson to become, in the space of a generation, the last emperor of the West worthy of that name, thus realizing the proud device of Frederick III: AEIOU (Austriae est imperare orbi universo).

THE ADVENTURER (1477–93)[1]

Right until his death in 1493, the cautious and thrifty Frederick III persisted in judging his son severely, refusing him any financial or military assistance. Maximilian had accumulated debts while rashly undertaking costly campaigns in Flanders and Hungary: his father had hoped to put an end to his prodigal son's adventures by cutting off his allowance, believing that this would force him to remain still. Maximilian had to wait until he was thirty-four before he came into possession of the Habsburg patrimony, itself but a modest sum. The successes of the first part of his career were entirely due to his marriage and his military talents.

His greatest stroke of good fortune was when, at the age of eighteen, he married Maria of Burgundy, whose patrimony was under threat following the premature death of Charles the Bold outside Nancy. His cousin Louis XI hoped to deprive the orphan Maria of the greater part of the lands which the cadet branch of the House of Valois had amassed in the course of a century: Burgundy (an apanage of the House of France), Franche-Comté (fief of the Empire), Flanders and Artois (fiefs of the crown of France), Hainaut, Brabant, Holland, Limburg, Gueldreland and Luxemburg (fiefs of the Empire).

Maximilian was able to cast himself in 'the role of the champion of the orphan under threat from her greedy relative' rather than the less attractive one of a 'chaser-after-dowries'. In addition to his ambitions, he brought to the court at Malines a genuine talent as an entrepreneur; his rank precludes his being considered a *condottiere*. A gifted captain as well as a talented organizer, he had the good sense to take advantage of the tactical innovations lately introduced by the Hussites in their struggle against the Teutonic Knights. Confronted by the French heavy cavalry, he skilfully deployed his German lansquenets (from the German *Landsknecht*). At the Battle of Guinegates in 1481 he repulsed the centre of the French army, a manoeuvre which led to the defeat of the French king's troops. Louis XI accepting defeat, was happy to negotiate and was finally satisfied with Artois and the duchy of Burgundy. Maximilian's effective intervention had saved the independence of the Netherlands and gave birth to a century of rivalry between France and Austria.

Maximilian's triumph was short lived: the death of his young wife following a fall from her horse left him in a false situation with regard to his new subjects for whom he was nothing more than the father of their little under-age duke, the future Philip the Fair. The archduke's exploits were insufficient to win him the loyalty of the Estates of Flanders and Brabant. Mindful of their political and tax privileges, they wanted to act as regents until 'their natural lord', Philip, attained his majority. The orders, dominated by the urban patriciate and landed aristocracy, did not want to prolong the war with France as to do so would be against their economic interests and so they refused to pay taxes to finance Maximilian's personal ambitions. Whether in Central Europe or the Netherlands, the orders presented the Habsburgs with a serious obstacle.

Still, in the long term, the Burgundian marriage constituted a brilliant connection for the future of the House of Austria. It had produced two children, Philip the Fair and Margaret, who as adults both played an important role in Maximilian's marriage alliances.

The peace agreement reached with Louis XI looked forward to the marriage of the young Margaret to the dauphin Charles (the future Charles VIII) to whom she would bring as her dowry Artois and the Franche-Comté. Although the treaty of Arras (1482) required Maximilian to sacrifice territory, it was a happy compromise and the House of Austria had laid its hands on the core of the Burgundian patrimony. The Habsburgs were firmly implanted in this wealthy part of middle Europe from which little by little they had earlier been driven; Flanders was certainly equal to the Swiss cantons, which had just rejected Austrian suzerainty. The Habsburgs, the heirs of the prestigious House of Burgundy, kept the Netherlands until the Peace of Campo-Formio in 1797. For three centuries the destiny of the

Flemings was directly linked to the European policy of the House of Austria.

Although Maximilian had worked in the interests of his descendants, the immediate benefits were slight and until 1490 his position in the Netherlands remained unstable. His successes were insufficient for him to win the unconditional obedience of the orders; indeed, in 1488 conflict turned to catastrophe: the burghers of Bruges in open rebellion held him prisoner in the house of the Grand'Place and threatened to hand him over to the people of Ghent, who spoke of executing him. He secretly sent a letter to the elector of Cologne, appealing for help as a man in desperate straits; however, neither the German princes nor his own father deigned to reply to his urgent demands for soldiers and money.

At the same time, Maximilian laid the groundwork for a marriage alliance which in the end did not yield any solid results: he negotiated his own marriage with Anne of Brittany, whose duchy had been under threat from Charles VIII since the disastrous rebellion of duke Francis II. In the fifteenth century Brittany, which was a French fief like Burgundy, pretended towards independence and made moves towards alliances with the enemies of France. By marrying the duchess, Maximilian would have acted once more in his role of 1477 – the champion of an orphan threatened by the wicked Valois – but more than that he would have inflicted real harm on the king of France by depriving him of a rich province of great strategic value. The projected union would have enabled him to resume war with France, which remained his chief enemy. The negotiations progressed to the point where the marriage took place by proxy; the contract is one of those curious items in the State Archives of Vienna which the Austrians delight in showing. Anne went against the general rules of feudal law, in particular the dispositions of the treaty signed between duke Francis II and the king of France: the heir to Brittany could not marry without the king's consent. The venture did not rest on any serious basis and revealed Anne's 'fiancé's' spirit of adventure. He did not provide the Bretons with military aid and did nothing to prevent their defeat at Saint-Aubin-du-Cormier (22 July 1488) since Matthias Corvinus's succession in Hungary had drawn him once again into the affairs of Danubian Europe. Order was restored in 1491 after the capture of Rennes by the French army and in the same year Charles VIII resigned himself to marrying Anne of Brittany, a princess with few physical charms and a melancholy disposition. Maximilian did not attempt to oppose this match and Charles VIII sent back to Malines the little archduchess Margaret, who harboured great bitterness over the whole affair. She was to marry in succession the *infante* Juan of Spain (1497), the duke of Savoy (1501) and finally served brilliantly as the governess-general of the Netherlands. Reason of state had prevailed and Maximilian limited himself to contesting in various pamphlets 'the proven treachery' of his Breton fiancée.[2]

During this period Maximilian had to defend his patrimony first and foremost from the recklessness of the other members of his House. He kept an eye on the Tyrol, which was being increasingly badly managed by his cousin, since he feared that it might fall into the hands of the duke of Bavaria. Relying on the orders, who had little desire to pass under the tutelage of the Bavarians, he persuaded the spendthrift prince to abdicate from the government of the Tyrol. He took advantage of the Swabian League and the internal quarrels of the Wittelsbachs and as compensation married his cousin Kunigunde to duke Albert of Bavaria – matrimonial alliances between the Wittelsbachs and the Habsburgs were promised a good future, until the very end of the monarchy.

The regency of the Tyrol finally presented the king of the Romans with a territorial base within the Holy Roman Empire which compensated for his personal defeat in the Netherlands. The Tyrol was now the centre of his – albeit modest – power and Innsbruck became his favourite residence: although he became master of Vienna, he spurned the Austrian capital for strategic reasons (it was too far from the Netherlands and Italy) and sentimental ones (he had bad memories of his stays at the Hofburg). The Tyrol on the other hand controlled the routes linking Upper Germany with Italy and was a country rich in copper, salt and silver mines which could provide him, with the help of the Fuggers, with the resources he had hitherto lacked.

Although Maximilian expected much to follow from the death of Matthias Corvinus in 1490, the real results were in fact modest. He raised an army of mercenaries which he paid with funds he had found in Germany. His troops freed Vienna and Lower Austria from the Hungarians, then laid waste to the region around lake Balaton before mutinying at the beginning of November 1490. The following year, the Hungarian Diet finally elected Władysław II Jagiełłończyk and Maximilian had to content himself with Lower Austria. The day of the Habsburgs had not yet dawned on the Pannonian plain.

MAXIMILIAN AND FINANCE[3]

Until 1493 Maximilian was obliged to survive on expediences and borrowed 500 000 florins from Sigismund and Heinrich Prüschenck, two brothers who made their careers at his side as advisers and treasurers. He also began the Habsburgs' collaboration with the illustrious House of Fugger, the merchant bankers from Augsburg, as part of his programme to improve the yield from the Tyrolean mines.

For the first time in their history, the Habsburgs' policies were dictated by their financial difficulties. Maximilian faced the problem posed by the employment of mercenaries, who were then the only truly efficient soldiers but were a great drain on the finances of princes with modest budgets. As

Fritz Redlich has shown,[4] a Swiss or German *Landsknecht* was a professional to a high degree who drew a large salary which could attract younger sons of the nobility. They had little in common with the 'proletarians' of the eighteenth-century armies who earned just sufficient to ensure a meagre ration. To the benefit of the public finances, however, manpower was still limited in Europe to several thousand men and armies were not truly permanent.

This did not stop Maximilian spending more than his ordinary sources of revenues brought him – more even than a booming credit system could provide him with. Contrary to the claims hitherto made by historians, Maximilian examined his accounts carefully and was not a spendthrift like Sigismund of the Tyrol. The situation that he faced was particularly harsh: his military expenditure always exceeded the loans he secured and the revenues of the hereditary lands (even after 1493 these were all that he had at his disposal), although he managed the peasants on his domains sufficiently strictly for discontent to increase among his subjects, who found themselves at the mercy of unscrupulous stewards.

The Fuggers gave him a great deal of assistance. From 1491 he granted the House of Ulrich Fugger and Cie of Augsburg the concession on the silver mines at Schwatz in the Tyrol, a concession previously held by the firm of Hans Vechlin and Cie of Memingen in Swabia. He immediately received 120 000 florins in advance during the period April to Christmas 1491, which kept him from bankruptcy while assuring the Fuggers an advantageous contract. From the sale of one silver mark fixed at 16 florins, 50 per cent went to the holder of the concession, 18 per cent to the king and 32 per cent to the producers, that is the small contractors who worked the mine and produced the ingots of silver. The Fuggers grew very rich in the process as did the rival Houses of Herwart and Baumgartner from Augsburg, who held the concession on the Tyrolean copper mines. The height of collaboration between the large capitalist firms of Augsburg and the House of Austria was reached at the end of Maximilian's reign, when in 1518 he began negotiating the election of his grandson as king of the Romans. The death of the emperor was followed by much bidding and counter-bidding on the part of the electors but Jakob Fugger's resolution – he was hostile to the French candidate – enabled Charles V to emerge victorious in the face of Francis I, the wealthiest sovereign in Christendom. The Fuggers made a decisive contribution to the imperial election, advancing more than 1 million florins.

MAXIMILIAN AND THE HOLY ROMAN EMPIRE
(1493–1519)

From 1493 Maximilian tried to strengthen imperial power, reorganizing the archaic institutions of the Empire where a measure of anarchy prevailed. The princes still believed that they were safe from the French, whose ambitions were not yet blatant, and from the Ottomans, who they mistakenly thought were a distant threat. The Netherlands, Alsace, Austria and, in particular, Hungary protected them and the Estates of the Empire jealously safeguarded their liberties. In the course of his reign, Maximilian summoned twenty-two sessions of the imperial Diet and was able in person or through the commissioners, his intermediaries, to wage a long campaign of threats and flattery in an effort to summon forth a measure of national sentiment among peoples whose only concern was their own interest. In fact, his only achievement was to enhance his own reputation, and then only briefly.

To add to his problems, he had a competitor in the archbishop of Mainz, Berchtold of Henneberg, who also wished to reform the Empire but in the interests of the princes. The princes formed what amounted to an oligarchic government with real authority and having direct control over the emperor's activities. A member of a family of counts from Franconia, the elector of Mainz also exercised the office of imperial chancellor and was one of the most able politicians of his day. He knew that an element within public opinion desired liberty, order and justice, in short for the system to be improved rather than to submit to an all-powerful monarch. As at the time of the Hohenstaufens, the German princes did not want to become drawn into escapades on the other side of the Alps or into European wars. Henneberg had a coherent plan which would guarantee good administration of justice, furnish a federal executive and procure regular resources for the Empire – all within a 'republican' perspective which anticipated the situation in Germany after the treaty of Westphalia but which left little place for the emperor and his grandiose schemes for foreign policy. The result was a conflict between Maximilian's moral authority, which was unchallenged, and the power which the princes possessed. Maximilian tried several times to win them over, convinced that he did not defend the particular interests of the House of Austria but those of the whole of Germany: 'My honour is the honour of Germany, the honour of Germany is my honour'.

The end result was a compromise which satisfied no one and proved in practice ineffective at a time when the other Western nations were strengthening their state apparatus (the Valois in France, the Tudors in England and in Spain the Catholic kings). After a number of serious crises, Germany limited itself to a skilfully balanced system under which the emperor's power, while certainly not non-existent, was carefully reined in.

From 1495 the Diet decreed perpetual peace (*ewiger Landfrieden*) and formally condemned private wars; this decree later provided the judicial basis for the formal censure of rebel princes and the imposition upon them of a ban of the Empire.

No less important was the creation, during the same session, of the imperial chamber court (*Reichskammergericht*, Germany's supreme court) which until 1689 sat at Worms then, following the devastation of the Palatinate, at Wetzlar until 1806. It was an appeal court modelled on the great council of the Valois, which judged in the final instance in trials referred from the particular courts of the Estates of the Empire. The court's jurisdiction emanated from the Diet, which appointed the judges; it totally escaped the control of the emperor, who thus lost his function as supreme judge, a prerogative which within the feudal perspective was fundamental.

To satisfy Maximilian, the Diet as compensation agreed to the principle of a general tax, the common penny (*gemeines Pfennig*), which was voted by the Diet and was divided among the Estates in proportion to their resources, just as the individual Diets (*Landtage*) in times of need voted and shared contributions among the orders of the different countries. These resources were collected and managed by an office dependent upon the Estates, the *Reichspfennigamt*.

In 1500 the imperial Diet sitting at Nürnberg attempted to create a genuine federal administration (*Reichsregiment*) according to the elector of Mainz's plan. The executive was to have consisted of twenty members, to be called regents (*Regenten*), who would have resided at Nürnberg, a free town of the Empire, and would have had at their disposal powers so extensive that even the emperor would have been tied by their decisions. The scheme was never realized because Maximilian conducted a campaign of passive resistance against the reform which would have limited the authority powerful princes like the electors of Saxony and Brandenburg exercised over their patrimonial lands.

In 1500 the Diet of Worms organized the German territory on the federal model: the Empire was divided into twelve circles (*Kreise*) modest in size and easy to administer. The hereditary lands of the Habsburgs formed a single circle; the Netherlands, with Franch-Comté restored by Charles VIII, formed the Burgundian circle. The other circles were governed by a Diet (*Kreistag*) charged with levying the *gemeines Pfennig* and recruiting the contingents of soldiers which every prince was obliged to supply should the imperial Diet declare war. The organization of the circles, often criticized for its delays, was nevertheless effective during the whole of the modern era, especially in particularly fragmented regions like Swabia, Franconia and Lower Saxony. The basis of this system was the 'imperial register' (*Reichsmatrikel*) where each state was charged with providing a certain number of knights and footsoldiers in addition to contributing to their pay, all in proportion to the population of the territory concerned.

The advantage of this organization was that it preserved the autonomy of the more modest states but its disadvantage was its cumbersome mechanism, difficult to set in motion and hard to control. The Estates of the Empire, as in the past, remained vassals anything but docile and ill-disposed towards the House of Austria. The German national state, despite the dreams of humanists like Ulrich von Hutten, was not yet born and the Holy Roman Empire would for a long time still preserve its confederal structure and its universalist vocation.

Maximilian for his part introduced a change to the institution of emperor. In 1507, blocked by the Venetians in northern Italy and sensing that pope Julius II was reluctant to crown him in the traditional way, Maximilian assumed the title emperor on his own authority and modified the German sovereign's title, adopting the formula which lasted until 1806, 'We Maximilian, by the grace of God, elected Roman emperor'. In so doing, as a good Renaissance prince, he kept his distance from the Church and the Holy See. Freed from the coronation at Rome, the king of the Romans was henceforth a German sovereign and the universal brilliance of the imperial title thereby lost a little of its lustre.

MAXIMILIAN AND THE HEREDITARY LANDS[5]

In 1493, because of Sigismund of the Tyrol's abdication, Maximilian was able to gather under his direct authority all the hereditary lands (*Erblande*) of the House of Austria. These comprised, besides Lower Austria and the Tyrol, Inner Austria (Styria, Carinthia, Carniola), the bishoprics of Brixen and of Trent, the county of Gorizia, eastern Swabia, the lordships around Augsburg and the remaining possessions on the upper Rhine known as the *Vorlande*, and Further Austria (Upper Alsace, Breisgau, the 'forest towns', with its capital at Ensisheim and its economic and cultural centre at Freiburg).

Like the Holy Roman Empire, the hereditary lands had grown accustomed to being self-governing, partly through inclination and partly through necessity given the power vacuum existing after Ferdinand III's accession. Maximilian's relations with the Estates of the Tyrol were good, while his relations with the Estates of Lower Austria showed the limits of royal power; at Linz, the orders rejected the appointment of Sigismund Prüschenck as governor (*Landeshauptmann*, literally captain of the country) of Upper Austria and Maximilian complied with their wishes even though Prüschenck was one of his favourites. In Vienna the Diet refused to vote Maximilian the contributions which he demanded, but, as Lower Austria had great strategic importance, he avoided inflaming conflict while installing, nevertheless, the Prüschencks there in the feudal lordship of Hardegg so that they could keep a watchful eye on the northern boundary of the land and the general behaviour of the orders.

Styria, with its iron mines and its metallurgy industry, was one of the bases of Maximilian's power. It furnished him with good artillery and exported its hardware throughout Renaissance Europe. Maximilian readily surrendered the government of Styria to the orders, who exploited their peasants harshly, and he seemed quite indifferent as long as the Diet voted him subsidies. He let his favourites brazenly exploit the monopolies that he had leased to them. Consequently he had to face numerous peasant rebellions and being more concerned for the defence of his dynastic interests than the well-being of his subjects, he crushed the rebels brutally. Even in the eulogies cobbled together by the most fawning humanist writers, he never became, unlike his adversary Louis XII, 'the father of the people'.

He proposed constitutional reforms which were accepted with some reservation and were later useful to his grandson Ferdinand I. Following the historian Gerhard Benecke, one may speak of 'proto-absolutism' in so far as Maximilian created a form of bureaucratic government modelled on that of the Burgundian and Parisian Valois. Contrary to the image left to posterity, Maximilian was given to study and wrote much; he served as a model for all the Habsburgs right until Francis-Joseph. A bureaucrat at heart, he studied the documents day by day, paying attention to detail. Unlike his famous predecessors, he did not let matters linger as he believed that where he could intervene personally, an immediate and appropriate solution would be effected.

His itinerant life – even his visits to Innsbruck were brief – forced him to create permanent bodies which could keep him informed, carry out his decisions and oversee the administration put in place by the orders. His nomadic life was customary for a medieval ruler and he was well acquainted with the Brabant, Rhineland, Alsace, Swabia, Tyrol and Austria. As the years advanced and his failures increased, his travels became the necessary outlet for his restless and blundering character. For the final ten years of his life, he rarely spent more than one night in the same castle, avoided large towns and stayed more often than not in hunting lodges or simple country inns.

He provided the hereditary lands with two governments, one for the Tyrol and the *Vorlande*, the other for Lower and Inner Austria. His wish had been to establish a single government to administer all the hereditary lands but this project was defeated by the vehement opposition of the orders, who were unwilling to see their privileges undermined by a prince inspired by Roman Law. Loyal in principle to their natural lords of the House of Austria, the nobles were without any 'Austrian national consciousness' – if one may risk such an anachronism – and lived only within the narrow framework of the land (*Landschaft*), not sensing any particular affinity with the orders of the neighbouring lands, although they had a common lord. Such – to a French reader at least – senseless particularism, not to say insularity, was a basic characteristic of German political culture where with respect to the Holy Roman Empire there was a strong sense of attachment to a very small country and an attenuated sense of belonging to a larger whole. The minds of Maximilian's subjects were not yet ready for such reforms and it is to his great merit that he nevertheless managed to introduce at least some of them.

In the Tyrol a collegiate system of government had been imposed since 1481 in order to restrict the havoc wrought by the archduke Sigismund's disastrous mismanagement. Responsibility was entrusted to a college of eight counsellors, who controlled the prince's excesses. In 1487 the counsellors were elected by the Estates, who had no doubt that they wanted to remain vassals of the Habsburgs. The government put in place by Maximilian in 1490, the *Regiment*, continued the existing system. In addition there was the college of four councillors subordinate to the government who were responsible for finance; since the Estates had every interest in the rigorous administration of their funds, the council had particular control over the steward who until then administered the Estates' treasury.

The other lands, however, resented an administration which appropriated to its own authority what they themselves had established. Since Maximilian needed the contributions which the Diets condescended to accord him, he practised caution when introducing reforms. The 'government' instituted in 1493, composed of a governor and counsellors, was simply a regency modelled on that in the Tyrol, to which Maximilian in time added a treasurer (*Schatzmann*) and a chamber of accounts which were installed at Vienna and took on the appearance of a government financial commission which in a very modern way distinguished finance from politics. In 1496 Maximilian created at Innsbruck a general treasury responsible for all the hereditary lands and made subordinate to it the chamber of accounts at Vienna. This move was without question directed against the reforms introduced in 1495 by the imperial Diet, but it also ended worries over the good administration of public funds.

The third phase of reform took place in 1501–2. The regency of Lower Austria was turned into a permanent institution with a governor at its head assisted by lieutenants and counsellors; a chamber of accounts (*Raitkammer*) controlled all financial affairs while a court chamber (*Hofkammer*) administered the whole of the prince's domain. Justice was entrusted to a tribunal of the court and of the chamber which consisted of twelve judges, the majority of jurists applying the rules of Roman Law. An Aulic Council represented the supreme jurisdiction and was responsible for the revision of trials. All these institutions did not sit at Vienna: the government was installed at Linz, the tribunal at Wiener Neustadt, while the chamber of accounts and the Aulic Council were established at Vienna.

Maximilian knew that these institutions went against the privileges of the Estates. The Styrian nobles considered Lower Austria a foreign country and refused to go there to seek justice, appealing to 'their liberties and privileges'. Necessity prompted them to create executive bodies dependent upon the Diet. The equivalent of the French Estates General, the general Diet of the five lands (Upper and Lower Austria, Styria, Carniola and

Carinthia) met at Wiener Neustadt in 1502 and ended in an accommodation: contact with the Estates of the *Vorlande* and even of the Netherlands was envisaged. Maximilian made a series of concessions. He authorized the codification of customary law, a task which was completed in 1514 with the edition of a code of procedure; for the orders it was preferable to the general use of Roman law which was hated by the lords, burghers and peasants alike. Maximilian was obliged to restore the court of the marshal of the land (*Landmarschall*) and accepted the strengthening of the Diets which were established for good in the capitals of each land.

After the session of the imperial Diet at Augsburg in 1510, the destiny of the institutional reforms was sealed. The court tribunal and the *Hofkammer* were swept away, the government or 'regency' was established at Vienna and absorbed the tribunal's personnel. No more ambitious reform from the year 1501 remained besides the 'regency' and the chamber of accounts. The first attempts to unify the hereditary lands had failed. The orders had nevertheless been introduced to the notion that they belonged to the same territory.

In 1518, a year before his death, Maximilian summoned to Innsbruck a general Diet of the Austrian lands which ended in the various lands promising to unite in the event of an external threat. Fortunately for the dynasty, the orders were incapable of coming together to impose a constructive scheme which would have made the Habsburgs feel the weight of their formidible power. They demanded the creation of an Aulic Council (*Hofrat*) responsible for justice, finance and administration which they would be able to inspect at any time. They also wanted to exclude the five counsellors from the Holy Roman Empire, a demand which Maximilian could not accept because he was also the elected sovereign of the Holy Roman Empire. This desire to exclude them nonetheless revealed the advance of a pronounced particularism with regard to the Empire which would presently fade away; right until the end of the monarchy in 1918 Germans from the Empire were free to pursue a career at Vienna without any discrimination with respect to their place of birth.

It is interesting to note that Maximilian at this time dreamt of establishing Austria as an autonomous kingdom within the Holy Roman Empire (the outlines for two projects have been preserved, one of which is in the humanist Conrad Peutinger's hand). Charles V had a similar idea when he ceded the hereditary lands to his brother Ferdinand. Such a reform would have had the advantage of placing Austria on a strictly equal footing with the kingdoms of Hungary and Bohemia within the framework of the Danubian monarchy. At the beginning of the sixteenth century, the Habsburgs dreamt of possessing the universal monarchy rather than creating a Central European state: Maximilian had done much to advance these dreams by his various marriage alliances.

MARRIAGE ALLIANCES[6]

It was through a series of marriage alliances rather than through institutions that Maximilian exerted a lasting influence upon the destiny of his House. Unable to create a German national state or even to give Austria a strong structure capable of directing the evolution of the Holy Roman Empire, he instead illustrated the famous motto:

> *Alli bella gerant*
> *Tu, felix Austria, nube.*
>
> Let others wage wars,
> You, happy Austria, marry!

The last twenty years of his life had a decisive effect on the history of the Habsburgs and the destiny of Europe since it was during those years that he created the necessary conditions for the formation of the universal monarchy of Charles V.

Maximilian's frantic activity was animated by three guiding principles: hatred of the French monarchy, the search for money vital for waging war, and imperialism in Italy.

After the comic-heroic episode of the Breton marriage, Maximilian believed that he had made a brilliant match in 1494 by taking as his second wife Bianca-Maria Sforza. In theory a vassal of the emperor, Ludovico Sforza (*Il Moro*) was one of the richest princes in Europe and one of the most powerful sovereigns in fifteenth-century Italy. However, his authority was challenged by Louis d'Orléans, the heir presumptive of Charles VIII who claimed the duchy of Milan in the name of the Viscontis, who had been ousted from the feudal lordship by the Sforzas. Here was a new source of conflict with the Valois and the old hostility was revived after 1489 when the duke of Orléans succeeded his cousin under the name Louis XII and used his kingdom's resources to gain possession of what he saw as his legitimate inheritance.[7]

Maximilian had married Bianca-Maria for the considerable dowry which she brought with her – 1 million florins in cash – but the marriage was a failure. The empress was undistinguished, incapable of taking the least decision and far from the magnificent regal figure that Maximilian needed to support him. Quarrels over money soon cast a shadow over the marriage. Self-centred and mean, Bianca-Maria filled her letters to her imperial husband with recriminations. A spendthrift who was used to the luxuries of life on the other side of the Alps, she was troubled by her creditors: she never had the 50 000 florins, interest on her dowry but only the 12 000 florins which the emperor was content to give her for her personal expenses. After 1498 she lived as a recluse at Innsbruck in the palace put at her disposal (*Hinterer Hof*) where she found consolation in the pleasures of the table. The union was sterile and oppressive. The empress took revenge on her husband by keeping systematically to her room. She died from indigestion at the age of thirty-eight (1 January 1511). Maximilian for a long time consoled himself with a series of brief liaisons which gave him some dozen or so bastards whose mothers' names are unknown.[8]

At the time of his engagement to Anne of Brittany, he had undertaken negotiations with the Catholic kings to arrange the marriage of his two children Margaret and Philip to the Spanish *infante* and *infanta*, Juan and Juana. The engagements took place in 1495 when the infanta was sixteen and the archduke seventeen. The marriage was solemnized the following year. The union was completed by the marriage of the *infante* don Juan, heir to the crowns of Castile and Aragón, to Margaret of Austria. The alliance had important consequences as it strengthened the alliance of the Austro-Burgundian state with the Iberian state and marked a rearrangement of traditional alliances: Castile had hitherto been allied with France (like the Habsburgs before 1477), while the interests of the crown of Aragón, like those of Flanders, placed its lands in the anti-French camp. The tragic destiny of the heir of the Catholic kings would swiftly change a clever diplomatic alliance into a windfall for the House of Austria.

Don Juan, always frail, did not survive more than a year of marriage: rumour claimed that he was worn out by the demands of the marriage-bed. A childless widow at eighteen, Margaret of Austria was happy to marry duke Philibert of Savoy. The death of the Spanish *infante* made Juana the only heir of the Catholic kings. She was mentally unstable but fell genuinely in love with Philip the Fair and gave birth to six children, all assured a brilliant future: Charles V, Ferdinand I, Maria, Eleanor and Elizabeth, the future queens of Hungary, France and Denmark respectively, and Philip's posthumous daughter Catherine, the future queen of Portugal. Philip the Fair's death in 1506 was a blow which toppled the delicate mental balance of the young queen. Although pregnant, Juana accompanied her husband's body from Bruges to Grenada, where it was buried. She survived him by half a century, shut away in the castle of Tordesillas in Castile. After giving birth to Catherine in 1507 she became mentally ill, for which reason she is popularly known as Juana the Mad. According to Castilian public law, she should have succeeded her father Ferdinand in 1517 and the investiture of her son Charles was considered tantamount to a *coup d'état*. It is questionable whether the queen really was incapable of ruling.

The emperor, after the death of his son the archduke Philip, tirelessly pursued his matrimonial policy. In 1507 he entrusted the regency of the Netherlands to his daughter Margaret, who was then a widow for a second time; she proved to be a remarkable stateswoman and a good tutor for her all but orphaned nephews, Charles and Ferdinand. Margaret of Austria, latterly the duchess of Savoy, left posterity the magnificent church at Brou, at the gates of Bourg-en-Bresse and seems one of the most attractive princesses from the House of Austria, combining intelligence with affection and genuine religious faith characterized by the *devotio moderna*.[9]

Maximilian resumed relations with the court of France and suggested to Anne of Brittany, whose second husband was Louis XII, that her daughter, Claude of France, should marry his grandson, then known simply as Charles of Ghent. The fundamental laws of the kingdom of France excluded women from the succession and even forbade transmission through the female line, with the result that the rights of the king's cousin, François d'Angoulême, to the kingdom could not be challenged. However, Breton custom allowed the transmission of inheritances through women and Claude was the heiress of her mother's duchy; the future Charles V had the chance, a quarter of a century later, to realize the scheme attempted by his grandfather – to acquire Brittany and to encircle France. Anne of Brittany, who had never made any secret of her hatred of the French in general and the Valois in particular, did all she could to involve Louis XII in this strange alliance. The marriage between Charles of Ghent and Claude of France appeared all the more threatening because Ferdinand of Aragón had strengthened the Anglo-Spanish alliance by marrying his daughter Catherine, the sister of Juana the Mad, to Henry VII of England's son, Arthur the prince of Wales. Soon widowed, Catherine of Aragón then married her late husband's brother, the future Henry VIII, their subsequent divorce being the origin of the Anglican schism of 1531.

All these marriage projects, as tedious as they may be, simply demonstrate how the destiny of monarchical states was linked to marriage alliances, frequently confounded by premature deaths, and that public affairs still bore a remarkable resemblance to the scheming of private citizens. These unions, where the personal feelings of a prince scarcely counted, favoured alliances and transformed emerging states into conglomerations of provinces without any link save loyalty to a common prince.

Maximilian's last marriage alliance was perhaps the most successful and had the most important long-term consequences for Danubian Europe. If Maximilian failed to join Brittany, England, the Netherlands and Spain in a league of maritime powers directed against French dreams of hegemony, he did at least lay the foundations of the Austrian monarchy, concluding in Vienna in 1515 a pact of mutual succession with Władysław II Jagieł-łończyk;[10] it was at the time a dangerous gamble. By this treaty the Habsburgs and the Jagiełłons both promised each other their patrimony, the surviving House inheriting the patrimony of the two Houses combined. The pact was accompanied by the promise of a double marriage: the archduke Ferdinand was to marry Anne Jagiełłon, daughter of Władysław II, while Maria of Habsburg was engaged to Louis Jagiełłon, son of the king of Bohemia and Hungary. The Habsburgs recovered a right to the crown of St István but it was a right of little value because the crown, like that of St Václav, was elective. As far as the two kingdoms were concerned, it was a simple 'option' which took care of the future.

The reign of Maximilian, despite his weaknesses and failures, constituted a turning-point in the history of the House of Austria. Although he did not truly renounce the Holy Roman Empire, he was able to effect there only reforms of little import, as he had to take account of the wishes of the great feudal lords while freeing the imperial crown of papal tutelage. He had, however, given the hereditary lands a parallel administration, that of the prince only running alongside that of the Estates. While he curtailed the immense ambitions of the orders, he was unable to stop a duality that lasted more than two centuries.

Neither a medieval sovereign nor yet quite a modern one, Maximilian was, according to the expression of the historian Benecke, a 'proto-modern' prince who had not created a state apparatus worthy of that name, but rather had gambled successfully with a series of marriage alliances. He had been able to assemble the mass of countries and kingdoms which became Charles V's patrimony in the face of the Valois's firm monarchy. This patrimony was no longer medieval Christendom nor yet a nation-state, but rather a confederation spread across Europe whose only bond was the person of the monarch, or more exactly the sovereign House. It was a novel construction but fragile at the level of the Estates, at a time when it was relatively easy for the aristocracy to gather together estates and to manage them through loyal stewards. This ambition turned the Habsburgs away from their Central European patrimony; the gravitational centre of their new power lay in the rich plains of Flanders, the leading centre for culture, art, religion and material wealth, while Upper Germany dealt like for like with the House of Austria and Italy remained rebellious towards its foreign protector.

For the future destiny of the Habsburgs, Maximilian's life's work was a success: who could have predicted that the *condottiere* of 1477, the 'chaser after dowries', as penniless as he was daring, would leave his grandsons an Empire over which the sun never set?

NOTES AND REFERENCES

1. Hermann Wiesflecker, *Kaiser Maximilian I*, 5 vols, Vienna, 1971–86.
2. Bernard Quilliet, *Louis XII*, Paris, 1984, pp. 278–94.
3. Richard Ehrenberg, *Le Siècle des Fugger*, Paris, 1957.
4. Fritz Hartung, *Deutsche Verfassungsgeschichte vom 15. Jahrhundert bis zur Gegenwart*, Berlin, 1922.
5. E. C. Hellbling, *Œsterreichische Verfassungs und Verwaltungsgeschichte*, Vienna, 1956.
6. Alphons Dopsch, 'Die Westaatspolitik der Habsburger im Werden ihres Grossreiches', *Gesamtdeutsche Vergangenheit*, Vienna, 1938.
7. Quilliet, *Louis XII*.

8. Gerhard Benecke, *Maximilian I (1459–1519): An Analytical Biography*, London, 1982, pp. 26–7.
9. E. Winker, *Margarete von Oesterreich: Grande Dame der Renaissance*, Munich, 1966.
10. Jörg K. Hoensch, *Geschichte Böhmens: von der slavischen Landnahme bis ins 20. Jahrhundert*, Munich, 1987, pp. 174–5.

CHAPTER ELEVEN

The Empire of Charles V and the Universal Monarchy

Elected emperor in 1519 and heir to a patrimony 'where the sun never sets', Charles V made a final attempt to realize the unity of Christendom, the old medieval dream which in the era of the affirmation of national monarchies seemed an insane undertaking and the manifestation of a quite unacceptable imperialism. In short, Charles V was accused of wanting to exercise his hegemony over Europe and of aspiring to create a universal monarchy. Attacked in turn by the Italian potentates, the kings of France and of England and by his own German vassals, he suffered a series of resounding failures and bore the consequences himself, surrendering all his powers in 1556 in order to withdraw to the monastery at Yuste in Castile. Bolstered by his inheritance and the imperial title, he had believed that Christendom when confronted with the Turkish menace would face up to the threat, immediately recover its unity and recognize at least the nominal authority of the emperor. He had, however, misjudged the spirit of the age, the determination of the Valois and the balance of power between France and Spain.

A BURGUNDIAN PRINCE[1]

Elected emperor at the age of nineteen, Charles of Ghent (1500–58) was without any strong national roots. By virtue of his education he was first and foremost a Burgundian prince whose mother-tongue was French and who perhaps became Castilian in his later years; he never thought of himself as a German prince. He had been even less subject to the influence of his parents than other contemporary rulers: when he was six, his father Philip the Fair had died and his mother, Juana the Mad, the heiress of Castile, lived shut up in her castle at Tordesillas. For this reason he had been brought up by his remarkable paternal aunt, Margaret of Austria, the widow of the duke of Savoy. She inculcated in him the aristocratic ideal of the Burgundian court: he acquired a taste for pomp, for hunting and for tournaments but proved no less an assiduous scholar and diligent sovereign, finding pleasure in the business of ruling. He was always travelling: although he preferred to stay in the Netherlands or in Castile, the demands of war took him to Germany, Italy and even Hungary. He never had a capital and was content to direct affairs with a limited team of ministers, leaving a large measure of autonomy to countries under his rule and making full use of the services of all the princes and princesses of the House of Austria: his aunt Margaret, his sister Maria of Hungary, his brother Ferdinand, his sister Eleanor and his son Philip.

Charles V had an aristocratic – and medieval – conception of patrimony. When Maximilian died in 1519, he found himself at the head of an even greater inheritance, because following the death of his maternal grandfather, Ferdinand of Aragón, he had held the Mediterranean domains of the Aragonese kings. He possessed a miscellaneous collection of states and provinces quite unconnected save by the loyalty of their subjects to their legitimate sovereign.

Charles V might truly boast that the sun never set on his states: they stretched from the Carpathians to Gibraltar, from the river Meuse to Calabria, and as king of Spain he had operational bases in North Africa while in America he held the Antilles; his Castilian subjects were embarking on the conquest of the Mexican high plateaux.

In Germany, he inherited the hereditary lands, a long band of territories stretching from the Vosges to the Carpathians. The Habsburgs' original patrimony included the feudal lordships in Upper Alsace (excluding Mulhouse and Colmar) and Breisgau, although in the fifteenth century the Swiss cantons had rejected the tutelage of the House of Austria. Added to these was Lower Austria, which controlled the middle valley of the Danube and with its capital at Vienna became the heart of the Austrian monarchy. Vienna, with its 50 000 inhabitants, its fortifications, its university and its international market, appeared like a capital city. Its patricians harboured pretensions to autonomy just like the nobles of the other hereditary lands who through the Diets enjoyed a very great measure of administrative autonomy. To the south of Lower Austria lay Inner Austria, which basically consisted of Styria, Carinthia and Carniola but through the country of Gorizia extended as far as the Adriatic. The acquisition in the fifteenth century of the county of Tyrol and its dependencies proved vital for communications between the Netherlands and Austria but most importantly for the route between central Germany and northern Italy. Like his grandfather Maximilian, Charles V stayed several times at Innsbruck. Through the bishoprics of Trent and Brixen, the Tyrol already had a foothold in Italy which the Habsburgs coveted. With the exception of the Slovenes of Carniola and some Italians, the majority of his subjects in the hereditary lands were German and, as long as the sovereign respected their extensive privileges, remained loyal. They represented an element of power over the German exchequer and on the level of Central Europe but counted for very little in comparison with Italy and the Netherlands. The 'countries on this side' were a continuous creation of the House of Burgundy; in 1419 Philip the Good, master of Burgundy, Artois and Flanders, acquired Limburg, Brabant and Antwerp. From 1430 he controlled twelve of the seventeen provinces: Flanders, Artois, Malines, Brabant, Limburg, Antwerp, Hainaut, Utrecht, Holland, Zeeland, Friesland and Luxemburg. Charles the Bold had conquered Guelders but it fell to Charles V to give the Burgundian state its final form, uniting with it the provinces which until then had been only loosely linked, securing its independence from France and the Holy Roman Empire and giving it a firm form of central government. In 1529 (by the treaty of Cambrai) Flanders and Artois ceased to be French fiefs. After 1512, the Burgundian states were freed of all obligations towards the Empire and formed a circle within it. Even so Charles V was very cautious about strengthening his monarchical authority; in 1548 a 'pragmatic sanction' assured the descendants of the House sovereignty over each province.

Required to be absent permanently from the Netherlands after 1520, Charles V chose to appoint governors-general drawn from the House of Habsburg – first his aunt Margaret of Austria, then his sister Mary,[2] and finally after 1549 his son Philip – as the unity of the country was fragile, the southern provinces being French-speaking and the northern ones (Flanders, Holland, Zeeland, etc.) Dutch-speaking. Furthermore the large towns were, just like the nobility, jealous of their privileges. The Netherlands at that time were one of the richest and most densely populated countries in Europe. Antwerp soared to eminence because of the rise of maritime trade and for half a century was Europe's leading centre for banking. The agriculture of the Netherlands gave the best yield in Europe while its textile industry remained one of the foremost on the continent.

Italy, where Charles V followed the policies of his grandfathers (Maximilian of Austria and Ferdinand of Aragón) was very different from the Netherlands. The kingdom of Naples with Sicily, still famed as the wheat granary of Europe, had been inherited by Ferdinand of Aragón. At that time, Naples had the largest population of any town in Italy and teemed with its wretched masses. Solidly girded with fortresses, it was to remain within the Spanish sphere for a further two centuries. Charles also inherited from Maximilian claims to the state of Milan which for the whole of his reign set him at variance with the Valois; it would take half a century of warfare to establish Spanish hegemony over the peninsula. In 1519 all that Spain had in Italy were the *presidios* on the Tyrrhenian coast and the alliance with Genoa.

The other bastion of Charles V's power was Spain, which was still not unified and where Catalonia was in decline while Castile seemed a rising star in the European firmament. Despite a fragile economy based on the profits from the Mesta (association of transhumant shepherds) and on the cultivation of cereals, which yielded poor returns, the Castilian state rested on a firm basis and its subjects were used to being obedient and to paying tax without too much muttering. Castile itself was a reservoir of good soldiers who ventured forth and got killed in America and in Germany for the glory of their king. Even if the kingdoms on the periphery (Navarre, Valencia and Aragón) had to be handled with consideration, the centre of the Iberian peninsula was secure and never ceased to support its king, albeit without much enthusiasm.[3]

All these patrimonies still did not satisfy the young king of Spain, who needed the imperial crown in order to outrival the other European sovereigns. The crown remained elective, however, and Maximilian had been unable to secure the election of his successor during his own lifetime. His death opened a political and diplomatic crisis throughout Europe as the election was contested between the king of France and the king of Spain, Francis I and Charles of Habsburg. The 1519 election was, in one sense, exemplary in so far as it was enacted against the background of the religious crisis initiated two years earlier by Luther.[4]

The stake was high and constituted the first episode in the confrontation between Francis I and Charles V. The Germans, if they chose the French candidate, risked losing their German liberties and seeing the implementation of the government reforms that Maximilian had been unable to achieve within the Empire. On the other hand, with Charles V they had the chance of witnessing the realization of the universal monarchy that had always been the Holy Roman Empire's vocation and the greatest threat posed by the young prince as a good Catholic was the rather brutal re-establishment of religious unity. There was, however, a strong possibility that he might maintain the government of the Holy Roman Empire in the state of impotence in which he found it. Moreover, neither Charles nor Francis spoke German, but the Habsburg candidate had the advantage of being the grandson of the late emperor and descended from a German House, albeit one which had become very cosmopolitan.

In practice, the election of 1519 became a vulgar matter of bribery and exposed the weakness of certain institutions. The seven electors were for sale and the two candidates decided to pay. National sentiment worked in Charles's favour: he was seen as a German, and he was also assisted by the diplomatic support of his aunt, Margaret of Austria, but above all by the unconditional help of the banker Jakob Fugger. In 1523 Fugger wrote to him, 'It is widely known and as clear as day that Your Imperial Majesty could not have secured the Roman crown without me'. Indeed, the electors had confidence in the House of Fugger alone, regardless of whom it backed. The operation cost Charles almost 1 million florins, an enormous sum at that time: it amounted to the Austrian annual budget during war or six years' worth of revenue from the Tyrolean mines. He obtained his initial financial aid on the Antwerp market with the support of his aunt, but it was the bankers from Augsburg, Welser and Fugger, who financed 80 per cent of the operation, while Genoa gave 15 per cent and Florence 5 per cent. Half a million florins had to be spent to buy the votes of the seven electors; according to the accounts made in 1520, only the elector of

Brandenburg, who had concluded a treaty with France, received nothing. The two most costly votes were that of the archbishop of Mainz, Albrecht of Brandenburg, which cost 113 000 florins, and that of the elector Palatine, who received 184 500 florins. Not only the princes but also their advisers had to be bought: the Swabian League was given 171 000 florins to abandon duke Ulrich of Wurtemberg and to recognize Habsburg suzerainty.[5]

The imperial coronation took place at Bologna ten years after the election and was the last in history to be carried out by the sovereign pontiff. Clement VII conferred upon Charles V the prestige of a true Roman emperor and the ambitions of a head of Christendom.

AN ANACHRONISTIC PROGRAMME

The emperor's conception of Christendom was oddly anachronistic. This is apparent from two important texts, a letter of 1519 to the electors and a memorandum from 1521 addressed to the princes assembled at the Diet of Worms. In 1519 Charles emphasized the struggle against the infidel:

As you know, it has pleased God our Creator through good, true and legitimate succession to have us succeed to the kingdoms forsaken by our late good lord and grandfather the king don Ferdinand of Aragón. And since for forty or fifty years there has been neither a king nor a Christian prince who has waged a war of honour to the benefit and advantage of Christendom against the infidels and enemies of our faith besides the aforementioned king of Aragón, we wish to follow in his steps.

Since nothing is so evident nor more true than that God has given us this grace of succeeding to the imperial dignity and majesty so that we might all the more easily make use of the goodwill which we enjoy; for that which our said grandfather, king of Aragón, achieved in many years against the infidels with the aid and might of this noble German nation, we shall carry out a great exploit against these said infidels in a short time with the aid of the subjects of the kingdoms and other lands which we at present possess. For our true intentions and our wish are to nourish and return to peace the whole of Christendom and to direct all our force and strength to the defence, preservation and increase of our Faith.

In 1521 it was the struggle against heresy that he emphasized:

You know that I am descended from those very Christian emperors who have ruled over the noble German House, the Catholic kings of Spain, the archdukes of Austria, the dukes of Burgundy, all of whom unto very death have been the faithful sons of the Roman Church, the defenders of the Catholic faith, of the sacred customs and practices of divine service which they have bequeathed to me and whose example I have hitherto followed. I am therefore resolved to remain faithful to all that which has been fixed since the Council of Constance. It is clear that a solitary brother is in error when he contradicts the opinion of the whole of Christendom unless Christendom has been in error for a thousand years and more. Therefore I am resolved to commit my kingdoms, possessions, friends, body and blood, life and soul. Since it would be to your shame and mine, members of the German nation, if during our lifetime and through our negligence, the appearance of a single heresy, of a fallacy stemming from the Christian religion were to penetrate into the hearts of men.

To achieve these ends, Charles V wanted to be the head of Christendom. He based his authority both on the supranational character of imperial power and on the possession of a patrimony which extended over a great part of Europe. Matters of government and matters of family were for him closely connected. It was he, for example, who managed the conclusion of the 1515 treaty of Vienna to his advantage and arranged the double Habsburg–Jagiellon marriage in 1521. There was a curious analogy between the Burgundian model and Charles V's collection of possessions. The Burgundian state still rested on feudal service, the loyalty of the nobility to their natural feudal lord and the alliance of its nobles among themselves. Charles V made use of this system without creating any loyalties himself. When he organized his government, he did not rely solely on Burgundians, who did not support a complete restructuring of the government. In politics, he was the pupil of a great Burgundian nobleman, Guillaume de Croÿ, lord of Chièvres, but as emperor he misapplied the principles which the latter had inculcated in him. The control exercised over creditors turned into avarice, the concern for peace into an immoderate love of justice that entailed endless conflicts. As for his decisiveness, this was blocked by the desire to know everything which was in turn paralyzed by his anxious and irresolute character, quite typical of the Habsburgs. He was not a sufficient realist and, like his grandfather Maximilian, confused the honour of his House, the interests of the Holy Roman Empire and the need for a crusade against the infidels. Also, as Karl Brandi notes, 'at the moment when the German nation desired a king who would embody its aspirations, it was presented with a young sovereign who did not forge any link with the inner-being of the people but rather was more inclined to oppose the individual nationalities, fortified as he was by the idea of hereditary universal empire.'

To these two goals – the fight against the infidel and the fight against heresy – he added the defence of his patrimony without really engaging in imperialism in the modern sense of the term. Did he yield to the lure of universal monarchy which his Piedmontian chancellor Mercurino Gattinara proposed to him as early as 12 July 1519?

Sir, since God has conferred upon you this great grace of raising you above all the kings and princes of Christendom to a power which hitherto only your predecessor

Charlemagne has possessed, you are on the path to universal monarchy, you will unite all Christendom under one sceptre.[6]

This was pure illusion. The spirit of the age no longer favoured the union of Christendom, not even just the Western half, under the authority of the emperor and the pope, and experience would show that even the threat from the Turks could not succeed in uniting all the nations in a joint defensive action. France assumed leadership of the resistance to Charles V's enterprise but found allies in Germany, Italy and sometimes even the king of England. The conflict between the House of Habsburg and the House of Valois continued after Charles V's abdication in 1553. Gattinara's analysis was, moreover, objectively inaccurate: in 1520, the balance of power was more in the favour of Francis I than Charles V. While Charles V's resources, when added together, exceeded those of the king of France, the distances between his possessions diminished the imbalance of power between the two opponents so that France and the Habsburgs constituted two equal forces. A logical process had engendered these two rival monarchies; in the second half of the fifteenth century, a powerful state was formed on the periphery of the kingdom of France which set in progress the process of consolidation from which emerged the confederation governed by Charles V.

According to Pierre Chaunu, the ordinary revenue of Castile under the Catholic kings amounted to 3 tonnes of silver, and the total revenue was in the region of 5 tonnes. These figures may be compared with the sum total of tax in France, which rose from 92 tonnes of silver in 1523 to 115 tonnes in 1547. The average annual sum of royal tax during the reign of Henry II, from 1547 to 1559, slightly exceeded 200 tonnes of silver a year. It was the precious metals from America which enabled the Habsburgs to finance their wars. According to Pierre Chaunu,[7] in the last twenty years of Charles V's reign, the Castilian state received from America 300 tonnes of money-equivalent or 15 tonnes annually in the form of around 7 tonnes of *white metal* and 0.8 tonnes of gold. In the course of the first twenty years, America had yielded only 90 tonnes of money-equivalent, that is approximately 4.8 tonnes of raw silver. The Spanish historian R. Carande published in 1949 the accounts of the ordinary of Castile: what is striking is the small increase after 1504 and in particular the low level of the final revenue which, far from increasing, hardly kept pace with the rise in prices. In Castile as in France, the rise in prices absorbed the apparent rise in revenue and the tremendous gap between the two kingdoms did not show any tendency to diminish. Charles V partly financed the war through the credit he obtained from the German bankers he found on the Antwerp market. It was less the treasure of the American Eldorado than the tangible riches of the Netherlands which enabled him to wage war and then only on a limited scale.

In reality, for Francis I as for Charles, a campaign represented 10 000 men on the pay roll in battalions with the same number in reserve. The manpower of the armies, it should be noted, doubled between 1550 and 1560. In 1552, the year of the siege of Metz, the French army stood at around 35 000 men; five years later Philip II's army, which was victorious at Saint-Quentin, had 50 000 men, and that of Henry II, 40 000. However, this display of might brought about the bankruptcy of the latter and robbed the former of the chance to follow up his victory by marching on Paris. Ferdinand Lot sums up the situation: 'Philip II had won the battle but he had missed the unhoped for chance of seizing Paris and destroying Henry II's last remaining forces.'[8] This failure nullified his success and without doubt he should have followed the routine procedure, which advises against advancing deep into enemy territory without securing possession of the strongholds encountered on the way. The king of Spain lost a valuable chance to make himself master of Saint-Quentin, du Câtelet, de Ham, de Chauny, but the underlying cause of his final failure rested in his army's too great numerical superiority. Even before the siege, he did not know how to feed it; victorious, he could not pay it.

THE BIRTH OF THE DANUBIAN MONARCHY

One of the principal triumphs of Charles V's reign was the moderate but lasting achievements in Central Europe of his younger brother, Ferdinand I, who was the true creator of the Danubian monarchy and one of the most remarkable Habsburgs.[9] Practically an orphan, Ferdinand was brought up in Spain by his grandfather, Ferdinand of Aragón, who entertained great expectations of his grandson and would have liked to have made him king of Spain. Maximilian and the future Charles V had, however, decided otherwise and in 1517 it was Charles who came into possession of the kingdom of Castile. With Juana the Mad in retirement in her castle at Tordesillas and incapable of ruling, Charles was proclaimed king alongside his mother but exercised power alone. For the Castilians, though, he was an outsider and Ferdinand attracted around him a party of supporters. When Charles V arrived in the Iberian peninsula, one of his first actions was to dispatch his younger brother to Flanders. Apparently he intended to compensate him once he had become emperor and had consolidated his authority in Spain. On the other hand, the orders meeting in Innsbruck in 1519 had expressed a desire to have Ferdinand as prince in the hereditary lands. The vast extent of the possessions of the House of Austria and the obstacles to communications between Vienna, the Netherlands, Valladolid or Seville fully justified the sharing of responsibilities, a sharing which was in keeping with family tradition. Charles was prepared to hand over the hereditary lands to his younger brother if only to keep Ferdinand from the kingdom of Naples to which he had rights through Ferdinand of Aragón's will.

The first treaty of division was signed in April 1521 during the session of the imperial Diet at Worms, with Charles V reserving for himself the Tyrol, Friuli and Trieste which he thought essential for communications with Italy. In accordance with the treaty of Vienna (1515) Ferdinand married Anne Jagiellon, sister of Louis II Jagiellon, king of Hungary and Bohemia (26 May 1521), thus the destiny of the emperor's younger brother was clear: Ferdinand was to represent the interests of the House in Central Europe, a region that Charles V viewed as quite marginal.

Complete victory came for Ferdinand the following year; in February 1522, by the treaty of Brussels, Charles surrendered to him the government of the whole of the Habsburgs' German patrimony, including the Tyrol and its mines, the *Vorlande* (Upper Alsace, Breisgau, Vorarlberg) and the fiefs of Wurtemberg. His possessions thus stretched from the Vosges to the Carpathians, reviving the tradition of the fourteenth century and finally establishing German Austria – especially as the hereditary lands' privileges with regard to the Empire were confirmed. It would be inaccurate to view this as the creation of an Austrian state separate from Germany; on the contrary Ferdinand became the emperor's proxy in German affairs in the event of Charles V's absence from Germany. Despite the developments of the Lutheran Reformation, Charles was absent from Northern Europe for many years while he restored order to Spain, which was shaken by the revolt of the *Comuneros*. The German patrimony of the House of Austria would henceforth give the young archduke Ferdinand sufficient authority within the Empire.

Ferdinand was no longer simply his brother's representative within the Empire but appeared as his most loyal supporter in the face of the German princes and the Lutherans. At the same time, he had the means to defend Habsburg interests in Hungary. After 1522 two distinct branches of the House of Austria appeared: the senior branch, with its universal vocation, and the German branch, with a more modest calling. This book is concerned with the latter but the interests of both branches were intertwined and Ferdinand was obliged to take full account of his brother's strategic options and only ever had a narrow margin in which to manoeuvre. Almost to the very end he paid heavily for the conflicts in which his brother was embroiled, without ever, it would seem, having very great means at his disposal. He represented a regional power which found itself involved in the conflicts of the great powers. This was the beginning of a situation that lasted two centuries and loyalty to the senior branch would often cost the Viennese Habsburgs dearly. In the front line in the conflict with the Ottoman empire or in the internal quarrels of the Holy Roman Empire, they received only the slightest trickle from their Spanish brethren's American hoards.

The treaty of Brussels in 1522 was, then, decisive for the future of Danubian Europe. While Louis II Jagiellon was in himself a thoroughly unremarkable sovereign, his tragic death in 1526 had truly remarkable consequences; the 1515 treaty of Vienna was applied at once and Ferdinand was elected to the thrones of Hungary and Bohemia at the moment when Charles V was completely occupied with the so-called 'Italian Wars'.

THE ITALIAN WARS[10]

The Italian Wars were an unedifying chapter in French history and the Valois's transalpine policy has been judged severely. The reader quickly gets lost in the political-diplomatic imbroglio of Renaissance Italy where some large cities achieved the status of territorial states (Venice, Milan, Genoa and Florence) and assiduously preserved the equilibrium – hence the disconcerting changes of camp and alliances. The French coveted Italy not simply on account of straightforward dynastic pretensions to Milan or Naples but rather because in the field of culture Italy was the richest and most prestigious country in Europe; a generation which was rediscovering the pleasures of Antiquity was not going to abandon to its Spanish rivals hegemony over so irresistibly attractive a peninsula. Besides, as Pierre Chaunu has pointed out in *L'Espagne de Charles Quint*, France in 1520 was probably the most powerful state in Europe and its bellicose nobility was looking for room to expand.

Charles VIII's ventures, although they finally ended in failure, provided a model for his successor, Louis XII, who while far from being belligerent, nevertheless stubbornly pressed home his rights to the duchy of Milan. Defeated in 1512 by a European coalition, he lost all his conquests and allowed Ferdinand of Aragón to seize Navarre. If death had not prevented him, Louis XII would have dreamt of venturing once again into Italy in spring 1515. This was the reason why, from the time of his accession (1515), the young Francis I did not hesitate to realize his father-in-law's scheme to recover Milan from the Sforzas. After the victory at Marignano, the French once again found themselves in a strong position in Italy. For the Habsburgs it was vital that they should possess Milan and consequently conflict was inevitable between Francis I and Charles V over this part of their respective patrimonies. Milan guaranteed the Habsburgs' links between the hereditary lands, Naples and Spain; for Francis I it was a bridgehead on the other side of the Alps.

That the French had fielded a candidate in the imperial election of 1519 had roused deep resentment in Charles V, who considered the crown of the emperors part of his patrimony and thought that the Habsburgs had a vocation to govern Christendom. Any accommodation with the Valois was thus impossible. At the end of three successive campaigns, the French were defeated at Pavia (1525). Francis I was captured, the flower of the French cavalry killed or captured. On this occasion, however, the emperor showed his limitations and did not follow the recommendations of his chancellor Gattinara:

Instead of swiftly taking action, in keeping with the circumstances, the emperor this time, by fault of his stubbornness and hesitation, lost even more time than usual. He gave proof of a singular indifference in the face of the powers of the opposition which immediately appeared in France, England and Italy; this quite simply put into question the success at Pavia.

The Peace of Madrid (1526) was imposed upon Francis I but the king of France never carried out its terms. Charles V succeeded in removing Artois and Flanders from French suzerainty but he wanted to use his victory to recover his patrimony, in particular the duchy of Burgundy which he thought of as the cradle of his family. Francis I took refuge in the feelings of the Burgundians and the inalienable character of the royal domain and refused to fulfil the terms of the treaty. Burgundy was never restored to the emperor, who dismissed his adversary as a perjuror who departed from the most basic rules of chivalry. The misunderstanding was total and the war was resumed from 1527, but France now had allies who had regrouped to form the League of Cognac. After the sack of Rome by the imperial troops (1527), pope Clement VII was obliged to make a treaty with Charles V and crowned him solemnly at Bologna; it was the last time the medieval Christian ritual was carried out.

Some months before the coronation, Margaret of Austria had engineered a compromising peace with Louise of Savoy, mother of Francis I. This was the Peace of Cambrai, the 'Ladies' Peace' concluded in 1529. Charles V renounced Burgundy, but the king of France abandoned all suzerainty over Artois, Franche-Comté and Flanders and any claim to Naples and Milan. He was obliged to pay an indemnity of 2 million golden écus to obtain the liberation of his two sons, whom Charles held hostage at Madrid.

A further thirty years, however, would pass before the Valois finally accepted this compromise and renounced any Italian ambitions. Right until the Peace of Cateau-Cambrésis (1559) the Milan affair remained a bone of contention. To make valid his rights, the king of France allied with the Turks and the German Lutherans.

THE FRANCO-OTTOMAN ALLIANCE[11]

A new element in the conflict emerged when the French king, who was a devout Christian, proved prepared to countenance a formal alliance with Süleymân the Magnificent and to unite his own forces with those of the sultan according to a plan set out in 1535 by the chancellor Duprat, in an order which was given to Jean de La Forest, the French ambassador at Istanbul. The goal was a general peace in Europe under the terms of which Charles V would restore to France Milan, Asti, Genoa and suzerainty over

Flanders, and Ferdinand I would abandon Hungary to Süleymân. To force the Habsburgs to give in, military pressure had to be applied not on Hungary but on Sicily and Sardinia in order to avoid alarming the German princes and driving them into Ferdinand's camp.

This was a reversal of principles: national interest went before the defence of Christendom (the author of the scheme was a cardinal of the Holy Church). It resulted in a combined operation during which the French and the Turks devastated the coastlines of Italy. The spirit of the crusades was far away.

THE ALLIANCE WITH THE GERMAN PRINCES

Charles V was deeply involved in the affairs of Germany. What is most surprising is his and his brother's moderation with respect to the Lutherans. Before 1530 the emperor was detained in Spain and preoccupied with Italian affairs and let matters rest in order to avoid involvement with the princes of the Empire who were jealous of their autonomy, in the confessional as well as other domains. A good Erasmian, he entertained the idea that heresy could be halted by summoning a general council, a suggestion which the Roman Curia greeted with extreme hostility because such a council would impinge on the prerogatives of the sovereign pontiff.

Having brought the confessional debate into the political arena, Charles V found himself confronted by an organized party led by the Saxon princes and the landgrave of Hesse and supported by the free towns (Strassburg, Ulm, Nürnberg and Frankfurt). Following Ferdinand's election as king of the Romans in 1531, the Protestant princes organized themselves into the League of Schmalkalden and sought patronage from the king of France. It was a classic scenario: German princes, vassals of the emperor, allied with the sovereign of a foreign power in order to oppose the Habsburgs. In the Empire, Francis I found natural allies against the House of Austria and, ever a political realist, he took advantage of confessional differences. The Most Christian King allied with heretics and rebels, just as he allied with the Turks who were spreading alarm among his German allies.

After the Peace of Crépy-en-Laonnois (September 1544) Charles V decided to take action. In 1545 the General Council met for the first time at Trent. In 1546, strengthened by the support of Maurice of Saxony, the emperor gathered together an army in Germany to wipe out the League of Schmalkalden, specifying that he was waging war only against rebels and not against Lutherans in general. He joined Maurice of Saxony and won a great victory at Mühlberg on the banks of the Elbe (26 April 1547) where he captured the elector of Saxony, Johann Friedrich. A few days later he defeated the landgrave Philipp of Hesse while Ferdinand I crushed the rebellion of the Bohemian Estates. Like the victory at Pavia, the triumph at Mühlberg was more apparent than real and did not have profound repercussions upon the history of Germany.

Charles V was at variance with pope Paul III, who transferred the Council to Bologna, then sabotaged its proceedings. The emperor believed that he was strong enough on his own to settle the religious question in the Empire. After exhibiting much patience, he summoned the Diet at Augsburg and imposed the Interim of 1548: while waiting for the decrees of the General Council to be promulgated, Catholicism was re-established throughout Germany while the Lutherans were granted communion in both kinds and their clergy were allowed to marry. Many Protestant princes accepted these terms, the towns submitted and, thirty years after his election, Charles V for a while appeared to be the master in Germany.

The state of mind of the members of the Diet, the subtle balance of political forces which regulated the German world and the orders' attachment to their liberties had been badly misunderstood. The Protestant princes turned to the king of France, Henry II, whose hatred of the Habsburgs was bred of personal experience following his captivity at Madrid after his father's defeat at Pavia. He was thoroughly determined to resume the conflict with the House of Austria and in 1552 signed at Chambord a treaty of alliance with the German Protestant princes. It was these princes who in spring 1552 allowed the king of France to occupy temporarily the bishoprics of Metz, Toul and Verdun, then fiefs of the Empire, and provided him with financial help. Maurice of Saxony, who had received the title of elector in recognition of his services in 1547, did not hesitate to desert the emperor and in the same year assumed leadership of the army which marched on Innsbruck where Charles V was residing. The emperor, without money and without troops, fled to Austria. In the autumn, he again assembled an army and marched on Metz, which was defended in a spirited fashion by the duke of Guise and held out against the imperial troops; the ailing sovereign was obliged to raise the siege in January 1553 in order to return to the Netherlands. It seems that this failure was decisive in driving the emperor to take a step unheard of for a hereditary monarch; Charles V abdicated and formally divided his patrimony between his son Philip and his brother Ferdinand.

The emperor's weariness can be better understood if it is remembered that Henry II had resumed the traditional policy of the Valois in Italy. In 1551 the king of France used troops to intervene against Jules III at Parma, supported the people of Siena in their revolt against the Medicis of Florence, who were allies of the Habsburgs, and then gave his assistance to the Corsicans, who were rising against the Republic of Genoa, also one of Charles V's allies. In the age of galleys, Corsica was the key to the western Mediterranean. Henry II was quick to breathe new life into the alliance with Süleymân and the Turkish fleet openly collaborated with the French to ease their conquest of Corsica.

THE PEACE OF AUGSBURG (1555)

Relations between Charles V and his brother Ferdinand had meanwhile grown worse. Ferdinand did not want to surrender the imperial crown to his nephew Philip and to be condemned for ever to play second fiddle with the title king of the Romans. Neither the emperor nor his son had lightly renounced the imperial crown which would have given them a formal supremacy in Europe but the electors were hostile to the election of 'a stranger', especially since Ferdinand had progressively become 'one of them'; the mediation of Maria of Hungary, the governess of the Netherlands, had no effect and Charles V abdicated in 1555 to avoid signing the peace of Augsburg.

As for Ferdinand, he was determined to find a compromise with the Lutheran princes, although he was personally devoted to Catholicism. He negotiated and signed in the same year the peace that sanctioned the defeat of his brother's religious policy.

The churches of the Augsburg Confession were then officially recognized to the exclusion of all other Protestant denominations (the Reformed, and with much better reason the Anabaptists and Unitarians). In each territory of the Empire, the prince (and he alone) chose, according to his own conscience, his confession in virtue of the *jus episcopale* (episcopal right) which legalized the existing state of affairs. His subjects were obliged to follow him and were given permission to emigrate if they belonged to another confession. The secular status of ecclesiastical property secularized before 1552 was recognized but henceforth if a bishop converted to Lutheranism, he could only administer the material wealth of his bishopric, not secularize it to his own profit.

The Peace of Augsburg thus settled the final separation of the two confessions: Bavaria and the Rhineland (with the exception of the Palatinate) remained Catholic, the north (with the exception of the bishopric of Münster) was Protestant. In Franconia, the bishoprics of Wurzburg and Bamberg remained faithful to the Roman Church. In short, the old Roman *limes* marked the boundary: the lands long ago Romanized remained faithful to the traditional religion, although Austria would receive the Augsburg confession favourably. The hereditary lands remained Lutheran with a Catholic sovereign, contrary to the provisions of the Peace of Augsburg.

THE DIVISION OF 1556[12]

Charles V's abdication put a final end to the project of a universal monarchy because the division of the House of Austria, which had been sketched in 1522, was finally sanctioned. For a century and a half, the

Habsburgs' patrimony was divided into a senior branch – the Spanish monarchy where Castile remained the federative component and was supported by its American empire then at the peak of its development – and a cadet branch – the Austrian monarchy, which kept the imperial title, the hereditary lands and the Central European domains.

Material wealth and power accrued to the senior branch but yet more important was the drive for the Spanish nation-state, following from the changes in effect after 1540. The visible sign of this pre-eminence, the order of the Golden Fleece, founded in 1429 by Philip the Good, remained the privilege of the senior branch which cornered the Burgundian heritage. To the cadet branch fell responsibility for affairs in Central Europe with, as compensation, the imperial title. The Habsburgs of Vienna, relying on Germany for support, were obliged to continue the fight against the Turks in the Balkans, while Philip II reigned over Italy, the Netherlands and Spain, then the three finest regions in Europe.

This change was significant: the Habsburgs renounced the universal monarchy, impossible to realize in a 'modern' Europe where confessional antagonisms and national aspirations were emerging. They divided their patrimony into two 'monarchies' which were still not nation-states but rather geo-political conglomerations, one under Castilian domination, the other under German, while the Germans in Austria still remained incapable of ruling the Danubian monarchy as the Castilians wished to rule the Spanish empire.

Be that as it may, the division of 1556 set the seal on the provisions of the 1520s and at the same time constituted the consecration of Ferdinand I's achievement and the second birth of the Austrian monarchy.

EPILOGUE

It would fall to Philip II to put an end – a little less provisional than usual – to the conflict with the Valois.

After 1555, Henry II threw himself into an ambitious policy beyond the Alps, allying with pope Paul IV, the sworn enemy of the Spanish. He sent a great army to Italy under the command of Francis, duke of Guise to reconquer the kingdom of Naples, a move which had the effect of weakening French defences on the Picardy front and so helped the Spanish victory at Saint-Quentin on 10 August 1557. Was the treaty of Cateau-Cambrésis (1559) unnecessary as France was already torn apart by the wars of religion? Henry II renounced Savoy and all his Italian claims but kept Calais, Metz, Toul and Verdun. The era of Spanish preponderance in Italy was unfolding and Philip II, although he did not have the title of emperor, seemed the most powerful king in the world.

The year before Cateau-Cambrésis, Charles V had died in his Castilian retreat, conscious of having failed to achieve his dream of uniting Christendom. At least, he had allowed his brother to lay the foundations of the Austrian monarchy, of the real Habsburg Empire.

NOTES AND REFERENCES

1. Karl Brandi, *Kaiser Karl V*, 2 vols, Munich, 1937, translated into French as *Charles Quint et son temps*, Paris, 1951; Brandi's work still remains the classic biography.
   Peter Rassow, *Karl V: der letzte Kaiser der Mittelalters*, Göttingen, 1963.
   Manuel Fernandez Alvarez, *Karl V: Herrscher eines Weltreiches*, Munich, 1977.
2. Ghislaine de Boom, *Marie de Hongrie*, Brussels, 1956. Jane de Jongh, *Mary of Hungary*, London, 1959.
3. Pierre Chaunu, *L'Espagne de Charles Quint*, 2 vols, Paris, 1973 (hereafter Chaunu).
4. Émile G. Léonard, *Histoire générale du protestantisme*, 3 vols, Paris, 1957–61, vol. 1, *La Réformation*.
5. Léon Schick, *L'élection impériale de 1519*, Paris, 1959.
6. Hugo Hantsch, 'Die Kaiseridee Karls V', *Charles Quint et son temps*, proceedings of the 1958 symposium, Paris, 1959.
7. Chaunu, vol.2, p.445.
8. Ferdinand Lot, *Recherches sur les effectifs des armés françaises des guerres d'Italie*, Paris, 1962, p.171.
9. Franz von Buchholtz, *Geschichte der Regierung Ferdinands I*, 9 vols, Vienna 1831–9, reissued Graz, 1971.
   Paula Sutter-Fichtner, *Ferdinand I, Wider Türkennot und Glaubensspaltung*, Graz and Vienna, 1986.
10. Pierre Renouvin (ed.) Histoire des relations internationales, 8 vols, Paris 1951–8, vol. 2, *Les Temps modernes* by Gaston Zeller, pp. 90–121.
11. Jean Bérenger, 'La collaboration militaire franco-ottomane à l'époque de la Renaissance', *Revue internationale d'histoire militaire*, no. 68, 1987, pp. 55–70.
12. H.G. Koenigsberger, 'The Empire of Charles V in Europe', *New Cambridge Modern History*, vol. 2, chapter 10, 1958.
    Bernard Vogler, *Le Monde germanique ... à l'époque des Réformes*, 2 vols, Paris, 1981, vol.1, pp.179–98.

CHAPTER TWELVE

The Formation of the Austrian Monarchy (1525–7)

During the sixteenth century, Danubian Europe was shaken by far worse upheavals than Western Europe. The era of independent states came to an end, the Austrian monarchy was formed and the region fell into two zones of influence divided between the Holy Roman Empire and the Ottoman empire; the Turkish occupation of Hungary turned Central Europe from being the very heart of Europe into a frontier region. The Reformation affected the region no less than the rest of Latin Christendom and violent social conflict erupted as the agrarian economy was transformed and the so-called 'second serfdom' emerged. Despite this difficult combination of circumstances, for the Habsburgs the era marked the realization of the dream they had nurtured since the thirteenth century – an Austro-Bohemian monarchy stretching from Saxony to the Adriatic and the acquisition of Hungary. The year 1527 marked the final establishment of what is known as the Habsburg empire based around the central nucleus which at the present time constitutes Austria.

PROBLEMS OF DEFINITION

It is very difficult to put a precise name to this collection of territories. Right until 1804, neither Austria nor an Austrian empire officially existed; rather a common sovereign was shared by the kingdoms of Bohemia, Hungary and the hereditary lands situated within the Holy Roman Empire the archduchy of Austria, the duchies of Styria, Carinthia, Carniola, the county of the Tyrol, etc. As this common sovereign was, through the imperial election, also Roman emperor and king of Germany (this was his official title), out of courtesy he was referred to as 'the emperor' but, in the official acts of Hungary and Bohemia, he was simply the 'king'. All that existed was a common sovereign, the symbol of a personal union which progressively turned itself into a confederation of states. This confederation had as its head and essential link a monarch belonging to the House of Austria, and consequently a historical tradition was born whereby the whole collection of territories was called 'the Austrian monarchy', just as 'the Spanish monarchy' is used to designate the complex of states in the seventeenth century ruled by the Habsburgs of Madrid. To refer to Austria is inaccurate because the German-speaking hereditary countries closely corresponding to the modern Republic of Austria did not annex Bohemia and Hungary and, moreover, the different states were freely associated on an equal footing.

The true creator of the monarchy was Charles V's younger brother, Ferdinand I, who was one of the most remarkable Habsburgs. The first task facing the young sovereign – he was just twenty – was to restore order to the hereditary lands, which since Maximilian's death had been governed by the Diets. The members of the Diets had seized the opportunity to strengthen their claims to much greater autonomy and the real master of the country was the *Bürgermeister* of Vienna, doctor Siebenbürger. Reciprocal mistrust characterized Ferdinand's relations with his new subjects during the early years of his reign. Nothing could endear the young 'Spaniard', without experience or reputation, to the Germans of Austria. Besides, the prince's favourites were also foreigners: the bishop of Trent, Bernard Clae, the president of the Privy Council, but more particularly the Spaniards among whom the most prominent was the general treasurer, Salamanca, the king's friend and confidant.[1] Ferdinand's entourage was scorned as *Welschen* just as the Flemings in Charles V's retinue were despised by the Castilians; the country's resources were being squandered for the benefit of a bunch of grasping, high and mighty foreigners. The object of envy and at the same time hatred, the luxurious grandeur of the court failed to impress; the new government was seen as marking foreign domination and was accordingly resented by both the nobility and the people.

Ignorant of the ways of his new states, Ferdinand wanted to affirm his authority just as the Catholic kings had lately done in Spain. He considered the orders' resistance unjustified and a form of rebellion which had to be vigorously opposed. For this reason he had Siebenbürger tried and executed at Wiener Neustadt in 1522, as well as other burghers of Vienna who had supported the *Bürgermeister*'s ambitions. Vienna was deprived of the municipal autonomy which it had gradually acquired in the course of the Middle Ages. The municipal tribunal passed into the hands of the prince and the merchant bankers lost the right to mint money.

Ferdinand meanwhile received envoys from the king of Hungary, his brother-in-law, asking for support against Süleymân the Magnificent, for ever since the fall of Belgrade (1521) the sultan had becoming increasingly more of a threat. Louis II Jagiellon realized that he could not rely only on Hungary, which was divided by internal conflicts, and Ferdinand swiftly understood that the *Reich*, which was no less rent by religious and social conflict, was quite incapable of providing substantial assistance. The king of Hungary would have to rely on his own resources.

Mohács, 29 August 1526: few battles have had such great importance for the history of Hungary and the Danubian lands. The facts are known: the feudal host of Louis II met the Turkish army in open country, in the south of the land, and the janissaries quickly got the better of the heavy Hungarian squadrons, which became entangled in their charge. The king tried to flee but was captured and killed. The Hungarians no longer had either king or army. They had lost a battle and the orders were going to make them lose the war. The disaster can be explained as much by the weakness of the Hungarian state as by the superiority of the Ottoman army.

Young and weak, Louis II Jagiellon was challenged by the governing class. Part of the aristocracy and the gentry remained on principle hostile to a foreign king, even though Louis II had allowed the orders to recover their political power. This party gathered around the *vojvode* of Transylvania, János Zapolya, whose family had risen under the patronage of Matthias Corvinus. The king lived in isolation in the castle at Buda, without money and surrounded by foreigners – Germans and Italians – while his queen Maria was hated because she was a Habsburg. Hemmed in by powerful magnates blinded by their own self-interest, the young couple found feeble supporters in the bishop of Eger, the chancellor of Hungary, and the archbishop of Esztergom (Strigonium), the primate of Hungary. The orders, while they were relatively well disposed towards the Jagiellons (they had let them govern Hungary since 1491), sensed the gravity of the threat posed by the 1515 treaty because the young royal couple did not have a child. In addition, the repression which had followed the peasant rebellion of 1514 had dug a deep division between the orders and the peasant masses: nine-tenths of the population no longer seemed to care about the defence of the country. Like the rural masses of the Balkans at the end of the fifteenth century, the Hungarian peasants awaited the arrival of the Turks with complete indifference. The king, on the other hand, no longer possessed a permanent army because he could not afford to pay mercenaries. In 1526 he had to be content with an *insurrectio* which brought him an army that was large but ill-fitted to fight the disciplined and seasoned troops of Süleymân the Magnificent. These difficulties were compounded by the series of bad diplomatic blunders on the part of Louis II, which drew the sultan's attention towards Hungary which since the fall of Belgrade lay open to attack. Without doubt, he was the victim of the international situation as to all outward appearances he was the ally of Charles V; there can be no doubt that the French government put pressure on Süleymân to attack Hungary. For Louise of Savoy and Francis I, who signed the Peace of Madrid, Mohács came as a measure of revenge for Pavia although Danubian Europe was for Charles V a marginal field of operations when compared with Italy.

The threat posed by the Turks should not have been treated so lightly as under Süleymân the Ottoman empire was at the height of its power. The principal reasons for its success have long been known: centralized administration, financial order, tolerance towards Christians and Jews, and an army which was well trained and well disciplined in combat. The Ottoman state was organized for war and the sultan was first and foremost the military chief who each year led his troops to victory, the source of booty and riches. By its very nature the Ottoman empire was condemned to perpetual war and indefinite expansion. Its immediate neighbours feared it all the more because Turkish society was still a slave society and the market at Istanbul had an enormous need for captives which it acquired on the borders of the empire during wartime or most frequently through straightforward raids. The use of 'renegades', Christians who had gone over to the service of the Great Turk, put at Süleymân's disposal all the Western technical innovations in the fields of artillery, the navy and the art of fortification. The janissaries constituted the elite of the army: every five years children of non-Muslim subjects were gathered together at various points in the empire, were raised in the Muslim religion and Turkish customs and were assembled in the barracks at Adrianople and Istanbul; they did not have the right to marry but escaped from ordinary jurisdiction. Under Süleymân, their number reached 51 000. The cavalry was made up of *sipahis*, the holders of *timars* or benefices, a type of fief which was granted to them for a fixed period. Finally there were the irregulars (Tartars, Moldo-Wallachians) who were responsible for pillaging and went to make up the great battalions. This was how Süleymân came to have at his disposal for the 1526 campaign 100 000 men and 300 cannons.[2]

Curiously, Süleymân did not exploit his victory at Mohács; he entered Buda on 10 September, but did not remain there, satisfying himself instead with sacking the plain and retaking Belgrade in the autumn. The Hungarians, however, did not use this respite to collect themselves. Instead they used the king's death as the opportunity to form two parties. Louis II's death also raised questions over the future of the kingdom of Bohemia and its dependencies (Moravia, Silesia and Lusatia). The problem of who should succeed the Jagiellons was raised but what Maximilian somewhat naively had presented as a simple matter (the union of Bohemia and Hungary with Austria) proved a Herculean task which Ferdinand with his tenacity and domineering spirit nevertheless brought to a successful conclusion.

First, he settled the question of Bohemia. The three orders of the kingdom of Bohemia (lords, knights and towns) imperiously demanded respect for their electoral right and produced whole chests of documents to support their claims. Ferdinand very quickly realized that state-right was not a myth and that for the orders, the treaty of 1515 hardly counted. There was no shortage of candidates for the Bohemian throne – the dukes William and Louis of Bavaria and the king of France. Ferdinand, though, had able ambassadors – Puchheim, Starhemberg and Sigismund Dietrichstein – who were able to implement a combination of concessions and claims. Also in his favour was the fact that he was brother-in-law and son-in-law of the last two Jagiellon kings; the orders had the impression that by favouring his candidature, they were remaining faithful to the dynasty. Ferdinand was elected king unanimously in the chapel of St Václav in the Hradčany on 23 October 1526 and was crowned in February 1527. Thus the idea of gathering together the forces of Christendom against Islam had triumphed. The kingdom of Bohemia had freely chosen a Habsburg and union with the hereditary lands.[3]

The question of the Hungarian succession was much more difficult. Queen Maria, a widow at a very early age, did not surrender to misfortune but rather busied herself on her brother's behalf. She showed an abundance of the political genius characteristic of her family and which she later proved in the service of Charles V in the Netherlands. But János Zapolya's hour had come. Since he had arrived at Mohács after the battle, the Transylvanian contingent which he commanded had not been destroyed. Zapolya had always been leader of the 'national' party which refused a foreign sovereign, especially a Habsburg one. Carried away by the general enthusiasm, he was elected and crowned on 10 November 1526 at Szekesfehérvár. Ferdinand seemed to have lost Hungary. Faced with the fait accompli, he had to refuse the orders the right to designate their king in a country where the crown was elective. Resting his claims on the 1515 treaty, he was forced to denounce Zapolya as a usurper because he, Ferdinand, had been elected in opposition to him and had had himself proclaimed king by an assembly of notables which the queen had summoned at Pressburg on 17 December 1526, when he confirmed the privileges of the orders contained in the Golden Bull of András II.[4]

Ferdinand had the wit to rally the Croatian nobility to his cause: they were only too happy to affirm their autonomy and to consolidate their state-right by electing him king of Croatia-Slavonia at Četin on 1 January 1527. This was more than a minor episode in the formation of the monarchy because it marked the beginning of an alliance that would last four centuries, uniting the Croats and the Habsburg king in common cause against the Hungarian nobility. The Croats, who feared the influence of the Hungarian magnates in Slavonia, sought to strengthen their distinct position within the Hungarian state. This was the reason why they supported royal power providing the Habsburgs with faithful subjects and excellent soldiers; it was for the same reason that they remained Catholic in the face of the Hungarian Protestants.

Ferdinand's chances remained slight: Zapolya was not only leader of the national party, which was growing in strength, but also of the whole political class; entire regions, Transylvania and eastern Hungary in particular, rejected the authority of a king who was a foreigner. Only the magnates and the higher clergy supported Ferdinand while Zapolya fled to Poland, married a Jagiellon and engaged in negotiations with Süleymân and Francis I in order to realize his legitimate rights; he had, after all, been properly elected and crowned king according to the provisions of the Hungarian constitution and Ferdinand, not Zapolya, might appear the anti-king. The struggle for power, long and indecisive, led to new alignments in Eastern Europe. Arrayed against the Habsburgs was the Hungarian-Ottoman coalition allied with the king of France. The defeat at Mohács perhaps had less serious consequences for Hungary than the incapacity of its ruling class to choose a successor to Louis II Jagiellon. A division was revealed which would dominate Hungarian history until the end of the Habsburg Empire and which irremediably compromised national independence. By making Süleymân the arbiter in their disputes, the Hungarians had introduced a wolf into the fold and renounced the role of 'the paladins of Christendom' which a certain school of historiography has wrongly attributed to them. Hungarian national interest was perhaps linked to the Ottoman alliance, but it would be foolish to hide the frequent complicity between the Hungarians and the Turks, which time and again was encouraged by French diplomacy.

Having inherited the crown of St Stephen from off the head of his young and weak brother-in-law, Ferdinand found himself faced with a long-term conflict for which he was ill-provided with resources. Two extraordinary taxes, the Turkish tax (*Türkensteuer*) and the poll tax, had already been introduced in Lower Austria in 1523 shortly after the fall of Belgrade.[5] The Turkish tax was a tax on liquid and fixed capital and was charged at the rate of 0.5 per cent, each inhabitant being obliged by the terms of the decree to declare all his goods. For the poll tax, the population was divided into 'classes': everyone, including children over twelve years and agricultural workers, was obliged to pay. These financial sacrifices, however, made it possible to enlist no more than 5 000 mercenaries and in 1525 the tax receipts from Austria provided only two months' army pay. Ferdinand had to find a way to meet the expenses of the other four months and for winter quarters and so had to resort to a loan; in 1529 he owed the Fuggers almost 1 million florins, about five times the amount of his ordinary annual revenue.

The hereditary lands clearly could not defend the eastern frontier of the Holy Roman Empire alone and Ferdinand had to appeal to Germany and Bohemia for support. By electing a Habsburg, Bohemia had implicitly recognized that it was becoming part of a much larger entity, that it was bound by a certain solidarity to its neighbours and that it therefore risked becoming involved in conflicts which did not directly concern it; it had acquired the status of a great power but was without control over the confederation's general policy. The Czech ruling class seems not to have been mentally prepared for such an evolution and even the very moderate school of Czech historiography criticizes the Habsburgs for having made Bohemia the monarchy's pack-horse (an accusation which is also made by Hungarian historians).

Ferdinand immediately applied himself to the task of reorganizing his new states and in this area his achievement was of prime importance: he gave the monarchy institutions which, with some modification, lasted until the revolution of 1848.[6]

The royal elections in the autumn of 1526, although they had negative aspects and involved the Habsburgs in centuries-long conflict with the Ottoman empire, transformed the destiny of Austria, which was no longer simply a mark of the Holy Roman Empire but the centre of a geo-political complex assured of a splendid future once the Turkish threat had receded. These acquisitions, as marginal as they might seem to Charles V, allowed the Habsburgs to establish their position in Germany and confirmed their vocation to dominate Central Europe. Ferdinand's powers were singularly limited by the terms on which the 1526 union had been realized, however it was neither a matter of conquest by the Habsburgs nor a matter of annexation by Austria. The king was bound by his obligations to the nobilities of Hungary, Bohemia and Croatia.

NOTES AND REFERENCES

1. Alfred Stern, 'Gabriel Salamanca, Graf von Ortenburg', *Historische Zeitschrift*, no. 131, 1925, pp. 19ff.
2. Gilles Veinstein, 'L'Empire dans sa grandeur', in Robert Mantran (ed.) *Histoire de l'empire ottoman*, Paris, 1989, pp. 159–226.
3. Ernest Denis, *La Fin de l'indépendance bohême*, Paris, 1890, vol.2, *Les Premiers Habsbourgs*. The whole question is raised anew by Winfried Eberhard, *Monarchie und Widerstand: zur Ständischen Oppositionsbildung in Herrschaftsystem Ferdinands I in Böhmen*, Munich, 1985.
4. Stanislaus Smolka, 'Ferdinands I Bemühungen um die Krone', *Archiv für Œsterreichische Geschichte*, no. 57, 1878.
5. Karl Oberleitner, 'Œsterreichs Finanzen und Kriegswesen unter Ferdinand I', *Archiv für Œsterreichische Geschichte*, no. 22, 1860.
6. Thomas Fellner and Heinrich Kretschmayr, *Die Œsterreichische Zentralverwaltung*, no. 1, Vienna, 1907.

CHAPTER THIRTEEN

The New State after 1527

A fundamental task confronted Ferdinand I; he had to impose upon his new subjects a common administration and the minimum requisite royal authority. Inevitably he clashed with the national traditions of the kingdoms of Hungary and Bohemia and their oligarchies who were identical with the nation and identified themselves with their personal privileges and public liberties. Having enjoyed a period of omnipotence after 1490, these oligarchies constituted a weighty opponent for the young king who, bolstered by his early successes in Austria, did not hesitate to apply the principles taught him by his grandfather Ferdinand of Aragón. Intelligent and resolute, Ferdinand I bravely tackled the problems of reorganization, creating a central government, establishing order in Bohemia and struggling to reduce the Diets' power.

REFORM OF THE ADMINISTRATION IN BOHEMIA AND HUNGARY[1]

To begin with, the union of the lands of the crown of Bohemia with the hereditary lands did not entail any noticeable modification of the country's administration, still less its Germanization, as the Czech historian Josef Macek has remarked.

In Bohemia, the grand burgrave of Prague (*Oberstburggraf, nejvyšší purkrabí*) possessed the same powers as the marshal of Lower Austria. In the sixteenth century, when the sovereign was absent, the grand officers administered the affairs of the kingdom according to the king's precise instructions, but as these officers were elected by the Diet and belonged to the order of lords, the country's autonomy was not in danger. It was only in 1577 that Rudolf II appointed a council of lieutenancy (*Statthalterei*) composed of various grand officers of the kingdom and presided over by the grand burgrave. In Silesia, Ferdinand entrusted the executive to an upper council (*Oberamt*), which was later named the council of lieutenancy and sat at Glatz.

It was only the revolt of the Estates in 1547 that allowed Ferdinand, after his victory, to deal a decisive blow to the government of the orders: the king proclaimed his exclusive right to nominate the officers of justice and to make all political appointments. He confiscated the property of those nobles who had rebelled and for the first time proclaimed his hereditary right to the crown. Finally, he appointed the royal judges in the free towns (known as 'captains' in Malé Strana, Staré Město and Nové Město, the towns which formed the city of Prague). In fact, in the sixteenth century the number of royal officers in Bohemia was greatly reduced and even in the case of royal institutions the influence of the orders remained considerable, particularly in the four principal (and also the lesser) courts.

The supreme court consisted of the grand burgrave, the grand chamberlain, the supreme judge and a dozen judges who were appointed by the king from the order of lords and knights. The grand burgrave presided at the supreme court when the king was absent. The court was essentially a criminal one but it also had jurisdiction to judge inheritance disputes involving the nobility. The lower court, made up of middle-ranking officers, had jurisdiction to judge cases involving sums less than 200 rixdales. The court of the table conducted cases concerning landed estates belonging to the nobility and registered in the 'table' of the kingdom, the record of property held by the orders. The court of the grand burgrave where he sat with six noble assessors had the jurisdiction to judge civil trials. All these courts sat only three or four times a year.

Ferdinand I created for all the Czech lands (Bohemia, Moravia, Silesia and Lusatia) two government councils based on the model of the Austrian councils. The chamber of Bohemia was the court of the highest instance in financial matters for the Czech lands. The king evidently was inspired by the chamber of accounts of the hereditary lands and in the instruction of 1527 gave the chamber a precise goal – to restore order to the finances which were burdened with debt. The chamber of Bohemia was also concerned with administering the ordinary revenues or *regalia*, the royal domain which was still extensive and included magnificent feudal estates such as Mělnik, customs and tolls, mines (very important in Bohemia) and coinage. Through the chamber, Ferdinand I, until 1560, was able to exploit to the utmost and in a quite 'brutal' manner the silver mines at Kutná Hora and most importantly those at Jachýmov, which were a considerable source of precious metal both for him and for the economy of the whole land. The chamber of Bohemia was composed of a president and a dozen councillors most of whom were nobles, the members of the orders disdaining any involvement in business, in contrast to what was happening in Western Europe. The councillors were assisted by secretaries and bookkeepers.

As the chancellor, who was appointed by the king, had to belong to the order of lords and had to follow the person of the sovereign in every circumstance, the chancellery was a kind of higher organ of government for the whole of the Czech lands; because its personnel was generally recruited from the kingdom of Bohemia, the incorporated provinces thought that they had been wronged. Besides the Czech section, the chancellery included a German-speaking section for Lusatia and Silesia. It served as the ministry of the interior, the supreme court of law and was the intermediary under obligation to the Viennese authorities, in particular for the raising of contributions. No royal patent had force of law in the Czech lands if it had not been countersigned by the chancellor and a secretary of the chancellery, who also took part in diplomatic correspondence with the countries of Eastern Europe (Poland and Russia).

Ferdinand created the Prague royal court of appeal in 1548, after crushing the revolt of the orders, in order to deprive the towns of Prague and Litoměřïce of their appeal tribunals. The new court judged on appeal the non-nobles of the kingdom and the incorporated provinces. It played the role of court of the highest instance as well as the source of jurisprudence. In civil trials, if the court of appeal confirmed the judgment of the lowest court, the affair was judged final. In criminal trials, on the other hand, the condemned could always appeal to the king, or rather in practice to the Bohemian chancellery. The court of appeal was composed of a president, six judges belonging to the nobility, four doctors of law and four burghers from Prague. The judges were all subject to three searching entry examinations, and the nobles who envisaged making their careers in the court had to attend schools of law to learn jurisprudence. Serious examinations eliminated incompetent candidates.

In Hungary,[2] Ferdinand I was faced by a government that was medieval in character and made up of grand officers belonging to the order of lords or the order of prelates. The office most to be feared by a foreign sovereign was that of the palatine, who was elected by the Diet and served as the intermediary between the orders and the king. The palatine led the government in the king's absence, was head of the army and possessed extensive judicial powers. Ferdinand I kept the post vacant in 1531 after the death of István Báthory and it was only force of circumstances that obliged king Matthias in 1608 to agree to the election of István Illésházy. Throughout the sixteenth century, the powers of the palatine were divided among a number of officers who, while it is true that they were of Hungarian nationality, were nevertheless appointed by the king: a governor (locumtenens regis) who represented the king, two 'captains', both of whom were in fact generals, one for Upper Hungary and one for Lower Hungary, and the palatine's proxy in tasks that were properly judicial. Ferdinand likewise suppressed the office of treasurer (thesaurarius) in 1528, replacing it with a Hungarian chamber (camera hungarica) which had jurisdiction over all matters connected with the royal revenues. The share of the contributions, however, was still lower in Hungary than in the other countries and was a question of managing the ordinary revenues – domain, tolls, customs, coinage and mines. These mines were even more important than the Bohemian mines, although the copper and silver mines of Slovakia were still in the hands of the Fuggers who had closed them. The Hungarian chamber also had authority over the royal free towns and judged on appeal the trials brought before the municipal magistrates. The chamber was made up of a president and six councillors belonging to the nobility; the fiscal procurator was the only legal instance in a position to defend the rights of the king, while all the other courts consisted of magnates. Thus the Habsburgs very often entrusted him with tasks far exceeding his original jurisdiction. Ferdinand I kept a tight hold on the other senior officers; the supreme judge (*judex curiae regiae*) had jurisdiction to judge on appeal trials involving the nobility of the counties. In Croatia-Slavonia, the king was represented by the ban, who also presided over the noble tribunal and commanded the armed forces there. As for the chancellor, ever since the foundation of the Hungarian state, he had been a clergyman, most often a bishop. Attached to the person of the king, after 1527 he acted as the intermediary under obligation to both the government at Vienna and the Hungarian government, the authorities at Pressburg systematically rejecting all correspondence that had not passed under his scrutiny. The language of the chancellery remained Latin throughout the modern period.

The district administration by contrast totally escaped the Habsburgs' control. While the prefect was a magnate named by the king to a title for life or to a hereditary title, the assistant prefect (*vice-comes*) was an officer whose job grew in scope during the sixteenth century. He was elected from among the nobility of the county which met at least once a year in the chief town of the district. The county assembly was the basis of Hungarian political life and was dominated by simple country gentlemen from whose midst emerged various families of the middle nobility, sometimes quite long-established and in every case better provided with landed property than the others. It was generally from among the gentry that judges and the county notary were recruited. The county notary was head of the still rudimentary district administration. The assistant prefect was responsible for maintaining order, levying troops and the contributions voted by the Diet, in particular the *dica*, the direct tax raised upon peasant families when occasion demanded. This political personnel was Hungarian, frequently xenophobic and nearly always ignorant of Latin and German: Ferdinand could make few changes.

The judicial administration was also unchanged. The king's court (*Curia regia*) remained the court of highest instance. It was made up of two chambers or 'tables': the 'septemvirale table' was the supreme court for the whole kingdom, presided over by the palatine or the grand judge; it was made up of the treasurer, the archbishop of Esztergom and judges drawn from among the magnates and the nobles. The royal table, presided over by the *personalis* and sixteen assessors (two prelates, two magnates, etc.) played the role of court of appeal for all the tribunals of the county; Croatia-Slavonia had its own court of appeal, the ban's court, over which the ban presided. In contrast to the case in Bohemia and Austria, a case could not be summoned before the king as the Hungarians, who derived strength from the distinctive character of their legal system, wanted to be judged by none but their compatriots.

CENTRAL GOVERNMENT[3]

Ferdinand I wanted to create administrative, legal and financial systems common to all three countries. He promulgated a decree on 1 January 1527, completely reorganizing the central government of his states: it was now to consist of an Aulic Council, a Privy Council, a court chancellery and a chamber of accounts. Its jurisdiction extended over the whole of the monarchy, without distinction between countries and particular privileges.

The Aulic Council (*Hofrat*) essentially had jurisdiction over legal matters and was the court of appeal of the monarchy. It was made up of eight councillors for the hereditary lands, two for the Empire, five for the Czech lands, two for Hungary and two doctors of law. The grand officers of the court were authorized to sit with the councillors, who were responsible for day-to-day business. One may imagine the moral prestige that a sovereign would have who was the supreme judge of all his subjects. It was also a means of harmonizing the different legislatures, in short, of centralizing the monarchy. For this reason, in 1537 Bohemia and Hungary succeeded in having the jurisdiction of the Aulic Council limited to the hereditary lands and the Reich. In 1556, after Charles V's abdication, this court became the Aulic Council of the Empire (*Reichshofrat*), which until the end of the eighteenth century served the Habsburgs as a means of strengthening their moral authority within the Empire.

The Privy Council (*Geheime Rat*) was attached to the person of the sovereign and was charged with directing general policy. It was also concerned with financial affairs (for example it made the large decisions connected with the budget). In matters of feudal justice (problems over inheritance within the Empire, etc.), it constituted a higher court than the Aulic Council and was not really concerned with any one specific field since any question of importance could be brought before it. It was not a cabinet council in the modern sense but was a convenient means for the prince to consult the grand officers of his house. The sovereign was free to summon whomsoever he wished but the council's advice was quite without any force of law in any part of the monarchy. Every decision took the form of a patent expedited by one of the chancelleries responsible to the chancellor. The Privy Council consisted of the Aulic dignitaries, the principal chiefs of the ministerial departments and various distinguished men. In addition to the high steward of the court (*Obersthofmeister*), also generally invited were the chief of the council, the grand marshal of the court, the vice-chancellor of the Empire (representing the arch-chancellor, the archbishop of Mainz), the court chancellor and an Aulic councillor. In the sixteenth century, the Privy Council was dominated by lawyers of burgher origin. In the seventeenth century the majority were drawn from the aristocracy and the 'new men' were immediately ennobled. Under Ferdinand I there was a division of power between gentlemen and 'experts' whose role was analagous to that of the Castilian *letrados*.

The Privy Council met every day, in fact whenever the sovereign summoned it. It operated in a rather perfunctory fashion. Meeting early in the morning, it listened to a report read by a secretary of the chancellery or by the chancellor himself; without the councillors having had time to study the issue, the high steward then gave his opinion, the chancellor received the opinions of the other councillors and finally the prince gave his decision, most often adopting the opinion of the majority. This was why the high steward was in effect prime minister, as the councillors voted as he did. Unless one of them had a serious reason for expressing a different opinion, it was in practice the opinion of the high steward that the sovereign followed.

From the reign of the emperor Matthias onwards, the Privy Council increased its personnel, reaching thirty under Ferdinand III and a hundred at the beginning of the eighteenth century, so prestigious was the title. The difficulties that this caused were remedied by summoning only a limited number of councillors to sessions; after 1665 the secret conference, which was an offshoot of the Privy Council, served as the organ directing the Habsburgs' general policy.

The chamber of accounts was intended to replace the treasury which Maximilian had founded. It was made up of a limited number of personnel – a president, four councillors, a master of accounts and two secretaries assisted by an ever increasing number of clerks – while the number of councillors reached more than a dozen in the seventeenth century. Around 1550 the chamber of accounts was granted two bookkeepers – the paymaster of the court for civil expenses and the paymaster of wars for military expenses. It was never a ministry of finance in the modern sense. It administered the ordinary revenues and regulated civil expenses, the military expenses being covered by the contributions voted by the Diets: these were the 'extraordinary affairs'. In 1527 the chamber of accounts had to pay the court's staff and running costs; it negotiated loans, saw that there was always money and controlled the chambers of the different lands. In particular it had to take care of the domain while redeeming those sources of revenue that were burdened with mortgages. It did not have its own revenues but had at its disposal the profits from the other financial bodies. This was why it never knew precisely what sums it had to hand and rather blindly issued assignments out of the chamber of Bohemia or the salt works of Upper Austria which might well go unpaid. It was completely bypassed by the contributions. The military and after 1556 the Council of War made their demands for the year and the chamber of accounts was content to pass them on to different chancelleries. These fixed, in the instructions that they sent to the royal commissars, the total sum judged necessary and the Diets debated their propositions. Once the credits were voted, the taxes were shared and raised by the administration of the orders. Twice a week the councillors met to deal with business handed to them by the subordinate chamber of accounts. All current business was dealt with by the secretaries, who presented their report to the Council, which voted; if it could not decide the matter, the issue was passed to the sovereign, who made a decision on his own or with the help of the Privy Council.

TAX REFORMS[4]

Ferdinand I's attempts at reorganization yielded some positive results. The ordinary revenues reached 1 million florins. The military expenditure, including the garrisons in Hungary and the tribute paid to the sultan, reached 625 000 florins and as court expenditure exceeded half a million florins (530 000), Ferdinand was faced with a permanent deficit and had to appeal for contributions which, after stormy negotiations, were voted by the Diets of the different countries. In 1542 a session of the Estates General of the monarchy decided to share the burden of taxation according to the wealth and population of each country and the proportions which were decided upon were maintained until the eighteenth century. The kingdom of Bohemia and its dependencies were invited to pay two-thirds of the total invoice, the hereditary lands the remaining one-third on the following basis:

Lower Austria 6/54 or 11 per cent
Upper Austria 3/54 or 5.5 per cent
   that is 9/54 or 16.5 per cent for the archduchy of Austria while Inner Austria
   (Styria, Carinthia, Carniola) also gave 9/54 or 16.5 per cent in total;
Bohemia 16/54 or 30 per cent
Moravia 8/54 or 18 per cent
Silesia 12/54, 22 per cent

The fraction 1/54 roughly corresponded to 100 000 inhabitants. The basis chosen in 1542 was, as it had lately been in Lower Austria, the sum of the rent from a feudal estate. It is noticeable that neither the Tyrol with Further Austria (Upper Alsace and Breisgau) nor Hungary were included in this distribution of the tax burden. Further Austria enjoyed practically complete fiscal autonomy while the kingdom of Hungary benefited through its nobles' fiscal privileges from almost total tax immunity, the Habsburgs collecting only the *regalia* (revenues of mines, customs and crown domains) and the exceptional tax voted by the Diet, the *dica*.

During Ferdinand I's long reign the classic fiscal system of the Habsburg

168

Empire was established within which Hungary's special status was for centuries set in contrast to the general status of the Austro-Bohemian complex. The stance taken by Czech historians is not totally unjustified as their lands suffered many gross injustices. Just as in the Spanish monarchy during the 'Golden Century' Castile bore the heaviest taxation, so the central nucleus – Austria and the Czech lands – was more heavily burdened than the periphery.

The direct tax levied on the rent from feudal estates became permanent and in the seventeenth century was voted without debate. It remained moderate because the total sum of the rent was under-evaluated. After 1545 in Lower Austria and after 1567 in Bohemia, direct tax was levied on the peasant holdings (provided, however, that the feudal lord had not arranged to pass the tax on to the tenant and to make him pay the direct tax on the estate's rent). This direct tax was the hearth tax (*Rauchfangsteur*) paid by every household-head and levied at one florin a year. In the course of a century it doubled, reaching two florins *c.*1640, which amounted to 1–2 écus per tenure of 10–20 acres of arable; it was a moderate tax. Added to this 'ordinary' tax were the 'extraordinary' taxes, the poll tax and the 'Turkish tax' but the latter was suspended after 1568 when peace was signed with the Ottoman empire and reinstated only in 1683.

Besides direct taxation, the Habsburgs readily had recourse to tax on consumption. The tax on drinks had the advantage of affecting all the taxpayers in those countries which were great beer producers (Bohemia) and wine producers (Lower Austria). In Bohemia, the tax on beer was first voted by the Diet in 1534, suspended and then repeatedly reinstated until it assumed its final form in 1552. In each circle, the royal authorities appointed a tax collector; every noble who wanted to manufacture beer had to declare his intention and then pay a tax of 2 groschen per barrel (in 1583 raised to 6 groschen per barrel). The imperial regiments alone enjoyed exemption. The tax was extended to wines in 1575 and to spirits in 1583 but it was difficult to collect because distilling was carried out everywhere in Bohemia.

In Lower Austria the tax on drinks (*Tranksteuer*) was imposed only in 1556 and in practice was chiefly placed on wines. It was levied at 10 per cent *ad valorem*. It brought in 50 000 florins in 1564 and 150 000 florins ten years later. The Estates were in charge of its collection.

The *Salzregal* was introduced in Bohemia only in 1628 but in Austria it had been established far longer, because the prince possessed salt mines at Hallstatt which had been worked since neolithic times. The monopoly was farmed out to a manager of a salt-warehouse who was generally a banker. Seven salt-granaries guaranteed its sale to the feudal lords who had to transport and sell it to their tenants.

The excise was a tax on widely consumed products, meat and flour. It was levied only at times of grave crisis when the orders shrunk from an increase in direct taxation. Under Ferdinand I, the tax was resorted to but then abandoned and reinstated towards the end of the Thirty Years War

(1618–48) and again at the time of the Vienna War (1684–1699). According to circumstances and the type of comestible, the tax was levied at 10–30 per cent and was a heavy burden on the poorer people in the towns. The introduction of the excise, which was greeted with strong resistance from the orders, could be provisional only in lands where the tax burden was, in all, moderate in comparison with that in Western Europe. Faced with the threat of Ottoman conquest, momentary sacrifices had to be made; this government thesis was cheerfully expounded in the preambles to the 'propositions' made to the Diets.

THE EXECUTIVE: THE CHANCELLERIES

To coordinate the councils' actions, Ferdinand I created a court chancellery, which had the task of putting into effect the acts and conducting correspondence but, unlike the Bohemian and Hungarian chancelleries, did not have the power to take decisions. Three secretaries (one for the Empire, one for finances and a third for judicial affairs) were placed under the authority of the chancellor.

This attempt at centralization was too advanced and was accordingly short-lived. Ferdinand had wanted to add secretaries for Bohemia and Hungary to the chancellery but the chancellors of the two kingdoms were afraid of being subordinated to the court chancellery and so the sovereign had to abandon his project.

In 1556, after Ferdinand had become Holy Roman Emperor, the court chancellery became the chancellery of the Empire and was reorganized and placed under the authority of the vice-chancellor of the Empire. The archbishop of Mainz remained the arch-chancellor but because he was too far away to carry out his duties, he was content to appoint jointly with the emperor a vice-chancellor who was drawn from the nobility of the Empire but not an immediate subject of the Habsburgs. The vice-chancellor had a very important role as he was responsible for diplomatic correspondence and relations with the princes of the Empire. For this he had offices divided in two sections, the German section for the affairs of the kingdom of Germany and the Latin section for diplomatic correspondence and affairs concerning Italy and the Netherlands.

It was not until 1620 and the reign of Ferdinand II that an Austrian chancellery was established on an equal footing with the Bohemian and Hungarian chancelleries.

THE AULIC WAR COUNCIL (*Hofkriegsrat*)[5]

Ferdinand I's reforms in the military field were more successful since the Turkish wars made a measure of centralization essential. In 1556 he created an Aulic War Council which was responsible for administration, the conduct of operations remaining the business of the sovereign and his generals.

Until then, military affairs had been entrusted to the authorities within each land (government and chamber of accounts) and the disorder which ensued was comparable to the mayhem that France suffered under the Valois. After an earlier and short-lived attempt to create a specialized council, Ferdinand I finally issued a directive in 1556; he named five councillors and a president whose jurisdiction extended to the whole monarchy, including Bohemia and Hungary. The Hungarians, however, challenged the principle behind the creation of such a council and refused to sit in it, thereby losing the chance to exert an influence on an administrative body which concerned them chiefly; subsequently, they took great pleasure in denouncing in the Diet's grievances the interference of foreigners in Hungarian affairs, but their stormy nationalism was never troubled by such contradictions.

All the military authorities of Lower Austria (the superintendent of fortifications, the administrator of the arsenal of Vienna, the grand master of the quartermaster corps, the grand master of artillery, the chief of the Danube fleet, etc.) were placed under the authority of the war council. This had its own chancellery with two secretaries, editors, clerks and a Hungarian interpreter, who was later joined by Turkish interpreters. The council's area of responsibility was vast but it was in charge of logistics for the whole imperial army rather than the direction of operations.

The Aulic Council was responsible for recruitment, armament and the supply of troops as well as the maintenance of *matériel*; in particular it had to supply the arsenals and warehouses. It enjoyed financial autonomy since a war-paymaster (*Kriegszahlmeister*) was authorized to regulate the current expenses – in the beginning a sum less than 150 florins. Although when the situation demanded, it had to take care of troops in the ranks, its principal purpose remained to support the Austro-Turkish military frontier, which after 1522 was established in the part of Hungary under Habsburg rule in order to protect the Austrian lands from Ottoman raids. In 1556 the Military Frontier consisted of a line of castles, forts and posts stretching for a thousand kilometres from the Adriatic to the Ukraine. The strength of these posts lay solely in their garrisons, which were made up of Germans, Hungarians and Croats with Walloon and Italian mercenaries and were all paid out of the contributions raised in the hereditary lands. They gradually grew in numbers to 10 000 men. They were a vitally important safeguard against the Ottomans since the sultan's army lost valuable time in each campaign laying siege with varying degrees of success to one of these posts after another: Köszeg in 1529, Szigetvár in 1566 and Eger many times.

The efficiency of the war council has often been questioned, as much by the Hungarian Diet, which relished supplying in its grievances a catalogue of its administrative shortcomings, as by Central European historiography which has found in its delays and inadequacies an easy explanation for the imperial army's defeats. Its task, though, was hardly an easy one. To feed its budget, the war council depended on the vote and return of taxes. Civil and military personnel pursued their careers side by side and, as the French experienced under the *ancien régime*, the pen and the sword did not always live together in harmony. It was only in the seventeenth century under Montecuccoli that the administration of war was put on a steady footing when a general war commissariat was created with responsibility for all the problems of the quartermaster corps and an inter-ministerial commission, the Deputation, which carefully prepared the military budget.

The army was the only institution directly dependent upon the emperor, escaping the direct control of the orders, although it was they who supplied the taxes necessary for recruitment and the maintenance of mercenaries.

THE LIMITS OF THE WORK OF FERDINAND I[6]

In his attempts at reorganization, Ferdinand I showed the full extent of his qualities as a statesman. Faced with the task of constructing a great monarchy at so unfavourable a time, under constant fear of a fresh Turkish advance, the new solutions that Ferdinand tried to impose were in part inspired by the reform projects of his grandfather, Maximilian I, but above all by Western models. There has recently been much debate among scholars about the influences acting upon the directive of 1 January 1527. The main influence was clearly the 'Burgundian model', the government of the Netherlands which was an adaption of the French model of the late Middle Ages made to fit an aristocratic society and a decentralized state. It should not be forgotten that in England at the same period, Henry VII and his son Henry VIII, when strengthening their royal power, borrowed much from the Valois of Malines and Paris.

The institution of the Privy Council was vital since it enabled the prince to call upon anyone who struck him as likely to make a valuable contribution to the direction of general policy. By inviting Aulic dignitaries, in particular the high steward, Ferdinand was able to bypass the grand officers of the crown. The Aulic Council, raised to the Aulic Council of the Empire in 1559, enabled him to act as supreme justice which under the *ancien régime* was seen as inseparable from the power of the monarchy in the minds of the *ancien régime*. Ferdinand and his successors were thus able to put a check on the court of the Empire, which was the embodiment of the orders. He was also able, as sovereign, to settle legal suits over fiefs and to judge appeals coming from those territories which did not yet have the privilege of *non appellando*. The Grand Council of Paris but also the *Groote rad* (Grand Council) of Malines undoubtedly served as models.

Another change in keeping with the spirit of the times was the systematic recourse to jurists, who were the products of the German universities then at the peak of their development, and to educated nobles who had studied at Padua or Bologna. It is significant that Ferdinand reserved places in each council for such men in preference to prelates. These arrangements eased the social rise of the personnel of the chancelleries but most importantly they made it possible to employ men whose talents had already been proven within the Empire, even if the loyal services of a chancellor or secretary had to be purchased with his ennoblement.

Mention has already been made of the existence of a strict hierarchy of offices from the concierge and the heating-clerk (the maintenance of earthenware stoves was a considerable task), right to the secretaries of the councils. There were the clerks responsible for keeping records and most importantly the editors who prepared the dossiers and edited the minutes of reports. The summary of each affair was set down in registers by the 'registrars' whose work, to the great delight of historians, has in part survived to the present day.

It would, however, be wrong to conclude that the famous Austrian bureaucracy was already in place in 1540 since there were only a hundred qualified members of the personnel, solely in the service of the councils of central government, while within each country the orders kept the upper hand in the administration and at the local level essential tasks were carried out by the lords, their bailiffs, judges and stewards. Very few enjoyed the privilege of being judged at the first instance by the royal courts and even appeal at the final instance was beyond the reach of the peasant masses. The prince was truly master only over his domain, the mines and in the administration of customs and coinage. For this reason, Ferdinand was not embarrassed to fill these offices with officers of German origin who were thought to be the most devoted to the interests of the state and dynasty. It was not until the reign of Maria-Theresa two centuries later that a true bureaucracy and class of officials came into being.

Ferdinand made a major concession to the nobles by maintaining and developing the collegiate system that would remain a fundamental feature of Austrian government right until 1848. A minister or bureaucrat did not make any decisions, rather each issue was studied by a councillor who edited a report and presented it before a full session of the council, which alone was authorized to make a decision. Contrary to what happened in France, it was the most senior official at the highest grade who gave his opinion or *votum* which often provoked long discussions and tedious objections. The report was not adopted as a matter of course and government by council proceeded slowly. Much time was consumed: the directives made provision for meetings two or three times a week and office hours were long. As there were numerous factions and cabals, the government was easily brought to a halt, but the eclectic recruitment of councillors gave the elites the impression that they were associated with the government. Most striking is the Hungarians' systematic refusal, from the reign of Ferdinand I onwards, to be integrated into the system; the impression given is that Austria-Hungary existed from the very beginning, i.e. a kingdom of Hungary on the one hand and the Austro-Bohemian lands on the other.

Ferdinand of his own will limited attempts at centralization, quickly realizing the danger of impinging on the prerogatives of the national Estates. He achieved a measure of success in his undertakings and exploited the opportunities that came his way, as, for example, the meeting of the Estates General in 1542 and when he defeated the Bohemian orders in 1547.

Noticeable at the social level is the formation of an 'Austrian' aristocracy, that is a court aristocracy which was drawn together by service to the prince. The prince employed lords originally from the different lands of the monarchy. The noble families of the court came together and acquired through purchase or inheritance domains outside their country of origin: the Auerspergs and Starhembergs in Austria, the Perény, Báthory and Török in Hungary, the Žerotins and Wallensteins in Bohemia, the Pethö, the Kollonich and the Zrinski families in Croatia. By contracting marriages and alliances these families stepped outside the national framework which was traditionally theirs.

NOTES AND REFERENCES

1. See E.C. Hellbling, *Œsterreichische Verfassungs und Verwaltungsgeschichre*, Vienna, 1956. Also Anton Gindely, *Böhmen und Mähren im Zeitalter der Reformation*, 2 vols, 1861, reissued Osnabrück, 1968.

2. The only complete study is in Hungarian: Gyözö Ember, *A magyar közigazgatas története* (1526–1711), Budapest, 1946.

3. Thomas Fellner and Heinrich Kretschmayr, *Die Œsterreichische Zentralverwaltung*, no. 1, Vienna, 1907.

4. Jean Bérenger, 'Fiscalité et économie en Autriche, XVI–XVII siècles', *États, fiscalités, économes*, Acts of the 5th Congress of the French Association of Economic Historians, 1983, Paris, 1985, pp. 13–25.

5. Oskar Regele, *Das œsterreichische Hofkriegsrat*, Vienna, 1956.

6. Heinrich Bidermann, *Geschichte der œsterreichschen Gesamtstaatsidee*, Innsbruck, 1867.

CHAPTER FOURTEEN

Ferdinand I and the Reformation

Ferdinand I, while attached by temperament and education to traditional religion, was conscious, like his brother Charles V, that the Church had need of reform. An Erasmian also, he thought that an ecumenical council and debate with Luther's supporters would pave the way for the restoration of order within the Western half of Christendom and would satisfy even the most exacting of the faithful. In keeping with family tradition, he was pious but not fanatical and did not believe that force was the way to return heretics to the bosom of Mother Church; besides he was without the means for such coercion. Yet, he avoided departing from his principles. As king of the Romans and heir presumptive to the imperial throne, he could not sacrifice the ideological basis of the Holy Roman Empire on the altar of modernity: a Lutheran emperor would have been an absurdity and would have forfeited the moral authority that was the basis of his power. Ferdinand I was always in a position to make concessions and as a tolerant and pragmatic prince to use tactical retreats, but there was never any chance that he would be won over to the Protestant camp. The gathering strength of the Reformation further complicated his task and bolstered opposition to the Habsburgs. Apart from a few regions (Croatia, the Tyrol), the Austrian monarchy was won over swiftly and deeply to various forms of the Protestant Reformation and Ferdinand I appeared as the reluctant overseer of the bankruptcy of Catholicism.

THE LANDS OF THE CROWN OF BOHEMIA[1]

Since the Hussite revolution, the kingdom of Bohemia had been, for the most part, lost to traditional religion and had even served as a model for the Lutheran Reformation. In the sixteenth century, the Catholics accounted for only one third of the total population: foreigners included, they represented less than 5 per cent of the inhabitants of Prague. All accounts, from that of Aeneas Silvio Piccolomini in c.1460 to that of the nuncio Caraffa in c.1580, reveal the abandoned state into which the Catholic Church had fallen. 'For a noble', wrote Caraffa, 'to profess the Catholic Faith is almost a source of shame and its followers are scorned and ridiculed by the dregs of humanity'.

The archbishop's seat at Prague remained vacant for almost a century from the death of Jan Rokycana in 1471 until the appointment in 1561 of the Catholic prelate Antun Brus of Mohelnice. The Utraquists, of course, did not have a seminary but a university for training priests. They and the Lutherans between them administered the majority of parish churches and urban schools. In Bohemia, at least, the aristocracy had taken into its own hands the ecclesiastical property thanks to the Hussite revolution and there no longer existed the wherewithal to furnish and endow Catholic benefices.

The situation was not quite so bad in Moravia, which had been less deeply affected by the Hussite revolution. Church structures had survived better and the episcopal see at Olomouc was not left to fall vacant but at the same time Moravia served as a refuge for all the sects and the towns with their German colonists became Lutheran.

While the official Church was being erased, the mendicant orders maintained a Catholic presence; they were influential in western Bohemia and the area around Plzeň as well as Česky Krumlov and the Bavarian and Saxon enclaves remained loyal to the traditional faith. The minor religious orders played an active role in the spiritual life of the nobles and Catholic burghers but their success could not stem the tide of religious disaffection which stemmed from the weakness of Church institutions and the doctrinal confusion reigning in Utraquist circles.

The Utraquists enjoyed a real revival with the birth of Lutheranism. While the most traditional among them now felt close to the Catholics, a section was radicalized by Lutheran doctrines and the two parties became rivals in the Diet and in public life. The 'lower' Consistory sat in the Old Town of Prague and served as the fundamental organ of religious life since the Compactata of Basle (c.1471) had become an element of the Bohemian constitution. The Consistory and its administrator took the place of the archbishop as the archiepiscopal seat was vacant. In the course of the sixteenth century, the authority of the Consistory diminished as the old Utraquists weakened in the face of the Protestant churches. The influence of its decisions was diminished by the spread of Lutheranism and the Unity of Czech Brethren.* Some of its members were themselves crypto-Lutherans. The Utraquist clergy lacked instruction even though the university of Prague, in principle, took care of their formation. Little is known of the Utraquist clergy, the strength of its manpower and its pastoral work. Gradually it went over to Lutheranism and after 1540 the greater part was

*Translator's note: there are several current English renditions of *Jednota Bratrská* or *Unitas Fratrum*; for justification of the addition of 'Czech', see the discussion by R.J.W. Evans, *Rudolf II and his World*, p.31.

declared 'neo-Utraquist', i.e. Lutheran. A number of its priests lived, notoriously, in concubinage or were even married. Pastors and teachers readily went to Wittenberg and so promoted a measure of Germanization among the elites, particularly in Moravia and Silesia.

Calvinism proper made only a few converts in the kingdom of Bohemia, although the third element making up the Czech religious landscape, the Church of the Unity of Czech Brethren, the heir of the radical Hussite movement, came close to the doctrinal position of the Calvinists. Despite its reformed sympathies, the Unity of Czech Brethren maintained its practices and autonomy,[2] although until the Letter of Majesty of 1609 it was without any legal status. The Brethren took hold in various parts of Bohemia, were well organized and played an educational and cultural role which extended even into neighbouring Poland. Although a minority, they exercised a profound influence through the elementary instruction they gave in their schools and by their emphasis on the vernacular. The books which issued from their printing-press at Litomyšl had an impact throughout the whole Czech world. In Moravia they had the benefit of the patronage of the Žerotins, the most powerful house in the margravate. Elsewhere they suffered systematic persecution because of a narrow interpretation of the Compactata of Basle, which allowed only Utraquists and Catholics in Bohemia. Before 1526, many Brethren were burnt at the stake. The Lutherans, through their numerical superiority, managed to escape all persecution and so were able to play ambiguously with the 'Utraquist' name; they were dubbed the new-Utraquists and called themselves the party 'in both kinds' (in Czech *pod oboje*).

Foreign travellers were struck by the numerous sects settled in northeast Bohemia and Moravia. Adamites and Anabaptists rubbed shoulders with Nicolaites and heretics who had fled from Italy. In a letter to Jaroslav of Pernštejn, Ferdinand I mentioned those 'who believed in neither God nor the devil, nor in the sacraments any more than the resurrection of the dead'. They lived principally in Moravia; Ferdinand added that he could 'no more suffer them in his states than the supporters of Luther or of Zwingli suffer such sects and seeming errors in their midst'.

After 1526, the lands of the crown of Bohemia were characterized by confessional pluralism. There were five main currents – Catholic, Utraquists, Lutherans, Moravian or Czech Brethren and converts to the countless sects. This situation continued until Ferdinand II's victory at the Battle of the White Mountain (1620). Confessional pluralism was linked to the orders' retention of political power because the orders saw such pluralism as an expression of their privileges; were not the exercise of the right of patronage and the guarantee of secularized Church property the basis of feudal lordship?

Within the monarchy, the lands of the crown of Bohemia were the first in which the monopoly of the Church of Rome was subject to such questioning. By reason of the monarchy's character, Ferdinand I found himself confronted by a similar challenge in Austria and Hungary.

THE REFORMATION IN AUSTRIA³

Shortly after Ferdinand's arrival in Austria, it became clear that the hereditary lands would not escape the great movement which was turning the Empire upside down, the same causes producing the same effects.

The idea of death haunted the Christian masses; in Austria *danses macabres* multiplied. The decline of the Church and the Empire was bemoaned and held to be a punishment sent by God; Christ the Man of Sorrows became the object of widespread devotions while cynics made haste to enjoy the goods of this world.

The Church itself was deeply affected in so far as it distributed benefices as rents to the privileged while some priests who were poorly educated and badly paid had, through necessity, to charge for the sacraments. They then found themselves accused of simony by the faithful who were all the more angry since their spiritual needs were growing. Alongside those with benefices swarmed a crowd of poor and ignorant assistant clergy whose pastoral activity left much to be desired. Even if a benefice had escaped the greed of a prelate or a monastery, it might be swallowed up by one of the lay feudal lords who often enjoyed the right of patronage. The regular clergy also underwent a crisis from the end of the fifteenth century. Monasteries, while serving as a veritable refuge for the offspring of the impoverished nobility, received postulants who were not always stirred by a deep vocation and so lacked the strength to withstand the spirit of the age.

As for the people in the countryside, they felt frustrated by the agricultural revolution (to be discussed later) which was reflected in the cultural field by the substitution of Roman Law for the old German customary law. The peasants understood nothing of the Latinized jargon of the new school of jurists and saw themselves progressively robbed of the advantages they had acquired. From 1515 onwards, numerous local revolts served as a prelude to the great peasant revolt of 1525–26. The peasants, naturally, did not know that this was an irreversible process, that the market economy was in the process of transforming society and that imperial power was incapable of preserving their privileges. Society was being divided into two camps, the creditors and the debtors and the harshness of the former roused the implacable hatred of the latter. In the hereditary lands, tensions were less violent than in the *Reich* because Vienna was the only large commercial town. As early as 1520, Luther's great writings (*On Christian Freedom, To the Christian Nobility of the German Nation, On the Babylonian Captivity of the Church*) had been brought by merchants to Vienna where they enjoyed great success; the authorities did nothing to prohibit the works as in the fifteenth century Hussite propaganda had won few converts among the Viennese. Upper Austria, the market towns (Steyr the iron town and Gmuden the salt town), were receptive to Luther's ideas. At Vienna, the preacher Paulus Speratus thundered from the throne of the cathedral of St Stephen against monastic vows and justification by works while the Swiss humanist Vadiamus spread abroad Lutheran doctrine. The propaganda of the Anabaptists found an echo among the artisans of the hereditary lands where they were attacked simultaneously by the Roman Church, the propertied classes and the disciples of Luther. Balthasar Hubmaier, one of the most heeded of Anabaptist preachers, founded a community at Nikolsburg in southern Moravia but was beheaded at Vienna in 1528 after taking an active part in the Peasants' War.

The peasant insurrections certainly undermined the position of the Church but the Turkish threat contributed equally to its decline as the sovereign, with the sanction of the Holy See, seized Church goods to pay for the expenses of war; one-quarter and later one-third of the Church's landed capital was put up for sale with the nobility as the chief beneficiary. The nobles took advantage of the Turkish menace to extort religious toleration and the confirmation of their privileges in return for subsidies. The first order, that of the prelates, quickly found itself in a difficult situation. The abbots considered their monasteries' goods as their personal property. With this swift expropriation of Church goods, the position of the clergy in the parishes became almost untenable. The priests deserted their flocks, who lapsed into total ignorance of the elementary precepts of religion. In many cases, it was not a question of conversion to Lutheranism but reversion to paganism.

Ferdinand's attempt to arrive at a compromise in the confessional domain was in vain since the era when reconciliation was possible had long passed; such were the illusions of Charles V and his brother Ferdinand.

The Peace, grounded in compromise, that was concluded at Augsburg between the emperor and the Lutherans was to Ferdinand's advantage because the choice of religion depended on the prince and not on the local Diets. All, then, was not lost for the Habsburgs in the hereditary lands, at least at the legal level. In 1566, although when faced with representatives of the various Diets, he refused to give ground on this matter of principle, the majority of the orders remained no less commited to the Reformation and the 1561 commission of inquiry only confirmed the conclusions of previous commissions. Only in Carniola did the majority remain Catholic, while Styria and Upper Austria appeared bastions of Lutheranism in the hereditary lands. Vienna itself was three-quarters Protestant. The first signs of Catholic revival only emerged once the Jesuits had begun their work in earnest. Summoned to Vienna by Ferdinand, the Jesuits founded a college there in 1552 and installed themselves at the Clementinum in Prague ten years later. Through their modern teaching methods, their dedication and their solid education, the disciples of St Ignatius would go on to win the spirits of the young nobles and to prepare the ground for future developments.

HUNGARY[4]

Lutheran ideas very quickly reached Hungary. As early as 1521 many professors at the college in Buda were teaching in the spirit of Luther and the following year students left for Wittenberg. The magistrates in the most important towns patronized preachers who supported the Reformation. Even though the primate Szatmari published the papal bulls issued against heresy, queen Maria did not hide her sympathies towards the new ideas, ideas which her young husband Louis II Jagiellon seemed incapable of opposing. Paradoxically it was the gentry who remained best disposed towards Catholicism out of hatred for the 'German queen'. The Diet of 1525 issued some measures against heretics and a few stakes were lit but it was the defeat at Mohács that determined the course of the Reformation in Hungary. Defending Catholicism was the least of the two rival kings' priorities as they handed out Church property to their loyal supporters in order to swell the ranks of their parties. Ferdinand's mercenaries were Lutheran; the Turks, in principle indifferent, were more inclined towards Protestantism; the towns which were inhabited by the Germans had gone over to the Reformation as had most of the aristocracy. The moral authority of the Church had been strongly shaken. The upper classes, who early on had been open to the influences of the Renaissance, were won over to the ideas of Erasmus and the humanists while the masses were touched by Hussitism. As for the national party, it abandoned its pro-Rome orientation when the excommunication of János Zapolya was upheld by pope Clement VII who was allied with the French king, Francis I, and the sultan. Moreover, the aristocracy counted on monopolizing Church property while the people in the countryside saw the Reformation as promising the end of feudal oppression and the dawn of a new world.

By 1550, the Catholic Church had practically ceased to exist as an institution in Hungary. The majority of the lower clergy had accepted the Augsburg Confession. The revenues from ecclesiastical properties were most often pocketed by the magnates. In eastern Hungary, the state seized the domains of the bishoprics of Oradea (Nagyvárad) and Alba Julia (Gyulafehérvár) while, in the Great Plain, Church property was handed out to the 'timariots'. The prelates, however, continued to survive, but they had taken refuge alongside the king at Vienna and Prague and lived at the Habsburgs' expense. Around 1580, the apostolic nuncio observed that Hungary was lost to the Church. Only 300 Catholic priests and religious remained, most of whom lived in Croatia, the last bastion of Catholicism. In the rest of the kingdom, 80–85 per cent of the population was Protestant with the remainder belonging to the Orthodox Church (Romanian peasants, Ukrainians and Serbs).

The change was, in general, accomplished without violence and bloodshed. The priests who had been won over to the Reformation tirelessly criss-crossed the country, rousing the inhabitants of whole regions with their preaching and installing priests who had been won over to the new ideas. They had the moral and material support of the magistrates of the towns and of certain great families who appropriated the right of patronage, thereby usurping one of the principal rights of the king. The radical reformation preached by Thomas Muntzer and the Anabaptists appeared around 1530. At first it spread among the urban masses before winning the peasantry. Although this was the passive wing of the movement, in 1548 it was nevertheless condemned by the Diet. Anabaptism continued its activity in the heart of eastern Hungary where, in 1570, it stirred up a large peasant revolt which had a millenarian character. In 1569 the serf György Karácsony had declared 'holy war' against the Turks and all oppressive powers and the leaders of the rising promised the coming of the reign of the peasants and social equality. They attacked the Turks, then turned against the feudal lords, holding to ransom the town of Debrecen. The revolt was short-lived, the magistrate of Debrecen had Karácsony arrested and executed, and the 'holy army' was crushed by the royal troops. The Anabaptist movement found refuge in the principality of Transylvania.

The Lutheran Reformation's hegemony was first challenged by some disciples of Zwingli, then after 1540 by the Calvinist Reformation which in the space of twenty years became the religion of almost all the Hungarians. Calvinism, more radical than Lutheranism in its doctrinal as much as its social programme, at first attracted the well-to-do peasantry of the small towns who were hostile towards the great landowners. Its presbyterian orientation made possible the removal of the Church administration and the absolute authority of the lords. Whether Calvinism really was revolutionary is open to question since it did not envisage the overthrow of the seigneurial regime. As the preachers taught that the great grasping feudal lords too could be forgiven by God if they repented and turned from sin, the nobility also adopted Calvinist doctrines. From 1560 the moderate tendency represented by the young bishop of Debrecen, Péter Juhász, began to take the lead ahead of the radical section represented by the preachers of the small towns. Juhász went so far as to defend openly the established social regime, professing obedience to the princes and recommending the payment of taxes and the tithe. In 1567, the adoption of the second Helvetic Confession by the Calvinist synod at Debrecen marked the beginning of a United Reformed Church in Hungary. All the Calvinist tendencies in fact had need to ally against a common enemy, the anti-Trinitarians or Socinians who were established in Transylvania and had won to their cause prince Zsigismund János II, some large families and the urban patriciate. With Ferenc Dávid, the prince's chaplain, they denied the divinity of Christ, the immortality of the soul, rejected feast days and the sacraments. Persecuted after 1571 by the new prince of Transylvania, the Catholic István Báthory, the majority of Unitarians re-embraced the Reformed Church but some emigrated to Poland. The situation around 1580 was as follows; 50 per cent of the Hungarians were reformed, 25 per cent belonged to the Augsburg Confession (Germans in Transylvania and Upper Hungary, Slovaks) and the remaining 25 per cent was made up of Unitarians, Catholic and Orthodox.

The underlying reasons for Calvinism's success in Hungary are not always clear, especially since it was very much a sweetened form of the doctrine, adapted to the political and social conditions of the country, which took root there. Was it a national reaction, at once anti-German and anti-Habsburg? Was the austerity of Calvinism naturally compatible with the Hungarians' religious instinct? The debate remains open. Certainly the Reformed Church, governed by its pastors and the nobles, represented a weighty force in Hungarian political life. The Calvinists were fierce defenders of the national language, culture and independence.

Under the influence of the Reformation, Hungarian writers adopted the vernacular, using the regularized form of Hungarian which had lately been established by philologists at the university of Krakow who had been inspired by the ideas of Jan Hus and Erasmus of Rotterdam. The movement in favour of the national language grew towards the end of the sixteenth century when Protestant schoolmasters demanded teaching in the vernacular alongside Latin. This literature, most of which was in verse, was concerned with the theological interpretation of the Hungarian-Turkish conflict. A. Farkas explained in a poem entitled 'On the Jewish and Hungarian nations' that the Turk was the instrument chosen by God to punish the country for its sins and to reconcile it to the Lord. He established a parallel between the history of the Jews and the history of the Hungarian people. Just as God, to punish the Jews, had their country invaded by the Romans, so He had had Hungary overrun by the Turks. If the Hungarian people accepted the Reformation and abandoned their sinful ways, God would deliver them from the Turks. As in the other Protestant countries, Holy Scripture was the source of the whole of religious life. After some partial translations of the Bible published before 1540, the first complete Hungarian Bible appeared in 1590 in a translation by Gáspár Károlyi. The most effective weapon of Protestantism, however, remained education. Schools in the villages taught the young peasants the basics of the Hungarian language necessary for reading the Bible, while the town schools and academies followed a humanist programme based on that of the German schools. Hungary did not have a university and the young went abroad to study, the Lutherans to Wittenberg, the Calvinists to Leiden, Strassburg, Heidelburg, Geneva or England. In this way Hungarian intellectual circles remained in contact with Northern Europe.[5]

Hungarian intellectual life was not dominated solely by the Reformation, however, even if twenty-nine out of the thirty printing-presses in the country were in Protestant hands. Humanism ceased to be the preserve of a cosmopolitan elite and passed to the urban patriciate and the gentry, social groups which were more deeply rooted in the national culture and land than the upper aristocracy. While literary mannerisms developed among the gentry, the towns of Upper Hungary experienced their own intellectual life, witnessing the establishment and development of literary Slovak as a language distinct from Czech and Polish. The humanists who followed the German school, turned from the study of natural sciences and took refuge in the study of historical sources, philology and theology. The clergy who had been trained at Wittenberg, however, stopped this tendency. Once the Lutheran patriciate sent their sons to study in Germany, the burghers of Upper Hungary cut themselves off from the melting-pot of ideas represented by sixteenth-century Italy. They needed pastors and school-masters to instruct the people, not scholars, philosophers and distinguished poets. German-inspired humanism found expression in two fields especially, school drama and neo-Latin poetry, which are currently being researched by Slovak historians.

As paradoxical as it might seem, the most brilliant figures and most interesting works appeared in those parts of Hungary less protected from Turkish incursions because there the humanists maintained direct links with Italy. The return to the aristocratic ideal of the Italian Renaissance was manifest in two poets belonging to the new class of magnates: Péter Bornemisza (1535–85) and Bálint Balassi (1554–94), who was considered the greatest Hungarian poet of his age.

In 1564 at the death of Ferdinand I and one year after the promulgation of the decrees of the Council of Trent, the Austrian monarchy appeared a bastion of Protestantism where all the churches stemming from the Reformation lived side by side, from the very conservative Utraquists of Bohemia to the Unitarians of Transylvania via the converts to the Augsburg Confession and to the teachings of Calvin and Zwingli. Such a picture is far removed from the classic image of 'Catholic Austria'; *pietas austriaca* might be applied to the sovereign but not to his subjects who saw confessional differences as the means to strengthen their autonomy. That the Croats remained preponderantly Catholic is revealing; their steadfast Catholicism was a way of expressing their identity in the face of the Hungarian nobility and at the same time of setting off to advantage their loyalty to the House of Austria.

When Ferdinand negotiated the Peace of Augsburg in the Empire and when he imposed it on a rather hesitant Charles V, he displayed his spirit of openness and his pragmatism in so far as even before the closure of the General Council the compromise perpetuated the breach with Germany. When he confirmed the German princes' right to exercise the *jus episcopalis* and gave them the choice between Lutheranism and Catholicism, Ferdinand made a major political concession to the Estates of the Empire, while settling the future of the hereditary lands; in virtue of this principle it was the Habsburgs who made decisions in Lower Austria, Styria and Carniola and not the lesser feudal lords who did not have any particular privilege written into the Peace of Augsburg. This is why the king of the Romans never yielded on the judicial level nor accorded any confessional privileges to the Austrians or the Hungarians. Henceforth there was a considerable difference between practice, which was very liberal, and the law which remained oppressive and obsolete but unrepealed. This apparent contradiction is explained by the fact that Ferdinand was totally dependent upon the Diets for military and financial aid to pursue the war with the Turks which seemed the more urgent concern, the conflict against the external threat postponing until better days the fight against heresy and the re-establishment of confessional unity.

NOTES AND REFERENCES

1. Ferdinand Seibt (ed.) *Bohemia Sacra: das Christentum in Böhmen* 973–1973, Düsseldorf, 1974.
2. R. Rican, *Die böhmischen Brüder: ihr Ursprung und ihre Geshichte. Mit einem Kapitel über die Theologie der Brüder von Amedeo Molnar*, Berlin, 1961.
3. Grete Mecenseffy, *Geschichte des Protestantismus in Œsterreich*, Graz, 1956.
4. Jean Bérenger, 'L'Europe du Nord et de l'Est', in Pierre Chaunu (ed.) *L'Aventure de la Réforme: le monde de Jean Calvin*, Paris, 1986, pp. 223–30.
5. Jean Bérenger, 'Les caractères originaux de l'humanisme hongrois', *Journal des savants*, 1973, pp. 257–88.

CHAPTER FIFTEEN

The Struggle against the Ottoman Empire (1527–68)

VIENNA: THE FRONTIER POST OF CHRISTENDOM

The reorganization of the monarchy was an enormous and difficult task and the restoration of traditional religion in all its splendour seemed a wild dream. The event from Ferdinand's reign that is best remembered by the Viennese is the first Turkish siege; a brief drama – it lasted only a month from mid-September to mid-October 1529 – but significant. The town discovered that it was no longer safe, that in the heart of Europe it was no longer protected by Belgrade and the Hungarian bulwark but had become the foremost fortress of Christendom. For the Turks, Vienna was the focus of their mythology of conquest. They did not cease to dream of the city, 'the golden apple', its treasures and the symbol which it represented.[1]

For the next two centuries, the geo-strategic role of the capital changed radically: previously the crossroads of the Austrian monarchy's communications and commerce, Vienna was now a frontier post; a metropolis, it had to be enclosed within a ring of walls still to be seen in the Ringstrasse, the ring of roads built in 1860 on the foundations of the earlier fortifications. The sixteenth-century Italian engineers employed on the project displayed their genius to the full in modernizing the medieval ramparts. For want of space, they had to build high and the arsenal presently occupied more room than the university.

There was another consequence. Despite the promises he had made to the Estates of Bohemia, Ferdinand moved his capital and made only occasional visits to Prague, setting up his government and residence at Vienna in order to be much closer to the Hungarian field of battle. His sojourn was a long one as he died without having been able to reach a lasting peace with Süleymân the Magnificent.

THE FORCES CONFRONT EACH OTHER

The two sides seemed quite unequal in strength: the Ottoman empire was a world power at the peak of its expansion whereas the Austrian monarchy would have been only a middling power had it not mobilized the resources of the Holy Roman Empire or the Spanish Monarchy. The Sublime Porte, however, had many theatres of operation of which the Hungarian front was not, perhaps, the most pressing. Indeed, Süleymân was in difficulties: in the Near East he was in dispute with the shah of Persia over Eastern Anatolia and Mesopotamia and he also sought control of the Mediterranean at the expense of Venice and especially Spain. His reign coincided with the development of Turkish naval power which dominated the eastern Mediterranean and in partnership with Francis I and the Barbary corsairs appeared in the western Mediterranean; Khair ad-Din Barbarossa, captain pasha of the Porte, laid siege to Nice in order to assist the French army to take the town then belonging to the duke of Savoy, an ally of Charles V.

In theory, Süleymân's resources were clearly superior to those of Ferdinand; the population of the Habsburg lands amounted to 6 million–7 million while the Ottoman empire after the annexation of Syria and Egypt in 1517 had perhaps 18 million–20 million inhabitants. As well as the imbalance in population sizes, the sheer might of the Ottoman state, then at the peak of its efficiency, also weighed against the interests of the Austrian monarchy. The sultan was a great captain who commanded his army in person. The state structure was that of an army camped over a vast territory. The *sipahi*, the basic cavalryman received a military fief, a *timar*, which he held neither as the proprietor nor the hereditary tenant, although tendencies towards the formation of Ottoman feudalism were already apparent. These timariots, who were regularly mobilized, wanted to wage war as a means of acquiring booty and glory. The Turkish nation which dominated the Empire never hid its military vocation. The Islamic notion of *jihâd* against the European infidel or the heretic shi'ites of the Near East further strengthened the *sipahis'* motivation; in 1521, Süleymân, as a gift to mark his succession, offered them the conquest of Belgrade and there was hardly a year when he did not suggest a campaign.[2] The Ottoman monarchy retained its imperialist vocation even though the sultan's ardour was sometimes moderated by diplomacy and pragmatism and he was able to draw lessons from his defeat in front of Vienna in 1529 and Malta in 1565.

Through the *devşirme*, the 'tithe on children' the sultan could recruit the healthiest offspring of the Balkan Christians. Raised in the Islamic faith, these children became Muslim fanatics and zealous servants of the commander of the believers. They formed not only the elite corps of the janissaries but also the permanent administrative establishment. Carefully nurtured, they were harshly punished for the slightest fault, dismissed or even executed on the orders of the sultan who, unlike his Western adversaries, did not have to deal with nobles jealous of their liberties and in a position to dominate the people and resist their ruler.

As sixteenth-century Western observers noted, a despotic state like the Ottoman state was in every respect very different from the society of orders and the patrimonial monarchy to which they were accustomed as a political model. The sultan also recruited, indirectly through renegades, men of talent from Italy and so he could benefit from European technological innovations. The financial administration was efficient and the Porte was rich. In 1543 Süleymân did not hesitate to spend 1 million ducats to arm Barbarossa's fleet which took part in the siege of Nice. Western observors were mightily impressed by the arsenal of Pera at Istanbul, which Barbarossa reorganized after 1535. The empire's resources enabled the sultan to arm 200 galleys; by contrast it was with great difficulty that Francis I was able to put just 20 galleys at his Ottoman ally's disposal.

Süleymân's army was unquestionably the foremost in Europe both in terms of its manpower and its organization. At its core were 12 000 to 15 000 janissaries who fought on foot and abandoned the bow for the arquebus. They passed for invincible on the field of battle where they formed the centre of the disposition and detachments could be dispatched on the sultan's galleys where their expertise worked wonders. In addition to these there were *c.* 50 000 *sipahis*, the cavalry corps which determined the outcome of great battles such as that at Mohács in 1526. The Turks also accorded a great place to their field artillery. There was a corps of artillerymen paid directly by the treasury and a corps of sappers essential for siege-warfare. The number of troops in the ranks was hardly more than 50 000 to 60 000 men, not the fantastic number of 100 000 to 200 000 readily trotted out by contemporary chroniclers and which can be explained for two reasons. First, the sultan took the lead with his auxilliary troops consisting of the Moldo-Vlach or Transylvanian contingents who had been pressed into the Ottoman war effort, and the Tartar auxiliaries who, by contrast, were the key element in Turkish strategy. Their mission was to operate in advance of the regular army, pillaging, burning and reducing the civilian populations to slavery, in short to demoralize the enemy so that it might all the more readily capitulate, even before any engagement. Then, when face to face with regular troops, the Tartars' mission was precise; by launching surprise attacks, they drove the enemy to break ranks and so smoothed the way for the decisive charge of the *sipahis*. With their mandate for psychological warfare they served to terrorize civilians and military alike who saw the Ottoman army as a multitudinous and invincible horde. The Ottoman army had numerical superiority in all areas. It is often quoted as astonishing that in 1557 Philip II of Spain was able to put together 60 000 men, an army so large that after its victory at Saint-Quentin, want of supplies prevented it from marching on Paris: a link has been made between this undertaking and the Spanish national bankruptcy of the same year. Süleymân though had long since invented logistics, a vital factor during combat on the dry steppes of Eastern Anatolia. Convoys of camels brought essential food and drink for the soldiers who by nature and by training were men of moderation. These basic precautions (unknown in the West) and the air of exoticism surrounding the camels all served to strike terror into Süleymân's European enemies.

Ferdinand could scarcely field ranks of more than 25 000 against the sultan as mercenaries were costly. In 1529 he had only 21 700 footsoldiers and 2 200 cavalrymen to defend Vienna. In 1541 he mobilized 40 000 footsoldiers and 8 000 cavalry. After 1542, he maintained in Hungary a permanent army of 4 000 men-at-arms, 3 000 light cavalry and 4 000 footsoldiers, who cost around 1 million florins a year. Only in the campaign of 1532 did he field a comparable force against Süleymân of almost equal strength to the sultan's: 10 000 men-at-arms, 20 000 light cavalry and 60 000 foot soldiers of whom 18 000 came from the king of Spain and 32 000 were lancers and 10 000 harquebusiers; the imperial Diet of its own accord voted to maintain 48 000 soldiers. As for Charles V, he was content just to show his strength rather than use it, and it is known that the two most powerful rulers of the day in their final encounter in 1532 studiously avoided engagement.

As formidable as Süleymân's military apparatus was in the case of frontal assault, it nevertheless suffered from serious failings. Although it had very modern logistical support, good strategy required that its lines of communication were not extended indefinitely. There were weaknesses also in recruitment. The timariots would demand to return home at the end of a campaign. The army was mobilized according to a strict calendar, especially if timariots from Anatolia were called upon for an offensive in Hungary. The Spanish and Italian intelligence services, by observing the earliest troop concentrations around Adrianople, knew as early as January in any year that a summer campaign was being prepared – information which would be confirmed in the spring by a march on Belgrade. In practice, the sultan had no more than four summer months in which to operate in Central Europe. If he had not obtained a decisive result by mid-September, he had to withdraw and wait until the following summer so that the timariots could return to their firesides. Unless a decisive success came in early summer, any real follow-up was hindered by the seasonal character of campaigns; the victory at Mohács came at the end of August and was followed by only a short-lived military advance, despite the collapse of the Hungarian state and military apparatus. Even in the sixteenth century, the sultan could not employ his 'active' army, the janissaries and *sipahis* on two continents simultaneously, for example in Hungary and Azerbaidjan.

Finally, the objectives of Süleymân's wars were not clear and probably changed in the course of his long reign (1520–66): as heir to the Byzantine emperors, did he want to reunite the then defunct Roman Empire; or by leading a holy war, to extend Islam's domain; was his aim quite simply to make Hungary a protectorate?

THE PRINCIPAL ENGAGEMENTS[3]

The Austro-Turkish hostilities, which ended only in 1568 with the Peace of Adrianople, were a heavy burden, politically and psychologically, on the development of continental Europe. The Turkish armies' crushing victories demoralized Ferdinand's soldiers and the civilians whose greatest dread was being captured and sold as slaves on the market at Istanbul. Within the empire, a whole body of literature evolved with the purpose of rousing spirits and turning Christendom into a united front against Turkish Islam; these calls were often quite fruitless despite pressure from the Holy See which feared for the security of the Italian peninsula.

Ferdinand's success in 1528 and the Franco-Turkish alliance provoked a renewal of hostilities. János Zapolya, who had fled to Poland in 1527, returned to Hungary in 1529 with Süleymân's backing. The sultan took Buda and then wanted to besiege Vienna,[4] but he was hindered by the autumn rain and the first cold; on 14 October he was forced to abandon the siege without having taking Ferdinand's capital. The events of that year had been a grave warning; Charles V, lost in his Italian dreams, had sent hardly any help and Austria had but narrowly escaped the fate of Hungary. German opinion was overcome with fear. In 1532, when Süleymân undertook his fourth campaign in Central Europe, Charles V felt obliged to put together an army at Vienna but Süleymân lingered on the outskirts of the little town of Köszeg on the Austro-Hungarian frontier and nothing happened. When Andrea Doria the Genoese admiral in the emperor's service, seized Patras and Lepanto, the two powers concluded an armistice in 1533 which enabled Süleymân to turn his arms against Persia (the occupation of Baghdad and Azerbaijan). Hostilities were resumed in 1538 over the principality of Moldavia, which paid tribute to the Porte but whose prince had allied with Ferdinand. In the same year an agreement was finally reached between Ferdinand and János Zapolya with the goal of reuniting Hungary after the latter's death and compensating his heir, János Zsigmond Zapolya. This agreement in fact precipitated events. Zapolya died in 1540 and so Süleymân no longer was obliged to defend him; it seems that between 1527 and 1540 the Grand Turk had wanted to make Hungary a protectorate rather than a province. In 1541 Ferdinand sent troops to seize Buda in accordance with the terms of the 1538 settlement with Zapolya. However, Süleymân then ordered the occupation of the Hungarian capital, built a mosque and placed János Zapolya's under-age son, János Zsigmond, under his protection.

The occupation of Buda marked the beginning of Hungary's annexation by the Turks and its division into three zones, a division which lasted until the end of the seventeenth century: first, Royal Hungary to the north and east, embracing modern Slovakia and Croatia as well as a more or less straight band of the Great Plain; second, Turkish Hungary, a straightforward frontier province of the Ottoman empire, dependent on the pasha of Buda, including the greater part of the Great Plain and forming a wedge carved out between Royal Hungary and Transylvania; third, the principality of Transylvania, which would gradually gain its independence and play an important role in the politics of south-east Europe and in the development of the Hungarian nation.

The fall of Buda also marked the resumption of hostilities on a large scale. In 1542 Ferdinand tried to take Pest, which was then completely independent of Buda and situated on the left bank of the Danube. The attempt failed. In 1543 Süleymân undertook his fifth Hungarian campaign in the course of which he seized Pécs and Esztergom. Four years later, Ferdinand was obliged to sign a truce, agreeing to supply an annual tribute of 30 000 gold florins. He persisted in trying to effect the terms of the 1538 agreement with the late János Zapolya and tried to seize Transylvania, which was governed by the prelate Georg Mönch Martinuzzi in the name of the young János Zsigmond Zapolya. The Turks once again responded, seized Temesvár in 1552, but ran aground outside Eger because of the heroic resistance of István Dobo and his garrison. They continued localized attacks until 1556 but their defeat before Szigetvár (Siget), a fortress in Slavonia, put an end to hostilities for ten years. In 1566 Süleymân, despite the treaty concluded in 1562, led his last Hungarian campaign. He laid siege to Szigetvár, which was defended by Croat and Hungarian troops under Nikola Zrinski (Miklós Zrinyi), the captain-general of the Transdanubian frontier. Zrinski and his men resisted heroically until September and when all was lost, made a final sortie during which they all perished, weapons in their hands. For the Hungarians and the Croats the defence of Szigetvár assumed great symbolic value and became the theme of numerous poems and even a baroque epic in Hungarian, *Szigeti Veszedelem*, composed in 1654 by Nikola Zrinski, the ban of Croatia and grandson of the hero of Szigetvár. Süleymân died during the siege and the Turks, having lost heart, beat a retreat. In 1568 the new sultan, Selîm II, who was less inclined towards war, signed the Peace of Adrianople with Ferdinand's son, Maximilian II. The latter continued to pay 30 000 florins in annual tribute, recognized the independence of Transylvania and agreed to the existence of a frontier zone where the peasants paid tribute both to the Turks and to the royal authorities. Prey to raids and the source of later conflicts, this border region, the Military Frontier (*Militärgrenze*), had a character all of its own.

THE MILITARY FRONTIER[5]

The Hungarian–Turkish Military Fróntier consisted of a chain of fortresses stretching about a thousand kilometres from the Dalmatian coast right to the frontier of Transylvania. On the Turkish side, these fortresses were sparse but equipped with strong garrisons. On the Hungarian side, the frontier consisted of a large number of small fortresses, often built of earth and wood using local resources and manual labour furnished by the royal *robot*. Some were made of stone, built in the Italian style by military engineers. The most powerful fortress, Györ, was protected by the marshes of the confluence of the Rába and the Danube. These fortresses sheltered the cavalrymen, the famous Hussars who launched frequent raids into the Turkish-occupied zone. When one of these small forts fell into the hands of the Turks, usually after a long siege, it was immediately replaced by another. In 1556 the frontier garrisons amounted to 16 000 men, who were German or Hungarian and paid by the king. The money came essentially from the contributions voted by the Estates of Styria, Lower Austria, Moravia and Bohemia, who saw the Military Frontier as their best defence against the Turkish peril. A frontier society evolved as much among the Turks as the Christians. Often a refuge for peasants fleeing from serfdom, the frontier was populated by military colonies exempt from the *robot*, obedient to their officers alone and living off raids against the enemy; the best defence against Ottoman expansion, it also served to limit abuse within the manorial system.

THE PRINCIPALITY OF TRANSYLVANIA[6]

The situation in the state of Transylvania was no less unusual. Its ruler, who held the title 'prince', was elected by the country's Diet, confirmed by the Sublime Porte and solemnly crowned at Alba Julia (Gyulafehérvár, Weissenburg), in the presence of a *tchaouch*, an extraordinary envoy of the Grand Turk. Transylvania paid the sultan an annual tribute of 10 000 florins and, in time of war, limited quantities of grains and forage. While the prince of Transylvania maintained a permanent representative at the Porte, the Porte was content to send an extraordinary mission to the prince of Transylvania in times of need. The prince enjoyed all the prerogatives of a ruler except in external policy where the prince's initiatives (the declaration of war, the conclusion of an alliance) were approved by the Porte before being acted upon. The prince was helped by a council of twelve members headed by the chancellor. In the seventeenth century its princes, notably Bethlen Gábor and György I Rákóczi, displayed tendencies towards absolutism and like the Habsburgs sought to appoint their successors and clashed with a Diet jealous of its prerogatives.

The Diet was made up of around 150 members, some named by the prince, others elected by the orders who made up the three 'nations'. Following the compromise of Torda (1568) 'four religions' were allowed: Catholicism, the Augsburg Confession, the Helvetic Confession (or

191

Reformed Church) and the Unitarians. The 'nations' were privileged groups: Hungarians, Saxons and Szeklers or Sicules. The absence of Romanians both as an ethno-linguistic group and as a religious one (Greek Orthodox) is noticeable. This was because the Romanian nobility had assimilated to the Hungarian nobility, the Hunyadi (the family of Matthias Corvinus) being a notable example. Lacking a nobility to defend and represent them, the Romanians found themselves reduced to the rank of the servile masses, *misera plebs contribuens*. The Orthodox Church also did not receive any privileged status. The 'four religions' and the 'three nations', the privileged orders, had a political status right until 1848. The Diet was dominated by the prince's men – delegates from the towns, the commanders of fortresses, magistrates, mines and customs officers – with the result that the assembly played a merely consultative role and could never take vital political decisions. Moreover the orders only ever sent notables, members of the Hungarian, Saxon or Szekler nobility, or the 'religions' who only nominated the prelates (all the Protestant Churches had adopted an episcopalian structure). The Diet was convoked each year in a different place according to where the prince was then residing.

Transylvania, as the description of its political regime might suggest, was a society of orders subject to a manorial regime much harsher than in Hungary or Bohemia. The serfs, who accounted for the greater part of the peasant masses, owed 50–100 days of *robot* a year as well as the tithe and dues (*census*), which were variable. Most importantly, they had lost the right to run away: if they left the domain they could be followed and returned to their master. In the seventeenth century, there was no longer even a time limit for the offence of flight. The peasant was subject to justice meted out by the feudal lords and totally escaped the prince's authority. During the same period, a number of peasants lost their hereditary holding and fell into the lower category of manual labourers who existed in conditions more precarious than those of the hereditary tenants; on the Rákóczis' domains, 26 per cent of the peasants no longer had any draught-animals and 56 per cent possessed fewer than four, the number necessary to make up a team. Certain aristocratic families came increasingly to dominate the Transylvania nobility. The middle and lower ranks were impoverished, with a family having only three or four tenures, sometimes only one or even just a simple parcel of land, the remains of the old domain. The phenomenon of the 'noble *plebs*' was less pronounced than in Poland because the lesser nobility in order to avoid becoming too tied to the clientage of the great nobility gave their support to the prince, supported his absolutist tendencies and demanded the development of the army and state apparatus. In Transylvania, even more so than in Hungary, landed wealth was concentrated in the hands of the great families such as the Bathorys and the Rákóczis while the towns had an even more restricted role. Despite the prince's efforts, the social structure remained characteristic of Eastern Europe. The great landowners enjoyed greater domination than elsewhere and still had considerable weight in the twentieth century with the Szeklers alone able to preserve relative freedom.

The final distinctive element in Hungary in the sixteenth century was the Turkish party. Military occupation and annexation during almost a century and a half greatly altered the composition of the population. In law the sultan as chief of war personally possessed all the lands, ceding usufruct to his warriors for a fixed period of time; this was the famous *timar*, the concession of a right to usufruct. As the possession of a domain was never hereditary and sometimes did not last more than two or three years, the timariot wanted to draw the maximum profit and therefore put pressure on his peasants to the point where he drove them into flight. Only the sultan's properties, or *hass* domains, were exploited with moderation by stewards, and so attracted runaway peasants. This was the origin of the large towns of the Great Plain, like Kecskemét. The countryside emptied and the peasants regrouped, practising extensive rearing of cattle and goats which they exported to Germany and Italy. Hungarian beef cattle were found in Venice and Strassburg and guaranteed the vital meat supply to Vienna. It was at this time that the Hungarian plain assumed its steppe-like character which has remained to the twentieth century.

Taxation in Turkish Hungary was moderate. Christians paid a poll tax (*haraç*) at the rate of one florin a year in return for the protection which they received while in Islamic territory. In addition, they were obliged, as in the past, to pay the tithe and some extraordinary taxes collected through tax-farmers. There was no *robot*, but the 'tithe on children' was felt keenly by the Christian population.

The Turks themselves rarely settled in lands where they dreaded the climate or felt out of place. They maintained just sufficient garrisons in some fortresses which served as administrative capitals. Buda was occupied by soldiers and Turkish officials for whose benefit the churches were turned into mosques, and the old town was dominated by minarets while the ancient palaces of the nobility fell progressively into ruin. The outskirts where the artisans and traders lived were inhabited by Bosnians, Serbs and Greeks. The Hungarians, except for rare exceptions, did not convert to Islam and the Turks really felt that they were camping in a hostile land where, despite peace treaties and truces, the state of war was endemic.

THE PEACE OF ADRIANOPLE (1568)

The situation at the time of Ferdinand's death in 1564 was unstable. Nothing was settled and it fell to Ferdinand's successor, Maximilian II to sign with Süleymân's son and successor, Selîm II, a peace granting mutual concessions, the Peace of Adrianople. The death of Süleymân during his last Hungarian campaign served as a symbol; his army once again had been held up by a small frontier fortress, Szigetvár, defended by a garrison which, though small in size, was determined and commanded by an energetic leader, Nikola Zrinski, a Croat assimilated into the Hungarian aristocracy. Süleymân was overcome by illness and his entourage carefully hid his death from the Turkish army so as not to demoralize it. The garrison, at the end of its resources, tried a final sortie and perished heroically. The place fell to the Turks who then retired. Zrinski's feat of arms became a national epic at the same time for both the Croats and the Hungarians.

Ferdinand had enjoyed partial success; he had not succeeded in sparing the Hungarian plain from Turkish occupation and the Peace of Adrianople was an inglorious compromise. During forty years, with the help of Hungarian loyalists and the hereditary lands, he had been able to develop an effective system of defence, a modernized version of the Roman *limes*, which forced Süleymân to curtail his ambitions. The great victim of the conflict was very clearly Hungary, transformed into a buffer zone for the Ottoman empire and a barrier for the Habsburg Empire: it would not be reconquered until the seventeenth century; Transylvania found itself separated from the kingdom of Hungary and under Ottoman protection; Royal Hungary was no more than a buffer protecting the hereditary lands and Bohemia against Turkish incursions. At the cost of the dismemberment of Hungary, the rest of the monarchy had been saved and Ottoman confidence had been shaken. The naval defeat inflicted on the Turks at Lepanto in 1571 by the fleet of the Holy League marked another arresting blow to their offensive spirit. The peoples of Europe, for the moment, ceased to live in a state of panic and fear of Ottoman aggression, slaving parties and invasion. The sorry memory of the siege of Vienna and the sacking of Lower Austria was gradually erased, while the imperial diplomats, never short of ingenuity, stirred the embers of the projected alliance with the shah of Persia, who was to have taken the common enemy, the *padischah* of Istanbul, from the rear. There is little point in describing in detail how such diplomatic missions to the shah never resulted in any concrete and coordinated military action; the psychological and geographical distance between Vienna and Ispahan was insurmountable.

Hungary played well the role of *antemurale christianitatis*, 'the bastion of Christendom' but in a different context from that envisaged by Pius II and János Hunyadi in the fifteenth century.

NOTES AND REFERENCES

1. Richard Kreutel, *Im Reich des goldenen Apfels*, Vienna, 1964.
2. J. von Hammer-Purgstall, *Histoire de l'empire ottoman*, French translation by Hellert, 18 vols, Paris, 1835–41.

3. Rudolf Neck, 'Œsterreich und die Osmanen', *Mitteilungen des Œsterreichischen Staatsarchivs*, 10, Vienna, 1957.
4. Ferdinand Stöller, 'Soliman vor Wien', *Mitteilungen des Vereins für die Geschichte der Stadt Wien*, 9–10, 1929–30.
    Walter Sturminger, *Bibliographie und Ikonographie der Türkenbelagerungen der Stadt Wien 1529 und 1683*, Graz and Cologne, 1955.
5. Erich Rothenberg, *The Austrian Military Border*, Chicago, 1964.
6. Laszló Makkai, *Histoire de Transylvanie*, Paris, 1946.

CHAPTER SIXTEEN

Economic Prosperity and Social Tensions in the Sixteenth Century

The Ottoman drive into the Pannonian plain did not automatically entail the ruin of the whole region, nor did the discovery of the New World and the Atlantic revolution completely marginalize that part of the Old Continent. The Turkish occupation of the Hungarian plain altered the routes of exchange and the lands spared from warfare developed their various activities, in particular mining. The quantity of precious metals mined was certainly modest when compared with the American silver which presently flooded Europe and in the second half of the century, with the opening of the Potosí mines in Peru, the gap would become yet greater. The output of the mines in Bohemia and Upper Hungary was, however, sufficient to strengthen the economy of the region, a modest echo of the 'world economy' dear to Fernand Braudel.[1]

There was another problem peculiar to the region: with the increase in taxation linked to the Turkish war, existing social structures were subject to tensions and changes which in the long term had heavy consequences.

FAVOURABLE ECONOMIC CIRCUMSTANCES

When working in the era before statistics, the economic historian has to be content with rather imperfect means of measurement such as the change in the price of cereals, an essential product which was increasingly integrated into the market economy although the greater part of the grain produced never reached the market, as it was consumed by the peasants who grew it. Patient research has made it possible to publish unbroken series of prices for the large towns, Frankfurt-am-Main, Gdansk and Vienna.

The price of a sextary of wheat on the market at Vienna, then the great metropolis of Danubian Europe with its 50 000 inhabitants, will serve as an example. From 11 kreuzers in 1470 the price had doubled by 1530 and continued to rise; in the period 1530–60 it stood at 30 kreuzers, then during 1578–80 it rose to its peak price of 50 kreuzers; between 1580 and 1610 prices settled at *c.*40 kreuzers before starting once again to climb. The price of wheat, then, had doubled between the beginning of the reign of Ferdinand I and that of Rudolf II, while the wages of artisans and agricultural workers remained almost the same, which shows that producers' profits had made a notable increase.[2]

The tendency already observed at the end of the fifteenth century was reinforced: the market economy developed to the benefit of the lords and the vast domains made their appearance at the expense of the towns and small agricultural holdings, that is to say, the artisans and peasants. As in Western Europe, the movement is explained by the influx of precious metals and the rise in population.

There is no precise numerical study of the increase in population in the Czech lands but it is almost certain that there was, despite the epidemics and plague and recurring famines, a slow and regular growth which led to 4 million inhabitants *c.* 1600 (1.5 million in Bohemia, 1.4 million in Silesia, 800 000 in Moravia and the rest in Lusatia). The whole of the lands of Bohemia covered 122 000 sq km, the average density of population was *c.* 33 inhabitants per sq km. Research into the case in Hungary, as István Hunyadi shows in his thesis,[3] is complicated by the movements of villagers fleeing the Ottoman invasion and returning home some years later after the danger had passed. Vera Zimányi,[4] starting with the partial census of 1598, hazards an estimate which may easily be compared with that of 1496 and which was made within the boundaries of 'historic Hungary', an area of over 350 000 sq km; it is difficult to attribute more than 3 million inhabitants to the whole of Hungary, including the 800 000 inhabitants in Transylvania. Hungary, then, had lost between 500 000 and 1 million inhabitants in the course of the sixteenth century, as much through epidemics – in particular malaria and dysentery – as through the Turkish wars. Zimányi refuses to accept the classic theory, based on the reports of some travellers; the density was less than 10 inhabitants per sq km with great regional variation. This shortage of manpower entailed the radical transformation of agriculture in the Great Plain. The great landowners tried to attract new colonists to the deserted lands, Croats in Royal Hungary, Serbs in Turkish Hungary. This development reached its peak in the eighteenth century and seriously affected the unity of the nation.

THE DEVELOPMENT OF MINING

One of the natural riches of Central Europe was its mines: the trend towards intense working favoured by Maximilian I and the Fuggers continued throughout the sixteenth century, despite the relatively low level of production and the great technical difficulties presented by great sheets of subterranean water; in some shafts more manual labour was engaged in pumping out the water than in digging galleries. Technicians – the term engineer is still inappropriate – from Bohemia and Upper Hungary enjoyed a good reputation and were highly valued. Often German in origin, some obtained contracts in mining enterprises in the New World and the treatise *De re metallica* by Agricola (the German humanist scholar Georg Bauer, 1494–1555), which was published in 1562, became the established authority on mining for more than a century.

To meet their financial difficulties, the Habsburgs followed the policy begun by Maximilian I in the Tyrol in 1493 and in return for substantial loans granted capitalists from Upper Germany the right to develop the mines commercially. The Fuggers and the Thurzos, a merchant family originally from Cracow, used these privileges to buy back a large number of mines and foundries from small entrepreneurs unable to make the necessary investments, especially for drainage. By the mid-sixteenth century all the Austrian monarchy's mines belonged to these capitalists from southern Germany, who had eliminated their Austrian and Hungarian competitors.

Since the end of the fifteenth century there had been a considerable increase in the demand for copper and this led the Fuggers to take an interest in the mines at Banská Bystrica, which were then experiencing technical and financial difficulties. Their marriage links with the Thurzos, who held the greater part of the capital, and the loans granted by Maximilian enabled the Fuggers to take control of copper working and most importantly to establish a real monopoly in the metal. In 1525 they invested 200 000 florins, followed in 1536 by a further 386 000. They increased efficiency and production and like a modern enterprise used waged labour. While the metal obtained was not of the quality for making wire, it was quite adequate for coins and weapons manufacture and as it contained silver its refinement brought some supplementary profits. Destined for the European market, some of the copper was refined at Fuggerau close to Villach in Carinthia and then sold on the market at Venice. It was also sent to Leipzig, Cologne, Frankfurt-am-Main and Nürnberg and also via Cracow to Gdansk, then to Antwerp which until 1570 was the largest outlet for Hungarian copper. The king of Portugal was the principal client who annually exported 5 000 to 6 000 tonnes of metal to his colonies.

In the period 1494–1546, the mines at Banská Bystrica produced in total 74 281 tonnes of copper and 119 tonnes of silver. Between 1526 and 1529 they exported 2 670 tonnes and were able to realize a net profit of more than 1 million florins. After 1546, the date at which the Fuggers withdrew from copper mining, the other Habsburg creditors obtained the monopoly for the working and sale of copper. They too were originally from Upper Germany, like Matthias Manlich, Ulrich Lik and Cie (in 1559) and in 1566 Melchior Manlich and Philipp Welser. At this time the mines were at their peak. They employed 200 waged workers each year, who cost 80 000–

90 000 florins and produced 1 300 tonnes of copper. The decline of Antwerp as a result of the revolt of the Netherlands and the Danish-Swedish war caused serious set-backs. The tariffs of the tolls on the Sund increased, other producers appeared, demand weakened, the price lowered and stocks piled up. Two merchants, Leonard Weiss and Wolfgang Paller, who in 1569 had leased the mines, in 1573 even stopped paying their workers, who then launched a series of violent strikes. Production rose after 1576 but never reached half the level it had been in 1560. In 1599, for the first time, the balance of working showed a deficit. In a century, the mines of Banská Bystrica had produced no less than 135 000 tonnes of copper of which 90 per cent had been exported.

Through the Thurzos, the Fuggers also had control of the mint and the production of gold of the 'Chamber of Kremnica'. Its annual average production in the period 1531–48 was 5.45 tonnes of silver (for 155 000 florins) and 0.245 tonnes of gold (worth 99 000 florins). Of the Central European silver mines under Habsburg authority, those in Upper Hungary were of secondary importance, the foremost being those at Schwatz in the Tyrol where the annual average production was 13 tonnes. The Bohemian mines' output was much more modest, with Jachýmov (Joachimstal), producing 3.5 tonnes and Kutná Hora (Kuttenberg), which reached its peak in the fifteenth century, just 1.7 tonnes.

The radical change took place after 1560 when the production of the Potosí mines in Peru flooded Europe via Spain. Their annual average production in the period 1560–80, was 151 tonnes to which were added 50 tonnes from the Mexican mines. Annually, between 1581 and 1600, Spanish America supplied a total of 330 tonnes of silver. Peruvian silver, which was excavated with the cheap slave labour provided by the *mita*, also profited from the process of amalgamation with mercury, with the result that its price became markedly lower than that of Central European silver. This inability to compete with American exports was the main reason why the Augsburg bankers were ruined and the Central European mines were left with only regional significance.

By contrast, the mercury mines of Idria, in Carniola, saw their importance grow in proportion to world demand, although they competed with the Spanish mines at Almaden for the supply of the American market.[5] The Idrian mines which had been annexed in 1509 by Maximilian I were worked by a company of merchants and nobles (the Auerspergs and Dietrichsteins among others) but in 1525 Ferdinand I granted the sales monopoly to the firm of Höchstetter from Augsburg. After the Höchstetters' bankruptcy in 1528, the monopoly was taken over by more German merchant bankers (Baumgartner, Herwart) until 1574 when the firm Haug and Cie declared bankruptcy. Mercury production retained its importance and was Inner Austria's only material for export. In 1528 annual production had already reached 100 tonnes. In the period 1539–1574 Idria delivered in total 3 350 tonnes valued at 1.1 million florins i.e. the average annual production remained at the level attained in 1528. However, while the producers in 1571 sold 100kg at 24 florins, the firm of Haug pocketed 40 florins per 100kg. For this reason, Ferdinand I's son the archduke Charles, then in charge of the administration of Inner Austria, decided to buy back the mines from their proprietors and to work them directly; it was a kind of 'nationalization' which came into effect in 1575. The archduke hoped that the operation would secure his own financial autonomy and free him from the control of Diets while doubling his own revenue which then did not amount to more than 300 000 florins.

The Austrian historian Helfried Valentinitsch has judged the whole venture a success because production quickly exceeded 140 tonnes; after 1620 the enterprise took advantage of the difficulties experienced by the Spanish mines to increase annual production to 440 tonnes. The sales monopoly was then leased to Italian businessmen and Idrian mercury passed through Venice. After 1594 the Habsburgs were happy to exploit the minerals and conceded to the Venetian merchant banker Bartolomeo Bontempelli del Calice the trade in mercury and cinnabar (a sulphide of mercury) which enabled Bontempelli to become Ferdinand of Styria's principal banker. Even if the prince's apparent profit was much less than that of the leaser, the mercury mines were the only serious guarantee that he could give a creditor and so were a means of procuring credit.

The iron mines of Eisenerz, on the borders of Styria and Lower Austria, were another focus of economic development. In 1561 the opening of a road between the Styrian iron mines and the Danube favoured the development of small-scale metallurgy, an advantage offset by the growing difficulties in the wood supply as the lords refused to exploit their forests rationally. The so-called Catalan forges were abandoned in favour of the construction of high furnaces. Iron production which was left to small entrepreneurs, was still subject to state control and in 1574 Maximilian II created the Chamber of Iron (*Eisenkammer*). Despite the absence of statistics, the impression is that production was at its peak around 1580 and showed a clear decline after 1620. Merchants supplied the miners with provisions and were paid in kind by the *Eisenkammer*. The centre for industrial processing was at Steyr in Lower Austria. About thirty merchants organized in a corporation operated the forges. The smiths were grouped in seven main workshops which attracted many specialists from Upper Germany. In the period 1470–1620, seven to ten new masters were registered annually. Around 1600, Steyr had about a thousand skilled cutlers while Waidhofen made scythes and sickles and Scheibbs specialized in the production of needles. Manufactured goods were traded at Vienna and were exported to Germany, Italy and the Ottoman empire where they competed with hardware dealers from Nürnberg.

Salt production was an important part of the Austrian economy during the modern era. It involved not only the working of the Habsburgs' mines but also the treatment of brine, the exploitation of forests, which were essential for wood supply, transport and marketing. When the lands of the crown of St Wenceslas joined the Austrian monarchy in 1527, the potential market for Austrian salt increased considerably. The only competition within the hereditary lands – and that very slight – came from the salt marshes of the Istrian coast which affected only Carniola.

In 1563 Ferdinand I created at Bad-Ischl in Upper Austria, a common administration (*Salzbergwerk, Salzkammer*) which joined the centres of salt production at Hall, in the Tyrol, Bad-Ausee and Hallstatt in Upper Austria. The extension of production required not only technical innovations but also administrative reforms, which were imposed by decrees in 1524 and 1563. These reforms were initiated by the *Salzkammergut*, the original department intended to provide the fuel necessary for the evaporation of brine extracted from beneath the ground. The reforms also protected the mine workers whose living conditions and supply of provisions were very uncertain. The miners were granted small plots of ground so that they could practise subsistance agriculture but an increase in their wages was out of the question since it would raise production costs and diminish the *Salzkammer*'s profits.

Since the sale of salt was a royal right, Ferdinand established a monopoly in his own interests. 'Salt officials' (*Salzamtmann*) were introduced in the hereditary lands and it was from them that the feudal lords or their agents had to buy salt to re-sell to the peasants. These offices were quickly leased by financiers and the *gabelle* – to use the name of its French counterpart – enabled the Habsburgs to guarantee the loans which they had to underwrite. In Bohemia, however, this monopoly was established only after the orders had been defeated in 1620.

THE GROWTH OF AGRICULTURE

While metal production stabilized before declining slightly in the seventeenth century, the production and export of foodstuffs were in full expansion at the time when the system of exchanges was established; Western Europe provided manufactured goods while Eastern Europe exported foodstuffs to the West where the population was growing rapidly. While Poland concentrated on exporting cereals, Hungary became the great supplier of meat on the European market and like Lower Austria sold wines while Bohemia specialized in beer and fish. This new situation supposed that the terms of exchange henceforth would be to the advantage of Danubian Europe and that more manufactured products could be bought in return for a certain quantity of exported wine or cattle. This development favoured certain specialized productions and so promoted the domain economy. The rise in prices was yet more noticeable in Hungary than on the Viennese market. By 1590 the price of cereals had multiplied six times since the beginning of the century while that of livestock tripled and wine quadrupled in the period 1520–80. By contrast, the price of cloth from Moravia remained unchanged throughout the sixteenth century as did the price of English cloth of comparable quality.

Hungary exported goats and large livestock, most importantly cattle – 200 000 head in 1575 alone. These were not the usual cattle, small in stature and used as draught-animals, but rather a long-horned breed with a grey-white coat. Originally from the steppe, they were different from the cattle widespread in the medieval West. Weighing 400 kg, they were raised on the Great Plain and in Royal Hungary by salaried 'keepers'. The rich peasants of the towns in Turkish Hungary had acquired the pasturage belonging to the deserted villages and little by little modified the rural landscape: while the dwellings were concentrated in the towns (Latin *oppida*), the farms were spread over the Great Plain; the cattle remained outside, even in winter when they were fed on hay and chopped straw, while in summer the grass was as high as they were. The vegetation and the low density of population favoured breeding; an average herd was around 150 head. These were sold at the great fairs at Debrecen or at Pest to merchants who took charge of exporting them to Nürnberg, Augsburg, Frankfurt am Main and Venice. The herds wandered about 20 km a day following the roads where resting places were arranged for them. The chamber of accounts in Vienna leased to a company the trade with Venice, which annually imported 15 000–20 000 Hungarian cattle, a move which provoked storms of protest from Austrian and German merchants but nevertheless guaranteed the Habsburgs a regular supplementary income. Customs rights at the Austro-Hungarian border alone brought them 180 000–200 000 florins. The Viennese butchers bought 50 000 Hungarian cattle a year and Upper Germany almost as much again until the beginning of the Thirty Years War (1618). In the towns the sale of dairy products grew, especially on the Viennese market.

In Hungary, countless fortunes grew through the trade in cattle; in 1542, according to the customs records, the principal exporters were the magnates, the Balassa, the Révay and the Nyáry. Some years later, another group of magnates, the Zays, Bornemiszas and Dobós, formed a company for the livestock trade while the Zrinskis exported cattle to Venice, using the Dalmatian port of Buccari. A fortune could also be made by enterprising commoners such as Szebásztián Thököly, an ennobled merchant from Upper Hungary, who was originally from a family of magnates and had one of the greatest fortunes of the modern era.

The development of viticulture was another source of profit. Two regions of Hungary – Sopron in Transdanubia and Tokay in Upper Hungary – would affirm their supremacy in this field. Tokay, especially its sweet variety, became celebrated in the second half of the sixteenth century because of the special attention paid to it. The vineyard workers were waged and not peasants compelled by the *robot*. The proprietors lived in town. The region of Tokay produced on average 60 000 hl a year of which half was exported to Poland. The vineyards of Sopron supplied 20 000 hl for Bohemia and Silesia at an average price of 10 florins per hectolitre.

According to Vera Zimányi, around 1580 Hungary exported wine worth 500 000 florins, to which were added the 2 million florins from the sale of cattle (200 000 cattle at 10 florins a head). In exchange, Hungary imported textiles (70 per cent of their consumption) from Bohemia, Moravia, Silesia, Lower Austria as well as Austrian hardware and spices from Venice and the Netherlands. The economy in the Austrian monarchy was set up so that while Hungary specialized in providing agricultural products, the other countries, Bohemia and Austria, devoted themselves to manufacture. It would, however, be wrong to describe this as a colonial economy with the Habsburgs exploiting Hungary, as the Hungarians had chosen to specialize in this role which placed them – like the Poles – in a marginal economy.

In Bohemia, sheep-raising was an essential source of revenue since the great flocks provided wool for the textile industry – according to an old Czech saying, a landowner's fortune rested in his forest, ponds and sheep. The lords in the south of Bohemia, a damp and marshy region, dug artificial ponds to raise carp, which came to compete with Baltic herring. For many centuries fish was a national dish and large fortunes were amassed from the sale of fish, for example the wealth of the Hradec and the Rožmberks. By building breweries on their domains, the lords could also use their surplus cereals and realize substantial profits as brewing was a monopoly. Added together, ponds and brewing represented one-third of the manorial revenues, almost as much as the feudal rights.

SOCIAL TENSIONS

It would be just as wrong to imagine that society in Danubian Europe was rigid and fossilized as it would be to imagine that the region had been reduced to a field of ruins, with its inhabitants put to flight by the Turkish and Tartar raids; quite the opposite was the case. In the sixteenth century the unrest which followed upon the wars and the Reformation made possible social advancement which roused nothing but indignation in the wealthy: the traditional social order was overturned. The deterioration in the condition of the peasantry was all the more badly received since it struck at the base of privileges which had been enjoyed since time immemorial. The society of Danubian Europe was deeply conservative and privileged – despite the precariousness of its biological and economic balance – and found itself faced with the enlargement of the state structure and integration into a market economy. Sometimes it reacted violently.

A considerable gulf existed between the great lord and the peasant; the Hungarian rural masses, however, were not an undifferentiated *plebs*, reduced to wretchedness. The villages of Danubian Europe had their own hierarchy and village notables as well as their wretches. As in a Western village at that time, three or four social levels are discernible. At the top was the judge (*Richter*), who represented the lord before the village community, still thriving in Lower Austria (*Taiding*); the judge was charged with the basic tasks of justice and the police. Immediately after him were the labourers possessing, in terms of the feudal dues, at least a taxable half-tenure, one or more teams, livestock, especially cows and pigs, and a house which was probably basic although wooden houses were then being replaced by stone. As proprietors of twenty hectares, labourers could feed a large family by following the system of three-year rotation with one year fallow. The third level was made up of the small independent workers who generally possessed a taxable quarter-tenure, a single team and livestock more modest than that of the labourer. Like the latter, he had to provide harnessed *robot* for his lord. Even so, with twelve hectares, he could survive a normal year; when the harvest was poor through bad weather, he was the first to be affected and had to feed himself from the market at precisely the moment when prices were rising.

The manual labourers were the real proletariat of the rural world but in the sixteenth century they made up only 20 per cent of the village population. They lived in shelters closer to a hut than a real house. In a single room, children, fowl, a goat and cow were crammed together with the labourers' most valued possessions. They were obliged to provide manual *robot* but in Austria they were fed – quite rightly – on days when they worked for the lord. The class of manual labourers grew since it served as a refuge for many labourers who could thus escape taxation; they evaded the state tax because they rented land from the manorial reserve, free of tax contributions.

Finally, the vineyard workers enjoyed a special status: in exchange for the payment of the tithe, they were exempt from other taxes. Viticulture developed further because it enabled the lords and the peasants to grow rich.

While the great revolts of the beginning of the sixteenth century first and foremost betrayed the peasants' discontent in the face of the heavier *robot*, they also strengthened egalitarian aspirations that challenged the feudal system; this was the case in the great peasant revolt of 1514 in Hungary and the Peasants' War (1524–5), which affected not only Germany but also the hereditary lands, Further Austria in particular and also the Tyrol and Upper Austria. Thomas Müntzer's presence in the 'forest villages' at the end of 1524 helped to radicalize the movement and gave it a pronounced revolutionary character. Ferdinand raised 5000 mercenaries who, under the command of Truchsess von Waldburg, crushed the peasant army near Ulm. But in the case of the Tyrolean uprising in 1526, the prince was forced to make some concessions. In 1549 the Hungarian Diet also foreswore turning their peasants into subjects 'attached to the glebe', for want of power to apply these legal dispositions. The *robot*, in the sixteenth century, remained within reasonable limits. In Lower Austria it was limited to thirty days, in Upper Austria to seventeen and in Bohemia to four days a year, while in Hungary it could reach fifty days and in Austria three days of 'royal *robot*' (*Landrobot*) came to be added for the maintenance of roads and most importantly fortifications; in addition there was sometimes an indemnity in kind, in principle paid as compensation for labour dues which the peasant had not provided.

In 1569 Maximilian II, as the legislator, intervened to put a stop to certain tendencies. The state tax grew heavier throughout the century. Needed at first to confront the Turkish threat, then to meet the expenses occasioned by building the Military Frontier (1 million florins a year *c.*1570), the state tax was necessary to clear the debts accumulated by Ferdinand I, which amounted to 10 million florins, or the equivalent of four to five financial years. The Peace of Adrianople, signed in 1568, did not restore the situation that had existed in 1520. The cost of servicing the debt according to the Venetian ambassadors rose to 1.5 million florins, the sum total of Bohemia's tax contribution. Of the 3.5 million florins in gross receipts scarcely 2 million remained and once the emperor had paid for the maintenance of the frontier he had only 1 million florins a year. Each fresh outbreak of the Turkish war signified a considerable additional effort for the subjects of the Austrian monarchy.

In 1542, the labourer paid tax in the form of the hearth tax at the rate of one florin and the poll tax at half a florin; thirty years later this had tripled to reach three florins a year. The pressure increased yet more after 1593, the date of the outbreak of the tax war. The seizure of Győr by the Turks in 1595 occasioned the 'levy of the tenth man' whereby one man in ten was mobilized and the nine others remaining in the village were obliged to pay his equipment and maintenance, i.e three florins each. The following year, the archduke Matthias, having been defeated once again at Mezőkeresztes, had to reassemble an army. On 29 September 1596, the government of Lower Austria then decreed the 'levy of the fifth man', who joined the 'tenth man'. The extraordinary tax contribution was raised to more than ten florins and one peasant in five had to go to Hungary to take part in a war from which he had little chance of returning. Those who did not die of illness (dysentery or malaria) risked being killed by the enemy or ending up on the slave market in Turkey. The 1596 decree provoked considerable discontent which added to the traditional complaints against feudal dues. The peasant revolt fed memories of the Peasants' War and the case of the Swiss. Following the classic scenario, the insurgents organized themselves, elected political leaders from among the labourers and chose former soldiers as military leaders. Addressing the emperor Rudolf at Prague and his brother Matthias at Vienna, they expressed their indignation at seeing the lords, who made loud claims about their military vocation, refusing to leave to wage war in Hungary and sending them in their stead. The most they were prepared to do was to fight at home to defend their own hearth. Despite the violence brought down upon those who were less than wholehearted, the movement was short-lived; the rebels pillaged some castles and were crushed by a cavalry regiment returning from Hungary.

The repression meted out by the orders was very harsh but the archduke Matthias ordered a reduction of the *robot* and the 'levy on the fifth man' was abandoned.

The 1596 revolt in Austria, despite its failure, was significant; the addition of manorial dues and the demands of the state had provoked the anger of the well-to-do elements in rural society whose prosperity had been threatened. The suppression of the revolt and the concessions made by central power at the expense of the needs of the feudal lords were sufficient to restore order. The *robot* remained moderate in Austria. In 1683 when the Turks threatened Vienna anew, the peasants were only mobilized within the framework of the 'royal *robot*' to repair in great haste the town's fortifications.

CHANGES IN SOCIAL STRUCTURE

The burden of taxation imposed by the Habsburgs also affected the orders, or at least the most exposed elements among them. Vienna, which around 1550 had 50 000 inhabitants, was beset by great financial difficulties since there was a decline in its economic activity. Like the 'Saxon towns' in Transylvania, it had lost the Balkan market through the Turkish conquest; the international trade in spices left the Danubian region and Vienna became a regional market. The capitalists of Upper Germany and Italy who had taken control of mine-working also shared with the aristocrats the great trade in livestock. As for the financiers, they enjoyed a privileged status as 'court merchants' (*Hofhandelsmann*) which freed them from taxation and the jurisdiction of the municipal magistrate. According to the agreement of 1542, the municipal magistrate paid 12.5 per cent of the total contribution of Lower Austria since only half of the towns' quota was paid to him and the nineteen other small towns (Krems, Klosterneuburg, Sankt-Pölten, etc.) paid the other half of the fourth order's contribution. After 1529 Vienna was forced to enclose itself within its ramparts for reasons of security and the outlying quarters destroyed at the time of the siege were not really reconstructed since all building activity was concentrated within the compact area taken over by the imperial palaces (the Hofburg, Stallburg, Schweizer Hof), the administrative buildings (chancelleries, the *Landhaus*), the arsenal, churches, some religious houses and above all the palaces of the nobility. From 1551 the number of burgher houses amounted to no more than 800, that is 25 per cent of the total built-up area, the other 75 per cent being filled by buildings exempt from charges.

Vienna ran into debt during the reign of Frederick III and after 1529 spent 300 000 florins strengthening and modernizing the fortifications and doubling the old medieval walls of the bastions built in the Italian way which alone were capable of resisting effectively the bombardments of siege artillery. These expenses entailed heavy taxation on the houses of burghers with the estimated value of the building determining the level of tax – 3–4 kreuzers a florin or 5–6.5 per cent of the capital value – which reduced to nil the profit which landlords could derive from their properties. Down-hearted, a number of burghers claimed it was better to rent lodgings than to be a property owner in Vienna. They also had to contend with the ploys of the *Hofquartiermeisteramt*, the office in charge of lodging the court which requisitioned the finest apartments to lodge diplomats and officers.

In a more general way, the privileged towns where the guilds practised a Malthusian policy did not attract industry as much as the manorial towns and the large domains, where the artisans escaped tax and the strict control of the guilds, with the result that these small towns and villages produced cloth at a better price.

The lesser nobility seems to have experienced a relative decline which benefited the great aristocrats who concentrated profits in their own hands. According to Gindely, the orders had been severely affected by the Habsburgs' tax policy. In the period 1527–66 they paid a tax on their fortune (*Vermögensteuer*): 1.2 per cent of capital or 24 per cent of revenue supposing that the average annual yield on landed capital was 5 per cent. The nobility managed since their properties were so undervalued that thay in fact paid only 12–15 per cent. But as this tax essentially affected rent from landed property, the lesser nobility, as well as the large proprietors who managed their lands badly or were content to rent them out, were very severely affected and were driven into debt. After 1550 numerous nobles who were unable to pay the tax were threatened with foreclosure. On six occasions between 1567 and 1592 they had to pay only a very moderate tax on their property but with the resumption of the Turkish War in 1593 this was raised to 15 per cent of the revenue from land rent.

The number of medium-sized properties (those with fewer than 100 tenants) declined from 1557 to 1620 and fell in Bohemia from 18 per cent to 16 per cent of the land being worked; however, large properties of more than 900 tenants rose from 25 per cent in 1557 to 42 per cent in 1620. Many impoverished country gentlemen took refuge in the towns while enriched commoners grabbed their lands; 300 new families, 120 of whom were of German origin, were admitted into the *Ritterstand*, which hides the third order's real decline. These new members were royal officers, doctors, lawyers and artists.

In Bohemia the order of lords strengthened its pre-eminence. In 1605 it possessed 45 per cent of the land under cultivation. In 1557 it consisted of 184 families and by 1605, the number had risen to 197. The old houses had died out (for example the Rožemberks and the Neuhaus) but the order renewed itself by admitting enriched knights such as the Trčka, Czernin, Kinský, Kollowrat, Kaunitz and Thurn families. In total, 53 families benefited from such a promotion and so secured confirmation of their rise into the heart of the Bohemian nobility which thus underwent considerable renewal in the course of the sixteenth century. The order itself was dominated by eleven houses (including the Lobkowitz family) who among them possessed 25 per cent of the lands of Bohemia while the king had just 10 per cent and the clergy 5 per cent.

The lesser nobles showed their uneasiness and discontent in 1547 when they joined the royal towns and rejected Ferdinand I's request for assistance against the Smalkaldic League, deciding instead to raise their own army to aid the Protestant princes who were in revolt against the emperor. When the elector of Saxony and the landgrave of Hesse were defeated at Mühlberg by the Habsburg army, the orders once again found themselves faced with a triumphant king. The rebel towns lost their privileges, thirty-five lords and knights were tried for treason and ten were condemned to death while the rest were punished with heavy confiscations. It was a general rehearsal of the great revolt in 1618, which ended in the disaster at the Battle of the White Mountain (1620).[6]

In Hungary the order of lords was renewed and reinforced but not to the detriment of the lesser nobility which was much stronger in number than in Bohemia, amounting to 3–4 per cent of the total population – 8 000–9 000 families possessing only a single tenure and 90 per cent having less than 150. Above the lesser nobility came the class of great landed proprietors. In 1580, just 28 per cent of lords owned among them 41 per cent of the land of Royal Hungary. The royal domain did not amount to more than 5 per cent of the land and the Catholic Church held just 0.2 per cent while twenty-two aristocratic families (including the Thurzos, Báthorys and Töröks) shared 27 per cent of the cultivable land, the rest having to be content with 52 per cent among them. The magnates, however, had grown rich not at the expense of the lesser nobles but of the royal domain and the lands belonging to the clergy. In 1526 and 1527 Ferdinand I had liberally distributed crown lands to secure support and had then surrendered to the magnates lands which were already mortgaged to pay for supplies for the royal army. This policy continued until the end of the sixteenth century. In Hungary, in marked contrast to what happened in Bohemia, the Turkish War, rather than costing the nobility money, brought them wealth. Zsigmond Rákóczy (acquired for 240 000 florins paid in several instalments) the domain at Munkács, which in 1588 yielded 120 000 florins; he had acquired it at one tenth of its value.

Some magnates used their colossal profits to acquire valuable objects. In 1580 Kristóf Báthory owned 250 kg of silver goods. The inventory of the Dobo family made in 1612 records a treasury of 120 000 florins in gold pieces in sacks and silver.

Impoverished nobles could find a lucrative situation employed in a magnate's private army and living amid the dangers of the Military Frontier like the peasants who fled the condition of serfdom on the manorial domain. They were all considered nobles and received land and formed a new social stratum. The Turkish war and the system existing in the Military Frontier both served to ease social claims. When the orders wanted to contest their privileges, these '*hajduks*' (free soldiers) supplied the great battalions for István Bocskai's revolt which first and foremost was political and religious in character.

The society of the Danubian lands, not only because of the Turkish wars and religious conflicts but also because of its integration into the 'world economy', presented opportunities for those prepared to take risks; it also helped to crush the middle strata and to increase the power of several hundred aristocrats who in many cases had been only recently promoted. Difficult to curtail, these changes help to explain the peculiar features of the baroque world so characteristic of the Habsburg Empire.

NOTES AND REFERENCES

1. Fernand Braudel, *Civilisation matérielle et Capitalisme*, 3 vols, Paris, 1979.
2. A.-F. Pribram and R. Geyer, *Materialien zur Geschichte der Löhne und Preise in Œsterreich*, Vienna, 1938, pp. 269–71. M.J. Elsas, *Umrisseiner Geschichte der Preise und Löhne in Deutschland vom ausgehenden Mittelalter bis zum Beginn des neunzehnjahrhunderts*, Leiden, 1936, pp. 462–5.
3. István Hunyadi, *Recherches sur la démographie et les structures sociales du comitat de Györ*, doctoral thesis, Strassburg, 1971.
4. Vera Zimányi, *Economy and Society in 16th and 17th Century Hungary (1526–1650)*, Budapest, Studia Historica 188, 1987.
5. Hellfried Valentinitsch, *Das landesfürstliche Quecksilbergwerk Idria 1575–1659*, Graz, 1981.
6. Winfried Eberhard, *Monarchie und Widerstand: Zur Ständischen Oppositionsbildung in Herrschaftsystem Ferdinands I. in Bohmen*, Munich, 1985.

CHAPTER SEVENTEEN

Philip II, Head of the House of Habsburg (1556–98)

The House of Austria had come to regard the Danubian lands as a marginal domain despite the region's evident vitality. For Ferdinand, the imperial crown carried an element of prestige but in reality the affairs of the Reich brought him more worries than genuine assistance in the fight against the Ottomans.

Charles V's abdication in 1556 confirmed this situation, formally disassociating the Habsburgs' German patrimony from their Atlantic and Mediterranean domains which were a source of genuine wealth, power and glory. This was why the old emperor, embittered, down-hearted, and ailing made his only son head of the House of Austria; had it not been for the unbending opposition of his family – Ferdinand and Maria of Hungary in particular – backed by German opinion, Charles V would have made his son head of the Holy Roman Empire. He had envisaged a clever alternation: Ferdinand emperor, then Philip II, to be succeeded by Ferdinand's son Maximilian II, then Philip's son, Philip III.

The Estates of the Empire had learnt from their experiences since 1519 to expect nothing from a Castilian emperor; they had warded off a foreign candidate in favour of the late emperor's grandson and the new emperor had proved to be no less a stranger to the Empire than the king of France, Francis I, would have been. It was no secret in Germany that Philip, like his father, nurtured dreams of universal monarchy, a costly utopia which the princes of the Empire did not find at all an attractive proposition. How would the ultra-Catholic faction have reacted to the Peace of Augsburg? It was well known that the Spanish *infante* cherished another dream – to erase heresy and so to restore the unity of Christendom which had been so decisively shattered since the dramatic exchange in 1521 between his father and Martin Luther at Worms.

Philip II's accession marked a further distribution of responsibilities within the House of Austria, with Ferdinand and the cadet branch holding the less substantial part of the patrimony. The notion of 'the House' – or as was said at the time *Casa d'Austria* – remained unshaken, with every archduke and archduchess obliged to add to the glory and grandeur of the Habsburgs either by marriage or by employment in the service of one or

210

other branch. The year 1556 did not mark the creation of a Spanish dynasty. The Habsburgs never felt themselves attached to one nation more than another, even though they were readily identified with the Castilian nation. They persisted in believing that they were a line superior to the rest of humankind by reason of divine election and they possessed their own rules, their own ethic. The House of Austria had to obey its head, who acted as cast director, distributing the parts in the higher interest of the dynasty. This outlook vexed Philip II's relations, as king of Spain, with his relatives in Danubian Europe. Developments at Madrid must be kept in view until the extinction of the Spanish branch of the Habsburgs in 1700, for it was Madrid that often imposed marriage arrangements, including those between blood relatives, that determined the direction of confessional policy, proposed alliances and sometimes gave material aid to its Viennese poor relative in order to attain the ends hoped for by both capitals.[1]

The German branch was not a 'satellite' of Madrid in the sense in which the term is used in current international relations. The very existence of a 'Spanish party' in the emperor's Privy Council clearly shows that voting was not unanimously in Madrid's interests and that the interests of the House of Austria and those of the Spanish monarchy were not always identifed as one and the same. The Spanish empire has already received masterly treatment from other historians; the present concern of this book is relations between the 'cautious' king and his Central European relatives. These relations remained strictly familial because the Holy Roman Empire, which had been at peace since the religious compromise of 1555, in the latter half of the sixteenth century studiously steered clear of the European conflicts that so troubled Spain, France, the Netherlands and England.

THE CAUTIOUS KING: PHILIP II (1527–98)[2]

Born in Spain of a Portugese mother and a 'Burgundian' father, Philip II (in marked contrast to his father) by temperament and education rapidly became Castilian. The abdication ceremonies at Brussels in 1556 set in relief the difference between father and son. Charles V, while prematurely aged, was still able to speak Flemish and identified with the great lords of the southern Netherlands, the Croÿs, Horns, Egmonts, and Nassaus, lovers of feasts, tournaments and the ceremonies and festivities of the court. The *infante* had adopted the black dress of his new subjects with only the collar of the order of the Golden Fleece for relief. This black dress set the tone for the European aristocracy for almost a century; to adopt it was to recognize the ideals of the Spanish monarchy, while to reject it, as the French and English courts did, was to display one's independence.

Philip II was a cautious man, stiff, proud and ill at ease with those to

211

whom he spoke, a type which his Flemish subjects neither liked nor understood. His moral rigour and obstinacy helped to nourish the black legend to which his memory has been victim, especially in the era of Romanticism; Verdi's *Don Carlos* (based on Schiller's work) clearly reflects current opinion, which saw Philip II as an insensitive monster, the slave of *raison d'état* with a thirst for power that did not spare his rebellious subjects, heretics and those close to him. In short, he had been presented as a bloody tyrant who channelled all his power into the service of religious fanaticism and Spanish imperialism. This legend, born in England amid an atmosphere of national conflict and nourished in the Netherlands where his rebellious subjects had reason to hate him, was expanded in the age of the Enlightenment – Goethe's play *Egmont* – and reached its peak in the age of liberalism: the Italians of the *Risorgimento* saw prefigured in Philip II the police tyranny exercised by Francis-Joseph in Milan and Venice in the neo-absolutist era (1849–59).

Such a portrait is both exaggerated and unjust and, it must be added, the name 'the cautious king' is only a partial reflection of the truth; in the 1580s he gave proof of his dynamism when he engaged in the affair of the Portuguese succession and especially in 1588 when he launched the Invincible Armada in the assault against England and Elizabeth I.

Philip II held his father in such great respect that he wanted to continue his work in all directions. But when emulating him, he acted more as his imitator than his real successor. He magnified his father's faults without having the human qualities which would have brought him popular support or endeared him to the aristocracy. Unlike his ancestors Rudolf and Maximilian, he was without any instinct for self-promotion and did not have his Burgundian forefather's taste for feasts and ceremonials; in contrast to Charles V his habits were austere and his tastes frugal.

Charles V had had a decided predilection for Madrid and had wanted to turn the small town into his capital; Philip II abandoned Valladolid and established Madrid as the centre of the Castilian state and the Spanish empire. Charles V had always dreamt of reforming the Church on the lines proposed by Erasmus (eradication of abuses, respect for dogma and traditional ritual); Philip struggled to defend traditional Catholicism, even to the point of opposing the innovations that the Holy See thought necessary. Charles V had wanted to make his universal monarchy governable; his son, whose Empire was now reduced – if that's the word – to the Iberian peninsula, America, the Netherlands and the possessions in Italy (Milan, Sicily, Naples, Sardinia and fortified posts in Tuscany), organized a centralized monarchy for the first time in the history of the Habsburgs. Whereas his father and Maximilian I became 'itinerant' sovereigns and so remained close to their people and directed their soldiers in battle, Philip II all but renounced travelling after 1559; after concluding the Peace of Cateau-Cambrésis with France, at the age of thirty-two he returned to the Iberian peninsula and made no more than short journeys within his kingdom, abandoning north-west Europe, where the destiny of his House was being enacted. His Flemish subjects felt that the Netherlands were no longer to be the heart of the monarchy but rather were to become a dependency and, according to contemporary satire, 'the Spanish milch-cow'. Their wealth, they claimed, had served to finance the imperial enterprises of their ruler. Even if this was a mistaken idea, it was certainly a disturbing one and Philip II despite renewed promises no longer travelled to Ghent and Brussels. For forty years he decided to direct everything from his Castilian residence. In 1580 cardinal Granvelle, his father's old Burgundian adviser, suggested that in order to give a pronounced Atlantic character to his monarchy, he should establish his residence at Lisbon, the capital of Portugal which he had but lately annexed. After a brief visit, the king preferred to return to the Escorial, which was more in keeping with his taste for solitude than the Portuguese capital.

THE ESCORIAL

There is no better symbol of Philip II's personality than the Escorial; erected at the foot of the mountains on the Castilian plain with its extremes of climate – scorching hot in summer, freezing cold in winter – this magnificent and austere residence was erected at the behest of the new king. Its plan was as symbolic as it was functional; it was a grid reminiscent of the grill on which had been tortured St Laurence, the martyr of the primitive Spanish Church for whom Philip II had a particular devotion. It was on the feast of St Laurence (10 August 1557) that the *tercios* had crushed the French army at Saint-Quentin in Picardy – the decisive victory that opened the way for the settlement, to Spain's advantage, of the seemingly interminable Valois-Habsburg conflict, the century of 'Spanish preponderance',[3] and the signing of the Peace of Cateau-Cambrésis.

The Escorial had many functions. It was first of all a mausoleum where Philip arranged the burial of Charles V, with provision for the other Spanish Habsburgs. It was also a monastery to which he invited the Hieronymites, a congregation of Augustinians, which was well established in Spain and had been favoured by Charles V. The building's central monument was the basilica and the royal residence was arranged so that Philip could see the main altar from his chamber. Alongside the king's apartments, the architect had planned offices and a library, but the modest character of the monarch's office comes as a surprise.

The 'cautious king' had inaugurated a new form of government, a way of managing affairs through a bureaucracy, a development made possible by the spread of literacy and the relative security of communication routes. Very conscious of the importance of written documents and personal testimonies, he ordered – much to the delight of historians – the creation of a central deposit of archives at Simancas.

He perfected the collegiate system introduced by the Catholic kings and later by the Burgundian sovereigns. He attached to the council of Castile a council for each part of his Empire – a council of the Indies, a council for Italy, a council for Flanders – surmounted by a council of state in charge of policy and a council of finance (*consejo de hacienda*). This system was almost identical to the one established more or less successfully by Maximilian I, then by Ferdinand I. Each council was made up of ten to twelve persons recruited either from the nobility or from among the graduates of the university of Salamanca (*letrados*). Discussion was free and criticism permitted but an essential difference from French practice was that the king did not assist in person at the council's deliberation and was content to sanction the written conclusions by a *yo el Rey* (I, the King) which was final and without appeal but not immediate in effect. The time taken to reach a decision might pass for caution but it was generally due only to delays in examining dossiers or still worse, the monarch's irresolution.

The reading of dispatches and of reports and the oral deliberations of the councils represented a crushing burden of work which entailed a total change in the kind of life led by the administrative head of the monarchy. This regular work considerably limited the time that the sovereign spent on the pleasures which, until late, had taken up the best part of his day. The king, as the 'first gentleman', was expected to live 'nobly', i.e. to do nothing. Philip II, however, agreed only occasionally to go hunting and his rare free moments were spent in religious devotions and with his family. The 'master of the world' lived like a patrician, engrossed in his dossiers without contact with his vassals; gone were the festivals of the Burgundian court and the interminable peregrinations of his father. The results were not equal to the efforts involved, however, for the system suffered from two failings – the slowness of the bureaucratic machine and the temperament of the king.

The transmission of news was surprisingly slow despite the presence of loyal agents in the different countries of the monarchy, competent informers abroad (the Spanish intelligence service was, with the Venetian, the best in Europe) and a high calibre of diplomatic representatives. While Brussels was positioned in the centre of the European postal system, Madrid was all the more remote because couriers, for reasons of security, avoided the most direct routes (i.e. across France or the sea-voyage from Flanders to Galicia), passing instead through Barcelona, Genoa and Milan. North-west Europe, where the most serious events were taking place, was therefore many weeks from the centre of decision-making. Besides, the system of councils, which guaranteed a certain impartiality, did not favour swift decision-making.

Philip II was afflicted with the Habsburgs' lack of resolution that had so hindered Charles V and was also evident in the Viennese branch of the family. Moreover, Philip stuck firmly to his resolutions from the moment he had settled upon a line of policy. Lacking confidence in his own ability to make decisions, he was too proud and too imbued with a sense of personal mission to consult advisers other than when he consulted clerics who would see the problem from a moral or theological standpoint. A man of great kindness – contrary to the assertions of the black legend – he was reluctant to withdraw his confidence from those he had chosen to work with him.

THE PORTUGUESE MARRIAGE

In 1543 Charles V had married his only son Philip at the age of sixteen to his first cousin, Maria, the Portuguese *infanta*. From this union, which lasted only five years, was born don Carlos, who brought his father more worries than joys in the years before his tragic death in 1568 at the age of twenty-three.

The royal House of Portugal was not very prolific and in 1578 there arose the question of succession. The last heir of the dynasty, don Sebastian, had undertaken a crusade against the Moroccans and was killed at the head of his troops in the Battle of Alczarquivir (Ksar el-Kébir) in Morocco. This was no less a disaster for Portugal than the Battle of Mohács had been for Hungary. The nobility was decimated, the army destroyed, the young king dead without a child. The only heir was the cardinal Henry of Portugal who reigned, 1578–80. Following the cardinal's death, the duke of Alba advised the 'cautious king' to make good his rights to the Portuguese crown, rights which he held through his mother and wife. Most of the Portuguese gave their support to Philip as a candidate while a small number supported Dom Antonio (the prior of Crato and illegitimate son of cardinal Henry's brother, Luis). An energetic campaign conducted by the duke of Alba and accompanied by the guarantee of the Portuguese Cortes entailed the fall of Lisbon and the rallying of the colonial empire. Portugal, in return for submission to the Habsburgs, benefited from a regime of personal union; even the council of Portugal which sat beside the sovereign had to be made up of Portuguese.

Both parties benefited from the arrangement. The Habsburgs placed under their authority the Portuguese colonies and trading stations in Asia, Africa and America; they thus had control of the entire world economy, the production of precious metals and the lucrative trade in spices, and put together the most powerful war fleet and merchant army. The Portuguese for their part had easier access to the American silver which they needed to pay for their purchases in the Far East; they still purchased more oriental goods than they sold European products and settled the deficit in their balance of payments with the massive export of precious metals. In addition, Philip II for the first time realized an old dream – the unification of the Iberian peninsula under one crown.

THE ENGLISH MARRIAGE

Philip II's second marriage was to another of his cousins, Mary I of England (Mary Tudor), and failed to bring him complete mastery of the sea. The daughter of Henry VIII and Catharine of Aragón, and so a first cousin – and at one time the betrothed – of Charles V, Mary had remained a loyal Catholic, like her mother. After her father had divorced his Aragonese first wife, Mary had experienced many difficult years. When she ascended the English throne in 1552, following the death of her half-brother Edward VI, she believed that the hour had come for her to take revenge and to re-establish Catholicism with the support of the numerous English who secretly had remained true to the faith of their fathers. Her reign was a brutal reaction to the innovations of the previous two kings and Mary I remains in the English collective consciousness as 'bloody Mary'. In 1554 she married Philip II, thereby renewing the old Anglo-Burgundian alliance. Her husband seems to have counselled moderation and caution – advice which, as Foxe's *Book of Martyrs* testifies, she chose to ignore. Philip made two visits to England – in 1554–5 and again in 1557 – but remained a stranger to his new subjects, who were afraid that their country might lose its identity. Philip involved England in the war against France and it was England that had to pay the price at the time of the negotiations at Cateau-Cambrésis, losing for ever Calais, its last bridgehead on the continent which the English had occupied for two centuries. Mary's death in 1558 put an end to their brief and sterile union. Elizabeth, the daughter of Henry VIII and Anne Boleyn, succeeded her half-sister. In order to save the Anglo-Spanish union, Philip II asked for Elizabeth's hand despite her Protestant upbringing, but the young queen declined, much to the relief of the 'cautious king'.

Philip was indeed cautious or prudent in his policy towards England: he waited thirty years before launching his ambitious campaign of conquest, the expedition of the Invincible Armada which counts among the most spectacular failures of his reign. The former allies would henceforth be divided in every respect, by their economic interests, their religious and patriotic loyalties.

The Catholics questioned the legitimacy of Elizabeth I as they did not recognize Henry VIII's divorce and still less his marriage to Anne Boleyn; in their eyes, the queen of England was quite simply illegitimate. Elizabeth I, with Parliament's complicity, renewed her father's religious policy, re-establishing the Act of Supremacy which made the sovereign the temporal head of the Church of England. With the new bishops' agreement, she reintroduced the *Book of Common Prayer*, which had a pronounced Protestant character. A substantial minority, however, remained loyal to Rome and the traditional religion, particularly in the north which was dominated by Catholic lords. While the Holy See remained hopeful, the period 1560–70 enabled the Anglican Church to grow in strength, its moderate position satisfying the mass of the faithful. Philip II also refused to get involved; even when the northern earls revolted in 1569, he rejected the duke of Alba's proposal that he should set out for England. He also possessed an objective ally in the person of Mary queen of Scots who, through her grandmother, had rights to the English crown. When pope Pius V excommunicated the queen of England, Philip and Elizabeth were thrown into opposing camps, not least because the queen discreetly supported the Dutch rebels in their revolt against the Spanish *tercios*.

The English resented Spain's colonial monopoly. Elizabeth supported the first English settlements in North America – Virginia was founded in 1584 – and at the same time turned a blind eye to the piratical ventures which were far more lucrative in the immediate future than colonial settlements, which required heavy investment. She even gave financial support to the adventurers from the south of England – Hawkins and Francis Drake – who sacked the American ports, captured the Spanish galleons filled with silver and so wrecked the security of the Caribbean. When the Spanish ambassador presented his master's complaints, the queen refused to denounce her sailors, let alone order their capture, and discreetly pocketed the proceeds.

Philip II then decided to put into action a plan worked out by Alexander Farnese, the governor of the Netherlands, to bear down on England from the Flemish coast, to conquer and annex it. The execution in 1587 of Mary queen of Scots, who had fled to England, served to make up Philip's mind as he was now the Catholic candidate with the most rights to Elizabeth's throne. He based his claims on his descent from Edward III (reigned 1327–77); the House of Lancaster and the House of York (which died out with Richard III in 1485) stemmed from Edward III's first and third marriages respectively; Edward III's fourth son, John of Gaunt (1340–99) had married Constance of Castile and their daughter Catherine was the grandmother of Isabella the Catholic, who was the great-grandmother of Philip II. Genealogy thus provided him with a somewhat tenuous argument for claiming the English crown. The English Catholics, though, were too conscious of their national identity to accept integration into the Habsburg monarchy and to play traitors by helping the Spanish to land. The king of Spain managed to put them in an impossible situation and the papists, although as patriotic as their fellow citizens, were suspect traitors in the eyes of the non-Catholic English.

The fate of the Invincible Armada was sealed in a few weeks in August 1588.[4] The superiority of the English galleon, so much swifter and easier to manoeuvre than its cumbrous Spanish counterpart, the superiority of the English naval artillery and the expertise of Elizabeth I's sailors and admirals, who limited themselves to a tactic of harassment, combined to inflict a series of defeats on Philip II's enormous fleet as soon as it entered the Channel. By the time the Armada reached the English Channel it was already in a difficult position. Moreover the invasion army, which was to have crossed the North Sea under its protection to disembark at Margate, was not ready. A storm effected the rest. Philip II's handsome ships, already severely damaged, did not find a port where they could shelter and be repaired and headed north to sail round Scotland and return to Galicia via the Irish Sea. It was a lamentable fiasco and many galleons sank on the reefs off the Orkneys or off the county of Donegal. Philip II, resigned not to say fatalistic, pardoned the commander-in-chief, the duke of Medina Sidonia, and was convinced that God did not favour the enterprise. The Spanish defeat, however, had great repercussions in Europe and confirmed the superiority of the English navy. Philip II prepared a fresh expedition but the reconstructed fleet never left the Iberian ports.

THE FRENCH MARRIAGE

Philip II's third marriage, this time to Elizabeth of Valois, provided him with claims to the French throne after the defeat of the Invincible Armada. After Elizabeth I had declined his offer of marriage at the beginning of 1559, Philip II had been happy to rally to the suggestion of the king of France, Henry II, who wanted to set the seal on the reconciliation between their two Houses by giving his daughter Elizabeth in marriage to Philip II.

The union was short-lived – less than ten years – and the young queen died at the age of twenty-three in 1568 after giving birth to a daughter, the *infanta* Isabella-Clara-Eugenia,[5] who was the consolation of the cautious king's old age. Gentle, pious and intelligent, the young *infanta* appears to have inherited her mother's qualities and brought the ageing sovereign, weighed down with care and sorrow, the human warmth which the Escorial had always lacked. Philip II wanted to secure a brilliant destiny for his daughter by procuring for her the crown of France.

The death of the duke of Alençon-Anjou, Henry II's last son, in 1584 had urgently raised the question of the Valois succession; Henry III did not have a child and his legitimate heir, according to the fundamental laws of the kingdom, was his brother-in-law, Henry of Navarre, head of the reformed party in France. The Catholics could not accept a Calvinist king – indeed to do so would be contrary to those very same fundamental laws. They were divided among themselves: the most fanatical formed the Holy League, which was led by the duke of Guise (known as le Balafré) and his brother, the cardinal of Lorraine. The Paris rebellion, the assassination of the Guises, then that of Henry III, in 1589 hastened in a dramatic fashion the problem of the succession. Philip II, who supported the members of the League militarily and financially, proposed as a candidate the *infanta* Isabella, who was, after all, the granddaughter of Henry II. However, her candidacy was contrary to another fundamental law, the Salic law, which had been introduced by French legal experts expressly to prevent the crown from falling into the hands of foreigners, as the crown might then be transferred if the queen took a foreign husband. As in the English affair, Philip II evidently had at his disposal more than arguments; the members of the League terrorized Paris while the army of the Netherlands (commanded by Alexander Farnese) had invaded France and held Henry of Navarre in check. The conversion of Henry at Saint-Denis in 1593 made it easier for the moderate Catholics, the *bons Français*, who did not wish to fall under Habsburg tutelage, to rally to him. The *infanta* Isabella remained at the Escorial until 1598.[6]

THE AUSTRIAN MARRIAGE

At his fourth wedding, in 1570, Philip II married his niece, the archduchess Anne, daughter of his sister Maria and the emperor Maximilian, who had earlier been intended for don Carlos. The latter's tragic death in 1568, the death in the same year of Elizabeth of Valois and the imperial need to have male heirs, all provoked this union of immediate blood relatives which the Church would not have countenanced among ordinary mortals. The marriage certainly tightened links with Vienna but initiated a foolish practice that would become more frequent in the sixteenth century culminating with a veritable disaster in the person of Charles II of Spain.

In 1578 queen Anne gave birth to the future Philip III, who in 1598 ascended the Spanish throne at the age of twenty.[7] When in 1617 the problem of who should succeed the emperor Matthias was raised, his father's Austrian marriage enabled Philip III to put forward his claim to the imperial crown and the patrimony of the German branch and so he was in a better position to negotiate a deal with the archduke Ferdinand of Styria and to obtain the cession of Alsace in exchange for a global renunciation; this was the treaty of Oñate (1617) which never came into effect, but was nevertheless sufficient to disquiet Richelieu and to give rise once more to the fear that France would be encircled by the House of Austria.

EMPLOYING THE FAMILY

The Habsburgs, unlike the Valois, who always distrusted their relatives and thought of them as subjects, did not hesitate to entrust important tasks to all members of the ruling House, whether legitimate or illegitimate. While still very young, don Philip, the Spanish *infante* and future Philip II, had represented his father in Castile while Charles V dedicated himself to German affairs. The Netherlands also demanded the permanent presence of a member of the House of Austria and in 1559 Philip II called upon the services of his half-sister Margaret of Parma, appointing her governor of the Netherlands, a position which had previously been held to everyone's satisfaction by her great-aunt, Margaret of Austria (1507–30) and then by her aunt Maria of Hungary, widow of Louis II Jagiellon (1531–58). The daughter of Charles V and a burgher woman from Ghent, Margaret of Parma was the widow of Ottavio duke of Parma, a bastard son of pope Paul III Farnese, and was the mother of Alexander Farnese. Endowed with undeniable political talents, handsome and cultured, she was responsible for a highly important political mission. Ghent-born, she understood the Flemish and tried to direct a conciliatory policy that did not preclude firmness when dealing with the arrogant Netherland aristocracy.

Surprised by the revolt of the 'Gueux' in 1566 and especially by the outburst of iconoclasm in the southern provinces, Margaret endeavoured to preserve the core while yet making some concessions to the Calvinists. For this she was denounced by Philip II who by temperament was intransigent in confessional matters. The king supported the policy of repression proposed by the duke of Alba and sent the duke to the Netherlands to re-establish order in a bloody fashion. Margaret withdrew after the arrival of the Spanish troops, leaving the duke of Alba entirely responsible for the acts of violence of which she so greatly disapproved.

Philip II also used the services of his half-brother, don John of Austria,[8] another bastard of Charles V whose talents lay in the military field. His most shining victory was the battle of Lepanto,[9] where he commanded the fleet of the Holy League – regrouping the galleys of Naples, Sicily, Genoa, Venice, Malta and those of the pope and the king of Spain. Despite difficult relations with the other admirals, especially the irascible Sebastiano Venier, future doge of Venice, on 8 October 1571 he was able to lead the Christian armada to victory, taking part in person in the assault on the chief Turkish galley. The adulation which don John received on his return offended Philip II but the king of Spain did not hesitate to make use of him once again in the Netherlands when the duke of Alba was relieved of his command in 1573, the excessive repression having pushed even the Habsburgs' most loyal subjects into the rebels' camp. In 1576, don John received both the command of the army and the government of the Netherlands with the precise mission of re-establishing the rule of law. His ambitions – to conquer England, marry Mary queen of Scots and to rule over a Catholic Great Britain – were foolish and contrary to the much more modest plans of Philip II, held in check by the 1575 bankruptcy; the re-establishment of peace in Flanders came at the expense of a general amnesty and a total withdrawal of the Spanish army. Don John achieved some military success and pursued a policy as harsh as that of his predecessors, Alba and Requesens. His death in 1578 did not greatly grieve his half-brother, Philip II.

At this juncture, Philip wanted to recall Margaret of Parma to show the Netherlands that he was prepared to make a fresh start, but in the end he sent Alexander Farnese, Margaret's son and his nephew. Farnese proved to be one of the best captains of his day and directed a coherent policy which relied on the Catholics of the southern provinces. Devoted to their religion above all else, these Catholics remained loyal to the Habsburgs as protection against the excesses of the Flemish and Dutch Calvinists. Through his military successes, in particular the taking of Antwerp in 1585, Alexander Farnese was able to secure a lasting reconquest of the southern Netherlands, but it was too late to crush the rebels in their bastions of Holland and Zeeland. At the time of his death, the division of the Netherlands was an accomplished fact. As for his campaigns against Henry IV, they led to brilliant tactical successes but without any real consequences. He was the originator of the expedition of the Invincible Armada as he was convinced that he would be able to triumph over the Dutch Calvinists only after they had been deprived of English support.

FAMILY DIFFICULTIES

It would be wrong to suppose that all the Habsburgs shared Philip II's political and religious ideas, his intransigent Catholicism, his dreams of an absolute monarchy and his imperialist programme.

Philip's eldest son, don Carlos (1545–68), was mentally and emotionally unstable, probably because he had been born from a series of marriages between blood relatives with the House of Portugal. He proved to be violent, anti-social and with homosexual tendencies and his father wondered whether he might not be obliged to alter the line of succession. The conflict between father and son became acute at the time of the revolt of the Netherlands, when don Carlos laid claim to the government there in order to direct a policy of appeasement contrary to that defined by the duke of Alba and approved by the king. Don Carlos did not hide his ambitions nor the hatred which he felt for his father. The king, stretched to the limit, after much hesitation, proceeded to arrest the *infante* and handed him over to ordinary justice 'for the service of Our Lord and for the public good'. The trial never took place, for on 24 July 1568 the young man died, exhausted by a series of hunger strikes and medical treatments. Philip II walled himself up in silence, as he was deeply affected by this tragic turn of events. The commentators lost no time as his son's death seemed suspicious to contemporaries, who had been surprised by the harshness with which a Spanish *infante* had been treated. Rumours of poisoning on the orders of the king began to circulate and were evidently taken up by William the Silent, the leader of the Dutch rebels, in his *Apologia* of 1581. These rumours formed a major part of the black legend of Philip II.

Philip II's relations with Maximilian II, his first cousin, brother-in-law and future father-in-law, were also very difficult. The archduke Maximilian was Charles V's favourite relative. The son of Ferdinand I and Anna Jagiellon, and eldest of a family of fifteen children, he received an education full of contradictions; destined to reign one day in Bohemia, during his childhood he had a Czech entourage that brought him into contact with the Hussite revolution and the Utraquist tradition. At fourteen, he took part in the battle at Mühlberg when the Smalkaldic League was defeated by the imperial troops (1547), and stayed in Castile, where the dry climate was more to his liking. He could not tolerate the haughtiness of the Spanish grandees nor their combative and crusading Catholicism; consequently he was nostalgic for his childhood spent at Innsbruck. On his return from Spain, he immersed himself in Luther's Bible which had belonged to the elector of Saxony, defeated at Mühlberg. When pressed by the apostolic nuncio, he replied, 'I am neither Catholic nor Protestant, I am Christian'. This openness of spirit pleased Charles V, who showed as much affection for Maximilian as he did for his son Philip, because through his nephew he could relive the passions of his own youth. As extrovert as Philip was introvert, Maximilian lived life to the full, relishing the company of lively women. Charles V wanted to draw him closer and arranged for him to marry his daughter Maria. Their marriage, whether happy or not, was certainly consummated and resulted in many children.

The young archduke's religious ideas led him into conflict with his father Ferdinand I and precipitated an internal crisis within the House of Austria. The evidence suggests a change in his troubled conscience; for example, the young prince refused to take part in the Corpus Christi Day procession when devotion to the Blessed Sacrament had been, since the days of Rudolf I, part of Habsburg family tradition. This 'crypto-Protestant' orientation was not slow to be recognized and appreciated by the Lutheran nobility of the hereditary lands, who showed their sympathy towards him. Maximilian obtained from the Holy See permission to receive communion in both kinds in private as well as medical certificates to support his absenting himself from High Mass according to the Catholic rite. Ferdinand I thought for a while about disinheriting his son as a Lutheran Holy Roman Emperor was inconceivable; he would become the head of an 'evangelical corps' which would include the German Protestant princes who refused to support him in 1562 in this risky path. Maximilian was elected king of the Romans and remained Catholic; Philip II, however, never trusted him.

Since Maximilian, still an archduke, had refused to entrust the education of his many children (eleven in total) to the Jesuits, Philip II persuaded his uncle Ferdinand I to send his grandsons to the Spanish court. The archdukes Rudolf, Ernest, Matthias and Albert derived some benefit from this strictly Catholic education and, contrary to what is sometimes written, they were never treated as hostages, but honoured as members of the House of Austria. The results of this education varied according to the personality of each archduke.

In the case of the future emperor Rudolf, the balance was entirely negative. Subjected to the influence of his cousin don Carlos, he left Castile with a strong aversion to women and was possible a latent homosexual. He obstinately rejected any suggestion of marriage, particularly to the *infanta* Isabella-Clara-Eugenia, a match which Philip II wanted to impose on him. The long negotiations with Elizabeth I likewise ended in failure and he had a liaison with an Italian burgher woman from Prague. He returned to Germany totally introverted, a veritable caricature of the 'cautious king'. Most importantly, he brought back a confirmed hatred of Philip II, of Castilian imperialism and the militant Counter-Reformation. During his reign (1576–1611), the German branch of the Habsburg dynasty was anything but a satellite of the Escorial.

The future emperor Matthias also seems to have been affected by his Spanish sojourn in an entirely negative way; it contributed to the disintegration of his personality, accentuating the erratic tendencies of a mediocre and unsatisfactory prince who was ever on the look out for opportunities likely to bring him power and which he only belatedly seized. As an ambitious younger son it was his destiny to side with the nobles against the higher interest of his House. He practised this ploy with Philip II's opponents in the Netherlands in 1581, when the Union of Utrecht was looking for a sovereign to direct the struggle against Madrid. But Matthias suffered a crushing checkmate and returned to Austria where he endeavoured to forget his Dutch escapade. Without employment for several years, in 1593 at the time of the renewal of Austro-Turkish hostilities, he was entrusted with the command of the imperial troops by his brother Rudolf. Later, at the turn of the seventeenth century, he played an equivocal role, relying on the orders in his attempt to oust his brother from power.

The archdukes Ernest and Albert on the other hand behaved like 'good' Habsburgs, loyal to their House and its head. In 1592, Philip II entrusted Ernest with the governorship of the Netherlands, left vacant by the death of Alexander Farnese. While serious and honest, the archduke Ernest was, however, neither a statesman nor as gifted a captain as his predecessor, the duke of Parma. He suffered a series of defeats at the hands of the prince of Orange, Maurice of Nassau, son of William the Silent, and the struggle became bogged down in siege warfare.

The archduke Albert truly benefited from his Spanish education. Quickly becoming known as 'Albert the pious', he embraced a career in the Church out of genuine vocation and his birth brought him, as early as 1577, the primatial see of Toledo. He was promoted to cardinal, but in 1596, when faced with the demands of the head of the family, he renounced his vocation and accepted the governorship of the Netherlands. Philip II, shortly before his death and after signing the Peace of Vervins with Henry IV (1598), tried to settle the question of the Netherlands and recognized the United Provinces, twenty years after their secession. To respect the sensibilities of his Flemish subjects, nostalgic for the Burgundian era and the government (idealized) of Charles V, and to try – twenty years too late – to rally the Dutch, Philip II decided to make a gesture; he granted independence to the Netherlands and placed the *infanta* Isabella-Clara-Eugenia at their head. In 1596, after the third bankruptcy of Philip's reign, the Spanish monarchy had need of peace. He married his daughter to the cardinal Albert of Austria. As the Holy See had no reason to refuse his Holy Catholic Majesty, for the sake of the cause, i.e. the triumph of the Counter-Reformation in the Netherlands, and in the higher interest of the House of Austria, it reduced the archduke Albert to lay status and permitted him to marry the *infanta* who, having failed to become either queen of France or empress, became ruler of the Netherlands.

Albert and Isabella are known in history as 'the Archdukes'. The head of the House of Austria's 'gift', however, brought with it restrictive clauses: the crown of Spain would recover the circle of Burgundy in the event of the couple not having a child, a clause which has led Belgian historians to suspect Philip II of deceit; did he know that the couple would not have children? After the archduke's death in 1621, Isabella continued as governor-general in the name of her nephew, Philip IV, and occupied this post to everyone's satisfaction until her death in 1633. Her thirty-five years of governorship had a profound effect on the development of modern Belgium. The *infanta* Isabella, who was very pious, devoted all her might to promoting the Catholic Reformation. Louvain became one of the foremost universities of the Catholic world, and its theology faculty entered into competition with the Sorbonne. Churches were rebuilt or redecorated. Jesuits and Capuchins, assisted by a dignified and capable clergy set on a solid footing a fervent people who showed their loyalty to the heiress of the House of Burgundy. Isabella for her part by the Twelve Years Treaty (1609) procured for her lands the peace with the United Provinces which was so desired, although she did not succeed in getting the port of Antwerp reopened to international traffic.

Philip II did not always find within his own House devoted assistants for his imperialist programme, which rested on a classic matrimonial policy and justified a combative Catholicism. Most importantly, however, his relatives in Vienna and Prague did not share his ideas and did not wish to be reduced to the role of satellites.

NOTES AND REFERENCES

1. Adam Wandruszka, 'Madrid und Wien', in *Das Haus Habsburg: eine europäische Dynastie*, Vienna, 1956, pp. 120–41.
2. Ludwig Pfandl, *Philip II*, Munich, 1938.
   Geoffrey Parker, *Philip II*, Boston 1978.

Peter Pierson, *Philip II of Spain*, London 1975.

3. Henri Hauser, *La Prépondérance espagnole (1559–1659)*, in the series *Peuples et Civilisations*, vol. 9, Paris, 1951, reissued in 1981 with a preface by Pierre Chaunu.

4. *Armada 1588–1988: An International Exhibition to Commemorate the Spanish Armada – the Official Catalogue*, London, 1988.

5. Charles Terlinden, *L'Archiduchesse Isabelle*, Brussels, 1943.

6. Michel Pernot, *Les Guerres de religion en France 1559–1598*, Paris, 1987.

7. John Lynch, *Spain under the Habsburgs*, 2 vols, Oxford, 1969, vol. 2, *Spain and America 1598–1700*.

8. Charles Pétrie, *Don John of Austria*, London, 1967.

9. Fernand Braudel, *La Méditerranée et le monde méditerranéen au temps de Philippe II*, 2 vols, Paris, 1966, vol. 2, pp. 223–517; published in English as *The Mediterranean and the Mediterranean World in the Age of Philip II*, 2 vols, trans. S. Reynolds, London, 1972.

CHAPTER EIGHTEEN

Catholic Reformation or Counter-Reformation?

On 4 December 1563, the General Council closed its third session held in the cathedral at Trent, a small episcopal city belonging to the Habsburgs. The assembly for which Charles V had incessantly called, finally, five years after his death, gave the Church a clear doctrine in the face of the diverse theological currents that issued from the Lutheran revolt. Catholicism from now onwards would strive to reconquer lost ground, gathering its faithful together in a disciplined and hierarchical society where there was no longer any place for individual states of soul and for taking an individual stance. Every Christian had to choose his or her camp since the unity of the traditional Church had been broken for once and for all. The faithful as a whole were no less nostalgic for the unity which had been lost and were convinced that their Church alone could guarantee personal salvation. There were, however, great differences in the methods employed to regain the 'errant flocks'. Some hoped to preach and convince simply by example while others employed constraints and even force, with the complicity of the state apparatus if need be.

Such coercion underpinned a combative policy which can only be termed 'Counter-Reformation', even if historians today, embarrassed by the excesses of fanaticism, prefer the more eirenic name of 'Catholic Reformation'. The horrors of the past should not be glossed over and certainly both the path of gentle persuasion and violent compulsion were followed in Danubian Europe as well as a third – that of toleration. In Hungary, Poland and Transylvania the exercise of the right of patronage by the nobility eased the way for the coexistence of more than one confession within the framework of the manorial estate.

In the second half of the sixteenth century, the Habsburg monarchy, where these three modes of religious life were juxtaposed, diverged markedly from the Spanish monarchy, which had furnished the archetype of combative Counter-Reformation. As long as Rudolf lived, a Spanish-style reconquest was out of the question; neither the orders, the majority of whom remained Protestant, nor the sovereign, who remained Catholic, would have allowed it.

From the Erasmian Ferdinand I to his grandson, the thoroughly original

Rudolf II, via the 'crypto-Lutheran' Maximilian II who described himself as a Christian refusing any label, the Habsburgs of Central Europe seem to have been remarkably consistent in their defence of a united Christian Church. This quest for lost unity and harmony proved entirely compatible with imperial ideology; while the division of 1556 isolated the clan of hardliners within the House of Austria, it eased the quest for reconciliation right until the beginning of the seventeenth century, as R. J. W. Evans has so brilliantly demonstrated.[1] This open attitude, though, did not mean that the Habsburgs were totally indifferent to the interests of Catholicism.

THE MEASURES OF FERDINAND I

Ferdinand I, amid the general disarray in which the Church found itself, took measures which prepared the way for the long-term success of the Catholic Reformation. In 1556 he summoned to Vienna and appointed as court preacher Peter Canisius, a Jesuit who brought distinction to the Society of Jesus. In Vienna Canisius published his great catechism, *Summa doctrinae christianae* before settling with a dozen of his German and Flemish colleagues at Prague in a former Dominican monastery, St Clement's, the *Clementinum*. While they themselves had no knowledge of Czech, they were succeeded by twenty-one novices of Bohemian origin, who underwent their formation in the *Collegium germanicum* at Rome, an institution tantamount to a real Jesuit university. In March 1562 the *Clementinum* was granted the status of a university with faculties of philosophy and theology and thus entered into competition with the old Caroline University directed by the Utraquist Consistory.

While there were only twelve students at the *Clementinum* in 1565, by 1598 the number had risen to eight hundred. The nobility of the kingdom, regardless of whether they were Catholic, were won over by the Jesuits' teaching methods, which had been developed precisely to train elites in an efficient and attractive way. The Jesuits placed emphasis on classical Latin, drama, physical exercise and religious devotions. Set up in opposition to the humanist model, which was orientated towards scholarship, it was an aristocratic ideal directed towards the education of the character, competitiveness and the formation of a man of the world. The Jesuits recruited not only among the nobles but also among the poorer classes in order to form future priests and to ensure the future of the holy orders.

The bishop of Olomouc (Olmütz) supported the establishment of the Society of Jesus in Moravia. In 1566 the Society settled in the bishop's town; in the following year the college was raised to university status and in 1572 another college was founded at Brno (Brünn). In 1578 the Jesuit university at Olomouc became the seat of the *Collegium nordicum*, the pontifical seminary set up specifically for the formation of missionaries for Scandinavia, Prussia and the Baltic lands as well as for Orthodox Christendom (Ukraine and Muscovy). It was, then, an element in the Counter-Reformation strategy of reconquest, like the Jesuit University at Douai in the Spanish Netherlands. After 1580, the great Catholic lords supported the foundation of other colleges in Bohemia – Česky Krumlov (1581), Chomutov (1589), Jindřichuv Hradec (1592) and Kladsko (Glatz, 1597).

The Jesuits organized numerous spiritual activities concurrent with their pedagogic work. They created Marian confraternities that extended the work undertaken among the pupils at the colleges and they took an active part in religious controversies, but without finding much response among enlightened opinion in the Czech lands. They preached in the urban areas in Italian and German, then in Czech. True to their policy of allurement, they welcomed poor students, even 'heretics', into their 'poor houses'. In 1600 they re-established two centres of pilgrimage, at the cave of St Ivan, according to tradition the first Czech hermit, and at the shrine of the miraculuous Virgin of Boleslav.

What effect did the Jesuits' patient activity have on the social elites and unquiet souls? The Society's own statistics quoted by Schmidl, the historian and apologist for the Jesuits, if they are to be believed, show that the Jesuits obtained 21 258 conversions in the twenty-two years from 1593 to 1615. At the end of this period (in 1615) there were 243 Jesuits in Bohemia. Despite their superior education system, their efficient organization and their practice of self-denial, they excited mistrust among their opponents. One of the first measures taken by the Protestant orders in 1618 was to expel the Society, as it no longer enjoyed the Habsburgs' protection. Those faithful to Rome made up 10 per cent of the population in 1576 and 10 per cent still in 1600. The Catholic Reformation, which probably had enjoyed some success among the elites, was not capable of regaining the ground lost in Bohemia during the fifteenth century; it required the direct intervention of monarchical power after 1620, force and a real policy of Counter-Reformation to recover a stronger position for the Catholic Church.

In 1561 Ferdinand I had taken a decision heavy with future consequences: a Catholic titular archbishop was appointed to the Prague archbishopric. This appointment represented the fruit of a patient policy which from 1537 to 1545 had met successive refusals from the Curia. In the end, however, pope Pius IV accepted a compromise; while refusing to recognize the Compactata of Basle he agreed to the institution of communion in both kinds for the laity and to a liturgy in the Czech language. The choice of archbishop for Prague augured well for a rapprochement with the Utraquists; Anton Brus of Mohelnice, the bishop of Vienna, was originally from Bohemia and was grand master of the Knights of the Cross, a local order of chivalry. After serving as Ferdinand's delegate at the Council of Trent, the new archbishop assumed his functions in 1564. The openings for pastoral action were limited to the 300 parishes out of a total of 1 300, which were still served by Catholic priests and situated on the estates of aristocrats faithful to the Roman Church and in the royal towns.

The restoration of the nunciature in 1581 strengthened the dynamism of the Catholic party. The nuncio Giovanni Francesco Bonomi, who remained in office at Prague until 1584, established links with the leaders of the great Catholic families – the Rožmberks, Pernštejns, Hradeces, Dietrichsteins and Lobkowitzes. In 1584 he elaborated a plan of campaign 'to root out heresy' based on pastoral visits, missions and an increase in the number of festivals and ceremonies. Here, for example, is the questionnaire issued in December 1584 during the conference held at the residence of the grand burgrave Vilém Rožmberk:

1. Are the parish priests steadfast in the Catholic faith? Are any of their number suspect?
2. Is communion taken in both kinds?
3. Were the parish priests and other priests ordained according to the rites of the Catholic Church?
4. Do they practise general confession?
5. Do they confess often?
6. Do those clergy in religious orders have letters of mission from their legitimate superiors?
7. What are their attitudes towards the sacraments?
8. Do all the parish priests and other priests possess a breviary? Do they say the offices at the canonical hours?
9. Do they live in concubinage?
10. Do they give instruction in the catechism on feast days?
11. Do they give sermons? If so, is it from Catholic books that they draw their sermons?[2]

The truth, however, is that this fine programme was not applied by Martin Medek, the new archbishop of Prague, and that pastoral visits did not take place before 1621, and then in a different context – that of triumphant Catholicism after the Battle of the White Mountain.

THE DIVISION OF THE INHERITANCE OF FERDINAND I (1564)

Already in 1552 Ferdinand had drawn up a will which established the broad outlines of his inheritance and divided the hereditary lands among his three sons, Maximilian, Ferdinand and Charles. Maximilian, the eldest, received only Lower Austria; Ferdinand, the middle child and the favourite of the king of the Romans, received the Tyrol and Further Austria

(*Vorlande*); Charles, the youngest, was entrusted with Inner Austria. These arrangements were confirmed several times and proved a millstone round the neck for those concerned: the heirs shared the debts accumulated by their father in the course of defending the common patrimony. These debts were a great burden, the weight of which is reflected in the increased taxation of the second half of the century. The cadet branch was not rich enough to pay for the successive bankruptcies that characterized the administration of the head of the House.

There have been many postscripts to this division of the hereditary lands which, after all, was simply a return to the medieval tradition still practised by certain other German princely houses, for example the Wittelsbachs of the Palatinate and of Bavaria and the Wettins of Saxony. The orders approved of the division as they did not wish to be swallowed up within an 'Austrian' conglomeration. Innsbruck and Graz in the future would have the status of regional capitals, each with a central government after the Viennese model, with Privy Council, chamber of accounts and, for Graz, a council of war responsible for the administration of the Croatian frontier. In common with every decentralized system, the number of offices increased, making it possible to satisfy a certain number of local vanities. For Innsbruck it marked the return to the privileged position that it had enjoyed in the reign of Maximilian I, while for Graz it was a welcome promotion which lasted formally until the accession of Ferdinand II but in fact continued until the reforms of the eighteenth century. At Innsbruck, even after the cadet branch died out in 1667, the emperor Leopold I, in order to satisfy the wishes of the Tyroleans, ensured that it maintained its regional government.

Maximilian received the best part of the inheritance: during his father's lifetime, he was elected king of Bohemia, king of Hungary and finally in 1562 king of the Romans. In this way the elective character of the various crowns was respected while the continuity of the Austrian monarchy founded by Ferdinand I was assured.

Ferdinand I had had an extraordinary and fruitful reign. Thought of as an intruder and an authoritarian prince dreaming of absolute government, after the great reforms of 1527, he had been able to harmonize with the aspirations of the local nobilities. Endowed with the same great political sense as his grandfather, Ferdinand of Aragón, he had turned bad fortune to good and had governed as a realist. But was this division of the hereditary lands advisable? Was there not a risk that the medieval quarrels might return which had so weakened the House of Austria before Frederick III? The situation had changed greatly: the weight of the Spanish monarchy – or even Bohemia linked to the imperial crown – had altered the balance of power to the detriment of the cadet lines. These, though, were in a better position to control the orders and to direct a confessional policy adapted to fit local realities. In the future, there would be three distinct confessional policies, with the Counter-Reformation first imposing itself in the Alpine lands.

Little is known of the feelings that the members of the House of Austria had for one another. Did Ferdinand I really distrust his son Maximilian? Were they not similar: they both favoured the unity of Christendom and neither was won over by the hardening of dogma exhibited by the Council of Trent in its final phase? The impression is that Ferdinand I felt defeated, like his brother Charles V. They both looked back, some time before their death, and judged the vanity of the task they had undertaken, Charles V considering universal monarchy an outmoded concept, Ferdinand seeing the Austrian monarchy as too modern an idea, unsuited to the realities of Danubian Europe. One can but think of Joseph II on his death-bed, destroying almost all his life's work, revoking the reforms which so little corresponded to the social, cultural and political realities of the Austrian monarchy.

THE TYROL

The position of Catholicism was clearly better in the Tyrol than in the rest of the hereditary lands. The peasant masses had hardly been touched by Lutheranism. The Anabaptists who had settled there had been harshly persecuted and those who had survived had taken refuge in Moravia. Most of the nobility had remained faithful to the Church. There were Protestants only in the towns and large villages, especially among the miners; the great entrepreneur Hans Stainperger made no secret of his leanings towards the Augsburg Confession.

From the very beginning, the archduke Ferdinand made it clear that he wanted to re-establish Catholicism in all its glory. He summoned to Innsbruck the Jesuits, who founded the college where Canisius stayed for a while, and invited the Franciscan Johannes Nas to be court preacher. The Catholic Reformation did not meet any opposition among the orders and only some crypto-Calvinist communities existed in the Vorarlberg through the discreet support of the Grisons. By 1595 at Ferdinand's death, every trace of this Protestant minority had disappeared.

The archduke Ferdinand, however, had not been a total conformist as he was the first in the illustrious House to contract a marriage contrary to aristocratic custom and the mentality of the *ancien régime*. He married a woman who, while thoroughly honourable, was of a clearly inferior rank which excluded the children from this quite legitimate marriage from any right to inherit. When, in 1557, Ferdinand had finally agreed to marry Philippina Welser, niece of the Augsburg banker, he did so on condition that the union remained secret. He was inspired more by personal sentiment than by interest, as the House of Welser was no more prosperous than it had been at the time of the election of Charles V. There were four children from this marriage, who were declared legitimate by the Curia in 1576. The eldest son, Andreas, was appointed bishop of Constance, while the second received the margravate of Burgau. Philippina died in 1580 and Ferdinand took as his second wife the princess Anne-Catherine of Mantua in the hope of having a male heir. However, the couple had three daughters. In 1611, the youngest, Anna, married her cousin, the emperor Matthias, but there were no children from the marriage. In the end, the Tyrol fell to the archduke Maximilian, grandmaster of the Teutonic Order. His nephew Leopold, bishop of Strassburg and Passau, received the governorship of the Tyrol in 1619, married Claudia of Medici and founded a new Tyrolean branch of the House of Austria which died out in 1665.

INNER AUSTRIA[3]

The archduke Charles, for his part, founded the Styrian branch, which was assured of a much better future as it did not die out in the male line until 1740, in the person of the emperor Charles VI, and survived to the present day through the marriage of the archduchess Maria-Theresa to duke Francis of Lorraine.

A convinced Catholic, the archduke Charles was yet further strengthened in his stance by the princess Maria, daughter of duke William V of Bavaria, whom he married in 1571. She was even more tireless and fanatical than the archduke, whose reign was a long battle on behalf of Catholicism.

Although Charles summoned the Jesuits to Graz to found a college there, he at first remained within the limits defined by law with respect to the orders who, for the most part, supported the Augsburg Confession. The orders wanted an extension of legal guarantees since the Peace of Augsburg did not apply, *stricto sensu*, to the hereditary lands. The balance between their forces was, nevertheless, favourable: as has been seen, they alone were capable of rescuing the archduke from his financial difficulties by voting him contributions.

In February 1572 the archduke Charles granted the nobility an 'edict of pacification' which was accompanied by a declaration before the Diet of Styria in which he proclaimed his unbending attachment to Catholicism. He granted the order of lords and that of the knights liberty of conscience. The edict, which was valid for their family, servants and peasants as well, also guaranteed liberty of worship and the right to maintain pastors and schools with the customary clause, 'as long as it does not affect the general, Christian and peaceful accord'. The towns and large villages that made up the fourth order were excluded from the Diet, although there were numerous Lutheran preachers and schoolmasters in the towns and the two confessions competed zealously to win over the youth. In 1576 the sovereign was obliged, against his will, to confirm the dispositions of the edict in order to secure the vote of subsidies.

Two years later, on 9 February 1574, in order to obtain fresh financial help for the defence of the Croatian frontier, the archduke Charles had to extend the edict by an oral declaration before the general Diet of Inner Austria; Lutheran preachers were authorized at Graz, Klagenfurt and Ljubljana and the burghers gained confessional liberty. The participants in the Diet, believing that the contest was won, published the Declaration of Bruck-an-der-Mur, setting out all the concessions made by the archduke since 1570. Violently criticized by the Catholic party, the archduke responded with a text from which the fourth order was excluded. This restrictive version was the work of the archduke's chancellor, doctor Wolfgang Schranz.

The general Diet of Bruck-an-der-Mur marked the break between the archduke and the orders, and in the future, the government applied legal means to furnish him with its own restrictive interpretation of the Declaration of 1578.[4]

In 1579 the archduke decreed the banishment of Lutheran preachers from the county of Gorizia, where they were sufficiently few in number for him to do so. The commissions of 'reformation', which enjoyed the energetic support of the bishops of Seckau and Lavant, then hounded out the pastors with a view to replacing them with parish priests. In 1585, on the very eve of the archduke Charles's death, the Jesuit college at Graz obtained the status of a university. Charles left an under-age son, Ferdinand (aged seven), who did not rule until 1595. Inner Austria was, in the mean time, administered by his cousins from the senior line, the archdukes Maximilian and Ernest, who, as has been seen, had carried out various other temporary offices in the service of the illustrious House.[5]

During this time, the young Ferdinand (the future Ferdinand II) was taken in hand by his mother's family and by the Jesuits at the Bavarian university of Ingolstadt, a bastion of the Counter-Reformation – the pupil would not disappoint his masters – while the Lutherans of Inner Austria enjoyed a ten-year reprieve.

THE REIGN OF MAXIMILIAN II (1564–76)[6]

The emperor Maximilian II had a short reign and disappointed a number of Protestants, who had imagined that he was waiting only for his father to die to show his true colours. The sovereign hated militant Catholicism but disdained no less the theological quarrels by which the Lutherans were riven. By temperament and by upbringing, he felt close to Melanchthon and his 'Philippist' disciples, who were persecuted by the intransigent theologians led by Flavius Illyricus.

Maximilian proved his authority in the case of a Lutheran prince, the duke of Saxony, Johannes Friedrich, son of the prince defeated at Mühlberg, who wanted to take revenge and to recover his electoral dignity. The duke had been involved in a conspiracy by a certain knight called Grumbach, who was motivated solely by interest. In 1567 the emperor besieged Johannes Friedrich at Gotha. Grumbach and the duke's chancellor were waylaid and the duke was led to Vienna under close guard. Maximilian sentenced him to imprisonment and the duke of Saxony ended his days in prison.

Faithful to the model of the Christian prince, Maximilian made more concessions to his Lutheran subjects than they expected.[7] Having ordered them to draw up an 'ecclesiastical ordinance' (*Kirchenordnung*) common to all the churches of Lower Austria, he had some amendments made to the final text (1568) elaborated by the pastor David Chytraeus, who was originally from Rostock (Mecklenburg). In the same year, he granted legal status to the evangelical orders, that is to say, to those nobles belonging to the Augsburg Confession. The lords and knights, their families, servants and their peasants acquired liberty of worship *in private*, that is to say in their castle and house, but the towns and large villages which made up the fourth order were excluded. In 1574 the emperor authorized the nobility to practise the Lutheranism in Vienna, which for many years became a Protestant town where Catholicism was ostensibly eclipsed and where some knights indulged in such acts of provocation as, for example, entering the cathedral of St Stephen on horseback, which in 1582 drove the emperor Rudolf to quit Vienna, to the benefit of Prague.

In Bohemia the orders used their political powers to obtain concessions in the confessional domain, especially after the departure of the archduke Ferdinand, who abandoned his post as governor in order to devote himself entirely to his Tyrolean apanage. Maximilian, because he depended upon the vote of subsidies to enable him to follow an active foreign policy (the Turkish War, his candidacy for the Polish throne), was forced to grant substantial religious privileges; the Catholic magnates, who occupied the positions of responsibility in the kingdom's government, associated with the other nobles rather than siding with the Habsburgs.

First of all Maximilian extended his control over the Utraquist Church, directly appointing the members of the Consistory. In 1571 he appointed as administrator a crypto-Catholic who was sympathetic towards the Jesuits, Jindřisch Dvorský. In the same year he also refused to recognize the legal existence of the Augsburg Confession while letting the bishop of Olomouc, Vilém Prusinovský of Vickov, persecute Protestant schoolmasters and magistrates in the royal towns of Moravia. The Protestants, ill at ease, united during the 1575 session of the Diet and proposed a resolution in twenty-five articles which accorded complete liberty of religion to the Utraquists, Lutherans and Unity of Czech Brethren. On 25 August the emperor granted just a verbal promise that non-Catholics would not be disturbed in the practice of their worship. The text set before Maximilian II, known as the *Confessio bohemica* (Bohemian Confession), was a synthesis of the Augsburg Confession, the confessions of faith of the Unity of Czech Brethren and Hussite texts. The new-Utraquists, united with the other Reform Churches of the kingdom of Bohemia, thus had control of the vast majority of the population. With the Consistory and the 'defenders of the faith' elected in the very heart of the orders, they found themselves given a solid organization in the face of the Catholic hierarchy re-established by Ferdinand I. Maximilian, however, proved to have as little understanding of the state as he had respect for confessional pluralism: he did not accord any written privilege to the followers of the *Confessio* of 1575, which included 116 out of 135 knights and 75 out of 90 lords who were members of the Diet.

In the Empire, the sovereign sought respect for the Peace of Augsburg, and showed himself less favourably inclined towards the Calvinists, who did not have any legal status. While he supported the Lutheran princes, he did not stop the Calvinist elector Palatine from being excluded at the time of the 1566 Diet, and did not recognize the secularization of the bishoprics in north Germany. He wanted reconciliation between the two Protestant confessions and respect for the status quo established in 1555. He found himself on the defensive because he wanted to spare the Empire the horrors of religious wars. This was why he forbade the raising of mercenaries to fight in France or the Netherlands. He resolutely and vigorously condemned the St Bartholomew's Day massacre and publicly blamed the king of France, Charles IX, his son-in-law, who two years earlier had married the archduchess Elizabeth.

Maximilian also proved critical of the policy followed by Philip II in the Netherlands but did not go so far as to break relations with his cousin and son-in-law. Maximilian recognized the weaknesses of the monarchy. Like many of his generation he believed that quarrels were appeased by time and that fratricidal conflicts should be avoided at all costs in expectation of the day when all Christians would again be united.

It was in the East that Maximilian followed an active policy. In 1566 he launched a final assault on the ageing Süleymân, who undertook a last campaign in Hungary to defend the interests of his protégé, János Zsigmond Zapolya, prince of Transylvania and pretender to the Hungarian throne. The heroic defence of Szigetvár and the death of Süleymân during the siege of this modest fortress in Slavonia had a profound effect upon the political situation in south-east Europe; Maximilian and Selîm II, Süleymân's son, buried the hatchet, signing the compromising Peace of Adrianople in 1568. Maximilian recognized the partition of Hungary into three territories, with János Zapolya's Transylvania receiving its peculiar status as an Austro-Turkish condominium, becoming in effect independent and governed by the Hungarian aristocracy. For more than a century, one of the major concerns of the Viennese court remained to regain control of Transylvania and to reincorporate it into the Austrian monarchy. Because of this long-term truce in the Balkan peninsula, the Sublime Porte turned its arms against Venice and attacked Cyprus in 1570. Maximilian II, just like Charles IX, studiously avoided rejoining the Holy League.

Maximilian took advantage of the restored peace to interest himself in the affairs of Poland, which from now onwards were a serious preoccupation for the Habsburgs. The Polish crown was elective and when the Jagiellons, who had reigned for two centuries, became extinct following the death of Zygmunt II Augustus, the Polish nobility was divided. Their choice finally rested upon a Frenchman, Henry of Valois, the future Henry III who accepted the throne despite the strict conditions which were imposed upon him, especially in matters of religion. After the death of his brother Charles IX, Henry left Warsaw and returned to France. The Polish crown was again vacant and Maximilian presented himself as a candidate but the majority of Polish nobles feared seeing the 'Republic' integrated into the Austrian monarchy and subject to the authority of a relatively strong external power. The Habsburgs, however, from now onwards would have supporters at each election in Poland. In 1576 Maximilian was elected but died before he could take possession of his new kingdom.

He had long suffered from heart disease and died during a session of the imperial Diet at Ratisbon on 12 October 1576. Maximilian had eleven children from his marriage to his cousin Maria and he had secured the election of his eldest son, the archduke Rudolf, as king of Hungary in 1572, king of Bohemia in 1575 and finally king of the Romans. The succession was thus assured without difficulty.

RUDOLF II, A MODERATE CATHOLIC[8]

The new emperor, Rudolf II, despite his education at the Spanish court, was not a champion of the Counter-Reformation and pursued the policies of his father and grandfather: defence of the position of the Catholic Church, respect for confessional pluralism with the reconciliation of Christians and the reunion of the Churches as a long-term goal. He was as far removed as his father had been from what German historians call 'confessionalism', that is the division of civil and religious society into clearly demarcated factions, foreign to each other.

Rudolf was as irresolute as Maximilian and his sympathies lay with Melanchthon and his disciples, the Philippists, who had been driven from the University of Wittenberg in 1570 because they desperately sought a middle way between strict Lutheran theology and tridentine Catholicism. It is interesting to note that the emperor Rudolf ceased every religious practice after 1590 and from 1600 lived in genuine fear of the sacraments; he refused to confess and died without receiving extreme unction. Despite the hopes of the Catholics and the fears of the Protestants, he did not play any part in the persecution of the Reformed Churches that took place during his reign. The intrigues against the Protestants were authorized by the archduke Matthias and his adviser, Khlesl, the future cardinal, while the archduke Ferdinand of Styria was personally involved in the scheming. As for the emperor, he was content to sign proclamations which, to the great distress of the papal nuncio, were never carried out.

Rudolf II's relations with the Catholics were strained: he envied them their authority and was anti-clerical; moreover, he considered that it fell to him and not to the pope to reunited Christendom. Among the Catholics of Bohemia, a movement arose which later culminated in Josephinism but which after the Battle of the White Mountain (1620) continued to be apparent in men such as cardinal Harrach, archbishop of Prague and the Premonstratensian Hirnhaim, abbot of Strahov (1637–87). The movement was the continuation of the Bohemian party of 'old Utraquists' within the Catholic Church, who condemned the Jesuits and submission to Rome. The emperor meanwhile continued to live in a morbid state of fear that the St Bartholomew's Day massacre might be repeated and that the Catholics might strike through the Holy League which, with Spanish support, was being organized around Bavaria.

Rudolf II was no more sympathetic towards the Protestant camp, even though he maintained good relations with Christian II, elector of Saxony. He hated sects, in particular the Unity of Czech Brethren, whom he saw as instigating trouble and – not without reason – as despising the established order. He had a lofty notion of his imperial mission and wanted to re-establish the unity of Christendom. The evidence shows that the practical measures he took were limited but by his presence alone he probably helped to delay the great confrontations within the Empire and Bohemia whereas Matthias's blunders and provocations in Hungary had started a crisis – the insurrection of István Bocskai which evolved into the rout of the Catholic party.

By practising a large measure of decentralization in favour of his brothers, Rudolf in fact had opened the way for a real policy of Catholic reconquest exemplified by Melchior Khlesl. Born at Vienna in 1554, the son of a baker of Moravian origin and a pupil of the Jesuits, Khlesl was won over by his masters to Tridentine Catholicism.[9] A canon of St Stephen's cathedral, then chancellor of the university of Vienna, intelligent and highly educated, a man of great character, he was appointed official of the bishop of Passau in 1579. In this capacity, Khlesl assumed direction of the Catholic Reformation in Lower Austria, where he progressively re-established episcopal authority. Later on, he was charged with presiding over the commission of the reformation intended to re-establish Catholic worship in those towns which depended directly on the Habsburgs. In 1582 he edited an *Instruction pastorale*, which served as a guide for the clergy. Later, Khlesl became the confidant and head of the council of the archduke Matthias. Judged too moderate by Ferdinand of Styria, he was arrested and imprisoned in 1617, some months before the death of his patron. But the real adherent of the Counter Reformation after the Spanish manner was an archduke who had never lived in Spain and had been educated by the Jesuits of Ingolstadt – Ferdinand of Styria. He it was who introduced among the Habsburgs of Austria the militant Catholicism which was the cement of the Spanish monarchy and one of the principal foundations of the policy of Philip II.

THE COUNTER-REFORMATION: POLITICAL DOCTRINE

Ferdinand of Styria was firmly resolved, whatever the cost, to effect the triumph of the Catholic cause and to re-establish religious unity in his patrimonial states. As early as 1579, his father, the archduke Charles, had signed an agreement with the duke of Bavaria, the champion of Catholicism in southern Germany: this was why Ferdinand was educated by the Ingolstadt Jesuits who turned him into a zealous soldier of the Catholic reconquest, first of all in Styria, then in Austria and Bohemia.

He made the conversion of his subjects a matter of conscience. All Catholics believed in good faith that the heretic was condemned to the fires of Hell for eternity; also that Christian charity ordered them to do everything to assure the salvation of the soul of their brothers and therefore their conversion to Catholicism. The first obligation of the prince, according to this contemporary paternalist concept, was to assure the eternal salvation of each of his subjects and he was morally obliged to promote the conversion of heretics or schismatics placed under his authority. When, as a youth, he had been a pilgrim to Our Lady of Loretto, Ferdinand of Styria made a vow to reign over a desert rather than over heretics. On one other occasion, he vowed to suffer death rather than the presence in his states of a single Protestant. He believed, moreover, in good faith that he risked his own damnation if he did not take seriously his role as the spiritual father of his subjects.

To this moral and paternalistic concept of the role of a prince, which the Jesuits had inculcated in Ferdinand, was added a more political vision of religion as the bond that maintained the unity of a sovereign's subjects. In Spain, under the Catholic kings, religious unity as expressed in France by the adage 'one law, one faith, one king', had become the basis of the state. From the sixteenth century, every Spaniard was obliged to become a Catholic or else to leave the country – hence the exile of Jews and Muslims, who in 1500 still represented substantial minorities in Spanish society. The Styrian branch of the House of Habsburg placed the same hopes in state religion; it would assure loyalty towards the prince and strengthen moral cohesion among his subjects, whatever their culture or nationality. In modern terms, the Styrian branch of the House of Habsburg sought 'ideological unity' but the Habsburgs as a whole were very tolerant with regard to nationality. Liberal historiography has been wrong to attribute to them Germanizing tendencies; Ferdinand II would have been content with a return to the 'true faith' and did not show any hostility towards the Czech and Hungarian nations. The Habsburgs were convinced that their Catholic subjects would be more loyal to their person and the dynasty and that their peoples would become increasingly united, while heretics would remain rebellious towards authority. Religion was still not a private matter but a political choice. The Habsburgs were not entirely mistaken as among the ruling classes rallying to heresy was often an act of defiance against the dynasty.

Ferdinand in the pursuit of his ends had at his disposal the support of the bishops and the religious orders, the Capuchins and Jesuits within his lands as well as external support from the papacy, the Spanish monarchy and the German Catholic princes. The nobles, by contrast, proved cautious of his policy but were not sufficiently strong to stop a prince who declared that he would 'sooner beg than rule over heretics'.

From 1596 Ferdinand resumed in Inner Austria the policy which his father, the archduke Charles, had undertaken. Assisted by bishop Brenner, who was untiringly active in the pastoral field, he did not allow himself to be intimidated by the orders' threats and enjoined the commission of the reformation to pursue its task in the towns. His action was legal because the right of reform (*jus reformandi*) belonged to the territorial prince. The commission pursued the Protestant preachers, sought to convince the half-hearted and undecided, and then installed Catholic priests while expelling the recalcitrant and recovering their places of worship. By 1600 the town of Graz had once again become entirely Catholic, with the exception of 115 who preferred to emigrate. At the same time, the commission extended its activity into open country and relied on armed force; this violent activity bore its fruits since 2 500 Lutherans chose to leave Styrian territory, taking with them their goods and money which they had been able to draw from the sale of their land or their house. The most famous victim of the archduke Ferdinand's fanaticism was the mathematician Johannes Kepler, who readily found refuge at Rudolf II's court at Prague. These emigrants belonged to an elite of artists and artisans. Ferdinand's policy, while harsh, still left the Lutherans a choice. There was some resistance in the mining districts, but not one death. As for the orders, they were content to make use of their confessional privileges in a limited way.

The way was free for the Jesuits and Capuchins, who enlisted new converts, but even so, they could not prevent the continuance of a certain clandestine Protestantism in the remote valleys. Ferdinand of Styria had found the model for an effective process of Counter-Reformation which he would later apply in the other patrimonial states.

THE BALANCE IN 1600

In 1600 the Habsburgs were yet to take a gamble in the Austrian monarchy. Tridentine Catholicism had touched only a minority and the position of the Catholic Church remained precarious, despite the Jesuits' resolute action and the protection of the Habsburgs, who themselves were not of one mind and for a long time remained faithful to traditional religion. The Erasmian ideal did not disappear with Charles V and Ferdinand I. After some expressions of sympathy towards the Augsburg Confession, Maximilian returned to that moderate path which his son, Rudolf, followed after him. While it is possible to speak of a Catholic Reformation with respect to confessional differences, what is also noticeable is the reluctance of monarchs to grant legal status to the Churches of the Reformation: the strangest case was Hungary, where there were almost no Catholics but where the different Protestant denominations were without any legal existence and the primate Oláh, a general without troops, had had the decrees of the Council of Trent published.

The rigorous tendency within Catholicism exemplified by Philip II was, though, imposed in the Alpine provinces and the hereditary lands, however, and Ferdinand of Styria took on the role of the champion of the Counter-Reformation. After the harsh confrontations of the period 1600–10 and the apparent triumph of the orders and the Protestant Churches, the succession crisis provided Ferdinand with the chance to impose a new political-religious model which had been elaborated in a Western Europe tired of confessional conflicts. Ferdinand of Styria's final success was aided by all that had been achieved deep down since 1560 for the sake of religious peace and the excess of certain Calvinist nobles like Erasmus Tschernembl who, while they were scarcely representative, were roused and wanted to impose the model provided by the United Provinces.

Meanwhile the long reign of Rudolf II (1576–1611) made possible the flowering of culture in parallel with the economic prosperity which is the subject of Chapter 19.

NOTES AND REFERENCES

1. R. J. W. Evans, *The Making of the Habsburg Monarchy*, Oxford, 1979.
2. Text quoted by Marie-Élisabeth Ducreux, 'La situation religieuse dans les pays tchèques à la fin du XVIe siècle', *Études danubiennes*, no. 2, 1986, pp. 116–28.
3. Joseph Hirn, *Erzherzog Ferdinand II von Tirol*, 2 vols, Innsbruck, 1885–7.
4. Joseph Loserth, *Reformation und Gegenreformation in den innen-österreichischen Ländern*, Stuttgart, 1898.
    Alexandre Novotny and Berthold Sutter (eds) *Innerösterreich 1564–1619*, Graz, 1967.

5. Viktor Bibl, *Erzherzog Ernst und die Gegenreformation in Nieder-Œsterreich*, 1901, 6 vols.

    Heinrich Notflascher, *Haus, Reich und Dynastie: Maximilian der deutschmeister*, Marburg and Lahn, 1987.

6. Viktor Bibl, *Maximilian II: Der rätselhafte Kaiser*, Dresden, 1929.

7. Otto Helmut Hoppen, *Kaiser Maximilian II und der Kompromisskatholizismus*, Munich, 1895.

8. Anton Gindely, *Rudolf II und seine Zeit*, 2 vols, Prague, 1862–5. R. J. W. Evans, *Rudolf II and his World*, 2nd edn, Oxford, 1984.

    Karl Vočelka, *Rudolf II*, Vienna, 1985.

9. J. von Hammer-Purgstall, *Khlesls, des Kardinals ... Leben*, 4 vols, Vienna, 1847–51.

CHAPTER NINETEEN

Rudolf II (1576–1611): the Triumph of Prague

Rudolf II was the only Habsburg to make Prague his residence – one of his several departures from customary Habsburg practice – although his grandfather Ferdinand I and others had made prolonged stays in the city. His decision to reside at Prague from 1582 onwards imparted to the Bohemian capital all the lustre of the capital of the Holy Roman Empire. Installed in the Hradčany, he made Prague an artistic and cultural capital to rival the great Italian cities and his Bohemian subjects were duly grateful. Rudolf II alone of their Austrian rulers has left a positive impression in the Czech mind, although Bohemian historians blinded by their nationalist passions have variously charged him with cosmopolitanism and with wanting to Germanize the country, accusations which denote a grave misunderstanding of both the man and the age.

His remarkable character has also given rise to another legend which has been cultivated by German historiography – Rudolf as a *dilettante* sidetracked into the imperial purple. Some historians have seen him simply as a weak monarch, unstable, incapable of assuming his duties as a bureacratic emperor with dignity, gradually becoming immured in the Hradčany like his cousin Philip II in the Escorial; a pale replica of the 'cautious king', Rudolf lost all grasp of reality and took refuge in the occult sciences. At the most these historians deign to credit him with a positive role as the patron and protector of Johannes Kepler and for making Prague one of the leading centres of European intellectual life at a time when the Parisians were interested only in the barricades of the League. But R.J.W. Evans, by trying to understand the mental world in which Rudolf II developed, has shown that he was instilled with a lofty sense of mission, and as a worthy successor of his great uncle Charles V, dreamt of re-establishing the unity of Christendom under his direction.[1] This dream of unity was not directed towards the creation of an ambitious universal monarchy, which no one any longer desired, but rather towards spreading peace in Europe and delivering Christendom from the Turkish menace.

If Rudolf II was without the means on the human or the material level to achieve his goal, nevertheless he helped to prolong the humanist dream and enabled Prague to have its hour of glory as the brilliant capital of the Holy Roman Empire which was then enjoying its longest period of peace in the modern era.[2]

AN UNPREPOSSESSING PRINCE

Unlike Charles V at the age of twenty, the archduke who returned from Spain in 1571 had about him little of the winning *cavaliere* and seemed a mockery of the ideal portrait of the perfect man of the world sketched at the beginning of the century by Balthazar Castiglione in his manual.[3] Rudolf II was ugly. The prognathism characteristic of members of the illustrious House of Habsburg was particularly pronounced in his case. It was not long before he lost his teeth, and his thick lips and bloated face rendered him unattractive. He had little taste for physical exercise, did not go hunting, and neglected the festivities and ceremonies of the court.

He nevertheless believed firmly in the eminence of the imperial title, a conviction grounded in his solid classical education and family tradition. Like Frederick III he was convinced that the House of Austria had been chosen by God and as such was superior to all other sovereign Houses. Consequently he disliked all manifestations of Castilian imperialism and had a perfect grasp of its ambiguities and contradictions. Philip II, he believed, served neither the interests of the House of Austria nor the cause of Catholicism by combining militant Counter-Reformation with Castilian expansion.

In his private life, Rudolf suffered a series of disappointments. He was jealous of his brothers Matthias, Maximilian and Albert and disapproved of the latter's marriage to the *infanta* Isabella. He liked Ernest alone. Despite his dissatisfaction with his kind, he still put them to work in Hungary and Austria. After his marriage negotiations with Madrid over the *infanta* failed for reasons that are still not known, he was again frustrated when Maria de Medici married Henry IV of France, as he had contemplated an Italian match. Much has been written about his sexual preferences; it has been claimed that he was attracted to young boys as well as very young girls. Rumour also has it that he suffered from syphilis which was then widespread. His attitude towards legitimate marriage was surprising, even scandalous, at a time when his first duty with respect to the House and people was to guarantee an heir, and thus forestall a crisis over the succession which might lead to civil war. Certainly he was not impotent: he had children by Barbara Strada, who belonged to a family of Italian patricians from Prague. Had he concluded a secret marriage like his uncle, the archduke Ferdinand? In this respect, as in many others, Rudolf was far from conventional.

He never suffered from mental illness in the clinical sense but during the period 1600–6 he probably had brief bouts of 'melancholy', spells of depression from which he quickly recovered. It was believed that while at Rome he had been bewitched by his chamberlain Hieronymus Makofski. Daniel Eremita, the envoy of the grand duke of Tuscany, in his report of 1609 gave a far more indulgent and promising account: an extraordinary prince – but not cut out for business, which bored him – and a magnificent patron.

RUDOLF II AND THE GOVERNMENT

Rudolf II received a good humanist education and, like all the Habsburgs since Maximilian, spoke several languages with ease; apart from Latin and German, he knew French, Italian and Spanish but, contrary to legend and unlike his father Maximilian II, he spoke Czech badly. He was happy to converse in Spanish and surrounded himself with a 'Spanish party' made up of Czech Catholic aristocrats. While he loathed his cousin and brother-in-law Philip II, he had, nevertheless, been won over by Spanish culture.

Rudolf established the practice of the administrative monarchy. His reign should be divided into two periods: the first phase until 1600, which was quite normal, and the second phase during which he caused everything to come to a halt. During this later period the emperor refused to receive ambassadors posted to Prague or granted them, after months of waiting, only a brief audience of a quarter of an hour's duration. Yet more serious was that he no longer summoned the Privy Council, which was responsible for the conduct of general policy. The state apparatus was paralyzed because, in a sudden assertion of his dignity, Rudolf refused to delegate his powers to a prime minister with full authority, who would have relieved him of the work of government and left him free to pursue his research and theorizing. In Rudolf's case, the tendency towards irresolution often found among the Habsburgs reached tragic proportions. Incapable of making up his mind when he did examine the dossiers of the council, he refused to take any decision; this explains his brothers' rebellion which clouded the final years of his reign and roused in him a surge of energy.

During the first part of his reign, Rudolf II governed quite rationally with the assistance of Bohemian Catholic nobles such as Vilém Rožmberk and the Chancellor Adam Vratislav of Hradec whose humanist ideals and political prudence made them hostile towards the Counter-Reformation. But in 1600 the existing team was ousted as it included Protestants, and was replaced by partisans of the 'Spanish faction' headed by the Chancellor Zdeněk Lobkovic and Karl Liechtenstein, who carried out the duties of the grand master of the court and found himself the president of the Privy

Council. Lobkovic, although Czech, was a confirmed supporter of monarchical absolutism, distrusted the Estates and installed a team composed of intransigent Catholics like Dietrichstein, Martinic and Slavata who would triumph under Ferdinand II. Even so, Lobkovic refused direct association with Spain and the Holy See.

Rudolf II's political programme was simple: internal peace and the resumption of the Turkish War with a view to reconquering Hungary and so adding to the glory of the House of Austria and recovering the lustre of the imperial title.

Within the Empire his desire for moderation was misunderstood at a time when 'parties' were being organized along confessional lines. Having refused to appropriate the duke of Wurtemberg's inheritance, Rudolf intervened, rather half-heartedly, in the dispute over the succession to Jülich and Cleves, two important duchies in the Cologne region which, it was feared, might pass from a Catholic house to the counts Palatine of Neuburg, who were then Protestant. He pronounced their sequestration, which was within his right as emperor, and let his fiery cousin, the archduke Leopold, bishop of Strassburg, occupy Jülich with a detachment of imperial soldiers, a move which risked upsetting the delicate strategic equilibrium in the lower Rhine and provoked a lively reaction from the French king, Henry IV. At the time of his assassination, Henry IV was preparing to call up his troops and to intervene with his army in the affair of the Jülich succession.

THE FIFTEEN YEARS WAR (1593–1608)[4]

In the historiography of Central Europe, this is the name given to the Austro-Turkish war that officially began in 1593 and ended with the Peace of Zsitva-Torok, the village in Hungary where negotiations were concluded between the imperial plenipotentiaries and the representatives of the Sublime Porte.

During the period 1568–93, the two powers had adhered fairly closely to the terms of the Peace of Adrianople, although border incidents had become increasingly frequent. The Sublime Porte turned its attention towards the Mediterranean, which it had abandoned after the conquest of Cyprus and the resounding defeat at Lepanto in 1571. The Ottoman empire had resumed its struggle against its avowed enemy, the shi'ite Persia of the Safavids. In the period 1576–90 the armies of Murad III led a series of campaigns in Azerbaïjan and Georgia, lands which the 1590 peace had given to him in perpetuity. These campaigns claimed the lives of many janissaries but Rudolf II did not take advantage of the Turks' difficulties and on the advice of Lazarus von Schwendi, a border general of Alsatian origin, the imperial court maintained a mood of cautious expectation, despite the numerous Turkish incursions into the Hungarian towns close to the frontier. Hungary took advantage of this respite to bind its wounds. Those peasants who had fled returned to their villages; local studies have established that the population of Transdanubia increased notably.

In 1593 the pasha of Bosnia, Hassan, who carried out endless raids against Croatia, was captured by the Croatian ban, set upon and killed. The Sublime Porte considered this incident a *casus belli* and broke the truce. The grand vizier embarked on a campaign with an army of 30 000 men in regular battalions supported by a considerable number of Tartar auxiliaries. The Turks' initiative was greeted with relief at the imperial court, where talk was already of 'Ottoman decline', a prelude to the inevitable and imminent collapse of their empire, which was epitomized by the sultan Murâd III, a fat pleasure-loving glutton, incapable of leading his janissaries. The 'experts' were a little premature in their judgement and the ensuing campaign showed that the enemy army remained formidable.

Rudolf II, while he was similarly incapable of heading his troops, nevertheless conceived a diplomatic plan of action of great scope. His treasurer Zacharias Geizkofler orchestrated a propaganda campaign to glorify the House of Austria as it undertook the reconquest of Hungary, while the emperor turned towards potential enemies of the Sublime Porte, namely Muscovy and shah Abbas the Great of Persia. Rudolf wanted to set in progress a counter-alliance involving the 'Austrian' faction in Poland in a project for a crusade. In 1595 he received at Prague a Muscovite embassy and responded in 1597 by sending count Abraham von Dohna to Moscow. But Russia at that time was experiencing great difficulties, which reached their climax in the 'Time of Troubles', and was no longer in a position to conduct an active foreign policy.

The project for an offensive alliance with shah Abbas was a scheme conceived on the grand scale: following the old dream of Charles V, the emperor was to have assumed leadership of a European coalition and, directly allied with Persia, would have taken the Turks from behind. The architect of the Persian alliance was an Englishman resident at Ispahan, Anthony Sherley, who in 1600 led a Persian embassy to Prague where it was received by the emperor. Whatever Sherley's true character – and he is often seen simply as an adventurer – Rudolf II gave the plan for military action his wholehearted approval and in turn sent to the Persian court an embassy led by István Kakas from Transylvania. Sherley returned to Prague in 1607 after the conclusion of the treaty of Zsitva-Torok, which Rudolf II had dismissed as unrealistic and not in accord with his plans. Meanwhile, the king of France did not at any time renounce the Turkish alliance, which was maintained by his ambassador at Constantinople, Savary de Brèves. He it was who in 1596 had forced Murâd III on the offensive in Hungary and obtained the renewal of the capitulations on particularly advantageous terms in 1604 after the accession of sultan Ahmed I (1603–17).

The conditions of the diplomatic game had, then, changed very little since the days of Süleymân the Magnificent, even if the indiscipline of the janissaries in the capital could give a misleading impression and rouse false hopes in the Christian camp. As for coordinating effective military action, whatever the Safavids' deep-seated hatred of the Ottomans, this proved a quite unrealistic fantasy given the obstacles to communications between Ispahan and Prague. In 1610, on the eve of Rudolf II's death, negotiations were still afoot as the emperor had not renounced his grandiose designs.

Among the Porte's vassals in Eastern Europe, Rudolf had found allies who were much closer and so much more useful than the Persians. The prince of Transylvania, Zsigmond Báthory, refused to campaign on the side of the Turks as required by his 'protégé' status. A Catholic Hungarian magnate and brother of the king of Poland, István Báthory, Zsigmond even married the archduchess Maria-Christina, sister of Ferdinand of Styria.[5] In 1594 he aligned himself resolutely with the Habsburg camp, bringing Rudolf II the support of the Danubian principalities, Moldavia and Wallachia which also rejected Ottoman suzerainty and fought in the Christian camp. When the Serbs seized the opportunity to revolt, the whole of south-east Europe stood ranged against the Porte. The Prague court meanwhile followed a short-sighted policy with the basic objective of re-establishing Habsburg authority in Transylvania while the *condottiere* Giorgio Basta, who commanded the imperial troops, misjudged who was the enemy: he went in hot pursuit of the Romanian prince Michael the Brave, who had been elected prince of Transylvania in 1600, and so had united under his authority for the first time Transylvania, Wallachia and Moldavia – a historic moment which would later nourish the dreams of Romanian patriots until the very end of the Habsburg monarchy. Michael the Brave was assassinated in 1601 on the orders of Basta, who believed that his removal would ensure that the imperial troops had the upper hand.[6] The revolt of István Bocskai would presently reduce to nothing the Prague court's plans for hegemony.

The war was drawn out in a series of sieges and brought only illusory results with losses and gains in equal measure. The Christian army generally enjoyed numerical superiority as it was made up of at least 50 000 regular soldiers, 10 000 Hungarians, 20 000 imperial troops and 20 000 Transylvanians, supplemented by Hungarian and Romanian auxiliaries. The imperial army counted Italians, Walloons, Czechs and Germans among its numbers and welcomed volunteers from other countries, especially England and, after the civil wars were ended, France; the duke of Mercoeur even received the command of the army in 1602. Some of the members of the League were drawn to the Hungarian war as much by its ideology – it had the allure of a crusade – as by the chance of employment now that peace had for the most part been restored to France. The war served as a practice ground for many future leaders in the Thirty Years War, the Walloon Johann Tserclaes von Tilly and the founder of Virginia, captain John Smith, who made his military début in the Hungarian campaign. It also allowed for the refinement of the system of war entrepreneurs, who were assured of a good future in Central Europe during the Thirty Years War.[7]

The army was, all the same, nothing more than a band of indifferently disciplined mercenaries: the only large battle, that at Mezökeresztes in October 1596, was lost through the indiscipline of the soldiers; after the initial success over the Ottoman troops who had given ground, the imperial troops became engrossed in pillaging the Turkish camp and were unable to withstand the counter-attack in which they were torn to pieces, the campaign ending lamentably. On another occasion, the garrison at Györ was seized by panic and forced the governor to surrender in the hope of escaping a massacre. The leaders were hardly any better than the troops. The archdukes Matthias and Maximilian were poor generals and it was the latter who was largely responsible for the defeat at Mezökeresztes. At so late a stage in the season the Ottoman army, faithful to its wonted timetable, was preparing to return towards Belgrade and Constantinople. In 1594 the count of Hardegg paid with his head for the capitulation of Györ which had imperilled the entire defensive system of the Military Frontier. He was brought before a war council, condemned and executed as an example.

The army was expensive and accordingly was badly paid, the financial demands it made far exceeding the ordinary capacity of the monarchy. The treasurer Zacharias Geizkofler had recourse to borrowing and the financier Lazarus Henkel, soon to become lord of Donnersmarck, made a fortune through this kind of operation. Taxes had to be raised. Among the peasants, the war effort gave rise to unbearable tensions which manifested themselves in Austria as popular revolts. Evidently the monarchy was still less than the Ottoman empire, capable of supporting a prolonged war. Despite the dreams excited by the early successes of the war, the hour had not yet come for the reconquest of Hungary.

When the imperial troops captured Esztergom and Visegrad, it became possible to believe that Buda, the historic capital and gateway to the Hungarian plain, would soon be recovered. But the Turkish counter-offensive and the fall of Györ in 1594 gave rise to serious misgivings. In 1596 sultan Murâd III, egged on by the French ambassador, took the head of his army and seized Eger despite the town's heroic struggle to defend itself. It was only in 1598 that Adolf von Schwarzenburg (forefather of the conqueror of Leipzig in 1813) succeeded in retaking Györ and filling the open breach in the defensive system covering Pressburg and Vienna. The net gains after ten years of warfare were meagre for both sides: the Turks had taken two important frontier towns, Kanizsa in Slavonia and Eger in Upper Hungary, while the imperial troops under general Basta had occupied Transylvania. The Hungarian orders, who had little enthusiasm for the war, were exasperated by the failures of the imperial troops who went on the rampage and seemed simply to be the secular arm of the Counter-Reformation. The auxiliary Hungarian troops, the *hajduks*, were ready to revolt in order to consolidate their social status. A few blunders on the part of the Prague court acting in Rudolf's name were sufficient to provoke rebellion in Hungary.

THE REVOLT OF ISTVÁN BOCSKAI (1604–6)[8]

Bocskai was a feudal lord from the east of the Tisza (Tiszántúl) region who had grown rich and led a political career in Transylvania. A mediocrity and an invalid, he was minister to his nephew Zsigmond Báthory, a mediocrity and an invalid. He drove him to ally with the Habsburgs and to fight the Turks but as the situation developed, he changed his mind and at the end of the war was an ally of the Sublime Porte, which he believed better disposed towards the Hungarian orders, their privileges and his country's religious liberties. It was then a politico-religious conflict that was brewing.

As early as 1580, the primate of Hungary, Miklós Oláh, had had the decrees of the Council of Trent published and had installed Jesuits, even though Catholicism, while it remained the only state religion in Royal Hungary, was now practised only in Croatia. The Lutherans and members of the Reformed Churches enjoyed legal status only in Transylvania, so the Prague authorities were in a position to bring the palatine Illesházy to trial, condemn him to death and pronounce the confiscation of his immense estates, which Lazarus Henckel von Donnersmarck especially coveted as reimbursement for the sums owed him by the chamber of accounts. Illesházy appealed in vain before the Diet, the supreme court of Hungary, and the class of great landowners felt threatened.

Matthias believed that occupation of the country by the imperial troops afforded a golden opportunity for hastening the Counter-Reformation. In 1604 he ordered Belgiojoso, a general originally from Milan in command of the army in Upper Hungary, to seize the large church at Kassa (Košice) and to restore it to Catholicism on the pretext that it was a royal town directly subject to the Habsburgs' authority. As 95 per cent of the population of Kassa was Lutheran, the Protestants all felt that this was an act of unwarranted violence. Belgiojoso, having occupied Illesházy's estates, wanted to seize Bocskai's land. The 1604 session of the Diet marked the break between the Habsburgs and the orders, who allied with the *hajduks*; the insurrection quickly assumed the character of a war of national liberation directed against the Habsburgs, the imperial troops and the Germans of Austria. The burghers of Kassa even stopped speaking German and adopted Hungarian to show clearly that they were natives of the kingdom.

The mainspring of the insurrection was Bethlen Gábor, a Hungarian nobleman and a Calvinist from Transylvania who took refuge in Turkey in protest against the occupation of his country by imperial troops. He called on Bocskai, who had withdrawn to the Oradea (Nagyvárad) region, to take the head of the movement and to negotiate an alliance with the Sublime Porte. Belgiojoso, who set in motion the Hungaro-Turkish machinations, wanted to occupy the east of the Tisza (Tiszántúl) region and, with the aid of Basta, to seize Transylvania. The orders had at their disposal only some private garrisons guarding various fortified castles. Bocskai, while he waited for help from the Turks, had the idea of appealing to the *hajduks* and so gave the insurrection a new dimension; from being a straightforward noble revolt, as legitimate as it was, it assumed the character of a national and social movement.

The *hajduks* were originally Balkan shepherds who had fought the Ottomans as irregulars, and whose movement later spread to Hungary. By the end of the sixteenth century they were peasants who had fled the feudal estates to escape the *robot*. Taking refuge in the Military Frontier, they made up auxiliary units of footsoldiers totalling 5000 in number, and supported the imperial troops during the Fifteen Years War. Always depicted in national costume, dressed in a cap decorated with three crow's feathers, they were Hungarian patriots hostile to the Habsburgs and the Catholic Church but – and this complicates matters – they possessed a measure of class consciousness and were equally hostile to the feudal regime. Having become professional soldiers they wanted to obtain full ownership of land without the constraints of the *robot*, even if this meant guaranteeing military service in return. These homeless wanderers, who generally had nothing to lose, excelled at guerrilla operations. The nobility were afraid of them because they were a bad example to the peasantry. The complaints set before the Diet always included a number of clauses against fugitive peasants and the frontier captains who protected them. A large landowner himself, István Bocskai was able to attract their sympathy and to obtain their cooperation against Belgiojoso.

Even the *hajduks* who served in the imperial army deserted and rallied to István Bocskai's camp. They all hoped to enjoy the status of freemen in a Hungary freed from Habsburg tutelage. The crushing of the insurrection in Lower Austria had shown them that the archduke Matthias, while himself not hostile to the peasants, would let the orders carry out a programme of repression that served their interests and (bad) feelings. As for the emperor Rudolf, in accord with the model of a good sovereign father to his subjects, he had received peasant delegations and had listened attentively to their complaints but had done nothing. Even if he had been so inclined, he would have encountered the opposition of the orders and at the same time would have upset the social equilibrium which tended to reinforce the power of the feudal lords.

Bocskai repulsed Belgiojoso's attack in the autumn of 1604, moved on to the counter-attack, took Debrecen and Kassa by assault and then invaded and liberated Transylvania. Presently Basta and Belgiojoso's armies were forced to withdraw into Transdanubia. In 1605 Bocskai was elected prince of Transylvania and received royal insignia from sultan Ahmed which included a magnificent crown, a masterpiece of the oriental goldsmith's art, which is now in the museum at Budapest. The Ottomans considered Bocskai to be king of Hungary, prince of Transylvania and a vassal of the Porte. His troops conquered Transdanubia while the Turkish army again took Esztergom from the imperial troops. The last conquest of the Fifteen Years War was thus lost once more.

In the Hungarian camp there were deep divisions. While the Transylvanian nobility wanted to continue the war on the Turkish side, the aristocracy of Royal Hungary were frightened by the idea of an Ottoman protectorate and wanted a compromise with the Habsburgs. In return for large concessions in the matter of confessions and respect for Hungarian autonomy, they were prepared to make peace with the Habsburgs and to remain in the Christian camp as they were even more afraid for strategic and cultural reasons of becoming an Ottoman protectorate. The Transylvanians, by contrast, because of their customs were much closer to the Turks and were in a much beter position to protect themselves from them because of the geography of their small *patria*, which resembled a natural fortress between the Danubian and Wallachian plains. But both parties agreed on one point – the immediate demobilization of the *hajduks* who were dangerous and embarrassing allies.

The Habsburgs were also ready to come to terms. Rudolf II delegated his powers to his brother Matthias, who resided at Vienna and proved to be better as a diplomat than as a general. Since a number of Hungarians led by Illesházy wanted peace also for reasons of self interest, namely the consolidation of the power of the orders and the neutralization of their Ottoman ally, negotiations were possible. The conference took place at Vienna and ended in an Austro-Hungarian compromise, the first – but not the last – in the stormy history of relations between the Habsburgs and their Hungarian subjects.

THE TREATIES OF 1606 (VIENNA AND ZSITVA-TOROK)[9]

The peace treaty with the Hungarians was signed at Vienna on 23 September 1606. It was not a short-term treaty but a fundamental text which listed the confessional and political liberties of the orders and served as a point of reference during all the conflicts of the seventeenth century. When the Hungarian orders formally presented their grievances they always referred to the Peace of Vienna, treating it as the founding text of a golden age. It is true that for the first time in Hungarian public law the Catholic monopoly was broken and the two Protestant confessions (Lutheran and Reformed) finally received religious liberty in Royal Hungary. The peace was invoked by the Protestant nobles and in 1681 enabled them to negotiate to their direct benefit at Sopron and to transform a tactical success into a political victory.

The office of palatine was re-established. The palatine exercised the functions of the head of government at Pressburg and supreme commander of the feudal army. He was elected by the Diet from among four magnates, two Catholic and two Protestant, who were put forward by the Habsburg king. The finances of the kingdom would in the future totally escape the control of the chamber of accounts in Vienna. All the civil and military offices were entrusted exclusively to Hungarians. The royal towns as well as the soldiers of the Military Frontier obtained total liberty in the confessional field.

The most important provision of the Peace of Vienna was article I, which decreed that no member of the Estates and the orders of the kingdom could be disturbed in the exercise of his religion. The Protestant peasants of a Protestant lord could practise their religion freely but if the lord converted, the peasants risked being forced to convert also since confessional liberty was extended only to the orders, that is the magnates and, by a truly generous extension, the royal free towns. Such religious toleration fell far short of that demanded by the eighteenth-century philosophers, who did not want toleration to be a privilege accorded only to the nobles and by extension, their subjects, but one which was enjoyed by everyone. Article I of the Peace of Vienna stated that the text nullified all previous laws which contradicted it in any way. Certainly it was a great victory for the Protestants and brought the Counter-Reformation to a decisive halt. Above all, it offered the orders serious guarantees.

István Bocskai was confirmed as prince of Transylvania, which gave his power the double legitimacy foreseen by the Peace of Adrianople; at the same time, he ceased usurping the title of king of Hungary, which was a victory for the Habsburgs. As compensation, he received a title for life, sovereignty over some counties in the Tiszáutúl region which were then *de facto* re-attached to Transylvania to become, in Hungarian history, the *Partium*. These provisions made Transylvania for a century the bastion of Hungarian liberties and the refuge of noble Protestants. Right to the end of the seventeenth century, it had an important part in the political and diplomatic game in Eastern Europe, providing rebels with troops and political cadres, no matter how little the Sublime Porte supported this game.[10]

The orders demanded that the Bohemian and Austrian Diets guarantee the treaty, a move which marked a clear withdrawal from monarchical authority and the beginning of a revision of the constitution which recalled the worst moments of Frederick III's reign. Was the Austrian monarchy on the verge of transforming itself into a confederation of noble republics?

As for the *hajduks*, they benefited from Bocskai's generosity of spirit and received recompense for their help to the cause of Hungarian liberty. Despite the orders' resistance, he granted the *hajduks* lands on his own states in the *Partium* (eastern Hungary) and the status of free peasants.

Their name lives on in the name of the modern Hungarian county of Bihar in the Debrecen region, which has become 'Hajdu-Bihar'. Their status as freemen was, naturally, disputed by the orders.

It was only in November 1606 that the preliminaries of the Peace with the Ottoman empire were signed, with the Hungarians playing the role of mediators. As the Porte had resumed the war with Persia in 1603, it decided to negotiate, but not at any price: although it allowed the emperor the pleasures of self-esteem (the transformation of the annual tribute into a 'gift' and the status of strict equality between the two empires), it refused to restore Kanisza, Esztergom and Eger but allowed the emperor to build new fortresses on the frontier. Rudolf, with much loathing, ratified these preliminaries on 9 December 1606 and promised to send a great embassy to Constantinople carrying 200 000 florins worth of presents.

The Porte abandoned the Vác region and was able to turn all its forces against Persia. The treaty was renewed and for more than half a century the sultan found himself at peace with the emperor, even though Royal Hungary was still subject to Turkish raids and incursions. The Peace of Zsitva-Torok revealed the relative weakness of the two adversaries and confirmed the *status quo*, in reality renewing the Peace of Adrianople, which reflected the balance between the forces of the two powers: the future 'sick man' was still sufficiently strong to keep the Danubian plain with the complicity of the Hungarians but was unable to advance beyond Buda.

THE 'BRUDERZWIST' AND THE TRIUMPH OF THE ORDERS[11]

Rudolf's grand scheme ended in a fiasco and the emperor found himself totally discredited by his failure in the face of the Turks and the total victory of the orders in Hungary.

The archduke Matthias found the role of governor of Lower Austria insufficient and egged on by his favourite, Melchior Khlesl, decided to seize the imperial throne.[12] The Golden Bull of 1356 allowed deposition in favour of a younger member of the family in the event of the oldest member becoming incapacitated but it is open to question whether Rudolf II really was incapable of exercising power. Matthias gathered his brothers together in Vienna and set out his plan; as head of the family he would have himself elected king of the Romans and would leave his brother Rudolf only the title of emperor, as had been the case with Charles V after his abdication in 1556. All this was plotted in secret, without the consent of Rudolf, who interpreted Matthias's plan as treason. Matthias made a double error which finally led the two brothers to armed conflict.

Matthias's first error was tactical: he made his plan public, presenting the emperor with the *fait accompli*. He then committed a grave political error: he relied on the orders who, as in the fifteenth century, became the arbiters of the situation and whose power and ambition had not ceased to grow. In the past the Habsburgs had negotiated with them separately, but in the future the orders would unite against the dynasty. Political Calvinism supplied them with theories founded on the sovereignty of the people:

the people choose a prince and consequently can dismiss him and although God bestows the crown upon princes, he does so only through the intermediary of the people who inhabit the land. That which has made hereditary sovereigns can just as well dismiss hereditary sovereigns.

Tschernembl, moreover, was in correspondence with English Puritans at the very time that Christian of Anhalt was leading a similar struggle in the Empire and founding the Evangelical Union (1608). In short, Matthias depended upon the worst enemies of monarchical power. What is more, he and Khlesl proved to be partisans of the Counter-Reformation, indeed violently so when the chance presented itself, while the orders of the different lands of the monarchy were Protestant.

From 1608 until his death in 1612, Rudolf found his power undermined by the intrigues of his brother Matthias. He spent the final year of his reign secluded in the royal castle at Prague with just the imperial title as he had been deprived of all his crowns.

Matthias allied with the Hungarian orders in order to consolidate the gains from the Peace of Vienna of which Rudolf and his entourage so disapproved. Without becoming emperor, Matthias summoned the Diets at Pressburg and had himself elected king of Hungary. In return, the articles of the Peace of Vienna were recognized as laws of the kingdom, and legislation was passed against the peasants; in the future they were to be subject to the authority of the royal courts and could raise an appeal only at the county court, which was made up of nobles. Other measures passed later made possible the establishment of 'perpetual serfdom' for the peasants, a local variant of 'second serfdom'. Three years after the Bocskai revolt, there was, then, an alliance between the Habsburgs and the orders aimed at preventing the extension of the privileged status accorded to the *hajduks* and consolidating the domain economy which rested on the *robot*.

In a new development, the orders with Matthias's complicity formed a confederation with the Estates of Upper and Lower Austria whose representatives were present at the Diet. Presently they were joined by the Estates of Moravia whose head, Karel Žerotin, belonged to the Unity of Czech Brethren but was nevertheless a moderate man. On 19 April 1608 the confederation of the Estates of Hungary, Austria and Moravia defined its programme: besides the execution of the treaties of 1606 (the Peace of Vienna and of Zsitva-Torok), it demanded respect for justice and legality and so formed a revolutionary opposition front. Matthias, at the mercy of the orders, suddenly found himself in open opposition to the emperor. It was, however, too late to retreat. A prisoner of the movement, he decided to take the head of an army and to march on Bohemia to seize the power still in Rudolf's hands.

Rudolf was saved by the orders of the kingdom of Bohemia and, indirectly, by the Evangelical Union, which mistrusted Matthias and preferred a weak emperor. The nobility of Bohemia hated the nobility of Moravia. Rudolf, after giving verbal assurances, signed what amounted to a treaty with the orders at Stará Libená on 26 June 1608. To keep his throne, he recognized the *Confessio bohemica* of 1575, the equal right of all to public office without confessional discrimination, the eviction of foreigners and even authorized the Estates to levy troops. Renouncing at the same time the throne of Hungary, he promised his brother Matthias the right to succeed to the throne of Bohemia. Rudolf had, in fact, lost all real power. The Austrian monarchy found itself divided between four archdukes: Rudolf, Matthias, Ferdinand and his brother Leopold, bishop of Passau (and of Strassburg), who administered the Tyrol and Further Austria.

The conflict between Rudolf and Matthias ended in an unhoped-for triumph for the orders. In Hungary, it was the palatine Illésházy, elected by the Diet according to the provisions of the Peace of Vienna, who really governed the executive. The right of resistance granted to the orders by virtue of the Golden Bull of András II, revived by the Calvinist jurists, was extended to cover Moravia as well as Hungary. The Estates arrogated for themselves the right to declare war, foreigners were excluded from public office in Moravia, Czech became the only official language, the Diet refused Matthias all legislative power and the captain of the country (*Landeshauptmann*) became the head of the executive, like the palatine in Hungary. In Austria, the homage paid to Matthias was a real capitulation and he revived and extended to the whole population the oral assurances granted by Maximilian II in 1568. In 1610 Matthias recognized the privileges of the towns, made them a fourth order and allowed them to sit with the nobility.

In Bohemia, Rudolf owed his throne solely to the loyalty of the orders, and the 'Spanish party', led by the chancellor Lobkovic, found itself running out of steam in the face of the 'party of the orders' led by Budovec. He created a military organization and entrusted its management to Matthias of Thurn and Leonard Colonna von Fels. Mediocre organizers and yet worse captains, these two were incapable of setting an efficient armed force on its feet. They created a directory of thirty members to which each order sent ten elected members. On 9 July 1609 Rudolf II gave in and granted the orders the Letter of Majesty which made them the virtual masters of the kingdom.

The Letter of Majesty, as brief as its period of application, has held a special position in the collective imagination of the Czech nation because it was an important landmark in the history of religious toleration. It granted the orders total and unlimited religious liberty. What is more, no lord was allowed to impose his confession on his vassals and in this respect the Letter went much further than the Peace of Vienna. The orders were finally

255

given control of the Utraquist consistory and the university of Charles IV at Prague. It was a severe set-back for the Catholic Reformation. Lastly, the Utraquists were permitted to build churches in the royal towns and on the royal domain.

The orders in Silesia obtained similar concessions on 20 August 1609. Budovec was fully aware that the orders had triumphed and in the future would alone hold legislative power. In the Empire the effect of these measures was disastrous, because the princes were under the impression that the office of emperor was vacant and accordingly organized themselves into hostile factions and drew support from foreign alliances.

Rudolf II reacted weakly and followed a yet worse policy: he appealed to the archduke Leopold and tried to make him king of the Romans so as to bar his brother Matthias's path to imperial power. Leopold raised troops among the veterans of the Hungarian campaign, seized the bishopric of Passau, entered Bohemia, marched on Prague and, with the emperor's complicity, occupied the Hradčany. The orders then appealed to Matthias whose mercenaries proceeded to commit the same kinds of outrages as the veterans of colonel Rammee, Leopold's infantry *condottiere*. The year 1611 long remained in the memory of the inhabitants of Bohemia and the 'people of the war of Passau' who, according to the Spanish ambassador, Zuñiga, did considerable harm to the Catholic cause. Leopold's mob merely took part in the general orgy of atrocities but its activities served to discredit the old emperor. Abandoned by everyone, including the king of Spain and the princes of the Holy League, Rudolf was obliged to surrender the throne of Bohemia to Matthias, who on 26 May 1611 was crowned king.

Matthias's coronation completed the process. Rudolf II had nothing but the imperial title, as the elector of Saxony refused to deprive him of it, and the Austrian monarchy became a federation of completely autonomous lands governed by the orders.

Rudolf II's death on 20 January 1612 put an end to the fratricidal war since the old sovereign had pursued Matthias with unrelenting hatred and did not cease to concoct schemes aimed at taking vengeance upon him. The Catholic and Protestant electors of the Empire duly elected Matthias king of the Romans on 13 June 1612, since they saw him as the lesser evil pending a final solution to the problem of the succession, for Matthias did not seem in a state to have legitimate heirs.

RUDOLF II, PATRON OF THE ARTS AND SCIENCES[13]

Rudolf II's failure on the political and military level should not obscure his role as a patron. When he installed himself in the Hradčany in 1582, he was faced with a collection of Gothic buildings built by Władysław

Jagiełłończyk and a small Renaissance palace, the Belvedere, which Ferdinand I had had built for his wife, Anna Jagiellon. Lacking money, Rudolf was not a great builder; he had an observatory constructed but he was content to remodel the existing buildings.

A true Renaissance prince, he preferred to devote his resources to the purchase of rare works, which he installed in four great rooms and the galleries of his palace. The palace became at once home to an ethnographical museum, an art and antiques gallery, a library of rare books and a collection of curiosities such as the table inlaid with precious stones representing trees, animals and flowers, and which, according to Bohuslav Balbin, so gave the illusion of reality that it passed for one of the wonders of the world.

An essential and specific task of his ambassadors at Rome and Madrid was to track down works of art on the market. They sent him catalogues of the most famous collections and when the collections of cardinal Granvelle and of Antonio Pérez, two ministers of Philip II, were dispersed, the imperial ambassador acquired a certain number of pieces and Rudolf, for want of ready money, had to appeal to the Fuggers for credit. The fruits of this collecting were on the grand scale and added to the imperial glory, as Rudolf desired. The catalogues of his collections have been preserved in the National Library at Vienna. The paintings accorded with current taste and included a large number of works by Titian and Corregio, as well as works by Raphael and Leonardo da Vinci, which were then prized pieces in every royal collection.

These treasures are now dispersed: in common with all that Rudolf undertook, his collections suffered a lamentable destiny. During the Swedish occupation in 1648, they were sacked, moved to Sweden and never returned. This is how the rarest manuscript, the *Codex Argenteus*, containing fragments of the Bible of Wulfila (the first translation made for the use of the Goths) was taken to Uppsala where it is now on display. This manuscript from the sixth century was discovered in 1553 and Rudolf had made it a point of honour to acquire the 187 leaves of purple parchment relieved by silver characters.

Rudolf was not only a collector but also a patron. The most celebrated of the artists at the Prague court was perhaps the Milanese Giuseppe Arcimboldo (1537–93), who had already worked for Ferdinand I and Maximilian II. The bizarre mode in which he composed portraits from fruits, flowers and vegetables has earned him a justifiable fame to the present day but Rudolf had also recognized his extraordinary merits, ennobling the artist a few months before his death in 1593. One of the central figures of the Prague court was Hans von Aachen, the painter and son-in-law of the composer Orlando di Lasso, who succeeded Arcimboldo after 1592. The other great mannerist painter was the Dutch artist Bartholomeus Spranger (1546–1611) who, after a spell in Italy, was summoned to the imperial court by Maximilian II and died at Prague in the service of Rudolf. There were also the Swiss artist Joseph Heintz and the

Flemish artists Roelandt Savery and Dirk de Quade Van Ravensteyn. These artists were all famed for their large allegorical compositions in the mannerist style, their skill at portraiture and the thousands of drawings that they produced.

Rudolf in common with his contemporaries showed great interest in the art of the goldsmith. Two exceptional pieces show how this particular art was directly linked to the lofty idea which the emperor entertained of his function and of his House: the ewer depicting an ancient triumph, a work attributed to Christoph Jamnitzer of Prague, and, of course, the imperial crown, now kept at Vienna, which became the imperial crown of the Austrian Empire after 1806.

With a particular enthusiasm for philosophical theorizing, the emperor and many of his contemporaries believed in the underlying unity of the universe. It is not surprising that Rudolf took a lively interest in astrology since it was considered one of the most direct ways of participating in the thoughts of the Supreme Being, the mind of God. A fluid emanated from God which through the stars acted on living beings with the result that observation of the stars allowed one to discern His designs. These speculations were different from the 'popular' astrology which was concerned with knowing the future destiny of individuals and which Albrecht Eusebius von Wallenstein was shortly to practise. Without making any distinction, Rudolf was also a patron of astronomy, then held to be an auxiliary science of astrology. According to the astronomers, observation of the vast reaches of the sky would lead to a better understanding of the universe. Rudolf spent hours in his observatory at the Belvedere, tracking the path of the stars; he fostered the research of Tycho Brahe, a Danish nobleman in exile for political reasons, and allowed him to work in peace at the head of a team of scholars.

He welcomed another victim of persecution to succeed Brahe, the Lutheran mathematician Johannes Kepler, one of the first casualties of the Counter-Reformation in the Austrian monarchy. Kepler immortalized the name of his patron and protector when he published the *Tabulae Rudolfinae*. Through his tireless labours, Kepler was able to calculate the trajectory of the then known stars and made possible later astronomical research as well as easing the task of the astrologers.

The royal castle had alchemical laboratories. Rudolf laboured in the search for the philosopher's stone, not to make gold, but to obtain what he believed would be the perfect substance. Tradition claims that the Hradčany long housed an inscription commemorating the emperor's great alchemical feat when he transmuted lead into gold through a substance supplied by an alchemist. He has also been charged with being obsessed with black magic; he engineered the visit to Prague of the magician Hieronymus Scotus,*

---

* Translator's note: confusion reigns over Scotus's Christian name and he is referred to as both Alessandro and Hieronymus Scotus as well as 'Odoardus Scotus'; see R.J.W. Evans, *Rudolf II*, p. 210.

who furnished him with the means of entering into communication with the Prince of Darkness, and in the seventeenth century there was still on display the armchair Rudolf had occupied during his interviews with the devil.

Rudolf's tragedy was that he refused to choose between the activities of doctor Faustus and those of an emperor. As a patron and protector of the sciences, Rudolf inclined towards late humanism – according to R.J.W. Evans he postponed the beginning of the great religious crisis which presently shook Central Europe – but it may also be asked whether a firmer hand might not have forestalled the short-lived triumph of the Protestant nobles, a triumph which engendered as its reaction militant Catholicism.

EPILOGUE: THE REIGN OF MATTHIAS (1612–18)[14]

After such a furious drive to seize power, Matthias did nothing and his brief reign was taken up with the problem of succession. Melchior Khlesl, the director of the Privy Council, was in favour of a political compromise, treading gingerly between the party of the orders and Lobkowitz's Spanish faction that was waiting in the wings. However, the hour had come for the archduke Ferdinand, the champion of the Counter-Reformation.

Since the archduke Albert was excluded, there were no other serious candidates for emperor apart from Philip III of Spain, Ferdinand and his brother Leopold. Leopold had left behind too many bad memories after his foolish escapade in 1611 and Philip III, head of the House of Austria, had no desire to reconstitute the empire of Charles V and was even prepared to purchase his exemption. Ferdinand might seem the perfect candidate: still young, he had children in good health, the archdukes Ferdinand and Leopold William, and he had been adopted by Matthias. His absolutist way of thinking and his religious fanaticism were known to everyone; he marked the end of the line of tolerant Habsburgs open to every current of Christianity.

Although the Protestant orders were powerful, the end was a compromise. Ferdinand, having promised Further Austria to Philip III by a secret convention (the treaty of Oñate, 1617), was elected king by the Diet of Bohemia in 1617 and by the Hungarian Diet in 1618. He was then obliged to swear to uphold the political and religious privileges of the two kingdoms, accepting without enthusiasm the Peace of Vienna and the Letter of Majesty. A religious man who respected the letter of the law and solemn oaths, Ferdinand II probably would have observed the laws which made him shudder so; but Bohemia's orders took the first step towards making the break and so launched the crisis that marked the beginning of the Thirty Years War.

NOTES AND REFERENCES

1. R. J. W. Evans, *Rudolf II and his World*, 2nd edn, Oxford, 1984.
2. From the Peace of Augsburg in 1555 to the defenestration of Prague in 1618, or sixty-three years of continuous peace.
3. Baldassare Castiglione, *Il Corteggiano*, Venice, 1522.
4. J.-L. Bacquet-Gramont, 'L'Empire dans sa grandeur', in Robert Mantran (*ed.*) Histoire de l'empire ottoman, Paris, 1989, pp. 139–58.
   Karl Nehring, *Adam Freiherrn zu Herbersteins Gesandschaftsreise nach Konstantinopel*, Munich, 1983.
5. Kálmán Benda, *Erdély végzetes asszonya: Báthory Zsigmondné Habsburg Mária Krisztierna*, Budapest, 1986.
6. P. Cernovodeanu (ed.) *Mihai Viteazul*, Bucharest, 1975.
7. Fritz Redlich, *The German Military Enterpriser and his Work Forces*, 2 vols, Wiesbaden, 1964.
8. Kálmán Benda, 'Der Haiduckenaufstand in Ungarn und das Erstarken der Stände in der Habsburgermonarchie 1607–1608', *Nouvelles Études hongroises*, vol. 1, Budapest, 1969, pp. 299–313.
9. Lothar Gross, 'Zur Geschichte des Wiener Vertrages vom 25 April 1606', MIOG, vol. 2, 1929.
10. Laszló Makkai, *Histoire de la Transylvanie*, Paris, 1946.
    Béla Kopeczi (ed.) *Erdély Története*, 3 vols, Budapest, 1986.
11. Hans Sturmberger, *Georg Erasmus von Tschernembl*, Linz, 1953.
12. Brigitte Hamann (ed.) 'Kaiser Mathias', in *Die Habsburger: ein biographisches Lexikon*, Vienna, 1988.
13. Evans, *Rudolf II*.
    Karl Vočelka, *Rudolf II*, Vienna, 1985.
14. Johannes Mulle, 'Die Vermittlungspolitik Khlesls von 1613–1616', MIOG, 5 vols, 1903.

CHAPTER TWENTY

Ferdinand II and the Thirty Years War

On 23 May 1618, a hundred Bohemian nobles climbed up the hill to the royal castle in Prague, which had been abandoned by the old emperor Matthias and his successor Ferdinand of Styria. They were the 'Utraquist orders' who had just convoked the 'defenders of the faith' instituted by the Letter of Majesty to regulate any confessional disputes that might arise in the kingdom of Bohemia. But the psychological climate had deteriorated since the election of Ferdinand II and the legal case which followed the construction of two Protestant churches on crown lands served to ignite the situation. The Protestant lords who had answered the appeal from the 'defenders of the faith' furiously blamed the lieutenancy council which was responsible for administering the kingdom in the king's absence. Having exhausted their supply of arguments, they resorted to force and took hold of counts Martinic and Slavata, both Czech Catholic lords and members of the council, and threw them with a young secretary out of the window. This incident is known as the 'Defenestration of Prague'.

The three victims fell into the rubbish piled high in the castle moat and, only slightly hurt, were able to take refuge in the palace of a great Catholic noblewoman, Polyxena of Perštejn; it was a fortunate turn of events which Catholic propaganda attributed to the intervention of the Virgin Mary. Ferdinand, intractable, refused to negotiate with the rebels and the Defenestration marked the break between the Habsburgs and the orders. The conflict soon spread, first to the whole monarchy, then the Empire and finally the whole of Europe, which had experienced a brief period of peace following the twelve-year truce in the Netherlands (1609–21).

THE ORIGINS OF THE CONFLICT[1]

Despite the praiseworthy efforts of contemporary Marxist historiography to explain the war in terms of economic crisis, the extension of the second serfdom or the decline of the lesser nobility, the conflict should first of all be seen as a conflict between Protestants and Catholics which was replicated as a confrontation between the sovereign and the orders; it was further complicated by the resumption of the conflict between the House of Austria and France where cardinal Richelieu feared that the Habsburgs were bent on hegemony.[2]

The European chancelleries continued to be preoccupied with Spanish imperialism even after the appeasement at the beginning of the century and the Franco-Spanish agreement sketched out under Henry IV, marked by the double marriage of Anne of Austria to Louis XIII and Elizabeth of Bourbon to Philip IV. The Madrid Habsburgs were not resigned to the final partition of the Netherlands of Charles V. The work of Michel Devèze and of Spanish historians has done justice to the legend of 'Spanish decadence' around 1620. Yet, despite Philip II's failures and the rise of Holland, Spain remained a power to be feared and was given a new impulse by Olivares, Philip IV's prime minister. The conflict, however, was born in the Empire where antagonism among Catholics, Lutherans and the Reformed Church grew worse since the Peace of Augsburg (1555) had given rise to much contention aggravated by the advance of the Counter-Reformation.

The parties had been trying to organize themselves since 1608. Some Protestant princes had formed the Evangelical Union, but the Lutherans and the Reformed hated each other heartily and had been unable to come together. The electors of Saxony and Brandenburg, out of loyalty to the emperor, had refused to form a party and the elector Palatine, who was a Calvinist, had assumed leadership of the Union with the encouragement of Christian I of Anhalt. The Catholics responded in 1609 by founding the Catholic League, which from the beginning was led by the duke of Bavaria. Both parties, then, had a Wittelsbach as leader. The Holy League united most of the ecclesiastical princes of southern Germany, in particular the archbishop-electors of Trier, Mainz and Cologne.

The affair of the Jülich succession set the two parties face-to-face and would have ended in open warfare had it not been for the assassination of the king of France, Henry IV, who was preparing to invade Germany in May 1610 to aid his Protestant allies. Eight years later, the political crisis in Bohemia provided the occasion for war.

THE POLITICAL CRISIS IN BOHEMIA[3]

Following the Defenestration, the dispute grew worse as before long there rose the question of the limits set to the Letter of Majesty. The confessional dispute grew into a rebellion. The nobles with count Thurn at their head rebelled once they understood that Ferdinand of Styria was determined to govern and that he was a supporter of absolutism: had he not taken as his motto *Princeps debet esse nulli subjectus* (a prince should be subject to no one)? Accordingly they did not hesitate to put together a provisional government of thirty members and to raise an army but since this involved open rebellion against the sovereign, many nobles in the kingdom and the annexed provinces (Moravia, Silesia and the Lusatias) were reluctant to join the side of the rebels; for this reason Karel of Zerotin remained loyal to Ferdinand while unable to prevent the orders of Moravia from following Thurn and his supporters.

The revolt quickly spread to the whole monarchy. In Upper Austria Tschernembl, a Calvinist, assumed leadership of the movement; he had pursued his advanced studies in Franconia and during a long tour of Europe, staying in Paris, London, Geneva, Strassburg and Poland (1584–91). The scion of two influential families, when he returned to Linz in 1593 he was quick to assert himself in the sessions of the provincial Diet as the leader of the Lutheran nobility, whom he encouraged to ally with the nobility of Bohemia in order to create the aristocratic republic of which he dreamt. Blinded by his hatred of Catholicism and the Habsburgs, he advocated the most radical solutions; an alliance with the Turks and, to obtain the support of the peasantry, the abolition of serfdom. It was he who urged the orders of Upper Austria to refuse homage to Ferdinand of Styria, a move which proved fatal to Upper Austrian Protestantism. The rebels presently turned to the prince of Transylvania, Bethlen Gábor, to assume leadership of the Hungarian nobility and create a real alliance of aristocratic republics, thereby giving Danubian Europe a new political structure.[4] Any compromise on the part of Ferdinand of Styria was impossible since the very future of the House of Austria was at stake. Giustinian, Venetian ambassador to Ferdinand, surmised that the real goal of these lands was to form a government on the lines of Switzerland or the United Provinces which would leave the Habsburgs with a choice between a purely nominal role or abdication. The question posed at Prague was essentially which of two models would be followed: the Dutch model with the nobility, or the Castilian model with Ferdinand.

The leaders of the Prague rebellion were neither good soldiers nor able diplomats. Thurn was quite without the qualities of a statesman and proved incapable of winning a swift victory over Ferdinand, although the latter was quite isolated in Vienna. In the spring of 1619, Dampierre's armed troops swarmed into the city, and when Thurn's men arrived in front of the Austrian capital, it was already too late. Ferdinand was able to leave for Frankfurt to have himself unanimously elected emperor on 28 August 1619. Not even the Protestant electors had believed that they should oppose the candidature of a Habsburg. As head of the Holy Roman Empire, Ferdinand II added a prestigious title to his patrimony.

The Prague rebels sought support from the German Protestants of the Evangelical Union and offered the crown of Bohemia to the young elector of the Palatinate, Frederick V, champion of the Calvinist cause.[5] Inexperienced, he was at the mercy of the whims of his minister, the fanatical Christian of Anhalt, while his wife Elizabeth, the daughter of James I of England, was full of ambition. The Bohemian revolt assumed European dimensions because it forced the German princes to take sides. The Evangelical Union and the Catholic League presently confronted each other while both sides sought support outside the Empire. Although James I, the champion of absolutism in Britain, refused to support his son-in-law, the latter could at least count on the support of the English Puritans and the Dutch Calvinists, while the free towns of the Empire showed themselves much more reserved. The Catholic powers, however, did not array themselves alongside Ferdinand II. Venice and the duke of Savoy in particular looked to take advantage of his difficulties, while Louis XIII, ever hesitant, ended by offering his mediation. Only the kings of Spain and Poland and the archduke Albert, prince of the Netherlands, gave their unreserved support.

In August 1619 the Diet of Bohemia elected the elector of the Palatinate as king, with just 10 per cent of the members of the orders taking part in the election. In any case, the new sovereign was without any power because the nobles retained the conduct of military, political and religious affairs. Despite countless warnings, Frederick V to his great misfortune accepted the crown offered to him, even though, by rebelling against the new emperor, he was putting himself *de facto* under a ban of the Empire. Frederick, even less so than Thurn, was not cut out for so difficult a situation. He brought with him Calvinist preachers whose zealous fanaticism disquieted the Lutherans and Utraquists and who did more harm to the Evangelical party than half a century of Jesuit preaching. In addition, he was neither an organizer, nor a man of war, nor one to take his moral obligations seriously. The nobility did not take arms, but contented themselves with putting together an army of mercenaries quite without experience and devoid of either patriotic or religious ideals. Some have wanted to turn the revolt, launched so unwisely and conducted so badly, into the last chance for Bohemian independence, but it is important to remember that aristocrats of German origin played a great role, that they looked to a German prince and that they were incapable of putting a national army on its feet. The nobility of Bohemia demonstrated its political incapacity and the military defeat at the White Mountain on 5 November 1620 was one of the bloodiest and most decisive battles in modern history.

The imperial troops, joined by the troops of the Catholic League, essentially the duke of Bavaria's army, marched on Prague under the command of the Walloon *condottiere*, Tilly. The orders did not field a battalion to oppose their offensive and it was only on the outskirts of Prague, at the White Mountain, that Christian of Anhalt set out a line of troops who, with the exception of some Czech battalions, scattered in the face of the first blasts of fire. The rout was general and there was no thought of establishing a second position or of defending the capital. The king, Frederick, was put to flight and abandoned his supporters to their sad fate, thereby paralyzing any inclination to resist. In the Catholic world, the victory at the White Mountain was celebrated as a miracle and was put on a par with that against the Turks at Lepanto half a century earlier. The victory is partly explained by the cohesion of Tilly's army, which was solidly staffed by preachers like the Dominican Carmelite Jesus-Maria, but it cost the emperor dear and he was obliged to mortgage Upper Austria to duke Maximilian of Bavaria, and the Lusatias to the Lutheran elector, Johann Georg of Saxony, who had rallied to Ferdinand II's cause and who tried to get back his expenses. Only Philip III and the Holy See gave their subsidies without accepting security.

Such was the price, but the victory enabled Ferdinand II to reorganize the kingdom of Bohemia according to the principles that he had always defended and to put an end to the aristocratic republic. He was at last master in his own house, completing three series of measures in the course of the following decade and deriving all that he could from the *Verwirkungstheorie*, the theory of forfeit. State right was a contract between the king and the orders; as the orders had unilaterally broken this contract the king was free of every obligation in both the political and confessional domain. The orders had gambled and had lost and the king felt authorized to punish the rebels, banish heretics and impose a new constitution.

The Repression[6]

Ferdinand II appointed Karl Liechtenstein governor and entrusted him with the task of restoring order. Twenty-seven Czech and German members of the Estates were condemned to death and were executed in front of the town hall at Prague on 21 June 1621. These executions left a deep impression and were long held up in reproach against the Habsburgs. The emergency court ordered a number of fines and confiscations which effected a significant social reversal. Many nobles compromised in the revolt had to sell for next to nothing or else abandon to the treasury one or more of their estates, a process which hastened the ruin of the *Ritterstand* underway since the sixteenth century. Royal authority had grown so greatly that the treasury was unable to retain these estates. Ferdinand II preferred to create his own clientele, giving or selling lands at a low price to those who had been the architects of the victory. The Kinskýs as well as old Czech families such as the Czernins were able to enrich themselves and passed into the order of lords while the Lobkowicz family further increased its fortune. Some Bohemian lords of German origin such as the Liechtensteins also profited from the emperor's generosity, as did Walloon and Italian officers who had served Ferdinand well, such as Tilly, Buquoy and Colloredo. The emperor's German favourites, such as the Eggenburgs, also received important estates, but it would be wrong to claim that the

Czech nobility was dispossessed to the benefit of German adventurers. More precisely, the old nobility, in particular the knights, who were Czech or German (Thurn was also ruined), had been dispossessed to the benefit of a new governing class which passed as loyal to the sovereign. The economic power and consequently the political power of the old families of Bohemia were crushed, all the more so since the religious patent of 1627 forced many nobles into exile.

The restoration of Catholicism

Ferdinand II swiftly restored the religious orders to their former grandeur and entrusted the university of Charles IV to the Jesuits. Protestant preachers were banished and non-Catholics relieved of their responsibilities. In 1627 the commissions of reformation were appointed by edict with the task of singling out, in a period of six months, all the members of the orders who still had not rallied to Catholicism. Two possibilities were offered – submission or exile – after which the party concerned was to sell his goods to Catholics. Many thousands of families were obliged to move. As for the peasants, they were provisionally forbidden to go into exile. The conversion of the masses to Catholicism lasted, just as in Lower Austria, until the end of the century and was felt more cruelly than the lack of parishes, aristocrats and prelates alike refusing to restore secularized Church tithes and goods.

The 'renewed' constitution of 1627
(Obnovené zřízení zemské: verneuerte Landesordnung)

The 'renewed' constitution affirmed the principle of royal authority but left the orders and their political voice, the Diet, with a large measure of autonomy. Far from depriving the country of all liberty, as liberal historians have averred, Ferdinand II brought the orders into partnership with the government of Bohemia. The vote of direct taxes remained within their competence and this allowed them to debate the total sum, or to refuse extraordinary taxes. While the king alone henceforth had authority to propose laws, the Diet, which was summoned each year, discussed proposals and its conclusions were promulgated in the 'articles of the Diet'.

The real innovations were in other areas – the election of the king, the banning of Protestantism, the modification of the composition of the Diet. The royal crown of Bohemia, hitherto elective, was declared hereditary in the House of Austria, a measure that freed the House from election-time haggling. The king convoked the Diet, exercised justice, alone determined foreign policy, proposed the admission of new members into the orders and, most importantly, appointed office holders within the kingdom. The chancellery of Bohemia, the administrative body and supreme judiciary of the kingdom, was transferred to Vienna and the Bohemian chancellor was henceforth chosen by the king from among the aristocracy. Although these measures served only to strengthen royal authority, they did not have a pronounced absolutist character.

Far more significant was the modification of the Diet's internal equilibrium: numerous knights left the country and those who remained were generally ruined and so found it difficult to defray the expenses of attending a session of the assembly (the cost of travelling and staying at Prague). They all but disappeared from the Diet and it became hard to fill the offices reserved for the *Ritterstand*. The clergy once again constituted the first order of the kingdom and were represented in the Diet by the prelates, that is bishops, abbots and deans of chapters, who were essentially recruited from the higher nobility: the Diet was in practice a manifestation of the order of lords. Unlike the Hungarian Diet, the Diet of Bohemia became an assembly of great lords who were in principle loyal to the Habsburgs but who were in a position to defend their own interests. It is possible to speak of absolutism in Bohemia only in so far as the knights and urban patriciate ceased to play a political role and dissension was muffled.

The aristocracy tried to compensate for its lost position by emphasizing its privileges as feudal lords and by strengthening its authority over the peasantry. The court aristocracy was no less powerful than the order of lords but it was, in principle, just as loyal and attached to the idea of the Austrian monarchy. It played a leading role in the development of baroque culture.

In the hereditary lands, it was Upper Austria which caused Ferdinand II the most difficulties. Occupied by the Bavarians, it was subjected like the rest to the edicts of reformation. The introduction of Catholic preachers led to disturbances directed against the Bavarians as much as the Catholic clergy. In 1625 a series of executions provoked a serious peasant revolt which had a social and religious character and lasted more than a year. Calm was finally restored in 1628 after harsh repression, some measures of appeasement and above all the departure of the Bavarians.

The demands of Bavaria and Spain, who occupied the Palatinate, involved Ferdinand II in an active policy in Germany. On the Hungarian side, however, he had been able to keep his hands free by reason of the truce that he had concluded with Bethlen Gábor in 1613. Although the Protestant-dominated Diet of 1620 had elected Bethlen king, it had the wisdom to make peace with Ferdinand II. By the treaty of Nikolsburg (1622), Bethlen renounced the royal title but kept not only the principality of Transylvania (which was the base of his power) but also seven counties in Upper Hungary for his lifetime; having become a prince of the Holy Roman Empire (*Reichsfürst*), he obtained the principalities of Oppeln and Ratibor in Silesia. The Peace of Pressburg of 1627 confirmed the provisions, which the Peace of Vienna in 1606 had withdrawn, and with the Jesuits' help, cardinal Pázmány, primate of Hungary, was able to continue his task of Catholic reconquest which was directed essentially against the members of the nobility and carried out within the bounds of complete legality. During this period Hungary was never a source of serious concern for the Habsburgs. However, Ferdinand II was unable to quell the disquiet in Europe to which the Battle of the White Mountain had given rise.

FERDINAND II AND THE EMPIRE[7]

Drawing upon the consequences of Frederick V's rebellion, Ferdinand placed him under a ban of the Empire and confiscated the Palatinate, his patrimony, which was occupied by Spanish troops under Spinola (Lower Palatinate) and Maximilian's Bavarians (Upper Palatinate). More importantly, he gave his electoral dignity to the duke of Bavaria without having summoned Frederick before the Diet or having consulted the college of electors. Even in the Middle Ages, a vassal accused of forfeiting his position was first of all summoned to appear before the Diet in order to justify his actions. He could be condemned only by default and the sentence of confiscation could be carried out only after he had been condemned. Ferdinand II failed to respect the forms of German civil law because he was under pressure from the ambitious Maximilian of Bavaria, who was well aware that he had saved the emperor and his army and had won the Battle of the White Mountain. Hindered by his allies' hesitation, Ferdinand granted him the electoral title for life by imperial decree in 1623, an act which for a long time blocked all prospects of an equitable settlement in the Empire.

The deposition of Frederick V shocked most of the princes of Europe. Having fled to the Hague to his uncle, the *stadhouder* Maurice of Nassau, and being deprived of his resources and his patrimony, the 'winter king' found more support than he had during his short-lived glory. He had at his disposal the armies of Mansfeld and Christian of Brunswick, who were still paid by the Estates General of the United Provinces. Mansfeld occupied eastern Friesland and Brunswick marched in the direction of Bohemia. Tilly, meanwhile, with the army of the Catholic League invaded Lower Saxony and crushed Brunswick at Stadtlohn on 6 August 1623. From then onwards the field of battle extended into northern Germany. Camerarius, adviser to Frederick V, spent without counting the cost in order to put on its feet a great Protestant alliance which included the Great Britain of James I, Gustavus Adolphus's Sweden, the United Provinces and even Richelieu's France, united by the common goal of reconquering the Palatinate.

The Palatine councillors had begun to despair until, at the critical moment, Christian IV, the rich and ambitious king of Denmark, decided to intervene to put an end to imperial action in northern Germany. Elected head of the Lower Saxon Circle, he engaged an army of 20 000 mercenaries in spring 1625 at a particularly inopportune moment, as he could count only on Mansfeld's small army, and James I's death deprived him of the active support of Great Britain. But more significantly, Ferdinand II engaged Wallenstein as 'general entrepreneur of war' and placed his own army alongside Tilly's.

Albrecht Eusebius von Wallenstein* was a Czech lord and Catholic convert from Protestantism, who in 1618 had sided with Ferdinand, raising troops for the king and subsequently profiting greatly from confiscations. He had put together a vast principality in the north of Bohemia, the duchy of Frýdlant which was the base of his economic power and of his activities as a war entrepreneur. Out of conviction and a taste for profit, he placed a good army at the emperor's disposal. He recruited, equipped and fed his regiments while granting credit to Ferdinand, who made over to him the revenue from the contributions.

A great scheme was elaborated for the 1626 campaign: Mansfeld was to rejoin Bethlen Gábor in Silesia and Christian IV would march on Vienna. The Danish king was beaten by Tilly in Lower Saxony on 26 August 1626, however, and it was to be the campaign of 1627 that bogged down the all-powerful imperial troops in northern Germany. After Bethlen had signed the Peace of Pressburg at the beginning of 1627, Wallenstein's army pursued Mansfeld and, after occupying Pomerania and Mecklenburg, invaded Jutland.

Ferdinand II was then at the peak of his power in the empire. His army overwhelmed the occupied lands with taxes, but Wallenstein was unable to take Stralsund or the Danish islands. The emperor believed that the moment had come to exact heavy penalties. The dukes of Mecklenburg, on the pretext that they had supported Christian IV, were, like the elector Palatine, sentenced to forfeiture and divested of their patrimony, while Wallenstein was invested with the duchy of Mecklenburg. The emperor demanded from Christian IV the cession of Jutland as well as the payment of heavy indemnities which earned the Danish king the support of Great Britain, the United Provinces and Sweden, and enabled him to sign an honourable peace at Lübeck in May 1629. Christian IV recovered all his lost territories but promised not to intervene any further in the affairs of the Empire.

The year served no less to confirm Ferdinand II's undeniable success in the military field. Christian IV was beaten and discredited, Charles I, the king of England and Scotland, ceased to participate in the war and Mansfeld and Bethlen, although unconquered, had stopped fighting shortly

---

* Translator's note: although the general is usually known as Wallenstein, the original form of his family's name was Waldstein (German) or Valdštejn (Czech).

before they died. The Protestant party seemed prostrated, while Wallenstein's army terrorized northern Germany. Ferdinand seemed very close to restoring his imperial authority, annihilating religious liberties and securing for the House of Austria a position of formidable power in Europe. In alliance with Philip IV's Spain, might not the House go on to establish its hegemony over the Baltic, or even realize the universal monarchy to its favour?

Ferdinand II, convinced that he was fulfilling a mission willed by God, in principle governed with the aid of his Privy Council which was presided over by the prince of Eggenberg and dominated by Anton Wolfrad, abbot of Kremsmünster, Stralendorf, vice-chancellor of the Empire, and the young Maximilian of Trauttmannsdorf, all of whom favoured a cautious policy. The emperor, however, was also under the influence of his confessor, the Jesuit Lamormain. Honest, wise and intelligent, originally from Luxemburg, Lamormain and the emperor were in agreement over more than just politics; he too dreamt of the restoration of Catholicism in the Empire and since 1624 had believed it within the realms of possibility. Ferdinand II was likewise subject to the influence of Wallenstein, who used his talents as an administrator in his duchy of Mecklenburg and pursued an active policy in the Baltic, while Collalto, president of the council of war, encouraged the emperor to intervene in Italy over the Mantuan succession. Lastly, Maximilian of Bavaria and the Rhine electors urged the emperor to apply the Peace of Augsburg of 1555 to the very letter. All these contradictory influences, which have been analyzed by the American historian Robert Bireley, led Ferdinand II to take a series of measures that quickly alarmed the German princes and foreign powers.

THE EDICT OF RESTITUTION (25 MARCH 1629)

The Edict was the result of the proposal made by the archbishop of Mainz and the German bishops, who demanded the restitution of Church goods secularized since 1552 in contravention of the dispositions of the Peace of Augsburg. Once the principle was established, it was to be applied by the Aulic Council of the Empire, which sat at Vienna and decided each individual case. Father Lamormain was enthusiastic about the project; Wallenstein and Collalto, being more realistic, opposed it, while the Privy Council, although far from being unreservedly in favour, did not believe that it should oppose it. The emperor, after consulting various theologians, was convinced that the Edict conformed to the imperial capitulation of 1619.

The Edict of Restitution, promulgated 25 March 1629 without either the Diet or the college of electors being consulted, guaranteed free exercise of the Augsburg Confession to lay princes, expressly condemned the reformed confession and foresaw the restitution of Church goods unduly confiscated since 1552, thereby putting into question the situation established in the Empire. Two archbishoprics, Magdeburg and Bremen, two bishoprics, Verdun and Halberstadt, and five hundred abbeys and monasteries were specific targets of the text. Some had been ceded, others annexed by the territorial Estates and in 1629 the owners felt threatened. The majority of Catholic princes had reservations; the Holy See, while approving in principle, did not hide its doubts, seeing the Edict only as the source of diplomatic complications. As for the elector of Saxony, Johann Georg, while a loyal ally of Ferdinand II and head of the evangelical corps in the imperial Diet, he protested energetically, all the more so since one of his sons, the administrator of the archbishop of Magdeburg, was directly touched by the Edict. The elector of Brandenburg, a Calvinist ruling over Lutheran subjects, hitherto an ally of the Habsburgs, did not hide his disquiet and dissatisfaction. Meanwhile, a Catholic work, *Pacis compositio*, edited by Laymann and published in spring 1629, gave cause for concern in Germany. It gave a narrow, Catholic interpretation of the Peace of Augsburg; every privilege which had not been expressly granted was to be withdrawn.

The imperial policy in the Baltic disturbed all those bordering on its shores, the majority of whom were Protestants, the Scandinavian sovereigns as well as the Hanseatic League and the elector of Brandenburg. Ferdinand II had named Wallenstein 'general of the Oceanic and Baltic seas' and did not hide his intention of building a war fleet. The Baltic was one of the vital centres of the sevententh-century European economy. It supplied raw materials, wood, hemp, iron, tar and in particular Polish grain and Swedish leather to Western Europe and imported in return salt, wines and manufactured goods. The Dutch, as clever diplomats as they were good merchants, exercised a monopoly in the Baltic which their natural enemies, Philip IV of Spain and his all-powerful minister Olivares, sought to ruin. It was Olivares who, counting on the foolish ambitions of Wallenstein, had inspired the emperor with this maritime policy. As the dukes of Mecklenburg had taken the side of the king of Denmark, Ferdinand II had dispossessed them on his own authority, without the Diet, and had given the two duchies to Wallenstein as security for his debts. In 1628 he made him duke of Mecklenburg with full possession. The port of Stralsund, however, eluded his grasp and fell into the hands of the king of Sweden, Gustavus Adolphus, who now possessed a bridgehead on the German bank of the Baltic. At the time of the Peace of Lübeck, which marked the final neutralization of Denmark, Ferdinand II was no less threatening because he possessed an army and a principality in northern Germany. Would Spain, through the power of its intermediary, finally control the Baltic and crush the economic power of the Dutch?

The electoral congress at Ratisbon was a failure for the emperor due in no small part to French diplomacy. The emperor wanted to have his son

Ferdinand, who was already king of Hungary, elected king of the Romans. He made no secret of his intentions of ensuring that the imperial crown became hereditary in the House of Austria in just the way that he had obtained hereditary succession in Bohemia. However, this was contrary to the basis of the 'German liberties' which Father Joseph, Richelieu's envoy, was employed to keep ever before the emperor's mind. Forgetting their confessional differences, the electors presented a common front and refused to elect the young Ferdinand.

The electors put pressure on the emperor to discharge his army, which he could not pay, and to dismiss Wallenstein. Ferdinand agreed and so deprived himself of the only real strength that he had at his disposal in the Empire. Wallenstein took this as an insult and harboured great resentment towards his master. The only reform that found favour with the electors was the Edict of Restitution as Ferdinand II, consoled by Father Lamormain, could not be moved on this point. His confessor explained to Maximilian of Bavaria:

The edict must remain in force whatever ill may come in the end. It matters little whether the emperor should for this reason lose not only Austria but all his kingdoms so long as he saves his soul which he could not do without applying this edict.

This confidence reveals the deep convictions of Ferdinand II, who believed that he was invested with a mission, namely to re-establish Catholicism throughout all his states. However, he seemed to forget that there was a great difference between his patrimonial states and the Holy Roman Empire. In wishing to erase this difference, he overturned a centuries-long tradition and began a revolution which even his Catholic vassals could not accept.

The assembly at Ratisbon, far from resolving the political and confessional problems posed in 1630, had served only to make them worse. Ferdinand II, in sacrificing Wallenstein, deprived himself of the only man whose talents and wealth could perhaps have enabled him to consolidate his recent gains and to unify a divided Germany under his direct administration. By confirming the Edict of Restitution, the emperor had alienated the northern electors and had exasperated the conflict between Catholics and Protestants. Instead of consolidating order and restoring peace, he relaunched the 'German War'. The most obvious result was a power vacuum: no one was any longer in a position to direct the destiny of the Empire.

THE INTERVENTION OF SWEDEN[8]

The intervention of Denmark in 1625 can be seen as an episode in the 'German War' in so far as Christian IV was duke of Holstein, a member of the circle of Lower Saxony and a relative of the Lutheran administrator of the archbishopric of Bremen. Gustavuus Adolphus was, in 1631, a stranger to the Empire, but he acted as the spearhead of a coalition which feared Habsburg hegemony as Ferdinand II had succeeded in provoking the enmity of Sweden, France and even Maximilian of Bavaria, all of whom for various reasons feared the transformation of the Holy Roman Empire into a unified monarchical state.

Gustavus Adolphus defended simultaneously two causes which were in reality directly linked – Swedish independence and Protestantism. For a long time, his principal enemy had been Catholic Poland: Sigismund II Vasa did not hide his intentions of conquering Sweden, which he claimed was part of his patrimony. A militant Catholic, the Polish king likewise did not hide his desire to lead his Lutheran subjects back to the 'true faith'. Not without difficulty, Richelieu manipulated the mediators and the Vasas signed a truce at Altmark in 1629, which left the king of Sweden with his hands free. Gustavus Adolphus possessed a modern army, which had proved itself against the Russians and Poles, and had also created a formidable navy and made no secret of his intention of imposing Swedish hegemony.

When he disembarked at Stralsund in July 1630, the 'Lion of the North' appeared to many German Protestants as the providential champion of a compromised cause. But the king of Sweden, even though he had the moral support of the German nation, was, unlike Christian IV, painfully short of money. The meagre resources of a poor and sparsely populated kingdom and the receipts of the Polish and Prussian ports were insufficient. For this reason he signed with the French diplomat Charnacé the treaty of Bärwald which sanctioned the Franco-Swedish alliance (23 January 1631). In exchange for the payment of an annual subsidy of 400 rixdales, or 400 000 écus by France, the Swedish king committed himself to raising an army of 36 000 men, to upholding the Catholic religion in those territories that he occupied and to respecting Bavarian neutrality. Richelieu thus at once linked himself to Gustavus Adolphus, the protector of the Protestants, and Maximilian of Bavaria, head of the Catholic League.

THE GENERAL WAR

It was an unexpected incident – the sack of Magdeburg by the troops of the League in May 1631 – which marked the beginning of the general war.

The destruction of a town of 20 000 inhabitants by Tilly's *Reiters* had symbolic value, even in the eyes of a world grown used, after ten years, to the horrors of war. Georg Wilhelm, elector of Brandenburg, concluded an alliance with Gustavus Adolphus in June; in September Johann Georg, elector of Saxony, abandoned the imperial camp. His 18 000 men joined Gustavus Adolphus's 23 000 veterans in order to bar Tilly's path and to protect Saxony from occupation by imperial troops, who had to combat a Protestant coalition which dramatically altered the ratio of forces.

The clash took place at Breitenfeld on the outskirts of Leipzig on 17 September 1631 and the imperial troops were completely routed. They lost half of their effective fighting force in the course of the battle where the tactics employed by Gustavus Adolphus triumphed. So complete a victory took the Swedish king by surprise. The emperor was disarmed. The Czechs in exile were already regrouping and returning to Bohemia, followed by the Saxon army, which took Prague after long having played a part in protecting the country and defending Ferdinand.

Gustavus Adolphus led his army into the Rhineland; after occupying Frankfurt, Heidelburg and Mannheim and after launching raids as far as Alsace (which started to alarm Richelieu) he spent the winter at Mainz. Gustavus Adolphus's army also unduly imposed periodic levies upon Franconia. In spring 1632, at Rain on the Danube, he defeated the veteran Tilly, who died there two weeks later. Gustavus Adolphus then ravaged Bavaria and occupied Munich. Historians have often wondered why the king of Sweden did not march on Vienna, but the 'strategy of capitals' was not yet in fashion in the seventeenth century; Gustavus Adolphus, rather than drive onwards into the heart of the hereditary lands, preferred to consolidate his positions in south Germany, besieging Nürnberg.

Ferdinand II's situation in the Empire was completely reversed in the space of a few months. He saw his authority in ruins, his patrimonial lands invaded, his capital threatened. His German allies had abandoned him and his principal support, Maximilian of Bavaria, found himself deprived of his army, while Bavaria was in ruins. For this reason, following Maximilian's advice, Ferdinand resolved to turn afresh towards Wallenstein. In April 1632 he charged him with recruiting a new army and entrusted him with full powers since the *generalissimo* had laid down his conditions. Embittered by the humiliation inflicted upon him eighteen months earlier, Wallenstein from now onwards had an equivocal attitude which has much intrigued historians of Central Europe. No longer showing any spirit of offensive, he did not cease negotiating with the emperor's enemies. To what end? Ever since Schiller, historians and poets have made countless contributions to the file on Wallenstein without giving any decisive explanation. Contemporaries were certain that the Bohemian aristocrat, more powerful than his master, pursued his own agenda. Did he want to have himself elected king of Bohemia as revenge for the affront of 1630? Did he dream of putting an end to ruinous war which was now without an objective? These speculations stem from the projects attributed to Gustavus Adolphus in the course of 1632: that he had wanted to tip the balance in the favour of the Protestant princes and to have himself elected emperor. These speculations at least prove one thing: Ferdinand II, by wanting to go too far, had ceased to be respected in the Empire and had harmed the cause of the House of Austria whose authority was in the future contested.

His recourse to Wallenstein had, at least provisionally, a positive result.[9] The imperial troops prevented the Swedes from taking Nürnberg and forced them to beat a retreat in the direction of Saxony, while Wallenstein considered turning to his winter quarters. However, Gustavus Adolphus did not let him and attacked Lützen on 16 November 1632. This was a fierce battle where the Swedes remained masters of the land but the death there of Gustavus Adolphus, killed at the head of his cavalry, was an irreparable loss for the Protestant cause: the 'Lion of the North' left only a little girl aged five years, Christiana, and it was open to question whether Sweden would continue the struggle. In fact, the regency was upheld by the Senate (*Riksråd*) which was governed with a firm hand by the chancellor Oxenstjerna, while Gustavus Adolphus's lieutenants, Horn and Torstensson, continued their master's work in Germany.

The Battle of Lützen, however, put an end to the wave of Protestant triumphs and Gustavus Adolphus's death stunned the supporters of 'the cause'. Ferdinand II, seeing in it a response from on high to his prayers and a sign of the workings of Grace, decided to found a monastery of Spanish Benedictines dedicated to the Blessed Virgin Mary.

After Breitenfeld and Rain, a third Swedish victory dealt the imperial cause an irremediable disaster. From then onwards, the two opposing camps found themselves on a par and forced to look for foreign assistance to tip the balance, the Swedes placing their hopes in an alliance with France, while the emperor had recourse to help from Spain.

The year 1633 was marked above all by the tightening of the alliance between Vienna and Madrid and by Wallenstein's negotiations, as bizarre as they were convoluted, with all the belligerents. He refused to execute the orders of the emperor, who enjoined him to resume operations and demanded from his colonels an oath of allegiance to his own person. Egged on by Father Lamormain, Ferdinand summoned Wallenstein to Vienna to render an account of himself and, when he refused, ordered some of his loyal officers, including Piccolomini and Leslie, to seize him in person. In conditions which remain mysterious, these officers killed him at Cheb on 25 February 1634. The emperor then entrusted command of the army to his son Ferdinand, king of Hungary, and finished with the entrepreneurial system of warfare. In the future, no colonel would be able to possess more than two regiments; the army had become truly an imperial one.

The victory of the imperial army over the Swedes at Nördlingen in Franconia on 6 September 1634 made it possible for a while to believe that the war was at an end. The Spanish troops of the cardinal-*infante*, combined with those of his cousin, the archduke Ferdinand, crushed Horn's army, the remnants of which fled towards Alsace under the command of Bernard of Saxe Weimar. The chancellor Oxenstjerna was dismayed at being abandoned by his German allies. A few weeks later, Johann Georg signed a temporary truce at Pirna.

Ferdinand II finally accepted Philip IV's advice to treat with the moderate Protestants in order to restore peace in Germany and to pursue the Swedes. He agreed not to apply the Edict of Restitution in the electorate of Saxony, accepting 1627 and not 1552 as the year of reference, and confirmed Johann Georg in possession of the Lusatias, which were crown lands of Bohemia, in payment for his loyal services at the beginning of the war. In addition, he guaranteed the free exercise of Lutheran worship in certain bishoprics in Silesia. The preliminaries were confirmed by the Peace of Prague, which was signed by the elector of Brandenburg, the landgrave of Hesse-Darmstadt and the majority of the Lutheran princes.

THE PEACE OF PRAGUE (1635)[10]

The Peace of Prague, which the Empire celebrated with much festivity, marks a turning-point in the Thirty Years War. For the Viennese government it represented the defeat of Father Lamormain and the victory of the politicians, symbolized by the accession of Trauttmannsdorf to the post of head of the council. The ultra-Catholics lost their monopoly of the direction of imperial policy. The government of Vienna had decided to make concessions in order to keep the advantages that it had gained in 1620.

On the eve of the restoration of peace, did the civil population really care so very much for the Empire? It seems to have been the case, as the only inveterates remained men such as the fugitive landgrave Wilhelm of Hesse-Cassel and duke Bernard of Saxe-Weimar, who had gone into French service, while Oxenstjerna had travelled to Compiègne to renew the treaty of alliance and subsidies with France. Louis XIII, at the very moment when he signed the Peace of Prague, declared war on Spain, which had come to the relief of its ally, the elector of Trier. German historians have judged severely Richelieu's initiative which relaunched war in the Empire. Was the move not intended, as Günther Barudio has recently observed, to defend German liberties in the face of the political hegemony of the House of Austria?

When, after 1622, Ferdinand II overturned the delicately balanced equilibrium within the Holy Roman Empire and deposed Frederick V, contrary to all the rules of German civil law, he exceeded his rights and provoked a conflict that would be difficult to end, especially while he applied absolutist methods which were so decidedly against the will of the body of Germans. He would not succeed so long as he played second fiddle to Spanish imperialism, still less while he was incapable of mobilizing the material resources at his disposal.

NOTES AND REFERENCES

1. V.-L. Tapié, *La Guerre de Trente Ans*, reissued Paris, 1989.
    Georges Pages, *La Guerre de Trente Ans*, Paris, 1938.
2. Arguments put forward by Georges Livet, *La Guerre de Trente Ans*, Paris, numerous editions.
3. Hans Sturmberger, *Aufstand in Böhmen: der Beginn des 30 jährigen Krieges*, Munich and Vienna, 1959.
4. Tibor Wittmann, *Bethlen Gabor*, Budapest, 1953.
5. Anton Gindely, *Friedrich V von der Pfalz*, Prague, 1884.
6. Günter Barudio, *Der teutsche Krieg, 1618–1648*, Frankfurt an Main, 1985.
7. Geoffrey Parker (ed.) *The Thirty Years' War*, London, 1984.
8. Michael Roberts, *The Sweden of Gustav-Adolph*, London, 1958.
9. Joseph Pekař, *Wallenstein*, 2 vols, Berlin, 1937.
    Golo Mann, *Wallenstein: sein Leben*, Frankfurt an Main, 1971.
10. J. Polišenský, *Documenta bellum tricenale illustrantia*, 7 vols, Prague, 1973–8.

CHAPTER TWENTY-ONE

The Peace of Prague to the Peace of Westphalia (1635–48)

In 1637, two years after the Peace of Prague, Ferdinand II died without having secured the election of his son Ferdinand as king of the Romans and so without ensuring continuity within the Empire. He had left a deep impression upon the destiny of the Austrian monarchy, bestowing upon it its character as the champion of Catholicism, which it maintained right until the end, and he had saved it from chaos and anarchy. It would never, for sure, have become a noble republic like Poland, yet his efforts at reorganizing the Empire ended in defeat. By his obstinacy, the late emperor had plunged Central Europe into a civil war which, at the time of his death, was in the process of expanding into a European war. It fell upon his successor to put an end to the conflict, but Ferdinand III's determination not to make concessions made the task all the more arduous and it took a crushing military defeat to bring him to compromise.

Little is known about the personality of Ferdinand III, who has never been the subject of a scholarly biography.[1] His mother was a Bavarian princess, Maria Anna, the sister of the elector Maximilian, and he was born at Graz in 1608. His education had turned him into a zealous Catholic and his father inculcated in him his own principles of government through the many 'political testaments' that were intended especially for his son. There was nothing moderate about Ferdinand's fervour. It was he who in 1647 officially dedicated Austria to the Virgin Mary and had a column in honour of the Immaculate Conception erected at Vienna.

Ferdinand III was a cultured man and a talented musician who left behind some interesting musical compositions. In contrast to his father, he displayed a real talent for the military art: the victory at Nördlingen (1634) can be attributed to him. After 1637 he showed much more flexibility and political intelligence than his father. He kept the team of ministers who had imposed the Peace of Prague, and after the death of the prince of Eggenburg made Trauttmannsdorf head of the Privy Council. Trauttmannsdorf passes for the most gifted diplomat ever to have served Austria; he led all the Westphalia negotiations on the imperial side. Ferdinand III also proved to the very end a faithful supporter of the Spanish alliance.

FRANCO-SPANISH RIVALRY[2]

The last phase of the Thirty Years War cannot be understood unless account is taken of the conflict which unfolded between France and the Spanish monarchy in the Netherlands, Italy and finally Catalonia. For Richelieu, the Empire was only a secondary theatre of operations where France's Swedish allies were to make the main effort. The cardinal was worried by Olivares's imperialist ambitions and, fearing Spanish hegemony in Italy, was concerned that France would presently become encircled by Spanish possessions. He was at war with the emperor only in so far as the emperor had a hand in Madrid's designs. He did not want the Habsburgs to establish a firm hold over Germany as the German states would then pass into Madrid's sphere of influence.

The resumption of the Spanish–Dutch war in 1621 had revived France's fears because Olivares still hoped to reconquer the northern provinces of the Netherlands which had ceded in 1576. A long war of sieges began under the direction of Maurice of Nassau on the Dutch side, and a Genoan, the marquis of Spinola, on the Spanish. In 1625 Spinola seized Breda, a spectacular success, immortalized by Velazquez in the painting *The Surrender of Breda*, but quite without any follow-up. However, the United Provinces were no longer alone after Richelieu's return to public affairs in 1624 and since the ultra-Catholic party in France, which favoured the Spanish alliance, had lost ground in the face of the advance of Castilian imperialism; Philip IV had recently laid hands on the duchy of Jülich, the Palatinate and then the Valtelline, all vital supporting links in the chain of communications between Milan and the Netherlands, and essential since the Spanish monarchy had abandoned its maritime links between the Cantabrian coast and Flanders. The fear was that Spain would establish hegemony over Italy, where a relative balance still reigned, and that it would take into its service the Swiss, who were excellent mercenaries.

This was why Richelieu, from 1624 to 1635, tried hard to oppose Spain without declaring war, using diplomacy or else having recourse, when necessary, to timely military operations in Piedmont. It is important, therefore, to explain French action in the affair of the Mantuan succession where France supported the claims of a French prince, Charles de Nevers-Gonzaga, against the Spanish and Savoyards and most importantly against the emperor, suzerain of Mantua.[3] The Spanish and the Savoyards had agreed to share Montferrat but Louis XIII's armed intervention in 1629 involved the formation of an alliance between Genoa, Venice and Savoy under the aegis of France. Ferdinand II's refusal to grant the duchy of Mantua as a fief to Charles de Nevers-Gonzaga provoked a diplomatic crisis between Paris and Vienna, which explains father Joseph's unshakeable determination at Ratisbon to thwart Ferdinand's election as king of the Romans. In 1631 the treaty of Cherasco, which was negotiated through the mediation of the pope and the personal engagement of the young Mazarin, restored Pignerol to France and returned to Charles de Nevers-Gonzaga the whole of his patrimony. Ferdinand II's mercenary soldiers, it is true, had meanwhile sacked Mantua beyond recovery; this was a venture comparable, from the point of view of Italian cultural history, to the sack of Rome in 1527 by the troops of Charles V. The treaty of Cherasco was a failure for both Philip IV and for Ferdinand II.

Until the Swedes' defeat at Nördlingen, the French and Spanish forced each other to observe an armed and malevolent neutrality. In 1633 Richelieu had occupied Lorraine whose duke, Charles IV, was a client of Spain. Since 1631 he had been negotiating with the Dutch the terms of an offensive alliance against the Spanish Netherlands but contented himself once again in 1634 with renewing the agreement to provide subsidies.

It was the Battle of Nördlingen and the Peace of Prague which forced Richelieu to throw off his mask, and the ousting by Spanish soldiers of Johann Philip von Sötern, archbishop-elector of Triers, provided him with a pretext. On 19 May 1635 Louis XIII declared war on his brother-in-law Philip IV in the traditional manner: the herald-of-arms of France went to Brussels to carry a challenge to the cardinal-*infante*, the victor of Nördlingen who had become governor of the Spanish Netherlands. Although the declaration of war did not directly concern the emperor, the pretext for the declaration was the defence of German liberties:

since you have been unwilling to restore liberty to Monseigneur, the archbishop of Trier and elector of the Holy Roman Empire who had placed himself under the Empire's protection when he cannot receive liberty from the emperor nor any other prince, and when, contrary to the dignity of the Empire and the rights of man, you keep prisoner a sovereign prince against whom you are not engaged in war, His Majesty declares to you that he is resolved to draw, by arms, satisfaction for this offence.

Not until 1636 did the advance of French troops into Franche-Comté provoke Ferdinand II's entry into the war and the attempted invasion of Burgundy by Gallas's troops, who were soon brought to a halt by the siege of Saint-Jean-de-Losne (Côte d'Or).

The war was indecisive for a long time after the short-lived success of the French in 1635 and the panic of 1636 (the year of Corbie) when Johann von Werth's Croat knights pushed as far as Pontoise and when Paris was threatened. However, the cardinal-*infante* no better exploited the fall of Corbie, which opened a breach in the lines of defence of the Somme, than Emmanuel Philibert of Savoy had followed up the victory of Saint-Quentin in 1557. The Parisians had fled for fear and the belligerents engaged in a long, costly and inconclusive war where a few resounding victories relieved the monotony of siege warfare.

Little by little, the French troops, who were great in number but little seasoned by reason of the long period of peace (1598–1635), acquired experience. Richelieu complained endlessly. They lacked leaders of vision as neither the prince of Condé, the father of the great Condé, nor the old marshal La Force and the cardinal La Vallete were great captains. They lacked tenacity and the officers, while courageous in action, soon lost heart and returned without leave to their lands. Above all, the public finances could not maintain troops at the same time in the Netherlands, Lorraine, the Rhineland, Piedmont and the Pyrenees without recourse to excessive taxation and costly expedients.

The French victory at Rocroi had a great psychological impact. The redoubtable *tercios*, the elite infantry of the king of Spain's army which for a century had been thought invincible, were torn to pieces by the duke of Enghien, the future great Condé. Just as serious for Philip IV as these military defeats were the separatist movements in Portugal, Catalonia and, later, Naples. Spain agreed to begin peace negotiations but on condition that France restored all its conquests, which neither Richelieu nor Mazarin were prepared to do since France had reconquered Artois and occupied the greater part of Catalonia. Olivares's disgrace in 1643 opened the way for lengthy negotiations.

France's later successes provoked a real reversal of alliances. The United Provinces in the future dreaded France rather than Spain and were particularly afraid that the armies of the young Louis XIV might conquer the Netherlands with the result that the doctrine founded on the adage *Gallus amicus sed non vicinus* (France as a friend but not as a neighbour) was elaborated little by little at the Hague. The Spanish diplomats, conscious of this change, drafted an agreement with their former Dutch subjects and proposed to them a separate peace. Spain then, by a calculated indiscretion, made it known that Mazarin had proposed to Philip IV the exchange of Catalonia for the Spanish Netherlands (Catalonia was placed under the protection of the king of France after the 1640 rebellion and had been conquered, with some difficulty, by the French). For Madrid it was an unhoped-for opportunity: in 1646 Philip II and Olivares's old fantasies of subduing the rebellious Dutch were abandoned and Spain, having made a treaty with the Estates General in January 1647, was free to turn the forces of the army of Flanders against France.

Despite this set-back, the French delegation gained confidence from Condé's victory at Lens over the army of the archduke Leopold William in August 1648 and refused to make a treaty with Spain, which still demanded the restitution of Artois and Catalonia. The delegation took care to exclude the circle of Burgundy and Lorraine from the provisions of the general peace (articles 4 and 5 of the treaty of Münster), despite the difficult situation in which Mazarin had found himself since the summer of 1648. The Spanish hoped that the Fronde would force him to make a treaty but the conflict continued for eleven years, until the Peace of the Pyrenees, which confirmed the Spanish monarchy's defeat and the beginning of its decline as a great power.

One of the objectives of Mazarin's war had been to break the direct alliance between Vienna and Madrid and to force Ferdinand III to come to terms at Münster.[4] One of the basic provisions of the Peace was the exclusion of the Spanish from Germany and the banning of the emperor from sending to the Netherlands regiments that he no longer needed.

THE FRANCO-AUSTRIAN WAR

The war in Germany was for the French government a secondary concern, probably far less important than the seizure of Savoy and the only high stake was the occupation and *de facto* annexation of Lorraine from 1633 while the French garrisons in Alsace covered the east of the kingdom. The stake was not territorial but political: it was necessary to bring support to the German princes and to maintain the Swedish alliance in the war. For this reason, France's principal adversary was not the emperor but his ally Maximilian of Bavaria who, with a first-rate army under the leadership of Mercy, held southern Germany and safeguarded the 'Bavarian sanctuary'.[5]

From 1636 Bernard of Saxe-Weimar with his mercenaries (often dubbed Weimarians) fought on the side of Louis XIII. Bernard was a true war entrepreneur. France promised him an indemnity of 3 million pounds in gold rixdales and food for his men. The seizure of Vieux-Brisach in December 1638 after a terrible siege guaranteed him control of the whole of Further Austria, but his premature death in 1639 changed the strategic facts and politics of the problem. While the Weimarians without difficulty renewed the contracts by which they were hired, they had to be provided with leaders, first the marshal of Guébriant until 1643, then Turenne. The annexation of the territories promised to the late duke of Saxe-Weimar was also vital for the creation of a buffer state across the upper Rhine.

From 1644 Turenne made the German army an offensive body with precise objectives. With Condé's support, he took Philippsburg, liberated the left bank of the Rhine, then laid waste Swabia and mounted joint operations with the Swedes.

The 1645 campaign was a disaster for Ferdinand III. Even so he refused to sign the peace. After having been defeated by the Swedes at Jankau in Bohemia in March, he almost lost Brno and Vienna, while the prince of Transylvania, György Rákóczi, led an anti-Habsburg rising in Hungary. At the same time, the Bavarian army was beaten by Turenne at Nördlingen and Mercy was killed in combat.

Turenne, exploiting his success and supported by Wrangel's Swedes, forced Maximilian in 1646 to sign an armistice in order to spare his 'Bavarian sanctuary', but the decisive campaign did not take place until 1648. After the victory at Zusmarshausen, in May, the French opened the route to Munich and the Weimarians gleefully sacked Bavaria. The old duke, chased from his states, did not have difficulty in convincing Ferdinand III to sign the Peace of Münster while the Swedes dismantled the collections in the Hračany without, however, being able to reach the inside of the Old Town of Prague. The emperor, without an ally, without resources and soon without an army, preferred to accept the Peace which on 24 October put a final end to the fighting within the hereditary lands.

The time had come, for the road to Vienna was practically open to the French after Turenne's victory at Zusmarshausen in Bavaria, while the defeat of the archduke Leopold William at Lens had destroyed the offensive power of the Spanish in the Netherlands. Ferdinand III judged that it was wisest to negotiate and to accept the compromise negotiated by Trauttmannsdorf, his plenipotentiary at Münster.

THE TREATIES OF WESTPHALIA[6]

The treaties of Westphalia were the result of the conferences at Münster, where the Catholic powers sat under the presidency of the mediator, the nuncio Chigi, and the conferences where Sweden, the Protestant princes and the representatives of the emperor Ferdinand III took part in negotiations. A history of the negotiations derived from the correspondence of the plenipotentiaries has been drawn up by a Jesuit, Father Bougeant, in his *Histoire du Traité de Westphalie*. The congress was truly European. Almost all the powers were represented with the exception of the tsar of Muscovy, the sultan and Charles I. Although the four principle belligerents – the emperor, the king of Spain, the queen of Sweden and the king of France – discussed the proposals, they did not have the power to make a treaty in the name of their allies, who were determined not to be forgotten. For four years (1644–8), the two towns were neutralized and occupied by a crowd of diplomats as each delegation was made up of plenipotentiaries, secretaries, courtiers and a crowd of domestic servants.

There were innumerable problems and the interests of the various camps often cancelled each other out, for example between France and Sweden, which represented respectively Catholicism and Protestantism in Germany, or between France and the United Provinces, which were divided over the fate of the Spanish Netherlands. Spain confronted the question of the independence of the United Provinces and the fate of Portugal and Catalonia as well as the delicate balance in northern Italy, the attribution of the Lower Palatinate, the fate of the French conquests in the Netherlands and in Catalonia. Within the Empire, the legal questions raised were yet more numerous. To what extent were the princes and orders to enjoy sovereign rights? What was to be the religious status of the Empire and the status of goods secularized since the Peace of Augsburg? What fate was in store for the elector Palatine, his electoral title, his confiscated patrimony? What rewards would France and Sweden be granted as the price of their intervention; in other words, what about Alsace and Pomerania?

The treaties finally confirmed what had been gradually admitted since the beginning of the sixteenth century, namely that Christendom as it had been conceived during the Middle Ages was at an end. The pope and the emperor were forced to accept this and to forswear the re-establishment of unity under Catholicism in fact as in law. Consequently the complete independence of the princes and the Estates had to be recognized. The failure of Charles V's ambitions and dreams and the division of the Holy Roman Empire into a collection of independent states was confirmed. The treaty of Münster in articles 64 and 65 in fact granted them only 'territorial lordship' (*Landeshoheit*) because sovereignty would be incompatible with the presence of an emperor at the head of the Empire. The states also had the hitherto unheard of right

to conclude treaties for their reciprocal protection and safety among themselves and with foreign powers with, it is true, the obligatory clause that they be 'of such a kind that they are not directed against the Empire and the Emperor nor against the public peace in the Empire.'

The princes naturally were not slow to conclude treaties which were far from compatible with the emperor's interests. Sweden and France were called in to safeguard 'German liberties', that is to say the independence of the princes and liberty of worship. This was a success because the unity of the Holy Roman Empire as it had been understood before the religious revolution scarcely existed any more.

Even if the powers of emperor and Diet had not been modified by the Peace of Westphalia, some dangerous 'innovations' appeared as the treaty of Osnabrück bestowed upon the Diet a programme of almost endless work. In 1663 the Diet turned itself into a perpetual Diet and took on the aspect of a permanent congress of diplomats.

In the religious field, the emperor had to renounce not only the Edict of Restitution but also the compromise established at Prague in 1635. The Edict was revoked and the legal status of confessions established by the treaties of Westphalia was more favourable towards the Protestants than the Peace of Augsburg had been. The Peace of Augsburg, enlarged to embrace the Reformed Churches, was recognized as the third confession and the Calvinist princes had the right to impose it on their subjects. There was no question of toleration. In each state there remained a single Church and a single prince, while the heterodox Protestants such as the Anabaptists and the Unitarians remained outside the law. Subjects refusing to conform to the prince's religion had no choice but to emigrate. The relaxation of the legal status of confessions within the Empire simply led to a growth of confidence among certain princes, such as the elector of Brandenburg. As for the property of the Church, the treaties took 1624 as the year of reference and confirmed the present status of the bishoprics, monasteries and religious foundations which had been secularized as well as the existing composition of cathedral chapters. Bishoprics which then had a Protestant administrator were not to be handed back to a Catholic bishop but rather the administrator was to be appointed by the emperor. In return, the emperor was free to regulate confessional questions according to his own discretion within the hereditary lands and Bohemia.

The new statute did not limit the power of the emperor as much as has been claimed. He had, it is true, to forswear for ever the establishment of absolute authority in Germany. The only real threat came – as of late – from a too restrictive electoral 'capitulation' such as the electors imposed on Leopold I in 1658. The emperor, however, retained undeniable prestige in the eyes of the Germans because he remained the defender of the German nation against the Turks or against attacks from outside. He was still the indisputable head of the Empire to whom the princes turned when threatened. Because of his judicial powers he remained the highest level of recourse for his subjects against a sentence perceived as unjust; the smooth running of the Aulic Council of the Empire contributed greatly to maintaining the emperor's prestige in the eyes of the German nation. The electors retained their privilege of designating the emperor, but the French plenipotentiaries could not prevent a clever sovereign from having his successor elected king of the Romans while he was still alive; the only title held by Ferdinand I during the period 1531–56 before his brother Charles V abdicated was king of the Romans. Since the electors were accustomed to electing a Habsburg, the House of Austria enjoyed a quasi-hereditary position with respect to the imperial title. The emperor remained influential within the Diet but only as the director of the second college of princes and by creating princes who in reality were members of his clientele, for example the Liechtensteins and the Auerspergs, and also through the existence of a clientele among the canons of the great Rhine chapters, for example the archduke Leopold William was bishop elect of Strassburg, Breslau and Halberstadt.[7]

The moderation with which the defeated princes were treated helped to restore calm. Their territories were given to the duke of Wurtemburg, the elector of Trier and the landgrave of Hesse-Cassel. Frederick V's son recovered the Lower Palatinate and the emperor created an eighth electorship in his favour. The elector of Bavaria kept the Upper Palatinate as compensation for all his expenses. This compromise altered the majority among the electors in favour of the Catholics. In 1693 the creation of a ninth electorate in favour of the duke of Hanover somewhat redressed the balance.

The treaties of Westphalia went some way towards making the hereditary lands a little more detached from the rest of the Empire. The emperor knew that in the future he would not be able to rule the Holy Roman Empire as a real kingdom. He tended to withdraw further into the Austrian monarchy and to strengthen it as a means of increasing his own power. Even so, he became the leading territorial prince and made his voice prevail with respect to the electors of Bavaria, Saxony and Brandenburg. The seventeenth century was not yet the era of Austro-

Prussian rivalry as the emperor was truly *primus inter pares*; after 1650 he was redoubtable only when supported by other German princes. This, moreover, was the view prevailing in Mazarin's entourage.

The Empire paid a high price for the peace and for the (almost) final resolution of its confessional conflicts. As compensation for the ruin and the cost in human lives, Sweden and France received all that they had coveted. Sweden for a long time claimed part of Silesia but finally was content with Pomerania which it had occupied since 1630, despite the claims of the elector of Brandenburg. Pomerania was divided into two with Brandenburg receiving the eastern part and Sweden receiving as compensation the secularized bishoprics of Bremen and Verdun, thus becoming a great power in northern Germany. By acquiring western Pomerania, Sweden was guaranteed a permanent base and strengthened its power in the Baltic, becoming a potential enemy of Brandenburg.

France expanded at the expense of the Empire and the House of Austria, which was forced to surrender its rights to Upper and Lower Alsace. However, articles 75–76, 79–85 and 89 of the treaty of Münster were deliberately left ambiguous. While the Austrian possessions passed to France, the other territories (the towns of Decapolis and the lay and ecclesiastical lordships) were the object of dispositions contrary to article 89 with the result that, in the words of the French plenipotentiary Abel Servien, 'everyone is left with his claims and explains the treaty as he understands it'. Georges Liviet has shown in his study of the stewardship of Alsace that French Alsace was in a state of continuous creation right until the surrender of Strassburg on 30 September 1681. The House of Austria, however, never renounced its Alsatian patrimony. The annexation of Alsace was a lasting cause of discord which relaunched the sixteenth-century dispute over Burgundy. The emperor took pains to ensure that France was excluded from the Diet. As for the rest, Trautmannsdorf, the imperial plenipotentiary, hoped that his master would enjoy a return of good fortune and would be able to recover his rights over the landgravate.[8]

It is questionable whether the compensation received by the kingdom of France was in the long term to its benefit. Richelieu longed to annex the whole of the duchy of Lorraine. Mazarin had at first wanted to obtain strategic points; Breisach with its bridge over the Rhine was a gateway into Germany just as Pignerol was into Italy. The annexation of territories totally alien to French culture and in part Protestant involved France in Rhine politics and increased the number of occasions when the king found himself in conflict with the German princes even though, for some at least, he was provisionally their ally. Through good administrators such as Charles Colbert, the intendant of Alsace, the king of France was able to make himself accepted by the people.

The Peace of Westphalia was a German peace and the principal benefit it conferred was to allow the reconstruction of the country which had been drained of its life-blood. An essential clause was the neutralization of the territory of the Empire, a clause that was renewed by the imperial capitulation in 1658, at the time of the troubled election of Leopold I, and sanctioned by the Rhine League, a masterstroke of diplomacy on the part of Mazarin that was negotiated by Hughes de Lionne during the Frankfurt Congress. The Rhineland princes wanted peace at any price, while Spain, now quite enfeebled, wanted to place the Burgundian circle (the Netherlands) under the Empire's protection and at the same time to recover the veterans of the imperial army in order to extract favourable terms from France while it was plunged into civil war.

Philip IV, isolated, his armies defeated in the Netherlands at the Battle of the Dunes in 1658, resigned himself to negotiating a settlement directly with a Franco-English coalition, for Mazarin had concluded an alliance with Cromwell. He avenged himself on the Viennese court, which was too cautious for his liking, by giving the *infanta* Maria-Theresa in marriage to Louis XIV. This change of mood did not endanger direct relations between the two branches of the House of Austria, both equally weakened but both incapable of renouncing their dreams of grandeur. The half-century ushered in by the Peace of Westphalia witnessed the reconstruction of the Austrian monarchy and its rise to power, while the Spanish monarchy, paralyzed by the crisis in its government and by lack of American silver, resumed for the worst the prolonged struggle which Philip IV's policy of aggrandizement had imposed upon it.[9]

The treaties of Münster, Osnabrück and the Pyrenees represented a defeat for the House of Austria because they marked not only the end of Spain's preponderance, but also the confirmation of German liberties. The Habsburgs clearly never imposed on Germany a real monarchical constitution in the moderate sense of the term, as Maximilian I had desired. This did not mean, however, that the Empire could be described as a concept devoid of substance and a 'monstrosity' as the jurist Samuel Pufendorf was shortly to aver. At Münster, the idea of Christendom, already well and truly outmoded, fell into splinters.

NOTES AND REFERENCES

1. R.J.W. Evans gives a good account of Ferdinand II in *The Making of the Habsburg Monarchy*, Oxford, 1979.
2. Michel Devèze, *L'Espagne de Philippe IV*, 2 vols, Paris, 1970.
   Geoffrey Parker, *The Army of Flanders and the Spanish Main Road*, London, 1967.
3. V.-L. Tapié, *La France de Louis XIII et de Richelieu*, 2nd edn, Paris, 1965.
4. Grete Mecenseffy, 'Habsburger im 17. Jahrhundert: die Beziehungen von Wien und Madrid während des 30 jährigen Krieges', AOG, 121, Vienna, 1955.
5. Jean Bérenger, *Turenne*, Paris, 1987.

6. Fritz Dickmann, *Der westfälische Frieden,* Münster, 1959, remains essential reading and should be supplemented by the *Acta Pacis Westphalicae*, in particular part I, *Instruktionen*, Münster, 1959.
7. Alfred A. Strnad, 'Wahl und Informativprozess Erzherzog Leopold-Wilhelms', *Archiv für schlesische Kirchengeschichte*, 26, Hildesheim, 1968.
8. Georges Livet, *L'Intendance d'Alsace sous Louis XIV*, Paris, 1956.
9. C. Hermann and J. Marcade, *La Péninsule ibérique au XVIIe siècle*, Paris, 1989.

CHAPTER TWENTY-TWO

The Task of Reconstruction

For Ferdinand III, in common with all the other princes of the Empire, the most urgent task was reconstruction. The beneficial provisions of the treaties of Westphalia made it easier to establish a lasting arrangement at the institutional level, while the application of *ius reformandi* offered the Habsburgs the chance to pursue with impunity the Counter-Reformation in the hereditary lands, even briefly presenting Leopold with the hope that he might finally apply his grandfather's programme and realize the unity of the Austrian monarchy through Catholicism. The states of the Empire for their part applied the constitution guaranteed by the Peace of Münster. From this compromise was born an Austro-German complex (quite alien to the French spirit) where the emperor was at once head of a powerful patrimonial state and sovereign of the Holy Roman Empire, using all the possibilities that German public law offered him and without which, contrary to what French historians affirm, Austria and Germany would have led a separate existence after 1648.[1] Saint Simon, a good judge of the peoples and realities of the world beyond the Rhine, understood this well and when writing of the emperor Leopold I asserted that in the end he was more powerful in Germany than Charles V had ever been at the height of his glory.[2]

The work of rebuilding went on long after the immediate aftermath of the war and continued well into the reign of Leopold I, the heir of Ferdinand III, who had died in March 1657 at the age of forty-nine thereby raising the important question of succession.[3] Ferdinand III had taken measures to ensure that the archduke Ferdinand would succeed him without difficulty. Ferdinand IV, however, having been elected king of Hungary in 1649 and king of the Romans in 1653, died horribly from smallpox the following year, making his younger brother, Leopold Ignace (aged fourteen), the heir presumptive. His death was a misfortune for the House of Austria because, like his cousin don Balthazar-Carlos, Ferdinand IV had seemed full of promise. His younger brother Leopold had been destined from his earliest days for a career in the Church so that he would inherit the benefices of his uncle Leopold William; he had had a moral and intellectual education fitted to a prince of the Church and not to a future head of the government and army. The development of his powers of resolution especially left much to be desired; Leopold I, like all the other Habsburgs, always had the greatest difficulty taking decisions, convinced as he was that it was beneath his dignity.

Ferdinand III, meanwhile, continued to put his trust in Maximilian von Trautmannsdorf, who had served him so well during the negotiations at Münster, as well as the surviving members of the 'Spanish faction', Martinic and Slavata. When Trautmannsdorf died, he replaced him with prince Weikhard Auersperg who was, like many others employed by the Styrian branch of the Habsburgs, originally from Inner Austria. Auersperg had all the powers of a prime minister in the manner of Richelieu or Olivares, governing the Privy Council, tightening links with Madrid – he has even been accused of having been bought by Spain – and relieving his master of the tasks of government. Ferdinand III, finding himself a widower, married Eleonora of Gonzaga-Mantua, who gave him a son, who died of epilepsy in 1662, and two daughters, one of whom, Eleonora, married duke Charles V of Lorraine in 1678. Eleonora proved a shrewd adviser to her stepson Leopold I after 1657 and was a patron of the arts. The young woman was, however, quite unable to raise the spirits of her husband, who sank into melancholy. Weighed down by the failures and ills of war, worn out by life in the camps, he took refuge in philosophy and alchemy, his other favourite pastime being music. He was the first Habsburg to leave a respectable body of work as a composer of scholarly music, but he did not achieve the renown of his son, Leopold I.[4]

Leopold, despite some youthful errors, was able to pursue the task undertaken by his father. He considered Auersperg to be arrogant and he crushed his power so that he could make his mentor, count Portia, prime minister. Blundering and indecisive, Portia was not a man of any great stature, but he nevertheless assured the continuation of the policy undertaken by Ferdinand III: reconciliation with the princes of the Empire, the rebuilding of the economy, the pursuit of the Counter-Reformation and the defence of the interests of the House of Austria.

POLITICAL RECONSTRUCTION WITHIN THE EMPIRE

While the numerous lay princes adjusted themselves to a reduction of power and were content to vote contributions through the permanent commissions of notables with the aim of establishing absolute power, the prince-bishops continued to be elected by the cathedral chapter. The canons, who had to give proof of sixteen quarterings*, belonged to the

* Translator's note: i.e. sixteen lines of noble ancestry.

290

better Houses of the Empire: the Wittelsbachs, for example, controlled the see of Cologne and the elector was a cadet of the House of Bavaria, while in contravention of the Tridentine decrees the Habsburgs occupied the bishopric of Strassburg and also the bishoprics of Passau, Halberstadt and Wroclaw (Breslau), until the death of Leopold William in 1662. The chapters were divided between the 'Spanish' or 'Austrian faction' favourable to the Habsburgs, and the 'French faction' at Trier led by Philipp von Sötern and later directed from Strassburg and Cologne by Franz and Wilhelm von Fürstenberg. The king of France maintained diplomatic agents at Mainz, Koblenz (the residence of the elector of Trier) and at Bonn (the residence of the elector of Cologne). There was nothing straightforward about the world of the baroque prelates who were attached to the Counter-Reformation movement but were also open to French pensions, while others, like Metternich of Manderscheid, had interests and relatives on the side of the Austrian monarchy. Their situation was a difficult one; too poor to maintain real armies and to defend themselves against the imperial troops or the troops of Louis XIV, they nevertheless possessed fortified palaces such as Ehrenbreitsten, close to Koblenz, or Philippsburg, opposite Landau, which brought them more worries than efficient protection. This was why they depended on diplomacy and, later on, imperial protection to defend what was most precious – peace.[5]

The centre of German political life was now the Diet of the Empire – where Louis XIV maintained an ambassador who played the role of informer and mediator – since the structure of the *Reich*, despite some modifications, remained complex. The 350 states directly in the Empire – the direct vassals of the Emperor – were not all represented and did not each have a voice. The Diet always included the three traditional colleges – the electors, princes and free towns. The electors, now eight in number (Mainz, Cologne, Trier on the one hand, Bohemia, Saxony, Brandenburg, Bavaria and the Palatinate on the other) would have liked to have been the emperor's privileged interlocutors and to exercise a kind of joint sovereignty (*Kondominium*) over the Empire, but they had been deprived of their claims during the negotiations at Münster; the perpetual Diet had put an end to their excessive pretensions. Conversely, the college of the free towns was in a state of disarray comparable to that of the fourth order in the Austrian monarchy. One resolution of the Diet in fact agreed that every measure voted by the two premier colleges could be sanctioned by the emperor without having to obtain approval from the college of the free towns. These towns were reluctant to maintain permanent delegations at the Diet; only some large cities such as Frankfurt-am-Main, Augsburg, Ulm, Nürnberg, Cologne and Aix-la-Chapelle still sat there, and then to little effect. Strassburg lost interest in the discussions at Ratisbon, and the little cities . ruined by war, such as Rothenburg-an-der-Tauber or Gengenbach, were absent from debates and were scarcely consulted.[6]

The electors' real partner was the college of princes, which was divided into three benches: the ecclesiastical princes (the bishops of Spire, Würms,

Bamburg, Würzburg, Passau, Münster, Osnabrück, Strassburg and above all the archbishop of Salzburg); the lay princes (Austria, Brunswick, Hesse, Wurtemburg, Mecklenburg, Baden, etc.); the third bench made up of counts all together carried as much weight in voting as the margrave of Baden alone. As for the knights, they were no longer represented at the Diet and had lost all political significance since the reign of Charles V.

The emperor was represented at the Diet by two commissioners: in so far as he was the archduke of Austria, his representative presided over the college of princes, alternately with the archbishop of Salzburg. He was also present in the college of electors as king of Bohemia. The imperial commissioners, a great lord and a jurist expert in German public law (for example Dr Hocher, who was originally from Alsace and a future chancellor of Austria), negotiated with the archbishop of Mainz, who governed the bureau of the Diet or *dictatura*. He had control of the agenda, edited the texts which, once approved by the two premier colleges and sanctioned by the emperor, had the force of law. These were the *recessus* which were generally easily passed and without coercion because they were discussed and approved in advance.

The Diet was summoned by Ferdinand III in 1653 to give the treaties of Westphalia the force of law in the Empire and was then convoked ten years later by Leopold I, who came in person to request financial and military assistance against the re-emergent Turkish threat; this was the last personal appearance by a Habsburg before the German Diet. The Diet agreed to the raising of a relief army, command of which was given to the prince of Waldeck, but then refused to dissolve and transformed itself into the perpetual Diet which sat right until the end of the Holy Roman Empire in 1806.

It was now an assembly of diplomats rather than, as before, a congress of sovereign princes. The princes' representatives acted on special instructions, negotiated in writing, put together their memoranda and gave account to their masters, with the result that the procedure was painfully slow and annoyed foreign diplomats. The princes' agents negotiated all important matters with the imperial commissioners: peace or war; the raising of the army of the circles; the voting of subsidies or the 'Roman months' (an expression which referred to the old equestrian processions that accompanied the emperor on his way to Rome for his coronation but which were destined, rather more prosaically, for the maintenance of the army of the circles); the appointment of generals for the army, etc. The Empire was not a coalition of independent princes, however: the monarchical structure remained and the emperor had at his disposal various powers that he had to exercise with tact and discretion, gradually regaining the authority lost by his predecessors and rendering null and void the humiliating imperial capitulation of 1658 which the enemies of the House of Austria had imposed on the young Leopold.

THE EMPEROR'S POWERS WITHIN THE EMPIRE

The emperor in keeping with the feudal tradition, retained extensive judicial powers and remained in the minds of the people the supreme judge. In all the states which, unlike Austria, had not obtained the privilege of *non appellando*, every legal decision could be brought to appeal before the Aulic Council of the Empire, which had found a new lease of life during the twenty-year presidency of prince Johann Adolf Schwarzenberg. The treaty of Münster had made provision for the Aulic Council to include Protestant judges alongside Catholic magistrates. These jurists were drawn from all the countries of the Empire and for the Habsburgs it was a way of calling upon the strengths of the whole of Germany. A real pool of talents, the council furnished the emperor with exceptional individuals who remained at Vienna in his service, sometimes at the cost of converting to Catholicism, like the chancellor Strattmann.

The Aulic Council's task was to deal with legal decisions of a feudal character and to decide questions of succession, as in the Oldenburg affair. Its jurisdiction extended also to northern Italy. In addition it prepared documents for the council which dealt at the political level with questions of enfeoffment.

It is often forgotten that the emperor directed the Empire's foreign policy, gradually organizing a modern diplomatic service in its name. The elector of Brandenburg, in accordance with the treaties of Westphalia, was authorized to send a representative to Paris and the emperor also maintained there a resident (for reasons of protocol, he was not an ambassador), who represented the interests of the Empire and the House of Austria. The emperor maintained ambassadors at Rome, Venice and Madrid, an internuncio at Constantinople, and residents at London, the Hague, Brussels, Florence, Warsaw and Stockholm.

In Vienna, as in France, it was not yet possible to make a career as a diplomat and the sovereign called as readily on men from the Empire as from the hereditary lands. He used jurists or chancellery clerks in minor offices – as secretaries or heads of secondary posts – while recruited aristocrats for the great embassies. In Madrid, Leopold sometimes maintained two envoys, an official ambassador and his own personal representative alongside the regent, his sister, queen Maria Anna. Often a diplomat left the service if a mission were not repaid with promotion within a council or to the court. In 1665 count Walter Leslie, who years before had been an accomplice in the assassination of Wallenstein, received the order of the Golden Fleece in return for his extraordinary embassy to Constantinople. In 1699 count Harrach, after his return from Madrid, became major domo at court. There was not, however, a real *cursus* as existed for the patricians in Venice.[7]

The head of the imperial diplomatic service was the vice-chancellor of the Empire, who directed the offices of the chancellery installed at Vienna in a wing of the Hofburg, which was extended in 1665. These offices dealt with correspondence from abroad and from the states of the Empire. The chancellery consisted of two sections, a German language section, which was the more important, and the Latin language section, which dealt with the affairs of the *welsch* lands of the Empire, that is northern Italy and the Burgundian circle. Each section or 'expedition' was directed by a secretary and included drafters of documents and forwarding agents as well as clerks. The imperial vice-chancellor, who was nominated by the archbishop of Mainz after prior agreement with the emperor, was always a German from the Empire. For a long time, the post was occupied by count Leopold Wilhelm von Königsegg, who was originally from Swabia and gradually won Leopold I's confidence to the point where he was admitted to the secret conference, for the imperial vice-chancellor did not belong to the highest institutions of the monarchy. Only relations with Muscovy and the Ottoman empire escaped the jurisdiction of these offices and depended on the council of war.

THE INSTITUTIONS OF THE EMPIRE

The princes did not trust the Habsburgs' policy, deduced that it was dictated by self-interest, and refused to finance the defence of the Spanish monarchy. They aimed at strengthening the Empire's own institutions, which had been put in place at the beginning of the sixteenth century. While continuing to finance the court of the chamber of the Empire, which sat at Spire until 1689, the states developed the administration of the circles created in 1512 and so practised a large measure of decentralization, particularly advantageous in Swabia and Franconia. The assemblies of the circle (the *Kreistag* or Diet of the circle) met periodically to manage the finances and the common army and this made easier the task of the heavy mechanism at Ratisbon.

More than anything else, the states wanted to create a permanent army of the Empire so as not to be dependent any longer on the imperial troops – in other words the Habsburg army – and to improve the efficiency of the system of contingents, in place since 1512, in order to confront the common enemy, the Turk or the king of France, when the integrity of the territory was threatened. For this reason, the Diet elaborated the project of an army of 40 000 men (60 000 in times of war) financed by contributions from the states; in any case, the treasury of the Empire no longer payed the 'Roman months' to the chamber of accounts in Vienna, criticizing its bad administration and corruption. This good project came to nothing in 1681, however, and the states had to be satisfied with the army of the circles made up of contingents in proportion to the importance of the states and set out by the 'register of the Empire'. These uncoordinated troops were difficult to manage and to command and were not always very effective in the face of the French army. They were commanded first by the prince of Waldeck and then by the margrave Louis von Baden, the *Türkenlouis* of German historiography. Beside the imperial troops and the troops of Bavaria and Brandenburg, there was, henceforth, an army of the Empire, or rather an army of the circles.

This effort, which cannot be dismissed despite French derision and the negative judgements passed upon it by traditional historiography, would not have been possible without the reconstruction of the economy and without a praiseworthy concern to avoid at all costs a return to the horrors of the Thirty Years War, which remained a collective traumatism on the German side of the Rhine.

'THE MISERIES OF WAR'[8]

The Thirty Years War, even when various uncertainties and revisionary theses are taken into account, constituted one of the most sombre periods in the history of Central Europe and the emphasis laid upon the 'miseries of war' has been justified. The classic witness of these woes is Simplicissimus, the hero of the novel by Grimmelshausen who left behind in baroque form a kind of autobiography; there is also the series of engravings by the French artist Jacques Callot which bears the title *The Miseries of War* and was published in 1633.

The countries most affected in the Empire were Mecklenburg, Holstein, the Rhineland, the lands of the crown of Bohemia and the Brandenburg Mark, which was drawn into the war in 1626 and remained the theatre of operations for over fifteen years. There is evidence of a sizeable drop in the population of Altmark – 40 per cent in the rural districts and 50 per cent in the towns. Of the 637 villages mentioned in pastoral visits 1650–2, 40 were completely destroyed and 68 had no more than one or two households. The centre of Brandenburg saw the urban population fall from 113 000 to 43 000 (Berlin-Kölln passed from 12 000 in 1618 to 6 200 in 1654, Berlin-Spandau 3 600 to 1 500, Frankfurt-an-der-Oder 13 000 to 2 400) while the rural population fell from 300 000 to 75 000. Mecklenburg was severely affected after Wallenstein's death. Gallas and the Swede Banér waged war there, the latter declaring:

nothing exists in this province save sand and air. Everything is razed right to the ground, the villages and countryside are full of dead beasts, the houses full of human corpses, the misery is impossible to describe.

After the war, only 25 per cent of agricultural land was returned to cultivation and Pomerania had experienced a 65 per cent drop in its population from the level of 1618. In the Rhineland which had been constantly crisscrossed by armies, the situation was catastrophic, especially in the Rhineland Palatinate, where people lived on nettle soup and where emigration to Prussia or North America seemed the answer. The country restored to the elector Karl Ludwig was a country drained of its life blood.

In Alsace, the losses varied, but the towns – Mühlhausen, Colmar and Strassburg – protected by their ramparts, were spared and even served as refuges for those abandoning the countryside. Breisgau and Wurtemburg were, on the other hand, severely affected. Freiburg fell from 10 000 inhabitants to 3 500 and Wurtemburg saw its population pass from 445 000 in 1622 to 97 000 in 1639. The hereditary lands, with the exception of Upper Alsace, Breisgau and Lower Austria, were all but spared the war.

Silesia, it seems, suffered the most from the passage of troops. It lost 200 000 of its 900 000 inhabitants, close to one-quarter of the population. Certain parts of Bohemia were affected more than others. The duchy of Frýdland was spared until 1634 while its duke Wallenstein was alive. Around Prague, as many as half the houses were abandoned, but losses over the whole of the country are estimated at less than one-fifth, and significantly, not until the end of the century did Bohemia recover its 4 million inhabitants of 1620. In Moravia the population dropped from 800 000 to 600 000 inhabitants.

The main reason for this depopulation was not the fighting: deadly as it was, it had involved forces of no more than around 20 000 to 30 000 combatants on each side. The ceaseless toing and froing of troops, searching for provisions during the summer months and quarters for 'refreshment' in autumn and spring, were devastating. The flat land was ruined, the villages burnt down, the harvests trampled underfoot and granaries pillaged. The peasants took refuge behind the walls of the town or in the forest. The passage of armies was accompanied by epidemics of plague and famine. The 'ills of war' seem to have been greatly exaggerated in so far as the peasant economies were extraordinarily resilient and deserted villages did not signify the total destruction of a population but rather its permanent migration.

Most often, the effects were cumulative. The peasants were hit by plague epidemics, infant mortality was high and famines made the situation yet worse. The higher rate of death among the male population condemned numerous women at the age of procreation to spinsterhood and there is a noticeable drop in the rates of birth and marriage, a phenomenon which was accompanied by an increase in the incidence of illegitimate births and abandoned children in garrison cities.

This is all explained by the character of armies in the Thirty Years War. Outside combat, discipline was relaxed in the extreme and the armies were really made up of outlaws, of the asocial who had passed almost beyond the point of being able to return to civil society. The soldier in this type of enterprise appears to have been an especially exploited labourer because the mercenary saw his pay reduced in comparison to that of the *lancequenets* of the sixteenth century. His nominal wages were at least equivalent to that of a mason, although he received a premium for a substantial engagement. In Wallenstein's army, two levels of soldiers were engaged for food and supplies which were rarely handed out. All the sources agree: the military life was one of misery punctuated by rare moments of relaxation – sacking a town, for example, as happened at Magdeburg in 1631. The simple soldier had become a pariah.

The Thirty Years War was the golden age of the war entrepreneur because most German princes, with the exception of the duke of Bavaria, did not have the means to raise an army. The war entrepreneur was a businessman who invested in one or more regiments; Gallas, for example, possessed four in 1643. This kind of speculation brought with it great risks: the possible loss of capital through the desertion of soldiers, the destruction of 'labour' when a battle was lost or when the prince and commander, quite simply, forgot to pay his debts. The entrepreneur was at the same time a war leader, like duke Bernard of Saxe-Weimar or the duke Charles IV of Lorraine; he ran the risk of imprisonment like the illustrious Montecuccoli at the start of his career, or dying prematurely in combat like the king of Sweden, Gustavus Adolphus, at the Battle of Lützen, for tactics demanded that the leader set the example in the brief but nonetheless deadly encounters. If he overcame all these difficulties, he not only invested his rewards in lands, like Wallenstein or Bernard of Saxe-Weimar, but also hoarded precious metals, jewels and coins so that he could dispose of his liquid assets in times of need. He might even lend money to the sovereign; in 1641 Arnim and Saxe-Lauenburg advanced 250 000 rixdales (the equivalent of 250 000 écus) to Ferdinand III at a time when the Estates of Bohemia were acting cautiously.

The war entrepreneur played a fundamental role with the Habsburgs. Ferdinand II was obliged to have recourse to the entrepreneurial system in order to escape the control over the conduct of the war exercised by Spain and Bavaria. In 1618 the imperial army was inadequate and Ferdinand called on the Spanish regiments of the Milanese and the army of the Holy League which was, in fact, Maximilian of Bavaria's army. He also used the credit given him by Prague merchant bankers, Bassevi and in particular Hans de Witte, who were sufficiently rich to make the necessary advances. The Venetian ambassadors remarked that the emperor was burdened with debt. Ferdinand, believing that he would get out of debt by inflating the economy, issued money by the billion and so provoked the grave monetary crisis of 1624 (the famous Münzcalada), a real bankruptcy which he escaped only by selling off at a cheap price the domains confiscated from the nobles in Bohemia. The real beneficiary of the whole operation was Albrecht von Wallenstein. With his first gains, he acquired vast domains in Bohemia and put together a principality, the duchy of Frýdland where he founded well-managed factories and enterprises. In 1624 he suggested to Ferdinand II levying an army and equipping and supplying it on condition that he also had command of it. Thus empowered, Wallenstein bled white northern Germany, levying contributions from the occupied towns and territories and appropriating Mecklenburg as the emperor was incapable of paying back the millions of rixdales for which Wallenstein sent him a bill. The lack of sufficient resources – in the next phase the Swedes were also without money – led to the principle that war should nourish war; the armies of the Thirty Years War were, with the exception of the French, without any organized system of supplies. When a battalion had 'eaten' a region, it moved a little further away to empty the cellars and granaries elsewhere and to raise new taxes on the rich. Turenne's Weimarians did the same after 1644 and although this allowed them to diminish the war contributions raised in Alsace, it brought devastation to Swabia, Franconia and Bavaria in 1648. It is easy to understand why, after 1648, the princes, nobles and peasants considered peace the greatest of all possible goods and why, time and again, those living in the country sought salvation in temporary, but all too often, permanent flight.

METHODS OF RECONSTRUCTION[9]

The methods of reconstruction were simple: as in France after the Hundred Years War, it sufficed to attract the peasants back to the devastated zones, offering them lands and tax advantages, generally three years of total exemption from feudal dues and state tax. For those who had remained, it was sufficient to reduce the tax burden by lowering contributions. The Viennese court took this course after 1665 when the international situation allowed it to discharge a large part of its army. These simple methods proved effective in the Rhineland, the Palatinate and in Alsace where a number of Swiss colonies were installed on land which had been abandoned.

In Bohemia and Austria, this policy was thwarted by the Catholic Reformation. K. Krofta estimates that 200 000 inhabitants left the territory of the kingdom of Bohemia to take refuge in Silesia and especially Saxony, Lusatia and western Poland (Posnania). These immigrants were, of course, Protestants, in particular Germanophone Lutherans who had settled in the peripheral zones and so found it easier to migrate to Saxony, where they compensated for the heavy losses of population caused by the war, especially in the Elbe valley, which had been the zone of passage of different armies. These migrations prove that the Habsburgs did not have any desire to Germanize Bohemia and show, on the contrary, that Ferdinand III followed his father's policy of Counter-Reformation whatever the immediate cost, and likewise preferred to 'reign over a desert rather than over heretics'. In

Lower Austria the measures of religious 'reform', which were combined for the peasants with the ban on their leaving the country, had a less disastrous effect on the demographic level.

At the social level, the reconstruction of Bohemia was accompanied by rigorous measures and a ban on peasants leaving the manor without authorization. One can speak of a 'second serfdom' because the peasants were truly 'attached to the glebe'. To marry, study or take a trade outside the estate, a peasant had to ask permission from the master, who might well refuse in order not to lose manual labour that had become valuable. Worse still, from the age of twelve until they reached their majority, children had to serve as domestic servants for little or no pay at the castle or on the dominical farm, while the *robot* which covered all types of agricultural activities easily reached 100 days a year. This situation affected the small cultivators far harder than the proprietors of 20 hectares, as J. Macek observes, in so far as a rich ploughman could send a farmhand and a supplementary team of draught-animals. An agronomist from Bohemia, a former steward, did not hesitate to write that the Czech peasant was so exploited that he represented a model of patience and resignation and underwent purgatory in this life if he carried out his obligations. The result of this state of affairs was a great peasant revolt in 1680 which was harshly suppressed and which resulted only in a yet stricter and more uniform royal ruling of 150 days' labour a year.

The other landowners tried to improve the yield in Lower Austria, introducing new speculative crops such as tobacco and forage crops to improve the rearing of cattle and the production of milk products, cheese and butter, which were easily negotiable on the urban markets. The sector that experienced the greatest expansion was the rational exploitation of the Austrian vineyards. The great abbeys built vast cellars to stock wines and to sell them at the most advantageous rate. These wines often came from the tithes collected on the abbey's far-flung plots, with the *robot* providing the necessary carriage for their collection. To guarantee outlets, the religious orders tried to eliminate competition, forbidding the import or transit of wines from modern Burgenland and Transdanubia, which provoked protests from the Hungarian Diet.

More trust, in general, was put in rational management of the large domains than in technological innovations. The aristocrats were persuaded that the supervision of managers, the careful examination of accounts and the reduction of general prices could clearly increase the yield of the land. Prelates had a reputation for excelling at this kind of activity. This is why they always occupied a choice place in the states' financial commissions, where they were always represented in these capacities. Leopold Kollonich, for example, built a towering reputation as a good financier thanks to the exemplary management that he exercised in the late 1670s over the Lower Austrian domains of the Order of Malta, of which he was commander. There was evidently a great gulf between the rigorous management of some estates, where the regular examination of accounts sufficed to assure the well-running of an enterprise, and the direction of public finances during wartime. Despite the trust shown in him by the emperor, cardinal Kollonich's passage to the head of the chamber of accounts was notoriously a disaster.

MERCANTILISM

From the beginning of his reign Leopold I showed great interest in mercantilism, the economic doctrine in favour in Western Europe, which French manuals named 'Colbertism', as the monarchy's principle resource remained agriculture.

Habsburg economic policy was the work of two groups of 'men in authority'; businessmen and Czech financiers who, impressed by the French and Dutch experiences, were disturbed by the economic depression prevailing in Bohemia and Moravia. From Malevsk to Boek, they demanded that industries be developed and that the restrictive policies of the guilds be combated and privileges granted to entrepreneurs. In addition, a group of foreign intellectuals in the hereditary lands involved the emperor in industrial development and large-scale trade. Leopold I, with his open-minded spirit and his concern for public well-being, was open to persuasion, being himself aware of the French example where the government succeeded in deriving enormous resources from the labour of peasants and artisans alone, without possessing gold mines. This was why he extended his patronage to Johann-Joachim Becher, Wilhelm Schröder and Philipp Wilhelm von Hörgnik who, in 1686, with his famous work *Österreich über alles, wann es nur will* (Austria above all others if only it so desires) fixed the official economic doctrine of the court of Vienna for more than a century. The administrators of the chamber of accounts, however, disapproved of Becher and his friends, who were personal advisers of the emperor.[10]

The policy adopted by Leopold I had been summarized in an ordinance at the end of his reign:

Nothing has been closer to our heart since the beginning of our government than to favour the general progress and improvement of my kingdoms, countries and peoples, and especially to maintain at every moment their prosperity by introducing to this end industries; in this way many thousands of men receive their bread in an honourable manner, the raw materials remain in the land, the subjects find work, people are turned from idleness and are led to find an honourable occupation; besides, contributions are easily paid, while money previously sent outside the country remains here and in this way the country can be rendered rich and populous.[11]

Achievements before 1683 were modest – some factories and a trade company with privileges. As early as 1650, vice-chancellor Khurtz had created a cloth factory on his lands at Horn in Lower Austria. In 1656 Ferdinand III installed at Wiener Neustadt an arms factory with engineers from the Netherlands, who were lodged with their families and workers in eighteen houses; from 1676 to 1700 the establishment enjoyed great prosperity through supplying the imperial army.[12] The president of the chamber of accounts, Sinzendorf, established on one of his domains in Lower Austria at Walpersdorf a silk factory which was ruined by the Turkish invasion in 1683. The manufacture of Tabor cloth at Vienna suffered a similarly lamentable fate in 1683, while that at Linz developed apace and had some 400 workers by the beginning of the eighteenth century. All these new enterprises were concerned with the manufacture of luxury goods which, with the exception of weapons, were not indispensable. The fate of the project of Jean Trehet in 1687 epitomizes the situation; an artisan of Parisian origin, he proposed to make tapestries at Vienna but, after studying the market, such an enterprise did not seem profitable since tapestries imported from Flanders were much less expensive.

If there was, in retrospect, a thriving industry within the monarchy, it is to be found not in the towns where the little that the guilds produced was poor and dear, nor in the prestigious enterprises intended to prove the theories of distinguished economists, but rather in the rural industries, scattered in the villages, on the domains of the aristocrats or in the towns on estates – fine examples of proto-industries.

The principal effort of the 'cameralists' (the Austrian name for the theoreticians of mercantilism) was directed towards international commerce and the recovery of the Balkan and Ottoman markets. The hope was to reach Salonika overland, or Istanbul by the Danube and the Black Sea, in order to compete there with the Venetians, Dutch and above all the merchants of Marseilles, who flooded the Ottoman Empire with manufactured products (linen and cloth especially).

The Peace of Vasvár in 1664 provided the opportunity: the Porte made a gesture by granting commercial facilities to the emperor's subjects while the emperor granted the Ottoman merchants the customs franchise in the hereditary lands and a 50 per cent reduction on Hungarian customs, which fell from 1/30th to 1/60th *ad valorem*. In 1667 an Eastern trade company was founded under the aegis of Triangl, a merchant from Fiume (Rijeka). The company acquired capital of 300 000 florins, which soon rose to 1 million in 1671. Until 1678 a convoy brought to Constantinople each year material from Silesia and hardware from Nürnberg and brought back raw silk from Persia, oil and oranges, but it was not until the Peace of Passarowitz (1718) that exchanges with the Ottoman empire really developed. The company concentrated on the trade in Hungarian beef and obtained the monopoly of the provisioning of Vienna at a guaranteed price of 3 kreuzers a pound.

This initiative ruined a number of Hungarian merchants, nobles and commoners; in 1681 the Diet of Sopron protested against the monopoly granted to Viennese merchants, a monopoly which placed Hungary in a dependent economic situation, a foreshadowing of the development that characterized the eighteenth century – the exploitation of Hungary as a reserve of raw materials, cheap food products and as an outlet for manufactured products from the hereditary lands, a veritable 'colonial pact'.[13]

Even though the results of Eastern commerce proved to be quite modest in the first period (the figure for business in 1675 was 600 000 florins, of which only 200 000 was in near-Eastern trade), the company's activity based on the Dutch and French model nevertheless began the great trade policy of the eighteenth century by restoring Austrian manufacturers to the traditional markets that had been lost since the beginning of the Turkish Wars.[14]

When the economic situation in the period 1648–83 is examined, it is apparent that, as in Western Europe, this was a period of recession. The results remained modest compared to the expansion that followed the siege of Vienna and the reconquest of Hungary. The outbreak of the plague in 1679 in Vienna and from 1680 in Bohemia struck with full force an organism that was still convalescent, the victim of a policy of Counter-Reformation combined with the evils of war and the financial strains imposed by the Habsburgs' grand policy.

This did not prevent the skilful policy of Leopold I, combined with French outrages in the Rhineland, from winning the Habsburgs the support of the German princes. Like the Czech countries on the other side, Austria also (to a lesser degree) experienced a long period of peace; the hereditary lands were able to recover their demographic and economic potential and so provided the emperor with the means for an active foreign policy. In short, at the end of a quarter of a century the reconstruction of the Austrian monarchy was successful, which helps to explain the emergence of Austria as a great power at the moment when the Spanish monarchy was experiencing yet worse difficulties.

NOTES AND REFERENCES

1. V.-L. Tapié, *The Rise and Fall of the Habsburg Monarchy*, London, 1971.
2. Louis de Rouvroi, duc de Saint-Simon, *Mémoires pour l'année 1705*, Paris, 1955, vol. 2, pp. 474–5.
3. Günther Barudio, *Der teutsche Krieg, 1618–1648*, Frankfurt am Main, 1985.
4. Gottlieb Eucharius Rinck, *Leopolds des Grossen ... Leben und Thaten*, Leipzig, 1708.
5. John T. O'Connor, *Negotiator out of Season: The Career of Wilhelm Egon von Fürstenberg, 1629–1704*, Athens, Georgia, 1978.

6. Charles Boutant, *L'Europe au grand tournant des années 1680: la guerre de la succession palatine*, Paris, 1985.

7. Klaus Muller, *Das kaiserliche Gesandtschaftswesen nach dem westfälischen Frieden (1648–1740)*, Bonn, 1976.

8. Günther Franz, *Der 30 jährige Krieg und das deutsche Volk*, 1st edn, Munich, 1938, and of course the celebrated collection of etchings of Jacques Callot, Paris, 1632.

9. Jean Bérenger, *Finances et absolutisme autrichien dans la seconde moitié du XVIIe siècle*, Paris, 1975.

10. Johann-Philipp von Hörgnik, *Œsterreich über alles wann es nur will*, Vienna, 1686.

11. *Codex Austriacus*, 2 vols, Vienna, 1705, vol.1, pp. 283–5.

12. Fritz Posch, 'Die Armaturmeisterschaft zu Wiener-Neustadt', *Unsere Heimat*, no. 21, 1950.

13. Jean Bérenger, *Les Gravamina: doléances de la Diète hongroise (1655–1681)*, Paris, 1973.

14. Herbert Hassinger, 'Die erste Orientalische Handelskompagnie', in *Vierteljahrschrift für Sozial und Wirtschaftsgeschichte*, Stuttgart, 1942.

CHAPTER TWENTY-THREE

The Counter-Reformation in the Seventeenth Century

The reconstruction of the economy, as successful as it was, was not the Habsburgs' chief preoccupation, even if Leopold I had been able to surround himself with intelligent and innovative advisers.[1] For Ferdinand III, as for his son, what came before all else was the task of completing the Catholic Reformation which had been undertaken by Ferdinand II at Graz in 1598. Religious unification, according to the theories expounded by the Flemish humanist Justus Lipsius (1547–1606), offered the dynasty faced with such powerful orders a means of strengthening its power, while maintaining a large measure of decentralization, pursuing collaboration with the orders and respecting the differences between national cultures. When writing of this period, Czech historiography has dubbed it 'the time of darkness', a totally misleading epithet if it leads to the period being seen as a phase of Germanization and deculturation. The Habsburgs committed plenty of injustices without historians adding more. Rather, the Counter-Reformation was the work of Czech Catholics, the 'Spanish faction' and others, and the Church. Although it imposed, in the spirit of the Council of Trent, a Latin liturgy just as in the rest of Christendom, it did not put a stop to preaching in the vernacular and even supported bilingual or trilingual publications.

The 'renewed' constitution of 1627 and the patent of reformation of the same year presented a model which Ferdinand III went on to apply to Lower Austria after 1648, by reason of the *jus reformandi* that the treaties of Westphalia had confirmed, and so came to realize an 'Austro-Bohemian' model which broadly corresponded to the political and religious ideal of Ferdinand II. But the task was not finished in 1657 when Ferdinand III died prematurely: it devolved upon Leopold I to pursue religious unification, applying this model to Hungary, although Hungary was protected by the Peace of Vienna of 1606 but more importantly by a nobility jealous of its liberties and confessional privileges.

THE AUSTRO-BOHEMIAN MODEL

Like Ferdinand II and Ferdinand III, Leopold I was personally devoted to militant Catholicism. It was his grandfather who, during a pilgrimage to Loretto in 1598, made a solemn vow to die rather than renounce the task of converting his subjects, a vow that he renewed for the Czech lands after the victory of his army at the White Mountain. Deeply influenced by family tradition and by the *princeps in compendio*, at the beginning of his reign Leopold declared to the nuncio that he would do everything to stop the public exercise of Lutheran worship in his hereditary lands for fear that the people would otherwise quickly return to Lutheran practices. He felt himself to be personally responsible for his subjects' salvation and 'he could not, at the risk of his soul, make himself the accomplice of similar non-Catholic meetings and religious worship in his hereditary lands'. He added on the same issue that he was inspired by the example set by his ancestors, 'who had taught him to beg rather than agree to the spread of heresy in his states' and that the defence of Catholicism was an integral part of his obligations. It is evident that, for him, there was no salvation outside the Catholic Church.

Although at the present time such an idea is shocking, it should nevertheless be conceded that Leopold was perfectly sincere in his fanatical determination. The spritual well-being of his subjects was not, however, the only basis for this policy: it was also an urgent political necessity. In a monarchy in which such diverse states, nations and cultures were juxtaposed, a common religion could supply an element of unity. Similarly, religion was not only a private affair but also a means of demonstrating opposition and of expressing particularist aspirations. In the seventeenth century the discontent of a social group was disclosed by a move to heterodoxy, whether within Christendom or in the world of Islam.

A good example is that of the Croat nobility of Slavonia, which remained Catholic because the magnates were rallying to Protestantism. Loyalty to Catholicism was a way of showing at the same time both loyalty to the House of Austria and hostility to the Hungarian magnates. By remaining Catholics, these nobles made a deliberate choice to side with the Germans against the Hungarian state. They demonstrated their distinct identity and helped to make a little more complicated the already very complex situation existing within the monarchy in general and the Hungarian state in particular. This is why the Viennese government, following Justus Lipsius, allowed Roman Catholicism to be a fundamental principle of unity in a political entity that encompassed so many peoples and states. Without it, the prince could not carry out his duties and there would be neither loyalty nor justice but only disorder: 'that religion might be the binding force and support of the state'. There was nothing new about this principle, which corresponded to the French adage 'one faith, one law, one king' and most markedly to the policy so resolutely followed by the

Madrid Habsburgs, who had expelled the Jewish and Muslim minorities from Spain, thereby realizing through Catholicism the unity of the Iberian peninsula. Inspired by this example, the Viennese Habsburgs would similarly have liked to realize unity in their states through Catholicism, knowing full well that, for the nobility, belonging to the Protestant Churches was a means of expressing their opposition to efforts to reorganize the state. The religious policy of the time should not therefore be understood only in terms of liberty of conscience, as religion then was far from being a private matter.

These were the conditions in which Leopold I had to complete the work of his grandfather and father. At Münster, Ferdinand III had obtained total freedom of action in the hereditary lands (except for Silesia) and made good use of it. After 1651 he renewed and extended legislative measures against non-Catholics, not only in the Czech lands but also in Austria where he was free to limit the nobility's freedom of worship while entrusting pastoral action to commissions which included the bishop of Wiener Neustadt and the abbots of Altenburg, Lilienfeld and Göttweig. The commissioners had at their disposal in each place 'instructors', namely monks charged with effecting through persuasion the conversion of Lutherans. In 1657 the commissions ceased their activities: the most important task was not the conversion of heretics but rather to ensure that new converts were regular in their religious practice. The general commission, which consisted solely of prelates (the abbots of Heiligenkreuz and of Seitenstetten, the provosts of St Andreas and of Dürnstein), ceased to exist and its powers were handed over to the official of Passau in 1670. From this date, Lower Austria may be considered as having become Roman Catholic once again, at least in so far as the masses were concerned, although some noble families remained faithful to the Augsburg Confession. According to the report of 85 parish priests, in 1675 there were no more than 354 Lutheran subjects and the last of these left in 1697. This rigorous policy was extended to the Jews in 1670, when 1 400 were expelled from Vienna, and settled in Bohemia and Moravia, and the synagogue was converted into a church and dedicated to St Leopold, margrave and patron of Austria. The empress Margarita-Teresa's confessor, a Spanish Franciscan, had particularly recommended this action but it was a measure that was also very much in accord with the wishes of the Viennese, who were fiercely hostile to the Jewish minority. Without over-estimating the depth of the Catholic restoration in the hereditary lands, it may be said that by around 1700 the Church and the House of Austria had obtained a certain measure of success.

The dangers of Protestant contamination seem to have been eliminated in the space of a generation: this is clear when a comparison is made between the reaction in 1666 of the government of Lower Austria, which banned non-Catholic foreigners from entering the country, and that, at the end of the century, of the Bohemian government which (without fear) planned to settle Protestant engineers. At the end of the seventeenth century, government circles considered the hereditary lands to have become Catholic. The vigilant policy of surveillance had borne its fruits.

The development of certain devotions, in particular the devotion to the Eucharist so favoured by the House of Austria, was manifest in the Corpus Christi Day processions, the adoration of the Blessed Sacrament and the practice of frequent communion. The addition of the cult of the Virgin Mary and of various saints was in keeping with this. Leopold paid homage to the Virgin in the name of the Empire in a pilgrimage to Altötting immediately after his election in 1658. Like his grandfather Ferdinand II at the shrine of Mariazell in Styria in 1676, he made the Virgin *generalissimo* of his armies and consecrated Austria anew to her. He favoured as well the cult of St Joseph extolled by St Teresa of Ávila and popularized by the Carmelite Dominicus a Jesu Maria; in 1675 he dedicated the hereditary lands to Christ's earthly father. By contrast, right until 1700, St Jan Nepomuk remained a Bohemian national saint, his international character coming later. The real significance of these cults in the popular consciousness is open to question. The historian Anna Coreth has too much confidence in 'baroque piety': she has not studied sufficiently the religious houses dedicated to various cults in the way that Y. Lasfargues has done in order to follow the progress of the cult of St Jan Nepomuk. The papal nuncio himself harboured doubts as to the solidity and depth of such beliefs as pastoral action was inadequate. The better parishes, in Germany as in Hungary, were given to noble beneficiaries and it proved almost impossible to change old customs.

The clergy, however, were not present in sufficient numbers among the masses to make themselves felt. In Vienna, as in Bohemia, the emperor had personally favoured the activity of the Society of Jesus, granting it generous material assistance in the form of pensions and tax exemptions. It is true that the Jesuits played an educational role among the ruling classes and endured the rigours of the missionary calling, but they did not themselves have the means to take charge of parishes. This is why the emperor had to appeal to the Estates (*Stände*) for assistance to complete his task of effecting Counter-Reformation.

In Austria the realization of this programme was especially complicated as the Lower Austrian nobility had retained its right to freedom of worship. A patent dating from 13 April 1651 repeated the provisions of previous texts (the patents general of 1634, 1638 and 1645), putting a stop to the peasants' practice of Lutheran worship. Non-Catholics were forbidden to go abroad to practise their religion – i.e. to the neighbouring Hungarian towns of Sopron and Pressburg (Poszony) – to eat meat on the days of abstinence prescribed by the Church, to read books by non-Catholics that had not received the censor's approval and to welcome or give lodgings to Protestant preachers. The first measures were intended to stifle all religious life among the Lutherans, who were deprived of preaching and sermons and similarly the sacraments, without going so far as to oblige them to convert to Catholicism. However, in 1652 the emperor created a general commission of the Reformation with the avowed goal of obtaining the conversion of non-Catholic subjects. The patent of 1652 in effect closed the frontiers since subjects could not move away without a passport issued by the local authorities. The commission sent into each district monks charged with 'instructing', that is to say, converting by persuasion. They stayed for six weeks, after which Lutherans could convert, request a delay for reflection, or emigrate. At Dürnstein, for example, out of fifty-five Lutherans, thirty-four converted, five asked for a delay for consideration and seven requested permission to emigrate, while nine were deemed 'undecided'.

These measures provoked a reaction from the Lutheran nobles within the Diet who, while they did not have the right to form Protestant Estates, reacted within each order, especially since they feared that their peasants would emigrate. This prospect did not give rise to concern among the Lutheran lords alone since, in Austria and Bohemia, every landed proprietor conscious of his interests feared seeing the working population pack up and go and finding himself faced with deserted houses and tenures. The session of 1652 was particularly stormy but Ferdinand III remained firm. The Lutheran lords acknowledged what was said and understood its import. From 1653 onwards, everyone took up the traditional clichés to contest the increase in the contribution; the ills of the age, the impoverishment of the country, the consequences of war. While these lines of argument were not unfounded, they should, however, be examined very critically in so far as they mask other antagonisms.

The Lutheran lords were a political and religious force which complicated the House of Austria's task since, even in the largest families like the Auerspergs, the Puchheims, the Starhembergs and Herbersteins, one still comes across Lutherans such as the count Leopold Christoph Herberstein who, when he died on 13 November 1667, left legacies of 300 florins to pastors and Protestant schools in Pressburg. These great lords who refused to convert, and so cut themselves off from the chance of employment at court, formed the nucleus of passive resistance to the work of Counter-Reformation desired by the imperial government. In particular, they maintained a measure of clandestine Protestantism among their peasants. In 1690 the administrator of an estate was accused of collecting together peasants in order to read Lutheran works to them while, in 1694, the Auerspergs still employed Protestant servants. The movement to convert was as slow in Austria as in Bohemia, though for different reasons: an investigation in 1675 revealed the existence of 354 heads of Lutheran families over the whole of Lower Austria, 242 in the Wienerwald alone.

The third point of the 1651 programme was yet harder to achieve. It was vital to install a priest in each parish to strengthen the sentiments of the recent converts as well as to develop the convictions of the longer-standing Catholics. It was thus essential to install or re-install priests able to carry out the day-to-day activities, administering the sacraments, celebrating mass regularly and instructing the faithful, in short, applying the directives of the Council of Trent. Although these demands now seem legitimate, they were achieved only with much difficulty, the Catholic clergy frequently retaining the outlook of beneficiaries and proving little mindful of the spiritual progress of their flock.

In fact, a parish could keep a priest only if it had sufficient resources to assure him an appropriate existence, much superior to that of the peasants and comparable with that of a country gentleman, a member of the third order. This was a question not only of the parish priest's well-being, but also essentially a matter of prestige. The poorly endowed parishes did not keep educated priests and if the priest wanted to take advantage of the perquisites which came with wearing a stole (*Stolageld*, fees for masses, etc.), he immediately lost the confidence of the newly converted. The real solution was the endowment of the parish with rents and especially with the recuperation of tithes, both of which had been taken over in the sixteenth century by lay lords who rarely restored them; even if they returned to being fervent Catholics. The House of Austria itself was powerless to resolve this economic problem quickly and efficiently. For example, in 1623 Ferdinand II re-installed a parish priest at Hollabrunn, but it was not until 1660 that that priest's successor was able to recover all the parish goods. The reluctance of the Catholic orders to restore the clergy's property was a general phenomenon throughout the Emperor's lands. According to the report of the commissioners appointed by the Bohemian Diet to inquire into the rebuilding of abandoned parishes, of the seventy-seven questioned during 1667–8, fifty did not reply at all, twenty-one declared that the matter was being pursued by the competent authorities (the archbishop's commission) and just three lords claimed to have re-established six parishes between them. Four of these, including Lobkowitz and Roudnice, had been rebuilt by prince Lobkowitz, who was hardly famed for his clericalism. The other two 'pious' lords were count Czernin and the grand prior of the Order of Malta. Conspicuous among those who displayed a splendid indifference to this vital aspect of the rebuilding of religious life are such mighty and devout lords as prince Johann Adolf Schwarzenberg and count Ignaz Sternberg and such very rich ones as the Liechtensteins and the Eggenbergs, as well as the chamber of Bohemia, which ought to have been keen to apply the sovereign's policy, and even the religious orders. Never mind that the Chapter of Prague Cathedral and the canonesses of the convent of St George in Prague – both well provided for and caring little for the spiritual needs of those in the country – did not deign to reply, but neither did the Dominicans nor the rector of the Jesuits at Glattau.

Here is proof that very few cared for anything but the most superficial activity among the peasant masses and that even the religious orders rarely had any taste for a vocation among the humble. The clergy, recruited among the wealthy or well-to-do, had no time for the ideal of poverty and in Bohemia as in Austria the monks preferred the holy discipline of their monasteries to a liberty which brought with it a diet of bread and water.

They made the work of Capuchins like Father Sinelli appear all the more worthy.

In purely political terms the 'renewed Constitution' had brought the Habsburgs some satisfaction, the significance of which has been greatly exaggerated by liberal historiography as it was a matter of real collaboration between the crown and the orders and not real absolutism.

For sure, after 1627 the crown of Bohemia was hereditary in the House of Habsburg which meant that there were no longer any negotiations between the king and the Diet at the time of the election as had last been the case in 1617. Above all there was no longer a contract limiting the powers of the monarchy (*Wahlcapitulation*). The crown henceforth had a firm hold on the real executive power because the king named the grand officers of the crown – grand burgrave, grand chamberlain, grand judge, land marshal, court equerry, etc. (*Oberstburggraf, Oberstkämmerer, Oberstlandrichter, Landmarschall, Hofstallmeister*) – who constituted the government and Lieutenancy Council in the event of the sovereign of Bohemia's absence. In practice, though, these dignitaries were always chosen from among the country's nobility, as were the judges of the court of appeal at Prague (*Appellationsgericht zu Prag*) and the chancellor. The Diet was no longer authorized to present grievances at the beginning of each session, however, as these never failed to be criticisms of the government's action.

The crown shared legislative power with the orders. It alone possessed the right to propose laws which it set out at the beginning of the session (*Landtagsproposition*), generally once a year. In Lower Austria the level of collaboration was so advanced that it was the orders who codified the laws in 1670 and the crown was content to sanction the Diet's proposals.[2]

Most importantly, the crown needed the permanent collaboration of the orders for the vote of the land tax (*Landtaxe*). The revenues of the *regalia* (demesne, customs, salt tax) represented scarcely more than 25 per cent of the king's resources and the remainder would be granted in the form of the land tax, voted and levied by the orders themselves. The emperor had to call a session of the Diet each year because he could not do without money from his subjects.

Finally, the crown did not control the local administration because since 1620 the power of the nobility over the peasants had been reinforced. It was the Diet that divided the tax among the different branches of the nobility and it was the lord's steward who collected the state tax from the peasants. In practice, the peasants never appeared before the royal tribunals unless on appeal, and then only in Lower Austria.

The application of the theory of forfeiture (*Verwirkungstheorie*), according to which the orders in 1618 had unilaterally broken the contract that bound them to the crown and had thereby given the crown authority to make Bohemia a patrimonial state (*Staat*), had limited results if the Czech or Austrian lands are compared with the France of Louis XIV. Even in the confessional domain, the apparent success of the Catholic Reformation was limited and the persistence of a hard core of crypto-Protestants is largely explained by the inadequacy of the framework of pastoral care linked to the egotism of the prelates and the aristocracy, a problem which would be resolved only much later by Joseph II when he secularized the monasteries and created parishes. For the moment it is important to show how Leopold I tried to apply the same policy of Counter-Reformation and restoration of constitutional order in Hungary.

THE FAILURE OF THE COUNTER-REFORMATION IN HUNGARY[3]

Even after the successes of cardinal Pázmány, the kingdom of Hungary supported by Transylvania remained a bastion of Calvinism in Europe and within the Austrian monarchy. Calvinism drew its support from the gentry (*középnemesség*), who were an important political and economic force and who used the sessions of the Diet particularly to present their grievances so that the government feared the violence of the debates. Until 1681 the emperor ceased summoning the Diet, believing that by doing so he would eliminate the gentry from political life. The gentry, however, were determined to defend their religous and political liberties and thereby made themselves the champions of the cause of Hungarian state independence.

The general tendencies of the Viennese government were expressed by one of Leopold's ministers at the time of the 1662 session of the Hungarian Diet: 'We might well need to treat the kingdom of Hungary in the way we treated the kingdom of Bohemia'. Hungarian state right hardly permitted the emperor to act directly, however, so he would have to be content to support the Catholic party, that is the prelates, magnates and the Jesuits.

The Catholic party in fact grew considerably in strength in the course of the seventeenth century. At the end of the sixteenth century, it was made up essentially of prelates who, for most of the time, had been deprived of their benefices and had taken refuge in the western part of Upper Hungary. The primate of Hungary, the archbishop of Strigonia (Esztergóm), withdrew to Trnava, not far from Pressburg. Determined supporters of the Counter-Reformation, they were still deeply entrenched in the society and government of the country. Traditionally, bishops occupied the important posts in the government at Pressburg. The chancellor of Hungary was always a bishop and, in the event of the office of palatine being vacant, the archbishop of Strigonia presided over the Lieutenancy Council. The clergy represented the first order of the kingdom and the prelates sat, like the magnates, in the upper chamber of the Diet. What is more, the higher clergy were related to the aristocratic families who sat in the government, for example the Forgáchs and the Pálffys. Besides, the magnates as a social group had made peace with the House of Austria in 1608 and were not

311

indifferent to the talents of cardinal Pázmány, who had brought back many a Hungarian aristocrat to the Catholic faith. In 1660 the upper chamber and the Hungarian government were made up of zealous Catholics who busied themselves with converting their Protestant peasants. The two most celebrated examples are those of Ferenc Nádasdy, lord chief justice of the kingdom (*judex curiae*) and Zsófia Báthory, widow of György II Räköczi, prince of Transylvania. Nádasdy ruined around 200 Protestant parishes in western Hungary through a combination of threats and persuasion while Zsófia Báthory chased the reformed pastors from her late husband's vast estates in eastern Hungary. Everywhere the Roman Catholic lords obtained the support of the Jesuits who founded houses subsidized by the king and higher clergy across the whole territory of Royal Hungary, the most important house being the university of Košice, founded in 1657.

The advance of the Counter-Reformation would thus have been assured if the crisis of 1664 had not put everything in doubt. It is well known that the Hungarians unanimously condemned the Peace signed by the emperor with the Turks at Vásvár. They accused the House of Austria of laying their country open to Ottoman incursions, although the Christian armies had been the victors, and criticized the emperor for sacrificing their country to German, that is to purely dynastic, interests. The Catholic magnates, the members of the government at Pressburg and the archbishop of Strigonia found themselves caught up in a great anti-Austrian conspiracy to which the palatine Ferenc Wesselényi gave his name. The Habsburgs thus, for the first time since 1526, succeeded in setting unanimously against them all the Hungarians, Catholics and Protestants alike, no matter to which order they belonged.

The movement became an open revolt only in 1670 because the leaders responsible, who wanted to give themselves either a national or a French king, were searching in vain for external support. Louis XIV let Grémonville play along with the conspirators right until 1668 at which point he decided it would be more in his interest to deal directly with the emperor. The ban of Croatia, Petar Zrinski, the main instigator of the conspiracy, had the ill-conceived idea of turning to the Turks for support and offering them a treaty by which Croatia would become a Turkish protectorate. Betrayed and exposed, he unleashed a serious political crisis. The kingdom of Hungary was occupied by imperial troops, all Hungarians thought to be rebels and the principal leaders of the conspiracy (Petar Zrinski, Fran Krsto Frankopan, Ferenc Nádasdy) were arrested, brought to trial, condemned and executed at Wiener Neustadt in April 1671. Through Zrinski's blunders, the very people who had wanted to spare their fatherland Bohemia's fate, put it in a situation similar to that of Bohemia in 1620. The Hungarians, by revolting, had broken the contract that linked them to their Habsburg king, who was not in a legal position to apply the *Verwirkungstheorie*. For once, the emperor had reacted resolutely and through the military occupation of the country, Leopold found himself in, for him, an unusually strong position.

Once the early anguish of the spring of 1670 passed, the event appeared to the government in Vienna as an unhoped-for windfall. First, the main body of the imperial troops was stationed in Hungary where it behaved like a real army of occupation. Second, the sovereign had become the *absolute* king through the Hungarians' own failure of duty. Until, then, he had had to respect the constitution of the kingdom, in particular the royal diploma which he had accepted before his election in 1655. Respectful of the letter of the law, the Habsburg king let the Catholic party continue its work and refused to hear grievances of a confessional character. In the future, however, he would show his true colours and apply the programme of the Hungarian clergy which bishop György Barsony had exposed in his book *Veritas toti Mundo declarata*, where he denied non-Catholics the right to freedom of worship, arguing that the Peace of Vienna of 1606, which remained the basis of Protestant privileges, did not have any value because it had been signed by the emperor Rudolph under duress.[4] Moreover, he argued, the kingdom of Hungary had been Catholic since the conversion of St Stephen and the king could not make any concession to heresy if he wanted to respect the fundamental laws of the state. This work fuelled much discussion among the Hungarian prelates and the Jesuits and was much debated by the Protestants.

The emperor's entourage had already been persuaded by these ideas. His Jesuit confessor, Father Müller, took care to study in depth István Werbczi's *Opus Tripartitum*, which remained the basis of Hungarian common law, and concluded that since the Hungarians were rebels, the Viennese government was justified in applying the *Verwirkungstheorie*.[5] In 1673 he declared to the Swedish minister Esaias Pufendorf that the Hungarians had lost their privileges and that they were now subjects like the rest. The Austrian chancellor Hocher was, for political reasons, very hostile to the Hungarians in general. As president of the emergency court that had condemned the leader of the rebellion to death, he thought that only conversion to Catholicism could turn them into subjects as obedient as the rest.

In the course of the winter 1670–1, Hocher expressed his point of view in a memorandum intended to be read before the Privy Council. It was, he said, necessary to take advantage of the opportunity to crush the rebellion, deprive the Hungarians of their liberty and occupy the country militarily. He also relied on the *Verwirkungstheorie* to justify the deep change which forced the Hungarians to accept German garrisons, then the German language, customs and dress. Montecuccoli insisted on the confessional aspect and urged the merits of religious unity. He reminded everyone that it was a matter of conscience for the 'emperor-king' to favour the 'true' religion and the salvation of his subjects' souls. Basing his views on Justus Lipsius, he considered especially that unity of religion made for unity of minds. This Catholic party had the support of the nuncio Buonvisi who urged a resolute policy of Counter-Reformation.

The government of Vienna's action was at first repressive in order to deprive the Protestant communities of their churches and above all their pastors. The latter were held responsible for the disorders and rebellion of 1670 and were accused of having roused spirits against the House of Austria, of having spread prophecies against the Habsburgs and of having openly hoped for a Turkish victory over the Christians at Candia (Crete) in 1669. The king appointed an emergency court presided over by the archbishop of Strigonia, György Szelepcsényi; in 1673 twenty-six pastors were condemned to the galleys, not as ministers of religion but as political agitators. In all, 733 Protestant intellectuals (pastors, university and school teachers) were rendered unable to practise, either through exile or imprisonment. It was an uncontestable victory for the Catholic Church since the Lutherans and Calvinists found their ranks considerably depleted. At the same time, the Catholic party was doing all it could to recover the Church's landed property and churches. At the Diet of 1655, the evangelical Estates supplied a list of churches recovered in contempt of the constitution. The king left the Hungarian prelates alone but these measures strengthened the hostility of the gentry towards the House of Austria. The occupation of churches became more frequent after the military occupation of Hungarian territory. Bishop Kollonich, president of the Royal Hungarian Chamber since 1672, expelled the Lutherans from the churches in the royal free towns and often led in person expeditions to seize churches in the country. The number of places of worship recovered by the Catholics between 1670 and 1680 is estimated at 800. The landed property belonging to the Church had to be recovered at the same time as the population was deprived of its ranks of Protestant clergy.

The government at Vienna also supported positive action, namely the conversion of the masses to Catholicism. The task of conversion was entrusted to the Jesuits, who numbered 354 in total and were divided between eight colleges, thirteen residences and six missions but for reasons of security, their apostolate was concentrated in the towns where the results were, at least in appearance, satisfactory. But what did such successes count for in a country as little urbanized as Hungary in the seventeenth century? The towns in fact did not represent very much in demographic, political or economic terms. In fact, the gentry largely escaped the efforts of the Jesuits whose successes, on the pastoral level, remained very modest.

However, this success was achieved at an exorbitant cost because the excesses employed to secure it roused the unanimous displeasure of the Hungarians, whatever their confession. The military occupation demanded by Leopold's counsellors roused the anger of even those best disposed towards the emperor. The imperial troops pillaged, raped and even committed acts of sacrilege against Catholic churches. These methods had been advocated by Montecuccoli and Hocher, who thought that the Hungarians would be broken by terror and would accept any reform in order to secure the retreat of the imperial troops. In fact, all those responsible for this policy had little knowledge of the land and imagined that the Hungarian nobles would react in the same manner as those of Bohemia after the Battle of the White Mountain. To think this, however, was badly to misjudge the mentality of the Hungarians, who little by little rose against the abuses of power of which they were the victims. From 1672 onwards, armed soldiers went underground, blocking the most important route, taking reprisals against priests and especially any Jesuits they could capture.[6] Recruited originally from among the nobles whose property had been confiscated by the Royal Chamber, these irregulars (*Bujdosok*, fugitives) were joined by countless soldiers who had been discharged for religious reasons or else were in straitened circumstances. The blunders of the Viennese government fuelled the rebellion. The Catholic clergy became more and more reticent in the face of bishop Kollonich's abuses of power and national unity tended to gain in strength in opposition to the House of Austria. Supporters organized themselves gradually and obtained outside assistance; from the very beginning Transylvania gave support, then after 1685 France and finally, from 1679 onward, the Porte.[7] With Thököly, the *kuruc* movement became a political and military force in Eastern Europe. The military occupation and repression, instead of getting rid of the Hungarian question, had only contributed to opening a second front, something the Viennese government especially feared.

From 1678 onwards, the most perceptive were reporting that the policy pursued for the previous eight years was not yielding the anticipated results and that a compromise with the Hungarians was a matter of urgency. The nuncio Buonvisi and Father Sinelli supported the idea of negotiation. Sinelli, who understood the facts of the case better than the emperor's other counsellors, had always preached moderation. Hocher himself was too intelligent not to accept a change of direction. Only prelates and the Jesuits remained intractable and defended a bad policy rather than lessen the force of the royal diploma of 1655; if the kingdom of Hungary could be reduced to obedience, the position of Roman Catholicism would be strengthened in the hereditary lands. In negotiating a compromise, Leopold would admit the failure of one of the essential goals of his government; the unification of the Habsburg monarchy by religion. If an accommodation was not reached, however, all of Royal Hungary risked passing under the authority of Thököly and being transformed into an Ottoman protectorate. Despite his personal feelings, the emperor therefore summoned a general Diet at Sopron in May 1681. Thanks to the tenacity of Father Sinelli, who had meanwhile become bishop of Vienna, the moderate party prevailed and the government granted substantial guarantees to Protestant Hungarians. Article I of the Peace of Vienna of 1606 was maintained and religious freedom was accorded to the orders and to Hungarian soldiers from the Military Frontier. Although Leopold did not return the Protestant churches confiscated since 1671, he did authorize the construction of a church in each county and allowed as well magnates and gentry to maintain oratories and chapels in their own residences.[8]

This compromise did not put a complete end to Catholic encroachments but, when the goals which the emperor had set himself in 1672-3 are considered, he had made an enormous concession, even if the Catholic

Church drew substantial benefits from the operation. In accepting the principle of confessional pluralism, Leopold renounced for ever the hope of unifying the monarchy through religion. Hungary kept its own particular status. This serious climb-down would have dire consequences for the future of the Habsburg monarchy.

The real significance of the failure of 1681 has perhaps been underestimated for want of a thorough appreciation of the fundamental importance which the Counter-Reformation held for the Habsburgs.

First of all, the conflict allowed the forces of opposition to crystallize; nobles and commoners mobilized in a war of opposition against the legitimate king. The 'Malcontents', as Louis XIV's contemporaries called them, organized themselves politically and militarily and had a courageous leader, count Imre Thököly, son-in-law of the late Petar Zrinski, and were supported by Transylvania, France and the Ottoman empire. In 1681 a clever French diplomatic move was enough to allow Thököly to break off negotiations with Leopold and to force the resumption of hostilities while the compromise at Sopron was being negotiated. Thököly's goal, Hungarian independence, was at the price of an Ottoman protectorate and furnished a pretext for Turkish intervention in 1682. After serious set-backs, the party for independence resumed combat at the beginning of the eighteenth century under the direction of Ferenc II Rákóczi and still with the blessing of Louis XIV, who was again at war with Leopold I. The Hungarian political landscape was for a long time divided between the moderate and extreme collaborators opposed to the House of Austria. Unconditional support for the Habsburgs was found, if anywhere, among the Roman Catholic clergy.

The result was that the only possible unifying bond between all the peoples of the House of Austria did not, and never did, exist. The patent of tolerance of 1681 was only a realistic admission of failure intended to avoid yet worse ills. Unification by religion, the governing notion of the Styrian branch of the House of Habsburg, would never be realized. Could an alternative be found? The future only showed this to be impossible.

For the moment, the compromise of Sopron ended in the re-establishment of the traditional constitution. The first measure of appeasement was in fact in May 1681 with the election of count, later prince, Pál Esterházy as palatine. Long portrayed as a loyal follower of the House of Austria, this Catholic magnate proceeded to defend the interests of the orders, especially the nobility's immunity from tax when, in 1696, cardinal Kollonich proposed a revised and by no means unreasonable sum of tax to be collected; the vote of an annual contribution of 4 million florins did not exceed the country's capacity and would have avoided the abuses provoked by the arbitrary levying of war contributions. The Pressburg government was re-established as well as the autonomy of the Hungarian Chamber. For sure, in the euphoria which followed the reconquest of the Great Plain and the retaking of Buda, the Habsburgs, in 1687, established the crown of Hungary as hereditary in their House and the abolition of the legal right of resistance, but this was a very slender victory when compared with the hopes that had been raised among Leopold's counsellors by the 'theory of forfeiture'.

Although, after an undeniable military victory and an advantageous peace with the Ottoman empire in 1699, Leopold I had indeed become the sole master of the countries of the crown of St Stephen, he had simply created, if the anachronism may be excused, an 'Austro-Hungary' rather than an Austrian monarchy on the road to unification.

NOTES AND REFERENCES

1. Jean Bérenger, *Finances et absolutisme autrichien dans la second moitié du XVIIe siècle*, Paris, 1975.
2. *Tractatus de juribus in corporalibus*, published in the *Codex Austriacus*, 2 vols, Vienna, 1705, vol. 1, p. 345.
3. Jean Bérenger, *Les Gravamina: doléances de la Diète hongroise (1655–1681)*, Paris, 1973.
   R. J. W. Evans, *The Making of the Habsburg Monarchy*, Oxford, 1979, pp. 168–92.
4. Georges Barsonyi, *Veritas toti Mundo declarata*, Sopron, 1681.
5. István Werboczi, *Tripartitum opus juris consuetudinarii inclyti Hungatiae*, 1st edn, Vienna, 1517.
6. Jean Bérenger, 'La Contre-Réforme en Hongrie', *Bulletin de la Société d'histoire du protestantisme français*, no. CXX, 1974, pp. 1–22.
7. Jean Bérenger, 'Le royaume de France et les Malcontents de Hongrie', *Revue d'histoire diplomatique*, 1975, no. 3, pp. 1–43.
8. Jean Bérenger, 'La Hongrie des Habsbourg au XVIIe siècle: république nobiliaire ou monarchie limitée?', *Revue historique*, no. 483, 1967, pp. 31–3.

CHAPTER TWENTY-FOUR

The Re-birth of the Turkish Peril and the Siege of Vienna

In the half-century following the Peace of Zsitva-Torok in 1606, Austro-Turkish relations verged almost on the cordial with hostilities limited to routine skirmishes over the Military Frontier, while the diplomatic crisis of 1645 was dealt with swiftly since the two antagonists had worries elsewhere. Ferdinand II, in marked contrast to Rudolf II, never dreamt of reconquering Pannonia and Thrace since his particular wish was to submit Germany to his authority. His principal adversary was not the infidel but the heretic. The Grand Turk had turned once again against his mortal enemy, the shah of Persia, retaking Baghdad and Mesopotamia. As Robert Mantran has shown so well,[1] the Ottoman Empire was then suffering a grave economic crisis, or, more precisely, downright impoverishment and the public treasury's difficulties gave rise to discontent among the janissaries which led to a series of *coups d'état* and lent credence to the myth of the 'sick man' of Europe. This thesis, which arose at the end of the sixteenth century, was complacently maintained by experts who mistook their desires for realities and so revealed only a superficial understanding of the Ottoman empire and misled men as clear-sighted even as Mazarin. Once the Albanian viziers came to power at Constantinople in 1656, the political crisis came to a close, a crisis which was simply a crisis of authority in central power. When the grand vizier Mehmet Köprülü inaugurated a period of firm government in the name of the young sultan Mehmed IV, Christendom, aghast, quickly realized that the Turks remained a force still to be feared.

The first victim of this renewal of Ottoman imperialism was the republic of Venice. Despite success at sea, the Most Serene Republic lost Crete, its last great possession in the eastern Mediterranean. The Turkish army quickly occupied the island and, although Candia (present day Heraklion) put up a long resistance, it ended by capitulating in 1669, despite the help supplied by the pope, the emperor and the king of France.[2] The second victim was Transylvania, which had ventured into the First Northern War, a hazardous enterprise that overstretched Transylvania's forces and presently landed it at the heart of the Austro-Turkish conflict.

The third victim was the Austrian monarchy: the period 1660–1700 was distinguished by a long Austro-Turkish conflict which ended with a brilliant Habsburg victory and the realization of one of Rudolf II's dreams – the reconquest of the Great Plain. Although Leopold I did not triumph over the heretic, after dramatic turns of fortune, he ended up triumphing over the infidel in the treaty of Karlowitz in 1699. However, this was the result of a series of lucky junctures rather than a premeditated plan on the part of the sovereign, who was less interested in the swift reconquest of Hungary than in the Rhine frontier and the Spanish succesion.

THE FIRST NORTHERN WAR

The origins of this new Austro-Turkish conflict are best understood if it is remembered that the House of Austria, although it had to abandon the Hungarian Plain to the Turks, never renounced Transylvania. Similarly, it is important not to forget that Maximilian II nurtured secret hopes of seizing the throne of Poland; finally it would be naive to believe that the Habsburgs, after the defeat of 1648, demobilized their army and withdrew into strict neutrality in order to dedicate themselves entirely to the material and moral reconstruction of their hereditary lands. Ferdinand II thought of himself as the defender of the interests of Catholicism in Poland and as being in some way Spain's political agent on the shores of the Baltic and the banks of the Vistula. Although respect for the letter and spirit of the treaties of Westphalia prevented Ferdinand III from assisting Philip IV in the Netherlands, he could still make himself the champion of the interests of the House of Austria and the Counter-Reformation in the face of the Protestant powers – something which his principal minister, the head of the 'Spanish party', the prince Auersperg, took it upon himself to keep ever to the forefront of his mind.

From 1655 Charles X Gustav of Sweden, who had succeeded queen Christiana, resumed Gustav Adolphus's policy, which had been suspended since 1629 through French mediation, and sought to seize, if not all, then at least a part of Poland. With the powerful Swedish war machine perfected during the Thirty Years War at his disposal, he gave assurances of his cooperation to the Great Elector, Frederick William of Brandenburg, who coveted western Poland in order to link Prussia and Brandenburg. Without a permanent army and caught up in the Cossack revolt in the Ukraine, Great Poland was quickly devastated and Warsaw occupied. These terrible years, which put an end to centuries of peace and prosperity, are remembered in Polish tradition as the 'Deluge'. In March 1657, a few days before his death, Ferdinand III decided to intervene to save Cracow, the historic capital of Poland, and sent an army under the command of Montecuccoli.

This military expedition was not unexpected since the Catholic Vasas were relatives and allies of the Habsburgs, and Poland, although officially neutral during the Thirty Years War, had shown itself well-disposed to the Habsburg cause. Wallenstein's ambitious project on the Baltic Sea, which was inspired by Spain, was intended to boost Poland with the goal of driving out the Dutch and so transforming this important economic region into a zone of Habsburg influence. In 1637 Władysław IV Waza had married an archduchess, Cecilia Renata, sister of Ferdinand III. After the defeat at Jankau in 1645, he had begged his brother-in-law for money to help put an army together again and to face up to the combined manoeuvres of the Swedes under Tortensson, and the Transylvanian troops.

The era of the 'Deluge' saw the reconstitution of the Hungaro-Swedish alliance of 1644. The prince of Transylvania, György II Rákóczi, who had been elected in 1655, let himself get involved in the war against Poland because the king of Sweden had promised him Galicia and Cracow. Combining passion and personal ambition and conscious of the memory of István Báthory and his father György I Rákóczi, he supported the idea of a Protestant coalition (Sweden, Brandenburg and Transylvania), a plan backed by French diplomacy.

In taking such an initiative, György II Rákóczi simply overlooked the precariousness of his own position. As a vassal of the Sublime Porte, he did not possess full sovereignty and should have taken such an initiative in foreign policy only with the prior consent of the sultan. He was careful not to ask for any such authorization since the Porte, already at war with Venice, did not intend to extend the conflict into Eastern Europe. Rákóczi had also failed to take full account of how radically the situation had changed since the appointment of the new grand vizier Köprülü, whose intention was to strengthen the sultan's power; Köprülü had rapidly restored the situation in the capital, Constantinople, carrying out mass executions, and was not disposed to let the sultan's authority be challenged on the periphery of the Empire. For this reason, he launched his Tartar allies into Transylvania and against the prince's army fighting the imperial troops in Poland. György II Rákóczi was killed in 1660 while the remains of his army retreated and painfully made its way back to Transylvania, sacked *en route* by Tartar raiding parties. By his ambitious undertaking, Rákóczi destroyed his tiny homeland's privileged position. What is more, his tragic end raised dramatically the problem of succession. From being an active agent, the principality suddenly became simply a passive object in European history.

THE TRANSYLVANIAN QUESTION

Transylvania was at one time capable of creating an illusion and of enjoying a role quite out of proportion to its real power. It had fewer than

1 million inhabitants and its economy, which was purely agricultural and limited entirely to great estates where the peasants' condition was very hard, was at a standstill. In the past the principality had been the passage through which international commerce passed but in the future it was bypassed by the great currents and 'Saxon' towns like Kronstadt (Brassov) withdrew into themselves. It still maintained its high level of culture through its Calvinist colleges and printing-presses and Italian musicians and actors were welcomed at the castles of some of the magnates. Bethlen Gábor's mercantilist policy had come to an abrupt halt and the prince's own resources were too modest to allow him to pursue a grand policy. The army, solid and effective, had difficulty in exceeding 10 000–12 000 men. The real strength of Transylvania rested in the state which has led some historians to speak of 'princely absolutism', but what is certain is that, once elected by the Diet and confirmed by the Porte, the prince escaped the orders' control. Even so, the principality had the character of a refuge for Hungarian nobility in the event of difficulties with the Habsburgs. Geography remained its true master. It was a natural fortress made up of two chains of mountains, the Carpathians and Transylvanian Alps, rearing up in the middle of the plains with easily guarded entries.

Transylvania, even more so than Bavaria in the Holy Roman Empire, was strong only by reason of the weakness of others and its power remained relative. The political class made up of various Hungarian magnates and their clientele was usually divided between Vienna and Constantinople.

After the death of György II Rákóczi, Leopold I and his prime minister Portia, encouraged by the Hungarian Diet, decided to intervene to secure the election of a candidate favourable to the Habsburgs as the first step towards the eventual reintegration of Transylvania into the Austrian monarchy, an achievement which would have served to strengthen the position of the House in Eastern Europe. The nomination of a Catholic magnate, János Kemény, provoked an angry response from the grand vizier Ahmet Köprülü, who once again launched the Tartars against Transylvania and gave orders to the pasha of Buda to intervene, a move which prompted Leopold to send an army under Montecuccoli's command to occupy the principality (1661). The autumn campaign was a disaster: the troops were decimated by dysentery and very few arrived at their destination. The sultan proceeded to secure the election of the candidate of his choice, Mihály I Apafi, a nonentity who, unlike Rákóczi, would not risk taking untimely initiatives. A pious Calvinist, Apafi divided his time between reading the Bible and paying his devotions to the bottle, and was manipulated by his wife and his chancellor Mihály Teleki, the country's real master until the end in 1690. This double election and the intervention of the imperial troops marked the break between the emperor and the Sublime Porte and the resumption of open war which had been suspended since 1606.

THE AUSTRO-TURKISH WAR (1661–4)[3]

The campaign of 1662 went very badly for the imperial troops. János Kemény was killed in combat with the Turks and the fortress of Nagyvárad (Oradea), the key to Transylvania, fell into Ottoman hands after a long siege. In mid-September 1663 the fortress of Ersekújvár (Nové Zámky in modern Slovakia), which protected Pressburg, fell to Ali Pasha; the surrender of the garrison commanded by count Forgách was thought as great a scandal as the capitulation of Györ during the Fifteen Years War. Vienna, throughout the whole summer within earshot of the rumble of cannons, was seized by genuine panic. The court, the emperor and the government fled to Linz while German and Italian government circles became extremely uneasy. For a while it was feared that the scenario of 1529 would be repeated, that Vienna under siege would be without extensive means, apart from a badly fortified rampart, to defend itself. The Ottomans, however, abided by the tactic taught them by experience and swiftly withdrew beyond Belgrade. Leopold I took advantage of the respite to organize in earnest the defence of the hereditary lands and to prepare for the forthcoming campaign.

He summoned the imperial Diet to Ratisbon in order to obtain the support of the German princes who were quick to grant him subsidies and military aid, while the circles' army was placed under the command of the prince of Waldeck. Despite Portia's misgivings, Leopold accepted the consignment of a French contingent which took part in the 1664 campaign in the name of the League of the Rhine. Made up of 6 000–7 000 veterans, this body of the French army was under the control of the count of Coligny, a protégé of Louvois. Meanwhile the ban of Croatia, Nikola Zrinski, conducted a brilliant winter campaign, bringing confusion to the Turkish rearguard and slowing down their preparations.[4]

The 1664 campaign was very different from previous ones and was rounded off by a resounding victory for Leopold. With Montecuccoli's imperial troops and the army of the circles, the French contingent defeated the janissaries at Szentgotthárd in Transdanubia (1 August 1664). This was a military success comparable to that at Lepanto; for the first time, the regular Turkish army was beaten in open country and the janissaries, overcome by the rolling fire of muskets, abandoned the field. However, this tactical success was exploited neither militarily nor diplomatically; because of the lack of Christian cavalry, the Turks were able to retreat in good order, but yet worse, the imperial resident at Constantinople, who accompanied the grand vizier, signed a botched Peace, the treaty of Vasvár (10 August 1664), which roused the indignation of the Hungarians and of the emperor's allies.

THE PEACE OF VASVÁR (10 AUGUST 1664)

The Turks renewed the treaty for twenty years and kept all their conquests, most importantly Ersekújvár and Nagyvárad, the loss of the latter placing Transylvania at the mercy of the pasha of Buda even though the imperial troops were authorized to construct a fortress opposite. Never before had the frontier zone which paid tribute to the Turks been so wide. It was the sultan, not the emperor, who strengthened his authority over Transylvania, whose 'golden age' seemed at an end.[5] Leopold I signed the Peace as if the victory of Szentgotthárd had never happened. The greatest losers were the Hungarians.

The Peace, however, only appeared to be disastrous for the emperor: he and the sultan, the two belligerents, both derived from it some personal benefit. The Ottomans escaped from a tight corner: as early as 1664, a sense of self-confidence gave rise to speculation that the reconquest of the Great Plain could be undertaken. They confirmed their rule over Transylvania, finally allowing it autonomy, and altered the equilibrium in Eastern Europe to their advantage. They were now in a position to renew the war in Crete and attack Candia; presently they would even be able to capture Polish possessions in the Ukraine.

The emperor, for his part, had his hands free in Western Europe where Philip IV, old and ill, might die any day, leaving the throne to a sickly young boy, don Charles, the king's son by his second marriage to Maria-Anna, Leopold I's sister. The vital interests of the House of Austria were at stake in this matter and took precedence over the reconquest of various fortified positions in Hungary. Besides, Portia did not have any confidence in France and thought that the aid brought by Coligny's army as occasional as it was, was only meant to break the old Franco-Ottoman entente; in his opinion, Louis XIV, at the first opportunity, would let the imperial troops face the janissaries alone. Finally, the Peace of Vasvár brought economic advantage to the monarchy because it opened up the markets of the Ottoman empire to merchants and manufactured products from the hereditary lands. A great embassy led by count Walter Leslie went in 1665 to ratify the treaty at Constantinople.

Mehmet Köprülü's successor, his son Ahmet, was firmly resolved to respect the treaty and Austro-Turkish relations remained good until his death in 1676. It was within the monarchy that the treaty of Vasvár had bad repercussions, as the Hungarian nation felt betrayed by its Habsburg king and sought to recover its independence with the help of France and Poland and, during the second phase, the Ottoman Empire. The government at Pressburg with the palatine Wesselényi at its head and the primate Lippay assumed the leadership of the movement known as the 'conspiracy of the magnates'. After the death of the palatine in 1667, the real leader of the movement was the ban of Croatia, Petar Zrinski. Catholics and Protestants, reconciled in a joint project against the House of Austria, dreamt of effecting the union of the land and re-establishing independence, even at the price of becoming an Ottoman protectorate. France ceased to support the movement in 1688 when Louis XIV ventured an agreement with Leopold I. Then the Hungarian project of a personal union with Poland faded away; Leopold was to have been declared deposed and the Diet would have elected as king the head of the republic of Poland, who was none other than the duke of Enghien, the son of the Grand Condé.

All these projects evidently lacked realism, given the distance and limited interest that Eastern Europe held for French diplomacy. Louis XIV was less concerned to accomplish any great scheme than to maintain a certain level of unrest in case of conflict with the emperor. Discrete contacts and some pensions were sufficient in peacetime. Petar Zrinski, therefore, prefered to make contacts with the Porte, using Transylvania as intermediary, and invited the Porte to establish its suzerainty over Croatia, while the nobility of Upper Hungary prepared for insurrection. The grand vizier, however, did not want to break the treaty for several reasons and not just because of a revolt at Mecca; he betrayed the conspirators and Leopold I was able to react brutally in Croatia and Hungary, as has already been shown.

THE REPRESSION AND THE KURUC REBELLION

Leopold took advantage of this unhoped-for situation to crush the Hungarian Protestants as well as the political power of the orders. Once the first alarm had passed, it was feared that the Turks might intervene on the side of the rebels; Leopold prolonged the military occupation in Upper Hungary, had Zrinski, Nádasdy and Frankopan condemned and executed (1671) and then named bishop Kollonich as president of the chamber at Pressburg. Kollonich, with the Jesuits, was the chief architect of the Counter-Reformation. Courageous and fanatical, he personally installed Catholic priests in towns or rural parishes while the Jesuits obtained conversions *en masse*. While he forgave the Croats easily, Leopold I by contrast accused the Protestant preachers of complicity in the revolt. Hundreds were brought before an emergency court, some were executed, others banished or condemned to the galleys.[6]

The major error made by this court was that it pursued hundreds of nobles and declared the confiscation of estates belonging to nobles who had not taken part in the revolt. Hungary was not Bohemia, however, and the Hungarians, instead of letting themselves be despoiled like the Czechs, fled to the mountains. From 1673 onwards, the insurgents multiplied and communications were no longer secure within Hungary. The *kurucok* made life hard for the Catholic clergy and the imperial troops. After 1675 the small towns and strongholds were no longer touched by the Counter-Reformation. The movement received support, at first from Transylvania, then from the French government, which sent subsidies and auxiliary troops. In 1676 it was clear that Thököly was at the head of the insurrection. As the provincial administration remained in the hands of the Hungarian nobility and as the Protestant nobles were well-disposed towards him, it was easy enough for Thököly to organize a principality in eastern Slovakia.

Thököly's activities were also helped by the development of the international situation which led Louis XIV to reactivate the conflict between the Porte and the House of Austria.

THE DUTCH WAR

The European war which was resumed in 1672 had driven France to put into play once again the counter-alliance against the Habsburgs. It was the Hungarian 'malcontents' who had been the prime movers in reviving this traditional policy with the Porte, which to begin with responded with caution. Constantinople did not look kindly on the aid furnished by France to the emperor in 1664 during the Hungarian campaign nor on the help brought to Venice during the siege of Candia, albeit under the cover of auxiliary contingents sent to the Rhine League or to the pope. However, after the renewal of capitulations in 1670, Franco-Ottoman relations improved but still remained complex.

The Porte was not interested in the Hungarian plain since it wanted to expand towards the Ukraine and was turning against the republic of Poland which was much more vulnerable than the emperor. The rebels meanwhile made it possible to open a second front in Hungary and to bring the imperial army there to a standstill so that 30 000 troops had to be recalled from operations in Germany. The Franco-Hungarian negotiations ended in a formal treaty signed between Akakia, French resident in Transylvania, and the Hungarian rebels (27 May 1677). Meanwhile, the marquis of Béthune, the French ambassador to Warsaw, arranged the passage into Hungary of a small auxiliary corps made up of four regiments of Cossacks recruited in the Ukraine who were placed under the orders of general Boham, a former staff-officer of Turenne. In return for the payment of regular subsidies, the Hungarians undertook to place a corps of 20 000 men in the alliance's service. In 1677 the French king paid out a total of 1 million *livres tournois*.

The Peace of Nijmegen ought to have put an end to the alliance, but Louis XIV did not respect the terms, hoping that the rebels would be abandoned after the peace treaty was signed. The French government was, in fact, already longing to pursue the policy of *réunions*, of peacetime annexations. The Peace did not signify a real reconciliation between Louis XIV and Leopold but rather a cession from direct armed confrontation from which France could benefit the most through the policy of *réunions*; diplomatic means of applying pressure were necessary to obtain concessions from the Viennese court. Louis XIV, in his instructions to Guillirague, the new French ambassador to Constantinople, set out his intentions precisely:

the peace which His Majesty has concluded with the Emperor does not permit him any longer to undertake openly their protection, but in the event that deputies from the Malcontents and the prince of Transylvania should have occasion to go to Constantinople and that they should see Monsieur Guillirague, he could make it known to them that, while His Majesty is no longer in a position to assist them against the Emperor, he still keeps for them always the affection with which he has honoured them.[7]

The task of the French agents was to prevent any reconciliation between the Viennese court on the one hand and the Transylvanian government and Hungarian malcontents on the other. From 1679 onwards, Leopold I sought compromise with the malcontents at any price in order to have his hands free over the Rhine and for this reason he decided to call a Diet which met at Sopron in spring 1681. The advice of the bishop of Vienna, Sinelli, had prevailed; the emperor re-established the ancient constitution suspended after the conspiracy of the magnates, and gave religious liberty to the Protestants. During the session of the Diet, however, the Transylvanians embarked on a campaign and Thököly refused to appear at Sopron. In September 1681 he attacked the imperial troops in Upper Hungary. The synchronization of operations was successful since the French troops were, at the same time, encircling Strassburg. The Viennese court was alarmed by the capitulation of the great Alsatian town, the councils were greatly agitated but the emperor did not move and his delegation did not leave the diplomatic congress then meeting at Frankfurt.[8]

From the beginning of December, Louis XIV relied on Thököly to whom he had promised 100 000 *écus* if he took up arms again in spring 1682. As for Mihály Apafi, he moved closer to Vienna.

OTTOMAN INTERVENTION

The Ottoman government was subject to diverse currents. Although Mehmed IV had attained his majority, he was not interested in business and passed a good part of his time hunting in Thrace or in Greece. His harem numbered 4 000 women and he left the business of governing to Kara Mustapha, the grand vizier, who had succeeded his father-in-law,

Ahmet Köprülü, in 1676. Originally from Anatolia, Kara Mustapha was a violent and uncouth man who despised Christians and foreigners. Ambitious and greedy, he sought to increase by all possible means his power and personal fortune and believed that he could realize his personal aims through a policy of great conquests as at the time of Süleymân the Magnificent. In fact, the government was divided and the imperialist party was opposed by the religious party, led by the mufti, which claimed that it squandered to no purpose the lives and resources of good Muslims in order to satisfy the egotistical visions of Kara Mustapha. It was, however, the views of the vizier which carried the day.

His decision in 1682 to give total support to Thököly completely changed the diplomatic game. The Porte obliged prince Apafi to break off negotiations with the emperor and to send a small army into Hungary to combat the imperial troops. Leopold I, meanwhile, sought to negotiate the renewal of the twenty-years' treaty concluded at Vasvár. Kara Mustapha entertained the inter-nuncio Caraffa, who had been ordered to conclude a treaty at any price because the majority of the Secret Conference dominated by the 'Spanish party', wanted to buy peace in Hungary in order to have its hands free in the Rhineland. Leopold also supported this course as did Viennese public opinion which wanted to declare war on Louis XIV in order to prevent the annexation of Luxemburg and to obtain the restoration of Strassburg which Louis XIV had occupied on 30 September 1681.

Kara Mustapha had granted Thököly royal dignity and a crown which was delivered to him, in the name of the sultan in August 1682. Hungary was then on the point of reunification but as an Ottoman protectorate: this prospect made the European chancelleries uneasy. Pope Innocent XI blamed the machinations of the French and drove Jan III Sobieski, king of Poland, to become reconciled with the emperor, while Thököly, protégé of the Great Turk, appeared cast as the 'enemy of Christendom'.[9]

Leopold's attitude was equivocal right until the end of 1682; if the Porte provided him with a good agreement, he would have preferred to get rid of his Hungarian subjects – whom he did not understand and who brought him nothing but worries – in order to be free to turn all his forces against France. These hopes collapsed after the diplomatic congress meeting at Frankfurt broke up in defeat because Louis XIV had refused to restore even a tiny piece of German territory annexed since the Peace of Nijmegen and because Kara Mustapha, lowering his mask, had broken negotiations with Caprara. It was necessary to wait for extensive action in the course of the campaign of 1683. The emperor found himself once again in the situation of the autumn of 1663.

Leopold I's propaganda and, consequently, Austrian historiography have always accused Louis XIV of launching the Turks against Vienna. The French were certainly not innocent of manipulation but they had as their only purpose to secure from the emperor and the German states recognition of the réunions. In the face of the emperor's obstinacy and Kara Mustapha's determination, this blackmail turned into a very serious operation; Turkish intervention in Hungary was made worse by a swift change of objective on the part of Kara Mustapha at the beginning of the campaign.[10]

THE SIEGE OF VIENNA[11]

While work on the fortifications at Vienna progressed and the court endeavoured to raise extraordinary taxes, the imperial diplomats concluded a treaty of alliance with Poland (20 March 1683) and the Curia raised funds to assist the emperor. The electors also ranged themselves on the emperor's side, including Leopold's son-in-law Maximilian Emanuel of Bavaria. Louis XIV adopted an attitude of strict neutrality, forbidding his young courtiers from going to serve with the imperial troops as simple volunteers which, nevertheless, was precisely what the prince of Conti and the abbot of Savoy, the future prince Eugene, did.

Everyone knew that Austria was about to undergo a severe trial, even though in spring 1683 the imperial army had 60 000 men in good units and leaders of merit, notably duke Charles V of Lorraine, who had refused to return to his patrimonial lands in 1679 because he judged as too humiliating the terms imposed on him by Louis XIV at Nijmegen. The first blow, however, fell while they waited for Polish and German auxiliaries.

The Ottoman army consisted of 110 000 men, of whom 40 000 were in the ranks and 70 000 soldiers from the provinces. The Crimean Tartar khan supplied 20 000 knights intended for missions of penetration while the prince of Transylvania furnished 6 000 soldiers; added to these were 6 000 Moldo-Vlachs and Thököly's 20 000 Hungarians. The artillery was average (160 field pieces) but only four were of great calibre for the Turks chiefly used sappers and miners and did not rely very much on heavy artillery to open a breach. The army was placed under the command of Kara Mustapha to whom the sultan solemnly delegated his powers and instructions. His mission was not to take Vienna, but to conquer positions on the frontier, most importantly Györ, in order to ensure the security of Turkish Hungary or, more precisely, the vassal principality entrusted to Thököly.

Charles of Lorraine took the offensive and laid siege to Ersékujvár in May 1683 in order to retrieve this position which had been lost in 1663. However, he was forced to beat a retreat before the Ottoman army, which after June 1683 controlled the Lake Balaton region. On 25 June, during a war council at Székesfehévár, Kara Mustapha took a serious decision against the advice of his more experienced lieutenants, the pasha of Buda and the Tartar khan, and in contradiction to the instructions of Mehmed IV; he determined to march immediately on Vienna, leaving behind him the strongholds controlled by the imperial troops, a move which was contrary to the principles of the art of war. The grand vizier's decision was his alone and may be judged bold or rash but was not a plan hatched in Paris and executed at Constantinople. Nor, contrary to the accusations regularly launched by Austrian historians, were there at any stage during the whole period of operations French 'military advisers' at the grand vizier's side. This, however, did not prevent the whole of Christendom, including France, from going through two months of anguish at the idea that Vienna might fall.

On 14 July 1683 the Turkish army arrived in front of Leopold I's imperial residence; the court and government had departed in great haste for Linz and Passau to prepare the counter-offensive while 60 000 civilians remained with the burgermeister Liebenberg inside Vienna. The garrison was made up of eleven infantry regiments, which saved the day and which were successfully put into position by the old general Kapliř, a cousin of Wallenstein, the burgher militia, which rendered great service, and an imposing artillery of 400 firearms of every calibre placed under the orders of general Kapliř and count Ernst von Starhemberg. The fortifications, which consisted of twelve bastions, were rather weak on the Danube side (the canal) and palissades protected the ramp while, just before the Turks arrived, houses in the suburbs were razed to the ground to ease the drawing of the artillery. Finally the city was properly provisioned and had more to fear from epidemics than from famine, even if the poor had to eat cats, renamed 'gutter hares'.

Starhemberg refused to surrender to the grand vizier's first demands and spared his forces in order to hold out for as long as possible while waiting for Charles of Lorraine's relief army. The latter remained intact but its leader did not want to rush lightly into an engagement before the arrival of Polish reinforcements. For this reason, pope Innocent XI sent 1 million florins to Poland to help Jan III Sobieski to mobilize and to collect together an army in accordance with the treaty of 30 March 1683. The Saxon and Bavarian contingents with 10 000 men apiece also had to be in a position to rejoin the imperial troops.

Kara Mustapha carried out the main assault in the direction of the Hofburg bastion and chiefly made use of miners whose task was to dig out a *camouflet* underneath the rampart and to blast it apart, thus opening up a breach through which the janissaries could make their attack. The vizier's real intention was to secure a surrender which would enable him to keep all the booty for himself, for if Vienna was taken by assault, he would have to allow the troops to pillage the city. As early as 12 August, the Turks seized the counter-escarpment while inflicting heavy losses on the garrison. Despite many sorties, the besieged did not manage to loosen the stranglehold. By 3 September the line of fortifications was on the point of being broken and street-fighting behind the barricades seemed likely. The supply of munitions was almost exhausted and Starhemberg launched desperate appeals because the garrison had run out of strength. The Turks also had suffered heavy losses and could not sustain their effort for many more weeks. The arrival of a relief army at the edge of the Vienna Woods was received by the city suffering from bombardments as nothing less than a providential sign.

It was on Sunday, 12 September 1683, that the Battle of Kahlenberg on the edge of the city put an end to an ordeal that had lasted fifty-nine days. Kara Mustapha was surprised by the allies' manoeuvre but their advance over slopes covered with vines was difficult. It was only in the evening that a charge of heavy Polish cavalry, the famous Hussars so feared by the Turks, swept over Mustapha's path, causing panic in the enemy camp. The grand vizier fled with his troops, abandoning the rich booty which still to the present day is in the museums of Vienna and Poland. The allied combatants have often been reproached for not having immediately exploited the brilliant victory at Kahlenberg, but it was very difficult to prevent the soldiers from laying hold of the most readily portable of the oriental treasures. It was a tradition; unfortunately, at Keresztes in October 1596, the pillage of the Turkish camp had even cost an imperial victory. The janissaries, it seems, drew back in formation, and prudence advised that they should be left to go away untroubled by further attacks in the evening of a bitter day. The Turks had lost 15 000 men, their artillery and their baggage, while the allies had only 1 500 men to lament.

This was no less a brilliant victory for the relief army which, besides the imperial troops, included the army of the circles, the Bavarian corps, the Saxon corps and 25 000 Polish, in total 65 000 in fresh units placed under the command of Jan III Sobieski, since Leopold had had the wisdom to leave this task to a real professional who had lately distinguished himself against the Turks in the Ukraine. It was the noble republic's last victory and its memory has remained in the Polish collective consciousness as much as in the Austrian. For the first time in a conflict between Islam and Christendom, the victory was not an isolated success but was methodically exploited. While singing the solemn *Te Deum* in the presence of the emperor in St Stephen's cathedral, the people of Vienna, bruised and battered, perhaps did not reckon that their city was about to swap its role as the thoroughfare of Christendom to become a grand metropolis situated in the heart of a vast continental empire and that the ramparts which it had saved for the second time would presently become a hindrance to its development.

THE FOLLOW-UP TO THE VICTORY

It was only on 18 September 1683 that the allies began their advance towards the East. They took Párkány by assault and Esztergom capitulated on 25 October. They retook Löcse (Levoča) in Upper Hungary, on 10 December, then the troops were sent to their winter quarters. Thököly soon found himself abandoned by his men, who rejoined the imperial armies; his political role was at an end. As for Kara Mustapha, he went no further than Belgrade since the sultan punished his defeat and disobedience by sending him a noose of black silk, a discreet invitation to commit suicide (Christmas Day 1683). *Vae victis!*

Leopold hesitated for a long time over the follow-up to the victory at Kahlenberg. Delivered from immediate danger, he intended to negotiate with the Porte as he had in 1664, since he had not abandoned his anti-French policy within the Empire. His allies and his entourage, however, forced him to continue the war. Innocent XI wanted to take advantage of this favourable turn of events to reconquer Hungary and to make Italy, for once and for all, secure from Ottoman invasion. He reacted not only as head of Christendom but also as temporal ruler of Italy. This was why he placed at the hesitant emperor's side Father Marco d'Aviano, a saintly Capuchin who swiftly came to exercise a decisive influence over a sovereign always ready to listen to private advisers. The conference was radically renewed and the Spanish ambassador, Borgomaneiro, lost much of his influence.

Finally, the diplomatic situation changed in the course of 1684. The Curia organized a Holy League intended to continue the struggle against the Ottoman empire. As well as the Holy See, which would continue to provide funds from Spain and Italy, it included the emperor and the republic of Venice which put its navy at the allies' disposal. While Poland retreated discreetly, its place was soon taken by Peter the Great's Russia. The princes of the Empire, meanwhile, took part in combat, fielding experienced troops, for the most part Bavarians and Brandenburgers, in exchange for subsidies and winter quarters. At the same time the situation within the Empire was simplified in so far as France signed the treaty of Ratisbon, the conclusion of the Congress of Frankfurt; the Empire recognized Louis XIV's occupation of the *réunions* for a period of twenty years. It was a compromise which can be interpreted as a partial defeat for France because the annexations were not recognized for ever. This was, of course, a result of the imperial victory at Vienna; since the emperor, even while the situation was precarious, had not accepted the 'principle of the *réunions*', he was not likely to agree to it at so favourable a juncture. Kara Mustapha's defeat should also be seen as a French defeat, since in the future the reverse alliance would operate much less easily. The Hungarians, rallying to the emperor, for the moment no longer counted on the international stage and Louis XIV took refuge in an attitude of well-advised neutrality, limiting himself to encouraging the Porte to continue the fight.

Despite this favourable situation, Leopold made a strategic choice, exactly the opposite of the decision he made in 1682: by engaging his forces in Hungary he made the House of Austria a purely continental dynasty, orientated towards the East, and risked disassociating himself from the affairs of Germany and Spain. Having earlier been disposed to place the Hungarians under Ottoman protection, would he not now go on to increase their position in the monarchy after having had to concede to them important religious and constitutional privileges in 1681? By choosing to pursue the war, he moved the monarchy's centre of gravity.

The fear that resources were insufficient to wage war in Hungary was soon dispelled. Some supplementary taxes (the Turkish tax and the poll tax), the swift reconstruction of Lower Austria which had been ravaged by the Tartars, the turn-around in the economic situation and the returning prosperity in the Czech lands, as well as the help of the Holy Roman Empire, combined to enable the emperor to conduct a prolonged campaign, a total of fifteen years of war (1684–99).

THE COUNTER-OFFENSIVE IN HUNGARY

After February 1684, Charles of Lorraine decided that Buda should be the objective of the following campaign, despite the misgivings of the Privy Council. The beginning of the operations was encouraging, and the imperial troops, after occupying Pest (8 July), undertook the siege of Buda (14 July). The historic capital of Hungary was situated on a hill and was strongly defended; the imperial troops, decimated by illness, especially dysentery, raised the siege at the end of October 1684 after losing 20 000 men. Viennese public opinion held the duke of Lorraine responsible for this failure.

The campaign of 1685 had less ambitious objectives but achieved the results necessary for a methodical reconquest. The duke of Lorraine persisted with the recapture of Ersékújvár which he took on 19 August, after a siege of five weeks and after crushing the Turkish relief army (Battle of Tothmegyer) on 16 August. It is an indication of the pitiless character of this war that the Turkish garrison was put to the sword.

Taking advantage of this success, the imperial troops continued fighting throughout the autumn and took control of eastern Upper Hungary, the bastion of the 'malcontents'. They seized Eperjes (Prešov) and Ungvár (Užhorod) and 17 000 kuruc made their submission. Only the fortress of Munkács (Mukačevo), which belonged to Ilona Zrinski, second wife of Thököly, still held out against the imperial troops. While Leopold refused the sultan's offers of peace, he negotiated with Apafi and especially with his chancellor, Mihály Teleki, proposing to recognize the independence of Transylvania in return for a treaty of alliance.

The campaign of 1686 turned the situation completely in the Habsburgs' favour. The Ottoman empire was then suffering serious internal difficulties (plague and famine), which brought into question an unpopular war and a government that had lost all prestige. Louis XIV gave a polite refusal every time to the grand vizier's demand for renewed military collaboration as at the time of Francis I and Süleymân, i.e. to intervene on the Turks' side by declaring war on the emperor. Charles of Lorraine decided to take advantage of the circumstances to strike a great blow by attacking Buda. He got the war council to agree that the army should reassemble early and on 13 June the army set out. The Turks were determined to defend themselves since Buda, besides its prestigious character, played an important strategic role being situated on the crossroads of all the routes across the Great Plain. Three assaults, those of 13 and 17 July and 3 August, ran aground, leaving the sultan leisure to send a relief army which arrived 8 August but attempted only limited action of little benefit to the besieged garrison. Charles of Lorraine decided to launch a second assault on 1 September. Buda was taken the next day and the bloody corpses of those put to the bayonet, a weapon used here for the first time, were piled up inside while Ali Pasha, governor of Buda, died in combat. The Christian victory degenerated into pillaging and massacre, the imperial troops 'putting to the sword all Turks and Jews'. After 145 years of occupation, Buda, which had undergone a profound transformation, became once more a Christian city and the event was celebrated as a great victory throughout the whole of Europe. Three years after the victory of Kahlenberg, the liberation of Buda showed that the balance of forces was in the process of changing, even if the Ottoman empire still possessed, as the French ambassador at Constantinople remarked, important reserves of soldiers in Anatolia.

The Turks, however, were everywhere in retreat; the Poles had reached into Moldavia, the Muscovite army (the young Peter the Great had joined the Holy League) took Azov from the Crimean Tartars who were allied to the Sublime Porte, while the Venetians advanced into the Morea. The imperial troops occupied the Great Plain, as the Ottoman command dreaded.

Although they rejoiced at the liberation of their capital, the Hungarians had to suffer the presence of imperial troops and the initiatives of the Viennese court where cardinal Kollonich proposed to the emperor that estates in the liberated region should be appropriated and repopulated with German, or at least Catholic, colonies. This was the notorious Hungarian 'reorganization project' which was put forward by the commission of *neoacquistica*. In 1687 the slaughter at Eperjes ordered by general Caraffa, a Neapolitan in the emperor's service, showed the rebels and the Hungarians in general, that the term 'liberation' was a euphemism supplied by Viennese propaganda and that they were in the process of swapping one yoke for another.

At the beginning of 1687 the Porte made offers of peace which did not reflect the new balance of forces as it proposed the renewal of a treaty on the conditions of the Peace of Vasvár. The offer was, of course, rejected by the Secret Conference (19 April). The imperial troops went on to extend their efforts into Slavonia in the south and Transylvania in the east. Charles of Lorraine wanted to seize Osijek which, with its pontoon bridge, controlled the crossing of the Sava. He clashed with the Turkish army on 20 July, and fell back west to Mohács. The second Battle of Mohács took place on 12 August 1687, and this time ended in a bloody defeat for the Turks who lost 30 000 men in the assault on the Christian barricades. The duke of Lorraine exploited his success by swiftly occupying Osijek and in the autumn Slavonia was liberated, after which Charles of Lorraine led his army towards Transylvania and occupied Kolozsvár (Cluj).

Prince Apafi and the Transylvanian Diet took refuge at Hermannstadt (Sibu): without Ottoman military support, they could not withstand the imperial troops. On 27 October 1687 Mihály Apafi signed what amounted to a protection treaty with Charles of Lorraine. He accepted the entry of imperial troops into Transylvania, handed over to them twelve fortresses, undertook their supply and promised to hand over 700 000 florins to the emperor. In exchange, the duke of Lorraine guaranteed the Transylvanian orders religious liberty and privileges as well as the security of the prince. This agreement, very advantageous for the Habsburgs, was the work of Mihály Teleki, who was generously rewarded. The treaty of Hermannstadt (9 May 1688) transformed Transylvania into an Austrian protectorate. The objective, pursued by Leopold I since 1661, was finally attained.

The gains in these four years of war were spectacular. The counter-offensive, led by the masterly hand of Charles of Lorraine, had pushed the Turks 350 kilometres south of Vienna. The goal of the next campaign was to capture Belgrade and so to close the Great Plain to any fresh Ottoman invasion. Charles V of Lorraine was seriously ill and was relieved of his command by Leopold, who in July 1688 entrusted the army to his son-in-law, the elector Max Emanuel of Bavaria, who led the imperial troops to victory and took Belgrade (6 September 1688), thereby opening the Balkans to the troops of the Holy League. In 1689 the imperial troops took Niš and Skopje, conquered Serbia and occupied Macedonia and Albania. They were received as liberators by the Balkan Christians, especially the Serbs. No hope seemed too wild and it did not seem impossible that the Habsburgs might go on to take Constantinople. In 1687 Morosini and the Venetians conquered Athens, but not without damaging the Parthenon; a Venetian bullet triggered an explosion inside this symbol of European culture, which the Turks had used as a powder magazine.

The resumption, however, of the war on the Rhine slowed the imperial 'troops' offensive and reduced to nil the hope of liberating the Balkans, as the emperor and his German allies did not have the means to lead a war on two fronts. By dividing his forces, Leopold I had again to make a choice and he gave priority to German affairs, despite the opposition of Charles of Lorraine who resumed his command in 1689.

THE WAR ON TWO FRONTS

The spirit of the treaty of Ratisbon was little heeded by French diplomacy and at the same time disputes over the succession arose in the Palatinate and at Cologne. Cardinal Fürstenburg, bishop of Strassburg, wanted to become archbishop-elector of Cologne but he was distrusted by the emperor who, even so, could not prevent the elector Maximilian Heinrich, uncle of Max Emanuel of Bavaria, from being elected as coadjutor. The Holy See refused to ratify the chapter's choice on the pretext that the candidate would thereby accumulate two bishoprics, which was contrary to the decrees of the Council of Trent. Following the death of Maximilian Heinrich, Louis XIV occupied Bonn, the electorate and then the Palatinate, in order to support the claims of the Madam Palatine, wife of the Master Palatine and daughter of the elector Palatine, Karl Ludwig. Feuquières, meanwhile, scoured Swabia and Franconia to levy war contributions, while French garrisons were installed at Mainz and Philippsburg, without war even having been declared.

The emperor then appealed to opinion, and as he knew how to win over the princes of the Empire, all those who had helped during the Turkish campaign did not prove stingy with their support, especially the champions of the Protestant cause. Leopold I had to do no more than reap the fruits of the defensive alliance concluded at Augsburg in 1686. Events in England, the Glorious Revolution and the accession of William of Orange to the Stuart throne brought him substantial and unhoped-for assistance. The decision was as difficult to take as in 1682 since the Turks were regaining courage and prince Louis of Baden, then prince Eugene of Savoy, had to conduct strenuous campaigns in order to overcome their staying power. For the first time, the House of Austria was not obliged to sacrifice vital interests and was in a position to fight on two fronts.

The victory of prince Eugene of Savoy over the Turks at Zenta in 1697, and the return of peace in Germany, led the Porte to negotiate with the Holy League and to conclude the treaty of Karlowitz in February 1699.

THE PEACE OF KARLOWITZ

The Peace marked the complete reversal of the situation in the Habsburgs' favour and restored to them full sovereignty over the whole of the kingdom of Hungary, with the exception of the banat of Temesvár (Timişoara). The son of Mihály Apafi abdicated in 1691, and Transylvania was reintegrated into the Austrian monarchy in return for respect for its political and religious liberties. It kept its separate status and, to the great annoyance of the Hungarian nobility, it was administered by a chancellery separate from the Hungarian chancellery. In the same year, the *Diploma Leopoldinum* officially recognized confessional pluralism in Transylvania. The treaty of Karlowitz, of course, marked the abandonment by the Sublime Porte of any pretence that it was a principality. A commission was charged with marking out the new boundaries of Slavonia where Serbian refugees were installed under the direction of their Orthodox patriarch. They supplied soldiers for what was the new Military Frontier, the old one having become quite redundant.

The increase of territory enjoyed by the monarchy was spectacular because all of historic Hungary with its 350 000 sq km was henceforth a part of it. The Great Plain, however, ravaged by the 'war of liberation' would have to be repopulated and rebuilt. The new quarrels between the orders and the Habsburgs slowed down this necessary work.

Leopold I, crowned with the prestige of the conqueror, was henceforth called Leopold the Great, despite his frail appearance and his dislike of the military life. Although he had not succeeded in conquering the heretic, he had defeated the infidel; the Turks were no longer the object of fear for the Viennese but rather in the future would serve as inspiration for fancy-dress and other similar diversions.

By chasing the Turks from Hungary, Leopold I made the Austrian monarchy a great power, but he also put an end to the nightmare in Central Europe which had lasted since the beginning of the sixteenth century. This and the loss shortly afterwards of the Spanish succession transformed the vocation of the House of Austria.

Through the reconquest of the Great Plain, which had been more or less planned, Leopold I gave the monarchy the boundaries which it kept, roughly, until 1918. But if the Turkish peril was finally conjured away after the last manifestation of Ottoman power, and if Belgrade was taken only five years after the dramatic siege of Vienna, the Hungarian question, nevertheless, was not settled and the orders soon raised their heads after the 1687 Diet. Above all, the Spanish succession, a major problem for Europe in the second half of the century, was settled to the detriment of the House of Austria, or more precisely, of its universal vocation, the Viennese Habsburgs receiving only territorial compensation.

At the end of the reign of Leopold I, the monarchy had a budget of 60–70 million *livres tournois* (in France: 180), a permanent army of more than 100 000 men, a territory more vast than that of the kingdom of France and a population of 8–9 million inhabitants. In 1699 the Peace of Karlowitz confirmed its vocation as the leader in Eastern Europe. The concert of powers which succeeded Christendom had said 'yes' to the monarchy of Ferdinand I and 'no' to the empire of Charles V. Despite a long and ruinous war 1701–14, the Viennese Habsburgs submitted to this verdict inspired by the principle of European equilibrium, since the concepts of Christendom and universal monarchy now belonged to the past.

NOTES AND REFERENCES

1. Robert Mantran, *Istanbul dans la seconde moitié du XVIIe siècle*, Paris, 1962.
2. Jean Nouzille, 'La guerre de Candie', *Revue internationale d'histoire militaire*, no. 68, Paris, 1987, pp. 115–52.
3. Georg Wagner, *Das Türkenjahr 1664: eine europäische Bewährung*, 2 vols, Eisenstadt, 1964.
4. Jean Bérenger, 'Un émule hongrois de Turenne: le comte Nicolas Zrinyi', *Turenne et l'art militaire*, proceedings of a colloquium on Turenne held in 1975, Paris, 1978, pp. 288–98.
5. From the title of the historical novel by Maurice Jokai, *L'Âge d'or de la Transylvanie*.
    See Bérenger's article, 'Le droit d'état Hongrois dans la seconde moitié du XVIIe siècle' in *Études finno-ougriennes*, no. 2, 1967, pp.132–47.
6. Jean Bérenger, 'La Contre-Réforme en Hougne', *Bulletin de la Société d'histoire du protestantisme français*, no. CXX, 1974, pp. 1–22.
7. P. Dupare (ed.) *Instructions aux ambassadeurs et ministres de France*, Paris, 1974, *Turkey*, no. 23, p. 216.
8. Jean Bérenger, 'Louis XIV, l'Empereur et l'Europe de l'Est', *Revue XVIIe siècle*, 1979, pp. 173–94.
9. Béla Kopeczi, *Magyarorszag a kereszténség ellensége. A Thökölyfelkelés az Europai közvéleményben*, Budapest, 1976.
10. Jean Bérenger, 'L'Alsace enjeu de la diplomatie européenne au XVIIe siècle', *Bulletin de la Société d'histoire moderne*, no. 4, 1987, pp. 1–7.
11. Robert Waissenberger (ed.) *Die Türken vor Wien, Europe und die Entscheidung an der Donau*, exhibition catalogue, Vienna, 1983.
    Richard Kreutel and Karl Teply, *Kara Mustapha vor Wien*, Graz, 1982.

CHAPTER TWENTY-FIVE

Baroque Austria

The dramatic turn of events at the siege of Vienna and the Christian victory at Kahlenberg marked the beginning of a new era for the Habsburg monarchy: the end of the Turkish peril, economic prosperity, and the rebuilding of the capital on new foundations with the development of Hungary following the peace settlement of 1711. It is convenient, however, to pause near the beginning of the eighteenth century to appreciate the original character of the baroque civilization which was so intimately linked in its development to the progress of the Counter-Reformation and the success of the House of Austria. The real masters remained the nobles in whose hands economic and political power were concentrated as the monk from Franche-Comté, Camille Freschot, remarked in 1705,

The emperor is hardly the master in his states [Austria, Bohemia, Hungary, Croatia]. He is obliged to summon the Estates (Diets), to speak there himself and to present them with the reasons that have obliged him to have recourse to their help. After that they usually show their approval and agree to what is wanted of them.[1]

THE FEUDAL ESTATE AND ECONOMIC POWER[2]

The economic power of the aristocracy was symbolized by the large domain, which usually combined several estates. In the course of the seventeenth century, this concentration of property became a more pronounced phenomenon. Such was the wealth of the proprietor of the estate that whether he was an aristocrat at the court or a simple country gentleman, he enjoyed absolute authority over the peasants. Only the simple gentleman still administered his domain himself and maintained personal links with his servants, a situation that prevailed in Lower Austria, Hungary and Croatia. In contrast to this, the large domain

338

governed by a steward was usual in Bohemia where, in 1699, 85 per cent of cultivable land was held by the order of lords. The steward tried to grow rich on the backs of the peasants (who called him 'father flogger') and exercised, in the name of his absent master, a real tyranny over the rural populations.

It was the manager who levied the estate dues in the form of the tithe (8–10 per cent of the harvest) and saw to it that the *robot* (between 50 and 100 days of free labour a year) was carried out. The *robot* enabled the lord to cultivate the reserve or the farm belonging to the castle (German *Meierhof*) while the product of the tithe was sold on the market or even consumed by the servants and soldiers of the lord, thereby largely excluding the peasant from the market economy.

In Lower Austria the clergy must be mentioned as the monasteries continued to be large landed proprietors possessing estates and subjects, just like the lay nobility. Prelates had mastery over the western part of the province, northern and southern Wienerwald, while the Waldviertel had only one large abbey, Zwettl, whose possessions were scattered over 91 localities and embraced 1 146 peasant tenures. The principal ecclesiastical estates of Lower Austria had a large number of tenants:

the college of Sankt Pölten (621)
the benedictine abbey of Melk (852)
the benedictine abbey of Göttweig (1 096)
the abbey of Lilienfeld (1 492)
the abbey of Herzogenburg (826)
the abbey of Gaming (783)
the Bavarian bishop of Freising, lord of Waidhofen (690)
the bishop of Passau (1 021)
the bishop of Ratisbon, lord of Pöchlarn (361)
the archbishop of Salzburg, lord of Traismaner (458)
the abbey of Klosternenburg (1 469)
the Cistercian abbey of Heiligenkreuz (563).

Most of these monasteries were situated in forested zones and their wealth lay in wood, vines and tithes. They resembled the largest domains of the laity; for example the wealthy estate of Walpersdorf, which belonged to the Jörgers, had only 790 tenants. Following the crises of the 1530s, when monasteries were deserted wholesale, in the seventeenth century the policy of Catholic Reformation encouraged by Ferdinand I bore its fruits and the large abbeys were well managed on the economic as well as the spiritual level. At the end of the century, vast wine cellars were constructed which allowed the monastery of Göttwerg to lay down its wine, keep it from one year to the next and to sell it at a good price in years of poor harvest. Originally from bourgeois backgrounds, the abbots and provosts proved clever managers, and made the religious orders as a whole benefit from their financial experience. The Viennese monasteries did not cease to grow in number and the ancient foundations, like the benedictines of Schotten, possessed many houses in the capital.

The situation in Styria and Inner Austria was similiar for the same historical reasons. The little bishopric of Gurk, a late foundation, could not counterbalance the archbishop of Salzburg, outside the province, nor the prelates whose monasteries had not fallen victim to the policy of secularization.

In Lower Austria the most important order was that of the lords, who in the seventeenth century acquired an overwhelming preponderance in the Diet. The symbol and the base of their power remained the large domain. The estate of Trauttmannsdorf in Lower Austria which, after 1576, was part of the patrimony of the Windischgraetz family, serves as an example to illustrate this. The centre of the domain was the small town or *burg* with a fortified castle which could withstand a Turkish cavalry raid since it possessed thirteen cannons and a small garrison. In 1530 the tax declaration covered fifty inhabited houses in the town: twenty-six tenants were labourers at the head of important farms (with nine peasants) or average farms (with seven peasants) while the other twenty-four were those of small-scale cultivators (vintners or brewers); the servants did not possess separate houses. Joined to these town houses were 350 other tenures divided between three other villages – Sarasdorf, Höflein and Deutsch Brodersdorf – each of which included 100 houses, and three other places of lesser importance. The lands were divided into *Dominikalländer* (the dominical directly worked by the owner) and *Rustikalländer* (rustical or peasant lands worked by 400 tenants).

The estate reserve was only 6 per cent of the total land (298 acres or 170 hectares) while the lands which were rented stretched over 2 700 hectares or 4 684 acres. The reserve was worked by means of the *robot*, the limits of which were determined not by law but by the needs of the estate farm. In addition to the work there, there was labour on the 1 100 hectares of rented vineyards and on the 44 hectares of the estate reserve, which devoted over 120 hectares of meadow to the raising of sheep. The core of the revenue, at the end of the period, was still provided by the estate dues; the tithe (57 870 florins in 1750 against 1 800 in 1570), the *robot* (2 025 florins), rights of succession, the 'minor services' (604 florins) and eight other kinds of estate dues each of which brought on average 100 florins a year. On the other hand, the rent derived from the lands of the *Rustikalland* could not be re-evaluated and the Windischgraetzes drew their clearest revenues from their estate dues (close to 10 000 florins in the eighteenth century under Maria-Theresa). It is noticeable that, in contrast to what happened in Bohemia and Hungary, the aristocrats in the alpine lands hardly practised agriculture by farming their own land and preferred to transform the *robot* into an indemnity paid by the tenant.

It should be explained that the members of the order of lords generally possessed several domains of this importance and that through the estate courts and local administration they exercised a quasi-absolute sovereignty over the peasant world. In Lower Austria, a dozen families (like the Starhembergs) enjoyed particular prestige because they were descended from lines established in the country in the early Middle Ages, before the Habsburgs even arrived. Others, like the Jörger family, were able to take advantage of the economic development of the sixteenth century to enlarge their possessions.

By contrast, the order of knights saw its relative importance diminish. A pamphlet from 1696, signed under the pseudonym Cosmophilus and dedicated to the emperor, seems to give a good account of the end of a development which had been under way for two centuries:

without speaking of the misery of the noble who, with his wife and children, has been transformed into a peasant, and your old nobility which, because of the extraordinary public offices (through which their subjects and their wealth are ruined) ought to be identified with a new class of peasants.

The inflated and dramatic style of this German text ought not to hide the irrefutable reality that the fortune and existence of a simple country gentleman were henceforth inseparable from that of the well-to-do peasant. Two examples serve to illustrate this decline: Otto Achaz von Hohenfeld, who survived the torments of the Thirty Years War, and Wolf Helmard von Hohberg, the subject of a masterly study by Otto Brunner[3].

Achaz von Hohenfeld belonged to an old family from Upper Austria and cut a privileged figure among his equals in the *Ritterstand*. Even after the catastrophe of 1621 he lived in a real castle; his lands in Upper Austria were occupied and sacked by the Bavarians. A timely conversion to Catholicism, however, allowed him to recover Aistersheim, his domain in Lower Austria which had been sequestered. This land yielded a net annual income of 3 000 florins and while it was administered by the chamber of accounts the gross income rose to 15 000 florins. Achaz von Hohenfeld was able to serve in the administration of the orders in Lower Austria and even received the distinction of being an imperial counsellor, which put him in a good position in relation to the other simple country gentlemen. It is significant that he derived his most certain income from the estate dues received in kind (1 852 florins after the depression of 1621) and in natural produce (tithes and champart) which, in years when the harvest was mediocre, put him in a favourable economic position.

Von Hohberg's income, by contrast, did not exceed 500 florins a year which he drew from two estates in the Waldviertel. He had sixteen tenants at Oberthumeritz and fourteen at Süssenbach, which brought him 23 florins in kind and what was owed him as *robot* (12 days a year from each tenant). The topography of Matthias Vischer gives a view of von Hohberg's residence – a large building, solid but only to be distinguished from a simple farm by its single tower.* There is a marked contrast with von

* Translator's note: Matthias Vischer, author of *Topographia Ducatus Styriae, 1681*.

Hohenfeld, who lived in a real castle, or with the Windischgraetzes who possessed a fortified castle at Trauttmannsdorf which is also described in Vischer's topography. Rather it was the nature of his income that placed von Hohberg economically and socially above a wealthy labourer. A simple country gentleman, he was obliged to manage and regulate his expenses out of his income. Furthermore, the order of knights remained associated with political power through its links with the assemblies of the estates.

The wealth of the aristocracy is measured by the loans which it granted the emperor and the chamber of accounts, backed by solid guarantees furnished by the revenues from the domain. The aristocracy negotiated either individually or collectively through the intermediary of the estates when the estates, as in Lower Austria, possessed their own treasuries; prince Ferdinand Schwarzenburg, who was heir to the largest fortune in Bohemia, that of the princes Eggenberg, was capable of making several loans of 100 000 florins to the emperor Leopold I at the time of the reconquest of Hungary. Wills, at least among the court aristocracy, reveal colossal fortunes; prince Pál Esterházy, the palatine of Hungary in 1681, created in favour of each of his three sons an entailed property (*majorat*) worth 300 000 florins. Prince Wenceslas Lobkowitz, head of Leopold I's council 1665–73, possessed two towns and sixty-five villages in northern Bohemia. He was so rich that in the eyes of the French ambassador, the knight Grémonville, he appeared beyond the reach of corruption. This was not the case with the president of the chamber of accounts, count Georg Ludwig von Sinzendorf, who was accused of embezzlement by his political enemies, removed from office in 1681 and following his trial was sentenced to pour back 1 million florins into the imperial treasury. Even this heavy fine did not ruin his family and, at the beginning of the eighteenth century, his son Philip-Ludwig had a good ministerial career.

The only other fortunes which can be assessed, besides those of the members of the order of lords, are the fortunes accumulated by tax farmers who were the beneficiaries of a 'fisco-financial' system. For example the farmer of the mines of Upper Hungary, Joannelli, who in 1665 was able to advance the 500 000 florins needed to reimburse the king of Poland and to pay off the mortgage on the duchies of Oppeln and Ratibor in Upper Silesia. The collectors of customs or the salt taxes were obliged to put down security and to agree to loans to the Viennese chamber of accounts if they wanted to obtain their post. These transactions were simply a way of disguising the sale of public offices. Outlines of careers show men beginning with the modest offices of finances and ending with the post of counsellor to the chamber of accounts. In the world of tax farmers, the most spectacular case is evidently provided by Samuel Oppenheimer, a Jewish banker originally from Spire, who began his career as supplier to the imperial troops during the Dutch War. Charles of Lorraine brought him to Vienna where he developed his business in a prodigious fashion during the war of the League of Augsburg, despite the opposition of the anti-Semitic lobby led by cardinal Kollonich. Oppenheimer guaranteed the supply and transport of provisions for the army operating in Hungary and also financed a good part of the budget deficit, which was approaching 5 million florins. Tolerated at Vienna, he was able to install a meeting place for prayer in his own private residence and obtained the privileged status of 'Court Jew', which was also later enjoyed by his son-in-law Samson Wertheimer after Oppenheimer's bankruptcy and death in 1703. His bankruptcy made prince Eugene despair and at the very beginning of the War of the Spanish Succession placed the monarchy's finances in a dramatic position.[4]

THE MIDDLING KIND

These fortunes, whether ephemeral or lasting, were in marked contrast to the average legacies of the burghers and the poverty of the agricultural workers. While for several dozen families it is a matter of counting in millions of florins, for the mass of the Habsburgs' subjects it is a question of thousands or just hundreds.

The personnel of the chancelleries received annual salaries of 600–1 000 florins – when, that was, they received any payment at all. The salary of a councillor of state only just reached 1 200 florins. Generally a member of the personnel was a noble who had other sources of income, while the concierge collected just 120 florins in wages. The emperor was anything but generous to his servants, which partly explains the endemic corruption that so pleased foreign diplomatic missions, as the secrets of the conference were secretly sold to the highest bidder.

As for the peasants, the study of notary acts and tax registers shows the situation in which the majority found themselves. Two examples can be quoted – the estates of Hardegg and Schlosshof in Lower Austria.

Hardegg belonged to the Khevenhüllers, aristocrats of the court who were originally from Styria. The estate was estimated at 236 000 florins and its annual yield at 4 500 florins (tithe and purchased exemption from the *robot*). The wealthiest person of standing, Johann Keller, the miller and also the judge (*Richter*) of the town of Hardegg possessed a fortune of 3 000 florins. Within Hardegg there were thirty-nine household proprietors, among them a well-to-do peasant, Jakob Brückner, who left his widow and eight children a legacy of 320 florins, out of which 60 florins had to be paid in debts, 10 florins in tax and about 10 florins for the honoraries for twenty masses. His capital consisted of a house valued at 90 florins, four oxen, a cow and its calf, ten stooks of rye and five of wheat. By contrast the inventory of a 'poor peasant' shows that he left as his bequest about three-quarters of a hectare of reclaimed land valued at 34 florins, out of which he had to pay 15 florins in debts and 2 florins in tax. He had only 17 florins in total to share among his heirs.

In the neighbouring village of Markesdorf the fifty-five inventories made after death show that there were thirty-seven labourers and eighteen agricultural workers. Thirty-six peasants bequeathed less than 100 florins, sixteen possessed capital of 100–250 florins while only three left more than 250 florins.

Should these modest resources be taken to imply wretchedness? As in France at the same period, everything depended on the yield of the harvest, and thus on the weather. Too severe a winter, a bad spring and summer could make the production of cereals fall and cause the price of grain on the markets to rise sharply so that prices doubled or tripled between March and July when the family stocks were exhausted. Then, to feed his family, the peasant had to make large purchases to tide himself over. In average years, though, the situation appears to have been bearable.

On prince Eugene of Savoy's estate of Schlosshof in the fertile plain of Marchfeld, the average tenure was ten acres of good workable land, which allowed the labourer to harvest on average 30 sextaries a year and supplied food for five adults (a sextary of grain made sixty 2 lb loaves, that is to say, sixty daily rations for a strong labourer). The labourer possessed a negotiable surplus and in addition the income which he derived from stock-rearing practised on communal pastures and on arable land when lying fallow. The profits were substantial: a milk cow brought on average 7 florins 30 kreuzers from 50 lb of butter at 6 kreuzers and 100 lb of cheese at 1 kreuzer, the Viennese market providing Schlosshof with a huge outlet. This estimate does not take into account the produce from vines, a crop which, since the beginning of the seventeenth century, had expanded greatly in Lower Austria.

These impressions, however, should be tempered with pessimism when regional diversity is borne in mind, and also with a certain optimism when favourable economic circumstances are taken into account.

The condition of the peasant in Lower Austria was quite good. There the *robot* was always limited in practice and in 1679 it was fixed by princely legislation (*Tractatus de iuribus in corporalibus*, §V), at twelve days a year. Moreover, the *robot* was often converted into a redemption in cash because the estate reserves were limited in extent and the large landowner often came simply to rent out land, on average tripling his income from rent between 1540 and 1740. However, the peasant in Bohemia was, according to Sébeville, Louis XIV's ambassador at Vienna, 'treated like an animal': he was required to provide not 12, but 150 days' *robot* a year. It might be said that he was really a day labourer and a provider of a team working half-time for the estate reserve. In 1666 the Czech agronomist J.E. Wegener in his *Oeconomia Suburbana* observed that 'if the peasant from his country paid all the dues and carried out all the *robot*, he might be counted among the martyr saints'.[5]

In Hungary a distinction should be made between increasingly harsh legislation and practice. After 1548 the tenants owed their lord fifty-two days of annual *robot* or two to three days a week at the busiest periods (haymaking, harvest). At the end of the seventeenth century, the phenomenon was still worse and there were practically no more waged labourers on the great domains. The dissatisfied labourer, however, could always clear out – illegally of course. He might take refuge in the Military Frontier or with a less demanding master; the Diet's books of grievances collected complaints against those far from scrupulous officers who 'forgot' to return runaway peasants, choosing to disregard a law which was in fact their obligation, for manual labour was welcome where the density of population was low.

A FAVOURABLE COMBINATION OF CIRCUMSTANCES

The long-term economic situation was everywhere favourable and would remedy the abuse of the estate regime which, in Bohemia and Hungary, had taken on the appearance of a 'second serfdom'. Contrary to the case noted in Western Europe, the period is characterized by a regular rise in the price of grain.

The archives of the civil hospital in Vienna (*Bürgerspital*) supply a continuous series of prices, for example for wheat and rye, provisions which involved major transactions.[6] From the curves established for the period 1640–1720, it is not an exaggeration to conclude that this was a phase of expansion despite the brief crises due to bad harvests or political events. Sharp rises are located in 1663–4 and in 1683–5 when the Turks threatened or besieged Vienna, and in 1679 at the time of the great outbreak of plague and in 1709 when a particularly harsh winter beset the Danube basin. The periods when prices collapsed (1657–60 and 1691–3) corresponded to the monetary disorder brought about by the influx of base coinage but the monetary readjustments of 1659 and 1693 restored order.

Most importantly the prices on the Viennese market show the trend and allow four periods to be distinguished:

1. From the end of the Thirty Years War right until 1659 was a period characterized by decline linked to economic stagnation, because reconstruction took place slowly.
2. In the course of the period 1665–75, the situation was healthy without being very brilliant; the price of a setier never attained the levels of the years 1640–50.
3. After settling at an average, the period 1678–93 was one of serious swings; a setier passed from 40 kreuzers to 120, the destitution of the poor helping to make the fortunes of the large landowners; after 1688, the rate went down, the rocketing of prices was nothing but an illusion for some and a nightmare for the rest.

4. After the monetary stabilization of 1693 (ordinances of 28 November 1692 and 21 March 1693), these were the genuinely good years which followed until 1720, with a slow and regular rise that allowed substantial profits.[7]

If the crisis years 1688–93 are disregarded, two periods can be set in opposition: before 1680, the Austrian economy experienced relative prosperity, then after 1693 it was in a state of full expansion. This division into three 'plateaux' was a phenomenon common to all the hereditary lands, Bohemia (archives at Mnichohradec) and western Hungary (Sopron).

The reverse of trends which followed after 1683 is confirmed by the rise of real wages at Vienna, where the wage of a manual labourer increased by 25 per cent and that of a mason by 33 per cent. The raising of the siege and the reconquest of Hungary clearly mark the turning-point made manifest in the flowering of baroque monuments and also in the pre-eminence of the aristocracy.[8]

THE SOCIAL ETHOS OF THE ARISTOCRACY

The real governing group at Vienna consisted of a hundred Austrian and Bohemian houses while the Hungarians of their own accord kept their distance, residing at Pressburg or in their castles, an arrangement which made a deep impression on all foreign travellers:

The persons of quality at Vienna are all counts or barons, but, although the counts of Austria might be very obstinate in their nobility which they make the essence of all their merit, there are nevertheless many new counts because of the readiness with which the emperors give this title to persons who have risen in the finance departments or the chancelleries. Those who are rich and who come from such families often marry daughters from old families, but it is quite rare to see men from the old nobility marry beneath their station for fear of losing the benefits of placing their children in the chapters whence the ecclesiastical electors and prince-bishops are taken. All the knights have a particular care in their youth for travelling, of taking their exercise in foreign lands, of learning foreign languages and it is rare to find one who, besides his mother-tongue, does not also speak Latin, French, Italian and sometimes Spanish, but after such good beginnings, the greater part applies itself to nothing and leads a very useless life. Few among them venture out to war, and if some are to be found in service, they are young men who, while the war lasts, have taken companies in order to subsist, the rest of the army officers are for the most part foreigners or soldiers of fortune. The Germans' lack of interest gives plenty of opportunity to the Italians to come looking for employment in the emperor's regiments. As these are industrious and naturally dedicated to their fortunes, they easily enter into the favour of the dowager empress, Count Montecuccoli and the Spanish ambassador and one can say that this nation makes up a sizeable party at this court.

With the exception of the Hungarian nobility, the governing class had no military ethos which made possible the constant renewal of the army officers and, for the more able, integration into the landed aristocracy. Montecuccoli, from a good Italian family, was engaged as a simple armourer in 1631; half a century later, he died rich, president of the council of war and covered in honours (prince of the Empire, knight of the Golden Fleece, *generalissimo*).

Towards the end of the century, Eugene of Savoy also carved out a brilliant career. Having been unable to find work at the French court, he was engaged as a simple knight in 1683 and soon inherited a regiment from his brother Louis, then a commander in Hungary. The victor at Zenta, he entered into ministerial service in 1701 as president of the war council. A brilliant *generalissimo* during the war of the Spanish Succession, when his opponent was the marshal de Villars, and negotiator of the Peace of Rastatt (1714), he became the principal minister of the emperor Charles VI and one of the greatest Austrian patrons of the arts.[9]

The rise of the baroque civilization was linked indissolubly to the wealth of the aristocracy as much as to the triumph of the Counter-Reformation, to direct links with Italy or to the economic situation. The great lords, lay and ecclesiastical, showed an unbridled taste for building which was, perhaps, a subtle form of tax evasion: in answer to the pressing requests of the impecunious Habsburgs, the reply given, through the intermediary of the Diet, was simply that one lacked liquid assets.

BAROQUE ARCHITECTURE[10]

The first wave of baroque buildings appeared in Bohemia, especially in Prague, where the large families had constructed palaces on the Malá Strana, the aristocratic quarter close to the Hradčany, the royal town and administrative seat of the kingdom. It was Wallenstein first and foremost who set the precedent for this need for pomp, palaces and conventual churches which appeared essential for sustaining the honour of a great name. His palace at Prague was not so very innovative since the façade is reminiscent of the style of the German Renaissance, the *sala terrena*. The palace of the Gonzagas at Mantua and the stone grottos in the garden recall the Munich residence of Maximilian of Bavaria. Thirty years later, the Czernin palace built by the Italian Carrati and inspired by Venetian and Palladian architecture, but on a colossal scale, marked the definitive victory of Italian taste. At the same time, the churches were rendered baroque in style, the oldest structures, Roman or Gothic, were covered in stucco while the façades received flat decoration surmounted by a pediment: the Carmelite church, which had formerly been Lutheran, was transformed in this way, and the chapel of the Jesuit college was rendered baroque by the Italian Lurago. After receiving their training in Italy, Czech artists like the painter Skréta or the sculptor Bendl applied their talents to the service of the traditions of the country. In the next generation, it was another Wallenstein, the archbishop of Prague, Johann-Friedrich, who played a decisive role in the evolution of Czech baroque, employing an architect of French origin and trained at Rome, Jean-Baptiste Mathey. He constructed the fine Church of the Knights of the Cross, redesigned the archbishop's palace, the Buquoy palace and the palace of the dukes of Tuscany. The capital of Bohemia in this way found itself transformed little by little, in particular the hills on the left bank of the Vltava which, through the accumulation of palaces and gardens, took on the remarkable character that they have kept to the present day.

The second baroque wave showed itself at Vienna in 1683. While it cannot be denied that the university church, run by the Jesuits, adopted in 1627 a style which was unquestionably Roman (flat façade with pediment) and that similarly the Dominican church (1631) and Am Hof (1662) are works in the baroque style, only a few palaces were renewed before the siege of Vienna (the Collatto palace, the Rottal and Abensperg-Traun palaces). After 1683 the aristocrats vied with each other, building at the same time a winter palace in the Roman style in the centre of the town (the present-day 1st district), and a summer palace as a secondary residence in the immediate neighbourhood of the capital. The first monuments were the Dietrischstein and Esterházy palaces, built by Tancala, and the Liechtenstein palace (the work of D. Martinelli), the monumental character of which served as the model for numerous other buildings in Vienna. The old streets of the town changed their appearance between 1690 and 1740; the Herrengasse, which led to the Hofburg, was edged with elaborate façades. While the Italians kept their position, the period was dominated by three great Austrian architects who had been trained in Italy: Johann-Bernard Fischer von Erlach (1656–1723), Johann Lucas von Hildebrandt (1668–1745) and Jakob Prandtauer (1658–1726). These three perfectly illustrate the great era of Austrian baroque (the *Hochbarock* of the German art historians). But between Fischer von Erlach and von Hildebrandt, there existed the same contrast in temperament as between the two masters of Italian architecture of the *Seicento*, Borromini and Bernini. Fischer von Erlach, formed in the studio of Fontana, possessed more power than von Hildebrandt, whose subtle genius had more invention and grace. He constructed the Kinský palace and the summer residence of prince Eugene of Savoy, the famous Belvedere, providing pavilions and gardens of subtle elegance.

How far can one speak of imperial baroque? Leopold I, for want of financial means, limited his orders to the administrative buildings of the

Hofburg (the wing of the chancellery, the work of D. Carlone) and to the summer palace of La Favorite, but with respect to Schönbrunn, had to content himself with the grandiose plans of Fischer von Erlach. In the last years of his reign, he brought to Vienna a great decorative artist, father Pozzo, whose art of *trompe-l'œil* began a decorative tradition greatly honoured in Austria during the eighteenth century. It was Charles VI who really played the role of patron of the arts. He entrusted to Fischer von Erlach the restoration of the Hofburg, a heterogeneous collection of buildings which had developed around the medieval castle. It is to him that the world is indebted for the admirable library which at the present time houses the Austrian National Library, while his son Joseph-Emanuel was responsible for the great Spanish Riding School. He was also the author of the plans for the new Bohemian chancellery outside the Hofburg which was destined to house the agencies of this highest organ of Czech government. At the same time, Fischer von Erlach designed the castle at Schönbrunn which, much more modest than the original project, can still be seen. At Charles VI's request, he built outside the city fortifications, the church of St Charles Borromeo (the Karlskirche). Here, the most diverse references are blended together and, if it is possible to speak of imperial baroque, then the term is surely most appropriate when referring to this church, which symbolizes the triumph of the Counter-Reformation and the House of Austria. The façade recalls in a minor way that of St Peter's at Rome and the two columns placed in front are without question an evocation of past and present imperial glory. Fischer von Erlach also worked for the aristocracy and among other projects constructed the winter palace of prince Eugene, a master work of power and majesty (currently the Austrian Ministry of Finances).

It was in the country that the aristocracy kept its seat of power, covering the province with churches and castles. Each large monastery, as a landowner, felt bound to renew its church and monastery buildings. Better management of fortunes, the development of vineyards and the increase of profits through the sale of wine allowed the abbeys of Lower Austria to render their Gothic churches baroque, like the Cistercians at Göttweig, or to reconstruct the whole building as the Benedictines did at Melk. On a promontory towering over the Danube, Prandtauer built the finest abbey church in Austria where the terraces, wings and the church with its two *Zweibeltürme* and its vast dome produce an effect which is grandiose and at the same time elegant, in harmony with the surrounding countryside. To these large monuments, which have held the attention of art historians, should be added innumerable churches in the countryside where the architecture and decoration share the same taste for a religion both approachable and miraculous, triumphant and consoling.

This baroque art is in fact an essential element of the civilization of the Habsburg monarchy. The Catholicism of the Counter-Reformation which is the dominant intellectual element within it, served to inform and to console the masses exploited by the large landed proprietors and the royal fiscus. In accordance with the recommendations of the Council of Trent, the statues of saints, the church decorations, the music, festivals, processions and pilgrimages had as their goal to develop the fervour of the masses while at the same time instructing them. Through the cults of new saints, the clergy likewise acted on their mental outlook. Besides the worship reserved for the Blessed Sacrament, the Church favoured devotions to royal saints (Leopold in Austria, Václav in Bohemia, István in Hungary) and ended by recognizing St Jan of Nepomuk, who had been the object of Czech popular fervour before he was canonized in 1722 through the personal intervention of the emperor Charles VI. The clergy and the dynasty, hostile to all intellectualism, favoured a culture that was essentially plastic in style, at the same time pompous and familiar and of which the theatre was probably the favourite expression.

If indeed a court art can be said to have existed at Vienna, then it is necessary to look at the opera, which was originally reserved for the emperor and his intimate circle. Although Leopold I spent little on buildings, it was because he reserved his modest resources for music, for his 'chapel' for which nothing was too fine nor too costly. He paid musicians, singers and *italiens* decorators highly – far more than the councillors of state, who received only 1200 florins a year. He had a theatre built from wood on the site of the present-day National Theatre. This building was formally opened for the performances of the *Pomo d'Oro* of Cesti which were given on the occasion of the marriage in 1666 of Leopold I to the *infanta* Margarita-Teresa. The *Pomo d'Oro* was an *opera seria* in the Venetian style and was intended to equal in its staging the contemporary fetes at Versailles. It marked the birth at Vienna of Italian opera which would dominate the musical life of the court right until Salieri. While the staging was ostentatious and called for machinery which could create the impression of miraculous happenings, the public was made up of invited guests of the highest rank carefully chosen by the major-domo of the court, the Viennese bourgeoisie being systematically excluded.

The emperor was himself a composer. Leopold I followed the example set by his father and was never parted from his spinet so that he could note down every musical idea that came into his head. In the first years of his reign, he refused to receive ministers or ambassadors while he was compos-ing a ballet or directing a rehearsal. He confided one day to a visitor that 'he would gladly have been master of the Chapel had he not been emperor', but, he added with a touch of humour, 'the trade is not too bad'. He left an impressive series of sacred and profane compositions which are interesting in style and are for the most part unedited. Masses and motets, sung once again at the present time through the efforts of musicologists, show that, while he was without the genius of a Monteverdi or a Lully, Leopold I had a gift for composition.

This phenomenon, whatever its importance, remained confined to certain levels of society and baroque music had a public limited to the court, some aristocratic circles and grand abbeys with some extension into Bohemia. It did not have an impact on the common masses or the bourgeoisie and did not open up any intellectual horizons.[11]

During the brief period of peace between the Austro-Turkish war and the Dutch War (1665–72), the court organized a series of fetes, especially at *Fasching*, the festival which preceded the period of penitence during Lent. The number of theatrical performances increased and there were balls and sleigh races in the snow-covered Prater and secular processions during the great religious spectacles.

Anna Coreth has shown the great importance assumed by the procession of the Blessed Sacrament. The most grandiose of all, the Corpus Christi procession, saw the bare-headed emperor follow on foot the dais on which was carried the monstrance enclosing the consecrated host. This ceremony bound together the court and the town, the emperor and the people in a common devotion which solemnly reaffirmed one of the fundamental dogmas of the Council of Trent, the real presence of Christ in the host. It was the sign of religious unity recovered in the face of the heretic and the infidel, the Protestant churches and the Turks, the two enemies of the House of Austria.

The imperial court also indulged in hunting, a particularly royal diversion, and the town of Vienna surrounded by vast forests lent itself to this recreation. Leopold I went hunting several times a week. An excellent horseman, despite his small stature and his frail physique, he took part in horse-ballets or carousels which also delighted the French court.

In addition to these large official fetes, there was a highly developed social life of balls, receptions and banquets in the great palaces of the aristocracy which forced diplomats to make great outlays in order to keep up their status. At the beginning of the eighteenth century, Montesquieu and prince Eugene both caricatured the frivolous character of those aristocrats who, once their educational travels were over, did nothing but feast and amuse themselves – although they conducted their idle chatter in French.

It would, however, be a serious error to take these harsh criticisms literally. Certainly, baroque civilization emphasized festivals, cared for decoration and appearances, gave more importance to gestures than to ideas and prized sentiment more than reason. Austrian baroque showed a pronounced taste for staging and theatre but it would be false to continue to believe that intellectual life was non-existent at Vienna and that the political personnel recruited from within the aristocracy was totally incompetent. How could one account for the Habsburgs' success at the beginning of the eighteenth century and the emergence of Austria as a great power be explained if the government was in the hands of a team of dull and dim-witted nonentities?

INTELLECTUAL LIFE

Ernest Denis boldly claimed that after the Battle of the White Mountain, intellectual life in Bohemia was wrecked and all the men of letters went into exile. The rigour of the censorship which was solidly maintained by the Jesuits until 1760 lends support to this thesis. It is true that published works and higher education were orientated towards Aristotelian philosophy and ultra-orthodox theology, and that there was no opening in the direction of rationalism, Cartesian philosophy and research in the field of the natural sciences.

As for the people, of their own free will they remained in a genuine obscurantism and were subject to the propaganda of preachers, the most famous and perhaps the most burlesque of whom was the Swabian cleric known under the name of Abraham à Sancta Clara. From the lofty pulpit in the Augustinian Church, he launched his invective against the Viennese or else galvanized them, as in 1683, with his sermon 'Arise, arise ye Christians!' (*Auf, auf Ihr Christen!*) at the time when the Turkish peril seemed especially menacing.

A pupil of the Jesuits and the Benedictines, the son of a country innkeeper, he is considered the best writer of the Austrian baroque age. A canon regular of St Augustine, after 1677 court preacher, he was unquestionably a long-winded and effective orator: he left fourteen volumes of *Complete Works* where he never referred to Francis Bacon, Descartes, Spinoza or Leibniz but most often to the *Summa Theologica* of St Thomas Aquinas. Abraham à Sancta Clara indulged in superficial criticism of the vices of Austrian society but above all he displayed a savage, visceral hatred of Turks (that is, the Muslims), Jews and Protestants. Despite the confusion, the irrational character of his discourse and the distressing poverty of his thought, he has been held up as the grandest master of the German language between Luther and Goethe, while his chauvinism and anti-Semitism rank him among the precursors of the Christian Socialists of Karl Lueger. Even though R.A. Kann saw in him the ultimate representative of the moralizing satire struck in the coin of great 'good sense' which was begun two centuries earlier by Sebastian Brant in the *Ship of Fools* (*Narrenschiff*), and even if Schiller found in him a measure of inspiration, Abraham á Sancta Clara was in reality a lamentable author. He was nonetheless a representative of the narrow culture of the Viennese petit-bourgeoisie whom he knew how to touch through his rhetorical artifices and whom he flattered while stirring their imagination.

Higher culture existed but it was the preserve of a narrowly restricted elite; the emperor himself, a small circle at court, some inquisitive aristocrats and the large monasteries between them possessed all the libraries. It was a Latin or neo-Latin culture conforming to the ideal of the Counter-Reformation and according to the pioneering work of R.J.W. Evans, completely foreign to that of Western Europe. During the 1660s a circle was formed around Leopold I and his librarian Peter Lambeck. It gathered together scholars from Germany, known primarily as the theoreticians of mercantilism: Johann Becher, Wilhelm Schröder and Philip Wilhelm von Hörgnik were Protestant converts who had studied in Holland and who were interested in alchemy as much as economics. Particularly revealing is the emperor's private library, where the Bible sat next to the *Complete Works* of Justus Lipsius. The Hungarian magnates like Ferenc Nádasdy, Pál Esterházy and especially Nikola Zrinski put together, at great expense, rich libraries. Zrinski, at the same time as being a political scientist, general and epic poet, was also a great writer. His *Siege of Szigetvár* remains a classic of Hungarian literature and a master work of baroque letters. Zrinski acquired at Venice all the French works as soon as they were translated into Italian.

The philosopher who served as the point of reference remained Aristotle. As in the Mannerist era, the universe was imagined as a whole where humankind was a microcosm corresponding to the macrocosm. This was why astrology and alchemy, far from being pleasant pastimes, were placed at the centre of scholars' preoccupations. Ferdinand III maintained with his brother Leopold-Wilhelm a copious correspondence concerning the occult sciences; he ennobled an alchemist banker, Conrad Richthausen, making him baron 'von Chaos'. His son Leopold offered protection to alchemists like Borri, considered in Italy as a dangerous charlatan. Ferdinand III, however, was curious about mathematics and took a personal interest in the problem, yet to be discredited, of squaring the circle. In private, he also took seriously the works of Galileo despite the Holy Office's condemnation of the scholar. Even so, the Viennese doctor Paul Sorbait, who showed so much devotion during the plague of 1679, had adopted Harvey's theory of the circulation of the blood at the time when the faculty of medicine at Paris showed itself more hesitant.

Modern ideas had made some advance particularly at the periphery of the monarchy. At Prague, Irishmen like Donovan and William O'Kelley made no mystery of their attachment to Augustinianism nor their interest in nascent Jansenism. Count Sporock, the son of a general enriched during the Thirty Years War, went to France to complete his education, frequented Arnauld and Nicole with the result that he took Jansenist ideas with him back to Bohemia. In his castle at Kuks, a masterpiece of baroque architecture, he installed a printing-press in order to spread Jansenism. Only his status as a great aristocrat allowed him to escape serious trouble during the reign of Charles VI. The aristocratic system allowed free spirits to escape the restrictions of the conformism surrounding them. A yet more elevated social position permitted prince Eugene to collect forbidden books and to gather together at Vienna a circle of free-thinkers, but the great man always felt himself superior to the German aristocracy.

The Hungarian Protestant intellectuals were especially open to the influences of the Dutch universities and to German modernist currents since they were obliged to carry out their advanced studies abroad. The ideas of Descartes, Bacon and Gassendi were studied at Debrecen and Kolozsvár and puritans like János Apáczai tried to widen the breach opened in the tradition. It should be counted a great misfortune that Transylvanian independence was lost at the very moment when the 'wars of liberation' in Hungary brought about the ruin of the academies at Debrecen and Sárospatak.

This brief sketch can be, as R. J. W. Evans has stressed, only an introduction to the study of intellectual life in the baroque age.[12] Although it was not non-existent, it was very different from what has been thought 'normal' since the age of the Enlightenment, with the result that it has been obscured or totally forgotten. Be that as it may, its main seats were, apart from the imperial palace, the castles and the monasteries. It cannot be understood without the Counter-Reformation, nor without a thorough understanding of the triumphant orders. In strengthening its preponderance, the landed aristocracy gave an original character to the civilization of Danubian Europe. Allied with the Catholic Church and the House of Austria it knew how to reinvest intelligently its profits from rented land and rural manufacture, but its high culture remained limited to the circles of the 'happy few'.

The Jesuits saw to it that the bourgeoisie and the peasant masses remained strangers to the great currents of thought which, little by little, were transforming Western Europe. Everything had to advance the salvation of souls and the success of the Catholic Reformation. Books and ideas judged subversive had only marginal impact while the vast sums invested in rebuilding churches and castles served to exalt the triumph of the Church and the dynasty.

Such was the success of this policy that Austria remains to the present day a country of large baroque monasteries and sumptuous Viennese palaces. This success cannot be denied, but the social basis of this brilliant civilization remained very narrow, much more so than in England, Holland or in the France of Louis XIV. The success of the Habsburgs' cultural policy stamped for once and for all an aristocratic character on Austrian civilization. Without a significant bourgeoisie open to the world, every initiative depended on some non-conformist nobles or religious orders desirous of opening a breach in the intellectual monopoly of the Jesuits.

Baroque Vienna, the castles of Bohemia and the monasteries of Lower Austria betray no less the prosperity recovered after 1683 and are the witnesses of a prestigious civilization which yielded nothing to its Italian model or its French contemporary. This model not only served, more or less consciously, as the point of reference right until the collapse of the monarchy, but also contributed to perpetuating the monarchy's backwardness.

NOTES AND REFERENCES

1. Camille Freschot, *Relation de la Cour de Vienne*, Cologne, 1705.
2. Helmut Feigl, *Die nieder-österreichische Landherrschaft*, Vienna, 1965.
3. Otto Brunner, *Wolf Helmard von Hohberg: Adeliges Landleen und Europäischer Geist*, Linz, 1959.
4. Jean Bérenger, 'Les Juifs et l'antisémitisme dans l'Autriche du XVIIe siècle', *Études européennes*, Paris, 1973, pp. 181–93.
5. J.E. Wegener, *Oeconomia suburbana*, Prague, 1966.
6. A.-F. Pribram and R. Geyer, *Materialen zur Geschichte der Preise und Löhne in Osterreich*, Vienna, 1938.
7. *Codex Austriacus* 2 vols, Vienna, 1705, vol. 2, pp.35–40.
8. J. Bérenger, 'Le redressement économique autrichien sous le règne de Léopold I', *Études danubiennes*, no.1/1, 1985, pp. 5–24.
9. Derek MacKay, *Prince Eugene of Savoy*, London, 1977.
10. V.-L. Tapié, *The Rise and Fall of the Habsburg Monarchy*, London, 1971.
    V.-L. Tapié, *Baroque et classicisme*, Paris 1957.
11. Robert A. Kann, *A Study in Austrian Intellectual History, from late Baroque to Romanticism*, New York, 1960, p.40.
12. R.J.W. Evans, *The Making of the Habsburg Monarchy*, Oxford, 1979.

Chronology

1273	Rudolf of Habsburg elected king of Germany.
1278	Battle of Dürnkrut.
1308	Murder of Albert of Habsburg.
1315	Victory of the Swiss at Morgarten.
1322	Victory of the Swiss at Mühldorf.
1348	Election of Charles IV of Luxemburg to the imperial throne.
1356	Charles IV promulgates the Golden Bull.
1363	Rudolf IV unites the Tyrol with Austria.
1365	Rudolf IV founds the university of Vienna.
1378	Death of Charles IV of Luxemburg, emperor and king of Bohemia.
1415	Meeting of the Council of Constance.
1419	Beginning of the Hussite revolution in Bohemia.
1439	Albert II of Habsburg, king of the Romans and king of Bohemia.
1440	Election of Frederick III of Habsburg as emperor.
1444	Victory of the Turks at Varna.
1453	Mehmed II seizes Constantinople.
1456	János Hunyadi brings the Turks to a halt outside Belgrade.
1458	Matthias Corvinus becomes king of Hungary.
1471	Death of Jiří of Poděbrady, king of Bohemia.
1477	Charles the Bold dies outside Nancy; his only daughter, Maria, marries Maximilian of Austria.
1482	Death of Maria of Burgundy.
1490	Death of Matthias Corvinus.
1493	Maximilian of Austria elected king of the Romans.
1500	Birth of Charles V.
1514	Peasants' Revolt in Hungary.
1515	Treaty of Vienna between Maximilian and Władysław Jagieł-łończyk.
1517	Charles V king of Spain. Luther nails up his '95 theses' at Wittenberg.
1519	Election of Charles V as emperor.

356

1522	Treaty of Brussels: the division of the Habsburg patrimony between Charles V and his brother Ferdinand.
1526	August: death of Louis II Jagiellon at the Battle of Mohács. October: Ferdinand of Habsburg elected king of Bohemia. November: Ferdinand elected king of Hungary.
1527	January: Ferdinand elected king of Croatia, he promulgates an ordinance creating the central government of the Danubian monarchy.
1529	The Ladies' Peace. First siege of Vienna by the Turks under Süleymân the Magnificent.
1531	Ferdinand of Habsburg elected king of the Romans.
1538	Treaty of Nagyvárad (Oradeà) between Ferdinand and János Zapolya.
1541	Süleymân annexes Buda.
1544	Peace of Crépy-en-Laonnais.
1545–63	Council of Trent.
1546–55	Schmalkaldic War.
1547	Bohemian revolt. Victory of Charles V at Mühlberg.
1548	Interim of Augsburg.
1551	Seizure of Temesvár (Timişoara) by the Turks.
1552	Treaty of Chambord. Occupation of the three bishoprics (Metz, Toul and Verdun) by Henry II.
1554	Ferdinand makes provision for the division of the hereditary lands.
1555	Peace of Augsburg.
1556	Abdication of Charles V. Accession of Philip II (1556–98). Creation of the War Council.
1558	Creation of the Aulic Council of the Empire.
1559	Peace of Cateau-Cambrésis between France and Spain.
1564	Death of Ferdinand I. Accession Maximilian II.
1565	Defeat of the Turks before Malta.
1566	Death of Süleymân the Magnificent before Szigetvár. Beginning of the revolt in the Netherlands.
1567	Confessional privileges accorded by Maximilian II in Austria.
1568	Peace of Adrianople. Religious toleration in Transylvania.
1571	Defeat of the Turks at Lepanto.
1572	St Bartholomew's Day massacre in Paris.
1576	Death of Maximilian. Accession of the emperor Rudolf II.
1578	Death of the archduke Charles.
1578–80	Beginnings of the Counter-Reformation within the monarchy.
1579	Pacification of Ghent in the Netherlands.
1582	Prague becomes the imperial residence.
1585	Sack of Antwerp by Spanish troops.
1588	Defeat of the Spanish Armada.

1593–1606	Austro-Turkish war.
1604	István Bocskai's revolt in Hungary.
1606	Peace of Vienna; Peace of Zsitva-Torok.
1608	Diet of Pressburg. The archduke Matthias elected king of Hungary.
	Formation of the Evangelical League within the Empire.
1609	Creation of the Holy League.
	Rudolf II concedes the 'Letter of Majesty' in Bohemia.
1612	Death of Rudolf II.
1614	General Diet at Linz.
1617	Ferdinand of Styria elected king of Bohemia.
1618	May: Defenestration of Prague.
1618–48	Thirty Years War.
1619	Ferdinand II elected emperor. Frederick V elected king of Bohemia.
1620	Battle of the White Mountain.
1621	Philip IV king of Spain.
	Resumption of war in the Netherlands.
1621–22	Repression in Bohemia.
1623	Devaluation of currency (*Münzcalada*).
1624	Wallenstein general of the imperial troops.
1625	Revolt in Upper Austria.
	Danish intervention in Germany.
1626	Treaty of Monçon between Louis XIII and Philip IV.
1627	'Renewed Constitution' in Bohemia.
1628	Wallenstein admiral of the Baltic and the Ocean.
	Fall of La Rochelle.
1629	Edict of Restitution.
	War of the Mantuan Succession.
1630	Electoral assembly at Ratisbon.
	Wallenstein's dismissal as general.
	György I Rákóczi, prince of Transylvania
	Gustavus Adolphus of Sweden lands in Germany.
1631	Treaty of Bärwald.
	Sack of Magdeburg. Beginning of Swedish intervention.
	Victory of Gustavus Adolphus at Breitenfeld.
1632	Wallenstein returns as general.
	Death of Gustavus Adolphus at Breitenfeld.
1633	Louis XIII occupies Lorraine.
1634	Assassination of Wallenstein. Victory of the cardinal-*infante* at Nördligen. Preliminaries of Pirna.
1635	Signing of the Peace of Prague. Louis XIII declares war on Spain.
1636	Siege of Corbie by the Spanish. Imperial troops invade Franche-Comté.
1637	Death of Ferdinand II. Accession of Ferdinand III.

1638	Bernard of Saxe-Weimar seizes Breisach.
1640	Catalan revolt. Seccession of Portugal. Beginning of the civil war in England.
1642	Death of Richelieu
1643	Death of Louis XIII. Victory of the French at Rocroi. Victory of Mercy at Tuttlingen.
1644	Preliminary negotiations at Hamburg. Turenne's victory at Freiburg.
1645	Swedish victory at Jankau (Bohemia) and of Turenne at Nördlingen. Beginning of the negotiations in Westphalia. Signing of the Peace in Linz.
1647	Armistice in Ulm. Revolt in Naples.
1648	Victories of Turenne at Zusmarshausen and of Condé at Lens. Beginning of the Fronde in France. Signing of the Spanish–Dutch Peace (January) and the Peace of Westphalia (24 October).
1652	End of the Fronde. The French lose Catalonia.
1653	Meeting of the imperial Diet at Ratisbon.
1654	Death of Ferdinand IV king of the Romans. Catholic Reformation in Austria.
1655	French–English alliance. Beginning of the second Northern War.
1656	Invasion of Poland by the Swedes.
1657	Death of Ferdinand III. Intervention by imperial troops in Poland.
1658	Turenne's victory at the Battle of the Dunes. Election of Leopold I at Frankfurt. End of the League of the Rhine.
1659	Signing of the Peace of the Pyrenees between France and Spain.
1660	Signing of the Peace of Oliva ending the Northern War.
1661	Death of Mazarin. Ottoman intervention in Transylvania.
1663	Turkish intervention in Hungary.
1664	Christian victory at Saint-Gotthard. Peace of Vasvár. Beginning of the perpetual Diet at Ratisbon.
1665	Death of Philip IV. Beginning of the 'Conspiracy of the magnates' in Hungary (Zrinski, Frankopan, Wesselenyi).
1666	Leopold I marries *infanta* Margaret-Theresa.
1667	War of Devolution.
1668	Treaty of Grémonville. Peace of Aix-la-Chapelle.
1669	Election of Michał Korybut Wiśniowiecki to the throne of Poland.
1670	Rebellion in Hungary.
1671	Execution of Petar Zrinski. Franco-Austrian treaty of alliance.
1672	Beginning of the Dutch War.
1673	Break between the emperor and France.
1674	Invasion of Alsace by the imperial troops. Revolt at Messina.

1675	Death of Turenne.
1676	Marriage of Leopold to Eleonora of Pfalz-Neuburg.
1678	Signing of the Peace of Nijmegen.
1679	Creation by Louis XIV of the Chambers of Reunion. Plague at Vienna.
1681	Session of the Hungarian Diet at Sopron. Meeting of the diplomatic congress at Frankfurt. The surrender of Strassburg. Peasants' revolt in Bohemia. Thököly takes up arms in Hungary.
1682	Thököly a vassal of the Porte.
1683	Second siege of Vienna by the Turks. Christian victory at Kahlenberg (12 September).
1684	Formation of the Holy League. Signing of a twenty-years' truce at Ratisbon.
1686	Seizure of Buda by the imperial troops. Joseph I elected king of the Romans.
1687	Session of the Hungarian Diet at Pressburg at which Joseph I elected king.
1688	'Glorious Revolution' in England.
1688–97	War of the League of Augsburg, or 'the war of the Palatine succession'.
1689	Capture of Belgrade by the imperial troops. The French raze and burn the Palatinate.
1691	*Diploma Leopoldinum* guarantees liberties to Transylvania.
1693	Monetary regulation within the Empire.
1696	*Concursus palatinalis* (assembly of Hungarian notables) at Vienna.
1697	Victory of prince Eugene of Savoy at Zenta. Signing of the peace of Ryswick between France and the allies.
1698	First partition treaty to settle the Spanish succession.
1699	Signing of the Peace of Karlowitz between the Porte and the Holy League. Death of the prince-elector of Bavaria, heir presumptive to the Spanish crown.
1700	Third partition treaty.
	The will of Charles II of Spain in favour of the Bourbons (2 October).
	Death of Charles II. Louis XIV accepts the will (November).

Glossary of German Terms

Appellationsgericht zu Prag: supreme court of appeal at Prague created by Ferdinand I in 1548 following the rebellion by the orders.

Bruderzwist: literally 'fraternal discord', most commonly used of the discord between Rudolf II and his brother Matthias.

Bücherkommission: censorship committee established at Frankfurt at the time of the Counter-Reformation with authority throughout the whole of the Holy Roman Empire.

Bürgerspital: from the end of the Middle Ages, the city hospital at Vienna subject to the *Magistrat* and serving as a hospice and charitable institution.

Dominikalland: the manorial reserve within an estate under the system of land-holding prevailing before 1848; generally the *Dominikalland* was worked directly by the estate owner and was exempt from taxation.

Donaumonarchie: the Danubian monarchy, the name given by Austrian historians to the Habsburg monarchy after 1526 and the union of Austria, Bohemia and Hungary.

Edler von: literally 'nobleman of . . .' title accorded with ennoblement.

Eisenkammer: institution established in Styria (Austria) responsible for the supply and marketing of metal goods.

Gasse: street in a city or town, generally narrow as opposed to a *Strasse* or road.

Geheimer Rat: a privy council (rather than a 'secret' council) tied to the person of the sovereign. It was created in 1527 by Ferdinand I and survived in various forms until the 1848 revolution, when it was replaced by a council of ministers.

Gemeines Pfennig: central treasury of the Holy Roman Empire filled by the subsidies voted by the Diet, in particular by the 'Roman months'.

Grundherrschaft: a landed estate based on the collection of rents and manorial rights.

Gutsherrschaft: a landed estate based on the working of lands directly and the use of the robot; the peasants whose tenures were reduced had to pay taxes as labour and not in kind.

Hochbarock: the high point in baroque art reached between 1680 and 1740 and coinciding with the reigns of Leopold I, Joseph I and Charles VI.

Hofburg: the imperial palace at Vienna consisting of a series of buildings erected between the fifteenth (the chapel) and the beginning of the twentieth centuries (Neue Hofburg in neo-baroque style). The principal elements are the *Stallburg*, the Schweizer Hof, Reichskanzlei and the library.

Hofhandelsmann: merchant-banker to the court holding special privileges, free from all territorial jurisdiction and answerable only to the marshal of the court.

Hofkammer: literally, 'chamber of the court' or chamber of accounts; it was created in 1527 by Ferdinand I to control the chambers of accounts of the different Estates of the monarchy; it played the role of minister of finances within the monarchy until 1848.

Hofkriegsrat: Aulic War Council created in 1556 by Ferdinand I to manage army administration; its powers were analogous to those of the secretary of state for war under the French *ancien régime* and continued to operate until 1848.

Hofrat: Aulic Council created by Ferdinand I in 1527; it became the Aulic Council of the Empire in 1556 and played the role of privy state council, judging in the last resort trials called on appeal from throughout the whole of the *Reich*; it was also a distinction granted to distinguished officials and still conferred under the Austrian Republic.

Hofstaat: all the imperial Aulic institutions.

Hofstallmeister: grand court equerry, responsible for the horses, carriages, carts, stables and travel arrangements for the court; it was an important Aulic office.

Kaiser: Roman emperor until 1806; the Germanized form of Caesar.

Kavaliertour: educational tour made abroad (Italy, Germany and later extended to France and the Netherlands) undertaken by young aristocrats; it included visits to universities.

Kreis: 'circle'; administrative district of the Empire but also of the kingdom of Bohemia (Czech, *kreš*).

Kreistag: Diet of a circle which ran the circles of the Empire created in 1512.

Kriegszahlmeister: war treasurer responsible for the war chest.

Landeshauptmann: literally 'captain of a country', i.e. head of the executive in the hereditary lands.

Landeshoheit: territorial sovereignty limited only by imperial authority.

Landhaus: palace of the Estates where the Diet and the provincial administration dependent on the orders met and were housed.

Landmarschall: marshal of the Diet and chief of the administration of the provincial Estates.

Landrobot: like the *corvée royale* in France which could be demanded of the peasants for work of public benefit, e.g. the repair of roads or fortifications.

Landschaft: community of Estates and orders which constituted the country and found its political expression in the provincial Diets.

Landtag: provincial Diet or Diet of the kingdom (Bohemia).

Landtagsproposition: the bills proposed by the king and presented at the beginning of a session of the Diet; once discussed and approved they had force of law within the country.

Meierhof: leasehold farm worked as part of the manorial reserve.

Militärgrenze: Austro-Turkish military frontier guarding the confines of the monarchy; created in 1522 to protect Austria, it was finally dismantled in 1878 after the occupation of Bosnia-Hercegovina by the imperial army; its garrisons were made up of *Grenzer* (i.e. 'borderers' who enjoyed special status.

Oberstburggraf: grand burgrave of Bohemia, the first of the grand officers of the crown and president of the council of lieutenancy – in fact the governor of Bohemia from 1620 to 1848.

Oberstkämmerer: grand chamberlain, another grand officer of the kingdom of Bohemia.

Oberstlandrichter: supreme judge in Bohemia, one of the grand officers of the crown which made up the council of lieutenancy.

Prunksaale: ostentatiously magnificent reception rooms in the royal palace or the palace of an aristocrat.

Raitkammer: first version of the chamber of accounts instituted by Maximilian I.

Rauchfangsteuer: hearth-tax, literally chimney-tax.

Rechsstaat: state-right.

Reich: Holy Roman Empire of the German nation; abolished in 1806.

Reichsfürst: 'prince of the Empire'; the *Reichsfürsten* constituted the second college of the German Diet immediately after the college of electors (*Kurfürsten*).

Reichshofrat: Aulic Council of the Empire; created by Ferdinand I, it was reorganized in 1648 by the treaty of Osnabrück; it was the supreme court of appeal for the whole Empire and its judges were appointed by the emperor.

Reichskammergericht: the court of the imperial chamber, the supreme court of appeal dependent on the authority of the Estates, who appointed and paid the judges; the court first sat at Spire, then after 1689 at Wetzlar.

Reichsmatrikel: the number of soldiers and the share of the contribution which each prince was obliged to furnish on the occasion of the Diet declaring war.

Reichspfennigamt: treasury of the Empire responsible for managing the sums collected for the Diet.

Reichsregiment: government of the Empire established by the reforms of the emperor Maximilian I.

Reichsstadt: free town in the Empire; the free towns constituted the third college of the imperial Diet.

Reichstag: the Diet of the Holy Roman Empire until 1806.

Richter: judge, but also the manorial officer placed at the head of a village where he carried out administration and justice.

Riksrad: Swedish equivalent of the council of state, often referred to as 'the Senate' by contemporaries.

Ritter: 'knight'; member of the second order of the nobility, the first being the order of 'lords' (*Herren*).

Ritterstand: the order of knights; the second order of the nobility which included the simple country gentlemen.

Rittmeister: captain of the cavalry in the imperial army.

Römerzug: 'the Roman journey'; originally the armed expedition undertaken by the medieval kings of Germany in order to be crowned at Rome; it was to finance this expedition that the Diet of the Empire voted the so-called 'Roman months' (*Römermonate*) which continued to give their name to the contributions paid by the princes to finance the army of the circles.

Rustikalland: lands give to a peasant in return for the payment of a certain number of dues in money, kind and labour (*robot*).

Salzamtmann: the manger of a salt warehouse.

Salzbergwerke: saltworks.

Salzkammergut: region of Upper Austria where the saltworks fell within the Habsburg domain.

Schatzmann: treasurer.

Stände: orders or estates and by extension the assemblies of the Estates or Diets.

Statthalter: literally the sovereign's 'lieutenant', i.e. the governor of a province or a country; in the Netherlands, the *stadhouder*.

Statthalterei: the government, the offices collectively dependent on the governor.

Stolageld: the money paid to a parish priest for certain offices.

Taiding: village community.

Tranksteuer: tax on alcoholic drinks.

Türkenlouis: name given to the margrave Louis of Baden (1655–1707), general of the imperial troops in recognition of his victories over the Turks in Hungary.

Türkensteuer: literally 'Turk-tax', the extraordinary tax raised to finance the war against the Turks.

Vermögenssteuer: tax on capital.

Verwirkungstheorie: the theory of forfeiture according to which the orders had unilaterally broken the contract binding them to the crown which was thereby absolved of all its obligations towards them.

Vorderösterreich or the *Vorlande*: 'Further Austria' including all the western part of the hereditary lands; approximately the Sundgau, the Breisgau and the city of Freiburg, Vorarlberg, the countries of Hohenberg and Sigmaringen, the landgravate of Nellenburg, the margravate of Burgau and the *Landvogtei* in Upper and Lower Swabia as well as, until 1648, Upper Alsace.

Wahlkapitulation: electoral contract; the contract negotiated with the orders before the imperial election in Germany and before the royal election in Bohemia and Hungary until the monarchy was established as hereditary rather than elective.

Welschen: the name, not necessarily derogatory, given by German-speakers to those speaking Romance languages; *Vlach* and *Welsh* are derived from the same root.

Winterkönig: the winter king, the name given to the elector of the Palatinate, Frederick V, who reigned at Prague for a year (1619–20) as king of Bohemia.

Zwiebeltürn: the characteristic onion-shaped tower surmounting many baroque churches.

Guide to Further Reading

This bibliography, which is restricted to books in English, is intended to assist the reader who now wishes to pursue particular subjects within the wide field opened up by Bérenger's introductory history. Most of the works listed have extensive bibliographies which will direct the confirmed Habsburg enthusiast towards original sources, articles in learned journals and the vast body of scholarly literature in other European languages for it is certain that the deficiencies of the present list will convince readers that life will be the richer for the acquisition of a reading knowledge at least of German.

1. The Habsburgs
2. The constituent nations
    (a) The Czechs and other Western Slavs
    (b) The Hungarians and Croats
    (c) The Germans and the Holy Roman Empire
3. Social and economic history
4. The Ottoman empire

THE HABSBURGS

For years, three broad surveys have served to introduce the English reader to Habsburg history. None covers precisely the same timespan as Bérenger but all three are thorough if rather dull: the reader may like to compare Bérenger's account with the admirably concise account of his acknowledged master V.-L. Tapie, *The Rise and Fall of the Habsburg Monarchy* (Paris, 1969; Eng. trans. London, 1971); C. A. Macartney, *The Habsburg Empire* (London, 1969) is more detailed while Robert Kann, *A History of the Habsburg Empire 1526–1918* (California, 1974) offers the chance to consider in English Habsburg history from the perspective of a Central European scholar.

The history of medieval Europe whence the Habsburgs made their remarkable rise is set out clearly in two general and informative accounts by G. Barraclough, *Eastern and Western Europe in the Middle Ages* (London, 1970) and *The Crucible of Europe: The Ninth and Tenth Centuries in European History* (London, 1976). For medieval Austria, from the settlement to the last Babenburg dukes, there is A. W. A. Leeper's study, *A History of Mediaeval Austria* (Oxford, 1941). Works covering the medieval history of the other later constituent lands of the Habsburg Empire are listed in the next section, 'The constituent nations'.

A good history of early modern Europe which refers at length to the Habsburgs is Roger Lockyer, *Habsburg and Bourbon Europe, 1470–1720* (London, 1974); as Bérenger supposes some understanding of French history, any reader feeling at a disadvantage when reading the sections on French–Habsburg relations would do well to turn to Lockyer's straightforward account.

Of the individual Habsburgs, it is the more extravagant figures who have attracted the most interest. Among the studies of Maximilian I, that by Gerhard Benecke, *Maximilian I 1459–1519: An Analytical Biography* (London, 1982), rather than presenting a narrative, deals with themes and sets out to place Maximilian in the context of contemporary European society and politics; individual chapters cover, among other concerns, Austria, its land and population, the standard of living, rural and urban life, mining and the court and at the end poses the question, 'What was the House of Austria?' L. Cuyler, *The Emperor Maximilian and Music* (Oxford, 1974) is not solely of interest to musicologists.

For the sixteenth century, the essays in the *New Cambridge Modern History* are, as always, a good starting-point: vol. II, H. G. Koenigsberger, 'The Empire of Charles V in Europe' (ch. x); F. C. Spooner, 'The Habsburg–Valois struggle' (ch. xi); R. R. Betts, 'Constitutional development and political thought in Eastern Europe' (ch. xv) includes a discussion of Ferdinand I's attempts to centralize the administration.

This is not the place for an exhaustive bibliography for sixteenth-century Habsburg Spain; however, Robert Lynch, *Spain under the Habsburgs* (vols 1–2, Oxford, 1981) and J. H. Elliott, *Imperial Spain 1469–1716* (London, 1963) are crisp, clear and stimulating works by two most eminent scholars. The *New Cambridge Modern History* is thorough in its coverage of Spain: vol. I, J. M. Balista and I Roca, 'The Hispanic kingdoms and the Catholic kings' (ch. xi); E. E. Rich, 'Expansion as a concern of all Europe' (ch. xvi) examines the effects of the Spanish Habsburgs' control of bullion; vol. III, H. G. Koenigsberger, 'Western Europe and the power of Spain' (ch. ix); vol. IV, H. R. Trevor-Roper, 'Spain and Europe, 1598–1621' (ch. ix); J. H. Elliott, 'The Spanish Peninsula, 1598–1648' (ch. xv).

Much has been written on Charles V and the following are among the most important studies in English: M. Fernández Alvarez, *Charles V: Elected Emperor and Hereditary Ruler* (London, 1975); K. Brandi, *The Emperor Charles V* (London, 1939) is still a standard work; J. M. Rodríguez-

Salgado, *The Changing Face of Empire: Charles V, Philip II and Habsburg Authority, 1551–1559* (Cambridge, 1988); J. M. Headley, *The Emperor and his Chancellor* (Cambridge, 1983) sets forth Charles V's relations with Gattinara. There is also a biography of Charles V's spirited sister, Jane de Iongh, *Mary of Hungary* (London, 1958), which is told in the romantic narrative tradition that the lives of so many royal women have attracted.

Two other sixteenth-century Habsburgs have been the subject of good individual studies: Paula Sutter Fichtner, *Ferdinand I of Austria: The Politics of Dynasticism in the Age of Reformation* (New York, 1982) is worthy and useful; in a different vein, R. J. W. Evans, *Rudolf II and his World* (Oxford, 1973) is respected as a model exercise in intellectual history with chapters devoted to Rudolf's politics and religion and more excitingly his patronage of the fine and occult arts. Rudolf's involvement in the arts and the formation of the circle of court painters at Prague are examined by Thomas Da Costa Kaufmann in *The School of Prague: Painting at the Court of Rudolf II* (Chicago UP, 1988), a superbly illustrated volume with accompanying authoritative text.

Several works span the sixteenth and seventeenth centuries. H. G. Koenigsberger, *The Habsburgs and Europe 1516–1660* (Cornell UP, New York, 1971) begins with the dream of universal empire under Charles V and traces its dissolution through the Thirty Years War to the Peace of the Pyrenees in 1559. T. V. Thomas and R. J. W. Evans (eds) *Crown, Church and Estates in Central Europe: Central European Politics in the Sixteenth and Seventeenth Centuries* (London, 1991) is chiefly concerned with the Habsburg monarchy but includes comparative material on Poland and the Holy Roman Empire; among the issues examined are the relationship between the Habsburg crown, the Estates and the Church from the Reformation to the Counter-Reformation and the character of Habsburg absolutism. This important collection of essays complements R. J. W. Evans, *The Making of the Habsburg Monarchy 1550–1700* (Oxford, 1979), which assumes a firm grasp of the political background but, while still concerned with the fundamental role of the Counter-Reformation and relations between the emperor and the great nobility, stresses the importance of a shared culture and intellectual world as a cohesive force within the monarchy: a lively and highly individual account which is persuasive from the first by force of its brilliance; precisely how clever this work is becomes apparent only with critical re-readings and closer acquaintance with the rest of the literature covering this period; a comprehensive bibliography and thorough index make it useful as a reference book which also serves as a convenient 'Who's Who' of the monarchy.

The New Cambridge Modern History offers: vol. IV, V. L. Tapie 'The Habsburg lands 1618–57' (ch. xvii); vol. V, R. R. Betts, 'The Habsburg lands' (ch. xx) ends with the reign of Leopold I and is informative on the economy and the Turks' involvement in Transylvania; vol. VI, J. W. Stoye, 'The Austrian Habsburgs' (ch. xviii).

The Thirty Years War will remain a rich field of historical controversy and the English texts include a wealth of literature. Among the important general works are G. Parker et al., *The Thirty Years War* (London, 1984); J. V. Polišenský, *The Thirty Years War* (London, 1971) which has a detailed account of the Bohemian phase of the war and bibliographical essay by its translator, R. J. W. Evans; perhaps more digestible is J. V. Polišenský's other work in English which is concerned with the same issues, *War and Society in Europe, 1618–1648* (Cambridge, 1978); *The New Cambridge Modern History*, vol. IV, E. A. Beller, 'The Thirty Years War' (ch. xi). Also of interest are Fritz Redlich, *The German Military Enterpriser and his Work Force: A Study in European Social and Economic History*, 2 vols (Wiesbaden, 1964–5) which is a fine work of scholarship; E. A. Beller, *Propaganda in Germany during the Thirty Years War* (Princeton, NJ, 1940); Golo Mann, *Wallenstein* (Eng. trans. New York, 1976); Robert R. Ergang, *The Myth of the All-Destructive Fury of the Thirty Years War* (Pocono Pines, Pennsylvania, 1956) which reassesses the war's impact. Any doubt as to the cruelty of the war is dispelled by the writings of one who witnessed at least some of its brutality; Hans Jacob Christoffel von Grimmelshausen's picaresque novel *Simplicius Simplicissimus* (1669) can be read in unabridged English translations by S. Goodrich, *Simplicissimus* (Sawtry, Cambridgeshire, 1989) and Monte Adair, *Simplicius Simplicissimus* (Landam, University Press of America, 1986).

With a wider scope but still relevant to the study of the Thirty Years War are Robert Birely, *Religion and Politics in the Age of the Counter-Reformation: Emperor Ferdinand II, William Lamormaini S. J. and the Formation of Imperial Policy* (North Carolina UP, 1981); Thomas M. Parker, *Army, Aristocracy, Monarchy; Essays on War, Society and Government in Austria 1618–1780* (New York, 1982).

Leopold I is the subject of a helpful and straightforward study by J. P. Spielman, *Leopold I of Austria* (London, 1977) which includes a chapter on the Wesselényi-Zrinski (Zrinyi) conspiracy and its aftermath in Hungary. This should be considered alongside the chapter by Jean Bérenger, 'The Austrian lands: Habsburg absolutism under Leopold I', in John Miller (ed.) *Absolutism in Seventeenth Century Europe* (London, 1990), which also has sections on Hungary and Bohemia. R. A. Kann, *A Study of Austrian Intellectual History: From Late Baroque to Romanticism* (New York, 1960) begins with the reign of Leopold I and has much of interest on Abraham á Sancta Clara. The broad theme of G. Dickens (ed.) *The Courts of Europe* (London, 1977) is the court as the prime focus of culture; Castiglione's work *I Cortegiano* (1514) is examined by S. Anglo in his essay, 'The courtier: the Renaissance and changing ideals', while other contributions include J. H. Elliott, 'Philip IV of Spain: prisoner of ceremony' and R. J. W. Evans, 'The Austrian Habsburgs: the dynasty as political institution', which focuses on the sixteenth and seventeenth centuries and argues for the importance of the court in binding together the Habsburgs' disparate possessions.

THE CONSTITUENT NATIONS

The Czechs and other Western Slavs

The following are very useful basic histories of the Czechs: R. W. Seton-Watson, *A History of the Czechs and Slovaks* (London, 1943) traces the origins of the Bohemian state until the Munich crisis which had added such urgency to the book's writing; less detailed but still an informative and scholarly account from the Přemyslids to the Czechoslovak Socialist Republic is J. F. N. Bradley, *Czechoslovakia: A Short History* (Edinburgh, 1971); S. Harrison Thomson, *Czechoslovakia in European History* (Princeton UP, 1965) is a straightforward history with a helpful bibliography.

The early history of the Slavs *c.* AD 500–1200, their migrations, settlement and Christianization is the subject of a solid work of scholarship by A. P. Vlasto, *The Entry of the Slavs into Christendom: An Introduction to the Mediaeval History of the Slavs* (Cambridge, 1970); there is also M. Simbutas, *The Slavs* (London, 1971).

The Cambridge Medieval History provides outlines of the medieval history of the Czechs: vol. II, J. Peisker, 'The expansion of the Slavs' (ch. xiv); vol. IV, Kamil Krofta, 'Bohemia to the extinction of the Přemyslids' (ch. xiii); vol. V, Austin Lane Poole, 'Germany 1125–1152' (ch. x) discusses German–Bohemian relations; vol. VII, Kamil Krofta, 'Bohemia in the fourteenth century' (ch. vi).

Jan Huss and the Hussites have attracted more attention than perhaps any other area of Czech history and there is a great quantity of historical but not necessarily critical literature available in English. As always, the *Cambridge Medieval History* serves the reader well: vol. VIII, W. T. Waugh, 'The Councils of Constance and Basle' (ch. i); Kamil Krofta, 'John Hus' (ch. ii) and 'Bohemia in the fifteenth century' (ch. iii); there is a discussion of warfare during the Hussite wars by Charles Oman, 'The art of war in the fifteenth century' (ch. xxi).

Euan Cameron's account of the Hussites in his remarkable scholarly synthesis *The European Reformation* (Oxford, 1991) is clear, brief and avoids making extravagant claims. Also to be recommended are R. R. Betts, *Essays in Czech History* (London, 1969), which is primarily concerned with cultural and intellectual developments within Bohemia during the fourteenth and fifteenth centuries but includes some discussion of political and constitutional changes during the Hussite period; F. M. Bartoš, *The Hussite Revolution, 1424–1437* (Columbia UP, New York, 1986) covers the period from the death of Jan Žižka to the death of king Sigismund and looks at the steps leading to the coexistence of the Hussites and the Catholic Church; Howard Kaminsky, *A History of the Hussite Revolution* (California UP, Berkeley, 1967) focuses on the period up to 1424 and is strong on the background to the movement with a discussion of the influence of John Wyclif; Otakar Odložilík, *The Hussite King: Bohemia in*

European Affairs, 1440–1471 (Rutgers UP, New Brunswick, NJ, 1965) is an example of scholarship coloured by national pride. Other studies which would have benefited from a more critical approach are Frederick G. Heymann, *John Žižka and the Hussite Revolution* (Princeton, NJ, 1955) and *George of Bohemia, King of Heretics* (Princeton UP, 1965); Count Lützow, *The Hussite Wars* (London, 1913) nevertheless has a useful fold-out map of the Bohemian crown lands from Charles IV to the Thirty Years War.

On later religious developments in Bohemia, Peter Brock, *The Political and Social Doctrines of the Unity of Czech Brethren in the Fifteenth and Early Sixteenth Centuries* (The Hague, 1957) begins with an account of Petr, Chelčiský and traces the schism between the Old and New Brethren.

The *New Cambridge Modern History* has two articles concerned with Bohemia and parallel developments in Hungary and Poland: vol. I, C. A. Macartney, 'Eastern Europe (ch. xiii); vol. II, R. R. Betts, 'The Reformation in difficulties' (ch. xi.).

Post-Mohács Bohemia is the subject of Kenneth J. Dillon, *King and Estates in the Bohemian Lands, 1526–1564* (Brussels, 1976), one of a series of studies presented to the International Commission for the History of Representative and Parliamentary Institutions; main themes within the work are the political, economic and social position of the Bohemian orders, the impact of the Turkish menace, the struggle over religion and the Counter-Reformation; the work has a good thematic bibliography. There is a vigorous survey of the political position of Bohemia and the process of its integration into the Habsburg Monarchy by R. J. W. Evans, 'The Habsburg monarchy and Bohemia, 1526–1848', in the generally excellent and stimulating collection edited by Mark Greengrass, *Conquest and Coalescence: The Shaping of the State in Early Modern Europe* (London, 1991). T. V. Thomas and R. J. W. Evans (eds) *Crown, Church and Estates: Central European Politics in the Sixteenth and Seventeenth Centuries* (London, 1991) includes essays based on important current research into the position of the Estates in the crown lands of Bohemia. Some appreciation of the flourishing cultural and intellectual life of the lands of the crown of Bohemia can be had from the essay by Josef Macek on Bohemia and Moravia during the Renaissance in R. Portner and M. Teich (eds) *The Renaissance in National Context* (Cambridge, 1992). J. Białostocki, *The Art of the Renaissance in Eastern Europe* (London, 1976) contains the texts of Białostocki's Wrightsman Lectures which focused on the castle, the chapel, the town and the tomb in Bohemia, Hungary and Poland. R. J. W. Evans, *Rudolf II and his World* (Oxford, 1973) and *The Making of the Habsburg Monarchy 1550–1700* are again to be recommended in this context, as is Thomas Da Costa Kaufmann, *The School of Prague: Painting at the Court of Rudolf II* (Chicago UP, 1988). Also useful and attractive are Milada Součková, *Baroque in Bohemia* (Ann Arbor, Mich., 1980) and B. Knox, *Bohemia and Moravia: An Architectural Companion* (London, 1962). Finally Karel Kuchař, *Early Maps of Bohemia, Moravia and Silesia* (Prague, 1961) contains many splendid reproductions with the text in English.

The Hungarians and Croats

Both C. A. Macartney, *Hungary: A Short History* (Edinburgh, 1962) and E. Pamlenyi (ed.) *A History of Hungary* (London, 1975) are good basic surveys of Hungarian history. They are supplemented by the stimulating collection of articles covering the history of Hungary from pre-Magyar times to 1990, Peter F. Sugar et al. (eds) *A History of Hungary* (Indiana UP, 1990); the articles on the Ottoman period and Transylvania are particularly welcome and a good bibliography is provided.

The *Cambridge Medieval History* covers the medieval history of Hungary in two essays: vol. VI (1968), Louis Leger, 'Hungary 1000–1301' (ch. xiii; vol. VIII (1969), Bálint Hóman, 'Hungary 1301–1490' (ch. xiv).

There is a small but worthy body of historical writing on medieval Hungary available in English: C. A. Macartney, *The Magyars in the Ninth Century* (Cambridge, 1930) is a substantial work of scholarship with translations of original texts, and a detailed discussion of a fundamental source for early history of Slavs and Magyars, the *De Administrando Imperio* of Constantine Porphyrogenitus; the scope of Z. J. Kosztolnyik's two studies is evident from their titles, *From Coloman the Learned to Béla III (1095–1196): Hungarian Domestic Policies and their Impact on Foreign Affairs* (Columbia UP, New York, 1987) and *Five Eleventh Century Hungarian Kings: Their Policies and their Relations with Rome* (Columbia UP, New York, 1981); Ferenc Makk, *The Árpáds and the Comneni; Political Relations between Hungary and Byzantium in the Twelfth Century* (Budapest, 1989) is an account of political contacts between the two ruling dynasties compiled chiefly from Byzantine Greek and Middle Latin sources; Erik Kügedi, *Kings, Bishops, Nobles and Burghers in Mediaeval Hungary* (London, 1986) is a collection of French, German and English articles, the latter including discussions of the aristocracy in medieval Hungary, the significance of the coronation ritual, the framework of kinship in Hungary, and oral culture and literacy among the medieval Hungarian nobility.

Early modern Hungary features in two articles in the *New Cambridge History* (1957): vol. I, C. A. Macartney, 'Eastern Europe' (ch. xiii) examines the complex ties binding the Poles, Hungarians and Czechs; vol. II, R. R. Betts, 'The Reformation in difficulties' (ch. xi) where religious developments in Hungary are discussed alongside those in Poland and Bohemia.

J. M. Bak and B. K. Király (eds) *From Hunyadi to Rákóczi: War and Society in Eastern Central Europe*, vol. III (Columbia UP, New York, 1982) offers good material on János Hunyadi and Matthias Corvinus with the emphasis placed on military history, the Ottoman advance and anti-Habsburg insurrections; there are articles not only on the siege of Szigetvár and Transylvania under Bethlen Gábor, but also on education and culture in Hungary during this period. The collection of essays edited by T. V. Thomas and R. J. W. Evans, *Crown, Church and State* (London, 1991) includes valuable contributions based on current research by László Makkai, 'The crown and diets of Hungary and Transylvania in the sixteenth century', by István Bitskey, 'The Collegium Germanicum Hungaricum in Rome and the beginning of Counter-Reformation in Hungary', Kálmán Benda, 'Habsburg absolutism and the resistance of the Hungarian estates in the sixteenth and seventeenth centuries', and Katalin Péter, 'The struggle for Protestant religious liberty at the 1646–7 diet in Hungary'.

Artistic, cultural and intellectual developments in Hungary are discussed in the following: L. Gerevich, *The Art of Buda and Pest in the Middle Ages* (Budapest, 1971); Tibor Klaniczay, 'Hungary' in R. Porter and M. Teich (eds) *The Renaissance in National Context* (Cambridge, 1992); J. Białostocki, *The Art of the Renaissance in Eastern Europe* (London, 1976) which has some discussion of Matthias Corvinus's activities as a patron of the arts; R. J. W. Evans, *The Making of the Habsburg Monarchy, 1550–1700* (Oxford, 1979).

Among the illuminating miscellanea available in English which bring the reader closer to original sources are János Thuróczy, *Chronicle of the Hungarians* (Indiana University Uralic and Altaic Series, vol. 155, Bloomington, Indiana, 1991); a best-seller from its first publication in 1488, Thuróczy's *Chronica Hungarorum* is worth reading not least for his portrait of Matthias Corvinus as a second Attila; this translation by Frank Mantello begins in 1387, omitting the earlier part of the original, and has a foreword and detailed commentary on the text by Pál Engel; also of interest is Gustav Bayerle, *Ottoman Diplomacy in Hungary: Letters from the Pashas of Buda 1590–1593* (Indiana UP, 1972), while it is much to be regretted that the letters themselves are not translated, the English synopses offer insight into the substance of contact at the official level between Ottomans and Christians with references to tribute paying and negotiations for the release of Ottoman officials held captive by the Christians; Marianna D. Birnbaum, *Humanists in a Shattered World: Croatian and Hungarian Latinity in the Sixteenth Century* (Los Angeles, 1985) likewise would have been useful to a wider audience if the substantial quotations had been translated but the text provides a readable (if rather prosaic) commentary on the attempts of contemporary Hungarian and Croatian scholars to make sense of their nations' suffering.

For the Croats and other South Slavs within the Habsburg monarchy, the best account by virtue of its clarity and absence of partisanship is that given by Ivo Banac in Part I of *The National Question in Yugoslavia, Origins, History and Politics*, (Cornell UP, New York, 1984). Of the general histories available, Stanko Guldescu, *A History of Mediaeval Croatia* (The Hague, 1964) and F. R. Preveden, *History of the Croatian People* (Chicago, 1949) are listed *faute de mieux*; it is hoped that this deficiency will presently be made up. G. E. Rothenberg, *The Austrian Military Border in Croatia 1522–1741* (Urbana, Ill., 1960) is an informative monograph on the defensive border with the Ottoman empire but its coverage of the early period is rather thin.

The Germans and the Holy Roman Empire

A good general history of Germany which emphasizes political, intellectual and cultural developments is H. A. Holborn, *A History of Modern Germany*, vols I–III (New York, 1959–69). The Longman History of Germany series, yet to be completed, should provide a much needed and more detailed alternative introduction to German history.

For the Middle Ages, the articles in the *Cambridge Medieval History* are a reliable starting point: vol. V, Austin Lane Poole, 'Germany 1125–1152' (ch. x) includes a discussion of German–Bohemian relations; vol. VII, P. J. Blok and W. T. Waugh, 'Germany 1272–1313' (ch. iv) and also W. T. Waugh, 'Germany under Charles IV' (ch. v); vol. VIII, R. G. D. Laffan, 'The Empire in the fifteenth century' (ch. iv).

Timothy Reuter, *Germany in the Early Middle Ages 800–1056* (London, 1991) is part of the Longman History of Germany series and is a clear and enjoyable account of the period from the coronation of Charlemagne as Holy Roman Emperor to the death of Emperor Henry III; it is a helpful introduction to the history of the Empire before Bérenger's main narrative.

Several chapters in the *New Cambridge Modern History* (1971) are devoted specifically to the Empire: vol. I, R. G. D. Laffan, 'The Empire under Maximilian I' (ch. vii); vol. III, G. D. Ramsay, 'The Austrian Habsburgs and the Empire' (ch. x); vol. IV, G. D. Ramsay, 'The state of Germany to 1618' (ch. x); vol. V, F. L. Carsten, 'The Empire after the Thirty Years War' (ch. xviii). Also to be recommended here is G. Benecke, *Germany in the Thirty Years War* (London, 1978), and again in the Longman History of Germany series, John Gagliardo, *Germany under the Old Regime 1600–1790* (London, 1991) which begins with an admirably clear account of the background and course of the Thirty Years War and continues with a good general survey of economic, political, social and cultural developments in Germany during the latter part of the early modern peiod.

The Renaissance in Germany is the subject of an essay by James Overfield in R. Porter and M. Teich, *The Renaissance in National Context* (Cambridge, 1992). Relations between Germany and the Habsburgs in the seventeenth century are discussed in R. J. W. Evans, *The Making of the Habsburg Monarchy 1550–1700* (Oxford, 1979).

SOCIAL AND ECONOMIC HISTORY

A good historical atlas is always an essential *vade mecum*; H. Kinder and W. Hildermann, *The Penguin Atlas of World History* (2 vols, Harmondsworth, 1974, 1978) is good and portable, *The Times World History Atlas* (London, 1980) is better but cumbersome.

Much valuable information on the geographical conditions of the lands of the Habsburg monarchy and their effect upon economic and social development are contained in the following: N. J. G. Pounds, *Historical Geography of Europe, 450 B.C.–A.D. 1330* (Cambridge, 1973) and *Historical Geography of Europe, 1500–1840* (Cambridge, 1979); also highly recommended is H. C. Darby's examination of the condition of Europe at the end of the Middle Ages, 'The Face of Europe on the Eve of the Great Discoveries' (ch. ii in the *New Cambridge Modern History*, vol. I) which surveys Central Europe, the Hungarian plain, Transylvania and Bohemia with sections on mining, urban development and trading activities. Two specific studies of Eastern Europe are David Turnock, *The Making of Eastern Europe, from the Earliest Times to 1815* (London, 1988), which is useful if patchy; W. H. McNeill, *Europe's Steppe Frontier, 1500–1800* (Chicago, 1964) offers many illuminating details.

A recent work strongly to be recommended is the collection of essays edited by A. Mączak, *East-Central Europe in Transition: From the Fourteenth to the Seventeenth Century* (Cambridge, 1985); focusing on Hungary and Poland with some comparative material on Bohemia, issues discussed include the demography of the region, agriculture and livestock production in Hungary, the 'economic landscape' from the fourteenth to the seventeenth century, towns, the circulation of capital and the Renaissance. A yet wider survey is S. Fischer-Galati (ed.) *Men, State and Society in East European History* (London, 1970) which begins with Eastern Europe before the fall of Constantinople and includes an account of the background to the Hussite revolution, has sections on the Ottoman and Habsburg empires with translations of interesting documentary evidence and ends with the 'Modernization of Eastern Europe (1918–41)'. Much the same timespan is covered in the collection edited by Daniel Chiot, *The Origins of Backwardness in Eastern Europe* (California UP, Berkeley, 1989), which examines afresh the divergence between Eastern and Western patterns of development from the fourteenth century to the early twentieth and includes articles on the effects of Ottoman occupation and the Balkans.

Urban development has been singled out as one of the key aspects of East–West divergence: R. Hodges, *Dark Age Economies: The Origins of Towns and Trade A.D. 600–1000* (London, 1982); E. A. Gutkind (ed.) *Urban Development in Central Europe* (New York, 1964) and *Urban Development in Eastern Europe* (New York, 1964) and *Urban Development in Eastern Europe: Poland, Czechoslovakia and Hungary* (New York, 1972); Maria Bogucka, 'The towns of East-Central Europe from the fourteenth to the seventeenth century', in A. Mączak (ed.) *East-Central Europe in Transition: From the Fourteenth to the Seventeenth Century* (Cambridge, 1985).

The so-called 'second serfdom' is discussed in Z. S. Pach, *Agrarian Development in Western Europe and Hungary from the Fifteenth to the Seventeenth Centuries* (Budapest, 1963).

OTTOMAN EMPIRE AND EUROPE

The evolution of the Habsburg Empire cannot be understood without due consideration of the role of the Ottoman empire as a cohesive force in its shaping. The following recommendations can serve only as an introduction to a highly specialized and stimulating body of historical literature some of the best of which is in French and German.

The *Cambridge History of Islam* (Cambridge, 1970) vol. I A, includes two articles by Halil Inalçik, 'The rise of the Ottoman empire' (part 3, ch. i) and 'The heyday and decline of the Ottoman empire' (part 3, ch. ii) both of which are especially relevant background to the period and themes touched on by Bérenger. The *New Cambridge Modern History* (1971) has much of use: vol. I, V. J. Parry, 'The Ottoman empire 1481–1520' (ch. xiv); vol. II, V. J. Parry, 'The Ottoman empire 1520–66' (ch. xvii); vol. III, V. J. Parry, 'The Ottoman empire 1566–1617' (ch. xi); vol. IV, J. Parry, 'The Ottoman empire 1617–1648' (ch. xx); vol. V, A. N. Kurat, 'The Ottoman empire under Mehmed IV' (ch. xxi); A. N. Kurat and J. S. Bromley, 'The retreat of the Turks 1683–1730' (ch. xix).

The following are all excellent general introductions by respected Ottoman scholars: V. J. Parry et al., *A History of the Ottoman Empire to 1730* (Cambridge, 1976); S. Shaw, *A History of the Ottoman Empire and Modern Turkey*, 2 vols (Cambridge, 1976–77); B. Lewis, *The World of Islam: Faith, People, Culture* (London, reprinted 1992) has good illustrations; H. Inalçik, 'Ottoman methods of conquest', *Studio Islamica*, vol. d, Paris 1954, *The Ottoman Empire: Conquest, Organization and Economy, Collected Studies* (London, 1978) and *The Ottoman Empire: The Classical Age, 1300–1600* (Eng. trans. London, 1973); K. Karpat, *The Ottoman State and its Place in World History* (Leiden, 1974); D. E. Pitcher, *A Historical Geography of the Ottoman Empire from Earliest Time to the End of the Sixteenth Century* (Leiden, 1970) gives an impression of the scale of the Ottomans' enterprise.

The government and administration of the Empire are the subject of J. Metin Kunt, *The Sultan's Servants: The Transformation of Ottoman Provincial Government 1550–1650* (New York, 1983); A. Lybyer, *The Government of the Ottoman Empire in the Time of Suleyman the Magnificent* (Cambridge, 1913); also very revealing is C. H. Fleischer, *Bureaucrat and Intellectual in the Ottoman Empire: The Historian Mustafa Âli (1541–1600)* (Guildford, 1987). There is a serviceable account of Süleymân by R. B. Merriman, *Suleiman the Magnificent, 1520–1566* (Cambridge, Mass., 1944) and an attractive exhibition catalogue with informative text by J. M. Rogers and R. M. Ward, *Süleymân the Magnificent* (British Museum, London, 1988).

On the Ottomans and Europe, the following can be recommended: Vera Zimány and Klára Hegyi, *The Ottoman Empire in Europe* (Budapest, 1986) is well illustrated with a lively text: B. Lewis, *The Muslim Discovery of Europe* (New York, 1982). On the 1683 siege of Vienna there are J. Stoye, *The Siege of Vienna* (New York, 1964) and M. Barker, *Double Eagle and Crescent: Vienna's Second Siege and the Historical Setting* (New York, 1967).

Bibliography

It is not possible to cite all the works and learned articles which have been used in this book: this bibliography simply serves to direct readers to supplementary texts.

PRINTED SOURCES

Acta Pacis Westphaliacae, first series: *Les Instructions*, vol. 1, *Frankreich-Schweden-Kaiser*, Fritz Dickmann (ed.) Münster-Westphalia, 1962; second series: *Les Correspondances*, section A: *Die Kaiserlichen Korrespondenzen*, vol. 1, 1645, W. Engels (ed.), Münster, 1968.

Barsonyi, Georges, *Veritas toti mundo declarata*, Sopron, 1682.

Bonfini, Antonius, *Rerum ungaricarum decades*, B. Ivanyi and L. Juhasz (eds), 4 vols, Szeged, 1935–41.

Codex Austriacus, 2 vols, Vienna, 1705.

Documenta bohemica bellum tricenale illustrantia, J. V. Polišenský (ed.), 7 vols, Prague and Vienna, 1971–4.

Documenta magistri Johannis Hus vitam, doctrinam, etc. illustrantia, František Palacký (ed.), Prague, 1869.

Ebendorfer, Thomas, *Kaiserchronik*, 1462, *Urkunden und Aktenstücke*, *Fontes Rerum Austriacarum*, Bachmann (ed.) II, 42, Vienna, 1879.

Gravamina (Les), Doléances de la Diète hongroise (1655–1681), Jean Bérenger (ed.), Paris, 1973.

Grillparzer, Franz, 'König Ottokars Glück und Ende' and 'Bruderzwist im Hause Habsburg', *Sämtliche Werke*, Vienna, 1855.

Herberstein, *Adam Freiherrn zu Herbersteins Gesandtschaftsreise nach Konstantinopel: Ein Beitrag zum Frieden von Zsitvatorok (1606)*, Karl Nehring (ed.), Munich, 1983, *Südosteuropäische Arbeiten*, 78.

Horgnik, Philipp von, *Œsterreich über alles, wann es nur Will . . .*, 1st edn, Vienna, 1686.

Iani Pannonii . . . opera omnia, Vienna, 1569, reissued Budapest, 1972.

Im Reich des Goldenen Apfels, Ottoman texts translated by Richard Kreutel, Vienna, 1964.

Instructions aux ambassadeurs et ministres de France (1648–1789): in particular vol. 1, *Autriche* A. Sorel (ed.), Paris, 1884 and vol. 22, *Turquie*, P. Duparc (ed. , Paris, 1974.

Kara Mustapha vor Wien 1683 aus der Sicht türkischer Quellen, published in German translation by Richard Kreutel and Karl Teply, Vienna and Graz, 1982.

Magyar orszaggyülesi emlékek ou Monumenta comitialia Hungariae (acts of the Hungarian Diet). To date, 14 volumes have been published and volumes 13 and 14, edited by Kálmán Benda, cover the 1607–8 session.

Magyar törvény tár (Corpus juris Hugarici), Dezso Markus (ed.), 14 vols, Budapest, 1897. This is the collection of all the laws passed by the Hungarian representative assemblies (Diet and Parliament) since the Middle Ages.

Materialien zur Geschichte der Löhne und Preise in Œsterreich, A. F. Pribram and Rudolf Geyer (eds), Vienna, 1938.

Monumenta Augustae Domus Austriae, Marquard Herrgott (ed.), published by Martin Gerbert, Order of St Benedict, Sankt Blasien im Schwarzwald, 3 vols, 1750–60.

Monumenta rusticorum in Hungaria rebellium anno MDXIV, A. F. Nagy (ed.) Budapest, 1979.

Princeps in compendio, hoc est Puncta aliquot compendiosa, quae circa Gubernationem Reipublicae observanda videntur, Vienna, 1632; Oswald Redlich (ed.), Vienna, *Monatsblätter des Vereins für Landeskunde Nieder-Œsterreichs*, 1906.

Privilegium majus, annotated edition and commentary by Alfons Lhotsky, Vienna, 1957.

Relationen der Botschafter Venedigs über Deutschland und Œsterreich im 17. Jahrhundert, J. Fieldler (ed.), Vienna, 1867, Fontes Rerum Austriacarum, II, vols 26 and 27.

Snémy ceské od léta 1526 az po nasi dobu (*die böhmischen Landtageverhandlungen und -beschlüsse vom Jahre 1526 bis auf die Neuzeit*), meaning 'Deliberations and decrees of the Bohemian Diet', 2 vols, Prague, 1877–1910.

Vita Karoli Quarti (Latin autobiography of Charles IV of Luxemburg), A. Blaschka (ed.), Prague, 1979.

Wegener, *Oeconomia suburbana*, Prague, 1666.

Werböczi, István, *Tripartitum opus juris consuetudinarii inclyti regni Hungariae*, 1st edn, Vienna, 1517.

Zredna, *Johannes Vitez de Zredna opera quae supersunt*, Ivan Boronkai (ed.), Budapest, 1980.

GENERAL WORKS

Bosl, Karl, *Handbuch der Geschichte der böhmischen Länder*, 4 vols, Stuttgart, 1967–73.

Bruckmuller, Ernst, *Nation Œsterreich: Sozialhistorische Aspekte ihrer Entwicklung*, Vienna, 1984.

Evans, R. J. W., *The Making of the Habsburg Monarchy, 1550–1700: An Interpretation*, Oxford, 1979.

Gonda, Imre and Niederhauser, Emil, *Die Habsburger: ein europäisches Phaenomen*, Budapest, 1978.

Hantsch, Hugo, *Die Geschichte Œsterreichs*, 2 vols, Graz and Vienna, 1955.

Herm, Gerhard, *Der Aufstieg des Hauses Habsburg*, Vienna and Düsseldorf, 1988.

Hoensch, Jörg K., *Geschichte Böhmens: von der slawischen Landnahme bis ins 20. Jahrhundert*, Munich, 1987.

Homan, Balínt and Szekfü, Gyulá, *Magyar Történet*, 7 vols, Budapest, 1935.

Kann, Robert A., *A History of the Habsburg Empire, 1526–1918*, California UP, 1974.

Kann, Robert A. and David, Zdenek V., *The Peoples of the Eastern Habsburg Lands, 1526–1918*, Vol. 6 of *History of East Central Europe*, Washington UP, Seattle and London, 1984.

Kopeczi, Béla; et al., *Erdély Története* (history of Transylvania), 3 vols, Budapest, 1986.

Lichnowsky, Prince, *Geschichte des Hauses Habsburg*, Vienna, 1839.

Macek, Josef, *Histoire de la Bohême des origines à 1918* (preface by Robert Mandrou), Paris, 1984.

Makkai, László, *Histoire de la Transylvanie*, Paris, 1947.

Mantran, Robert et al., *Histoire de l'empire ottoman*, Paris, 1989.

Pamlenyi, Ervin et al., *Histoire de la Hongrie des origines à nos jours*, Budapest, 1974.

Purs, Jaroslav and Kropilak, Miroslav, *Prehled dejin Ceskoslovenska*, 2 vols, Prague, 1980–2.

Wandruszka, Adam, *Das Haus Habsburg: Die Geschichte einer europäischen Dynastie*, Vienna, 1956 (English trans., *The House of Habsburg: Six Hundred Years of a European Dynasty*, New York, 1964).

Zollner, Erich, *Geschichte Œsterreichs*, 2nd edn, Vienna, 1961 (French trans., *Histoire de l'Autriche*, Roanne, 1966).

BIOGRAPHIES
(in chronological order of the subjects)

Hamann, Brigitte, *Die Habsburger: Ein biographisches Lexikon*, Vienna, 1988.

Allgemeine Deutsche Biographie, 54 vols, Leipzig, 1887–1910.

Redlich, Oswald, *Rudolf von Habsburg*, reissued Vienna, 1965.

Winter, Ernst Karl, *Rudolph IV von Œsterreich*, 2 vols, Vienna, 1934.

Strnad, Alfred, *Herzog Albrecht III von Œsterreich*, Vienna, 1961.

Seibt, Ferdinand, *Karl IV: Ein Kaiser in Europa, 1346–1378*, Munich, 1978.

Hodel, Günther, *Albrecht II: Königtum, Reichsregierung und Reichsreform 1438–1439*.

Fraknói, Vilmos, *Matthias Corvinus: König von Ungarn*, Freiburg im Breisgau, 1891.

Ackerl, Isabella, *König Mathias Corvinus: Ein Ungar, der in Wien regierte*, Vienna, 1985.

Benecke, Gerhard, *Maximilian I (1459–1519): An Analytical Biography*, London, 1982.

Wiesflecker, Hermann, *Kaiser Maximilian I*, 5 vols, Vienna, 1971–86.

Winker, E., *Margarete von Œsterreich, Grande Dame der Renaissance*, Munich, 1966.

Brandi, Karl, *Kaiser Karl V*, 2 vols, Munich, 1937 (French trans., *Charles-Quint et son temps*, Paris, 1951).

Alvarez, Manuel Fernandez, *Karl V: Herrscher eines Weltreiches*, Munich, 1977.

Boom, Ghislaine de, *Marie de Hongrie*, Brussels, 1956.

Sutter-Fichtner, P., *Ferdinand I*, Graz and Vienna, 1986.

Parker, Geoffrey, *Philip I*, London, 1979.

Pfandl, Ludwig, *Philipp II*, Munich, 1938.

Petrie, Charles, *Don John of Austria*, London, 1967.

Terlinden, Charles, *L'Archiduchesse Isabelle*, Brussels, 1943.

Bibl, Viktor, *Maximilian II: Der rätselhafte Kaiser*, Dresden, 1929.

Hirn, Joseph, *Erzherzog Ferdinand II von Tirol*, 2 vols, Innsbruck, 1885–7.

Evans, R. J. W., *Rudolf II and his World*, 2nd edn, Oxford, 1984.

Vocelka, Karl, *Rudolf II und seine Zeit*, Vienna, 1985.

Spielman Jr., John, *Emperor Leopold I*, London, 1977.

Ingrao, Charles W., *Emperor Joseph I and the Habsburg Monarchy*, Purdue UP, West Layafette, Indiana, 1979.

McKay, Derek, *Prince Eugene of Savoy*, London, 1977.

Braubach, Max, *Prinz Eugen von Savoyen*, 5 vols, Munich and Vienna, 1963–5.

INSTITUTIONS AND POLITICAL LIFE

Ember, Gyözö, *A magyar közigazgatás története 1526–1711* (history of Hungarian public administration), Budapest, 1946.

Hellbling, Ernst C., *Œsterreichische Verfassungs-und Verwaltungsgeschichte*, Vienna, 1956.

Fellner, Thomas, and Kretschmayr, Heinrich, *Die Œsterreichische Zentralverwaltung 1526–1848*, 2 vols, Vienna, 1925.

Bidermann, Hermann Ignaz, *Geschichte der österreichischen Gesamtstaatsidee 1526–1804*, Innsbruck, 1867.

Bireley, Robert S. J., *Religion and Politics in the Age of the Counter-Reformation: Emperor Ferdinand II, William Lamormaini SJ and the Formation of Imperial Policy*, North Carolina UP, 1981.

Bérenger, Jean, *Finances et absolutisme autrichien dans la seconde moitié du XVIIe siècle*, Paris, 1975.

ECONOMY

Zímanyi, Véra, 'Economy and society in 16th and 17th century Hungary 1516–1650', Budapest, *Studia Historica*, 188, 1987.

RELIGIOUS AND CULTURAL LIFE

Bohemia Sacra: Das Christentum in Böhmen 973–1973, Ferdinand Seibt (ed.), Düsseldorf, 1974.

Humanizmus a Renasancia na Slovensku, Holotik and Vantuch (eds), Bratislava, 1967.

Csapodi, Csaba, *The Corvinian Library: History and Stock*, Budapest, 1976.

Renaissance et Réforme en Pologne et en Hongrie, Gy. Szekzly (ed.), Budapest, 1966.

Seibt, Ferdinand, *Hussitenstudien*, Munich, 1987.

Kalivoda, Robert, *Revolution und Ideologie: Der Hussitismus*, Vienna and Cologne, 1976.

Mecenseffy, Grete, *Geschichte des Protestantismus in Œsterreich*, Graz, 1956.

Révész, Imre, *A magyarországi protestantizmus története* (a history of Hungarian Protestantism), Budapest, 1925.

Bucsay, Mihály, *A protestantizmus története Magyarországon 1521–1945*, Budapest, 1985.

Tapie, V.-L., *Baroque et classicisme*, Paris, 1958.

Tomek, Ernst, *Kirchengeschichte Œsterreichs*, 3 vols, Innsbruck, 1937.

Wodka, Josef, *Kirche in Œsterreich: Wegweiser durch ihre Geschichte*, Vienna, 1959.

INTERNATIONAL RELATIONS

Histoire des relations internationales (general editor, Pierre Renouvin), 8 vols, Paris, 1949–53. The reader will find volumes 2 to 3 by G. Zeller, volume 4 by A. Fugier and volumes 5 to 7 by P. Renouvin a useful introduction to the subject.

Lynch, John, *Spain under the Habsburgs*, 2 vols, Oxford, 1969.

Chaunu, Pierre, *L'Espagne de Charles Quint*, 2 vols, Paris, 1973.

Deveze, Michel, *L'Espagne de Philippe IV*, 2 vols, Paris, 1970.

Elliott, J. H., *Imperial Spain, 1469–1716*, London, 1963.

Parker, Geoffrey et al., *La Guerre de Trente Ans*, Paris, 1987.

Polišenský, J. V., *The Thirty Years War*, London, 1971.

Barudio, Gunther, *Der deutsche Krieg 1618–1648*, Frankfurt am Main, 1985.

Tapie, V.-L., *La Guerre de Trente Ans* (with a preface by P. Chaunu), Paris, 1989.

Dickmann, Fritz, *Der westfälische Frieden*, Münster (Westphalia), 1961.

Boutant, Charles, *L'Europe au grand tournant des années 1680: la succession palatine*, Paris, 1985.

Barker, Thomas E., *Double Eagle and Crescent*, New York, 1979.

Maps and Genealogical Tables

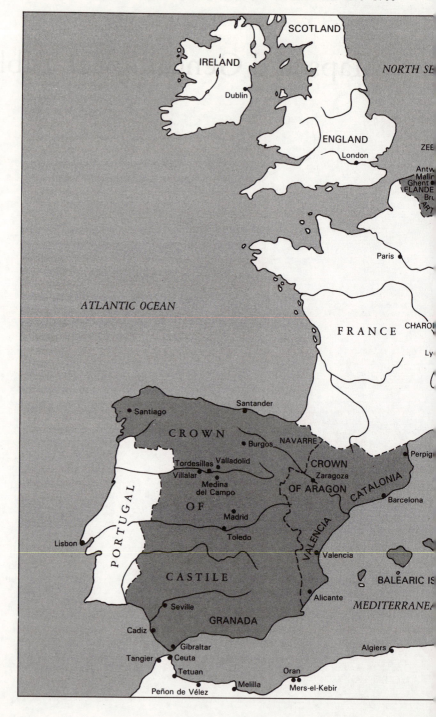

1. The Empire of Charles V in 1519

DENMARK

Lübeck

BRANDENBURG

FRIESLAND

Amsterdam
AND
HER-
DS

WESTPHALIA

BRUNSWICK

Leipzig

Mühlberg

LUSATIA

BANT

Cologne

Erfurt

SILESIA

T
EMBURG

Frankfurt

Prague

Glatz

Olomouc

Mainz

Bamberg

BOHEMIA

Brno

tz

Trier

Nürnberg

MORAVIA

PALATINATE

Ulm

Vienna

Pozsony

Danube

Augsburg

Buda

BREISGAU

BAVARIA

AUSTRIA

Sopron

KINGDOM

ANCHE
COMTE

Basle

STYRIA

OF

Mohács

SWITZERLAND

Innsbruck

CARINTHIA

HUNGARY

TYROL

Villach

Geneva

Brixen

REPUBLIC
OF
VENICE

CARNIOLA
CROATIA

Zagreb

SLAVONIA

Belgrade

DUCHY
OF
SAVOY

DUCHY
OF Milan
MILAN

Trent

Mantua

Venice

OTTOMAN

Pavia

EMPIRE

Nice

Genoa

Bologna

ADRIATIC SEA

Marseilles

Florence

Ragusa

PAPAL
STATES

CORSICA

Rome

KINGDOM
OF
NAPLES

Naples

CORFU

SARDINIA

Lepanto

SEA

Messina

Palermo

SICILY

Bona

La Goletta

Tunis

ALGERIA

Charles V's patrimony

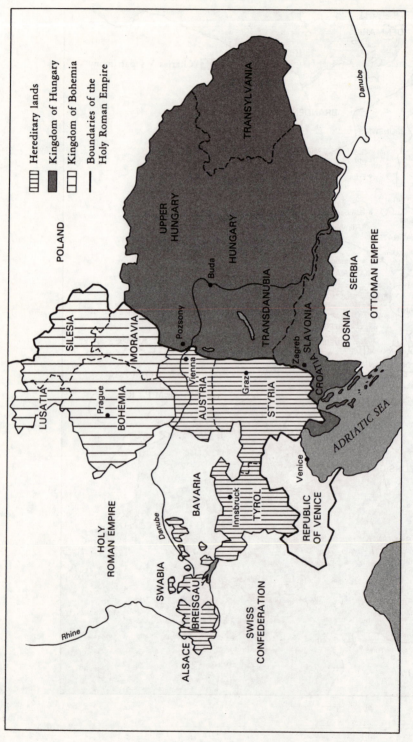

Hereditary lands
Kingdom of Hungary
Kingdom of Bohemia
Boundaries of the
Holy Roman Empire

POLAND

Danube

TRANSYLVANIA

UPPER
HUNGARY

HUNGARY

Buda

TRANSDANUBIA

SERBIA

BOSNIA

OTTOMAN EMPIRE

SILESIA

MORAVIA

Pozsony

Zagreb

SLAVONIA

CROATIA

LUSATIA

Prague

BOHEMIA

Vienna

AUSTRIA

Graz

STYRIA

ADRIATIC SEA

HOLY
ROMAN EMPIRE

Danube

BAVARIA

Innsbruck

TYROL

Venice

REPUBLIC
OF VENICE

Rhine

SWABIA

ALSACE

BREISGAU

SWISS
CONFEDERATION

2. The Austrian monarchy in 1526

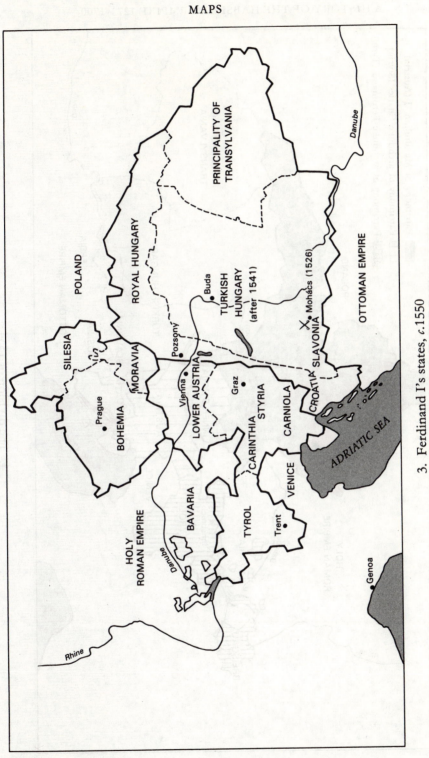

3. Ferdinand I's states, c.1550

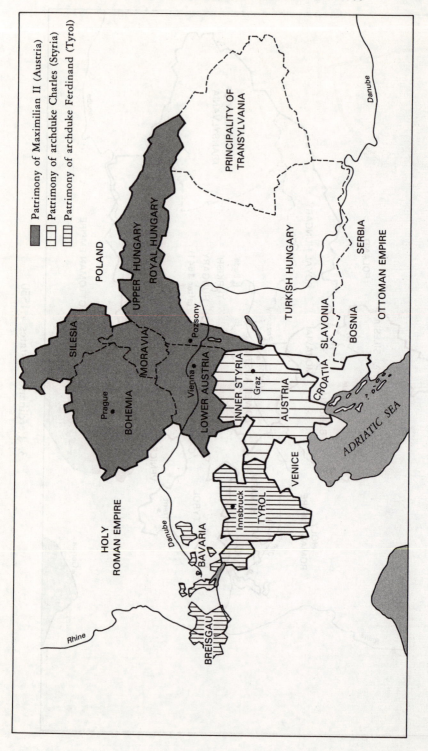

4. The division of 1564

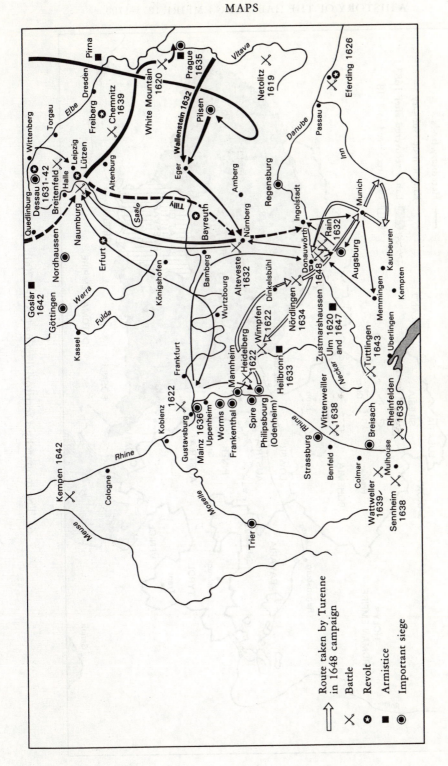

5. The Thirty Years War in Germany (1618–48)

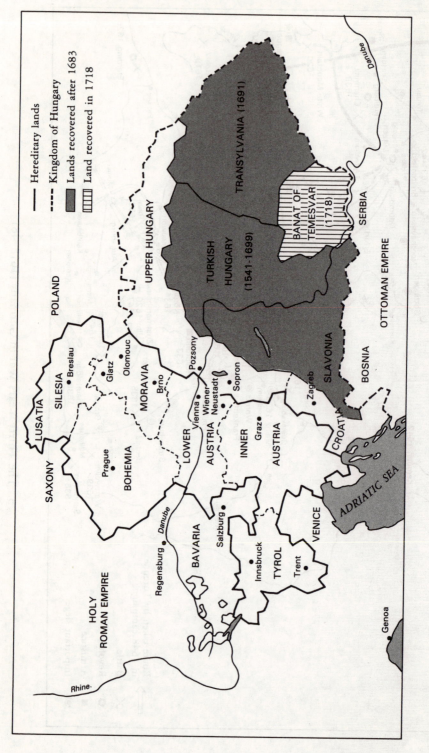

6. The monarchy's territorial gains (1650–1700)

1. **The Habsburg kings of Germany before Frederick III**

Rudolf I	1273 – 91
Albert I	1298 – 1308
Frederick (anti-king)	1313 – 22
Albert II	1438 – 9
Frederick III	1440 – 93

1. The Habsburg kings of Germany before Frederick III

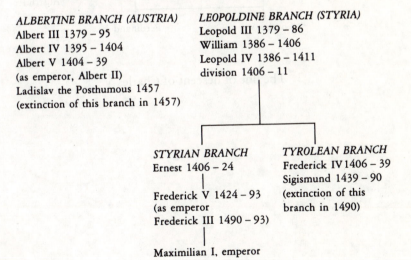

Rudolf IV the Founder 1355 – 65
Albert III and Leopold III (jointly) 1365 – 79
Treaty of Neuberg 1379 (division into two branches)

ALBERTINE BRANCH (AUSTRIA)
Albert III 1379 – 95
Albert IV 1395 – 1404
Albert V 1404 – 39
(as emperor, Albert II)
Ladislav the Posthumous 1457
(extinction of this branch in 1457)

LEOPOLDINE BRANCH (STYRIA)
Leopold III 1379 – 86
William 1386 – 1406
Leopold IV 1386 – 1411
division 1406 – 11

STYRIAN BRANCH
Ernest 1406 – 24

Frederick V 1424 – 93
(as emperor
Frederick III 1490 – 93)

Maximilian I, emperor

TYROLEAN BRANCH
Frederick IV 1406 – 39
Sigismund 1439 – 90
(extinction of this
branch in 1490)

2. The different branches of the House of Habsburg from 1365 to 1490

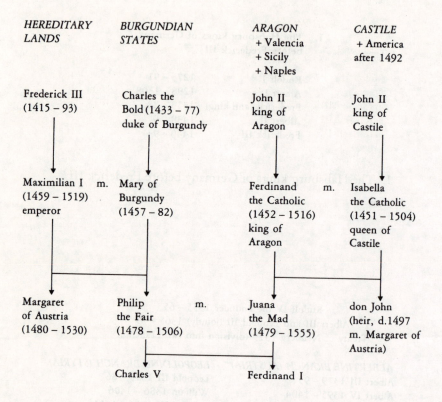

HEREDITARY LANDS	BURGUNDIAN STATES	ARAGON + Valencia + Sicily + Naples	CASTILE + America after 1492
Frederick III (1415 – 93)	Charles the Bold (1433 – 77) duke of Burgundy	John II king of Aragon	John II king of Castile
Maximilian I (1459 – 1519) emperor	m. Mary of Burgundy (1457 – 82)	Ferdinand the Catholic (1452 – 1516) king of Aragon	m. Isabella the Catholic (1451 – 1504) queen of Castile
Margaret of Austria (1480 – 1530)	Philip the Fair (1478 – 1506)	m. Juana the Mad (1479 – 1555)	don John (heir, d.1497 m. Margaret of Austria)
	Charles V	Ferdinand I	

3. The line of descent of Charles V

BOHEMIA		HUNGARY	
Ferdinand I	1526 – 64	Ferdinand I	1526 – 64
Maximilian	1564 – 76	Maximilian	1564 – 76
Rudolf II	1576 – 1611	Rudolf	1576 – 1608
Matthias	1611 – 17	Matthias II	1608 – 19
Ferdinand II	1620 – 37	Ferdinand II	1619 – 37
Ferdinand III	1637 – 57	Ferdinand III	1637 – 57
Ferdinand IV	(1654)	Ferdinand IV	(1654)
Leopold I	1657 – 1705	Leopold I	1657 – 1705
Joseph I	1705 – 11	Joseph I	1705 – 11
Charles II	1711 – 40	Charles III	1711 – 40
Maria-Theresa	1740 – 80	Maria-Theresa	1740 – 80
Joseph II	1780 – 90	Joseph II	1780 – 90
Leopold II	1790 – 2	Leopold II	1790 – 2
Francis I	1792 – 1835	Francis I	1792 – 1835
Ferdinand V	1835 – 48	Ferdinand V	1835 – 48
Francis-Joseph	1848 – 1916	Francis-Joseph	1848 – 1916
Charles III	1916 – 18	Charles III	1916 – 18

4. The Habsburgs as kings of Bohemia and as kings of Hungary

Philip I (of Castile)	1504 – 6
Charles I (V)	1516 – 56
Philip II	1556 – 98
Philip III	1598 – 1621
Philip IV	1621 – 65
Charles II	1665 – 1700
Charles III (VI)	1703 – 13

5. The Habsburg as kings of Spain (1504–1713)

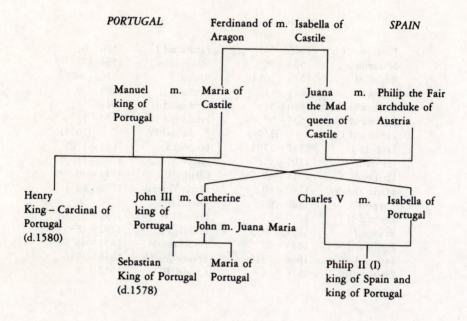

6. The Habsburgs in Portugal

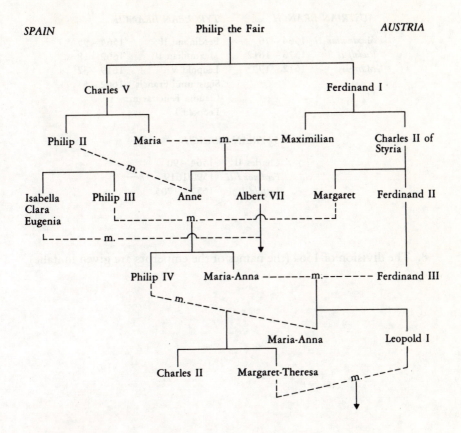

7. Marriages between the two branches of the Habsburgs

AUSTRIAN BRANCH

Maximilian II	1564 – 76
Rudolf II	1576 – 1612
Matthias	1612 – 19

TYROLEAN BRANCH

Ferdinand II	1564 – 95
Maximilian III	1602 – 18
Leopold V	1619 – 32
Sigismund-Francis	1662 – 5
Claudia Felicitas m.	
Leopold I	

STYRIAN BRANCH

Charles II	1564 – 90
Ferdinand II	1590/1619 – 57
Leopold I	1657 – 1705

8. The division of 1564 (the names of the emperors are given in italic)

Index